Lecture Notes in Computer Science 8665

Commenced Publication in 1973
Founding and Former Series Editors:
Gerhard Goos, Juris Hartmanis, and Jan van Leeuwen

T0224342

Gul Agha   Atsushi Igarashi
Naoki Kobayashi   Hidehiko Masuhara
Satoshi Matsuoka   Etsuya Shibayama
Kenjiro Taura (Eds.)

Concurrent Objects and Beyond

Papers dedicated to Akinori Yonezawa
on the Occasion of His 65th Birthday

 Springer

Volume Editors

Gul Agha
University of Illinois at Urbana-Champaign, Urbana, IL, USA
E-mail: agha@illinois.edu

Atsushi Igarashi
Kyoto University, Kyoto, Japan
E-mail: igarashi@kuis.kyoto-u.ac.jp

Naoki Kobayashi
Etsuya Shibayama
Kenjiro Taura
The University of Tokyo, Japan
E-mail: koba@is.s.u-tokyo.ac.jp
E-mail: etsuya@ecc.u-tokyo.ac.jp
E-mail: tau@eidos.ic.i.u-tokyo.ac.jp

Hidehiko Masuhara
Satoshi Matsuoka
Tokyo Institute of Technology, Tokyo, Japan
E-mail: masuhara@acm.org
E-mail: matsu@is.titech.ac.jp

Cover gure: US Post Office-Central Square, Cambridge, MA, USA

ISSN 0302-9743   e-ISSN 1611-3349
ISBN 978-3-662-44470-2   e-ISBN 978-3-662-44471-9
DOI 10.1007/978-3-662-44471-9
Springer Heidelberg New York Dordrecht London

Library of Congress Control Number: 2014946291

LNCS Sublibrary: SL 2 – Programming and Software Engineering

Typesetting: Camera-ready by author, data conversion by Scientific Publishing Services, Chennai, India

Printed on acid-free paper

Springer is part of Springer Science+Business Media (www.springer.com)

Yonezawa

Preface

It is with great pleasure that we present this Festschrift volume in honor of Professor Akinori Yonezawa, a towering figure in computer science who has made pioneering contributions to research, education, and service in the field over four decades.

Professor Yonezawa worked on both theoretical and practical aspects of concurrent object-oriented programming. He defined one of the first actor languages, developed methods for reasoning about concurrent object systems, and built the first high-performance compiler and run-time system for such a language. The language constructs he developed for communication have been incorporated in subsequent actor languages. His techniques for implementation demonstrated the suitability of using concurrent objects for high-performance computing. His work on reasoning techniques and computational reflection provided deep insights into the semantics of programming languages based on concurrent objects.

Professor Yonezawa's research on concurrent object languages not only spurred an enormous body of research, it laid the ground for the successful development of actor languages now widely used in academia and industry. Besides making ground breaking research contributions, Professor Yonezawa has been an extraordinarily influential educator and mentor. He trained a generation of students who are now well-known researchers in leading universities and industrial laboratories. It is fair to say that it is in no small part because of Professor Yonezawa's effort that Japan today is recognized as an important center for research in programming languages and high performance computing.

This Festschrift includes a collection of papers written by the participants to the symposium titled "Concurrent Objects and Beyond: From Theory to High-Performance Computing" to celebrate the accomplishments of Professor Yonezawa on the occasion of his 65th birthday in 2012. A few researchers who were regretfully unable to attend the symposium, were also invited to submit to the Festschrift volume. All papers went through a rigorous peer review process with one or more rounds of revision as needed. We have also decided to reprint two of Professor Yonezawa's early influential papers on the programming language ABCL. It is indeed a privilege to present this body of research as a tribute not only to Professor Yonezawa's long and distinguished career, but as an appreciation of his inspiring warmth and friendship which we have all cherished over the decades.

Acknowledgements. We would like to thank all the authors of the papers in this volume and also the speakers at and participants to the symposium. We are also grateful to Toshiyuki Maeda and Yoshiko Iwasa for everything about local arrangements of the symposium. Last but not least, we would like to dedicate this volume to the memory of Kohei Honda, one of the distinguished researchers in concurrency theory and also one of the speakers at the symposium and authors of the papers in this volume, who, very unfortunately, passed away in London in December 2012, just several months after the symposium.

June 2014

Gul Agha
Atsushi Igarashi
Naoki Kobayashi
Hidehiko Masuhara
Satoshi Matsuoka
Etsuya Shibayama
Kenjiro Taura

Papers in This Festschrift

We give brief summaries of the papers included in this Festschrift.

Birth of Concurrent Objects. The opening of the Festschrift is an essay titled *My Early Education and Concurrent Objects* by Prof. Yonezawa about his intellectual journey, including recollection of how he grew up intellectually and of how he came up with and developed the idea of concurrent objects. The next paper *Object-Oriented Concurrent Programming in ABCL/1*, originally presented at the first OOPSLA in 1986 by Akinori Yonezawa, Jean-Pierre Briot, and Etsuya Shibayama, introduces the programming language ABCL/1, which based on concurrent objects. In *Reflection in an Object-Oriented Concurrent Language*, originally presented at the third OOPSLA in 1988 by Takuo Watanabe and Akinori Yonezawa, the authors applied the notion of computational reflection by Smith and Maes to concurrent objects and developed ABCL/R, an extension of ABCL/1 with reflection.

Foundations of Concurrent Objects and Beyond. The paper *Building Safe Concurrency Abstractions*, by Ole Lehrmann Madsen describes how high-level concurrency constructs such as monitors and rendezvous can be built by using patterns, the unifying abstraction mechanism in Beta, and a rather low-level concurrency construct of test-and-set. *Structuring Communication with Session Types*, by Kohei Honda, Raymond Hu, Rumyana Neykova, Tzu-Chun Chen, Romain Demangeon, Pierre-Malo Deniélou, and Nobuko Yoshida reviews session types, emphasizing its historical background and design philosophies. It also demonstrates the use of session types and session programming through programming examples instead of going through formalities (such as the formal syntax and semantics of programs and types). *From Linear Types to Behavioural Types and Model Checking*, by Naoki Kobayashi gives an overview of a series of the work by him (and his colleagues) on linear and behavioral type systems for process calculi and higher-order model checking. Interestingly, the author also describes how these ideas relate to each other and evolved, mainly from a personal perspective.

Implementation of Concurrent Objects and Massively Parallel Languages. The paper *SALSA Lite: A Hash-Based Actor Runtime for Efficient Local Concurrency*, by Travis Desell and Carlos Varela presents SALSA Lite, a Java-like actor language for non-distributed environments. It introduces a notion of stages, an abstraction of a thread, and allocating actors to one of the stages in the system. The paper comes with performance comparison with other actor frameworks like Erlang, Scala, and Kilim, and shows that SALSA Lite demonstrates the best performance among them. *Past and Future Directions for Concurrent Task Scheduling*, by Robert Halstead reviews two important concepts and techniques for task scheduling systems, namely Lazy Task Creation and speculative computation based on sponsor model. This paper gives a valuable review about the root of the idea when we consider growing number of systems similar to Lazy Task Creation and a growing interest in parallel programming systems for multicores in general. The paper *Controlling Concurrency and Expressing Synchronization in Charm++ Programs*, by Laxmikant Kale and Jonathan Lifflander provides a good overview of work done on the Charm++ language library and subprojects, going into detail about different strategies for controlling concurrency and parallel program flow. It concludes with case studies for a set of related high performance computing applications (leanMD and a dense LU factorization for the high performance computing challenge). *MassiveThreads: A Thread Library for High Productivity Languages*, by Jun Nakashima and Kenjiro Taura describes the MassiveThreads library, which is a fine-grained thread library compatible with Pthreads. Unlike other fine-grained thread libraries, the MassiveThreads library allows thread switching upon blocking I/O operations. The paper presents the results of the micro-benchmarks. *On Efficient Load Balancing for Irregular Applications*, by Masahiro Yasugi is an essay on efficient dynamic load balancing for task based parallel programming languages. Topics covered include Cilk, Lazy Task Creation, and Tascell, which is the author's own work.

Concurrent Objects in the World The paper *Verifiable Object-Oriented Transactions*, by Suad Alagić and Adnan Fazeli proposes techniques to describe specifications of integrity constraints of OODB transactions and to statically verify that those constraints are satisfied by using Spec#. *Design and Implementation of a Mobile Actor Platform for Wireless Sensor Networks*, by Youngmin Kwon, Kirill Mechitov and Gul Agha summarizes the design and implementation of ActorNet, which is an actor-based language for embedded devices. The notable features of ActorNet include its lightweight implementation as well as intrinsic support of concurrency. *Objects In Space*, by Wolfgang de Meuter, Andoni Lombide Carreton, Kevin Pinte, Stijn Mostinckx and Tom Van Cutsem overviews extensions to AmbientTalk for writing mobile RFID-enabled applications. The extensions consists of storing objects in RFID tags, a mechanism to obtain object references from tags, and a support for reactive programming. Advantages of those extensions are discussed through a case study on an application that suggests cooking recipes for a given set of ingredients.

Beyond Concurrent Objects. The paper *Towards a Substrate Framework of Computation*, by Kazunori Ueda gives an overview of LMNtal (and its extension HyperLMNtal) that he designed and worked on for the past several years. The overview includes an introduction to the language, static analysis, and an encoding of lambda-calculus into LMNtal. *Event-Based Modularization of Reactive Systems*, by Somayeh Malakuti and Mehmet Akşit proposes an event-based language for implementing reactive systems in a modular way, i.e., separating the base- and reactive parts of the systems. *From Actors and Concurrent Objects to Agent-Oriented Programming in simpAL*, by Alessandro Ricci and Andrea Santi describes an agent-oriented programming language called simpAL, including some design philosophy, programming examples, and implementation issues as well as discussion on actors and concurrent objects.

We hope this volume demonstrates Professor Yonezawa's deep influence on a wide range of research on concurrent/parallel computing.

Symposium "Concurrent Objects and Beyond"

An international symposium titled "Concurrent Objects and Beyond: From Theory to High-Performance Computing" was held in Kobe, Japan to celebrate the accomplishments of Professor Yonezawa on the occasion of his 65th birthday in 2012. It was held during May 28 and 29, 2012 at Integrated Research Center of Kobe University, Kobe, Japan, located next to RIKEN Advanced Institute for Computational Science (home of the K Computer), where Professor Yonezawa serves as Deputy Director. The symposium, which attracted about 40 participants (see the group photo in Figure 1), included talks by prominent researchers, many of them colleagues and former students of Professor Yonezawa, who are working on topics related to concurrent objects and high performance computing. After the symposium, we had a tour to the K Computer as an excursion.

Fig. 1. Participants to the Symposium

We record the technical program in figures and the participants below:

Gul Agha	Mehmet Akşit	Suad Alagić
Kenichi Asai	Eric Chen	Shigeru Chiba
Andrew Chien	Pierre Cointe	Wolfgang de Meuter
Toshio Endo	Jacques Garrigue	Bert Halstead
Kohei Honda	Atsushi Igarashi	Takayasu Ito
Tomio Kamada	Takuya Katayama	Naoki Kobayashi
Ole Madsen	Toshiyuki Maeda	Naoya Maruyama
Hidehiko Masuhara	Motohiko Matsuda	Satoshi Matsuoka
Tsuyoshi Murata	Viet Ha Nguyen	Atsushi Ohori
Yutaka Oiwa	Yoshihiro Oyama	Mitsuhisa Sato
Etsuya Shibayama	Kohei Suenaga	Eijiro Sumii
Kenjiro Taura	Mario Tokoro	Kentaro Torisawa
Jan Vitek	Takuo Watanabe	Masahiro Yasugi

10:00–10:20   Opening

Session 1 (Chair: Toshio Endo, Tokyo Institute of Technology)
10:20–10:50   Suad Alagić (University of Southern Maine)
              Verifiable Object-oriented Transactions
10:50–11:10   Shigeru Chiba (University of Tokyo)
              Does modularity help high-performance computing?

Session 2 (Chair: Masahiro Yasugi, Kyushu Institute of Technology)
11:40–12:10   Gul Agha (University of Illinois)
              Dynamic Analysis of Concurrent Systems
12:10–12:40   Bert Halstead (Curl Corporation)
              Past and Future Directions for Concurrent Task Scheduling
12:40–13:00   Kenjiro Taura (University of Tokyo)
              MassiveThreads: A Lightweight Thread Library for Massively Parallel
              Machines

Session 3 (Chair: Kenjiro Taura, University of Tokyo)
14:30–15:00   Akinori Yonezawa (RIKEN AICS)
              Working for High Performance Computing
15:00–15:30   Andrew Chien (University of Chicago)
              Concurrent Objects in High-Performance Computing and Architec-
              ture: A Fundamental Theme
15:30–15:50   Mitsuhisa Sato (University of Tsukuba)

              Researches on Programming Environment for the K Computer in
              AICS

Session 4 (Chair: Eijiro Sumii, Tohoku University)
16:20–16:50   Kohei Honda (Queen Mary University of London)
              Structuring Communications with Session Types
16:50–17:20   Vijay Saraswat (IBM Watoson Research Lab)
              Building applications with X10
17:20–17:40   Atsushi Ohori (Tohoku University)
              Development of SML♯ and its Potential for Massively Parallel
              Computation

18:00–20:00   Reception

Fig. 2. Symposium Program, Day 1 (May 28, Monday, 2012)

Session 5 (Chair: Etsuya Shibayama, University of Tokyo)
10:00–10:30   Ole Madsen (Aarhus University)
              Concurrent object-oriented modeling and programming in BETA
10:30–11:00   Wolfgang de Meuter (Vrije Universiteit Brussel)
              Objects in Space
11:00–11:20   Satoshi Matsuoka (Tokyo Institute of Technology)
              Million Cores Now a Reality: Tsubame 2.0 and Beyond

Session 6 (Chair: Jacques Garrigue, Nagoya University)
11:50–12:20   Jan Vitek (Purdue University)
              Thorn: Objects, Scripts and more...
12:20–12:40   Naoki Kobayashi (University of Tokyo)
              Towards Model Checking of Concurrent Objects
12:40–13:00   Atsushi Igarashi (Kyoto University)
              Gradual Typing for Java

Session 7 (Chair: Takuo Watanabe, Tokyo Institute of Techonology)
14:30–15:00   Mehmet Akşit (University of Twente)
              From Object-Oriented to Event-Driven Programming
15:00–15:30   Pierre Cointe (École des Mines de Nantes)
              Designing Programming Languages: an Historical Perspective
15:30–15:50   Hidehiko Masuhara (University of Tokyo)
              Reflection on the Power of Pointcuts

Fig. 3. Symposium Program, Day 2 (May 29, Tuesday, 2012)

Brief Biography of Professor Akinori Yonezawa

Akinori Yonezawa was born in 1947 in Tokyo, Japan. He received his B.E., M.E. degrees from the University of Tokyo in 1970, and 1972, respectively, and Ph.D degree in computer science from Massachusetts Institute of Technology in 1978. From 1974 to 1978, he was a Research Associate at Laboratory for Computer Science and Artificial Intelligence Laboratory, MIT. After returning to Japan, he joined the faculty of Department of Information Science, Tokyo Institute of Technology, Japan as a research associate and was promoted to assistant professor and then professor. He moved to Department of Information Science, University of Tokyo as a professor in 1989. He was appointed Director of Center for Information Technology, University of Tokyo from 2006 for 4 years. In 2011, he left Tokyo and took office in RIKEN Advanced Institute for Computational Science as Deputy Director. He became a Fellow of ACM in 1999, cited as "a pioneer of concurrent object-oriented programming systems." He received AITO Dahl–Nygaard Prize in 2008 and Medal of Honor with a Purple Ribbon of Japan (Shijuhousho) in 2009.

Brief Biography of Professor Akihiro Kobayashi

Publications of Professor Akinori Yonezawa

Books

1. Goto, E., Furukawa, K., Nakajima, R., Nakata, I., Yonezawa, A. (eds.): RIMS 1982. LNCS, vol. 147. Springer, Heidelberg (1983)
2. Yonezawa, A., Tokoro, M. (eds.): Object-Oriented Concurrent Programming, pp. 1987–282. MIT Press
3. Agha, G., Wegner, P., Yonezawa, A. (eds.): Proceedings of the 1988 ACM SIG-PLAN workshop on Object-Based Concurrent Programming, 214 pages. ACM, San Diego (1988)
4. Tokoro, M., Anzai, Y., Yonezawa, A. (eds.): Concepts and Characteristics of Knowledge-Based Systems: selected and reviewed papers from the IFIP TC 10/WG10.1 Workshop, November 9-12, 511 pages. North-Holland, Mount Fuji (1989)
5. Ito, T. (ed.): UK/Japan WS 1989. LNCS, vol. 491. Springer, Heidelberg (1991)
6. Yuen, C.K., Yonezawa, A. (eds.): Parallel Programming Systems: Proceedings of a JSPS Seminar (Tokyo, Japan, 27-29 May 1992), 253 pages. World Scientific (September 1993)
7. Nishio, S. (ed.): ISOTAS 1993. LNCS, vol. 742. Springer, Heidelberg (1993)
8. Agha, G., Wegner, P., Yonezawa, A. (eds.): Research Directions in Concurrent Object-Oriented Programming, 532 pages. MIT Press (November 1993)
9. Ciancarini, P., Wang, J. (eds.): ECOOP-WS 1994. LNCS, vol. 924. Springer, Heidelberg (1995)
10. Ito, T. (ed.): TPPP 1994. LNCS, vol. 907. Springer, Heidelberg (1995)
11. Briot, J.-P., Geib, J.-M. (eds.): OBPDC 1995. LNCS, vol. 1107. Springer, Heidelberg (1996)
12. Bahsoun, J.-P., Baba, T., Briot, J.-P., Yonezawa, A.: Object-Oriented Parallel and Distributed Programming, 329 pages. HERMES Science Publications, Paris (2000)
13. Matsuoka, S. (ed.): Reflection 2001. LNCS, vol. 2192. Springer, Heidelberg (2001)
14. Okada, M., Babu, C. S., Scedrov, A., Tokuda, H. (eds.): ISSS 2002. LNCS, vol. 2609. Springer, Heidelberg (2003)

Chapters in Books

15. Shibayama, E., Yonezawa, A.: Distributed Computing in ABCL/1. In: Yonezawa, A., Tokoro, M. (eds.) Object-Oriented Concurrent Programming, pp. 91–128. MIT Press (1987)
16. Yonezawa, A., Shibayama, E., Takada, T., Honda, Y.: Modelling and Programming in an Object-Oriented Concurrent Language ABCL/1. In: Yonezawa, A., Tokoro, M. (eds.) Object-Oriented Concurrent Programming, pp. 55–90. MIT Press (1987)
17. Yonezawa, A., Briot, J.-P., Shibayama, E.: Object-Oriented Concurrent Programming in ABCL/1. In: Bond, A.H., Gasser, L. (eds.) Readings in Distributed Artificial Intelligence, pp. 434–444. Morgan Kaufman Publishers (1988)
18. Matsuoka, S., Yonezawa, A.: Analysis of Inheritance Anomaly in Object-Oriented Concurrent Programming Languages. In: Agha, G., Wegner, P., Yonezawa, A. (eds.) Research Directions in Concurrent Object-Oriented Programming, ch. 4, pp. 107–150. MIT Press (1993)

19. Yonezawa, A., Osawa, I.: Object-Oriented Parallel Parsing for Context-Free Grammars. In: Adriaens, G., Hahn, U. (eds.) Parallel Natural Language Processing, ch. 4, pp. 188–210. Ablex Publishing Corporation (1994)
20. Yonezawa, A., Briot, J.-P., Shibayama, E.: Object-Oriented Concurrent Programming in ABCL/1. In: Skillicorn, D.B., Talia, D. (eds.) Programming Languages for Parallel Processing, pp. 158–168. IEEE Computer Society Press (1995)
21. Masuhara, H., Yonezawa, A.: Reflection in Concurrent Object-Oriented Languages. In: Bowman, H., Derrick, J. (eds.) Formal Methods for Distributed Processing: A Survey of Object-Oriented Approaches, pp. 305–325. Cambridge University Press (2001)

Invited Talks

22. Object-Oriented Concurrent Programming and Its industrial Applications. International Conference on Theory and Practice of Software Development (TAPSOFT), Berlin (March 1985)
23. Object-Oriented Concurrent Computing. Department of Computer Science and Engineering, Technical University of Dresden, Dresden, East Germany (May 1985)
24. Object-Oriented Concurrent Programming - A Language ABCL -. AFCET Conference on Object-Oriented Languages, Paris, France (May 1986)
25. AI Parallelism and Programming. IFIP Congress, Dublin, Ireland (September 1986)
26. Object-Oriented Concurrent Computing. Fall 1987 Lecture Series, Department of Computer Science, University of Maryland (October 1987)
27. Reflection in an Object-Oriented Concurrent Language. School on Foundations of Object-Oriented Languages, Noorwijkerhout, Netherlands (May 1990)
28. Object-oriented Concurrent Computing. Five Lecture Series, Swedish Institute of Computer Science (June 1992)
29. Theory and Practice of Concurrent Object-Oriented Computing. International Conference on Theoretical Aspects of Computer Software (TACS 1994), Sendai, Japan (April 1994)
30. Object-Based Models and Languages for Concurrent Systems. 1994 Workshop on Models and Languages for Coordination of Parallelism and Distribution, Bologna, Italy (July 1994)
31. Mobile Objects and their Implementations. International Symposium on Future Software Technology, Hangzou, China, October 29 (October 1998)
32. Distributed and Concurrent Objects Based on Linear Logic. Third International Conference on Formal Methods for Open Object-based Distributed Systems (FMOODS 1999), Florence, Italy, Feburary (1999)
33. Message or Object? – Origin and Future of Concurrent/Mobile Objects –. The 7th International Workshop on Foundations of Object-Oriented Languages (FOOL 7), Boston, USA (January 2000)
34. Overview of the Japanese Inter-University Research Project on Software Security. 4th International Symposium on Theoretical Aspects of Computer Software (TACS 2001), Sendai, Japan (October 2001)
35. An Overview of a Mext funded Inter-University Software Security Research, Berkeley, California, USA. An NSF Agenda Meeting on computer security (August 2002)

36. An Overview on a 3.5-Year Japanese Inter-University Research on Software Security. Workshop on New Approaches to Software Construction - WNASC 2004, Komaba, Tokyo (September 2002)
37. Concurrent Objects - Introspect and Prospect -. European Conference on Object Oriented Programming, Paphos, Cyprus (July 2008)
38. Modeling and Simulating Real/Virtual Worlds with Concurrent Objects. The 4th Franco-Japanese Computer Security Workshop, Tokyo (December 2008)

Journal Articles

39. Yonezawa, A.: Comments on Monitors and Path-Expressions. Journal of Information Processing 1(4), 180–186 (1979)
40. Yonezawa, A., Hewitt, C.: Modelling Distributed Systems. Machine Intelligence 9, 41–50 (1979)
41. Yonezawa, A.: Specifying Software Systems with High Internal Concurrency Based on Actor Formalism. Journal of Information Processing 2(4), 208–218 (1980)
42. Yonezawa, A.: A Method for Synthesizing Data Retrieving Programs. Journal of Information Processing 5(2), 94–101 (1982)
43. Furukawa, K., Nakajima, R., Yonezawa, A.: Modularization and Abstraction in Logic Programming. New Generation Computing 1(2), 169–177 (1983)
44. Maruyama, H., Yonezawa, A.: A Prolog-Based Natural Language Front-End System. New Generation Computing 2(1), 91–99 (1984)
45. Yonezawa, A., Loeper, H., Jäkel, H.-J.: The Rendezvous Concept - a Programming Tool for Parallel Processing. Journal of Information Processing and Cybernetics 21(9), 429–440 (1985)
46. Matsuoka, S., Takahashi, S., Kamada, T., Yonezawa, A.: A General Framework for Bi-Directional Translation between Abstract and Pictorial Data. ACM Transactions on Information Systems 10(4), 408–437 (1992)
47. Yonezawa, A., Matsuoka, S., Yasugi, M., Taura, K.: Implementing Concurrent Object-Oriented Languages on Multicomputers. IEEE Parallel and Distributed Technology: Systems and Technology 1(2), 49–61 (1993)
48. Sugimoto, T., Yonezawa, A.: Multiple World Representation of Mental States for Dialogue Processing. IEICE Transaction on Information and Systems E77-D(2), 192–208 (1994)
49. Kobayashi, N., Yonezawa, A.: Asynchronous Communication Model Based on Linear Logic. Formal Aspects of Computing 7(2), 113–149 (1995)
50. Kobayashi, N., Yonezawa, A.: Towards Foundations of Concurrent Object-Oriented Programming-Types and Language Design. Theory and Practice of Object Systems 1(4), 243–268 (1995)
51. Matsuoka, S., Yasugi, M., Taura, K., Kamada, T., Yonezawa, A.: Compiling and Managing Concurrent Objects for Efficient Execution on High-Performance MPPs. In: Bic, L., Nicolau, A., Sato, M. (eds.) Parallel Language and Compiler Research in, pp. 91–125. Kluwer Academic Publishers (1995)
52. Nakaya, A., Yamamoto, K., Yonezawa, A.: RNA Secondary Structure Prediction Using Highly Parallel Computers. Computer Applications in the Biosciences 11(6), 685–692 (1995)

53. Asai, K., Matsuoka, S., Yonezawa, A.: Duplication and Partial Evaluation For a Better Understanding of Reflective Languages. Lisp and Symbolic Computation 9(2/3), 203–241 (1996)

54. Nakaya, A., Taura, K., Yamamoto, K., Yonezawa, A.: Visualization of RNA Secondary Structures Using Highly Parallel Computers. Computer Applications in the Biosciences 12(3), 205–211 (1996)

55. Nakaya, A., Yonezawa, A., Yamamoto, K.: Classification of RNA Secondary Structures Using the Techniques of Cluster Analysis. Journal of Theoretical Biology 183(1), 105–117 (1996)

56. Kobayashi, N., Shimizu, T., Yonezawa, A.: Distributed Concurrent Linear Logic Programming. Theoretical Computer Science (Linear Logic Special Issues), Elsevier Science 227(1-2), 185–220 (1999)

57. Oiwa, Y., Taura, K., Yonezawa, A.: Extending Java Virtual Machine with Integer-Reference Conversion. Concurrency: Practice and Experience 12(6), 407–422 (2000)

58. Masuhara, H., Yonezawa, A.: A Portable Approach to Dynamic Optimization in Run-time Specialization. New Generation Computing 20(1), 101–124 (2001)

59. Shibayama, E., Yonezawa, A.: Secure Software Infrastructure in the Internet Age. New Generation Computing 21(2), 87–106 (2003)

60. Kaneda, K., Taura, K., Yonezawa, A.: Virtual private grid: a command shell for utilizing hundreds of machines efficiently. Future Generation Computer Systems 19(4), 563–573 (2003)

International Conference Proceedings

61. Yonezawa, A., Hewitt, C.: Modelling Distributed Systems. In: Reddy, R. (ed.) Proceedings of the 5th International Joint Conference on Artificial Intelligence, Cambridge, MA, pp. 370–376. William Kaufmann (August 1977), Also in Machine Intelligence 9, Ellis Horwood Ltd., Chichester, Sussex (1978)

62. Yonezawa, A.: A Specification Technique for Abstract Data Types with Parallelism. In: International Conference on Mathematical Studies of Information Processing, Kyoto, Japan (August 1978), Also available as Research Report C-17, Department of Information Science, Tokyo Institute of Technology (April 1978)

63. Yonezawa, A.: A Formal Specification Technique for Abstract Data Types with Parallelism. In: Blum, E.K., Takasu, S., Paul, M. (eds.) Mathematical Studies of Information Processing. LNCS, vol. 75, pp. 127–150. Springer, Heidelberg (1979)

64. Yonezawa, A., Matsumoto, Y.: Object Oriented Concurrent Programming and Industrial Software Production. In: Mathematical Foundations of Software Development, Proceedings of the International Joint Conference on Theory and Practice of Software Development (TAPSOFT), vol. 2: Colloquium on Software Engineering (CSE), vol. 186 of Lecture Notes in Computer Science, pp. 395–409, Berlin, Germany, Springer (March 1985)

65. Yonezawa, A.: AI Parallelism and Programming. In: Kugler, H.J. (ed.) Information Processing 1986, IFIP Congress, pp. 111–113. North-Holland (1986)

66. Yonezawa, A., Matsuda, H., Shibayama, E.: An Approach to Object-Oriented Concurrent Programming – A Language ABCL –. In: Proceedings of AFCET Conference on Object-Oriented Languages, Paris, pp. 125–134 (1986)

67. Briot, J.-P., Yonezawa, A.: Inheritance mechanisms in distributed object-oriented languages. In: Conference on Software Science and Engineering (SSE 1986), RIMS, Kyoto University, Japan (September 1986)

68. Yonezawa, A., Briot, J.-P., Shibayama, E.: Object-Oriented Concurrent Programming in ABCL/1. In: Proceedings of the Conference on Object-Oriented Programming Systems, Languages, and Applications (OOPSLA 1986), Portland, Oregon, pp. 258–268 (November 1986), Also in SIGPLAN Notices 21(11), 258–268

69. Briot, J.-P.: Inheritance and Synchronization in Concurrent OOP. In: Bézivin, J., Hullot, J.-M., Lieberman, H., Cointe, P. (eds.) ECOOP 1987. LNCS, vol. 276, pp. 32–40. Springer, Heidelberg (1987)

70. Cottrell, G.W., Dey, P., Diederich, J., Reich, P.A., Shastri, L., Yonezawa, A.: Parallel processing in computational linguistics. In: Proceedings of the 12th International Conference on Computational Linguistics, Budapest, Hungary, pp. 595–598 (August 1988)

71. Honda, Y., Yonezawa, A.: Debugging Concurrent Systems Based on Object Groups. In: Gjessing, S., Chepoi, V. (eds.) ECOOP 1988. LNCS, vol. 322, pp. 267–282. Springer, Heidelberg (1988)

72. Yonezawa, A., Ohsawa, I.: Object-Oriented Parallel Parsing for Context-Free Grammars. In: Proceedings of the 12th International Conference on Computational Linguistics, Budapest, Hungary, pp. 773–778 (August 1988)

73. Watanabe, T., Yonezawa, A.: Reflection in an Object-Oriented Concurrent Language. In: Proceedings of Conference on Object-Oriented Programming Systems, Languages, and Applications (OOPSLA 1988), San Diego, CA, vol. 11, pp. 306–315 (September 1988), Also in SIGPLAN Notices 23(11) (November 1988)

74. Akinori Yonezawa, T.W.: An Introduction to Object-Based Reflective Concurrent Computation. In: Agha, G., Wegner, P., Yonezawa, A. (eds.) Proceedings of the 1988 ACM SIGPLAN Workshop on Object-Based Concurrent Programming, San Diego, pp. 50–54 (1989), Also in SIGPLAN Notices 24(4)

75. Watanabe, T., Yonezawa, A.: Reflective Computation in Object-Oriented Concurrent Systems and its Applications. In: Proceedings of the Fifth International Workshop on Software Specification and Design (IWSSD 1989), Pittsburgh, USA, pp. 56–58 (1989)

76. Shibayama, E., Yonezawa, A.: Optimistic and Pessimistic Synchronization in Distributed Computing. In: Ito, T., Halstead Jr., R.H. (eds.) US/Japan WS 1989. LNCS, vol. 441, pp. 257–260. Springer, Heidelberg (1990)

77. Yonezawa, A.: A Reflective Object Oriented Concurrent Language ABCL/R. In: Ito, T., Halstead Jr., R.H. (eds.) US/Japan WS 1989. LNCS, vol. 441, pp. 254–256. Springer, Heidelberg (1990)

78. Matsuoka, S., Yonezawa, A.: Metalevel solution to inheritance anomaly in concurrent object-oriented languages. In: ECOOP/OOPSLA 1990 Workshop on Reflection and Metalevel Architectures in Object-Oriented Programming, Ottawa, Canada (October 1990)

79. Ichisugi, Y., Matsuoka, S., Watanabe, T., Yonezawa, A.: An Object-Oriented Concurrent Reflective Architecture for Distributed Computing Environments (Extended Abstract). In: Proceedings of 29th Annual Allerton Conference on Communication, Control and Computing, Allerton Illinois (1991)

80. Ichisugi, Y., Yonezawa, A.: Exception Handling and Real Time Features in an Object-Oriented Concurrent Language. In: Ito, T. (ed.) UK/Japan WS 1989. LNCS, vol. 491, pp. 92–109. Springer, Heidelberg (1991)

81. Watanabe, T., Yonezawa, A.: An Actor-Based Metalevel Architecture for Group-Wide Reflection. In: de Bakker, J.W., Rozenberg, G., de Roever, W.-P. (eds.) REX 1990. LNCS, vol. 489, pp. 405–425. Springer, Heidelberg (1991)

82. Kobayashi, N., Matsuoka, S., Yonezawa, A.: Control in Parallel Constraint Logic Programming. In: Proceedings of Logic Programming Conference 1991, Tokyo, Japan. Lecture Notes in Artificial Intelligence. Springer (July 1991)

83. Matsuoka, S., Watanabe, T., Yonezawa, A.: Hybrid Group Reflective Architecture for Object-Oriented Concurrent Reflective Programming. In: America, P. (ed.) ECOOP 1991. LNCS, vol. 512, pp. 231–250. Springer, Heidelberg (1991)

84. Matsuoka, S., Furuso, S., Yonezawa, A.: A Fast Parallel Conservative Garbage Collector for Concurrent Object-Oriented Systems. In: Proceedings of IEEE International Workshop on Object Orientation in Operating Systems (I-WOOS 1991), Palo Alto, CA, pp. 87–93 (October 1991)

85. Yasugi, M., Yonezawa, A.: Towards User (Application) Language-Level Garbage Collection in Object-Oriented Concurrent Languages. In: Proceedings of the OOPSLA 1991 Workshop on Reflection and Metalevel Architectures in Object-Oriented Programming, Phoenix, USA (October 1991)

86. Takahashi, S., Matsuoka, S., Yonezawa, A., Kamada, T.: A General Framework for Bi-Directional Translation between Abstract and Pictorial Data. In: Proceedings of the Fourth ACM Symposium on User Interface Software and Technology (UIST 1991), Hilton Head, South Carolina, USA, pp. 165–174 (November 1991)

87. Wakita, K., Yonezawa, A.: Linguistic Supports for Development of Distributed Organizational Information Systems in Object-Oriented Concurrent Computation Frameworks. In: Proceedings of ACM Conference on Organizational Computing Systems (COCS 1991), Atlanta, pp. 185–198 (November 1991)

88. America, P., Milner, R., Nierstrasz, O., Tokoro, M., Yonezawa, A.: What Is An Object (panel). In: Zatarain-Cabada, R., Wang, J. (eds.) ECOOP-WS 1991. LNCS, vol. 612, pp. 257–264. Springer, Heidelberg (1992)

89. Matsuoka, S., Watanabe, T., Ichisugi, Y., Yonezawa, A.: Object-Oriented Concurrent Reflective Architectures. In: Zatarain-Cabada, R., Wang, J. (eds.) ECOOP-WS 1991. LNCS, vol. 612, pp. 211–226. Springer, Heidelberg (1992)

90. Yasugi, M., Matsuoka, S., Yonezawa, A.: ABCL/onEM-4: A New Software/Hardware Architecture for Object-Oriented Concurrent Computing on an Extended Dataflow Supercomputer. In: Proceedings of the 6th International Conference on Supercomputing (ICS 1992), Washington D.C., pp. 93–103 (July 1992)

91. Masuhara, H., Matsuoka, S., Watanabe, T., Yonezawa, A.: Object-Oriented Concurrent Reflective Languages can be Implemented Efficiently. In: Proceedings of Conference on Object-Oriented Programming Systems, Languages, and Applications (OOPSLA 1992), Vancouver, Canada, pp. 127–144 (1992), Also in SIGPLAN Notices 27(10)

92. Ichisugi, Y., Matsuoka, S., Yonezawa, A.: RbCl: A Reflective Concurrent Language without a Run-Time Kernel. In: Proceedings of IMSA 1992 International Workshop on Reflection and Metalevel Architectures, Tokyo, Japan (November 1992)

93. Miyashita, K., Matsuoka, S., Takahashi, S., Yonezawa, A., Kamada, T.: Declarative Programming of Graphical Interfaces by Visual Examples. In: Proceedings of the Fifth ACM Symposium on User Interface Software and Technology (UIST 1992), Monteray, CA, pp. 107–116 (November 1992)

94. Asai, K., Matsuoka, S., Yonezawa, A.: Model Checking of Control-Finite CSP Programs. In: Proceedings of the 26th Hawaii International Conference on Systems Science, vol. 2, pp. 174–183 (1993)

95. Kobayashi, N., Yonezawa, A.: Asynchronous Communication Model Based on Linear Logic. In: Halstead Jr., R.H., Ito, T. (eds.) US/Japan WS 1992. LNCS, vol. 748, pp. 331–336. Springer, Heidelberg (1993)

96. Taura, K., Matsuoka, S., Yonezawa, A.: An Efficient Implementation Scheme of Concurrent Object-Oriented Languages on Stock Multicomputers. In: Halstead Jr., R.H., Ito, T. (eds.) US/Japan WS 1992. LNCS, vol. 748, pp. 402–405. Springer, Heidelberg (1993)

97. Yonezawa, A., Matsuoka, S., Yasugi, M., Taura, K.: Efficient Implementations of Concurrent Object-Oriented Languages on Multicomputers (abstract). In: Proceedings of a JSPS Seminar: Parallel Programming Systems, pp. 50–52 (1993)

98. Taura, K., Matsuoka, S., Yonezawa, A.: An Efficient Implementation Scheme of Concurrent Object-Oriented Language on Stock Multicomputers. In: Proceedings of the Fourth ACM SIGPLAN Symposium on Principles and Practice of Parallel Programming (PPoPP 1993), San Diego, pp. 218–228 (May 1993), Also in SIGPLAN Notices 28(7) (July 1993)

99. Matsuoka, S., Taura, K., Yonezawa, A.: Highly Efficient and Encapsulated Reuse of Synchronization Code in Concurrent Object-Oriented Languages. In: Proceedings of the 8th Annual Conference on Object-Oriented Programming Systems, Languages, and Applications (OOPSLA 1993), Washington D.C., USA, September-October, pp. 109–126 (1993), Also in SIGPLAN Notices 28(10)

100. Miyata, T., Hasida, K., Yonezawa, A.: Plan Inferences in Dialogue under Dynamical Constraint Programming. In: Proceedings of the Fourth International Workshop on Natural Language Understanding and Logic Programming (NLULP,4), Nara, Japan, September-October, pp. 129–145 (1993)

101. Asai, K., Matsuoka, S., Yonezawa, A.: Duplication and Partial Evaluation to Implement Reflective Languages. In: Proceedings of OOPSLA 1993 Workshop on Reflection and Metalevel Architectures, Washington D.C., USA (October 1993)

102. Kobayashi, N., Yonezawa, A.: ACL – A Concurrent Linear Logic Programming Paradigm. In: Proceedings of the 1993 International Logic Programming Symposium, Vancouver, Canada, pp. 279–294. MIT Press (October 1993)

103. Masuhara, H., Matsuoka, S., Yonezawa, A.: Designing an object-oriented reflective language for massively-parallel processors. In: Proceedings of OOPSLA 1993 Workshop on Object-Oriented Reflection and Metalevel Architectures, Washington D.C., USA (October 1993)

104. Aksit, M., Wakita, K., Bosch, J., Bergmans, L., Yonezawa, A.: Abstracting Object Interactions Using Composition Filters. In: Guerraoui, R., Riveill, M., Wang, J. (eds.) ECOOP-WS 1993. LNCS, vol. 791, pp. 152–184. Springer, Heidelberg (1994)

105. Sekiguchi, T., Yonezawa, A.: A Complete Type Inference System for Subtyped Recursive Types. In: Hagiya, M., Mitchell, J.C. (eds.) TACS 1994. LNCS, vol. 789, pp. 667–686. Springer, Heidelberg (1994)

106. Hosobe, H., Miyashita, K., Takahashi, S., Matsuoka, S., Yonezawa, A.: Locally Simultaneous Constraint Satisfaction. In: Borning, A. (ed.) PPCP 1994. LNCS, vol. 874, pp. 51–62. Springer, Heidelberg (1994)

107. Taura, K., Matsuoka, S., Yonezawa, A.: ABCL/f: A Future-Based Polymorphic Typed Concurrent Object-Oriented Language – Its Design and Implementation –. In: Proceedings of the DIMACS workshop on Specification of Parallel Algorithms, May 1994. DIMACS Series in Discrete Mathematics and Theoretical Computer Science, vol. 18, pp. 275–291. Princeton, New Jersey (1994)

108. Yasugi, M., Matsuoka, S., Yonezawa, A.: The Plan-Do Style Compilation Technique for Eager Data Transfer in Thread-Based Execution. In: Proceedings of the IFIP WG10.3 International Conference on Parallel Architectures and Compilation Techniques (PACT 1994), Montréal, Canada, pp. 57–66 (August 1994)

109. Konno, K., Nagatsuka, M., Kobayashi, N., Matsuoka, S., Yonezawa, A.: PARCS: An MPP-Oriented CLP Language. In: Proceedings of the First International Symposium on Parallel Symbolic Computation (PASCO 1994), Linz, Austria, pp. 254–263. World Scientific (September 1994)

110. Kobayashi, N., Yonezawa, A.: Type-Theoretic Foundations for Concurrent Object-Oriented Programming. In: Proceedings of the 9th Annual Conference on Object-Oriented Programming Systems, Languages, and Applications (OOPSLA 1994), Portland, Oregon, pp. 31–45 (October 1994), Also in SIGPLAN Notices 29(10)

111. Takahashi, S., Miyashita, K., Matsuoka, S., Yonezawa, A.: A Framework for Constructing Animations via Declarative Mapping Rules. In: Proceedings of IEEE Symposium on Visual Languages, St. Louis, Missouri, pp. 314–322 (October 1994)

112. Kamada, T., Matsuoka, S., Yonezawa, A.: Efficient Parallel Global Garbage Collection on Massively Paralle Computers. In: Proceedings of the 1994 ACM/IEEE Conference on Supercomputing (Supercomputing 1994), Washington D.C, pp. 79–88 (November 1994)

113. Miyashita, K., Matsuoka, S., Takahashi, S., Yonezawa, A.: Interactive Generation of Graphical User Interfaces by Multiple Visual Examples. In: Proceedings of the 7th ACM Symposium on User Interface Software and Technology 1994 (UIST 1994), Marina del Rey, CA, USA, pp. 85–94 (November 1994)

114. Kamada, T., Matsuoka, S., Yonezawa, A.: An Algorithm for Efficient Global Garbage Collection on Massively Parallel Computers. In: Ito, T. (ed.) TPPP 1994. LNCS, vol. 907, pp. 346–355. Springer, Heidelberg (1995)

115. Kobayashi, N., Yonezawa, A.: Higher-Order Concurrent Linear Logic Programming. In: Ito, T. (ed.) TPPP 1994. LNCS, vol. 907, pp. 137–166. Springer, Heidelberg (1995)

116. Taura, K., Matsuoka, S., Yonezawa, A.: StackThreads: An Abstract Machine for Scheduling Fine-Grain Threads on Stock CPUs. In: Ito, T. (ed.) TPPP 1994. LNCS, vol. 907, pp. 121–136. Springer, Heidelberg (1995)

117. Kobayashi, N., Nakade, M., Yonezawa, A.: Static Analysis of Communication for Asynchronous Concurrent Programming Languages. In: Mycroft, A. (ed.) SAS 1995. LNCS, vol. 983, pp. 225–242. Springer, Heidelberg (1995)

118. Takahashi, S., Matsuoka, S., Miyashita, K., Hosobe, H., Yonezawa, A., Kamada, T.: A Constraint-Based Approach for Visualization and Animation. In: Montanari, U., Rossi, F. (eds.) CP 1995. LNCS, vol. 976, pp. 103–117. Springer, Heidelberg (1995)

119. Masuhara, H., Matsuoka, S., Asai, K., Yonezawa, A.: Compiling Away the Meta-Level in Object-Oriented Concurrent Reflective Languages Using Partial Evaluation. In: Proceedings of the 10th Annual Conference on Object-Oriented Programming Systems, Languages, and Applications (OOPSLA 1995), Austin, Texas, USA, October 1995, pp. 300–315 (1995), Also in SIGPLAN Notices 30(10)

120. Masuhara, H., Matsuoka, S., Asai, K., Yonezawa, A.: Efficient implementation technique for object-oriented concurrent reflective languages using partial evaluation. In: Proceedings of International Workshop on New Models for Software Architecture (IMSA 1995), Tokyo, Japan (October 1995)

121. Kamada, T., Yonezawa, A.: A Debugging Scheme for Fine-Grain Threads on Massively Parallel Processors with a Small Amount of Log Information - Replay and Race Detection. In: Queinnec, C., Halstead Jr., R.H., Ito, T. (eds.) PSLS 1995. LNCS, vol. 1068, pp. 108–127. Springer, Heidelberg (1996)

122. Taura, K., Yonezawa, A.: Schematic: A Concurrent Object-Oriented Extension to Scheme. In: Briot, J.-P., Geib, J.-M. (eds.) OBPDC 1995. LNCS, vol. 1107, pp. 59–82. Springer, Heidelberg (1996)

123. Sato, N., Matsuoka, S., Yonezawa, A.: Hierarchical Collections: An Efficient Scheme to Build an Obeject-Oriented Distributed Class Library for Massively Parallel Computation. In: Futatsugi, K., Matsuoka, S. (eds.) ISOTAS 1996. LNCS, vol. 1049, pp. 96–117. Springer, Heidelberg (1996)

124. Masuhara, H., Matsuoka, S., Yonezawa, A.: Implementing Parallel Language Constructs Using a Reflective Object-Oriented Language. In: Proceedings of Reflection 1996, San Francisco, pp. 79–91 (April 1996)

125. Hosobe, H., Matsuoka, S., Yonezawa, A.: Generalized Local Propagation: A Framework for Solving Constraint Hierarchies. In: Freuder, E.C. (ed.) CP 1996. LNCS, vol. 1118, pp. 237–251. Springer, Heidelberg (1996)

126. Hosoya, H., Kobayashi, N., Yonezawa, A.: Partial Evaluation Scheme for Concurrent Languages and Its Correctness. In: Fraigniaud, P., Mignotte, A., Bougé, L., Robert, Y. (eds.) Euro-Par 1996. LNCS, vol. 1123, pp. 625–632. Springer, Heidelberg (1996)

127. Asai, K., Masuhara, H., Yonezawa, A.: Partial Evaluation of Call-by-Value lambda-Calculus with Side-Effects. In: Proceedings ACM Conference on Partial Evaluation and Semantics-Based Program Manipulation (PEPM 1997), Amsterdam, pp. 12–21 (June 1997)

128. Taura, K., Yonezawa, A.: An Effective Garbage Collection Strategy for Parallel Programming Languages on Large Scale Distributed-Memory Machines. In: Proceedings of ACM SIGPLAN Symposium on Principles and Practice of Parallel Programming (PPoPP 1997), Las Vegas, pp. 264–275 (June 1997)

129. Taura, K., Yonezawa, A.: Fine-grain Multithreading with Minimal Compiler Support - A Cost Effective Approach to Implementing Efficient Multithreading Languages. In: Proceedings of the 1997 ACM SIGPLAN Conference on Programming Language Design and Implementation (PLDI 1997), Las Vegas, pp. 320–333 (June 1997)

130. Sato, N., Matsuoka, S., Jezequel, J.-M., Yonezawa, A.: A Methodology for Specifying Data Distribution using only Standard Object-Oriented Features. In: Proceedings of the 11th ACM International Conference on Supercomputing (ICS 1997), Vienna, pp. 116–123 (July 1997)

131. Sekiguchi, T., Yonezawa, A.: A Calculus with Code Mobility. In: Proceedings of Second IFIP International Conference on Formal Methods for Open Object-based Distributed Systems (FMOODS 1997), Canterbury, UK, pp. 21–36 (July 1997)

132. Oyama, Y., Taura, K., Yonezawa, A.: An Efficient Compilation Framework for Languages Based on a Concurrent Process Calculus. In: Lengauer, C., Griebl, M., Gorlatch, S. (eds.) Euro-Par 1997. LNCS, vol. 1300, pp. 546–553. Springer, Heidelberg (1997)

133. Masuhara, H., Yonezawa, A.: Reasoning-conscious Meta-object Design of a Reflective Concurrent Language. In: Proceedings of International Symposium on Biologically Inspired Computation (IMSA 1997), Tsukuba, Japan, pp. 42–56. ETL/IPA (October 1997)

134. Endo, T., Taura, K., Yonezawa, A.: A Scalable Mark-Sweep Garbage Collector on Large-Scale Shared-Memory Machines. In: Proceedings of ACM/IEEE High Performance Computing and Networking (SC 1997), San Jose, CA, USA (November 1997)

135. Takahashi, T., Ishikawa, Y., Sato, M., Yonezawa, A.: A Compile-Time Meta-Level Architecture Supporting Class Specific Optimization. In: Sun, Z., Reynders, J.V.W., Tholburn, M. (eds.) ISCOPE 1997. LNCS, vol. 1343, pp. 89–96. Springer, Heidelberg (1997)

136. Hosoya, H.: Garbage Collection via Dynamic Type Inference - A Formal Treatment -. In: Leroy, X., Ohori, A. (eds.) TIC 1998. LNCS, vol. 1473, pp. 215–239. Springer, Heidelberg (1998)

137. Masuhara, H., Yonezawa, A.: A Reflective Approach to Support Software Evolution. In: Proceedings of International Workshop on Principles of Software Evolution (IWPSE 1998), Kyoto, Japan, pp. 135–139 (1998)

138. Yamamoto, H., Taura, K.: Comparing Reference Counting and Global Mark-and-Sweep on Parallel Computers. In: O'Hallaron, D.R. (ed.) LCR 1998. LNCS, vol. 1511, pp. 205–218. Springer, Heidelberg (1998)

139. Masuhara, H., Yonezawa, A.: Design and Partial Evaluation of Meta-Objects for a Concurrent Reflective Language. In: Jul, E. (ed.) ECOOP 1998. LNCS, vol. 1445, pp. 418–439. Springer, Heidelberg (1998)

140. Oyama, Y., Taura, K., Yonezawa, A.: An Implementation and Performance Evaluation of Language with Fine-Grain Thread Creation on Shared Memory Parallel Computer. In: Proceedings of 1998 International Conference on Parallel and Distributed Computing and Systems (PDCS 1998), Las Vegas, USA, pp. 672–675 (October 1998)

141. Sugita, Y., Masuhara, H., Harada, K., Yonezawa, A.: On-the-fly Specialization of Reflective Programs Using Dynamic Code Generation Techniques. In: Proceedings of OOPSLA 1998 workshop on Reflective Programming in C++ and Java, Vancouver, Canada (October 1998)

142. Sekiguchi, T., Hansen, K.A.: A Simple Extension of Java Language for Controllable Transparent Migration and Its Portable Implementation. In: Ciancarini, P., Wolf, A.L. (eds.) COORDINATION 1999. LNCS, vol. 1594, pp. 211–226. Springer, Heidelberg (1999)

143. Taura, K., Tabata, K., Yonezawa, A.: StackThreads/MP: Integrating Futures into Calling Standard. In: Proceedings of the Seventh ACM SIGPLAN Symposium on Principles and Practice of Parallel Programming (PPoPP 1999), Atlanta, USA, pp. 60–71 (May 1999)

144. Masuhara, H., Yonezawa, A.: Generating Optimized Residual Code in Run-Time Specialization. In: Technical Report on Partial Evaluation and Program Transformation Day (PE Day 1999), Waseda, Tokyo, Japan, 20 pages (November 1999)

145. Masuhara, H., Yonezawa, A.: An Object-Oriented Concurrent Reflective Language ABCL/R3: Its Meta-level Design and Efficient Implementation Techniques. In: Object-Oriented Parallel and Distributed Programming, Paris, pp. 151–165. HERMES Science Publications (2000)

146. Oyama, Y., Taura, K., Yonezawa, A.: Executing Parallel Programs with Synchronization Bottlenecks Efficiently. In: Proceedings of International Workshop on Parallel and Distributed Computing for Symbolic and Irregular Applications (PDSIA 1999), Sendai, Japan, July 5-7, pp. 182–204. World Scientific (April 2000)

147. Yamauchi, H., Masuhara, H., Hoshina, D., Sekiguchi, T., Yonezawa, A.: Wrapping Class Libraries for Migration-Transparent Resource Access by Using Compile-

Time Reflection. In: Proceedings of Workshop on Reflective Middleware (RM 2000), New York, pp. 19–20 (April 2000)

148. Oyama, Y., Taura, K.: Online Computation of Critical Paths for Multithreaded Languages. In: Rolim, J.D.P. (ed.) IPDPS-WS 2000. LNCS, vol. 1800, pp. 301–313. Springer, Heidelberg (2000)

149. Tanaka, Y., Taura, K., Sato, M.: Performance Evaluation of OpenMP Applications with Nested Parallelism. In: Dwarkadas, S. (ed.) LCR 2000. LNCS, vol. 1915, pp. 100–112. Springer, Heidelberg (2000)

150. Hashimoto, M.: MobileML: A Programming Language for Mobile Computation. In: Porto, A., Roman, G.-C. (eds.) COORDINATION 2000. LNCS, vol. 1906, pp. 198–215. Springer, Heidelberg (2000)

151. Sakamoto, T., Sekiguchi, T.: Bytecode Transformation for Portable Thread Migration in Java. In: Kotz, D., Mattern, F. (eds.) MA 2000, ASA/MA 2000, and ASA 2000. LNCS, vol. 1882, pp. 16–28. Springer, Heidelberg (2000)

152. Hashimoto, M., Yonezawa, A.: A Context-based Higher-Order Typed Language for Mobile Computation. In: Proceedings of the International Workshop on Mobile Objects/Code and Security (MOCS 2000), Tokyo (October 2000)

153. Masuhara, H., Sugita, Y., Yonezawa, A.: Dynamic Compilation of a Reflective Language Using Run-Time Specialization. In: Proceedings of International Symposium on Principles of Software Evolution (ISPSE 2000), Kanazawa, Japan, pp. 125–134 (November 2000)

154. Sekiguchi, T., Sakamoto, T.: Portable Implementation of Continuation Operators in Imperative Languages by Exception Handling. In: Romanovsky, A., Cheraghchi, H.S., Lindskov Knudsen, J., Babu, C. S. (eds.) ECOOP-WS 2000. LNCS, vol. 2022, pp. 217–233. Springer, Heidelberg (2001)

155. Endo, T., Taura, K., Yonezawa, A.: Predicting Scalability of Parallel Garbage Collectors on Shared Memory Multiprocessors. In: Proceedings of the International Parallel and Distributed Processing Symposium (IPDPS 2001), San Francisco, CA, USA (April 2001)

156. Hansen, K.A.: Run-time Bytecode Specialization: A Portable Approach to Generating Optimized Specialized Code. In: Danvy, O., Filinski, A. (eds.) PADO 2001. LNCS, vol. 2053, pp. 138–154. Springer, Heidelberg (2001)

157. Oyama, Y., Taura, K.: Fusion of Concurrent Invocations of Exclusive Methods. In: Malyshkin, V.E. (ed.) PaCT 2001. LNCS, vol. 2127, pp. 293–307. Springer, Heidelberg (2001)

158. Hoshina, D., Sumii, E.: A Typed Process Calculus for Fine-Grained Resource Access Control in Distributed Computation. In: Kobayashi, N., Babu, C. S. (eds.) TACS 2001. LNCS, vol. 2215, pp. 64–81. Springer, Heidelberg (2001)

159. Nguyen, V.H., Taura, K., Yonezawa, A.: Parallelizing Programs Using Access Traces. In: Proceedings of the 6th Workshop on Languages, Compilers, and Runtime Systems for Scalable Computers (LCR 2002), Washington D.C., USA (March 2002)

160. Kaneda, K., Taura, K., Yonezawa, A.: Virtual Private Grid: A Command Shell for Utilizing Hundreds of Machines Efficiently. In: Proceedings of the 2nd IEEE/ACM International Symposium on Cluster Computing and the Grid (CCGRID 2002), Berlin, Germany, pp. 212–219 (May 2002)

161. Affeldt, R., Masuhara, H., Sumii, E., Yonezawa, A.: Supporting Objects in Runtime Bytecode Specialization. In: Proceedings of ACM SIGPLAN ASIAN Symposium on Partial Evaluation and Semantics-Based Program Manipulation (ASIA-PEPM 2002), Aizu, Japan, pp. 50–60 (September 2002)

162. Chen, E.Y., Fuji, H., Yonezawa, A.: Solution Deployment on Multi-Provider Networks. In: OPENSIG 2002 Conference Proceedings, Lexington, USA (October 2002)

163. Oiwa, Y., Sekiguchi, T., Sumii, E., Yonezawa, A.: Fail-Safe ANSI-C Compiler: An Approach to Making C Programs Secure: Progress Report. In: Okada, M., Babu, C. S., Scedrov, A., Tokuda, H. (eds.) ISSS 2002. LNCS, vol. 2609, pp. 133–153. Springer, Heidelberg (2003)

164. Tabuchi, N., Sumii, E., Yonezawa, A.: Regular Expression Types for Strings in a Text Processing Language. In: Proceedings of Workshop on Types in Programming (TIP 2002), Dagstuhl, Germany, vol. 75, 19 pages. Elsevier Science (February 2003)

165. Peschanski, F., Briot, J.-P., Yonezawa, A.: Fine-grained Dynamic Adaptation of Distributed Components. In: Endler, M., Schmidt, D.C. (eds.) Middleware 2003. LNCS, vol. 2672, pp. 123–142. Springer, Heidelberg (2003)

166. Taura, K., Kaneda, K., Endo, T., Yonezawa, A.: Phoenix: a Parallel Programming Model for Accommodating Dynamically Joining/Leaving Resources. In: Proceedings of the ACM SIGPLAN Symposium on Principles and Practice of Parallel Programming (PPoPP 2003), San Diego, pp. 216–229 (June 2003)

167. Chen, E.Y., Yonezawa, A.: Federation of Network Service Providers and Its Applications. In: Proceedings of the Eighth IEEE Symposium on Computers and Communications (ISCC 2003), Kemer-Antalya, Turkey (July 2003)

168. Maeda, T.: Kernel Mode Linux: Toward an Operating System Protected by a Type Theory. In: Saraswat, V.A. (ed.) ASIAN 2003. LNCS, vol. 2896, pp. 3–17. Springer, Heidelberg (2003)

169. Masuyama, T., Peschanski, F., Oyama, Y., Yonezawa, A.: Mobile Scope: A Programming Language with Objective Mobility. In: Proceedings of the 2nd International Workshop on Mobile Distributed Computing (MDC 2004), Tokyo, Japan, pp. 542–547 (March 2004)

170. Endo, T., Kaneda, K., Taura, K., Yonezawa, A.: High Performance LU Factorization for Non-dedicated Clusters. In: Proceedings of the 4th IEEE/ACM International Symposium on Cluster Computing and the Grid (CCGrid 2004), Chicago, USA (April 2004)

171. Kaneda, K., Taura, K., Yonezawa, A.: Routing and Resource Discovery in Phoenix Grid-Enabled Message Passing Library. In: Proceedings of the 4th IEEE/ACM International Symposium on Cluster Computing and the Grid (CCGrid 2004), Chicago, USA (April 2004)

172. Nagata, A., Kobayashi, N.: Region-Based Memory Management for a Dynamically-Typed Language. In: Chin, W.-N. (ed.) APLAS 2004. LNCS, vol. 3302, pp. 229–245. Springer, Heidelberg (2004)

173. Tatsuzawa, H., Masuhara, H., Yonezawa, A.: Aspectual Caml: an Aspect-Oriented Functional Language. In: Proceedings of Foundations of Aspect-Oriented Languages (FOAL), Chicago, USA (March 2005)

174. Oyama, Y., Onoue, K., Yonezawa, A.: Speculative Security Checks in Sandboxing Systems. In: Proceedings of The 1st International Workshop on Security in Systems and Networks (SSN 2005), Denver, USA (April 2005)

175. Maeda, T., Yonezawa, A.: Writing practical memory management code with a strictly typed assembly language. In: Proceedings of the 3rd Workshop on Semantics, Program Analysis, and Computing Environments for Memory Management (SPACE 2006), Charleston, South Carolina, USA (January 2006)

176. Marti, N., Affeldt, R., Yonezawa, A.: Verification of the heap manager of an operating system using separation logic. In: Proceedings of the 3rd Workshop on Semantics, Program Analysis, and Computing Environments for Memory Management (SPACE 2006), Charleston, South Carolina, USA (January 2006)

177. Unno, H., Kobayashi, N., Yonezawa, A.: Combining Type-Based Analysis and Model Checking for Finding Counterexamples against Non-Interference. In: Proceedings of the ACM SIGPLAN Workshop on Programming Languages and Analysis for Security (PLAS 2006), Ottawa, Canada (June 2006)

178. Ragab, K., Oyama, Y., Yonezawa, A.: K-Interleaving Rendezvous Overlay Network Construction Scheme. In: Proceedings of the 5th IEEE/ACIS International Conference on Computer and Information Science and 1st IEEE/ACIS International Workshop on Component-Based Software Engineering, Software Architecture and Reuse (ICIS-COMSAR 2006), Honolulu, Hawaii, USA (July 2006)

179. Marti, N., Affeldt, R.: Formal Verification of the Heap Manager of an Operating System Using Separation Logic. In: Liu, Z., Kleinberg, R.D. (eds.) ICFEM 2006. LNCS, vol. 4260, pp. 400–419. Springer, Heidelberg (2006)

180. Hansen, K.A., Endoh, Y.: A Fine-Grained Join Point Model for More Reusable Aspects. In: Kobayashi, N. (ed.) APLAS 2006. LNCS, vol. 4279, pp. 131–147. Springer, Heidelberg (2006)

181. Onoue, K., Oyama, Y., Yonezawa, A.: A Virtual Machine Migration System Based on a CPU Emulator. In: Proceedings of the 1st International Workshop on Virtualization Technology in Distributed Computing (VTDC 2006), Tampa, Florida, USA (November 2006)

182. Kosakai, T., Maeda, T.: Compiling C Programs into a Strongly Typed Assembly Language. In: Cervesato, I. (ed.) ASIAN 2007. LNCS, vol. 4846, pp. 17–32. Springer, Heidelberg (2007)

183. Onoue, K., Oyama, Y., Yonezawa, A.: Control of system calls from outside of virtual machines. In: Proceedings of the 2008 ACM Symposium on Applied Computing (SAC 2008), Fortaleza, Brazil, pp. 2116–1221 (March 2008)

184. Maeda, T., Yonezawa, A.: Writing an OS Kernel in a Strictly and Statically Typed Language. In: Cortier, V., Kirchner, C., Okada, M., Sakurada, H. (eds.) Formal to Practical Security. LNCS, vol. 5458, pp. 181–197. Springer, Heidelberg (2009)

185. Matsuda, M., Maeda, T., Yonezawa, A.: Towards Design and Implementation of Model Checker for System Software. In: Proceedings of the 1st International Workshop on Software Technologies for Future Dependable Distributed Systems (STFSSD 2009), Tokyo, Japan (January 2009)

186. Dun, N., Taura, K., Yonezawa, A.: GMount: An Ad Hoc and Locality-Aware Distributed File System by Using SSH and FUSE. In: Proceedings of the 9th IEEE/ACM International Symposium on Cluster Computing and the Grid (CC-Grid 2009), Shanghai, China, pp. 188–195 (May 2009)

187. Shimizu, M., Yonezawa, A.: Remote Process Execution and Remote I/O for Heterogeneous Processors in Cluster Systems. In: Proceedings of the 10th IEEE/ACM International Symposium on Cluster, Cloud and Grid Computing (CCGrid 2010), Melbourne, Australia, pp. 145–154 (May 2010)

188. Dun, N., Taura, K., Yonezawa, A.: ParaTrac: A Fine-Grained Profiler for Data-Intensive Workflows. In: Proceedings of the 19th ACM International Symposium on High Performance Distributed Computing (HPDC 2010), Chicago, USA, pp. 37–48 (June 2010)

189. Maeda, T., Yonezawa, A.: Typed Assembly Language for Implementing OS Kernels in SMP/Multi-Core Environments with Interrupts. In: Proceedings of the 5th International Workshop on Systems Software Verification (SSV 2010), Vancouver, Canada (October 2010)

190. Dun, N., Taura, K., Yonezawa, A.: Easy and Instantaneous Processing for Data-Intensive Workflows. In: Proceedings of the 3rd IEEE Workshop on Many-Task Computing on Grids and Supercomputers (MTAGS 2010), New Orleans, USA (November 2010)

191. Sawazaki, J., Maeda, T., Yonezawa, A.: Implementing a Hybrid Virtual Machine Monitor for Flexible and Efficient Security Mechanisms. In: Proceedings of the 16th IEEE Pacific Rim International Symposium on Dependable Computing (PRDC 2010), Tokyo, Japan, pp. 37–46 (December 2010)

192. Maeda, T., Sato, H., Yonezawa, A.: Extended Alias Type System using Separating Implication. In: Proceedings of the 7th ACM SIGPLAN Workshop on Types in Language Design and Implementation (TLDI 2011), Austin, USA, pp. 29–42 (January 2011)

193. Suzuki, T., Pinte, K., Cutsem, T.V., Meuter, W.D., Yonezawa, A.: Programming Language Support for Routing in Pervasive Networks. In: Proceedings of the 8th International IEEE Workshop on Middleware and System Support for Pervasive Computing (PerWare 2011), Austin, USA (March 2011)

Technical Reports

194. Yonezawa, A., Hewitt, C.: Symbolic Evaluation Using Conceptual Representations for Programs with Side-Effects. Technical Report 399, MIT Artificial Intelligence Laboratory, AI-Memo (December 1976)

195. Yonezawa, A.: Specification and Verification Techniques for Parallel Programs Based on Message Passing Semantics. Technical Report TR-191, MIT Laboratory for Computer Science, Ph. D Thesis (December 1977)

196. Yonezawa, A., Matsuda, H., Shibayama, E.: An Object Oriented Approach for Concurrent Programming. Technical Report C-63, Department of Information Science, Tokyo Institute of Technology (1984)

197. Yonezawa, A., Matsuda, H., Shibayama, E.: Discrete Event Simulation Based on an Object-Oriented Parallel Computation Model. Technical Report C-64, Department of Information Science, Tokyo Institute of Technology (1984)

198. Ichisugi, Y., Yonezawa, A.: Distributed Garbage Collection Using Group Reference Counting. Technical Report is-90-014, The University of Tokyo, Faculty of Science, Department of Information Science (1990)

199. Matsuoka, S., Wakita, K., Yonezawa, A.: Synchronization Constraints With Inheritance: What Is Not Possible - So What Is? Technical Report is-90-010, The University of Tokyo, Faculty of Science, Department of Information Science (1990)

200. Kobayashi, N., Yonezawa, A.: Asynchronous Communication Model Based on Linear Logic. Technical Report TR92-05, The University of Tokyo, Faculty of Science, Department of Information Science (1992)

201. Yasugi, M., Yonezawa, A.: An Object-Oriented Parallel Algorithm for the Newtonian N-Body Problem. Technical Report TR92-06, The University of Tokyo, Faculty of Science, Department of Information Science (1992)

202. Kobayashi, N., Yonezawa, A.: Logical, Testing, and Observation Equivalence for Processes in a Linear Logic Programming. Technical Report TR93-04, The University of Tokyo, Faculty of Science, Department of Information Science (1993)

203. Sugimoto, T., Yonezawa, A.: A preference-based theory of intention. Technical Report TR94-04, The University of Tokyo, Faculty of Science, Department of Information Science (1993)

204. Asai, K., Matsuoka, S., Yonezawa, A.: Roles of a Partial Evaluator for the Reflective Language Black. Technical Report TR94-11, The University of Tokyo, Faculty of Science, Department of Information Science (May 1994)

205. Kobayashi, N., Nakade, M., Yonezawa, A.: Static Analysis on Communication for Asynchronous Concurrent Programming Languages. Technical Report TR95-04, The University of Tokyo, Faculty of Science, Department of Information Science (April 1995)

206. Asai, K., Masuhara, H., Matsuoka, S., Yonezawa, A.: Partial Evaluator as a Compiler for Reflective Languages. Technical Report TR95-10, The University of Tokyo, Faculty of Science, Department of Information Science (December 1995)

207. Taura, K., Yonezawa, A.: Schematic: A Concurrent Object-Oriented Extension to Scheme. Technical Report TR95-11, The University of Tokyo, Faculty of Science, Department of Information Science (December 1995)

208. Asai, K., Masuhara, H., Yonezawa, A.: Partial Evaluation of Call-by-value lambda-calculus with Side-effects. Technical Report TR96-04, The University of Tokyo, Faculty of Science, Department of Information Science (November 1996)

209. Oyama, Y., Taura, K., Yonezawa, A.: An Efficient Compilation Framework for Languages Based on a Concurrent Process Calculus. Technical Report TR97-07, The University of Tokyo, Faculty of Science, Department of Information Science (July 1997)

Others

210. Agha, G., Yonezawa, A., Wegner, P., Abramsky, S.: OOPSLA/ECOOP 1990 Report, Panel: Foundations of Object-Based Concurrent Programming. In: Proceedings of the European Conference on Object-Oriented Programming Addendum, Ottawa, Canada, pp. 9–14 (1990)

211. Agha, G., Abramsky, S., Hewitt, C., Milner, R., Wegner, P., Yonezawa, A.: Foundations of Concurrent Object-Oriented Programming (Panel). In: Proceedings of OOPSLA/ECOOP 1990, Ottawa, Canada, p. 100 (October 1990), Also in SIGPLAN Notices 25(10)

212. Agha, G., Yonezawa, A., Wegner, P., Abramski, S.: OOPSLA panel on object-based concurrent programming. OOPS Messenger 2(2), 3–15 (1991)

213. Halstead Jr., R.H., Chikayama, T., Gabriel, R.P., Waltz, D.L., Yonezawa, A.: Applications for Parallel Symbolic Computation (panel). In: Halstead Jr., R.H., Ito, T. (eds.) US/Japan WS 1992. LNCS, vol. 748, p. 417. Springer, Heidelberg (1993)

214. Wada, E., Yonezawa, A.: Obituary: Professor Nobuo Yoneda (28 March 1930-22 April 1996). Science of Computer Programming 27(3), 215–216 (1996)

List of PhDs Supervised

Ichiro Osawa, *Fundamental Research on Natural Language Dialogue Systems*, 1989.

Takuo Watanabe, *Object-Oriented Models for Reflection in Concurrent Systems*, 1991.

Etsuya Shibayama, *An Object-Based Approach to Modeling Concurrent Systems*, 1991.

Yuuji Ichisugi, *A Reflective Object-Oriented Concurrent Language for Distributed Environments*, 1993.

Ken Satoh, *A Logical Formalization of Preference-based Reasoning by Interpretation Ordering*, 1993.

Satoshi Matsuoka, *Language Features for Extensibility and Re-use in Concurrent Object-Oriented Languages*, 1993.

Masahiro Yasugi, *A Concurrent Object-Oriented Programming Language System for Highly Parallel Data-Driven Computers and its Applications*, 1994.

Takeshi Fuchi, *New Methods to Analyze Japanese Morphemes and Dependency Structure AND Formalization of Rules to Derive Implied Meanings*, 1995.

Toru Sugimoto, *Formal Models of Dialogue Participants*, 1995.

Jacques Garrigue, *Label-Selective Lambda-Calculi and Transformation Calculi*, 1995.

Jeff McAffer, *A Meta-Level Architecture for Prototyping Object Systems*, 1995.

Shigeru Chiba, *A Study of Compile-Time Metaobject Protocol*, 1996.
(supervised with Prof. T. Masuda and Prof. G. Kiczales)

Naoki Kobayashi, *Concurrent Linear Logic Programming*, 1996.

Takashi Miyata, *A Study on Inference Control in Natural Language Processing*, 1996.

Kenichi Asai, *The Reflective Language Black*, 1997.

Naohito Sato, *Modularity and Composability in an Object-Oriented Library Framework for Parallel and Distributed Computation*, 1997.

Kenjiro Taura, *Efficient and Reusable Implementation of Fine-Grain Multithreading and Garbage Collection on Distributed-Memory Parallel Computers*, 1997.

Ken Wakita, *Continuations and Concurrent Transactions: Extensible Language Constructs for Concurrent Computing*, 1997.
(supervised with Prof. T. Masuda)

Hiroshi Hosobe, *Theoretical Properties and Efficient Satisfaction of Hierarchical Constraint Systems*, 1998.

Sachiko Kawachiya, *Analyses and Reduction of Operational Overhead in Computer-Assisted Drawing*, 1998.

Hidehiko Masuhara, *Architecture Design and Compilation Techniques Using Partial Evaluation in Reflective Concurrent Object-Oriented Languages*, 1999.

Tatsurou Sekiguchi, *A Study on Mobile Language Systems*, 1999.

Atsushi Igarashi, *Formalizing Advanced Class Mechanisms*, 2000.
(supervised with Prof. N. Kobayashi and Prof. B. C. Pierce)

Kentaro Torisawa, *Towards Practical HPSG Parsing*, 2000.
(supervised with Prof. J. Tsujii)

Yoshihiro Oyama, *Achieving High Performance for Parallel Programs that Contain Unscalable Modules*, 2001.

Haruo Hosoya, *Regular Expression Types for XML*, 2001.

Toshio Endo, *Scalable Dynamic Memory Management Module on Shared Memory Multiprocessors*, 2001.

Reynald Affeldt, *Verification of Concurrent Programs Using Proof Assistants*, 2004.

Eijiro Sumii, *Theories of Information Hiding in Lambda-Calculus: Logical Relations and Bisimulations for Encryption and Type Abstraction*, 2004.
(supervised with Prof. N. Kobayashi and Prof. B. C. Pierce)

Yutaka Oiwa, *Implementation of a Fail-Safe ANSI C Compiler*, 2005.

Eric Y. Chen, *Defending against Distributed Denial of Service Attacks*, 2005.

Toshiyuki Maeda, *Writing an Operating System with a Strictly Typed Assembly Language*, 2006.

Kenji Kaneda, *Middleware Systems for Enabling Users to Adapt to Dynamic Changes in Execution Environments*, 2006.

Kohei Suenaga, *Type Systems for Formal Verification of Concurrent Programs*, 2008.

Marti Nicolas, *Formal Verification of Low-Level Software*, 2008.

Hiroshi Unno, *Dependent Type Inference for Program Verification*, 2009.

Koichi Onoue, *VMM-based Systems for Enhancing Application Security*, 2010.

Masaaki Shimizu, *Operating System Structures for High Performance Computer Clusters*, 2011.

Dun Nan, *Rapidly Deployable, Scalable, and High-Performance Distributed File System for Data-Intensive Distributed Computing*, 2011.

Table of Contents

My Early Education and Concurrent Objects

Akinori Yonezawa

Riken Advanced Institute of Computational Science
7-1-26 Minatominami-cho Chuo-ku Kobe City, Japan, 750-0047
yonezawa@riken.jp

Forewords

Before attaining the mandatory retirement age of the University of Tokyo, I left the university and moved to the Riken Advanced Institute of Computational Science (AICS) in the spring of 2011. AICS is located in Kobe, which is 600 km to the west of Tokyo. It is the second city outside of Tokyo in which I have lived, with the exception of Boston in the USA. In addition to the location of AICS being new to me, the institute's missions for which I am partially responsible are also new. In May 2012, I had the honor of being a part of an international workshop that was organized by many of my ex-students and overseas-based colleagues to celebrate my 65th birthday.

Gul Agha suggested that I write this essay (in his words, it would be an account of my intellectual journey), which has turned out to be one of the most unique experiences I have had in my writing career, as I am the subject of this manuscript. I am very fortunate to have the opportunity to write such an essay. I would therefore like to thank Gul and the other editors of this volume, including the editor of Springer Verlag LNCS. An interesting chain of events have led me to publish this kind of essay in a Springer LNCS volume, as I have edited more than seven volumes in the series.

With their permission, I have included in this manuscript some nonacademic and personal experiences knowing that people tend to be quite receptive of a university professor's discourse in his final lecture. Actually, Professor Sigeiti Moriguti at the University of Tokyo, who is one of my mentors, gave a series of four talks (usually it is just one talk) at his final lecture, which I was unable to attend as I was in Cambridge, Mass. that time.

This essay has two parts. The first one sketches a personal trail of my intellectual growth. The second part summarizes my research on concurrent objects. It also contains an account of the development of my idea of mobile concurrent objects.

Part I My Early Education

1   Before Reaching University

Family Traditions
I was born in Japan in June, 1947. My family tradition was somewhat scholastic, and, consequently, I was always encouraged to study. Many of my ancestors also loved

G. Agha et al. (Eds.): Yonezawa Festschrift, LNCS 8665, pp. 1–17, 2014.

studying, and both of my grandfathers graduated from the University of Tokyo nearly one hundred years ago, one with a doctoral degree in medicine, and the other with a doctoral degree in engineering. My father also graduated from the University of Tokyo with a doctoral degree in engineering. My mother was literalistic and she often talked to me about her compositions in a Japanese short poetic form of 32 characters called "tan-ka."

As a child, I was always very talkative, with which my mother was extremely displeased. Once she scolded me, saying "Akinori, men do not talk much, and you are like a girl talking all the time." I believe, since that day, I have become less chatty and have retreated into being a reticent person, communicating in a cryptic manner. Eventually, I began to develop an aversion toward giving nontechnical talks and speeches, including public greeting speeches, which I am occasionally obliged to give. Actually, I am very clumsy when it comes to reading things aloud and composing sentences in speeches (and perhaps in writing as well) in both Japanese and English. Nevertheless, I have been always very interested in the literary field and linguistic phenomena, and this has reflected in my field of research, i.e., programming languages. It may be that my complex/mixed feelings toward speech and language in general emanated from my musing of my mother's words.

Travelling

My intellectual upbringing is something that is inalienable from my fondness of traveling. From the nascent stages of my life, I have been encouraged to travel. I recall that at around age 4, after having lunch one day, my paternal grandfather sat me down on his lap while squatting on a tatami-mattress in a room and said to me "Akinori, when you grow up, you should go to see other countries as I did." He also told me about his three lifetime goals that were planned and achieved. One of the goals was to study abroad. Actually, he stayed in London for more than three years early in the last century and studied mining. Another goal was to obtain a doctoral degree. I do not remember what I felt when my grandfather told me his story and how much I was directly influenced by his narrative, but it does appear that his words more or less determined the course of life.

My parents also encouraged me to travel, and they especially pressed me to travel alone. During my days of elementary school, almost every year my mother took my sister and I to Kyoto, where her parents had survived the war and were living simple lifestyles. Traveling by special express trains between Tokyo and Kyoto was a wonderful event and excited me a great deal. In those days, special express trains were steam-powered, which later became electric-powered.

When in secondary school, my solo travels included a trip to Kyoto and a one-week trip to the Tohoku area. I even visited a small town in Aomori prefecture, in which my grandfather was raised before he left for Tokyo to pursue higher education over a hundred years ago. Traveling by myself helped me feel liberated and matured.

Middle and High School Days (Age 12 to Age 17)

The Azabu middle and high school, in which I was enrolled, was somewhat unique with regards to teaching. The rules were not very stringent. A half of the teachers were very old (and often funny), and the other half were not professional teachers, but mostly graduate students pursuing doctoral courses in well-known universities, who were hired on an annual basis. The school's atmosphere was very relaxed. Some students worked diligently, while some partook only in sports or hobbies. Of course, the school did not use any of the government-issued textbooks. The teachers had their own styles of teaching, especially young teachers from graduate schools, who taught us the content that they believed was crucial and essential, and which is often beyond students' imagination at that age.

At an early stage in middle school, I subscribed to a popular science magazine called Kagaku Asahi, which had many science-related pictures, especially about astronomy. My interests in science piqued on account of this magazine. As mentioned earlier, my mother was a literary person, but while raising me, she did her best to avert me from following the same path. This magazine was not given to me by my mother, but I picked it up myself in a book store on the way back home. In a sense, she was successful in directing me to science and technology. The photos that impacted me the most in the magazine volumes were those of the far side of the moon. In the year 1959, these photos were taken and sent to the earth by a Russian space rocket called Luna 3, which traveled in an orbit to the other side of the moon and returned to the earth. At the time, the success of Luna 3 was another severe blow to US science and technology, following on the heels of the success of the satellite Sputnik in the year 1957, where the first artificial satellite in human history was launched by Russia. With this mental impression of Russian superiority, I chose Russian as my second foreign language in the university.

The classes that interested me throughout middle and high schools were those of Japanese classics, Chinese classics (Kanbun), Japanese history, English, Physics, and Mathematics. There were good teachers in Modern Japanese, but I never quite liked it. Chemistry teachers were uninterested in teaching, and practically all of the students lost interest in Chemistry. In contrast, the biology and mathematics teachers were really good. One biology teacher used to be a Professor of Biology at Taipei University before the war. His classes were always clear and steeped with intense biological knowledge. He talked about the functions of DNA and RNA, perhaps including the new scientific findings of the 50's.

A mathematics teacher, who was a graduate student at the University of Tokyo, and who was writing a PhD thesis in differential geometry, taught us vectors, matrices, and determinants, introducing the axioms of vector space and linear algebra. His class was enlightening to me, and it introduced me to axiomatic approaches of modern mathematics. Another mathematics teacher selected several smart students and gave them a series of lectures on the introduction of "functional analysis or complex analysis." I was not among the selected students initially, but I asked the teacher to permit me to join the class. There was a rumor that the teacher used to be a doctoral student in mathematics at the University of Tokyo, and that he ended his university studies after starting his new life as a teacher of mathematics in our high school. The goal of his lecture series was to prove the Cauchy-Riemann Theorem in complex analysis by the end of the series, which is to say that the integral of any "regular" (complex) function on a closed path on a complex plane is always equal to zero. I managed (with some difficulty) to follow his lectures to the end and learned that there is such a notion as Laurent expansion. About a year earlier, we had just learnt the Taylor expansion. I was quite impressed that the Laurent expansion contained the terms of negative powers of the variable, just as a Taylor expansion has only terms of positive powers of the variable. One of the students who followed the entire lecture series eventually became a professional mathematician after entering the graduate course of mathematics at the University of Tokyo. He was indeed much smarter than me in mathematics.

2   Undergraduate School in Japan (1966-1970)

Freshman and Sophomore Days – Chomsky and Mathematics (1966-1968)

In the spring of 1966, I was admitted to the University of Tokyo as a student of Science Category I, and while on the Komaba campus, I was truly liberated from the somewhat tedious high school studies in preparation for the university entrance examination. The first two years at the university were devoted mainly to general liberal arts education. The students of Science Category I were supposed to enter either the science (including mathematics) departments or engineering departments in the remaining two years, and the departments were located on a different campus called Hong Campus.

My second foreign language, Russian, was taught as a part of liberal arts education. While I like languages in general, I am not as good at learning them, including my mother tongue and English. Russian was therefore not an exception, but I was intrigued by the Russian (Greek borrowed) alphabet and its grammatical structures. Even after a two-year period of learning Russian, my command of the language was limited, and it was really difficult to prepare for the graduate school entrance examination, which at that time still required reading and writing competence of a foreign language besides English.

The Russian class was not of much practical benefit to me, but one experience has had a life-long impact upon me. I was introduced to the work of Noam Chomsky. One day in Russian class, the lecturer (Mr. Kurihara) mentioned the name of N. Chomsky when explaining Russian grammatical structures. Also, he mentioned "generative grammars." I was very much intrigued by the term "generative grammars." After the class ended, I followed him to his office and asked him for some more explanation of the term "generative grammars." He gave me reprints of his recent papers on an account of Russian grammar or morphological analysis in terms of generative grammars, and he also spoke a bit about "Syntactic Structures," which is the book form of N. Chomsky's Ph.D. thesis. Immediately after the conversation with Kurihara-sensei, I went to the book store called Maruzen, which was the largest seller of foreign books in Tokyo. I was very lucky to find the book, and I bought it right away. Of course, I began to read it the very next day. As far as I remember, what astonished me the most about "Syntactic Structures" was not its contents, but rather the clarity of the language used and the manner in which Chomsky wrote the book.

One of the marvelous things in the education at the Komaba campus was that they offered many special lecture/seminar series, where for each course, a maximum of 10 to 15 students were allowed to participate, and the advanced topics were taught by the professors, many of whom were from the Hongo Campus. The lecture/seminar series that I attended/participated in during the first three terms (18 months in total) were Advanced Lecture on Banach Space, Advanced Lecture on General Topology, Lecture on Molecular Orbital Methods, Reading of Watson's Molecular Biology of the Genes (1st Edition), and Introduction to Computer Architectures and Machine Languages. Actually, I did not participate in the reading of Watson's book as I drew a losing ticket in the lottery held to select the students who could take part. Had I won the lottery, my academic and research interests would, no doubt, have been different. Here I should add that in addition to pure educational motivations, many departments on the Hongo Campus wanted to attract good, motivated students (or to have imprinting of their disciplines on the students).

By the end of the third term, all sophomore students had to decide the department into which they wished to go for their junior and senior years. My initial wish was the pure mathematics department in the School of Science, after which I changed to the applied mathematics department in the School of Engineering. When I talked to my father about my first choice during the first bidding, he said to me, "Akinori, do you have mathematical talent?" His question reminded me of a small episode I witnessed in a class of the Advanced lecture on Banach Space. One of the classmates had pointed out an error in the proof of the Hahn-Banach Theorem, which was given by the lecturer. The student also appeared to have suggested the correction, and, with a perplexed expression, the lecturer appealed to us to pardon his error. Yes, there were many students who were smarter and more talented than I was. This episode brought me a sense of realization that may have saved my life.

Junior and Senior Days in University – Campus Strike and Travelling in Russia
My new student life in the Department of Applied Mathematics began on the Hongo Campus in April, 1968. The courses I took on the Hongo Campus included Automata & Computation Theory (by Prof. Eiiti Wada), Information Theory (by Prof. Shun ichi Amari), Numerical Analysis (by Prof. Sigeiti Moriguti), and Linear Programming (by Prof. Iri). I was deeply interested in those courses, and their lecturers were excellent. Among them, Amari's lecture on information theory was the one that I remember most clearly. His lecture started with a statement "Information is a reduction of ambiguity. The information carried by a message is the difference between the degree of ambiguity before and after the arrival of the message."

There was also a mandatory seminar where each student (about 15 students in total) was supposed to read and present a technical paper. Papers were assigned to students by teachers. Prof. Iri gave me an early paper written by a Russian linguist S.K. Shaumyan, who later became one of the authorities of Russian grammar with his Adaptive Grammar Theory, which is an opponent of Chomsky's generative grammar. Naturally, the paper was written in Russian. While I hesitated to accept Iri-sensei's assignment, he insisted, saying "You took Russian on the Komaba campus, so I will give you two weeks for reading." I presented what I had understood from those two weeks. From my recollection, Iri-sensei did not make many comments regarding my presentation.

Before the end of the first term (summer 1968), a radical student group blocked the access to the university's medical school using barricades. This marked the beginning of a university-wide student strike, which was significantly influenced by the late 60's global student movements including the Paris Quartier Latin demonstrations and anti-Vietnam War campaigns in the United States. Several months later, the School of Engineering was blocked too. For the next six months, there were no classes. At the time, I was a moderately radical student and an active participant in student demonstrations on the campus, but it never went outside the campus. One of the classmates was arrested and jailed during the final resistance against the police, who invaded the campus and removed the students who had fortified the university's monumental auditorium (Yasuda Kohdo) building. Some twenty years later, I found him teaching in a small university in the southern area of Japan. In my mind, I had felt a certain sense of remorse for a long period.

For about three weeks during the summer of 1968, I traveled within Russia by myself. This was my first trip outside of Japan. I implored my father for some money for the trip, and he gave it to me. Starting at the port of Yokohama, the ship sailed to the Russian port city of Nakhodka, after which I moved to Khabarovsk by train, and then flew to Moscow. I spent several days in Moscow, sightseeing popular places, and I also visited the building of the Moscow State University without knowing anybody there. After leaving Moscow, I flew to Leningrad (now called Sankt Petersburg) and spend three days there. I traveled aboard a very advanced Russian jet plane, Ilushin 62. At Hermitage Palace, I was pleasantly surprised to be able to be almost within a touching distance of paintings and designs by da Vince and Raphael without being intervened by the museum guards. My journey continued south when I flew to Tashkent, the capital of Uzbekistan, and then to Samarkand, an old town and the capital of the Timour Empire of the 14th century. The ruins of the Gur-Imir Mausoleum were extremely beautiful. At the airport in Tashkent, I met a professor from the Department of Applied Physics at my university. He was among a group of researchers on a tour after an International Conference on Semi-conductors held in Moscow a few days earlier. He kindly introduced me to Prof. Bardeen, one of the three cowinners of the Nobel Prize for "transistors." I shook hands with him and exhanged a few words. The event lasted just 15 seconds. Afterwards, the professor from my university confessed to me that he had felt nervous while traveling with Prof. Bardeen.

Before graduating from the university, students have to write a senior thesis. All students were supposed to choose a professor to supervise their theses. Without any second thought, I chose Prof. Amari on account of the clarity of his lecture. The period allocated for the writing of the senior thesis was about four months. We were not required to make any new findings or help conducting the research work being done by professors. Prof. Amari simply gave me two papers and told me to read and think. The two papers were "Computation In the Presence of Noise" (1958) by Peter Elias, and "Probabilistic logics and the synthesis of reliable organisms from unreliable components" (1956) by von Neumann. (I subsequently met Peter Elias at the beginning of my graduate studies at MIT). As expected, I did not come up with anything new, but I wrote a survey paper in English as my thesis after three months of reading related literatures.

3   Graduate School in Japan (1970-1973)

Master Course Days (1970-1972) – ALOGOL N, McCarthy, and Gentzen –

In the of Applied Mathematics, students were strongly encouraged to choose, as their supervisor,   a professor who was different from their supervisor for the senior thesis. On the basis of my grades in the graduate school entrance examination as well as my expressed preference, I was admitted to Professor Moriguti's group. While he was a senior faculty member, he was very active in mathematical programming and numerical analysis. Because I was interested in programming languages, Prof. E. Wada, who was an associated professor in Prof. Moriti's group, became my de facto advisor. He was working on programming languages and compilers. At that time, Prof. Wada was actively designing an extensible programming language called ALGOL N. ALGOL was one of the candidates being considered to replace ALGOL 60. Although it failed in this regard, it had many interesting features of extensibility. The idea was to have a core language that can be extended to become different kinds of languages such Fortran, Cobol, or PL/I. ALGOL N's extensible features allowed extensions of both the syntax and semantics. Under the supervision of Prof. Wada, two of the second year master students were designing and implementing an ALGOL N compiler. I was assigned to work together with them in the writing of many subroutines for the compiler implementation, and, consequently, I learned a lot of compiler writing.

During my two years as a Master's student, several great pioneering computer scientists visited Tokyo. They were John McCarthy, Patrick Winston, Andre Ershov, Rod Burstall, among others. Brief conversations with them gave me important information and greatly influenced me in various ways. McCarthy gave a talk including an overview of the research being carried out at the Stanford Artificial Intelligence Lab. He also showed us a film. It showed the scenes of a robot's hand solving an "Instant Insanity Puzzle." Solutions were generated by a theorem prover based on J.A. Robinson's resolution principle. A couple of days after McCarthy's talk, the professors hosting him went to the Tokyo airport to see him off. While I cannot recollect the reason, I did accompany the professors to the airport. At the airport, I saw John walking alone in a corridor. I walked up to him and spoke with him. I told him that I was planning to implement an automatic theorem prover for my master's study and asked him for his thoughts over it. His immediate response was to ask me the reason for which I was going to implement the theorem prover. In response, I mumbled something and could not give a clear reply, so I ended the conversation.

On another occasion, Electro-Technical Laboratory (belonging to Japanese MITI) invited several well-known AI researchers from abroad. Rod Burstall from Edinburgh gave a talk in a Tokyo hotel. While introducing the AI Lab at Edinburgh University, he explained a formulation of robot movement planning in terms of modal logic. However, I did not comprehend it entirely at that time. After he left Japan, I wrote to him requesting the additional details of his modal logic formulation. He was a very kind and sincere person, and several weeks later, he sent me a two page hand-typed letter with his explanations. The letter also said that I should read a book "An Introduction to Modal Logic" by M.J. Cresswell and G.E. Hughes. I read Cresswell's book and was very impressed by the semantics of modal logic based on the possible world model, which was first invented by Saul Kripke. Later, I learned that Kripke had published his possible world model at the age of 15. When I was at MIT as a graduate student, the Boston University Logic Colloquium invited him as a speaker, and I attended the lecture of this genius. The audiences were unexpectedly small in number, and his talk was not very interesting.

Theorem Prover and Herbrand's Decidable Case

Late in the spring of 1971, the ALGOL N compiler project ended. It was time to think about what should be the focus of my master's thesis. There was not much research on ALGOL N compiler to be carried out, and no suggestions were made by either Prof. Moriguti or Prof. Wada regarding my thesis research topic. Early in the spring of 1971, Professor T. Simauti (Rikkyo University), who was the main designer of ALGOL N and an accomplished logician, gave a series of four tutorial seminars in the office of Prof. Wada. This series was given at the request of Prof. Wada, who wanted to know the differences between classical logic and intuitionistic logic (and constructive logic). The master's students (including me) who had been involved in the ALGOL N compiler project attended the seminars. Prof. Simauti presented G. Gentzen's sequent calculus logics (LK ad LJ), the formalism of which clearly and elegantly distinguished between classical and intuitionistic logics. In this seminar, I learned Gentzen's Hauptsatz (the principal theorem), which guarantees that any provable first order logical formula can be proven without using modus ponens. In my opinion, this theorem appeared to be very profound, and the actual proof given by Genzten was very interesting. Because Simauti had devised an automatic theorem prover using Genzten style sequent calculus, he did not forget to explain his theorem prover. Because I had maintained my interest in automatic theorem proving, these seminars by Simauti led me to follow his line of study.

The entire summer of 1971 was filled with struggles and hardships. I was attempting to identify a new material for my thesis, and the implementation of Simauti's old ideas on a new and faster computer was not sufficient. I juggled and played around with various formal proofs and formulas in the sequent calculus. I read articles related to proof strategies that had been invented for theorem proving based on Robinson's resolution principle. By the end of August 1971, I had found that a class of first order formulas is decidable when proving them. In general, it was known that the proof procedures of the first order predicate calculus are semi-decidable, in that any true formula can be proven in a finite step, but some false formulas can be proven to be false in a finite step, while some cannot be proven to be false (in a finite step). In the class of formulas that I identified, all of the formulas could be proven to be either true or false. Using this discovery, I planned to implement an automatic theorem prover which first recognizes decidable cases of logical input formulas (to be proved), and treats decidable formulas separately from general formulas. After the summer of

1971, I visited Prof. Simauti's office and explained to him my plan for implementing a theorem prover as well as my proof of decidability of the formula class that I had found. Upon approval by Simauti of both my implementation and proof, I began   the implementation of the theorem prover.

At the time, Prof. Morituti's group did not have a suitable computer available for implementing an automatic theorem. The university computer center did have a large and fast machine, but it served only as a number cruncher, and not for system implementation. The two professors managed to find a Toshiba machine called TOSBAC 3400, which had a 32K word core memory and could be programmed in an assembly languages, Fortran and Cobol. The computer was owned by the library of the Tokyo Women's Christian University. For the next several months, I often visited the campus of the Women's University. I had no choice but to use assembly language to implement the theorem prover. I wrote I/O routines in Fortran as I did not fully understand the section of I/O in the assembly language manual. In the end, the program that I wrote was assembly code with more than 3000 lines.

While debugging my code, I tried to identify other decidable classes of logical formulas in order to incorporate other cases in my theorem provers. I searched old articles and found the book "Solvable Cases of Decision Problems"

(by W. Ackermann, 1954). I was unable to find the book in the university, so I ordered it from the Maruzen Book Store. They said that it would take a couple of months for me to obtain a copy of the book. Indeed, it arrived in December 1971, which was less than two months before the deadline of thesis. I skimmed through the book quickly, and was both surprised and disappointed to see that the class of decidable formulas was mentioned in the book. It had been discovered about 40 years earlier by Jacques Herbrand, who was a great logician and had died at a young age in the Alps. In addition to the mathematical logic community, he is well known for the term Herbrand Universe in the logic programming community. At a later date, in the winter of 1973, I found a biography (with an elegant cover) of Jacques Herbrand at the Crimson Book Store in a corner of Harvard Square. I bought it on the spot, paying a price which at the time was prohibitively expensive for a graduate student with an research assistantship.

Therefore, my discovery of the decidable class was in fact not new. I told my disappointing story to Prof. Simauti, adding that my proof was simpler than that of Herbrand's. He said that it was allowed for a master's thesis, as Herbrand is a great logician. During my thesis defense, I told the master thesis committee that Prof. Simauti had assured me that my discovery and theorem prover implementation were definitely worthy of a master degree. However, I was entirely aware that with my master thesis work, I had not answered the question that I was asked by John McCarthy at the airport. I was also convinced that automatic theorem proving may be useful for local or short reasoning, but it probably would not be effective for general AI problems.

Doctor Course Days in Japan – Winograd's SHRDLU and MicroPlanner –

Without a future insight, I entered the doctoral course in the Department of Applied Mathematics Department at the University of Tokyo and remained a part of the group led by Prof. Moriguti and Prof. Wada. The English version of my master's thesis contained material that could be published in a domestic computer science journal. I, therefore, submitted a draft (written in Japanese), and it was soon accepted and published in the fall of 1972. While writing the paper, I did not follow the line of research on automatic theorem proving. But the experience gained during my master work was very important for my future research. For example, when I was (with Naoki Kobayashi) attempting to present the semantics of the core of ABCL (my concurrent object-oriented language) in terms of Linear Logic, my understanding of Gentzen's sequent calculi (LK and LJ) helped me significantly as Liner logic is formulated as a sequent calculus. Also, my pessimistic view on the automatic theorem proving led me to Minsky's (as opposed to McCarthy's) approach to the representation of human intelligence in computers.

In early 1973, Pattick Winston from MIT's AI Lab was invited to give a series of talks hosted by Electro-Technical Laboratory. Winston gave a very insightful lecture series on his lab's research activities, focusing mainly on Terry Winograd's natural language understanding system called "SHRDLU," which was a significant landmark in early AI research. During his explanation of how English commands to a robot were translated into programs for execution by the robot, he mentioned Carl Hewitt's Micro-Planner Language. In Winston's account, (micro-) Planner is a language that describes procedural interpretations of logical formulas. I was very impressed, and I began to read about the Planner language of Carl Hewitt, who subsequently became my advisor at the MIT graduate school and my eventual boss at the Laboratory for Computer Science and Artificial Intelligence Laboratory, MIT.

I had no other choice but to go abroad for studies. I quickly prepared myself for this impending change, and applied to the doctoral courses of six graduate schools in the United States. I also obtained a nine-month scholarship from the Japan Society for the Promotion of Science (JSPS). The University of California (Berkeley campus), Cornell University, University of Illinois, and MIT all sent me acceptance letters by the beginning of April 1973. Naturally, I chose to go to MIT.

Part II Concurrent Objects[1]

In the summer of 1973, I spent six weeks at the University of Texas at Austin in preparation for my graduate studies in the States, which was a part of the support from the JSPS. In September, I joined the EECS department of MIT as a graduate student. During the fall and spring terms, I took courses and seminars by Albert Meyer, Patrick Winston, Carl Hewitt, Marvin Minsky, Barbara Liskov, Vaughn Pratt among others. The seminars by Carl Hewtt and Barbara Liskov were most exciting to me. At the time, Carl had begun to develop his idea of Actors[9]. Barbara had also started to develop her idea of data abstractions based on her language CLU[11]. By the end of the 1974 spring term, I had managed to pass the first stage of the qualifying examination. Almost immediately after the ending of the term, I took an inexpensive flight to

[1] Part II is an extended revision of my paper "Early Concurrent/Mobile Objects." In Proc. 2006 ECOOP Nantes, pp198-202, Springer LNCS No.4067, 2006.

Madrid, which marked the starting point of my nine-week European back-packer tour. In September 1974, I joined Carl Hewitt's group, and he became my academic advisor. He also hired me as one of his research assistants.

1 Some History and Motivations

In the early 70's (it may have been in the second half of 1973), research ideas were conceived in the group led by Carl Hewitt who was a member of the AI Lab and the Laboratory for Computer Science. Carl and his group member were interested in

–finding a universal model for *concurrent* computation, and

–the abstraction and simulation of activities for almost all entities which interact with each other and are able to move around in physical spaces.

The entire research group was convinced that the basic entities in the model should be process- or procedure-like things that mutually interact with *message passing*. Message passing is required to be *asynchronous* in the sense that an entity can send a message to another entity anytime, even when the destination entity is not ready or able to receive the message. This assumption was taken because maximum concurrency needs to be expressible at the modeling level[8]. Almost all of the members who were only concerned with computation/execution but not with modeling were uninterested in the *mobility* of entities. However, I had a keen interest in modeling the world, describing it in programs and running (simulating) it with large and powerful machinery. To me, it was natural to capture mobile aspects of entities that exist in the world.

Even in the early days of computer science, the term "object" was used in many CS subdomains. In particular, the group led by Barbara Liskov, which designed a structured programming language called CLU[11], was using the term "object" to refer to an instance of abstract data types being defined by the novel program module feature in CLU. CLU was not the first language system to use the term. Others included early Lisp systems, early Smalltalk systems, and the Hydra Operating System, which all frequently used the term "object." However, these notions of objects did not deal with *message transmissions* which take place among objects. Of course, the interactions among objects were called *message passing*, but they were merely meant to be dynamically dispatched method calls (or procedure calls). A more restricted formal calculus of modeling message passing objects was proposed by Robin Milner [7].

2 Concurrent Objects

After several trials of developing frameworks, I came up with my own notion of objects that abstract away and model entities that interact with each other in problem domains. To me, it was a very suitable approach to modeling things in the world. In explaining my notion of *concurrent objects*, I often used an anthropomorphic analogy. Things are modeled as autonomous information processing agents called "concurrent objects," and their mutual message transmissions abstract away various forms of communications found in human or social organizations. Also, such forms of communication need to be realized by the current computer technology without much difficulty.

In our approach, the domain to be modeled/designed/implemented is represented as a collection of *concurrent objects*, and the interaction of the domain components is represented as *concurrent* message passing among such concurrent objects. Domains in which our approach is powerful include distributed problem solving, the modeling of human cognitive process, modeling and implementation of real-time systems, and design and implementation of distributed event simulation. Although a mathematical account of the basic notion of concurrent objects has been given in [11], let me describe an intuitive characterization of concurrent objects (COs) below. Each CO

 –has a globally unique identity/name,
 –may have a protected, yet updatable local memory,
 –has a set of procedures that manipulates the memory,
 –receives a message that activates one of the procedures,
 –has a single FIFO queue for arrived messages, and
 –has autonomous thread(s) of control.

In each CO, memory-updating procedures are activated one at a time with the message arrival order. The contents of the memory of a CO, which is the local state of the CO, can be defined at the time of message arrival, owing to its single FIFO message queue. Each CO can send messages to the set of COs whose ids are known to the CO approximately at the time of sending. This means that communication is point-to-point, and that any CO can send messages as long as it remembers the names of the destination COs. Because the memory of a CO can be updatable, a CO can forget names of other COs. The set of objects to which a CO can send messages therefore varies from time to time. The communication topology is therefore dynamic, and any CO can dynamically create COs.

3 What Can Be Contained in Messages?

In my framework, message passing is the sole means by which information can be exchanged among COs. So we need to clarify the information that can be contained in messages. My design is as follows: Messages are allowed to contain the *names* and *ids* of COs, in addition to COs *themselves*. In implementation terms, this means that messages can contain both pointers to COs and the code of COs. This mechanism allows direct addressing of what has been called *code migration* or *code mobility*. In our framework, messages are sent by COs, and not by other kinds of entities. When a message contains a whole CO (not just its id), the CO is actually (forced to be) moved by COs. This mechanism is somewhat strong for modeling interactions among domain components. Therefore, I restricted message passing in such a way that a message containing a CO should be transmitted *only* when a CO sends the very CO itself, and not when other COs do so. This restriction allows a CO to move on its own accord, but it can never be forced to move by other COs. It should be noted that while a CO is moving, it can both send and receive messages.

4 Modeling Customers Coming to a Post Office

To observe the suitability of my concurrent object framework, I modeled concurrent activities in a simple post office following an example given in the book by Simula[3].

Activities in the post office include customers entering/exiting, interactions between post office clerks and customers (buying/selling stamps), and customers dropping letters in the mailbox. Figure 1 illustrates the post office. Post office clerks are collectively represented by the counter-section. First, we model customers as concurrent objects. We also need to model the post office building. Customers go into the post office through its main door. More than one customer can be inside the post office. It is therefore acceptable to model the building as a concurrent object D representing the entrance door. Now, two kinds of objects, the customer object and the door object, exist in our domain. The next step is to determine how to model the interactions of the two kinds of objects. In our message passing paradigm, arrivals or transmissions of messages are the sole event of interaction among COs. The event representing a customer C going through the door is naturally represented as the arrival of a message M at the door object D, where M *contains* the customer object C itself (not the id of C). Then, the door object D sends to the customer object C a message M' requesting that C moves to the counter-section object CS. As the customer object C does not know the location of counter-section object CS, the door object D should supply the information of the location/name of the counter-section object to CS. This information is provided in the message M' requesting the customer C to change its location.

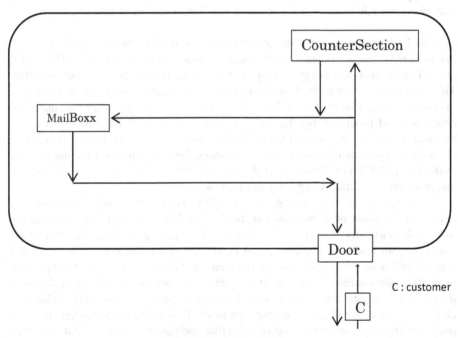

Fig. 1. Simple Post Office

5   Need for Autonomous Mobility and Ambients

When explaining the modeling of the post office above, the explanation of *how* a message M containing a customer object C arrives at the door object was somewhat vague. There are two possibilities: (1) Another concurrent object sends M containing C, and (2) C itself sends M. As noted earlier, I restricted the movement of objects in such a way that objects can only be moved by themselves. The second possibility is therefore the correct interpretation. This means that concurrent objects move by themselves, and are not moved by other COs. In turn, we need to provide a *Move*-instruction which is executed by any concurrent object C. When this instruction is executed, it is transformed into the transmission of a message containing C to a specific destination object.

Another point to note is that customers are not necessary local people who are familiar with the layout of the post office. Therefore, when a customer enters the post office, he needs to know the location of the counter-section or the mailbox. This information corresponds to what is known as an *ambient*. In our modeling, the locations (or names) of the counter-section and the mailbox are given to the customer object by the door object when the customer object arrives at the door object. In other words, the ambient information about the inside of the post office is given by the door object to the customer object. As the information contained in incoming messages can be stored, updated, and retrieved in the local memory of a CO, it can be said that that my framework has addressed issues associated with "ambients" of mobile objects [6].

6   ABCL, A Language for Concurrent Objects and Its Reflective Versions

We presented the first sketch of our concurrent object-oriented language ABCL [19] at the third French workshop on Object-Oriented Languages held in Paris in 1985. This workshop was organized by Pierre Cointe and Jean Bezivin. They graciously invited me. After that invitation, I became a member of the European community of object-oriented programming. This was a great opportunity for me to return to the international scene after several nonproductive domestic years in Tokyo. Henry Liebermann also presented his work at the workshop. This workshop was the predecessor of the first ECOOP (1987) and the first OOPSLA (1986). Much of my own research career on object-oriented computing owes this workshop.

The design of our full language ABCL/1[20], its prototype implementation, and several applications were presented at the first OOPSLA in 1986. My presentation was enthusiastically received by Kristen Nygaard, who was the Scandinavian/European leader of object-oriented computing. I was encouraged a great deal because of his strong support and encouragement. I distributed the ABCL language manuals at the conference site. In 1990, which was several years later, a thorough treatment of our concurrent object model was published as a book [21], which includes our work on reflective computation in the field of concurrent object-oriented programming. The whole purpose of reflective computation is to facilitate the self-evolution of systems. The original idea of computational reflection came from Brian Smith's work on LISP. Then, P. Maes and Luc Steels introduced the idea into an object-oriented knowledge representation language to design their reflective language 3-KRS. I thought that reflective computation was much more powerful and useful in parallel/concurrent computation than in sequential computation. To verify this view, I developed a reflective computation scheme which was formulated in our concurrent object-oriented framework, and T. Watanabe and I designed and implemented a reflective language ABCL/R[18]. Using ABCL/R, interesting applications of reflective object-oriented concurrent programming were identified. Examples of the applications include an object's dynamic acquisitions of methods, distributed time management, and the dynamic monitoring of object behavior. I still like this work and am proud of these accomplishments.

The semantic framework of our ABCL languages was given by N. Kobayashi and myself in 1994[6]. This semantics was based on the Linear Logic reported by Jean-Yves Girard. Novel language implementation techniques for high-performance computing machines were developed together with S. Matsuoka, K. Taura. and M. Yasugi [22]. In particular, Taura's idea of StackThread[17] was enlightening, and this techniques were proved to scale on Fujitsu AP1000, which is a multi-computer consisting of 512 Spark processors. The problems of inheritance mechanisms with concurrent object-oriented languages, coined *inheritance anomaly*, were found by J.-P. Briot, S. Matsuoka, and myself [4,12]. Furthermore, the work by T. Sekiguchi and myself on a very efficient implementation of our MOBILE object language called *Java-GO* [16] was published in 1999.

7 Large Scale Applications of Concurrent Objects

The ultimate goal of programming language research is that the central ideas in the languages being designed and implemented will be actually used in the real world. I am happy to report that the idea of concurrent objects has been extensively used in interesting large-scale applications including the following software systems.

-Charm++ and NAMD
-Twitter System
-Second Life (Linden Lab.)

Charm++[9] is a concurrent object-oriented programming and runtime system developed by Sanjay Kale and his group at the University of Illinois, and it has been extensively used to implement various high-performance computing applications. NAMD[13] is one of the most well-known applications of Charm++, and is a molecular dynamics simulation platform. It was developed jointly by Klaus Scholten's group and Kale's group. NAMD is one of the major molecular dynamics applications and the number of its users has been reported to be more than 7000. Also in 2000, 10~20% of the resources of two major US supercomputing centers were used for applications using Charm++.

It has been reported that the twitter system is being used by more than 200 million people worldwide. The idea of concurrent objects was used to implement the core part of processing incoming tweets. This implementation is highly efficient and reliable, and was succinctly written[15].

Also, Second Life is a very popular virtual world simulation (game) system developed by Linden Lab. With the Second Life system, users create program avatars, buildings and other such things by combining built-in software components that are constructed with concurrent objects[14].

Afterwords

Despite this educational journey, I feel I have not accomplished as much as I should have in my academic life, and I do reflect upon it with a certain sense of . bitterness. However, I would like to express my heartfelt thanks to the many people who were a part of this process. The following list is not exclusive: Makoto Kikuchi, Sigeiti Moriguti, Eiiti Wada, Takakazu Shimauti, Shun'ichi Amari, Masao Iri, Shigeru Igarashi, Makoto Nagoa, Kazuhiro Fuchi, Takuya Takuya, Yoshinori Morimura, Carl Hewitt, Kristen Nygaard, Barbara Liskov, Albert Meyer, Gerald Sussman, Vaughan Pratt, J.C.R. Licklider, Hirochika Inoue, Patrick Winston, Hilary Putnam, Mike Gordon, Gul Agha, Mehmet Aksit, C.A.R. Hoare, Robin Milner, Krishna Prasad, Takayasu Ito, Norihisa Suzuki, Jean Pierre, Ken kahn, Suad Alagic, Mario Tokoro, Atsushi Ohori, Hisao Miyauchi, Dennis Tsichritzis, Brian Smith, Gregor Kiczales, Guy Steele, Luc Steels, Pierre Cointe, Jean Bezivin, Ole Madsen, Wolfgang de Meuter, Jan Vitek, Reiji Nakajima, Kouichi Furukawa, Jun'ich Tsujii, Etsuya Shibayama, Akikazu Takeuchi, Kazunori Ueda, Satoshi Matsuoka, Kenichi Asai, Tsuyosh Murata, Naoki Kobayashi, Ken-jiro Taura, Hidehiko Masuhara, Vijay Saraswat, Ken-ichiro Torisawa, Kazuhiko Kato, Shigeru Chiba, Kohei Honda, Tomio Kamada, Takuo Watanabe, Atsushi Igarashi, Jacques Garrigue, Affeldt Reynaldt, Tatsuro Sekiguchi, Eijiro Sumii, Yoshihiro Ooyama, Eric Chen, Toshiyuki Maeda.

References

1. Agha, G.: Actor: A Model of Concurrent Computation in Distributed Systems. MIP Press (1986)
2. Agha, G., Wegner, P., Yonezawa, A.: Research Directions in Concurrent Object-Oriented Programming. MIT Press (1993)
3. Birtwistle, G., Dahl, O.-J., Myhrhang, B., Nygaard, K.: SIMULA Begin. Auerbach, Philadelphia (1973)
4. Briot, J.-P.: Inheritance and Synchronization in Concurrent OOP. In: Bézivin, J., Hullot, J.-M., Lieberman, H., Cointe, P. (eds.) ECOOP 1987. LNCS, vol. 276, pp. 32–40. Springer, Heidelberg (1987)
5. Cardelli, L.: Abstractions for Mobile Computation. In: Vitek, J. (ed.) Secure Internet Programming. LNCS, vol. 1603, pp. 51–94. Springer, Heidelberg (1999)
6. Kobayashi, N., Yonezawa, A.: Asynchronous Communication Model Based on Linear Logic. In: Halstead Jr., R.H., Ito, T. (eds.) US/Japan WS 1992. LNCS, vol. 748, pp. 331–336. Springer, Heidelberg (1993)
7. Milner, R.: The polyadic pi-calculus: a tutorial. Technical Report ECD-LFCS-91-180, Laboratory for Foundations of Computer Science, Edingburgh University (October 1991)
8. Hewitt, C., et al.: A Universal Modular Actor Formalism for Knowledge Representations. In: ACM Conf. on Principles of Programming Languages, Boston (1973)
9. Kale, S., Krishman, S.: CHARM++: A portable concurrent object oriented system based on C++. ACM SIGPLAN Notices 28(10), 91–108 (1993)
10. Kobayashi, N., Yonezawa, A.: Asynchronous communication model based onlinear logic. Formal Aspects of Computing 7(2), 113–149 (1995)

11. Liskov, B., Snyder, A., Atkinson, R., Schaffert, C.: Abstraction Mechanisms in CLU. Comm. of the ACM 20, 564–576 (1977)
12. Matsuoka, S., Yonezawa, A.: Analysis of Inheritance Anomaly in Object-Oriented Concurrent Programming in [2]
13. Nelson, M.T., Humphrey, W., Gursoy, A., Dalke, A., Kale, S., Skeel, R.D., Schulten, K.: NAMD: A parallel, object-oriented molecular dynamics program. International Journal of High Performance Computing Applications 10(4), 251–268 (1996)
14. Purbrick, J., Lentczner, M.: Second life: The world's biggest programming environment. Invited talk, OOPSLA 2007, Portland, Oregon (October 2007)
15. Pointer, R.: Kestrel system (August 14, 2009),
    http://github.com/robey/kestrel/tree/master
16. Sekiguchi, T., Hansen, K.A.: A Simple Extension of Java Language for Controllable Transparent Migration and its Portable Implementation. In: Ciancarini, P., Wolf, A.L. (eds.) COORDINATION 1999. LNCS, vol. 1594, pp. 211–226. Springer, Heidelberg (1999)
17. Taura, K., Matsuoka, S., Yonezawa, A.: An Efficient Implementation Scheme of Concurrent Object-Oriented Languages on Stock Multi-Computers. In: Proc. ACM Symposium on Principles and Practice of Parallel Programming, San Diego, pp. 218–228 (1993)
18. Watanabe, T., Yonezawa, A.: Reflection in ABCL/R. In: Proc. ACM Conference on Object-Oriented Programming, Systems, Languages and Applications, San Diego (1988)
19. Yonezawa, A., Matsuda, H., Shibayama, E.: An Approach to Object-oriented Concurrent Programming–A Language ABCL–. In: Proc. 3rd Workshop on Object-Oriented Languages, Paris (1985)
20. Yonezawa, A., Briot, J.-P., Shibayama, E.: Object-oriented Concurrent Programming in ABCL/1. In: Proc. ACM OOPSLA 1986, Portland, Oregon, USA, pp. 258–268 (1986)
21. Yonezawa, A. (ed.): ABCL: an Object-Oriented Concurrent System, 329 pages. MIT Press (1990)
22. Yonezawa, A., Matsuoka, S., Yasugi, M., Taura, K.: Implementing Concurrent Object-Oriented Languages on Multi-computers. IEEE Parallel & Distributed Technology 1(2), 49–61 (1993)

Object-Oriented Concurrent Programming in ABCL/1

Akinori Yonezawa, Jean-Pierre Briot, and Etsuya Shibayama

Department of Information Science, Tokyo Institute of Technology,
Ookayama, Meguro-ku, Tokyo, Japan, 152

Abstract. An object-oriented computation model is presented which is designed for modelling and describing a wide variety of concurrent systems. In this model, three types of message passing are incorporated. An overview of a programming language called ABCL/1, whose semantics faithfully reflects this computation model, is also presented. Using ABCL/1, a simple scheme of distributed problem solving is illustrated. Furthermore, we discuss the reply destination mechanism and its applications. A distributed "same fringe" algorithm is presented as an illustration of both the reply destination mechanism and the future type message passing which is one of the three message passing types in our computation model.

1 Introduction

Parallelism is ubiquitous in our problem domains. The behavior of computer systems, human information processing systems, corporative organizations, scientific societies, etc. is the result of highly concurrent (independent, cooperative, or contentious) activities of their components. We like to model such systems, and design AI and software systems by using various metaphors found in such systems[1–4]. Our approach is to represent the components of such a system as a collection of *objects*[5] and their interactions as *concurrent* message passing among such objects. The problem domains to which we apply our framework include distributed problem solving and planning in AI, modelling human cognitive processes, designing real-time systems and operating systems, and designing and constructing office information systems[6].

This paper first presents an object-based model for parallel computation and an overview of a programming language, called ABCL/1[7, 8], which is based on the computation model. Then, schemes of distributed problem solving are illustrated using ABCL/1. Though our computation model has evolved from the Actor model[9, 10], the notion of *objects* in our model is different from that of *actors*.

2 Objects

Each *object* in our computation model has its own (autonomous) processing power and it may have its local persistent memory, the contents of which represent its *state*. An object is always in one of three modes: *dormant*, *active*, or

G. Agha et al. (Eds.): Yonezawa Festschrift, LNCS 8665, pp. 18–43, 2014.

waiting. An object is initially dormant. It becomes active when it receives a message that satisfies one of the specified patterns and constraints. Each object has a description called *script* (or a set of methods) which specifies its behavior: what messages it accepts and what actions it performs when it receives such messages.

When an active object completes the sequence of actions that are performed in response to an accepted message, if no subsequent messages have arrived, it becomes dormant again. An object in the active mode sometimes needs to stop its current activity in order to wait for a message with specified patterns to arrive. In such a case, an active object changes into the waiting mode. An object in the waiting mode becomes active again when it receives a required message. For instance, suppose a buffer object accepts two kinds of messages: a [:get] message from a consumer object requesting the delivery of one of the stored products, and a [:put <product>] message from a producer object requesting that a product (information) be stored in the buffer. When the buffer object receives a [:get] message from a consumer object and finds that its storage, namely the buffer, is empty, it must wait for a [:put <product>] message to arrive. In such a case the buffer object in the active mode changes into the waiting mode.

An active object can perform usual symbolic and numerical computations, make decisions, send messages to objects (including itself), create new objects and update the contents of its local memory. An object with local memory cannot be activated by more than one message at the same time. Thus, the activation of such an object takes place one at a time.

As mentioned above, each dormant object has a fixed set of patterns and constraints for messages that it can accept and by which it can be activated. To define the behavior of an object, we must specify what computations or actions the object performs for each message pattern and constraint. To write a definition of an object in our language ABCL/1, we use the notation in Fig. 1. Fig. 2 shows a skeletal definition of an object. (state ...) declares the variables which represent the local persistent memory (we call such variables *state* variables) and specifies their initialization. *object-name* and the construct "where *constraint*" are optional. If a message sent to an object defined in the notation above satisfies more than one pattern-constraint pair, the first pair (from the top of the script) is chosen and the corresponding sequence of actions is performed.

```
[object object-name
   (state   representation-of-local-
memory... )
   (script
     (=> message-pattern where constraint
         ... action ...)

     (=> message-pattern where constraint
         ... action ...))]
```

```
[object Buffer
   (state ... )
   (script
     (=> [:put ... ] ... )

     (=> [:get] ...) )]
```

Fig. 1. Object Definition   **Fig. 2.** Buffer

An object changes into the waiting mode when it performs a special action. In ABCL/1, this action (i.e., the transition of an object from the active mode to the waiting mode) is expressed by a *select*-construct. A select construct also specifies the patterns and constraints of messages that are able to reactivate the object. We call this a *selective message receipt*. As an example of the use of

```
(select
    (=> message-pattern where constraint ... action ...)
        ⋮
    (=> message-pattern where constraint ... action ...))
```

Fig. 3. Select Construct

this construct, we give, in Fig. 4, a skeleton of the definition of an object which behaves as a buffer of a bounded size.

```
[object Buffer
  (state   declare-the-storage-for-buffer)
  (script
    (=> [:put aProduct]     ; aProduct is a pattern variable.
       (if the-storage-is-full
          then (select      ; then waits for a [:get] message.
             (=> [:get]
                remove-a-product-from-the-storage-and-return-it)))
       store-aProduct)
    (=> [:get]
       (if the-storage-is-empty
          then (select      ; then waits for a [:put ...] message.
             (=> [:put aProduct]
                send-aProduct-to-the-object-which-sent-[:get]-message))
          else remove-a-product-from-the-storage-and-return-it))  )]
```

Fig. 4. An Example of the Use of Select Constructs

Suppose a [:put <product>] arrives at the object Buffer. When the storage in the object Buffer is found to be full, Buffer waits for a [:get] message to arrive. When a [:get] message arrives, Buffer accepts it and returns one of the stored products. If a [:put] message arrives in *this* waiting mode, it will not be accepted (and put into the *message queue* for Buffer, which will be explained in Sec. 3. Then, Buffer continues to wait for a [:get] message to arrive. A more precise explanation will be given in the next section.

As the notation for a select construct suggests, more than one message pattern (and constraint) can be specified, but the ABCL/1 program for the buffer example in Fig. 4 contains only one message pattern for each select construct.

3   Message Passing

An object can send a message to any object as long as it knows the name of the target object. The "knows" relation is dynamic: if the name of an object T comes to be known to an object O and as long as O remembers the name of T, O can send a message to T. If an object does not know or forgets the name of a target object, it cannot at least directly send a message to the target object. Thus message passing takes place in a point-to-point (object-to-object) fashion. No message can be broadcast.

All the message transmissions in our computation model are asynchronous in the sense that an object can send a message whenever it likes, irrespective of the current state or mode of the target object. Though message passing in a system of objects may take place concurrently, we assume message arrivals at an object be linearly ordered. No two messages can arrive at the same object simultaneously. Furthermore we make the following (standard) assumption on message arrival:

[Assumption for Preservation of Transmission Ordering]
   When two messages are sent to an object T by the same object O, the temporal ordering of the two message transmissions (according to O's clock) must be preserved in the temporal ordering of the two message arrivals (according to T's clock).

This assumption was not made in the Actor model of computation. Without this, however, it is difficult to model even simple things as objects. For example, a computer terminal or displaying device is difficult to model as an object without this assumption because the order of text lines which are sent by a terminal handling program (in an operating system) must be preserved when they are received. Furthermore, descriptions of distributed algorithms would become very complicated without this assumption.

In modelling various types of interactions and information exchange which take place among physical or conceptual components that comprise parallel or real-time systems, it is often necessary to have two distinct modes of message passing: *ordinary* and *express*. Correspondingly, for each object T, we assume two message queues: one for messages sent to T in the ordinary mode and the other for messages sent in the express mode. Messages are enqueued in arrival order.

[*Ordinary* Mode Message Passing]
   Suppose a message M sent in the ordinary mode arrives at an object T when the message queue associated with T is empty. If T is in the dormant mode, M is checked as to whether or not it is acceptable according to T's script. When M is acceptable, T becomes active and starts performing the actions specified for it. When M is not acceptable, it is discarded. If T is in the active mode, M is put at the end of the *ordinary* message queue associated with T. If T is in the waiting mode, M is checked to see if it satisfies one of the pattern-and-constraint pairs that T accepts in *this* waiting mode. When

M is acceptable, T is reactivated and starts performing the specified actions. When M is not acceptable, it is put at the end of the message queue.

In general, upon the completion of the specified actions of an object, if the ordinary message queue associated with the object is empty, the object becomes dormant. If the queue is not empty, then the first message in the queue is removed and checked as to whether or not it is acceptable to the object according to its script. When it is acceptable, the object stays in the active mode and starts performing the actions specified for the message. If it is not acceptable, the message is discarded and some appropriate default action is taken (for instance, the message is simply discarded, or a default failure message is sent to the sender of the message). Then if the queue is not empty, the new first message in the queue is removed and checked. This process is repeated until the queue becomes empty. When an object changes into the waiting mode, if the ordinary message queue is not empty, then it is searched from its head and the first message that matches one of the required pattern-and-constraint pairs is removed from the queue. Then the removed message reactivates the object. If no such message is found or the queue itself is empty, the object stays in the waiting mode and keeps waiting for such a message to arrive. Note that the waiting mode does not imply "busy wait".

[*Express* Mode Message Passing]

Suppose a message M sent in the *express* mode arrives at an object T. If T has been previously activated by a message which was also sent to T in the *express* mode, M is put at the end of the *express* message queue associated with T. Otherwise, M is checked to see if it satisfies one of the pattern-and-constraint pairs that T accepts. If M is acceptable, T starts performing the actions specified for M even if T has been previously activated by a message sent to T in the *ordinary* mode. The actions specified for the previous message are suspended until the actions specified for M are completed. If so specified, the suspended actions are aborted. But, in default, they are resumed.

An object cannot accept an *ordinary* mode message as long as it stays in the active mode. Thus, without the express mode message passing, no request would be responded to by an object in the active mode. For example, consider an object which models a problem solver working hard to solve a given problem (cf. Sec. 7). If the given problem is too hard and very little progress can be made, we would have no means to stop him or make him give up. Thus without the express mode, we cannot monitor the state of an object (process) which is continuously in operation and also cannot change the course of its operation. More discussion about the express mode will be found in Sec. 5.3, Sec. 10.2, and Sec. 10.3.

As was discussed above, objects are autonomous information processing agents and interact with other objects only through message passing. In modelling interactions among such autonomous objects, the convention of message passing should incorporate a *natural* model of synchronization among interacting objects. In our computation model, we distinguish three types of message passing: *past*, *now*, and *future*. In what follows, we discuss each of them in turn. The following discussions are valid, irrespective of whether messages are sent in the ordinary or express mode.

[*Past* Type Message Passing] (send and no wait)

Suppose an object O has been activated and it sends a message M to an object T. Then O does not wait for M to be received by T. It just continues its computation after the transmission of M (if the transmission of M is not the last action of the current activity of O).

We call this type of message passing *past* type because sending a message finishes before it causes the intented effects to the message receiving object. Let us denote a past type message passing in the ordinary and the express modes by:

$$[T <= M] \quad \text{and} \quad [T <<= M],$$

respectively. The past type corresponds to a situation where one requests or commands someone to do some task and simultaneously he proceeds his own task without waiting for the requested task to be completed. This type of message passing substantially increases the concurrency of activities within a system.

[*Now* Type Message Passing] (send and wait)

When an object O sends a message M to an object T, O waits for not only M to be received by T, but also waits for T to send some information back to O.

This is similar to ordinary function/procedure calls, but it differs in that T's activation does not have to end with sending some information back to O. T may continue its computation after sending back some information to O. A now type message passing in the ordinary and express modes are denoted by:

$$[T <== M] \quad \text{and} \quad [T <<== M],$$

respectively. Returning information from T to O may serve as an acknowledgement of receiving the message (or request) as well as reporting the result of a requested task. Thus the message sending object O is able to know for certain that his message was received by the object T though he may waste time waiting. The returned information (certain values or signals) is denoted by the same notation as that of a now type message passing. That is, the above notation denotes not merely an action of sending M to T by a now type message passing, but also denotes the information returned by T. This convention is useful in expressing the assignment of the returned value to a variable. For example, [x := [T <== M]].

Now type message passing provides a convenient means to synchronize concurrent activities performed by independent objects when it is used together with the parallel construct. This construct will not be discussed in this paper. It should be noted that recursive *now* type message passing causes a local deadlock.

[*Future* Type Message Passing] (reply to me later)

Suppose an object O sends a message M to an object T expecting a certain requested result to be returned from T. But O does not need the result immediately. In this situation, after the transmission of M, O does not have to wait for T to return the result. It continues its computation immediately. Later on when O needs that result, it checks its special *private* object called *future object* that was specified at the time of the transmission of M. If the result has been stored in the future object, it can be used.

Of course, O can check whether or not the result is available before the result is actually used. A future type message passing in the ordinary and express modes are denoted by:

$$[T \; \texttt{<=} \; M \; \texttt{\$} \; x] \qquad \text{and} \qquad [T \; \texttt{<<=} \; M \; \texttt{\$} \; x],$$

respectively, where x stands for a special variable called *future variable* which binds a future object. We assume that a future object behaves like a queue. The contents of the queue can be checked or removed *solely* by the object O which performed the future type message passing. Using a special expression "(ready? x)", O can check to see if the queue is empty. O could access to the first element of the queue with a special expression "(next-value x)", or to all the elements with "(all-values x)". If the queue is empty in such cases, O has to wait. (Its precise behavior will be given in Sec. 6.2).

A system's concurrency is increased by the use of future type message passing. If the now type is used instead of the future type, O has to waste time waiting for the currently unnecessary result to be produced. Message passing of a somewhat similar vein has been adopted in previous object-oriented programming languages. Act1, an actor-based language developed by H. Lieberman[11] has a language feature called "future," but it is different from ours. The three types of message passing are illustrated in Fig. 5.

Though our computation model for object-oriented concurrent programming is a descendant of the Actor computation model which has been proposed and studied by C. Hewitt and his group at MIT[9, 10, 12, 11], it differs from the Actor computation model in many respects. For example, in our computation model, an object in the waiting mode can accept a message which is not at the head of the message queue, whereas, in the actor computation model, a (serialized) actor can only accept a message that is placed at the head of the message queue. Furthermore, now type and future type message passing are not allowed in the Actor computation model. Therefore, an actor A which sends a message to a target actor T and expects a response from T must terminate its current activity and receive the response as just one of any incoming messages. To discriminate T's response from other incoming messages arriving at A, some provision must be made before the message is sent to T. Also the necessity of the termination of A's current activity to receive T's response causes unnatural breaking down of A's task into small pieces.

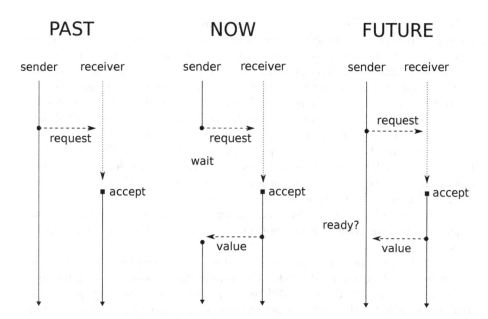

Fig. 5. The Three Message Passing Types

4 Messages

We will consider what information a message may contain. A message is composed of a singleton or a sequence of *tags, parameters*, and/or *names of objects*. Tags are used to distinguish message patterns. (In the buffer example mentioned in Fig. reffig:buffer-def, :get and :put are tags, and "aProduct" denotes a parameter in the [:put ...] message.) Object names contained in a message can be used for various purposes. For example, when an object O sends a message M to an object T requesting T to do some task, and O wishes T to send the result of the requested task to a specified object $C1$, O can include the name of $C1$ in the message M. Objects used in this way correspond to "continuation" (or customer) in the Actor computation model. Also, when O requests T to do some task in cooperation with a specified object $C2$, O must let T know the name of $C2$ by including it in the message M.

Besides the information contained in a message itself, we assume two other kinds of information can be transmitted in message passing. One is the *sender name* and the other is the *reply destination*. When a message sent from an object O is received by an object T, it is assumed that the name of the sender object O becomes known to the receiver object T. (We denote the sender name by "&sender" in ABCL/1.) This assumption considerably strengthens the expressive power of the model and it is easy to realize in the implementation of our computation model. A receiver object can decide whether it accepts or rejects an incoming message on the basis of who (or what object) sent the message.

When an object T receives a message sent in a now or future type message passing, T is required to reply to the message or return the result of the requested task (or just an acknowledgement). Since the destination to which the result should be returned is known at the time of the message transmission, we assume that such information about the destination is available to the receiver object T (and this information can be passed around among objects). We call such information the *reply destination*. To specify the object to which the result should be returned, the *reply destination* mechanism provides a more uniform way than simply including the name of the object in the request message. This mechanism is compatible with the three types of message passing, and enables us to use both explicit reply destinations in case of past type message as well as implicit ones in case of now or future type messages (cf. Sec. 6 and Sec. 9). Furthermore, the availability of the reply destination allows us to specify continuations and implement various *delegation* mechanisms[13] uniformly. This will be discussed in Sec. 8.

The fact that sender names and reply destinations can be known to message receiving objects not only makes the computation model powerful, but also makes it possible that the three different types of message passing: *past*, *now*, and *future*, be reduced to just one type of message passing, namely the *past* type message passing. In fact, a now type message passing in an object T can be expressed in terms of past type message passing together with the transition into the waiting mode in the execution of the script of the object T. And a future type message passing can be expressed in terms of past and now type message passing, which are in turn reduced to past type message passing. These reductions can be actually demonstrated, but to do so, we need a formal language. Since the programming language ABCL/1 to be introduced in the subsequent sections can also serve this purpose, we will give an actual demonstration after the explanation of ABCL/1 (cf. Sec. 6). The reply destination mechanism plays an important role in the demonstration.

5   An Overview of the Language ABCL/1

5.1   Design Principles

The primary design principles of our language, ABCL/1, are:

1. [Clear Semantics of Message Passing] The semantics of message passing among objects should be transparent and faithful to the underlying computation model.
2. [Practicality] Intentionally, we do not pursue the approach in which every single concept in computation should be represented purely in terms of objects and message passing. In describing the object's behavior, basic values, data structures (such as numbers, strings, lists), and invocations of operations manipulating them may be assumed to exist as they are, not necessarily as objects or message passing. Control structures (such as *if-then-else* and

looping) used in the description of the behavior of an object are not necessarily based upon message passing (though they can of course be interpreted in terms of message passing).

Thus in ABCL/1, *inter*-object message passing is entirely based on the underlying object-oriented computation model, but the representation of the behavior (script) of an object may contain conventional *applicative* and *imperative* features, which we believe makes ABCL/1 programs easier to read and write from the viewpoint of *conventional* programmers. Since we are trying to grasp and exploit a complicated phenomenon, namely parallelism, a rather conservative approach is taken in describing the internal behavior of individual objects. Various applicative and imperative features in the current version of ABCL/1 are expressed in terms of Lisp-like parenthesized prefix notations, but that is not essential at all; such features may be written in other notations employed in various languages such as C or Fortran.

5.2   Creating Objects and Returning Messages

In our computation model, objects can be dynamically created. Usually, when an object A needs a new object B, A sends, in a now or future type message passing, some initial information to a certain object which *creates B*. Then B is returned as the value (or result) of the now/future type message passing. This way of creating an object is often described in ABCL/1 as follows:

```
[object CreateSomething
  (script
    (=>  pattern-for-initial-info      ![object  ...  ] ) )]
```

where [object ....] is the definition of an object newly created by the object CreateSomething. The CreateAlarmClock object defined in Fig. 6 creates and returns an alarm clock object when it receives a [:new ...] message containing the person (object) to wake. The time to ring is set by sending a [:wake-me-at ...] message to the alarm clock object. It is supposed to keep receiving [:tick ...] messages from a clock object (called the Ticker and which will be defined in the next subsection). When the time contained in a [:tick ...] message is equal to the time to ring, the alarm clock object sends a [:time-is-up] message to the person to wake in the express mode. Note that the "Person-to-wake" variable in the script of the alarm clock object to be created is a free variable (it is not a state variable nor a message parameter). It will be "closured" when creating this object, which implies that the scope rule of ABCL/1 is lexical. The notation using ! is often used in ABCL/1 to express an event of returning or sending back a value in response to a request which is sent in a now or future type message passing. In the following fragment of a script:

$$(\Rightarrow pattern\text{-}for\text{-}request \ldots !\,expression \ldots),$$

where is the value of *expression* returned? In fact, this notation is an abbreviated form of a more explicit description which uses the reply destination. An equivalent and more explicit form is:

```
[object CreateAlarmClock
  (script
    (=> [:new Person-to-wake]

     ![object
        (state [time-to-ring := nil])
        (script
          (=> [:tick Time]
             (if (= Time time-to-ring)
                then [Person-to-wake <<= [:time-is-up]]))

          (=> [:wake-me-at T]
            [time-to-ring := T]) )] ) )]
```

Fig. 6. An Example of the Use of Select Constructs

$$(=> \; pattern\text{-}for\text{-}request \; @ \; destination \; \dots [destination \; <= \\ expression] \; \dots \;)$$

where *destination* is a pattern variable which is bound to the reply destination for a message that matches *pattern-for-request*, When a message is sent in a past type message passing, if we need to specify the reply destination, it can be expressed as:

$$[T \; <= \; request \; @ \; reply\text{-}destination \;].$$

Note that *reply-destination* denotes an object. In the case of now or future type message passing, pattern variables for reply destination are matched with certain objects that the semantics of now/future type message passing defines. (See Sec. 6) Thus the programmer is not allowed to explicitly specify reply destinations in now or future type message passing. So the following expressions [*target* <== *message* @ *reply-destination*], and [*target* <= *message* @ *reply-destination* $ x] are illegal.

There is another way to create an object. That is, an object can be obtained by copying some object. We can use the copy instantiation model[14] after defining a prototype[13], rather than defining a generator object (analog to a class). Each object can invoke a primitive function "self-copy" whose returning value is a copy of the object itself (Me), which will be exemplified in Sec. 9.

5.3   Ordinary Mode and Express Mode in Message Passing

The difference between the ordinary mode and express mode in message passing was explained in Sec. 3. The notational distinction between the two modes in message transmission is made by the number of "<", one for the ordinary mode and two for the express mode (namely <= and <==, vs. <<= and <<==). The same distinction should be made in message reception because a message sent in the ordinary mode should not be interpreted as one sent in the express mode. To make the distinction explicit, we use the following notation for expressing the reception of a message sent in the express mode.

> (=>> *message-pattern* where *constraint* ... *action* ...),

The reception of a message sent in the *ordinary* mode is expressed by the following notation as explained above:

> (=> *message-pattern* where *constraint* ... *action* ...)

This notational distinction protects an object from unwanted express mode messages because the object accepts only messages that satisfy the patterns and constraints declared after the notation "(=>>)". Express mode messages which do not satisfy such patterns and constraints are simply discarded.

Suppose a message sent in the express mode arrives at an object which has been currently activated by an ordinary mode message. If the script of the object contains the pattern and constraint that the message satisfies, the current actions are temporarily terminated (or suspended) and the actions requested by the express mode message are performed. If the object is accessing its local persistent memory when the express mode message arrives, the current actions will not be terminated until the current access to its local memory is completed. Also, if the object is performing the actions whose script is enclosed by "(atomic" and ")" in the following manner:

> (atomic ... *action* ...),

they will not be terminated (or suspended) until they are completed. And if the actions specified by the express mode message are completed and no express mode messages have arrived yet at that time, the temporarily terminated actions are resumed by default. But, if the actions specified by the express mode message contains the "non-resume" command, denoted by:

> (non-resume),

the temporarily terminated actions are aborted and will not be performed any more.

Note that, in the above explanation, the actions temporarily terminated by an express mode message are the ones that are activated (specified) by an ordinary mode message. When an object is currently performing the actions specified by an express mode message, no message (even in the express mode) can terminate (or suspend) the current actions.

To illustrate the use of express mode, we give the definition of the behavior of a clock object Ticker which sends [:tick ...] messages to all the alarm clocks he knows about (the value of its state variable "alarm-clocks-list"). The definition of the Ticker object is given in Fig. 7. The two state variables of Ticker, "time" and "alarm-clocks-list", respectively contain the current time and a list of alarm clocks to be "ticked". When Ticker receives a [:start] message, it starts ticking and updating the contents of "time".

> [alarm-clocks-list <= [:tick...]]

means sending [:tick ...] messages to each member of "alarm-clocks-list" simultaneously. We call this way of sending messages *multicast*. When Ticker receives a [:stop] message sent in the express mode, it stops ticking by the effect of (non-resume). This message must be sent in the express mode because Ticker always stays in the active mode to keep ticking (in the while loop). An [:add ...] message appends new alarm clock object to the "alarm-clocks-list" in Ticker. This message also should be sent in the express mode for the same reason. The definition of the CreateAlarmObject (which appeared in Fig. 6)

```
[object Ticker
  (state [time := 0] [alarm-clocks-list := nil])
  (script
  (=> [:start]
    (while t do
      (if alarm-clocks-list
        then [alarm-clocks-list <= [:tick time]])
      [time := (1+ time)]))

  (=>> [:add AlarmClock]
    [alarm-clocks-list := (cons AlarmClock alarm-clocks-list)])

  (=>> [:stop] (non-resume)) )]
```

Fig. 7. Definition of Ticker Object

should be slightly changed in order for a newly created alarm clock object to be known by Ticker. The description of an alarm clock object is the same as in Fig. 6, but when created it will now be bound to a temporary variable "AlarmClock". Then, after the created object is sent to Ticker to be appended to Ticker's "alarm-clocks-list", it is returned to the sender of the [:new ...] message as in the case of Fig. 6.

```
[object CreateAlarmClock
  (script
  (=> [:new Person-to-wake]
    (temporary
      [AlarmClock := [object description of an alarm clock object]])

    [Ticker <<= [:add AlarmClock]]
    !AlarmClock) )]
```

Fig. 8. New Definition of CreateAlarmClock Object

6 A Minimal Computation Model

Below we will demonstrate that

1. A now type message passing can be reduced to a combination of past type message passing and a selective message reception in the waiting mode, and
2. A future type message passing can also be reduced to a combination of past type message passing and now type message passing.

Thus both kinds of message passing can be expressed in terms of past type message passing and selective message reception in the waiting mode, which means that now type message passing and future type message passing are derived concepts in our computation model. (The rest of this section could be skipped if one is not interested in the precise semantics of "now" and "future" types message passing.)

6.1 Reducing Now Type

Suppose the script of an object A contains a now type message passing in which a message M is sent to an object T. Let the object T accept the message M and return the response (i.e., send the response to the reply destination for M). This situation is described by the following definitions for A and T written in ABCL/1.

```
[object A
   ...
  (script
     ...
     (=>  message-pattern  ...    [T <== M]  ...             ) ... )]
```

```
[object T
   ...
  (script
     ...
     (=>  pattern-for-M @ R ... [R <=  expression ] ... ) ... )]
```

** Note that the script of T can be abbreviated as:

$$(\Rightarrow \ pattern\text{-}for\text{-}M \ ... \ !expression \ ...)$$

We introduce a new object "New-object" which just passes any received message to A, and also introduce a *select*-construct which receives only a message that is sent from "New-object". The behavior of the object A can be redefined without using now type message passing as follows:

```
[object A
  (script
     ...
    (=>  message-pattern
```

```
(temporary [New-object := [object (script (=> any [A <= any]))] ])
   ...
[T <= M @ New-object]
(select
   (=> value where (= &sender New-object)
            ... value ... ))     ... ) ... )]
```

Note that the message M is sent by a past type message passing with the reply destination being the newly created "New-object." Immediately after this message transmission, the object A changes into the waiting mode and waits for a message that is passed by the "New-object". The constraint

$$\text{"where (= \&sender New-object)"}$$

in the select-construct means that the messages sent by New-Object can only be accepted. "New-object" serves as a unique identifier for the message transmission from A to T in past type: [T <= M @ New-object].

6.2   Reducing Future Type

Suppose the script of an object A contains a future type message passing as follows:

```
[object A
   (state ... )
   (future ... x ... )                    ; declaration of a future variable x.
   (script
      ...
   (=>   message-pattern
      ... [T <= M $ x] ...
      ... (ready? x) ... (next-value x) ... (all-values x) ...) ...)]
```

Then we consider the future variable x in A to be a state variable binding a special object created by an object CreateFutureObject. (In general, such an object, namely a future object, is created for each future variable if more than one future variable is declared.) Also we rewrite the accesses to x by now type message passing to x as follows:

```
[object A
   (state ... [x := [CreateFutureObject <== [:new Me]]] ... )
   (script
      ...
   (=>   message-pattern
      ... [T <= M @ x] ... [x <== [:ready?]] ...
      ... [x <== [:next-value]] ... [x <== [:all-values]] ...) ...)]
```

Note that the future type message passing [T <= M $ x] is replaced by a past type message passing [T <= M @ x] with the reply destination being x. Thus, the future type message passing is eliminated. The behavior of the future object is defined in Fig. 9. As mentioned before, it is essentially a queue object, but it only accepts message satisfying special pattern-and-constraint pairs. A queue object created by CreateQ accepts four kinds of messages: [:empty?], [:enqueue...], [:dequeue], and [:all-elements]. Note the fact that the contents of the queue

```
[object CreateFutureObject
  (script
    (=> [:new Creator]

    ![object
      (state [box := [CreateQ <== [:new]]])
      (script
        (=> [:ready?] where (= &sender Creator)        ; if [:ready?] is sent
          !(not [box <== [:empty?]]))          ; by the Creator,
                        ; and if the box is non-empty, t is returned.

        (=> [:next-value] @ R where (= &sender Creator)
          (if [box <== [:empty?]]
            then (select      ; waits for a message to come, not sent by the
                    (=> message where (not (= &sender Creator))) ; Creator.
                    [R <= message]))             ; it is returned
                    ; to the reply destination for a [:next-value] message.
            else  ![box <= [:dequeue]]))
        ; removes the first element in the queue and returns it.

        (=> [:all-values] @ R  where (= &sender Creator)
          (if [box <== [:empty?]]
            then (select      ; waits for a message to come, not sent by the
                    (=> message where (not (= &sender Creator))) ; Creator.
                    [R <= [message]]))             ; sends a singleton list.
            else  ![box <== [:all-elements]]))
        ; removes all the elements in the queue and returns the list of them.

        (=> returned-value
          [box <= [:enqueue returned-value]])~)] )~)]
```

Fig. 9. Definition of Future Object

object stored in "box" can be checked or removed *solely* by the object which is
bound to the pattern variable "Creator". Furthermore, if the queue is empty,
the object which sends messages [:next-value] or [:all-values] has to wait
for some value to arrive.

7 Project Team: A Scheme of Distributed Problem Solving

In this section, we present a simple scheme of distributed problem solving described in ABCL/1. In doing so, we would like to show the adequacy of ABCL/1
as a modelling and programming language in the concurrent object-oriented
paradigm.

Suppose a manager is requested to create a project team to solve a certain
problem by a certain deadline. He first creates a project team comprised of
the project leader and multiple problem solvers, each having a different problem solving strategy. The project leader dispatches the same problem to each
problem solver. For the sake of simplicity, the problem solvers are assumed to

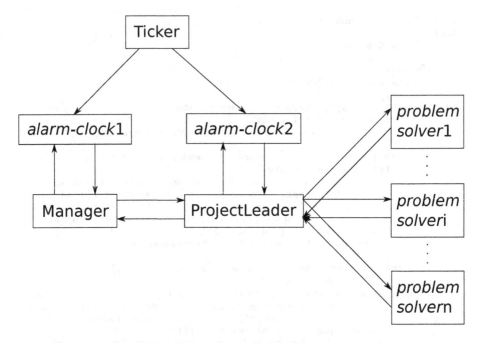

Fig. 10. A Scheme for Distributed Problem Solving

work independently in parallel. When a problem solver has solved the problem, it sends the solution to the project leader immediately. We assume the project leader also tries to solve the problem himself by his own strategy. When either the project leader or some problem solvers, or both, have solved the problem, the project leader selects the best solution and sends the success report to the manager. Then he sends a *stop* message to all the problem solvers. If nobody has solved the problem by the deadline, the project leader asks the manager to extend the deadline. If no solution has been found by the extended deadline, the project leader sends the failure report to the manager and commits suicide. This problem solving scheme is easily modeled and described in ABCL/1 without any structural distortions. (See Fig. 10.)

The definition of the project leader object is given in Fig. 11. Initially it creates an alarm clock object which will wake the project leader, and keeps it in a state variable "`time-keeper`". "`Me`" is a reserved symbol in ABCL/1 which denotes the innermost object whose definition contains the occurrence of "`Me`". We assume that the `Ticker` defined in Fig. 7 is now ticking. When the project leader object receives a [`:solve`...] message from the manager object, it requests its alarm clock (`time-keeper`) to wake itself at certain time. Then, the project leader object *multicasts* to the project team members a message that contains the problem description. Note that dispatching the problem to each problem solver is expressed as a *multicast* of the problem specifications and also the message passing is of *future* type. If a problem solver finds a solution, it sends the solution

```
[object ProjectLeader
  (state  [team-members := nil] [bestSolution := nil]
     [time-keeper := [CreateAlarmClock <== [:new Me]]])
  (future  Solutions)
  (script
     (=> [:add-a-team-member M]
       [team-members := (cons M team-members)])

     (=> [:solve SPEC :by TIME]
       (temporary  [mySolution := nil])   ; temporary variable

       [time-keeper <= [:wake-me-at (- TIME 20)]]
       [team-members <= [:solve SPEC] $ Solutions]
                              ; multicast in future type
       (while (and (not (ready? Solutions)) (null mySolution))
          do ...  try to solve the problem by his own
                    strategy and store his solution in  mySolution ...)
       (atomic
          [bestSolution := (choose-best mySolution (all-values Solutions))]
          [Manager <<= [:found bestSolution]]
          [team-members <<= [:stop-your-task]]))

     (=>> [:time-is-up] where (= &sender time-keeper)
       (temporary  new-deadline)

       (if (null bestSolution)
          then
             [new-deadline := [Manager <<== [:can-extend-deadline?]]]
             (if (null new-deadline)
                then [team-members <<= [:stop-your-task]]  (suicide)
                else [time-keeper <= [:wake-me-at new-deadline]])))

     (=>> [:you-are-too-late] where (= &sender Manager)
       (if (null bestSolution)
          then [team-members <<= [:stop-your-task]]  (suicide))) )]
```

Fig. 11. Definition of ProjectLeader Object

to the future object bound to "Solutions" of the project leader object. While the project leader engages himself in the problem solving, he periodically checks the variable by executing "(ready? Solutions)" as to if it may contain solutions obtained by problem solvers. Note that there is a fair chance that more than one problem solver sends their solutions to the future object bound to "Solutions". As defined in the previous section, solutions sent by problem solvers are put in the queue representing the future object in the order of arrival. "(all-values Solutions)" evaluates to the list of all the elements in the queue. Note that the sequence of actions from selecting the best solutions to terminating the team members' tasks is enclosed by "(atomic" and ")" in Fig. 11. Thus, the sequence of actions is not terminated (or suspended) by an express mode message.

If no solution is found within the time limit the project leader himself has set, a [:time-is-up] message is sent by his time keeper (an alarm clock object) in the *express* mode. Then, the project leader asks the manager about the possibility of extending the deadline. If the manager answers "no" (i.e., answers "nil"), it sends a message to stop all the problem solvers and commits suicide.

Though the definition of the manager object (denoted by "Manager" in Fig. 11) and problems solvers are easily written in ABCL/1, we omit them here.

8   Delegation

The *reply destination* mechanism explained in Sec. 4 and used in Sec. 6 is the basic tool to provide various delegation strategies[13]. The explicit use of pattern variables for reply destinations enables us to write the script of an object which delegates the responsibility of returning a requested result to another object.

Below we define an object A, and an object B which will delegate all unknown messages to A. The pattern variable "any" will match any message not matched by the other patterns in the script of B (this is analog to the last clause with predicate t in a Lisp cond construct). The variable R will match the reply destination. So any kind of message, namely past type with or without reply destination, or now type, or future type message, will be matched and fully delegated to the object A, which could in turn, also delegate it to another object.

```
[object A                    [object B
    (state ...)                  (state ...)
    (script                      (script
        (=>  patternA₁               (=>  patternB₁
        ... )                        ... )
        ...                          ...
        (=>  patternAₙ               (=>  patternBₚ
        ... ) )]                     ... )
                                     (=> any @ R   [A <= any @ R]) )]
```

This is illustrated by Fig. 12, showing an answer is delivered directly to the asker without coming back through B.

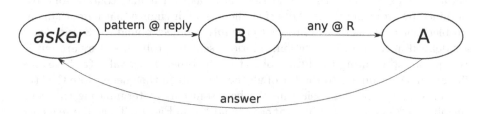

Fig. 12. Illustration of Basic Delegation

9   A Distributed Algorithm for the Same Fringe Problem

The same fringe problem is to compare the fringes of two trees (Lisp lists). We will present a solution of the same fringe problem in ABCL/1, which will permit us to illustrate the use of both *future* type messages and *reply destinations*.

Our approach to the problem is similar to the one proposed by B. Serpette in [15]. Basically, there are three objects in this model:

− two tree extractors, extracting recursively the fringe of each tree,
− one comparator, comparing the successive elements of the two fringes.

These three objects will work in parallel. (See Fig. 13.) The two tree extractors are linked to the comparator through two dashed arrows. Each one represents the data-flow of the successive elements of the fringe extracted by each tree extractor.

The Comparator object, defined in Fig. 14, owns two state variables: "Extractor1" and "Extractor2" binding the two tree extractors, and two *future* variables "input1" and "input2" which are used for receiving the fringes from these two extractors. "Extractor1" will be bound to the object TreeExtractor defined in Fig. 15, the second extractor ("Extractor2") will be created by requesting TreeExtractor to copy itself. When the Comparator object receives the [tree1 :and tree2] message, it will send a future type message [:fringe tree] to each TreeExtractor in order to request it to compute the fringe of each of the trees. Comparator assumes that Extractor1 and Extractor2 will

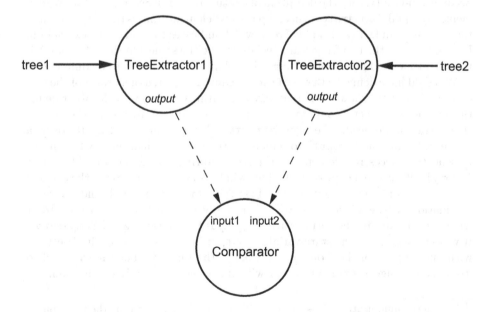

Fig. 13. The Same Fringe: Tree Extractors and Comparator

```
[object Comparator
    (state
      [Extractor1 := TreeExtractor]
      [Extractor2 := [TreeExtractor <== [:copy]]])
    (future    input1 input2)
    (script
      (=> [tree1 :and tree2]
          [Extractor1 <= [:fringe tree1] $ input1]  ; future type message
          [Extractor2 <= [:fringe tree2] $ input2]  ; future type message
          [Me <= [:eq (next-value input1) :with (next-value input2)]])

      (=> [:eq atom1 :with atom2]
          (if (eq atom1 atom2)
              then  (if (eq atom1 'EOT)
                        then  (print ''same fringe'')
                        else  [Me <= [:eq (next-value input1)
                                          :with (next-value input2)]])
              else (print ''fringes differ''))) )]
```

Fig. 14. The Same Fringe Comparator

reply the successive elements of the fringes, which will be enqueued in the future objects bound to input1 and input2, respectively. When two values from the two extractors become available to Comparator through input1 and input2, Comparator sends an [:eq (next-value input1) :with (next-value input2)] message to itself. Note that if one of the two queues (i.e., the future objects bound to variables input1 and input2) is empty, Comparator has to wait until both queues become non-empty. (See the definition of a future object in Sec. 6.2.) If the two elements are equal, Comparator will compare next elements unless they were equal to the special atom EOT (as End Of Tree), which indicates the end of the extraction. If both are EOT, the two fringes are declared to be the same. On the other hand, if the two elements differ, Comparator will declare the two fringes to be different.

We could have defined a CreateTreeExtractor object, as generator of the tree extractors, but (to show a different way of creating objects) we will rather define the prototype object TreeExtractor, and later copy it to create the second tree extractor we need. The TreeExtractor object, defined in Fig. 15, owns a single state variable "output" to remember the reply destination to which it has to send the successive elements of the fringe during the extraction. The script [:copy] will return a copy of itself. This will be a *pure* (exact copy of the original object) copy of TreeExtractor. The [:fringe tree] script will bind the reply destination to the variable "Pipe". This reply destination is a future object which was bound to the future variable "input1" or "input2" of Comparator. It will be assigned to the state variable "output", thus connecting[1] its "output" with one "input" of the Comparator (like in the Fig. 13). Then it will send to itself the message [:extract tree] with itself being the reply destination.

---

[1] Like the communication pipes in the ObjPive model[15], inspired by the Un*x pipes. In contrast, these "pipes" are virtual (no assumption of shared memory).

```
[object TreeExtractor
  (state output)
  (script
    (=> [:copy]     !(self-copy))

    (=> [:fringe tree] @ Pipe
        [output := Pipe]
        [Me <= [:extract tree] @ Me])

    (=> [:extract tree] @ C
     (cond
       ((null tree) [C <= [:continue]])
       ((atom tree) [output <= tree] [C <= [:continue]])
       (t   [Me <= [:extract (car tree)]
             @ [object
                 (state [Extractor := Me])
                 (script
                   (=> [:continue]
                       [Extractor <= [:extract (cdr tree)] @ C]))] ]) ))

    (=> [:continue]   [output <= 'EOT]) )]
```

Fig. 15. The Same Fringe `TreeExtractor`

To extract the fringe of a tree, the continuation-based programming style is adopted, which is in contrast to iterative or recursive ones. This model was initiated by Carl Hewitt[16], who gave a solution of the same fringe problem using continuations in a coroutine style. In contrast, our algorithm is fully parallel. The "[:extract tree] @ C" message script will bind the variable C to the reply destination, which represents the continuation, i.e., the object which will do the following:

- If the tree is null, the tree extractor just activates the continuation C, by sending it the message [:continue].
- If the tree is atomic, then this element is sent to the output, (so the corresponding "input1/2" of Comparator will receive a new element) and the continuation will be activated.
- The last case means that the tree is a node (a Lisp cons). We have to extract its left son (car), and then its right son (cdr). This second part to be performed later is specified in a dynamically created object (a new continuation), which will request the tree extractor to extract the cdr of the tree, when receiving the [:continue] message. The bindings of variables "tree" and "C" are memorized in the new continuation because of the lexical scoping of ABCL/1.

When the tree extractor receives the [:continue] message, that means the end of the extraction. So it will send EOT to the output, and stop there.

Note that in this algorithm if the two fringes are found to be different, the two extraction processes go on. Comparator could then send a *stop* message to either "freeze" or kill them. To deal with such a situation, we could devise various strategies which are related to the issues of objects' "capability" and garbage collection. This will be a subject for further study.

10   Concluding Remarks

10.1   Importance of the Waiting Mode

The computation model presented in this paper has evolved from the Actor computation model. One of the important differences is the introduction of the waiting mode in our computation model. As noted at the end of Sec. 3, without now type (and/or future type) message passing, module decomposition in terms of a collection of objects tends to become unnatural. Thus the now type message passing is essential in structuring solution programs. In our computation model, the now type message passing is derived from the waiting mode and the past type message passing in a simple manner as demonstrated in Sec. 6. In contrast, the realization of a now type message passing in the Actor computation model forces the unnatural decomposition of actors and requires rather cumbersome procedures for identifying a message that corresponds to the return (reply) value of now type message passing.

10.2   Express Mode Message Passing

We admit that the introduction of the express mode message passing in a high-level programming language is rather unusual. The main reason of introducing the express mode is to provide a language facility for *natural* modelling. Without this mode, the script of an object whose activity needs to be interrupted would become very complicated. When an object is continuously working or active, if no express mode message passing is allowed, there is no way of interrupting the object's activity or monitoring its state. One can only hope that the object terminates or suspends its activity itself and gives an interrupting message a chance to be accepted by the object. But this would make the structure of the script of the object unnatural and complicated. It should also be noted that the express mode message passing is useful for debugging because it can monitor the states of active objects.

10.3   Interrupt vs. Non-Interrupt

Our notion of *express* mode message passing is based on a very simple *interrupt* scheme. Even in this simple scheme, we must sometime protect the activity of an object from unwanted interruptions by using the "(atomic ...)" construct. (See the script of ProjectLeader in Fig. 11.) Appropriate uses of this construct sometimes requires skills.

An alternative scheme might be what we call the *mail priority* model. In this model, objects are not interrupted during their activities. An express mode message sent to an object arrives at the express queue without interrupting the object. When the object is ready to check its message queues, it always first consult its express queue (with first priority), and consult its ordinary queue only when there is no (more) message in the express queue. Now there is no fear of *bad* interruptions that the programmer has to take care of. But, on the other hand, as noted in the previous subsection, the activity of an object cannot be stopped or monitored when it is in progress. To alleviate this situation, we can introduce a built-in primitive, say "(check-express)", with which an object can check to see whether an express mode message has arrived while the object is carrying out its actions. "(check-express)" can be placed in the script of an object and it is invoked as one of the actions performed by the object. When it is invoked, if a message is in the express queue and it satisfies one of the pattern-and-constraint pairs in the script, the execution of the actions specified for the message pattern intervenes.

Since both schemes have various advantages and disadvantages and they depend on the application areas of our language, we need more experiments to draw a firm conclusion.

10.4   Parallelism and Synchronization

Let us review the basic types of parallelism provided in ABCL/1:

1. Concurrent activations of independent objects.
2. Parallelism caused by past type and future type message passing.
3. Parallelism caused by the *parallel* constructs [7] (we did not explain in this paper) and *multicasting* (cf. Sec. 5.3 and Sec. 7).

Furthermore, ABCL/1 provides the following four basic mechanisms for synchronization:

1. Object: the activation of an object takes place one at a time and a single first-come-first-served message queue for ordinary messages is associated with each object.
2. Now type message passing: a message passing of the now type does not end until the result is returned.
3. Select construct: when an object executes a select construct, it changes into the waiting mode and waits only for messages satisfying specified pattern-and-constraint pairs.
4. Parallel construct: see [7].

10.5   Relationship to Other Work

Our present work is related to a number of previous research activities. To distinguish our work from them, we will give a brief summary of ABCL/1. Unlike CSP [17] or other languages, ABCL/1 has characteristics of *dynamic* nature: objects can be created dynamically, message transmission is asynchronous, and the "knows"-relation among objects (i.e., network topology) changes dynamically. An object in our computation model cannot be activated by more than one message at the same time. This "one-at-a-time" nature is similar to that of Monitors [18], but the basic mode of communication in programming with monitors is the call/return bilateral communication, whereas it is unilateral in ABCL/1.

10.6   Other Program Examples

A wide variety of example programs have been written in ABCL/1 and we are convinced that the essential part of ABCL/1 is robust enough to be used in the intended areas. The examples we have written include parallel discrete simulation [19, 20], inventory control systems [21, 22] à la Jackson's example [23], robot arm control, mill speed control [24], concurrent access to 2-3 trees and distributed quick sort [20].

Acknowledgements. We would like to thank Y. Honda and T. Takada for their implementation efforts on Vax/11s, Sun workstations, and a Symbolics.

References

1. Smith, R.G.: Report on the 1984 distributed artificial intelligence workshop. AI Magazine 6(3), 234–243 (1986)
2. Special issue on distributed problem solving. IEEE Transactions on Systems, Man, and Cybernetics, SMC 11(1) (1981)
3. Yonezawa, A., Tokoro, M. (eds.): Object-Oriented Concurrent Programming. The MIT Press (1987)
4. Brodie, M., Mylopoulos, J., Schmidt, J. (eds.): On Conceptual Modelling. Springer (1984)
5. Stefik, M.K., Bobrow, D.G.: Object-oriented programming: Themes and variations. AI Magazine 6(4), 40–62 (1986)
6. Tschritzis, D. (ed.): Office Automation. Springer (1985)
7. Yonezawa, A., Shibayama, E., Takada, T., Honda, Y.: Modeling and programming in an object-oriented concurrent language ABCL/1. In: Yonezawa, A., Tokoro, M. (eds.) Object-Oriented Concurrent Programming, pp. 55–89. The MIT Press (1987)
8. Shibayama, E., Yonezawa, A.: ABCL/1 User's Manual (1986), Internal Memo
9. Hewitt, C.: Viewing control structures as patterns of passing messages. Artificial Intelligence 8(3), 323–364 (1977)
10. Hewitt, C., Baker, H.: Laws for parallel communicating processes. In: IFIP Congress Proceedings, Toronto, pp. 987–992 (1977)
11. Lieberman, H.: A preview of Act-1. AI-Memo AIM-625, Artificial Intelligence Laboratory. MIT (1981)
12. Yonezawa, A., Hewitt, C.: Modelling distributed systems. In: Machine Intelligence, vol. 9, pp. 41–50. Halsted Press (1979)
13. Lieberman, H.: Delegation and inheritance - two mechanisms for sharing knowledge in object-oriented systems. In: Bezivin, J., Cointe, P. (eds.) 3rd AFCET Workshop on Object-Oriented Programming, Paris, France. Globule+Bigre, vol. 48, pp. 79–89 (January 1986)

14. Briot, J.P.: Instanciation et héritage dans les langages objets (thèse de 3ème cycle). LITP Research Report 85-21, LITP - Université Paris-VI, Paris, France (December 1984)
15. Serpette, B.: Contextes, processus, objets, séquenceurs: FORMES. LITP Research Report 85-5, LITP – Université Paris-VI, Paris (October 1984)
16. Hewitt, C., et al.: Behavioral semantics of nonrecursive control structures. In: Proceedings of Colloque Sur la Programmation, Paris (April 1974)
17. Hoare, C.A.R.: Communicating sequential processes. Communications of the ACM 21(8), 666–677 (1978)
18. Hoare, C.A.R.: Monitors: An operating system structuring concept. Communications of the ACM 17(10), 549–558 (1974)
19. Yonezawa, A., Matsuda, H., Shibayama, E.: Discrete event simulation based on an object oriented parallel computation model. Technical Report C-64, Dept. of Information Science, Tokyo Institute of Technology (1984)
20. Shibayama, E., Yonezawa, A.: Distributed computing in ABCL/1. In: Yonezawa, A., Tokoro, M. (eds.) Object-Oriented Concurrent Programming, pp. 91–128. The MIT Press (1987)
21. Kerridge, J.M., Simpson, D.: Three solutions for a robot arm controller using pascal-plus, occam and edison. Software – Practice and Experience 14, 3–15 (1984)
22. Shibayama, E., Matsuda, M., Yonezawa, A.: A description of an inventory control system based on an object-oriented concurrent programming methodology. Jouhou-Shori 26(5), 460–468 (1985)
23. Jackson, M.: System Development. Prentice-Hall (1983)
24. Yonezawa, A., Matsumoto, Y.: Object-oriented concurrent programming and industrial software production. In: Ehrig, H., Floyd, C., Nivat, M., Thatcher, J. (eds.) TAPSOFT 1985 and CSE 1985. LNCS, vol. 186, pp. 395–409. Springer, Heidelberg (1985)

Reflection in an Object-Oriented Concurrent Language

Takuo Watanabe and Akinori Yonezawa

Department of Information Science, Tokyo Institute of Technology,
Ookayama, Meguro-ku, Tokyo, Japan, 152

Abstract. Our work is along the lines of the work of B. Smith and P. Maes. We first discuss our notion of *reflection* in object-oriented *concurrent* computation and then present a reflective object-oriented concurrent language ABCL/R. We give several illustrative examples of reflective programming such as (1) dynamic concurrent acquisition of "methods" from other objects, (2) monitoring the behavior of concurrently running objects, and (3) augmentation of the time warp mechanism to a concurrent system. Also the definition of a meta-circular interpreter of this language is given as the definition of a meta-object. The language ABCL/R has been implemented. All the examples given in this paper are running on our ABCL/R system.

1 Introduction

Reflection is the process of reasoning about and acting upon itself[1, 2]. A reflective computational system is a computational system which exhibits reflective behavior. In a conventional system, computation is performed on data that represent (or model) entities which are external to the computational system. In contrast, a reflective computational system must contain some data that represent (or model) the structural and computational aspects of the system itself. And such data must be manipulable within the system itself, and more importantly, changes made to such data must be causally reflected/connected to the actual computation being performed.

B. Smith[3] and other researchers(e.g.,[4–6]) investigated the power of computational reflection and emphasized its usefulness. In particular, P. Maes has proposed a reflective system in the framework of object-oriented computing[7] and made good contributions to the fields of object-oriented programming and reflective computation. Her work, however, confined itself to sequential systems, and did not consider systems where more than one object can be active simultaneously.

Our present work proposes a reflective system in the framework of object-oriented *concurrent* computing. This is one of our research results in the paradigm of "Object-Oriented Concurrent Programming"[8, 9]. We expect that reflective facilities will become increasingly more important in concurrent computational systems such as (distributed) operating systems, realtime systems,

G. Agha et al. (Eds.): Yonezawa Festschrift, LNCS 8665, pp. 44–65, 2014.
© Springer-Verlag Berlin Heidelberg 2014

distributed simulation systems, distributed problem solving systems, robot planning/controlling, etc. For reflective capabilities are indispensable when one tries to make the behavior of these systems more powerful and intelligent as well as controllable by the user.

In this chapter, we first discuss our notion of reflection in object-oriented concurrent computing and then present a reflective object-oriented concurrent language ABCL/R. We give several illustrative examples of reflective programming such as

- dynamic concurrent acquisition of "methods" from other objects,
- monitoring the behavior of concurrently running objects, and
- augmentation of the time warp mechanism[10] to a concurrent system.

Also the definition of a meta-circular interpreter of this language is given as the definition of a meta-object. This language ABCL/R is an extension of our previously proposed language ABCL/1 [11] and has been implemented. All the examples given in this paper are running on our ABCL/R system. The summary of our present work is given in the final section of this chapter.

2   Object-Oriented Concurrent Computation Model

In order to present the framework of our work, we first introduce an object-oriented concurrent computation model. This model is basically a submodel of our existing object-oriented concurrent computation model ABCM/1[11].

2.1   Overview of the Computation Model

In our computation model, a system is a collection of *objects* — autonomous information processing agents. Each object has an individual serial computation power, and may have local persistent memory called a *state memory*. Functions and properties of a conceptual/physical entity in the problem domain are modeled and represented as such an object. In order to use the functions and properties, a request *message* is sent to the object. When an object receives a message, if the message is acceptable to the object, it starts the sequence of actions which are requested by the message.

Actions performed by an object are combinations of inquiring/updating the object's local state memory, sending messages to other objects (including itself), creating new objects, and other symbolic/numerical operations. Basically, sequences of actions by objects in the system proceed asynchronously. This means that many objects perform their computation in parallel. In our model, the unit of concurrency is an object. Communication among objects and the synchronization of their computation are done only by message passing. Any two objects don't share any data other than the names (addresses, or pointers) of other objects. The state memory of each object cannot be accessed directly by other objects, and only indirect accesses through message passing are permitted.

Each object is always in one of two modes: *dormant* and *active*. The mode of an object is dormant at creation time. It becomes active when it accepts a message and starts executing a sequence of actions for the message. When the execution completes, and if no subsequent message has arrived, the object becomes dormant.

From the programming point of view, an object is the basic building block of program. A program is written as the behavior description of objects — what actions to perform when received messages. The description of the behavior of an object is a collection of *scripts* (often called *methods* in other object-oriented languages), which consists of a message pattern and a sequence of actions. A script prescribes the sequence of actions by the object invoked when received a message that matches the message pattern of the script.

2.2   Structure of an Object

Since each object has a single serial processing power, it executes a script one at a time. Although messages can be received by an object which is in active mode, the execution of the scripts for the messages must be postponed until the current script execution completes. Therefore each object has a *message queue* to store incoming messages. (This message queue can be viewed as a part of the receiver memory state.)

The structure of an object consists of a serial evaluator, a set of scripts, a state memory, and a message queue. The structure itself can be regarded as a serial computational system. This structure of an object is a basic one. As will be seen in the subsequent sections, we can build different structures for objects, and such structures can dynamically be changed by using *reflective* language facilities.

2.3   Message Transmission

All message transmission is *asynchronous*. There is no need for any handshaking to send/receive messages. This means that one can send messages whenever it wants, regardless of the current condition (mode) of the target object. When a message is sent to an object, it will be treated by the receiver object in the following way.

1. *Arrival*: First, the message arrives at the receiver object. This event is called the *arrival* of the message. The receiver starts processing the message. It is assumed that once a message is transmitted, it is guaranteed to arrive at the receiver (as long as the receiver exists).
2. *Receiving*: Next, the receiver object enqueues the arrived message in its message queue — this is the event of *receiving*. If the receiver is in dormant mode, it starts trying to accept the messages in the queue (see next).
3. *Acceptance*: If the receiver is in dormant mode, it dequeues the first message in the queue, and checks to see whether the receiver can process it. To be more precise, the receiver tries to find an appropriate script for the message

by pattern-matching. *Acceptance* of the message is the event in which the appropriate script for the message is found. If the receiver accepts the message, it starts executing the script for the message. Otherwise, the message is simply ignored (in the language ABCL/R, a warning message is issued).

4. *End of Processing a Message*: When the evaluation finishes, the receiver checks the queue to process subsequent messages. If the queue is empty, the receiver becomes dormant.

2.4   Types of Message Transmissions

Our model has the following two types of message transmissions (ABCM/1 also has three types including the *future type*).

- *Past type*: Suppose an object x sends a message to y in the course of computation. Then x does not wait for the message to be received by y, and continues the rest of computation immediately. Using the notation of our reflective language ABCL/R, this type of message transmission is written as:

$$[T \text{ <= } M] \qquad \text{or} \qquad [T \text{ <= } M \text{ @ } R]$$

where T, M, and R are the target object, message, and *reply destination*, respectively. The reply destination is an object to which the receiver can send a reply message. If the reply destination is not specified, the receiver regards NIL as the reply destination. (Sending messages to NIL causes no effect.)

- *Now type*: When an object x sends a message M to T, x waits for the message to be received by y and further waits for a reply from T to come, blocking the current script execution. A now type message transmission is written in ABCL/R as:

$$[T \text{ <== } M]$$

A now type message transmission looks similar to an ordinary remote procedure call, but it is different. In the case of now type, after sending the reply to x, T may continue its computation, and furthermore, T can ask another object y to send a reply to x.

3   Reflection in Our Model

To realize reflection in a system based on our computation model, the causally connected self representation[1, 2] of the system must exist within the system. Since reflective computation depends on the way in which the self representation is described, choosing the formalism for the self representation is the primary concern of building a reflective system.

There are at least two approaches to build the self representation of an object-oriented concurrent computational system. One is to assume the existence of a datum which is the causally connected self representation of the *whole* system, and the other is to introduce the self representation of each object in the system individually. Our approach is the latter one. The remarks on the former approach will be found in the concluding section.

As explained in the previous section, we can regard an object as a serial computational system. Thus we can build a representation of an object as a representation of a serial computational system. The representation of an object contains the representations of the message queue, the state memory, the set of scripts, and the evaluator of the object. Besides this structural aspect, the computational aspect of the object — arrival, receiving, and acceptance of a message and the execution of a scripts — must be represented. Our approach is to represent each object as an *object* called a *meta-object*.

For each object x, there exists a meta-object $\uparrow x$, which represents both the structural and computational aspects of x. $\uparrow x$ contains the meta-level information about x. Meta-object $\uparrow x$ represents the object x in a similar way that usual objects represent entities in the problem domain. x is called the *denotation* of $\uparrow x$. The structure of x is represented as the data in the state memory of $\uparrow x$, and the computational aspects of x is described as the scripts (methods) of $\uparrow x$. The following points should be noted.

- An object x and the information about x in $\uparrow x$ are causally connected. Thus the data stored in $\uparrow x$ always represent the current status of x, and operations on the data cause the isomorphic effect on x.
- $\uparrow x$ is an object. So $\uparrow\uparrow x$ also exists. This means that operations on $\uparrow x$ are allowed. Thus, there is an infinite tower of meta-objects $\uparrow x$, $\uparrow\uparrow x$, $\uparrow\uparrow\uparrow x$, ... for each object x. In the actual implementation, meta-objects are created when their access takes place (by lazy creation).
- If one knows the name of x, it can always get the name of $\uparrow x$, and vice versa.
- The correspondence between objects and their meta-objects is one to one. That is, for each object x, y, $x \equiv y \iff \uparrow x \equiv \uparrow y$ holds ($\equiv$ is the identity relation).

The concept of meta-objects in our model is similar to that of meta-objects in 3-KRS[2, 7]. In 3-KRS, structural/computational aspects of an object is also represented in its meta-object. But the way of modeling an object as its meta-object is different, because an object is a unit of concurrency in our computation model.

In our model, the causal connection link between an object x and its meta-object $\uparrow x$ is implicit — the changes in x cause the isomorphic changes to the data in $\uparrow x$ not by the message transmission from x to $\uparrow x$ (and vice versa). The reason is that the message transmission takes time, which requires the synchronization of x and $\uparrow x$. As we will see in the later section, $\uparrow x$ is used as the "implementation" of x.

Reflective computation in an object x is performed by x sending messages to its meta-object $\uparrow x$. This enables x to inquire/modify itself through $\uparrow x$, because the structural/computational aspects of x is represented in $\uparrow x$ in a causally connected way. Note that appropriate scripts for operations on x must be prepared in ⇑x. If ⇑x doesn't have such scripts, it is possible to modify ⇑x using ⇑⇑x to acquire such scripts. Such examples are found in Sec. 5.

Of course a meta-object can receive messages from objects (other than its denotation). In a system that consists of a collection of many objects, we can regard the meta-object of an object as the partial representation of the system. Thus the reflective computation in the system is realized by sending messages to each other's meta-object. Note that such message transmissions may take place concurrently in our computation model.

4   Meta-Objects and Reflective Language ABCL/R

The notion of *meta-objects* is the key concept for the reflection in our computation model. ABCL/R — the description language of our model — is an object-oriented concurrent language with reflective architecture based on the notion of meta-objects. The syntax and basic features of the language are adopted from the language ABCL/1[11, 12]. In this section, we describe the definition of meta-object in details in terms of the language ABCL/R.

4.1   Object Definition in ABCL/R

In ABCL/R, an object definition is written in the following form. The value of the form is a newly created object the name of which is *object-name*.

```
[object object-name
  (state variable-declaration...)
  (script
    (=> message-pattern @ reply-destination-variable
                        from sender-variable
        (temporary variable-declaration...)
        behavior description)
    ...)]
```

object-name is optional in the above definition. (state ...) is the local state variable declaration. *variable-declaration* is either [*variable* := *initial-value*] or *variable* which is equivalent to [*variable* := nil]. [*variable* := *expression*] is the expression for assignment of the value of *expression* to *variable*. Each (=> *message-pattern* ...) is the description of a script. The object defined in the above form accepts a message which matches a *message-pattern*. The reply destination and the sender object of an incoming message are bound to the variables *reply-destination-variable* and *sender-variable*, respectively. These two variables are optional. *behavior description* in each script description is a sequence of actions, which are described as expressions of either object creation, message transmission, inquiring/modifying state memory (through state variables), or some other symbolic/numerical calculation (as Lisp expressions). (temporary ...) is the declaration of temporary variables used in the script.

4.2   Definition of a Meta-Object in ABCL/R

As explained in Sec. 3, a meta-object ↑x is an object which models the structural and computational aspects of an object x, and x is called the *denotation* of ↑x.

Modeling the Structure of an Object. Since an object x in our computation model consists of a set of scripts, a state memory, a local serial evaluator, and a message queue, the structural aspect of x is represented as the values of ↑x's state variables `scriptset`, `state`, `evaluator`, and `queue`, respectively. Using the ABCL/R notation, this structural aspect is described as the `state`-part of the definition of the meta-object ↑x given in Fig. 1.

```
[object ; a meta-object
  (state [queue := a message queue]
         [state := a state object]
         [scriptset := a set of scripts]
         [evaluator := an evaluator object]
         [mode := either :dormant or active])
  (script
   (=> [:message Message Reply-Dest Sender] ; message arrival & receiving
       [queue := (enqueue queue [Message Reply-Dest Sender])]
       (if (eq mode ':dormant) then
           [mode := active]
           [Me <= :begin]))
   (=> :begin ; acceptance & script execution
       (temporary mrs scr newenv [object := Me])
       [mrs := (first queue)]
       [queue := (dequeue queue)]
       [scr := (find-script (first mrs) scriptset)]
       (if scr then ; acceptance
           [newenv := [env-gen <== [:new (script-alist mrs scr) state]]]
           ;; pattern variables, reply & sender variables have been bound in newenv
           [evaluator <= [:do-prg (scr$body scr) newenv [den Me]] @
                         [cont ignore ; the value of the evaluation is ignored
                               [object <= :end]]]]
        else ; cannot accept
           (warn ''Cannot handle the message ~A'' (first mrs))
           [Me <= :end]))
   (=> :end ; termination of the execution
       (if (not (empty? queue)) then
           [Me <= :begin]
         else
           [mode := :dormant]))
;; The following scripts are examples of special scripts for meta-level operations.
   (=> :queue ; inquiring about the message queue
       !queue) ; returns the value of queue
   (=> [:script Message];inquiring about the script whose pattern matches Message
       !(find-script Message scriptset)) ; returns the found script
   ...)]
```

Fig. 1. Definition of A Meta-Object

Each element in the value of `scriptset` is a script (represented in a certain data structure, say, character strings), and the values of `state` and `evaluator` are *objects* which represent the state memory and the evaluator. The value of `mode` indicates the current mode of the denotation object, which is either `:dormant` or `:active`.

Modeling the Behavior of an Object. Besides the structural aspect, the meta-object ↑x models the computational aspect of its denotation — *arrival*, *receiving*, and *acceptance* of messages, and execution of scripts. This aspect is described in the ABCL/R notation as the `script`-part of the definition in Fig. 1.

The following is a more precise description of what was explained in Sec. 2.3 in terms of the ABCL/R notation. Suppose a message M is sent to an object x.

1. *Arrival of a Message*: The arrival of a message M at the object x is represented by acceptance of a message [`:message` M R S] by ↑x. R is the reply destination of M, and S is the sender object of M.

2. *Receiving a Message (See the script for* [`:message` ...]*)*: When ↑x accepts the message [`:message` M R S], it enqueues the triple [M R S] to its message queue — the value of the variable `queue`. This represents the situation where the object x receives the message M. If x is in dormant mode — the value of the state variable `mode` in ↑x is `:dormant`, then ↑x sends a message `:begin` to itself.

3. *Acceptance of a Message (See the script for* `:begin`*)*: ↑x dequeues one triple [M R S] from the queue. If there is an appropriate script σ for M in `scriptset` (acceptance), ↑x executes the body of σ (see next). If there is no script for M, it just ignores this and sends `:end` to itself after issuing a warning message.

4. *Execution of a Script*: First, ↑x creates a new environment — which binds the contents of M to the pattern variables of σ, R to the reply variable of σ, and S to the sender variable of σ —, then evaluates the body of σ under the new environment using the `evaluator` object.

5. *After a Script Execution (See the script for* `:end`*)*: When the execution of the script completes, a message `:end` is sent to ↑x. Then ↑x checks the queue, and starts processing of subsequent messages if the queue is not empty (by sending a message `:begin` to itself).

Let us look at the script execution more closely. A new environment is created by the environment generator object `env-gen` from the a-list of pattern variables/values and the state object. The evaluator object `evaluator` is activated by receiving a message [`:do` *Exp Env Me-ptr*], where *Exp* is the expression to be evaluated, *Env* is the environment object, and *Me-ptr* is the object in which the evaluation takes place. The following expression in Fig. 1 is executed at the end of the execution of the script for `:begin`.

```
[evaluator <= [:do-prg (scr$body scr) newenv [den Me]]
           @ [cont ignore [object <= :end]]]
```

Message [:do-prg ...] is used instead of [:do ...], and this is used to evaluate the list of expressions (the value of (scr$body scr)) and the result is the value of the last expression of the list (like **progn** of Lisp). The value of the variable Me is the meta-object itself (such variables are often named "self" in other languages), and [den Me] (this form is explained in a later section) is the denotation of the meta-object.

Since a *past* type message transmission is used, the execution of the script for :begin immediately completes after the execution of the above expression, and the mode of the meta-object becomes dormant. The result of the evaluation is passed to the reply destination of the message, which is expressed as [cont ...]. Note that the form

$$[\text{cont } message\text{-}pattern \ script\text{-}description]$$

is syntactically equivalent to the following form.

```
[object
    (script (=> message-pattern script-description))]
```

The notation [cont ...] is intended to be used as the continuation of the evaluation which accepts the evaluation result and does the rest of the task. The result of the script evaluation is bound to a variable ignore and just ignored (the variable ignore is not used in the body), and the rest of the task is to send a message :end to the meta-object which is bound to a variable object.

Inherent Concurrency. Suppose the meta-object $\uparrow x$ has accepted a message :begin and the evaluation of the corresponding script has been started by evaluator. Since this evaluation is triggered by a past type message transmission, now $\uparrow x$ changes to dormant mode and stays in dormant mode until a message :end is sent to $\uparrow x$ from the continuation object ([cont ...]) of the evaluator. (Note that if the evaluator object is executing a script, the mode of x can be active even when $\uparrow x$ is in dormant mode.) Thus $\uparrow x$ can accept the next [:message ...] without waiting for the completion of the current script execution.

This corresponds to the fact that x can receive messages while x is in active mode (*asynchrony* described in 2.3). The fact is called the *inherent concurrency* of the object x.

To model the behavior of an object correctly, it must be guaranteed that the execution of the object's scripts takes place one at a time. We can see that this is guaranteed by the meta-object definition: once a message :begin is sent to the meta-object $\uparrow x$, the next :begin message will not be sent until a message :end is sent to $\uparrow x$. (The value of variable mode becomes :dormant only after the script for :end has been executed.)

The definition in Fig. 1 also says that messages arriving at the denotation x are simply enqueued when x is in active mode, and the search of the scriptset by $\uparrow x$ is postponed until the current script execution completes. For more detailed explanation, see [13].

4.3 Meta Circularity of Objects

In ABCL/R, to satisfy the requirement of the causal connection between an object x and its meta-object $\uparrow x$, $\uparrow x$ is used as the actual implementation of x. That is, the contents of the state variables of $\uparrow x$ — a message queue, a set of scripts, a state object, and an evaluator object of x — are used for the actual computation of x. The arrival, receiving and acceptance of messages are performed as we have seen before. Moreover, the evaluation of scripts is carried out by the evaluator object, which is also an ordinary object of ABCL/R. Thus every object of ABCL/R is implemented in a meta-circular way as its meta-object.

The definition of the meta-object in Fig. 1 is used in default. In ABCL/R, we can specify other meta-object instead of this in the object definition. An example of a non-default meta-object is described in Sec. 6.4.

A message transmission to an object x is defined in terms of its meta-object $\uparrow x$. The form

$$[x \ \text{<=} \ m \ @ \ r]$$

in the script of an object y, which is the sender of the message m, will be reduced to (interpreted as)

$$[\uparrow x \ \text{<=} \ [\text{:message} \ m \ r \ y]]$$

when the above form is evaluated by the evaluator of y. In the definition of the evaluator object, the part for the evaluation of a message transmission expression is actually defined as above. (Of course, it is possible to access the meta-object of the evaluator object.)

Because a meta-object $\uparrow x$ is also an object, there exists an object $\uparrow\uparrow x$ which is a meta-object of $\uparrow x$. This implies that $\uparrow x$ is implemented in $\uparrow\uparrow x$ in the same way as x is implemented in $\uparrow x$. This situation induces an infinite tower of meta-objects for each objects, but in the actual implementation, we can avoid the infinite tower by the lazy creation of meta-objects.

5 Reflective Programming Facilities in ABCL/R

This section explains language facilities for reflection in ABCL/R using simple examples.

5.1 Sending Messages to Meta-Objects

In ABCL/R, $\uparrow x$ can be accessed as the value of the special form [meta x], and the value of [den $\uparrow x$] is x. Thus, for each object x, [meta [den $\uparrow x$]] $\equiv$ $\uparrow x$ and [den [meta x]] $\equiv x$ always holds. Access to $\uparrow x$ enables the inquiry and/or modification of components of x if $\uparrow x$ has scripts appropriate for those operations (e.g., scripts for :queue and [:script Message] in Figure 1).

Let us look at a small program example in which meta-objects are accessed. Suppose that there is a group of objects consisting of the manager object M

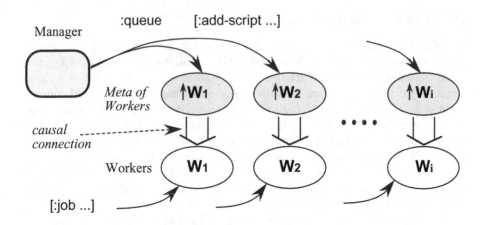

Fig. 2. Manager and Workers

and some worker objects $W_1, W_2, \ldots$. Each W_i can receive a message of pattern [:job *job-type* :param *parameter*], which is the request for a job of *job-type* with *parameter* (Fig. 2).

M constantly monitors each worker W_i, and if M notices that W_i receives requests of a particular job type (e.g., job 1) very frequently, M gives W_i a new script for [:job 1 :param *parameter*] which is an optimized script for the job type 1. This is realized by accessing $\uparrow W_i$ from M. For example, to know the messages received by W_i, M can simply send a message to $\uparrow W_i$ as

$$[[\text{meta } W_i] \texttt{ <== } \texttt{:queue}]$$

and also to add the new script for the job type 1, M can send a message to $\uparrow W_i$ as

```
[[meta Wi] <= [:add-script
        '(=> [:job 1 :param parameter-var]
            body of the script)]]
```

Note that this script extension of W_i by M can be done while W_i is executing its jobs — the performance of the whole system is gradually improved while the system is working.

5.2   Reflective Functions

Beside [meta ...] and [den ...], there is another language feature which facilitates reflective programming in ABCL/R. That is *reflective functions*, which are similar to the *reflective procedures* in 3-Lisp[3]. In 3-Lisp, the unevaluated call-time arguments (as in **fexprs** of the old-fashioned Lisp), call-time environment, and call-time continuation can be accessed in arbitrary place/time using reflective procedures. The triple (arguments, environment, and continuation) represents the "snapshot" of a serial computation of 3-Lisp.

The number of the formal parameters of a reflective function in ABCL/R is always five, and they are bound to the list of call-time (unevaluated) arguments, the call-time environment (as an object), the call-time continuation (as an object), the caller object which has invoked the reflective function, and the evaluator object, respectively.

As an example of the use of (user-defined) reflective functions, let us look at the following definition of a reflective function. This function is actually a definition of a now-type message transmission, namely, the invocation of this function, (now-send T M), is equivalent to the execution of [T <== M].

```
(define (now-send args env cont caller eval) reflect
   [eval <= [:do-seq args env caller] @
       [cont [Target Message]
         [[meta Target]
             <= [:message Message cont caller]]]])
```

The evaluation of the form (now-send T M) is performed at the level of the evaluator as in 3-Lisp. Let E_x be an evaluator object of an object x. Since E_x is an object, there is a meta-object $\uparrow E_x$. So $\uparrow E_x$ has an evaluator, and it is an evaluator of E_x, namely E_{E_x}. If the above expression is invoked as the part of a script of x, then the formal parameters are bound to the following values: args=(T M), env=*environment object in* $\uparrow x$, cont=*continuation object*, caller=x, and eval=E_x. First, the value of the args is evaluated and the elements of the result is bound to Target and Message. Then a message containing Message, cont and caller is sent to the meta-object of Target. Note that the abbreviation form [cont ...] explained in Sec. 4.2 is used.

6   Reflective Programming in ABCL/R

In this section, we will present several characteristic examples of reflective programming in ABCL/R. First, we explain the basic methods for dynamically modifying objects. Then we will show that the dynamic acquisition (or dynamic "inheritance") of scripts from other objects are concisely programmed at the user-level by using the means of dynamic modification. Furthermore, we illustrate how an object can monitor other concurrently running objects' behavior. In this example, the meta-object of the meta-object of an object is involved. Also we will briefly explain the implementation of the timewarp mechanism[10] using reflective features of the language ABCL/R. The reader should be reminded that all the computations illustrated by these examples are performed in the framework of *concurrent* computation.

6.1   Dynamic Modification of Objects

As we have seen, the internal structure of an object can be manipulated as data in the meta-object of the object. In the default meta-object of an object, some special scripts which manipulate the internal structure of the denotation object (queue, scripts, state, and evaluator) are provided. For example, the following messages can be acceptable by the default meta-object.

- [:add-script s] : Adds a new script s to the denotation object of the target meta-object.
- [:script m] : Returns a script whose message pattern matches m.
- [:delete-script m] : Deletes a script whose message pattern matches m.
- :state : Returns the object which represents the state memory of the denotation of the target object.

Let us look at how these messages are used. First, to add a new script to the object x:

[[meta x] <== [:add-script '(=> [:foo X] *body-of-script*)]]

Now x can accept messages that match the pattern [:foo X]. Before adding this script, if x already has a script whose pattern matches [:foo X], this newly added script is used instead of the old one. But the old script still remains and when the new one is deleted, the old one will be used again.

[[meta x] <== [:script [:foo 1]]] $\Longrightarrow$ (=> [:foo X] *body-of-script*)

(The right hand side of "$\Longrightarrow$" is the value of the expression on the left hand side.) The result is the script added before. The execution of the following form deletes it.

[[meta x] <== [:delete-script [:foo 1]]]

In addition, it is possible to access the object which represents the state memory by:

[s := [[meta x] <== :state]]

Variable s is bound to the state memory of x represented as the state object of x. To know the value of a variable, a message [:value *variable-name*] is used as follows.

[s <== [:value 'X]] $\Longrightarrow$ 1

In this example, the value of the state variable X of x is 1. To create a new variable binding in the state memory, the following will do.

[s <== [:add-binding 'Y 100]]

Then x has a new state variable Y with its value being 100. If the binding of Y already exists before adding, the old one is hidden by the new binding. The old binding remains but cannot be accessed until the new one is deleted.

Using these special scripts of the default meta-objects and state objects, we can write the code to modify the scripts and the state memory of an object dynamically, and such modification can be done while the object being modified is running. The examples described below use these special scripts effectively.

6.2   Dynamic Acquisition (Inheritance) of Scripts

Suppose an object x has received a message M, but x does not have any script for M. If x has the following script:

> (=> *message-pattern-for-M* @ *reply-var* from *sender-var*
>   (inherit *msg-pattern-for-M reply-var sender-var y* t))

x can inherit (acquire) the script for the message M from another object y. (What really happens when the above script is executed is: ↑x gets the script dynamically from ↑y and then ↑x starts execution with the environment (state memory and evaluator) of x as if the script were x's local one.)

inherit is a reflective function whose caller object acquires (inherits) scripts from a specified object. The first, second, and third arguments of inherit are the message, reply destination, and the sender, respectively. The fourth argument is the source of inheritance, which is an object (y) from which the caller (x) inherits a script. If the last argument is a non-nil value, the script inherited is stored in the caller object as its own script. Then the caller object can process the subsequent messages of the same pattern using the newly acquired script, and now it doesn't need to inherit the script for the same message pattern. The following is the definition of the function inherit.

```
(define (inherit args env cont caller eval) reflect
  [eval <= [:do-seq args env caller] @
    [cont [Message Reply Sender Inherit-Source Cache?]
      (let ((scr [[meta Inherit-Source]
                     <== [:script Message]]))
        (if scr then
          [eval <= [:do-progn (scr$body scr)
                    [env-gen
                        <== [:new (script-alist
                                    [Message Reply Sender]
                                    scr) env]]
                    caller]
            @ [cont Value
                (if Cache? then
                    [[meta caller]
                        <== [:add-script scr]])
                  [[meta caller] <= :end]]]
        else
          (warn "No script found: ~A ~A" Message Inherit-Source)
          [[meta caller] <= :end]))]])
```

First, all the call-time arguments are evaluated by the evaluator object eval, and the values are bound to Message, Reply, Sender, Inherit-Source, and Cache?. The message [:script ...] explained above is used to try to get, from the source of the inheritance (the value of Inherit-Source), a script whose pattern matches the message (the value of Message). If found, the body of the script is evaluated using the environment of the caller object as if it were the caller's local one.

Let us look at a simple example of using the function inherit. Objects bird and emu are defined as follows:

```
[object bird
  (script
    (=> :has-feather? !t)    ; returns t
    (=> :can-fly? !t)        ; returns t
    (=> Any @ Reply from Sender
        (inherit Any Reply Sender animal nil)))]

[object emu
  (script
    (=> :can-fly? !nil)      ; returns nil
    (=> Any @ Reply from Sender
        (inherit Any Reply Sender bird nil)))]
```

These objects model simple knowledge about birds and emus. Since an emu is a bird, the object emu inherits all the scripts from bird except for :can-fly?. In the second script of emu, the single pattern variable Any can match any messages. When a message :can-fly? is sent to emu, it answers using its local script. In the case of :has-feather?, emu inherits the script from bird, and answers using it.

In this example, the fifth argument of inherit is nil. So emu can always answer correctly being consistent with the changes made to the definition of bird, because the scripts acquired are not cached in emu.

The function inherit will be used in the examples below. It should be noted that the object-based inheritance scheme in [14] and the proxy-query inheritance in [15] can easily be implemented using our inheritance scheme.

6.3   Monitoring Running Objects

The behavior of an object can be monitored from outside through its meta-object. For example, let us consider how an object can monitor what messages have been received by a specified object while the specified object is running. Below we will show how simple reflective programming in ABCL/R implements this monitoring facility.

Let Monitor be an object which monitors messages accepted by an object x. To do so, Monitor modifies the behavior of x so that whenever x *accepts* a message m from s with reply destination r, x sends a message [:has-accepted m r s] to Monitor. See Fig. 3.

To start monitoring of x, the following will do:

```
[Monitor <= [:monitor x]]
```

Now, whenever x accepts a message m with reply destination r from s, Monitor receives a message [:has-accepted m r s]. To stop this monitoring:

```
[Monitor <= :stop-monitoring]
```

We can start/stop monitoring whenever we want — even when the object being monitored, namely the subject of monitoring, is executing its script. The

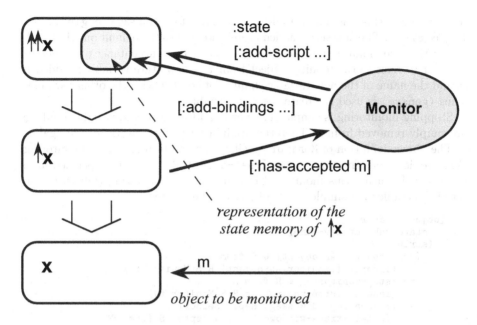

Fig. 3. The monitor object

inherent concurrency explained in 4.2 guarantees that the meta-object can receive and accept messages when its denotation is executing the script.

The definition of the monitor object `Monitor` is as follows:

```
[object Monitor
  (state subject new-name)
  (script
    (=> [:monitor An-object]
        [subject := An-object]
        [new-name := (gensym)]
        [[meta [meta subject]]
           <== [:add-script
                 ‘(=> :begin
                      ...
                      (if scr then
                          [,new-name
                             <= [:has-accepted . mrs]]
                          ...))]]
        [[[meta [meta subject]] <== :state]
           <== [:add-binding new-name Me]])
    (=> :stop-monitoring
        [[meta [meta subject]]
           <== [:delete-script ’:begin]]
        [[[meta [meta subject]] <== :state]
           <== [:remove-binding new-name]]))]
```

When the monitor object receives the message [:monitor x], the monitor object modifies ⇑x so that ⇑x may send the monitored information, namely, a message [:has-accepted m r s] when x accepts a message m (from s with reply r). To do this, the monitor adds a new script for a message :begin through ⇑⇑x (see Fig. 1). The new script added is almost equal to the default one (in Fig. 1) except that the monitored information is sent to x upon acceptance of a message. In order to refer to the monitor object from x, a new state variable is added in x, and the name of the new variable should not conflict with the other variables. Thus ⟨gensym⟩ is used to create the new variable.

Stopping monitoring is simple. The newly added script and variable bindings are simply removed from x. Then the original script for :begin is used again.

The above definition of Monitor specifies just the framework for monitoring. What to do when a message comes [:has-accepted ...] is not specified in its definition. By using this monitor object, actually by acquiring (inheriting) its scripts, the following simple tracer object can be defined.

```
[object tracer
  (state subject new-name)
  (script
    (=> [:monitor An-object] @ R from S
        (inherit [:monitor An-object] R S Monitor t))
    (=> :stop-monitoring @ R from S
        (inherit :stop-monitoring R S Monitor t))
    (=> [:has-accepted Message Reply Sender]
        (format *trace-window* "~&~S accepts ~S from ~S"
                subject Message Sender)))]
```

The object tracer monitors an object and displays the trace of message acceptances on *trace-window*.

6.4 Time Warp Mechanism

A simple *Time Warp* mechanism based on the *Virtual Time* concept[10] has been implemented using the reflective language constructs in ABCL/R.

Object-oriented concurrent programming offers the natural framework for distributed discrete event simulation. Each entity in the simulation domain is modeled as an object, and events among entities are represented as transmission and reception of messages by such objects. The essential problem in this framework is how to manage the *temporal consistency* among events. Our computation model does not assume the existence of the *global clock*.

In [16], this problem is solved with ABCL/1 using a *rollback* mechanism based on the notion of the virtual time. Messages transmitted by objects (which model or represent simulation entities) explicitly contain *timestamps*, and if *time conflict* is detected by an object (i.e., the timestamp τ of a message is older than the time according to the local clock of the object), the object performs undoing of its execution (rollback) to τ. That is, it sends *anti-messages* to objects to which the object has already sent messages since τ, and undoes the execution so far.

As in [16], this roll back mechanism is usually explicitly specified in the scripts of an object mingled with the description of simulation activities. But this explicit specification of roll back severely decreases the modularity of the simulation program and it is very cumbersome and error-prone because the programmer has to write the code for roll back everywhere necessary in the script.

Since the rollback mechanism (of handling anti-messages and undo operations for state variables) is meta-level to the simulation of activities, our implementation explicitly separates the two levels and describes the general roll back mechanism in the definition of the meta-object of an object doing simulation activities.

To define an object which has the Time Warp mechanism, the meta-object specification facility of ABCL/R can be used as in the following object definition.

```
[object a-simulation-object
  (meta TW-meta-gen)
  (script
    (=> message-pattern @ reply from sender
        description of simulation activities)
    ...)]
```

(meta TW-meta-gen) in the above definition specifies the generator (TW-meta-gen) of the meta-object of *a-simulation-object* explicitly. (The definition of TW-meta-gen is described in Appendix.) When the above expression is evaluated, TW-meta-gen, instead of the default meta-object generator, is actually used in creating a new object.

The Time Warp mechanism is fully handled by the meta-object. Thus the programmer of *a-simulation-object* does not need to write the code for rollback. The Time Warp mechanism part and the simulation part are completely separated. Of course, it is possible to use TW-meta-gen for defining of other simulation objects. It can be used as library code. Introducing this type of modularity is an important feature of languages with reflective architecture.

7   Concluding Remarks

7.1   Summary

We designed and implemented an object-oriented *concurrent* language ABCL/R which has a *reflective* architecture based on the notion of meta-objects. The following is the summary of our present work.

- Each object is represented/implemented by its *meta-object*. The meta-object incorporates the meta-level representations of structural and computational aspects of the object in a meta circular way. A meta-object is also an object of ABCL/R. This implies the infinite tower of meta-objects. (For its implementation, see below.) An evaluator (interpreter) of the language is also an object. In our computation system, a number of such objects may work in parallel.
- Reflective computation is performed by *message transmissions to meta-objects* and such message transmissions take place concurrently. Reflective computation can be performed in meta-objects of any level because of the infinite tower of meta-objects. Sending messages to a meta-object makes it

possible to inquire and alter the structure and behavior of the object. It is possible to send messages to the meta-object of an object while the object is performing its jobs. Thus, a concurrent system can gradually modify itself by means of objects and (their) meta-objects in the system sending messages each other.

- The dynamic modification of running objects in a concurrent system can be described by using reflective language constructs of ABCL/R. We have presented programming examples of dynamic (concurrent) modification such as acquiring (or inheriting) scripts from other objects, and monitoring a running object by modifying its meta-object through the meta-object of the meta-object.

- Enhancement of program modularity can be attained by using meta-objects. The example of a simple Time Warp mechanism has demonstrated this. In a simulation program using this mechanism, the meta-level part is separated from the object-level part by specifying a non-default meta-object for each simulation object.

7.2   Current Status of ABCL/R

So far, we have built a prototype implementation of ABCL/R written in ABCL/1 (written in Kyoto Common Lisp on UNIX and Symbolics Common Lisp on Symbolics Lisp Machines). All the examples described in the preceding sections are actually tested on this implementation.

The primary concern of implementation is how to represent the infinite tower of meta-objects. In our implementation, meta-objects are created in the lazy way. A meta-object $\uparrow x$ is actually created when the access to $\uparrow x$ takes place — when the evaluator first evaluates an expression [meta x].

7.3   Future Work

This work is our first attempt to build concurrent reflective systems. As we mentioned in Sec. 3, there are at least two approaches to building the causally connected self representation of an object-oriented concurrent system. To completely represent the whole concurrent system as a single datum is difficult because of the causal connection. To do so, we need a good formalism and an appropriate modeling of a concurrent system as a whole, as well as techniques to establish the causal connection.

A possible approach is that the system is divided into some groups of objects in such a way that each group contains objects that are related each other. Then we describe an approximate (or partial) self representation of the computational aspect of each group and make the representation accessible from all the members of the group.

References

1. Smith, B.C.: Reflection and semantics in a procedural language. Technical Report TR-272, Laboratory for Computer Science, MIT (1982)
2. Maes, P.: Computational reflection. Technical Report 87-2, Artificial Intelligence Laboratory, Vrije Universiteit Brussel (1987)
3. Smith, B.C.: Reflection and semantics in Lisp. In: Proceedings of ACM Symposium on Principles of Programming Languages (POPL), pp. 23–35 (1984)
4. Friedman, D.P., Wand, M.: Reification: Reflection without metaphysics. In: Proceedings of Lisp and Functional Programming, pp. 348–355. ACM (1984)
5. Weyrauch, R.: Prolegomena to a theory of mechanized formal reasoning. Artificial Intelligence 13(1,2), 133–170 (1980)
6. Batali, J.: Computational introspection. AI Memo AIM-701, Artificial Intelligence Laboratory. MIT (1982)
7. Maes, P.: Concepts and experiments in computational reflection. In: Proceedings of ACM Conference on Object-Oriented Programming Systems, Languages, and Applications (OOPSLA), pp. 147–155 (1987)
8. Yonezawa, A., Tokoro, M. (eds.): Object-Oriented Concurrent Programming. The MIT Press (1987)
9. Hewitt, C.: Viewing control structures as patterns of passing messages. Artificial Intelligence 8(3), 323–364 (1977)
10. Jefferson, D.R.: Virtual time. ACM Transactions on Programming Languages and Systems 7(3), 404–425 (1985)
11. Yonezawa, A., Briot, J.P., Shibayama, E.: Object-oriented concurrent programming in ABCL/1. In: Proceedings of ACM Conference on Object-Oriented Programming Systems, Languages, and Applications (OOPSLA), pp. 258–268 (1986)
12. Yonezawa, A., Shibayama, E., Takada, T., Honda, Y.: Modeling and programming in an object-oriented concurrent language ABCL/1. In: Yonezawa, A., Tokoro, M. (eds.) Object-Oriented Concurrent Programming, pp. 55–89. The MIT Press (1987)
13. Watanabe, T.: Reflection in object-oriented concurrent systems. Technical Report (Master Thesis), Department of Information Science, Tokyo Institute of Technology (March 1988)
14. Hailpern, B., Nguyen, V.: A model for object-based inheritance. In: Shriver, B., Wegner, P. (eds.) Research Directions in Object-Oriented Programming, pp. 147–164. The MIT Press (1987)
15. Briot, J.-P.: Inheritance and synchronization in concurrent OOP. In: Bézivin, J., Hullot, J.-M., Lieberman, H., Cointe, P. (eds.) ECOOP 1987. LNCS, vol. 276, pp. 32–40. Springer, Heidelberg (1987)
16. Shibayama, E., Yonezawa, A.: Distributed computing in ABCL/1. In: Yonezawa, A., Tokoro, M. (eds.) Object-Oriented Concurrent Programming, pp. 91–128. The MIT Press (1987)

A   Code for Simple Time Warp Mechanism

TW-meta-gen is the generator of meta-objects in which a simple time warp mechanism is implemented. The structure of an object consists of a *local clock*, an *input message queue*, and an *output message queue*, a set of scripts, a state memory, and an evaluator. The local clock and input/output message queues are implemented as values of variables lvt, input-messages, and output-history, respectively.

The arrival of a message is represented as the acceptance of the message (in meta-level) which matches [:message Message Reply-Dest Sender Timestamp] where the argument Timestamp is the timestamp of the message. Messages which match the pattern [:anti-message Message Reply-Dest Sender Timestamp] are *antimessages*.

In this program, the rollback works only for the past type message transmissions. The retrieval of the state value is not implemented. In the script description of an object whose meta-object is created by TW-meta-gen, timestamps must be specified explicitly in message sending expressions like following:

[*target* <= *message* @ *reply-destination* :time *receive-time*]

receive-time is the virtual receive time[10] — the time at which the target object receives the message *message*.

The definition of TW-input-queue-gen, TW-output-history-gen, and TW--evaluator-gen is omitted. See [13] for details.

```
;; Meta-object generator with Time Warp mechanism
[object TW-object-gen
  (script
   (=> [:new State-Vars Lexical-Env Scripts & Creation-Time]
       ![object TW-object     ; scope of this name is local to TW-object-gen
         (state [input-queue := [TW-input-queue-gen <== :new]]
                [output-history := [TW-output-history-gen <== :new]]
                [state := [state-gen <== [:new State-Vars Lexical-Env]]]
                [scriptset := Scripts]
                [evaluator := [TW-eval-gen <== :new]]
                [mode := ':dormant]
                [lvt := (or Creation-Time 0)])   ; Local Virtual Time
         (script
          (=> [Message-Type Message Reply-Dest Sender Timestamp]
              where (member Message-Type '(:message :anti-message))
              [input-queue
                 <== [:enqueue
                       [Message-Type Message Reply-Dest Sender
                                     Timestamp]]]
              (if (eq mode ':dormant) then
                  [mode := ':active]
                  [Me <= :begin]))
          (=> :begin
              (match [input-queue <== :dequeue]
                ;; positive messages whose timestamp is equal to or newer than LVT
                (is [:message Message Reply-Dest Sender Timestamp]
                    where (>= Timestamp lvt)
                    (case (find-script Message scriptset)
```

```
            (is [Message-Pattern Script-Body]  ; a script is found
                [lvt := Timestamp]
                [evaluator
                    <= [:do-prg Script-Body
                            (newenv Message-Pattern
                                    [Message Reply-Dest Sender]
                                    state)
                            [den Me] lvt output-queue]
                    @ [cont ignore
                        [TW-object <= :end]]])
            (is []                                  ; script is not found
                (warn "Cannot handle the message: ~S" Mesg)
                [Me <= :end])))
    ;; Messages whose timestamp is older than LVT
    (is [Message-Type Message Reply-Dest Sender Timestamp]
        where (< Timestamp lvt)
        [lvt := Timestamp]
        [input-queue <== [:rollback-to lvt]]
        ;; Sending anti-messages
        (case-loop [output-history <== :last]
            (is [Message Reply-Dest Target Timestamp]
                where (> Timestamp lvt)
                [[meta Target]
                    <= [:anti-message
                            Message Reply-Dest [den Me]
                            Timestamp]]
                [output-history <== :drop]))
        [Me <= :end])))
(=> :end
    (if (not [input-queue <== :empty?]) then
        [Me <= :begin]
    else
        [mode := ':dormant])))]])))]
```

Building Safe Concurrency Abstractions

Ole Lehrmann Madsen

Department of Computer Science, Aarhus University and the Alexandra Institute
Åbogade 34, DK-8200 Aarhus N, Denmark
ole.l.madsen@{cs.au.dk,alexandra.dk}

Abstract. Concurrent object-oriented programming in Beta is based on semaphores and coroutines and the ability to define high-level concurrency abstractions like monitors, and rendezvous-based communication, and their associated schedulers. The coroutine mechanism of SIMULA has been generalized into the notions of concurrent and alternating objects. Alternating objects may be used to start a cooperative thread for each possible blocking communication and is thus an alternative to asynchronous messages and guarded commands. Beta like SIMULA, the first OO language, was designed as a language for modeling as well as programming, and we describe how this has had an impact on the design of the language. Although Beta supports the definition of high-level concurrency abstractions, the use of these rely on the discipline of the programmer as is the case for Java and other mainstream OO languages. We introduce the notion of *subpattern (including subclass) restrictions* as a mechanism for defining safe concurrency abstractions. Subpattern restrictions have been implemented in a new experimental version of Beta, called **xBeta**.

1 Introduction

Concurrent object-oriented programming, and concurrent programming in general, is a discipline that despite many years of research still is difficult to master. And no model for concurrent programming has been established as the one to be used. In practice, concurrent programming is often based on threads, locks, and/or monitor-like mechanisms. It is well known that these styles of programming in mainstream languages such as Java[27], C++[53] and C [34] give rise to many problems with race conditions, deadlocks and non thread-safe libraries.

In 1999 Per Brinch-Hansen, the designer of the first high-level concurrent programming language Concurrent Pascal [12], wrote the following [13]:

> Gosling [1996, p.399] claims that Java uses monitors to synchronize threads. Unfortunately, a closer inspection reveals that Java does not support a monitor concept. . . .
>
> The failure to give an adequate meaning to thread interaction is a very deep flaw of Java that vitiates the conceptual integrity of the monitor concept. . . .

G. Agha et al. (Eds.): Yonezawa Festschrift, LNCS 8665, pp. 66–104, 2014.

It is astounding to me that Java's insecure parallelism is taken seriously by the programming community, a quarter of a century after the invention of monitors and Concurrent Pascal. It has no merit. ...

If programmers no longer see the need for interference control, then I have apparently wasted my most creative years developing rigorous concepts, which have now been compromised or abandoned by programmers.

Today one may conclude that Brinch-Hansen was right in the sense that Java as a concurrent programming language has a number of problems that Concurrent Pascal did not have. On the other hand, Concurrent Pascal has a number of other shortcomings as also expressed by the work of Brinch-Hansen himself [11].

In the literature, there are many proposals for concurrent OO programming languages that do not suffer from the problems of Java. These include Actors [29,2,3], CSP [32], Ada [1], ABCL[61], Concurrent Smalltalk[59], Erlang [6], and Timber [51].

Recently there has been a growing interest in using Actor-like languages like Erlang as an alternative to Java. One reason for this is that in Erlang concurrent processes are completely encapsulated and there is no way two or more processes can access the same data items. The language Dart [26] is a new OO language that also supports processes as 'isolated' units.

In most of the above-mentioned languages, communication is based on messages between processes. A process may send a message (using an *output command*) and/or receive a message (using an *input command*). A message may be a simple or structured value or a method activation depending on the language.

There is a standing issue regarding the use of synchronous versus asynchronous messages. With synchronous messages, the caller is blocked until the receiver is ready to accept the message. The proponents for asynchronous messages argue that these reduce the likelihoods for deadlocks just as the calling process may do other things while waiting for the answer. Some authors [2,51] also argue that asynchronous messages are more fundamental than synchronous messages.

With pure asynchronous messages, return values have to be passed back by another message call, as in CSP. To improve on this, so-called futures [52] are often used to hold return values. However, this to some extent often just delays the point where the process may be blocked waiting for a value.

Proponents for synchronous messages argue that this style makes programs more readable compared to control flow with sending messages and receiving answers, even using futures, that may be difficult to follow.

A process may be involved in communication with several other processes and because the order of arrival of messages from different processes is nondeterministic, most languages have a select mechanism (based on guarded commands as proposed by Dijkstra [25]) that makes it possible to wait for more than one message at a given point of execution. This may be combined with Boolean expressions that further may control which messages are accepted.

A disadvantage of the select-mechanism is that in most languages there is an asymmetry between sending and receiving messages since a select may only contain input commands. There are proposals [7] in the literature for allowing both input and output commands in a select, and Hoare mentions this in his original paper on CSP. As we will discuss below, the lack of symmetry between input and output commands and the use of Boolean expressions may blur the control flow of the process.

In this paper, we present the Beta [36,39,42] approach to concurrent object-oriented programming. Beta is a language designed for modeling as well as programming, following the tradition of SIMULA. For the concurrency part, the original goals for the design of Beta were:

- In contrast to SIMULA, full concurrency should be supported.[1]
- It should be possible for the programmer to define high-level concurrency abstractions using the basic mechanisms. This should include the ability to define an associated scheduler.
- The concurrency mechanisms should support modeling as well as programming.

SIMULA [22,20,23], the very first object-oriented programming language, was originally designed as a language for describing simulation systems motivated by work in operations research at the Norwegian Computing Center in Oslo, Norway. The goal for SIMULA I was to devise a language for modeling as well as programming systems to be simulated.

Since SIMULA was supposed to model real-life systems, it was necessary to be able to describe concurrent processes from the application domain. SIMULA did not have true concurrency, but did have so-called quasi-parallel systems based on coroutines. Later full concurrency was added in the Lund SIMULA system [46,56], by introducing a mechanism for enforcing suspend on a coroutine from, say, an external process, like a clock.

One of the strengths of SIMULA is the ability to define schedulers for concurrent processes based on the mechanism for scheduling active objects (coroutines) in a simulation program. An example of a simulation scheduler was described by Dahl and Hoare [19]. In the Lund SIMULA system, this mechanism may be used to define schedulers for real concurrent objects.

Beta is based on the coroutine mechanism of SIMULA and further generalizes and simplifies it. SIMULA has symmetric (resume) as well as semi-coroutines (call, detach). Beta only has semi-coroutines, but symmetric coroutines may be defined as an abstraction. In Beta, objects may execute concurrently or alternatingly (see below).

In an early version of Beta, communication between concurrent objects was supported by a rendezvous mechanism as in Ada, and a select-mechanism with Boolean expressions but allowing both input and output commands. It was, however, soon realized that it was complicated to implement a symmetric select, and the concept of alternation was developed as a replacement.

At a later stage, experience with the rendezvous mechanism was found to be too heavy for a number of concurrency problems — often monitors were much

---

[1] As mentioned below, full concurrency was later added in the Lund SIMULA system.

clearer. Jean Vaucher introduced the concept of prefixed procedures [55] inspired by subclass and the inner-mechanism in SIMULA, and he showed how to define a monitor abstraction using subprocedures and inner.

The experience with using rendezvous and monitors was that different concurrency mechanisms were needed for different kinds of problems. This was apparently also a requirement for C++: "I considered it crucial – as I still do – that more than one notion of concurrency should be expressible in the language" Bjarne Stroustrup in [54].

It turned out that in Beta it was possible to define high-level concurrency abstractions like monitor, Ada-like rendezvous, futures, asynchronous methods, etc. using a low-level mechanism for synchronization [42,62]. Semaphores were therefore chosen as the low-level synchronization mechanism.

Although it is possible to define high-level concurrency abstractions in Beta, there is nothing that forces a programmer to use them as intended. Beta thus has the same kind of problems as Brinch-Hansen has pointed out for Java. When Beta was designed, we either had to select a fixed set of safe concurrency mechanisms or include general mechanisms for defining concurrency abstractions.

Languages, such as Simula, Beta, C++, Java, Smalltalk, and C# suffer from the problem that they are primarily perceived as sequential languages. Concurrency is often presented and considered as an add-on. One just has to consult text books and reference manuals, and other course material, which in most cases start by presenting the sequential parts and at an (often) later stage introduce the concurrency part. This does not encourage/inspire programmers to think of their software systems as concurrent systems.

With languages like CSP, ABCL, and Erlang this is quite different, since these are inherently concurrent languages that force the programmers to think in organizing his/her program as a set of communicating concurrent processes.

In this paper, we present the Beta approach to concurrent object-oriented programming with focus on abstraction mechanisms for building high-level concurrency abstractions with associated schedulers. We also present the notion of alternating activities as an alternative to asynchronous messages and select statements.

To overcome the problems with unsafe concurrency mechanisms, we introduce a language mechanism called *subpattern restrictions* for restricting the use of a concurrency abstraction (class library). Subpattern restrictions make it possible to define safe abstraction mechanisms without compromising the generality of Beta.

A new experimental version of Beta, called **xBeta**, has been implemented in order to experiment with various improvements of Beta, including subpattern restrictions. In Beta, a pattern is a generalization of, e.g., class and method – subpattern restrictions thus also make it possible to enforce restrictions on subclasses and submethods (as we shall introduce later).

Other improvements in **xBeta** include a new module mechanism based on singular objects [44], and a new debugger based on a combination of object diagrams and message sequence charts [43].

The overall goal of this paper is to contribute to language mechanisms for concurrent object-oriented programming that are safe and help keep structure and overview of the code. We are not addressing efficiency issues of multi/many-core computers – for a large class of software systems, readability, structure and safety are major issues.

As mentioned, Beta is a language for modeling as well as programming. We start by a short introduction in section 2 to modeling in Beta and (some of) the implications for the (concurrent) parts of Beta. In section 3, we present two examples of concurrency abstractions defined in Beta: a monitor-based system and a rendezvous-based system. In section 4, we show how these systems may be defined (by the programmer) in Beta. In section 5, we present the language mechanism for expressing subpattern restrictions. Finally, section 6 is related work and evaluation and section 7 is the conclusion.

2   Modeling

Programming is modeling [21,41,47,60,49,38,45]), although some people do not think modeling is important. The critique [17,18] of the modeling aspect has been that (1) just a small percentage of the code relates to the "real world", and (2) there are many other means for modeling such as mathematical functions, algebras, processes, constraints, rules, and automata.

It is true that the ability to represent the real world may have been overemphasized. This is, however, a question of what is the "real world"? Any application domain may be considered the "real world" and independent of whether or not a given technical domain such as network protocol is considered the "real world", the domain has phenomena and concepts that may be represented using objects and classes.

It is of course also true that OO is not the only formalism for modeling (the "real world" / application domains), and depending on the purpose of the model, other formalisms may be better suited. However, when the purpose is programming software systems, we claim that a modeling approach to OO has a number of advantages as we shall argue below.

Software systems are complex entities and it is still a major problem to avoid errors just as they are often inefficient and difficult to maintain. By and large, we are still – and will continue to be – dependent on people's ability to understand the structure, interoperability and details of these systems. And for many systems no single person is capable of doing this. To quote Grady Booch [10]: "..., the complexity of such [industrial strength software] systems exceeds the human intellectual capacity."

We therefore claim that understandability of software systems is an essential requirement. The better people understand the software, the easier it is to ensure the right functionality, avoid errors, and ensure efficiency. There is a general acceptance that abstraction and modularization are powerful means for dealing with complexity just as simplicity (over smartness and tricks) should be a guiding principle. To quote Kristen Nygaard [42]: "To program is to understand".

This should be understood in contrast to: "To program is to get away with it" – Nygaard called this the Lisp-hacker's credo. These quotes appeared during (heated) discussions with (especially Lisp, Loops, Flavors) people about the purpose of (multiple) inheritance: for inheritance of code (code grabbing according to Nygaard) or for representing concept hierarchies.

In programming, abstraction is often about hiding details (information hiding and encapsulation) of the code and providing well-defined interfaces. Abstraction is, however, also about identifying and forming concepts (abstractions) representing knowledge about the application domain [30]. This form of abstraction requires an in-depth understanding of the application domain and this is what modeling is about.

Modeling is really about abstraction in the sense of identifying and forming concepts (abstractions). Any abstraction is a concept, and language mechanisms like procedure (method) or class are suitable for representing concepts/abstractions. Procedures and classes in a given program should therefore represent meaningful concepts in the application domain. And a class/subclass hierarchy should in general represent a concept hierarchy that is meaningful in the application domain.

There is no conflict between viewing abstraction as information hiding and/or encapsulation and concept formation, since the latter may provide guidelines for the former. And as mentioned, one of the advantages of a modeling approach is that the application domain is reflected in the programs [40,15]. A modeling approach thus provides design guidelines for identifying classes, subclasses, methods, data items, etc.

An important part of the Beta project was to develop a *conceptual framework* [42, Chap. 2, 18] for understanding and organizing knowledge about the application domain. The conceptual framework includes means for identification of relevant phenomena and their properties: objects, properties of objects, and related action-sequences and their properties. In addition, conceptual means such as various forms of composition, classification, and association are discussed.

An abstraction may be considered a model [14], but in the Scandinavian approach to OO, a model is considered a physical entity [41], and the program execution is viewed as such a physical model. This is in contrast to UML where the UML diagram is considered the model – this would correspond to the program text being the model. As argued in [41,38,45], the dynamic process generated during a program execution should be considered the model for the application domain. Of course, language mechanisms/languages for describing (the program text and/or UML diagram) are equally important.

Composition (*is-part-of* relation) and classification (*is-a* relation) are well-known conceptual means. In programming languages, we have support for composition of action sequences: an action-sequence may be composed of other actions by means of procedures (methods). For objects, class and subclass support classification by making it possible to represent a classification hierarchy of general and more specialized concepts as the one in Figure 1 for vehicles.

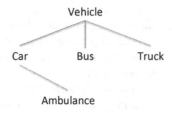

Fig. 1. Vehicle hierarchy

Beta and UML have direct support for composition of objects in the sense that an object may consist of other objects. In [9], a proposal for supporting part objects in Smalltalk is presented. Composition of objects is not directly supported by mainstream languages like C++, Java and C#. You may simulate composition using constant references, but this is only indirect support.

For concurrent action-sequences one may also claim that composition is supported since an action-sequences may be split into two or more concurrent action-sequences using mechanisms like parbegin/parend and fork/join.

Classification of action-sequences are, however, rarely supported by programming languages and not by mainstream languages. Mechanisms like procedure (method) and process do support simple one-level classification since action-sequences may be grouped and given a name as a procedure or process. It is, however, not possible to define procedure or process hierarchies – i.e. inheritance for methods.

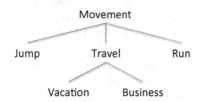

Fig. 2. Movement hierarchy

For people, composition and classification are used to understand and organize knowledge for all kinds of phenomena. Consider concepts like movement, travel, run, jump, business (travel), and vacation (travel). As shown in Figure 2, these may be organized in a classification hierarchy where jump and travel are more specialized action-sequences than movement, which on the other hand is a generalization. Another example is cooking in general and more specialized cooking as Italian cooking, French cooking, Chinese cooking, etc.

Beta supports classification of action-sequences [37]: a method may be a *sub-method* of another method just like a class may be a subclass of another class. And as we shall see later, a process may be a defined as a *subprocess* of another process.

2.1 Submethods in Beta

In this section, we give examples of how submethods may be defined and used in Beta. For the benefit of the reader, we will use a syntax in the style of C++, Java, and C# to avoid introducing Beta syntax.

In Beta there is no distinction between a class and a method – they are unified into the notion of a *pattern*. A pattern may be used as a class or method and instances of a pattern may be executed as method activations, or as coroutines. As we shall see later, coroutines may be executed concurrently or alternatingly with other coroutines.

A *class* in the following means a pattern intended to be used as a class. A similar terminology is used for *method, coroutine*, etc.

A class (pattern) has the following syntax:

```
MyClass: super{ attributes do statements }
```

Where **super** is the superclass of **MyClass**, **attributes** describes the attributes of objects and **statements** describes a sequence of statements.

As can be seen, a class pattern may contain a do-part in the form of statements to be executed. A method (pattern) has the following syntax:

```
returnType msg(arguments): super{ attributes do statements }
```

The structure of a method is the same as the structure of a class with respect to super, attributes and do-part. A class may in fact also have arguments and a return type, but we will not give examples of this in this paper.

Consider the following example of a submethod hierarchy:

```
void msg1(): { ... do S1; inner; S6 };
void msg2(): msg1{ ... do S2; inner; S5 };
void msg3(): msg2{ ... do S3; inner; S4 };
```

The methods msg2 and msg3 are submethods of msg1 and msg2 respectively, and msg1 and msg2 are *supermethods* of msg2 and msg3 respectively. Execution of msg1 implies that S1, inner and then S6 are executed, and in this case, inner is just a skip-statement with no effect.

Execution of msg2 starts by execution of the do-part of msg1, and in this case, execution of inner in msg1 implies that the do part of msg2 is executed. All together the following statements are executed: S1, inner (in msg1) S2, inner(in msg2), S5 and then S6. In this case, inner in msg1 has an effect whereas inner in msg2 is a skip-statement.

Submethods may form an arbitrary hierarchy - the method msg3 is a submethod of msg2 which in turn is a submethod of msg1. Execution of msg3 gives rise to the following statements being executed: S1, S2, S3, S4, S5, S6.

In Beta, it is possible to define *singular objects* – corresponding to anonymous classes in e.g. Java. In a similar way, it is possible to define *singular method activations*. A singular method activation may have the form:

```
msg2{ ... do S7 }
```

Execution of this statement implies that the do-part of the top supermethod, in this case msg1, is executed and the resulting statements being executed are: S1, S2, S7, S5, S6.

A singular method activation corresponds to a prefixed block in SIMULA, which in turn is a generalization of inner blocks from Algol 60 [48].

In Beta, control abstractions are defined using submethods. This includes iterators as shown in the example below of a List class:

```
List :
   { void insert(V: integer ): {...};
     integer head(): {... };
     void scan():
       { current: integer
       do current := first_element ;
          while current <> none then
            inner ;
            current := next_element ;
          endwhile
       };
       — representation of List
   }
void useList():
   { L: obj List ;
   do ...;
     L.scan{do current.print ()}
   }
```

The List has methods insert and head (returns and removes the head of the list). In addition, List has a control pattern scan that iterates through all elements of the list – none is the the same as null in Java. For each element of the list, the variable current holds the value of the next element and inner is executed. Execution of inner implies that the do-part of a submethod of scan is executed. Note that inner appears within a loop and is thus potentially executed several times.

The method useList defines a List object L, it scans the elements of L, and prints each element.

In Beta, a declaration like L: obj List defines a static object in the form of L being an instance of List. It is similar to final List L = new List() in Java.

Execution of the anonymous method activation L.scan{do current.print()} thus prints the elements of L. Note that L.scan is the supermethod of the anonymous method activation.

Control abstractions defined using submethods and inner have the advantage that you do not need to initialize the iterator and there is no state in the object

```
M:  obj Semaphore;
L:  obj List;
void entry(): { do M.wait(); inner; M.signal() }
void put(V: integer): entry{ do L.put(V) }
integer get(): entry{ do return L.get() }
```

Fig. 3. Supermethod ensuring exclusive access

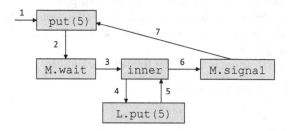

Fig. 4. Entry supermethod

keeping track of the progress of the iterator. This means that several instances
of the control abstraction (iterator) can be made.

Submethods are also useful for describing a general supermethod that ensures
mutual access to shared variables as shown in Figure 3. Here we have two objects:
a Semaphore M, a List L and three methods entry, put and get.

The method entry is a supermethod used by put and get, which are both
submethods of entry. Execution of the do-part of put and get is thus wrapped
by the do-part of entry. Figure 4 shows the actions executed for put(5). As
can be seen entry ensures the exclusive access to the variable L. Later we will
expand this example to show how a monitor abstraction may be defined.

3   Multi-sequential Action-Sequences

In Beta, the basic mechanisms for supporting multiple action-sequences are
coroutines and semaphores.[2] A coroutine may be executed concurrently with
other coroutines or alternatingly with the execution of other coroutines within
a concurrent object. These basic mechanisms are used for defining higher level
concurrency abstractions by means of patterns.

In this section, we will introduce some of the concurrency abstractions defined in Beta and in a subsequent section, we will show how these are defined
using coroutines and semaphores. We present these concurrency abstractions
as if certain patterns: system, process, monitor, activity, port, entry, etc. are

---

[2] In **xBeta**, semaphores are not primitives, but may be implemented as abstractions
– see section 5.

built-in mechanisms in Beta, and they are also marked as keywords (in bold). The implementation in Beta is shown in section 4.

In general, a Beta system may contain one or more modules[3] defining concurrency abstractions in the form of patterns and objects. The structure of such concurrency abstractions may vary, but they often have the following form:

A *system* is an object that may contain coroutines that are executed concurrently. A system object is a subclass of the pattern **system**. A *process* is a coroutine (an object) that may be executed concurrently with other processes. A process is an instance of a subclass of the pattern **process**.

If P is a process defined within a system S, then an action P.start(), implies that P is scheduled for concurrent execution within S. **Start** is defined as a virtual method in **process**.

A concurrent program may have the following structure:

```
MySystem: obj ConcSys.system
   { S1: process ...
     S2: process ...
     S3: process ...
   do S1.start(); S2.start(); S3.start()
   }
```

ConcSys is the module defining the concurrency patterns being used in the example. I.e. **system**, **process**, etc., are defined within ConcSys. In the next sections, we give examples of such modules. As can be seen, MySystem is a singular system object being a subclass of ConcSys.system.

3.1   The Monitor Abstraction

As mentioned, the abstraction mechanisms in Beta make it possible for the programmer to define new concurrency abstractions using the basic concurrency mechanisms. The Mjølner Beta System contains a number of such abstractions for well known concurrency mechanisms and the **monitor** class is one example. It is important to stress that the **monitor** class is defined completely within Beta and the programmer is free to define his/her own variants.

The example below shows how the monitor abstraction may be used:

```
monitorEx: obj MonitorSystem.system
   { producer: obj process{ do ...; buffer.put(exp); ...; }
     buffer: obj monitor
        { void put(V: integer): entry
          {
          do wait{do cond := L.full() };
             L.put(V)
          };
        integer get(): entry
          {
          do wait{do cond := L.empty() };
```

---

[3] In **xBeta**, a module is a singular objects – see [44].

```
                return L.get()
            };
        L: obj List
    }
    consumer: obj process { do ...; X := buffer.get(); ...}
do producer.start(); consumer.start()
}
```

The monitor pattern is defined in the object module MonitorSystem. The objects producer and consumer are declared as process objects and executed concurrently. The buffer object is a subclass of Monitor. The put and get methods of Buffer are submethods of the method pattern entry defined within Monitor. The pattern entry acts as a wrapper around the do-part of put and get and ensures mutual access to the buffer. The semantics of entry, put and get is as described in Figure 3.

The pattern wait is also defined within Monitor and delays execution of put and get if the buffer is full or empty respectively. The statement

```
wait{do cond := L.full(); }
```

is a singular method activation. Wait repeatedly executes cond := L.full and if cond (defined within wait) is true, execution of put (or get) is delayed. If cond is false, execution of the singular method activation terminates.

As an alternative to wait, the Monitor pattern also defines a queue pattern with operations signal and wait corresponding to the original primitives of Concurrent Pascal monitors. The main point here is not the actual monitor mechanism being used, but that the programmer is able to define whatever monitor abstraction (or other concurrency abstractions) that fits his/her needs.

Readers familiar with Concurrent Pascal may notice that the above example is quite similar to a Concurrent Pascal program except for the wait pattern. We will later show how monitor is defined in Beta – for now system, process, monitor, entry and wait may be considered primitives/keywords in the language.

3.2 Rendezvous

The Mjølner Beta System also has a concurrency abstraction that supports communication between processes in the form of rendezvous-based method invocations similar to Ada-style procedure entries.

The Port class defines objects that may be used to associate methods with processes. External processes may perform synchronous calls of methods attached to ports. Such methods can only be executed if the enclosing process has executed an accept on the corresponding port. This style of communication is thus similar to rendezvous as in CSP and Ada.

A process with ports and methods attached to ports has the following form:

```
S: obj process
 { P1: obj port
     { void m1(): entry{ ... do ... }
```

```
      void m2 (): entry{ ... do ... }
    }
P2: obj port
    { void m3 (): entry{ ... do ... }
    }
do ...; P1.accept (); ...; P2.accept ();...
}
```

S has two ports P1 and P2 declared as singular objects, each as a subclass of port. The methods m1, and m2 are nested within P1 and declared as submethods of the entry method of P1. The method m3 is similarly declared within P2. M1 and m2 are thus associated with the port P1 and m3 with P2.

The Port class also has an accept method that when executed makes it possible for external systems to execute methods attached to the Port. The system executing the accept method is blocked until an external system has executed a method attached to the Port. When the method returns, the execution resumes after the accept call.

In the example, a system, say R, may execute a method invocation of the form S.P1.m1(). R is blocked until S executes P1.accept(). S is similarly blocked until another system executes S.P1.m1(). When P1.m1() has been executed, S continues execution until P2.accept() and is blocked until some other system has executed m3.

The accept pattern exists in three different forms:[4]

- P.accept() – all processes may execute methods attached to P.
- P.accept(X) – only the process X may invoke methods on the port.
- P.accept(C) – invocations are accepted from all processes belong to the class C (instances of C or subclasses of C).

3.3   Alternation

Beta also has the ability to describe processes consisting of one or more alternating coroutines. The concept of alternation was identified in order to model/represent active entities that alternate between different activities, and also to understand coroutines from a modeling point of view.

Active entities, such as people, may be engaged in several activities, but at most one at a time. An agent working in a travel agency may be engaged in booking tours for several customers and in addition perform various administrative activities. At a given point in time, the agent is working on one of the tasks and the other tasks are temporarily suspended. The agent may decide to suspend the current task and resume one of the other tasks. An external event such as a telephone call may also imply that the current task is suspended and another one is resumed.

Cooperative scheduling may be considered an example of structuring a software system into two or more alternating activities. Each such activity may

---

[4] Beta does not have overloading, so there are three different method names.

consist of carrying out a task involving communication with other processes. Scheduling of the inner alternating activities may be explicit in the code or implicit depending on the communication with external processes. But at most one activity at a time is being executed.

A concurrent system may be engaged in communication with several external systems, and since it is unpredictable and non-deterministic when an external system is ready for communication, languages like CSP, Ada, Actor languages, ABCL, Concurrent Smalltalk, etc. introduced guarded commands (or select statements) to be able to specify accept of more than one external communication. In addition, these languages allow for Boolean expressions as part of the guard to be able to let the state of the system influence which methods may actually be accepted.

In the design of Beta, a number of deficiencies with guarded commands were identified. As mentioned, there is an asymmetry in most languages between input and output commands, since a select may only contain input commands (accept of method activations).

In addition, the use of Boolean expressions often blur the control flow in the sense that independent logical action sequences have to be mixed into one sequence and the sequencing has to be controlled by Boolean expressions.

Consider the following example where a process S may be engaged in an activity that involves communication with two external systems, S1 and S2. S alternates between accepting a method from S1 and invoking a method on S1. Similarly it alternates between invoking a method on S2 and accepting a method activation by S2.

A standard technique to guarantee the sequencing between S1 and S2, is to use Boolean variables. In this example, two Booleans B1 and B2 are introduced and S may be described in the following way using **select**:

```
S: obj process
    { P1: obj port{ void m1(): entry{ ... } };
      P2: obj port{ void m2(): entry{ ... } };
      do ...;
        cycle{
          select
              P1.accept(S1)    and B1       => stm1; B1 := not B1;
              S1.Px.f()        and not B1 => stm2; B1 := not B1;
              S2.Py.g()        and B2       => stm3; B2 := not B2;
              P2.accept(S2)    and not B2 => stm4; B2 := not B2;
          endselect
      }
      ...
    }
```

What we really would like to express is that S alternates between two logical action sequences:

```
cycle{ P1.accept(S1); stm1; S1.Px.f(); stm2 }
cycle{ S2.Py.g(); stm3; P2.accept(S2); stm4 }
```

We may express this in Beta by defining two inner alternating objects in S:

```
S: obj process
   { P1: obj port{ void m1 (): entry{ ... } };
     P2: obj port{ void m2 (): entry{ ... } };

     A1: obj activity
         { do cycle{do P1.accept (); stm1; S1.Px.f (); stm2 }}
     A2: obj activity
         { do cycle{do S2.Py.g (); stm3; P2.accept (); stm4 }}
     do ...; A1.start (); A2.start (); ...
   }
```

The class `activity` describes coroutine objects that may be executed as alternating with other activities in the same process. The process S thus consists of two alternating activities A1 and A2.

At most one of the activities may be executing at a given point in time. A suspended `activity` may be marked as either ready to be resumed or waiting for an external event.

The do-part of the process S is for initializations. The method `A1.start` implies that the activity A1 is scheduled for execution.

The execution of the activity continues until it either terminates or is blocked by an `accept` or method activation in another system. If blocked, it is temporarily suspended and marked as waiting for an external event. An activity marked as ready to be resumed will then be resumed.

The following is a possible scenario for S:

1. S a.o. executes `A1.start()`, and `A2.start()`, which implies that A1, and A2 are scheduled for execution.

2. A1 is selected for execution.

3. A1 executes `P1.accept()` and is blocked and thus suspended as waiting.

4. A2 is selected for execution.

5. A2 executes `S2.Py.g()` and is blocked and suspended as waiting.

6. Now the situation is that none of A1 and A2 are ready to be resumed. In this case no actions are executed by S and its inner activities.

7. An external event may imply that one of A1 and A2 becomes ready.

8. Let us assume that S2 executes an accept of g. Then A2 is resumed and eventually executes `P2.accept()` and possibly blocked and suspended as waiting.

9. Now either A1 may be resumed if S1 invokes m1 or A2 may be resumed if S2 invokes m2.

10. At any given point in time, one of A1 and A2 may be executing or they may both be waiting for communications with external systems.

11. ...

3.4   A Simple Shop Example

Consider a shop where a customer[5] may order some items that are delivered to the customer at a later stage. The shop in a similar way orders items from a supplier that delivers the items to the shop.

The example is similar to the sketchy example above, except that (1) we show how a `port` may be used to communicate values between processes, and (2) an example of using a conditional `wait` within an `activity` is shown.

The structure of the `Shop` system is as follows:

```
SimpleShop: obj RendezvousSystem.system
  { Customer: obj process{ ... };
    Shop: obj process{ ... }
    Supplier: obj process{ ... }
  do Customer.start(); Shop.start(); Supplier.Start();
  }
```

The module object `RendezvousSystem` defines the rendezvous based concurrency abstraction. The example defines `SimpleShop` as a subclass of `RendezvousSystem.system`.

The `Customer` has the following structure:

```
Customer: obj process
  { start()::< { do shopper.start() }
    mailBox: obj port
      { void deliver(item,quantity: integer): entry{ ... }
      };
    shopper: obj activity
      { itm,qua: integer
      do cycle
        {do Shop.orderBox.placeOrder(itm,qua); ...;
          mailBox.accept(); ...
        }
      }
  }
```

The `Customer` object is a process. It has a `port`, `mailBox`, which defines an `entry` method, `deliver`, for receiving items ordered in the `shop`.

It defines an activity, `shopper`, that repeatedly places an order at the shop (`Shop.orderBox.placeOrder(itm,qua)`) and then awaits that the order is delivered (`mailBox.accept()`).

The virtual `start` method from `process` is further bound (specified by `::<`) to start the `shopper` – this implies that the do-part of `start` in `Customer` is combined with the do-part of `start` in `Shop` in the same way as described for submethods in Section 2.1.

---

[5] To keep the example simple, we have only one customer.

The Shop has the following structure:

```
Shop: obj process
  { start()::< {do orderhandler.start(); importHandler.start() };
    orderBox: obj port
      { placeOrder(item,quantity: integer): entry
          { do itm := item; qua := quantity};
        (integer,integer) accept()::{ do return (itm,qua)};
        itm,qua: integer
      };
    importBox: obj port
      { void receive(item,quantity: integer): entry
          { do store.add(item,quantity) }
      };
    orderHandler: obj activity
      {
      do cycle
        { item,quantity: integer
        do (item,quantity) := orderBox.accept();
          wait{do cond := store.inStock(item,quantity) };
          Customer.mailBox.deliver(store.get(item,quantity));
        }
      }
    importHandler: obj activity
      { itm,qua: integer
      do cycle{do Supplier.request(itm,qua); ...; importBox.accept; ...}
      }
    store: obj { ... }
  }
```

The shop is a process. It defines two ports, orderBox and importBox for communicating with the Customer and Supplier respectively.

The orderBox defines an entry method, placeOrder, for receiving orders from the Customer. It has a (final) binding of the accept method[6] – in addition to executing the accept defined in port, the accept in orderBox returns two integers being the new order received by placeOrder.

The orderBox defines two variables, itm and qua, which are used by placeOrder to store the values of its item and quantity arguments. And itm and qua are subsequently returned by accept. The orderBox box is an example of using a port to communicate values.

The importBox has a method for receiving items ordered from the supplier. The entry method receive updates the store with the new items received. We do not show the details of this and the store object.

The Shop alternates between two activities. The orderHandler receives an order from the Customer. It then checks if the item and quantity is in stock. Otherwise it waits until they are in stock. When in stock, it delivers the items to the Customer.

The importHandler places orders at the Supplier and awaits delivery from the Supplier.

---

[6] accept in orderBox is a submethod of accept in port.

The Supplier has the following structure:

```
Supplier: obj process
  { start()::< {do orderHandler.start() };
    orderBox: obj port
      { void receive(item,quantity: integer): entry{ ... }
      };
    orderHandler: obj activity
      {
      do cycle
        {do orderBox.accept(); ...;
             Shop.importBox.receive(itm3,qua2); ...}
      }
  }
```

4 Implementation in Beta

In this Section, we show how the above concurrency abstractions may be defined as patterns in Beta. The implementation described here is for a processor with a single CPU/core. In Section 4.4 below, we describe what is needed to generalize the implementation to a multi-core CPU.

4.1 Coroutines

A Beta object may behave like a semi-coroutine in the style of SIMULA. Consider an object R defined as follows:

```
R: obj
  { void foo(): { do ... L3: R.suspend; L4: ... }
    ...
    do ...; L1: R.suspend; L2: ...; foo(); ...
  }
```

L1 - L4 are labels.

R may be executed as a coroutine by a statement of the form:

```
R
```

The first time R is executed, execution starts by the do-part of R – if R has a superclass, execution starts with the do-part of the topmost superpattern as for submethods. The execution of R may be temporarily suspended, and control then returns to after the R-statement. A subsequent statement, R, resumes execution at the point of suspension.

Consider the following method:

```
void callR():
  {
  do ...; A1: R; A2: ...; A3: R; A4: ...; A5:R; ...
  }
```

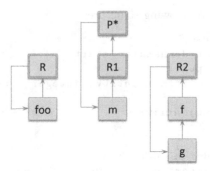

Fig. 5. Snapsnot of coroutines

Again A1 - A5 are labels. At A1, R is executed by the statement R. At the label L1, R.suspend implies that execution of R is suspended and control returns to the point of A2. When execution is at A3, the statement R resumes execution of R at the point of L2. R eventually executes foo and at L3, execution of R is suspended and controls returns to A4. In this situation R is suspended while executing foo. The final execution of R at A5 resumes execution of R at L4.

In Figure 5 is shown the state of execution of a program at a given point in time. The snapshot shows one active object, R1, and two suspend objects, R and R2. R1 is executing a method m. R is the coroutine from the above example – R is shown as suspended at the label L3 in foo. R2 is suspended in a method activation g called from f, where f is called from R2.

The boxes with a double line border show the objects being the head of the coroutine and the boxes with a single line border show method activations. The arrows show the return link of a method activation. The return link of an active coroutine refers to the calling object – here P*. For a suspended coroutine, the return link points to the top method activation. This notation was introduced by Dahl and Wang [24].

It is illegal to invoke an active coroutine and/or to suspend a coroutine that is already suspended.

Coroutines may be used to define control abstractions of objects as shown in the following example:

```
List:
  { void insert(e: integer): { ... };
    ...; — other methods
    traverse: obj
      { scan(current: ref node):
          {
            do if current <> none then
                V := current.elm;
                this(traverse).suspend;
                scan(current.next)
              else
                while true do
```

```
                    V := MaxInt;
                    this(traverse).suspend
                endwhile
            endif
        };
        V: integer
    do scan(head)
        };
    — representation of the List
    head: ref node;
    node: { elm: integer; next: node };
}
...
L1,L2: obj List

void merge():
    {
    do L1.traverse; L2.traverse;
        while (L1.V != MaxInt) and (L2.V != MaxInt) do
        if L1.V < L2.V then
            L1.V.print(); L1.traverse
        else
            L2.V.print(); L2.traverse
        endif
        endwhile
    }
```

A declaration like current: ref node defines a variable, current that may refer to instances of class node. It is similar to node *current in C++.

A traverse object has been added to the List class. Traverse is used as a coroutine and acts as a generator that supplies the elements of the list one by one. Traverse calls a recursive method scan that returns the next element in the List. The value is returned via the local variable V. When the list is exhausted, the value MaxInt is returned whenever traverse is resumed.

L1 and L2 are two List objects. We assume that the two lists are sorted with the smallest value appearing first in the list. The merge method prints a merged sequence of the two lists. It starts by invoking traverse for L1 and L2. L1.V and L2.V are then the smallest elements of L1 and L2, respectively. If L1.V is smaller than L2.V then L1.V is printed and L1.traverse is executed to get the next element of L1, etc.

As mentioned, Beta coroutines are semi-coroutines in the style of SIMULA. SIMULA has also *symmetric* coroutines where control is transferred to another coroutine by an operation resume R. The coroutine executing resume R is suspended and R is resumed. This is the most common form of coroutines. In [42], it is shown that in Beta it is possible to define a symmetric coroutine abstraction using semi-coroutines.

Preemptive Suspend. A coroutine may also be invoked/resumed by the primitive operation R.attach(e), where e is an integer expressions. A *preemptive* *suspend* is enforced on R after e time units. This is in contrast to invoking/re-suming the coroutine using R as used above – in this case R continues execution until it executes R.suspend.

In Beta the Semaphore is a primitive in the language. A semaphore is, how-ever, a somehow high-level structure since it contains a queue for keeping track of possible waiting processes. For **xBeta**, semaphore is not a built-in primitive. Instead we use primitives for disabling and enabling preemptive suspend to im-plement say a semaphore, and below we describe implementations of two variants of a Semaphore pattern.

4.2   Monitor Abstraction

The MonitorSystem module has the following structure:

```
MonitorSystem : obj
  { System :
      { Process :  ...  —— superpattern for process objects
        Monitor :  ...  —— superpattern for monitor objects
        scheduler : obj ... — scheduler for process objects ;
        P_status : obj —— constants used for scheduling
          { ACTIVE = 1;
            WAITING = 2;
            RESUMED = 3;
            TERMINATED = 4;
          } :
        Semaphore :  ...  —— the semaphore pattern
      do inner ;
        scheduler
      }
  }
```

A System as defined by MonitorSystem starts by executing **inner** to allow for process objects to be started (see above). Then it executes the scheduler object, which handles the scheduling of Process objects.

The Process pattern is defined as follows,

```
Process :
    { void start (): < { do scheduler . add ( this ( Process )); inner };
      status : integer
    do status := P_status . ACTIVE ;
      inner ;
      status := P_status . TERMINATED
    };
```

The virtual[7] start method adds the Process to the scheduler. The do-part sets the status of the Process to ACTIVE, executes inner, and when the Process terminates, sets the status to TERMINATED. The object P_status defines con-stants used by the scheduler.

---

[7] A virtual method is declared using :<.

The `Monitor` pattern is defined as follows:

```
Monitor:
    { M: obj Semaphore;
      Monitor():< { do M.init(1)  -- initially open }
      void entry(): { do M.wait(); inner; M.signal() }
    }
```

The `Monitor` pattern is encapsulating the code in Figure 3 in appropriate patterns. The constructor[8] assures that the M-semaphore is properly initialized.

Finally, we may show the definition of the `scheduler`:

```
scheduler: obj
    { void add(P: obj Process): { do SQS.insert(P) };
      Process next(): { do return SQS.next(); };
      active: ref Process;
      SQS: obj Queue;
   do loop:
         cycle
           {
           do active:= next();
              if active <> none then
                 active.status := P_status.ACTIVE;
                 active.attach(100);
                 if active.status = P_status.ACTIVE then
                     add(active)
                 endif
              else
                 leave loop
           endif}
    }
```

The `scheduler` has a FIFO-queue, `SQS`, of `Process` objects ready to be scheduled. The `scheduler` is a simple round-robin scheduler that takes the first process in the queue and executes it.

The primitive operation `active.attach(100)` resumes `active` as a coroutine and a preemptive suspend is enforced on `active` after 100 time units.

A `Semaphore` may be implemented in **xBeta** in the following way:

```
Semaphore:
    { cnt: integer;
      Q: obj Queue;
      void init(c: integer): {do cnt := c };
      void wait():
        {
        do disable();  -- disable preemption
           cnt := cnt - 1;
           if cnt < 0 then
               scheduler.active.status := P_status.WAITING;
               Q.insert(scheduler.active);
```

---

[8] Beta does not have constructors, but **xBeta** does.

```
            enable ();  — enable preemption
            scheduler . active . suspend
        else
            enable ()  — enable preemption
        endif;
    };
  void signal ():
    { P:  ref Process
    do disable ();
        cnt  := cnt + 1;
        if cnt >= 0 then
            P  := Q . next ();
            P . status := P_status . RESUMED;
            scheduler . add (P );
        endif;
        enable ();
    }
}
```

The method **signal** moves a waiting **Process** from the queue (**Q**) of the **Semaphore** to the queue of active processes in the **scheduler**. The **scheduler** will then eventually pick it up for execution. Note that **Semaphore** is a local pattern of **MonitorSystem**, which means that **scheduler** is visible within **Sempahore**.

As can be seen, **xBeta** has no basic patterns with built-in structures like queues – they are all defined as abstractions. And the programmer is free to define his own abstractions. This makes it possible to implement/tailor concurrency abstractions to the actual needs. For semaphores there may be alternative implementations – one example is to suspend the active process in **signal**.

4.3   Imlementing Rendezvous System

The implementation of the rendezvous system is a bit more complicated than the monitor system. The definition has the following structure:

```
RendezvousSystem : obj
  { System:
      { BasicProcess:  { ... };
        Process: BasicProcess{ ... };
        Port:  { ...};
        Semaphore:  { ... };
        scheduler: obj { ... };
        P_status: obj { — same as for Monitor }
      do inner; scheduler
      }
}
```

The BasicProcess and Process patterns have the following structure:

```
BasicProcess:
   { status: integer
   do status:= P_status.ACTIVE;
      inner;
      status := P_status.TERMINATED
   };
Process: BasicProcess
   { void start():< { do scheduler.add(this(Process)); inner };
      Activity: { ... }; ...
      ActivityScheduler: { ... };
      myAS: obj ActivityScheduler
   do inner;
      myAS;
   };
```

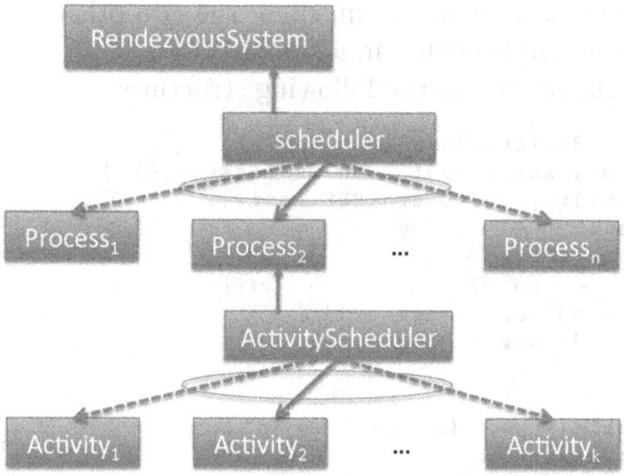

Fig. 6. The two levels of scheduling of processes and activities within processes

A Process has a start pattern that adds the Process to the scheduler queue. It has a local pattern Activity that defines possible alternating activities of the Process. It has a scheduler object, myAS, defined as an instance of class ActivityScheduler, for scheduling inner alternating Activities. It executes an inner that allows for initializations and then it executes the myAS.

Scheduling of coroutines takes place at two levels. At the outer level, the scheduler schedules concurrent process objects and is similar to the scheduler for MonitorSystem. Each process has an ActivityScheduler, which takes care of the scheduling of its inner activities. The two levels of scheduling are illustrated in Figure 6.

An Activity has the following structure:

```
Activity: BasicProcess
   { void start():< {do myAS.add(this(Activity)); inner };
      sch: ref ActivityScheduler
   do inner;
      }
```

An `Activity` has a `start` method that adds the activity to the `ActivityScheduler`, myAS.

A `Port` has the following structure:

```
Port :
  { m,mutex: obj Semaphore ;
    Port ():< {do m.init (0); mutex.init (0)  };
    entry: {do m.wait (); inner; mutex.signal ()  }
    accept:< {do m.signal (); mutex.wait (); inner}
  }
```

A `Port` has an `entry` and an `accept` method that controls access to the methods in the `Port`. The m-semaphore guarantees that at most one `entry`-method at time may access the `Port`. The `mutex`-semaphore similarly handles termination the `entry`-method and resumption of `accept`-method. (We only show the implementation of `accept` without arguments – the two other variants described in Section 3.2 may be implemented in a similar way.)

The `ActivityScheduler` has the following structure:

```
ActivityScheduler : BasicProcess
  { void add(P: obj Activity): { do SQS.insert(P) };
    Activity next (): { do return SQS.next (); }
    SQS: obj Queue;
    active: ref Activity;
    now: integer; -- no of waiting activities
    incrWaiting: {do now := now + 1};
    decrWaiting: {do now := now - 1}
  do loop:
      cycle{
        do disable (); -- disable preemption;
           active:= next ();
           if active <> none then
              active.status := P_status.ACTIVE;
              enable ();
              active; -- no preemptive suspend
              disable ();
              if active.status = P_status.ACTIVE then
                 add(active)
              endif;
              enable ();
           else
              if now > 0 then -- waiting activities in this process
                 enable ();
                 scheduler.active.suspend; -- the process is suspended;
              else -- no more active activities
                 enable ();
                 leave loop
              endif
           endif
      }
  }
```

The `ActivityScheduler` invokes `active` using `active`. This implies that `active` cannot be preemptively suspended. In this way, the `ActivityScheduler` differs from the process scheduler, which invokes coroutines that may be preempted. Note that preemption is disabled during scheduling of activities.

If there are no scheduled activities in SQS (active = none), but waiting activities (now > 0), the ActivityScheduler suspends execution of the Process (scheduler.active.suspend) that initially invoked it. This Process then returns to the scheduler in the enclosing System, and since it is still active, it is added to scheduler.SQS for a subsequent scheduling.[9] It will then eventually be executed and if some of the waiting activities have become active, they will be executed. Otherwise it will suspend execution again.

When there are no more activities in SQS and no waiting activities, the ActivityScheduler terminates (through leave Loop). It then returns to the Process, which initially invoked it. And then this Process object terminates.

The Semaphore pattern defined here differs from the one defined for the monitor system. In the monitor system, a semaphore interacts with the scheduling of process objects. For the rendezvous system, a semaphore interacts with the scheduling of activities.

```
Semaphore:
  { cnt: integer;
    Q: obj Queue;
    void wait ():
     { P: ref Process
      do disable ();
         cnt := cnt − 1;
         if cnt < 0 then
             P := scheduler.active;
             P.activityScheduler.active.status := P_status.WAITING;
             P.activityScheduler.active.sch := P.activityScheduler;
             P.activityScheduler.incrWaiting ();
             Q.insert(P.activityScheduler.active);
             enable ();
             P.activityScheduler.active.suspend
         else
             enable ();
         endif;
     };
    void signal ():
     { A: ref Activity
      do disable ();
         cnt := cnt + 1;
         if cnt >= 0 then
             A := Q.next ();
             A.status := P_status.RESUMED;
             A.sch.add (A);
             A.sch.decrWaiting ();
         endif;
         enable ()
     }
  }
```

This completes the definition of the rendezvous system.

---

[9] As pointed out by one of the reviewers, this may waste CPU time since there is no need to add a process for rescheduling until one of the waiting activities of the process is signaled.

4.4 Summing Up

As shown above, it is possible in Beta to define high-level concurrency abstractions. It is, however, fairly complicated and it requires a lot of work to validate the correctness of such abstractions.

The important message here is that it is possible to design a programming language that with the right primitives and abstraction mechanisms makes it possible to define a broad range of concurrency abstractions including associated schedulers.

The basic primitives used here are (semi-)coroutines that may be executed in a cooperative way as in SIMULA together with a preemptive suspend R.attach(t), R.suspend, and primitives for disabling and enabling preemptive suspend. In addition, the ability to define submethods using the pattern/subpattern mechanism and method combination using inner is essential.

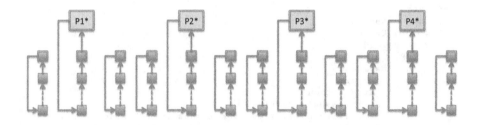

Fig. 7. Snapshots of coroutines in multi-core implementation

Multicore Implementation. The implementation described above is for a processor with a single CPU/core. There has also been an experimental implementation of Beta on a SPARC multiprocessor with 4 cores[10]. In this implementation, the basic environment for Beta was extended with a predefined array of coroutines representing the cores of the available platform:

    Processors: [noOfCores] ref Processor

The coroutines Processors[1], Processors[2], ..., Processors[noOfCores] are attached to threads in the operating system and thus representing potentially noOfCores coroutines executing in parallel.

A Beta coroutine, S, may be attached to a processor by the primitive operation S.attachTo(Processors[i]).

The implementation of Semaphore as described in this paper was adjusted to handle the situation with possible true concurrent coroutines accessing the semaphore at the same time.

In this implementation, we experimented with attaching different types of schedulers to the processors using different kinds of strategies for organizing the queues of active coroutines to be scheduled.

---

[10] The SPARC implementation is no longer maintained.

Figure 7 illustrates a situation with 4 predefined **Processor** coroutines (P1, P2, P3, P4). Each Processor coroutine has a Beta coroutine attached. In addition, the figure shows a number of suspended coroutines.

5   Subpattern Restrictions

As shown in the previous section, the abstraction mechanisms in Beta make it possible for programmers to define a variety of concurrency abstractions. Beta, however, suffers from the same deficiencies as Brinch-Hansen has pointed out for Java. As long as the programmer follows a discipline where all concurrent activities and shared data are encapsulated in appropriate abstractions, the code is safe. There is, however, no way the compiler can prevent or warn a programmer if he/she by accident or incidentally bypasses the abstractions. This may e.g. happen by declaring methods in a monitor that are not submethods of **entry**.

In addition, Beta is a block-structured language, which means that classes, methods, processes and objects may be arbitrarily nested. And inner methods may access global variables. Nesting thus makes it possible for two concurrent processes to share global variables without interference control.

In the design of Beta, it was considered important to be able to unify all abstraction mechanisms into the pattern concept and avoid specialized mechanisms. This was on the sacrifice of e.g. interference control by the compiler, and safety of concurrent processes was relying on the discipline of the programmers.

One straightforward solution to this is of course to introduce some of the above concurrency abstractions (monitor, process activity, port, etc.) as built-in mechanisms, and appropriate language-defined restrictions. In this way, the compiler may check and enforce interference control. This is indeed a viable alternative and such a version of Beta will then be similar to other languages with built-in high-level mechanisms for concurrency. The price will be that the generality of the one-pattern approach and the ability to define new concurrency abstractions will be degraded, but this is no worse than other specialized languages with classes, processes and methods. In fact, a version of Beta with built-in mechanisms for rendezvous and alternation and process objects as isolated objects would in our opinion be a usable alternative to e.g. Java in the sense that the basic OO mechanisms are available. Concurrent objects are closed and only values can be communicated, and the compiler can enforce interference control.

We do, however, think it is useful to be able to define new concurrency abstractions from the basic primitives.

In this section, we will propose a new language mechanism called *subpattern restrictions*, which makes it possible to define *safe* concurrency abstractions without compromising the concept of one pattern. By means of subpattern restrictions it is possible to define restrictions on the use and scope of subpatterns of a given pattern.

Most OO languages have mechanisms for controlling the access to methods and data-items of objects. In SIMULA, C++, Java, C# and others, a method or data-item may be declared as private, public or protected. In Smalltalk all data items are private and all methods are public.

Subpattern restrictions complement public, private and protected. For the latter, the programmer on a class-by-class basis defines the accessibility of data-items and methods. With subpattern restrictions, the programmer defines restrictions that make the pattern function as a wrapper for all of its subpatterns.

5.1   Restrictions

A pattern with subpattern restrictions is described in the following way:

```
MyPtn: [R1, R2, ... , Rn] super{ ...}
```

where R1, R2, ... Rn are restrictions imposed on subpatterns of MyPtn. A given restriction, R, can only be imposed if it holds for the superpattern as well.

One example of a restriction is immutable. A pattern restricted by immutable can only be used to define immutable objects. For such a pattern and its subpatterns, it is not possible to change the state of its instances.

The pattern Complex is an example of how to declare a pattern defining immutable objects:

```
Complex: [immutable]
  { Complex(x,y: real) { do re := x; im := y};
    re,im: real;
    ...
  }
```

As recognized by several authors [8], immutable objects are useful in the case of concurrent and distributed objects. For this reason, an object restricted by immutable may not refer to or return mutable objects, since this will make it possible (indirectly) to pass a reference to a mutable object to two or more processes.

The restriction globals [P1,P2,..., Pn] where each Pi is a pattern, and $n \geq$ 0 limits the types of global data-items that may be referred. Only subpatterns of Pi may be referred. If $n = 0$, i.e. globals[], then no global data-items in enclosing objects may be referred. A pattern restricted by globals[] is called a *closed pattern*.

The globals restriction apply both directly and indirectly. If a global variable is accessed directly it must be of one of the types Pi. And for indirect access to global data-items, a (global) pattern used within a subpattern restricted by globals may also not access data-items that are not of type Pi. A pattern defining the behavior of a function may be defined as follows:

```
Function:
  [globals [] , signature [immutable] , kind [method]]
  { do inner }
```

The restriction signature[immutable] means that only immutable objects may be passed as arguments to subpatterns of Function. In addition, only immutable objects may be returned. Subpatterns of Function will thus behave as functions in the sense that the result will depend only on its input arguments just as it can have no side effects. An example of a Function is:

```
Complex fromPolar(magnitude,angle: real): Function
  { re,im: real;
  do re := magnitude * cos(angle);
     im := magnitude * sin(angle);
     return new Complex(re,im);
  }
```

The function `fromPolar` has local variables `re`, and `im`, which are instances of the closed pattern `real` and it calls two closed functions `cos`, and `sin`.

The restriction `interface[P1,P2, ..., Pn]` implies that all externally visible methods must be submethods of one of `Pi` just as no data-items may be accessed remotely. The `Monitor` class may e.g. be declared as follows:

```
monitor: [interface[entry]] { ... }
```

which implies that all methods in subclasses of `Monitor` must be submethods of `Entry`.

In Beta, a pattern may be used as a class, method or superpattern. And a class pattern may be used to generate a dynamic object by means of `new` or as a static (part) object using `obj`. An object's *kind* refers to how its is generated. In Beta, we thus have the following kinds: method, dynamic, static, and super. The restriction `kind[K1,K2,...Kn]` makes it possible to restrict the use of a pattern.

The pattern `Entry` in `Monitor` may e.g. be restricted in the following way:

```
Entry: [kind[method]] {... }
```

which means that subpatterns of `Entry` may only be used as methods.

5.2 Monitor System

The `MonitorSystem` presented above is subject to a number of restrictions in order to be similar to e.g. Concurrent Pascal(CP).

All communication between processes must be via monitors and only values (immutable objects) may be communicated. Processes cannot access global variables and no methods can be invoked on processes.

A monitor cannot access global variables and all remote-accessible methods defined within the monitor must be submethods of `entry`. And such submethods may only be used as kind method.

In CP, classes may be used to define abstract data-types. CP does not have references to objects – all instances are in-lined and copied when passed as arguments to methods. Here we use immutable objects instead of copying.

Data-items / variables are not meaningful in the outermost system object, since neither processes nor monitors may access them.

It is meaningful to define global classes to be used within processes and monitors as long as the classes do not break the restrictions on processes and monitors with respect to globals.

We may thus specify the restrictions for `MonitorSystem` as follows:

```
MonitorSystem : obj
  { System: [interface [] , globals []]
      { Monitor : [interface [entry] , globals []]
          { Entry :
              [signature [immutable] , kind [method]]
              { ... }
          }
        Process :
          [interface [] , globals [Monitor]]
          { do inner }
          —— Semaphore and scheduler should be declared private
        do inner
      }
  }
```

A `System` object can have no remote-accessible methods (`interface[]`) and it is closed (`globals[]`).

All remote-accessible methods of a `Monitor` must be submethods of `entry` (`interface[entry]`), and it is closed (`globals[]`). Submethods of `Entry` can only have immutable arguments and return types (`signature[immutable]`). In addition, `Entry`-methods can only be of kind method (`kind[method]`).

5.3 Rendezvous System

The restrictions to be imposed upon the `RendezvousSystem` are similar to the ones for `MonitorSystem`:

```
RendezvousSystem : obj
  { System: [interface [] , globals []]
      { Process :
          [interface [port . entry] , globals [Process]]
          { Activity : [ ] { ... };
            Port :
              { entry :
                  [signature [immutable] , kind [method]]
                  { ...
                  do ... Inner ...
                  }
              }
          }
      }
  }
```

One difference is that processes may communicate directly – this is expressed by `interface[port.entry]`, which means that a `process` may invoke `entry`-methods within arbitrary `port`-objects of `processes`.

`Processes` may also refer to other `Processes` (`[globals[Process]]`).

For an `Activity` there are no additional restrictions since activities cannot refer to data-items outside their enclosing process and no external process may access an `Activity`. The same holds for `port` where no additional restrictions are needed.

5.4 Summary of Subpattern Restrictions

Figure 8 shows a grouping of the restrictions that we may impose upon subpatterns of a given pattern:

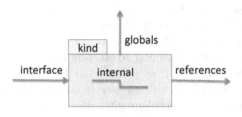

Fig. 8. Subpattern restrictions

- *Interface*: This group contains the restrictions `interface[...]`, and `signature[...]`. It may be considered to have a special property `returns[...]` for restricting the return values of a pattern and not coupling this with the signature restriction. However, they seem to go pair in pair.
- *Globals*: This group contains the restriction `globals[P1,P2,...,Pn]`, i.e. the restrictions enforced on accessing global data-items
- *References*: A restriction of the form `references[P1,P2,...Pn]` is being considered – to restrict the type of objects that may be referred from an object.
- *Internal*: Restrictions on the internal behavior of an object. It includes: `immutable, exclude:primitives[p1,p2,...pn]`,
- *Kind*: Here we have the restrictions of type `kind[K1,K2,K3]` where Ki is `method, dynamic, part` or `super`.

6 Evaluation and Related Work

Concurrent programming languages, including concurrent object-oriented programming languages has been an active research area for more than 40 years. With respect to concurrent object-oriented modeling and programming, there are a number of proposals for modeling of concurrent processes including Petri Nets, CCS, CSP and similar for concurrent programming [11]. There is very little work on combined object-oriented modeling and programming. One example is ABCL where modeling as well as programming were important for the design of the language [60]. Except for SIMULA, we are not aware of other languages than Beta where modeling requirements have had a direct influence the programming language in the form of the inner-mechanism, submethods, subprocesses and concurrent and alternating process objects.

Regarding alternation, we are not aware of a similar mechanism in other languages. The pros and cons of synchronous and asynchronous communication have been extensively discussed in the literature [3,51].

Alternation makes it possible to use synchronous method invocation and, in our opinion, this makes it easier to follow the control flow of concurrent processes. In addition, the input- and output commands are handled in a symmetric way - as opposed to the select-mechanism in most languages.

Some authors, e.g. Nordlander et al [51], mention that in order to avoid blocking on a synchronous communication one may start a thread for each new communication. In some way, this is similar to starting a new alternating activity as presented here for Beta. However, as pointed out by Nordlander et al., if concurrent threads are used, there is still an issue of coordinating the computations of these threads. This is not a problem with alternation, since at most one alternating activity is executing at a time, and each activity may safely update shared data in the enclosing process.

A number of language mechanisms have been proposed for synchronization and communication of concurrent processes. This includes simple enable/disable of interrupts, testAndSet operations, locks, semaphores, message passing, rendezvous, guarded commands, public subscribe, Actors, etc.

For Beta, a goal has been to identify a few simple basic mechanisms that do not imply unnecessary overhead and structures like queues. In Beta, the basic mechanism for synchronization was the semaphore, which does require a queue as part of the implementation. In **xBeta**, semaphores have been replaced by enable/disable of interrupts.

Coroutines in the style of SIMULA are the basis for threads. SIMULA has symmetric coroutines and semi-coroutines, whereas Beta has only semi-coroutines, but as mentioned earlier, the abstraction mechanism in Beta makes it possible to build an abstraction for symmetric coroutines. In SIMULA, all objects are coroutines. In Beta, a pattern may be instantiated as a simple object corresponding to objects in C++, Smalltalk, Java, etc. or as a coroutine object. In **xBeta**, all objects may be used as coroutines.

Most (OO) languages, like Java, and C#, have concurrent tasks built into the language. Other languages like C++ provided task libraries. Coroutines were originally proposed by Conway [16]. There are few languages based on coroutines, but some languages have a notion of generators that essentially are coroutines – the language Icon [28] is an example of such a language. Modula 2 [57] is an example of a language that has direct support for (semi) coroutines. And according to [58], "...it was decided that only the very basic notion of coroutines would be included in Modula-2, and that higher abstractions should be programmed as modules based on coroutines".

In SIMULA, Beta and **xBeta**, the scheduling of coroutines may be cooperative or preemptive, and coroutines may be executed concurrently. And as shown in this paper, it is possible to implement schedulers in these languages. We are not aware of other languages where it is possible to implement schedulers to the same extent.

The main concern for the design of Beta and **xBeta** is, however, not the choice of basic primitives, but the ability to define higher-level concurrency abstractions directly in the language. In almost all modern programming languages, it is possible to define new abstractions from the primitives of the language, but we are not aware of languages that to the same extent as Beta/**xBeta** can define new concurrency abstractions from simple synchronization primitives like enable/disable of interrupts.

In [62], Kasper Østerbye and Wolfgang Kreutzer describe how to build high-level synchronization abstractions using Beta patterns using examples from BetaSIM [35], a high-level framework for discrete event simulation.

Concurrent object-oriented languages have a problem passing references to mutable objects between processes. In the current design of **xBeta**, a notion of immutable object has been introduced in order to handle this problem. This is a well-known restriction in many concurrent OO languages [8].

During the design of Beta, a mechanism like subpattern restrictions was discussed as a possibility for restricting the use of a pattern – and was named *local language restriction*. The main purpose was to be able to define patterns that define abstraction mechanisms like procedure (method), function, class and process as specializations of the pattern concept.

Originally, the main idea with unifying abstraction mechanisms like class and method into one abstraction mechanism – the pattern – was to ensure a uniform treatment of all abstraction mechanisms. It might still be useful to distinguish between class and method patterns – however, in practice programmers do not seem to have difficulties of just using one pattern.

The problems with lack of interference control for concurrent objects was recognized but not discussed in the light of local language restrictions.

The original idea of local language modifications was to impose restrictions on the use of a pattern similar to the kinds [...] restriction and to exclude the use of certain syntactic categorizes in a given subpattern. The working proposals were: ExcludedIn – constructs where this subpattern cannot be used, and Exclude - constructs excluded in subpatterns. A concrete proposal for such a mechanism was, however, never completed.

Subpattern restrictions are analogous to islands, balloons, and ownership types [33,5,50,4] that also try to put restrictions on the use of objects, but primarily to avoid aliasing. In **xBeta**, aliasing is possible within a process, but for the inter-process situation this may only be the case for immutable objects.

7 Conclusion

We have presented the Beta/**xBeta** approach to concurrent object-oriented programming. We have shown how coroutines and preemptive suspend combined with patterns and subpatterns, especially in the form of submethods and method combination using inner, are powerful means for defining high-level concurrency abstractions. This is exemplified by showing how to define a monitor-based system and a rendezvous-based system.

The rendezvous-based system further includes the notion of alternating activities, which may be used as an alternative select-statements (guarded commands) and asynchronous messages to handle non-determinism.

We have furthermore shown that it is possible to define an associated scheduler as part of a concurrency abstraction.

We have introduced the notion of subpattern restrictions as a means to restrict the use of a given pattern in order to control interference control and insecurity and not rely on programmer discipline – cf. the comments made by Brinch-Hansen on Java in the introduction. Subpattern restrictions complement access control mechanisms like public, private and protected and make it possible to define patterns that define general rules for access to attributes of subpatterns.

In the literature, there are many proposals for supporting concurrency and no model has gained widespread acceptance. Concurrency on mainstream languages like Java, C++, and C# makes use of insecure threads, locks, etc.

For this reason we think that it is useful to be able to define libraries of concurrency abstractions in a given language including schedulers. Few languages to our knowledge support this.

In [31], Tony Hoare wrote the following about Algol 60: "Here is a language so far ahead of its time, that it was not only an improvement on its predecessors, but also on nearly all its successors." Bertrand Meyer has made a similar statement about SIMULA. The SIMULA notions of object, class, subclass, virtual and the ability to define frameworks like class Simulation have been widely adapted. The notions of objects as active coroutines and the ability to define schedulers have been overlooked.

In Beta and **xBeta**, we have further generalized the SIMULA notions of coroutine and preemptive suspend and demonstrated their usefulness to support concurrency abstractions.

xBeta retains the power of object-orientation and at the same time provide safe concurrent processes. Concurrent objects may be defined using the standard OO mechanisms, and communication between concurrent processes is not reduced to simple messages.

There is of course a restriction that only immutable objects may be passed between concurrent processes. As for processes, we may use the full power of OO to define immutable objects.

For **xBeta**, we have thus not been forced to downgrade support for concurrent objects to asynchronous messages and simple values.

It may still be an issue if **xBeta** will be considered an inherently concurrent language. As of now, there is nothing that prevents the programmers from using **xBeta** as a sequential language and adding concurrency by need. In the outset, we believe that the new organization of modules as objects [44] and the ability to offer safe concurrency abstractions may improve on this. In some sense, it may be a matter of presentation. In practice, programmers may freely choose their language – so concurrency modules should be offered as languages. In the real world the programmer is free to choose between e.g. Java, Erlang and C. With **xBeta**, we provide the option of choosing an inherently concurrent language.

The final issue relates to the generality of the proposed language mechanisms. The notions of coroutine and preemptive suspend should be easily adapted to languages like Java, C++, and C#. The same holds for submethods and inner — being central in order to define the kind of abstractions presented here.

Adapting submethods and inner to a given OO language may require a major change in language philosophy and programming style. In most languages, a method may be completely redefined and method combination is done by means of a super-mechanism. Submethods and inner provides more structure and security, but at the expense of flexibility. We do, however, believe that in software development, structure and security should be prioritized.

Acknowledgements. Beta was developed as a joint effort with Bent Bruun Kristensen, Birger Møller-Pedersen, and Kristen Nygaard. Boris Magnusson taught us about a deficiency of the SIMULA suspend mechanism and introduced us to preemptive suspend. I am grateful to Eric Jul, Birger Møller-Pedersen, and the anonymous reviewers for giving useful comments on this paper, especially for pointing out a number of errors in the first version of this paper. I would also like to thank the editors of the Festschrift for professor Akinori Yonezawa, especially Atsushi Igarashi for their assistance with this paper and making it possible for me to attend the Symposium in Honor of Professor Akinori Yonezawa's 65th birthday. And, finally, a warm thank you to Akinori Yonezawa for his significant achievements in computer sciences including concurrent objects – Aki and his work has always been of great inspiration to me.

References

1. Ada. Ada reference manual. proposed standard document (1980)
2. Agha, G.: Actors: a model of concurrent computation in distributed systems. MIT Press, Cambridge (1986)
3. Agha, G.: Concurrent object-oriented programming. Communications of the ACM 35(9), 125–141 (1990)
4. Aldrich, J., Chambers, C.: Ownership Domains: Separating Aliasing Policy from Mechanism. In: Odersky, M. (ed.) ECOOP 2004. LNCS, vol. 3086, pp. 1–25. Springer, Heidelberg (2004)
5. Almeida, P.S.: Balloon Types: Controlling Sharing of State in Data Types. In: Akşit, M., Matsuoka, S. (eds.) ECOOP 1997. LNCS, vol. 1241, pp. 32–59. Springer, Heidelberg (1997)
6. Armstrong, J., Virding, R., Williams, M.: Concurrent Programming in Erlang. Prentice Hall (1993)
7. Bernstein, A.J.: Output Guards and Nondeterminism in "Communicating Sequential Processes". ACM Transactions on Programming Languages and Systems (TOPLAS) 2(2), 234–238 (1980)

8. Black, A., Hutchinson, N., Jul, E., Levy, H.: Object Structure in the Emerald System. In: OOPLSA 1986 – Object-Oriented Programming Systems, Languages and Applications, pp. 78–86. ACM SIGPLAN (1986)

9. Blake, E., Cook, S.: On Including Part Hierarchies in Object-Oriented Languages, with an Implementation in Smalltalk. In: Bézivin, J., Hullot, J.-M., Lieberman, H., Cointe, P. (eds.) ECOOP 1987. LNCS, vol. 276, pp. 41–50. Springer, Heidelberg (1987)

10. Booch, G.: Object-Oriented Analysis and Design with Applications. Benjamin/Cummings, Redwood City (1991)

11. Brinch-Hansen, P.: The Origin of Concurrent Programming: From Semaphores to Remote Procedure Calls. Springer (2002)

12. Brinch-Hansen, P.: The Programming Language Concurrent Pascal. IEEE Transactions on Software Engineering SE-1(2) (1975)

13. Brinch-Hansen, P.: Java's insecure parallelism. ACM SIGPLAN Notices 34(4), 38–45 (1999)

14. Budd, T.: An Introduction to Object-Oriented Programming, 3rd edn. Addison Wesley (2002)

15. Coad, P., Yourdon, E.: Object-Oriented Analysis. Prentice-Hall, Englewood Cliffs (1991)

16. Conway, M.E.: Design of a Separable Transition-Diagram Compiler. Communications of the ACM 6(7), 396–408 (1963)

17. Cook, S.: Object Technology – A Grand Narrative? In: Thomas, D. (ed.) ECOOP 2006. LNCS, vol. 4067, pp. 174–179. Springer, Heidelberg (2006)

18. Cook, W.R.: Peak Objects. In: Thomas, D. (ed.) ECOOP 2006. LNCS, vol. 4067, pp. 180–185. Springer, Heidelberg (2006)

19. Dahl, O.-J., Hoare, C.A.R.: Hierarchical Program Structures. Academic Press (1972)

20. Dahl, O.-J., Myhrhaug, B., Nygaard, K.: SIMULA 67 Common Base Language (Editions 1968, 1970, 1972, 1984). Technical report, Norwegian Computing Center (1968)

21. Dahl, O.-J., Nygaard, K.: SIMULA—a Language for Programming and Description of Discrete Event Systems. Technical report, Norwegian Computing Center (1965)

22. Dahl, O.-J., Nygaard, K.: SIMULA: an ALGOL-based Simulation Language. Communications of the ACM 9(9), 671–678 (1966)

23. Dahl, O.-J., Nygaard, K.: The Development of the SIMULA Languages. In: ACM SIGPLAN History of Programming Languages Conference (1978)

24. Dahl, O.-J., Wang, A.: Coroutine Sequencing in a Block Structured Environment. BIT 11, 425–449 (1971)

25. Dijkstra, E.W.: Guarded Commands, Nondeterminacy and the Formal Derivation of Programs. Communications of the ACM 18, 453–457 (1975)

26. Google. Dart – Build HTML5 Apps for the Modern Web. Technical report (2011), http://www.dartlang.org/

27. Gosling, J., Joy, B., Steele, G.: The Java (TM) Language Specification. Addison-Wesley (1996)

28. Griswold, R.E., Hanson, D.R., Korb, J.T.: Generators in Icon. ACM Trans. on Programming Languages and Systems 3(2), 144–161 (1981)

29. Hewitt, C., Bishop, P., Steiger, R.: A universal modular ACTOR formalism for artificial intelligence. In: IJCAI 1973 – 3rd International Joint Conference on Artificial Intelligence, pp. 235–245 (1973)

30. Hoare, C.A.R.: Notes on Data Structuring. Academic Press, London (1972)

31. Hoare, C.A.R.: Hints on Programming Language Design. Technical report, Computer Science Department, Stanford University (1973)
32. Hoare, C.A.R.: Communicating Sequential Processes. Communications of the ACM 21(8) (1978)
33. Hogg, J.: Islands: Alisasing Protectio in Object-Oriented Languages. In: OOPSLA 1996 – Object-Oriented Programming Systems, Languages and Applications (1991)
34. Kernighan, B.W., Ritchie, D.M.: The C Programming Language, 2nd edn. Prentice Hall, Englewood Cliffs (1978)
35. Kreutzer, W., Østerbye, K.: BetaSim - a framework for discrete event modeling & simulation. Simulation - Practice & Theory (1999)
36. Kristensen, B.B., Madsen, O.L., Møller-Pedersen, B., Nygaard, K.: Abstraction Mechanisms in the BETA Programming Language. In: Tenth ACM Symposium on Principles of Programming Languages (1983)
37. Kristensen, B.B., Møller-Pedersen, B., Chepoi, V.: Classification of Actions or Inheritance also for Methods. In: Bézivin, J., Hullot, J.-M., Lieberman, H., Cointe, P. (eds.) ECOOP 1987. LNCS, vol. 276, pp. 98–107. Springer, Heidelberg (1987)
38. Kristensen, B.B., Madsen, O.L., Møller-Pedersen, B.: The When, Why and Why not of the BETA Programming Language. In: Hailpern, B., Ryder, B.G. (eds.) History of Progamming Languages III. SIGPLAN (2007)
39. Kristensen, B.B., Madsen, O.L., Møller-Pedersen, B., Nygaard, K.: Multisequential execution in the BETA programming language. ACM SIGPLAN Notices 20(4), 57–69 (1985)
40. Krogdahl, S., Olsen, K.A.: Modular and Object-Oriented Programming. Data Tid 9 (1986)
41. Madsen, O.L., Møller-Pedersen, B.: What Object-Oriented Programming May Be—and What It Does Not Have to Be. In: Gjessing, S., Chepoi, V. (eds.) ECOOP 1988. LNCS, vol. 322, pp. 1–20. Springer, Heidelberg (1988)
42. Madsen, O.L., Møller-Pedersen, B., Nygaard, K.: Object-Oriented Programming in the BETA Programming Language. Addison Wesley (1993)
43. Madsen, O.L.: Defining Object Semantics using Object Sequence Diagrams – or just another high-level debugger. Technical report, Aarhus University (2012)
44. Madsen, O.L.: Modularization and Browsing – an Integrated Design. Technical Report, Dept. of Computer Science, Aarhus University, Aarhus (2012)
45. Madsen, O.L., Møller-Pedersen, B.: A Unified Approach to Modeling and Programming. In: Petriu, D.C., Rouquette, N., Haugen, Ø. (eds.) MODELS 2010, Part I. LNCS, vol. 6394, pp. 1–15. Springer, Heidelberg (2010)
46. Magnusson, B.: Using the simioprocess library on Unix Systems. Technical report, Lund Software House AB, Sweden (1997)
47. Meyer, B.: Object-Oriented Software Construction. Prentice Hall (1997)
48. Naur, P.: Revised Report on The Algorithmic Language ALGOL 60. Communications of the ACM 6 (1963)
49. Nierstrass, O.: Ten Things I Hate About Object-Oriented Programming – Banquet speech given at ECOOP 2010. Maribor 2010. The JOT blog – Journal of Object Technology (June 24, 2010)
50. Noble, J., Vitek, J., Potter, J.: Flexible Alias Protection. In: Jul, E. (ed.) ECOOP 1998. LNCS, vol. 1445, pp. 158–185. Springer, Heidelberg (1998)
51. Nordlander, J., Jones, M.P., Carlsson, M., Kieburtz, D., Black, A.P.: Reactive Objects. In: Fifth IEEE International Symposium on Object-Oriented Real-Time Distributed Computing, ISORC 2002 (2002)
52. Halstead Jr., R.H.: Multilisp: A language for concurrent symbolic computation. ACM Transactions on Programming Languages and Systems 7(4), 501–538 (1985)

53. Stroustrup, B.: The C++ Programming Language. Addison-Wesley, Reading (1986)
54. Stroustrup, B.: Evolving a language in and for the real world: C++ 1991-2006. In: History of Programming Languages III. ACM (2007)
55. Vaucher, J.: Prefixed Procedures: A Structuring Concept for Operations. INFOR 13(3) (1975)
56. Vaucher, J., Magnusson, B.: SIMULA Frameworks: the Early Years. Wiley (1999)
57. Wirth, N.: Programming in Modula-2. Springer, New York (1982)
58. Wirth, N.: Modula-2 and Oberon. In: Hailpern, B., Ryder, B.G. (eds.) History of Progamming Languages III. SIGPLAN (2007)
59. Yokote, Y., Tokoro, M.: Experience and Evolution of Concurrent Smalltalk. In: OOPSLA 1987– Object-Oriented Programming Systems, Languages and Applications, pp. 406–415. ACM SIGPLAN (1987)
60. Yonezawa, A.: Early Concurrent/Mobile Objects. In: Thomas, D. (ed.) ECOOP 2006. LNCS, vol. 4067, pp. 198–202. Springer, Heidelberg (2006)
61. Yonezawa, A., Briot, J.-P., Shibayama, E.: Object-Oriented Concurrent Programming in ABCL/1. In: OOPLSA 1986 – Object-Oriented Programming Systems, Languages and Applications, pp. 258–268. ACM SIGPLAN (1986)
62. Østerbye, K., Kreutzer, W.: Synchronization Abstraction in the BETA Programming Language. Computer Languages 25, 165–187 (1999)

Structuring Communication with Session Types

Kohei Honda[1], Raymond Hu[2], Rumyana Neykova[2], Tzu-Chun Chen[1],
Romain Demangeon[1], Pierre-Malo Deniélou[2,3], and and Nobuko Yoshida[2]

[1] Queen Mary,
University of London
[2] Imperial College, London
[3] Royal Holloway, University of London

Abstract. Session types are types for distributed communicating processes. They were born from process encodings of data structures and typical interaction scenarios in an asynchronous version of the π-calculus, and are being studied and developed as a potential basis for structuring concurrent and distributed computing, as well as in their own right. In this paper, we introduce basic ideas of sessions and session types, outline their key technical elements, and discuss how they may be usable for programming, drawing from our experience and comparing with existing paradigms, especially concurrent objects such as actors. We discuss how session types can offer a programming framework in which communications are structured both in program text and at run-time.

1 Introduction

This paper illustrates a structuring method for distributed computing based on session types [19, 20, 29]. We take the standpoint that communication is an essential building block for concurrent and distributed computation and that there is a strong prospect that both software and hardware engineers need to position this notion as a foundation of their design activities. Under this assumption, we seek a general principle for structuring communications as a basis to facilitate the development of correct and efficient programs. Computation based on communication is so rich – it certainly includes the whole of sequential and shared variable computation – that it looks hopeless to identify a principle which may apply to its different realisations. There is also a difficulty inherent in communication as we discuss in the next section. Given these potential difficulties, instead of looking for general principles, we may be content with having different techniques depending on different classes of use cases and different levels of expertise. But we believe this difficulty should not deter us from our quest towards a unifying foundation since only with such a foundation we can start to harness the richness of the large class of behaviours realisable through communication and concurrency, providing a guide for individual problems and giving a basis upon which different techniques can be positioned and integrated with greater benefits than isolated solutions.

G. Agha et al. (Eds.): Yonezawa Festschrift, LNCS 8665, pp. 105–127, 2014.

A central idea for structuring communications in session types is to divide them into chunks of inter-related interactions forming logical units, called sessions. Each session, in its own temporal-spatial confine, consists of messages which are clearly identifiable as belonging to that session. The term "session" comes from the networking community where such a classification has been practised for a long time, albeit informally. Each session is associated with its protocol, specifying how its participants may interact with each other, which gives a type for the session in the sense that it classifies interaction structures, and that they are directly linked to programming primitives as a formal specification, just as types for functions and methods are directly linked to their underlying primitive. This is how protocols arise as types when programming with sessions. We illustrate this framework more concretely in Section 2.

The study of session types over the past two decades has extensive interactions with other threads of research. Session types were born from a desire to articulate the abstract structures arising from idioms that repeatedly occur when we encode high-level data types and programs in the asynchronous version of the π-calculus [23], which in turn was influenced by actor model. Theories of concurrency, in particular process algebras such as ACP [3], CCS [21] and CSP [16], offered mathematical foundations of session types: the research on concurrent languages based on actors and concurrent objects also played an important role in the inception of session types. These languages include the ABCL family of programming languages starting from [32], developed by Akinori Yonezawa and his team, which is one of the prominent accomplishments in the study of concurrent languages and formed a cultural background of the initial introduction of session types.

This paper is intended for a concise presentation of key ideas as well as some of the open topics. We also provide comparisons with related programming and software development methodologies. For technical details, we hope the reader can consult citations in each section. Section 2 gives the background of session types. Section 3 introduces its programming methodology informally through examples. Section 4 discusses one of its application examples. Section 5 compares our approach with other framework for concurrent programming with a focus on concurrent objects and actors, and concludes.

2 Background

2.1 Structuring Sequential Programs

Computing in its modern sense started from the discoveries in 1930s and 1940s of abstract and concrete machines which are in nature sequential. Among them, the abstract machine by Turing and its crystallisation as an engineering design by Von Neumann offered the combination of striking simplicity and universality with a finite state automaton as the processing unit and a linear array of memory cells as the workspace for the automata (designated as a "tape" containing many squares in Turing's model: symbols are read from and written to these squares by an automata). This simple machine model was to be explored extensively by generations of engineers, developing faster processing units and larger memories with high-bandwidth for reading and writing. By Turing's result, engineers know that, just by focusing on these two key elements (the processor and the memory) and enlarging their capabilities, the machine can simply get better.

It is on this stable hardware model that the fundamental programming abstractions for sequential computing were developed, from assemblers to a simple notion of control flows and data types, to procedures and the structured programming discipline, to dynamically created data structures with multiple operations (objects), to higher-order procedures. The stable and universal hardware model makes it possible, assisted by other fundamental theories including, among others, the λ-calculus and its type theories, to incrementally build up layers of abstractions that assist designers and programmers to describe the intended behaviour with clear structures understandable by the programmer and his/her fellow colleagues, as well as by compilers which perform static checking of programs. Without good structures, it is hard for both humans and machines to understand programs' semantics.

This point is well-articulated by Dijkstra, when he advocates the structures programming discipline in his famous communication [13]:

> Our intellectual powers are rather geared to master static relations. [...] For that reason we should do (as wise programmers aware of our limitations) our utmost to shorten the conceptual gap between the static program and the dynamic process, to make the correspondence between the program (spread out in text) and the process (spread out in time) as trivial as possible.

Implicit in this observation is that the dynamic process realisable by the structured presentation of programs has the same expressive power as the "unstructured" method. Another observation underlying Dijkstra's remark is the fact that a formal basis for the structuring method, such as Hoare logic for structured programming constructs, can pinpoints the status of the method.

The quote above also indicates a crucial element for any effective structuring method for programming: we obtain abstraction and good structure so that we can map the resulting program text tractably into efficient code, since without the existence of such a mapping, it is hardly expected that we can make the correspondence between program text and how it will be executed "as trivial as possible."[1] And for this correspondence to be judged to be effective for a high-level programming language, we needed a stable machine model which not only underlies the existing hardware products but also would underlie for potential ones.

---

[1] Note that this correspondence is preserved, albeit not too trivially, even for dynamic data structures such as objects, by a stable compilation strategy based on class tables. Such a basic correspondence is a basis for individual optimisations for architectures.

2.2   Communication and Concurrency

Communicating processes are at the heart of computing since early days of computing. While, as we have just discussed, computing has been based on the most effective sequential model, scientists and engineers quickly found the use of networking in combination with computing machinery, especially in the shape of packet-switching networks that deliver digital data throughout networks with effective use of the capacity of wires and flexibility which is not possible through circuit-based networks. This is done through the help of intermediate nodes which act as exchanges of data packets.

On this basis, at the network engineering level, we saw the emergence of the idea of inter-networking, which links multiple networks, born and crystallised as the TCP/IP combination of protocols [7]. This protocol was later split into the two components as we know now based on the understanding on the end-to-end principle [26], leading to the scalable inter-network infrastructure now known as Internet, which was eventually to span the globe. Around the time when TCP/IP was being engendered and incorporated as part of the then nascent Internet, many studies on communicating processes, in abstract models, programming languages and verifications were initiated, on which we shall discuss later.

In Internet, after several notable applications had been developed such as electronic mails based on corresponding application-layer protocols, we saw an invention of a simple but useful idea to implement hyperlinks over Internet, embodied in the document format HTML and the application-layer protocol HTTP. HTTP, a simple protocol based on server-client interactions performed in a TCP-connection, has turned out to be a great medium for providing services to users, by which the user base of Internet has undergone an explosive growth. Later we found other applications of Internet, such as Internet Telephony as well as social networking, leading to the proliferation of web services, where many businesses become Internet-based and have global presence, be they bookshops, music or flower delivery. The resulting socio-technical complex is to be called World-Wide Web.

Global services in the World-Wide Web need to cope with a large number of clients. This in turn necessitated the development of server technologies, to be used for the backend of these web services. Combined with virtualisation technologies of OSes and networks, this has led to a set of technologies by which multiple users can share a gigantic interconnected network of commodity hosts as if each has its own network and computing resources, leading to cloud computing. Cloud computing is giving at least three impacts. First it allows every user an opportunity to use large amount of computing resources economically. Second, it allows diverse networking technologies to be experimented without interfering with other users. Thirdly, it offers users an economical platform where an embarrassing amount of concurrency and distribution are the norm rather than a marginal concern.

The cloud computing has become prominent in the first decade of the 21st century. Not neglecting other factors, an insight which the cloud computing may give us is that, to share computation, that computation had better be distributed. This is a physical problem, having the same root as the following observation by Hoare on multi-processor architecture several decades ago [16]:

> [...] Where the desire for greater speed has led to the introduction of parallelism, every attempt has been made to disguise this fact from the programmer [...]. However, developments of processor technology suggest that a multiprocessor machine, constructed from a number of similar self-contained processors (each with its own store), may become more powerful, capacious, reliable, and economical than a machine which is disguised as a monoprocessor.

In brief, there is a limit to share a large amount of computing power in the sequential form (or, in Hoare's words, to "disguise" it to be sequential), due to the existence of latency. In spite of all the engineering efforts to achieve the contrary, we see a clear slowing-down of sequential performance of representative CPUs at the beginning of the 21st century, fulfilling Hoare's prediction in a globally aware form. Since then, the architectural development centres on increasing parallel performance through many cores. This is also in line with the architectural evolution of super computers, which, after prominent instances such as Bluegene showed their performance merits, have turned into communication-centred designs.

2.3   Structuring Communication

Thus, in all scales of computing, communication is becoming one of the major elements. And theoretical results such as Milner's embedding of the λ-calculus into the π-calculus [22] confirms their status as an expressive computing primitive. However, as Hoare himself observed when he introduced CSP, communication is hard to harness, in both design and formal verifications, which is one of the reasons why Hoare and Milner have chosen synchronous interaction. Can we find a tractable way to specify and manage communication in program texts and runtime?

There is however subtlety in this question itself: what is it to which we aim to give a good structure? Sequential computation has a stable execution basis, in the abstract models and in concrete machine instructions. But communication is different. Either inside a chip, among different machines in a cluster or across continents, communication is always mediated by intermediate infrastructure, be it on-chip interconnect and buffering facilities in a manycore chip, Ethernet bus and drivers, or IP routers. Communication is not a hardware primitive at the same level of assignment, and never will be. Thus it is hard to determine and agree on what would count as basic *primitives* for communication. And if we cannot identify primitives, how can we think of the structuring method for them?

Answering this problem is hard because communication is useful, after all, because it is between two computing machines: there may not be only one way to realise it. Session types started from a theory of processes based on asynchronous communication based on the π-calculus which is also close to the actor model.

This theory, introduced in [5, 18], is interesting in that it is a sub-set of the π-calculus, which itself is based on synchronous, handshake computation, but just by taking its subset, now represents asynchrony. This also suggests all theories developed in CSP, CCS and the π-calculus are now applicable to asynchronous theory. These theories show that, at the foundational level, we can indeed have a rigorous theory of asynchronously communicating processes, with an exact notion of behaviours, their equivalence, and logical specifications. But having a general theory does not dispel the theoretical intractability, and accompanying mental intractability, of asynchrony: assuming we use large or infinite buffering in communication, it looks hard to reason about behaviours (consider model checking interactional behaviours with infinite buffering).

It is here that the notion of protocols and session types comes in, on which we shall discuss in the next section.

3   Multiparty Protocols and Sessions

3.1   Session Types

One of the outcomes of using very large-scale integration for implementing a central processor of a computer is that, to link "remote" areas of a single chip (since we want different cores to share data), we need to rely on asynchronous communication. This is for the following simple reason: if we need to have two computations to be not too closely synchronised, that is (as we want when two different cores to calculate two parts of computation) if we want their computations to proceed independently unless absolutely necessary, the only way is to link them with a buffered communication medium, which an on-chip interconnect in VLSI readily provides. Note that a relative independence in processing also means that we can overlap computation and communication, which is a major method to make the most of distributed computing resources.

But this very asynchrony also poses a problem in understanding computation: the "dynamic process", as Dijkstra called it, of asynchronously communicating processes looks hard to harness, because, simply put, all different ways in which the messages can be buffered add new states in potential computations, making the reasoning extremely difficult. For example, if a process changes its state on each occasion when a new message is received, and each sending action depends on this state, then unbounded buffering means unbounded states and behaviours.

It is to harness this untenable nature of asynchronous communicating processes that has led to the birth of the structuring method for communications programming based on sessions and session-based primitives (creating sessions and communication through sessions), together with the underlying types which offer a way to specify protocols for sessions as types, drawing from the study of the π-calculus and its type theories as well as the foregoing studies on types in programming languages. By restricting asynchrony by protocols, we can reduce the size of state space to be considered, for each session and interleaved sessions, ensuring safe interactions by static checking and giving a basis for understanding and verifying behaviour. It has the equivalent expressive power as the original primitive of the π-calculus, which is known to possess a universal computing power for interactions in a certain technical sense.

The original session typed π-calculi are based on synchronous communication primitives, assumed to be compiled into asynchronous interaction: later researchers found that, if we assume *ordered* asynchronous communications for binary interactions inside a session, the original synchronous theory of safety can be preserved while directly expressing asynchronous interaction. This safety theory includes the simple fact that the type of a message by a sender coincides with what a receiver expects inside a multiparty dialogue, which is practically important because such an error costs a lot more in asynchronous communicating processes than in sequential computing.

3.2   Writing Protocols

Session types describe a way, or a pattern, in which interactions can take place in sessions. Session types have been called *protocols* for many years in network and other engineering disciplines which need to treat such patterns. For this reason, and because session types are sufficiently different in nature from data types, we know in sequential computing (although the former share the key principle from data types as we shall discuss later), hereafter we often use the term "protocols" instead of "session types" when discussing their use for programming.

One of the key ingredients of session-based programming is the use of protocols as an essential element of design and programming, because a clear understanding of an interaction scenario is an essential ingredient of communications programming. For this reason, one of the key features of programming with sessions is a *protocol description language*, the language with which engineers read and write their protocols. They are close to types in sequential programming: like data and function types, there is a tight linkage to language primitive. Like data and function types, protocols may be inferred from programs or declared by programmers so that programs may be checked against them. A difference is that a protocol describes interactions for a session, and that, for this reason, each session involves a sequence of interactions (which may not necessarily be contiguous, since interactions in other sessions or internal computation may interleave).

A Simple Protocol. To illustrate how we can specify a protocol, we take a simple scenario, and show how the corresponding protocol can be specified using an experimental protocol description language we are developing, called Scribble [17,27,28] (the name comes from our desire to create an effective tool for architects, designers and developers alike to quickly and accurately write down protocols).

A key feature of Scribble is that all of its constructs are fully founded on the formal theory of multiparty session types, starting from the core language features for message passing, choice and recursion [4,20], to more advanced features, such as parallel [10], interrupts [6], sub-sessions [9] and run-time monitoring [8],

```
1   type <ysd> "ListingFormat" from "ListingFormat.ysd" as Format;
2
3   protocol ListResources(role client as cl, role resource_registry as rr) {
4       request(resource_kind:String) from cl to rr;
5       rec loop {
6           choice at rr {
7               response(element:Format) from rr to cl;
8               continue loop;
9           } or {
10              completed() from rr to cl;
11          }
12      }
13  }
```

Fig. 1. A protocol for the List Resources use case

and studies relating session types to alternatives such as communicating automata [10]. The development of Scribble is a collaboration between researchers and industry partners [24,27]. Most of the examples presented in this section are supported by the current working version of Scribble [28], with a few exceptions that we note as being planned for future release.

The initial scenario we treat is called "List Resources", where a Client obtains a list of resources of some kind from a Resource Registry. This is a basic use case applicable to many environments where a user may be provided with a variety of resources by the infrastructure, e.g. remotely operable instruments or systems resources such as bandwidth. The scenario consists of two steps:

Step 1: Client asks Registry to send her a resource list, specifying the kind of resources it is interested in.

Step 2: Registry responds by sending the list of the resources of the kind specified, until the list is exhausted.

It is a simple elaboration of a remote procedural call. Note, however, that Step 2 involves a repetition of sending actions. This use case may be further elaborated in various ways, but this simple version is sufficient for our first exercise.

Writing down a protocol goes through a natural flow, practised for decades in the networking community. We first list the *message formats*, followed by the participating *actors* (and other parameters). Then we scribble away the structure of the *conversation* between the actors. The result for our mini use case is given in Figure 1.

Line 1 starts from importing an message type `ListingFormat`, specified in YAML (`ysd`), from the external source (file) `ListingFormat.ysd`. This message type can then be referred to in this Scribble protocol specification by the given alias `Format`. (In the coloured presentation of this paper, the `import` and `as` are coloured **blue**, signifying they are keywords.) Message type imports allow Scribble to be used in conjunction and orthogonally with externally defined message formats: here we are using a YAML schema, but any data format given in a well-defined schema/type language may be used as far as the protocol validator is notified. Data format is of course fundamental in protocols to ensure interacting parties understand what the other is saying.

In Line 3, we give the name to the protocol, ListResources, followed by its parameters. The parameters consist of the names of the two actors roles which participants can play, client and resource_registry, aliased as cl and rr (short names are often good for scribbling away protocols). This completes the header of the protocol.

The remaining lines (Lines 4–13) constitute the *protocol body*, which describes the structured flow of the conversation in a session. We have the first interaction described in Line 4, which reads:

> A request *message whose content, annotated as* resource_kind *and typed as* String, *is sent from* cl *to* rr *asynchronously.*

In Line 4, request is the message *operator*; String (which is a built-in type for strings) is a message *payload* type, and resource_kind is the payload annotation (a simple name). Finally from and to specify the source and destination, respectively.

Line 4 is reminiscent of a method/function declaration found in APIs and modules of high-level sequential programming languages: an interaction signature is a symmetric, peer-to-peer version of the familiar notion of "interface" of functions and objects. As such, Line 4 does *not* specify constraints on *concrete values* a message may carry, but specifies only the *type* of an interaction. For this reason, we call the description in Line 4 as a whole, an *interaction signature*.

Registry now responds through a sequence of one or more messages: in the protocol, we use a light form of labelled recursion for such repetition. Line 5 declares the *recursion label* loop that names the *recursion body* starting from Line 6 and reaching Line 12. The recursion body consists of a single *choice* statement.

The choice construct starts from Line 6, which first declares the choice: at rr says that it is the Registry who will be the deciding party of this choice, through a subsequent send action.

Lines 7–8 and Line 10 are respectively two distinct *branch*es of the choice, separated by or on Line 9. In the first branch, Line 7 says that Registry sends a response message to Client, with message content annotated as (list) element and typed as Format. Again we specify only a sender, a receiver and a message signature. This is followed by Line 8, a *recurrence* denoted by the continue keyword, which says that the protocol flow at this point returns to the start of the recursion body labelled by loop, i.e. to Line 5.

The other branch consists of a single interaction, Line 10, where a completed message with an empty payload is sent from Registry to Client, indicating the end of the list, i.e. the end of the recursion – since there is no recurrence, the loop terminates if this branch is chosen. As described in Step 2 above, at the level of the application logic, the repetition should terminate only when all the resource data for the specified kind has been sent by Registry: our protocol description again abstracts from exactly how this may be determined in the program logic (although the protocol assertions we discuss later can constrain this behaviour in some way or another). After this action, the flow exits

```
1   protocol ListResources<type ListingFormat as Format>
2       (role client as cl, role resource_registry as rr) {
3       request(resource_kind:String) from cl to rr;
4       rec loop {
5           choice at rr {
6               response(element:Format) from rr to cl;
7               continue loop;
8           } or {
9               completed() from rr to cl;
10          }
11      }
12  }
```

Fig. 2. A refined List Resources protocol (1)

the choice and the recursion, and (since no further interactions are specified) the session terminates.

Nature of Protocols. We have seen a simple but self-contained protocol (session type), `ListResources`. Even from this simple example, we can find unique features of protocols. First, a protocol is like an API in that it defines a *contract*, but this contract is not just between a function and its user, but among conversing agents. Further, a protocol describes a *series* of interactions, with conditional and repeated segments, because conversations among distributed agents will often involve more elaborate structures than call-return. Like APIs, a protocol only offers a bare minimal behavioural specification, without constraining values nor conditions for actions. This paucity has a practical merit: minimal notations are needed for reading and writing basic protocols; they are amenable for efficient validation at both compilation time and at runtime; and they can serve as a minimal sufficient basis for elaborating them with refined behavioural constraints through, among others, assertions.

Elaborating Protocols. For protocols to assist computer software development, be it a newly built system or an upgrade of an existing system, they had better be *reusable*, i.e. once you author a protocol, it should be able to be used for many concrete applications. From this viewpoint, the `ListResources` protocol in Figure 1 may not be fully satisfactory. In particular, it works only for the message type defined in the specification by the concrete `ListingFormat` YAML schema. Even if only one listing format is known now, new formats may arise later. Why should we write different protocols for all different formats, given the structure of interactions is identical? We use a basic technique from programming theory, *parametrisation*, to solve the problem.

There are at least two different, and natural, ways we may employ parametericity in the protocol of this example. The first approach, supported in the current version of Scribble, is given in Figure 2. Here, we directly abstract the message type as a parameter to the protocol. In Line 1, the protocol has gotten an additional parameter, `<type ListingFormat>`, as well as dispensing with the "import" statement. This additional parameter means, with the keyword `<type>`,

```
1   protocol ListResources(role client as cl, role resource_registry as rr) {
2       request(resource_kind:String, type ListingFormat) from cl to rr;
3       rec loop {
4           choice at rr {
5               response(element:ListingFormat) from rr to cl;
6               continue loop;
7           } or {
8               completed() from rr to cl;
9           }
10      }
11  }
```

Fig. 3. A refined List Resources protocol (2)

that `ListingFormat` (again aliased as `Format`) is now a type name to be instantiated each time this protocol is instantiated as a whole into a run-time session.
Later, in the **response** interaction in Line 6, Registry is obliged to send the list
elements according to the concrete type known at run-time, while the Client
should be ready to receive them. The protocol again gives a contract among
participants, while now flexibly catering for arbitrary data formats.

A second approach, based on a dynamic form of parametrisation [25, 30], is
presented in Figure 3. This time, we elaborate the initial **request** interaction, in
Line 2 (the **import** clause is again dispensed with), so that the type `ListingFormat`
is now explicitly communicated from the Client to the Registry as the *value* of
a message, signifying its kind as **type**. This communicated type is then used
in Line 5, specifying that Registry should send the datum using the format it
has received from Client in Line 2. Scribble may be extended to support this
alternative technique for achieving the necessary parametrisation in a future
release, as the underlying theory is already well established.

Nested Protocols. Consider the protocol given in Figure 4. It has two actors,
a Requester and an Authority. In Lines 2–3, Requester sends a **check** message
to query on whether a subject is permitted to do an operation on a resource,
carrying the identities of a subject and a resource, the name of an operation, and
the certificate of Requester (for authentication, possibly validated via a separate
protocol) in its payload. In Lines 4–10, Authority responds, saying the operation
is allowed or not, or else by saying **other**, to deal with cases when the answer
cannot be delivered for some reason, such as an unqualified Requester.

Now consider the following elaboration of our original "List Resources" use
case:

Step 1: Client asks Resource Registry to send a resource list (as before).
Step 2: Registry checks if Client has sufficient privileges.
Step 3: If everything is fine, the Registry replies by a sequence of data for
resources of the specified kind to Client.

This use case incorporates a privilege check as part of the protocol, as an extension to the original use case. Note this use case composes two previous use cases,
by nesting a protocol inside another protocol. Can we realise such composite use
cases as a protocol?

```
1    protocol CheckPrivileges(role requester as req, role authority as au) {
2      check(subject:URI, resource:URI, operation:String, certificate:String)
3        from req to au;
4      choice at au {
5        allowed() from au to req;
6      } or {
7        not_allowed(reason:String) from au to req;
8      } or {
9        other(reason:String) from au to req;
10     }
11   }
```

Fig. 4. A protocol for the Check Privileges use case

In Figure 5, we show how such a composition is done in Scribble, by combining the previously specified CheckPrivileges and ListResources (the Figure 1 version). In Line 5, we use the introduces keyword to indicate that Registry will "introduce" a new actor, authority. After this preparation, the CheckPrivileges protocol is launched (spawn) by Registry (at rr) in Line 6. Note the arguments include Authority which has just been introduced, as well as Registry (who will play the requester role in the spawned session). We call the nested CheckPrivileges session spawned during the execution of the ListResources protocol a *child session*, or a *sub-session*, of the *parent* ListResources session. The lifetime of a child session is, in the standard run-time semantics [9], dependent on its parent (e.g. if a parent session aborts, its child session(s) should also abort). Where such causal dependency is not desired, these unrelated protocols may well be specified separately, to be instantiated into distinct sessions at run-time.

Returning to Figure 5, after the CheckPrivileges sub-session is carried out, Registry, now knowing the qualification of Client for this query, responds to Client with either an ok or an error message with the reason (a String payload). When ok, the remainder of the protocol is the same as in Figure 1 (and also Figures 2 and 3). Note that the result of running CheckPrivileges is likely to be related to whether ok or error is selected at the application logic but, at this type level, we do not specify such detailed constraints.

As mentioned earlier, there are other constructs in Scribble, and in session types in general. Among them are parallel composition, where two concurrent threads of conversations can occur; interrupts, where a participant can asynchronously interrupt an ongoing session using a message with one of the declared signatures; and other modes of interactions beyond simple unicast. Additional features supported by Scribble, and founded on formal theory, include nested protocols, which is based on recent work introduced in [9] studying a general form of nesting and instantiating session types.

3.3   Writing Programs with Sessions

We next take a brief look at how we can use the proposed concept of protocols and sessions to implement clear and understandable communication programs, taking a Python implementation of the List Resources protocol from Figure 1

```
1   import Authentication.CheckPrivileges as CheckPrivileges;
2
3   protocol ListResources(role client as cl, role resource_registry as rr) {
4       request(resource_kind:String, type ListingFormat) from cl to rr;
5       rr introduces au;
6       spawn CheckPrivileges(rr as requester, au as authority) at rr;
7       choice at rr {
8           ok() from rr to cl;
9           rec loop {
10              choice at rr {
11                  response(list:ListingFormat) from rr to cl;
12                  continue loop;
13              } or {
14                  completed() from rr to cl;
15              }
16          }
17      } or {
18          error(reason:String) from rr to cl;
19      }
20  }
```

Fig. 5. A refined List Resources protocol (3)

as an example. We cannot give a full implementation in its entirety here, but we hope the reader can get the flavour.

Preliminaries. A protocol describes interactions among two or more agents. While the running agents are often distributed in terms of run-time locality, the implementation of the agent programs is also often "distributed" in terms of development. Indeed, one of the primary purposes of protocols is to provide a minimal interface against which each agent program may be independently implemented, by different parties using different languages and techniques, while ensuring full interoperability when global application is executed as a whole. Therefore, the basic but general protocol- and session-oriented methodology for developing programs is based on designing and implementing one program for each endpoint. These programs interact with each other inside run-time conversations via asynchronous messages following the specified protocols.

At run-time, a multiparty session functions like a network of TCP connections between the multiple endpoints, enabling them to communicate with each other following the stipulated protocol. However, the concept of session also insulates interactions among its participants from the underlying concrete transport mechanisms, so that developers can (mostly) stay unaware of the particular networking technologies that may be employed at run-time. Our session-oriented programs are constructed using "socket" abstractions that can be seen as standard TCP sockets generalised for multiparty messaging. Explicit structuring of conversation flows makes the description of multiple flows of interactions within an endpoint implementation clear with regards to the dependencies within each flow and between flows. Since interactions in a session are ensured to never violate the underlying protocol, either by static checking [4,20] or through run-time monitoring (by protocol machines) [8], each endpoint knows what kinds of messages are coming from which other participants at each stage of a conversation.

```
1    protocol RequestResponse(role Client as cl, role Server as sr) {
2       choice at cl {
3          GET() from cl to sr;
4          choice at sr {
5             sc200(s:String) from sr to cl;
6          } or {
7             sc500(reason:String) from sr to cl;
8             ...
9       } or {
10         POST() from cl to sr;
11         ...
12      ...
13   }
```

Fig. 6. A HTTP-like request-response protocol (extract)

To demonstrate the description of multiple conversation flows, our example implementation shall integrate the List Resources protocol with a separately specified HTTP-like request-response protocol (simply called Request-Response). We first give the relevant part of the Scribble for Request-Response in Figure 6 before proceeding to the code. In the figure, "sc" in e.g. sc200 stands for the "status code" of a message.

Program. We now consider a Python program that uses the ListResources and RequestResponse protocols (the latter for transparently receiving user requests) in combination. The program is an implementation of a service proxy that obtains data from the Registry on behalf of the User. We call this endpoint program simply "Proxy" from now on. Proxy needs to carry out two kinds of conversations:

1. As a Request-Response server, it will engage in sessions with Users, accepting the User query and returning the results from the Registry.
2. As a List Resources client, it will engage in sessions with the Registry, passing on the User query and receiving the list of resources following Figure 1.

Proxy will return the results to User in HTML format, in a similar manner to a standard CGI application. The main Python code for Proxy related to implementing these sessions is given in Figure 7 (in the version with colours, the blue and red indicate Python keywords and conversation programming constructs, respectively).

Line 2 declares a try block for handling exceptions that may arise during session execution. In Line 3, Proxy (receives and) accepts an invitation to interact in the Request-Response session with User. The proxy_uri object represents Proxy as a network *principal*, and may roughly be considered as a conversation programming counterpart to a TCP server socket. Proxy can then accept an invitation through this interface, with respect to the RequestResponse protocol, playing the role of Server to User. Specifying the protocol and role for this endpoint prescribes the local programming interface for cl, by which Proxy will interact with User.

```
1    c1 = None
2    try:
3        c1 = proxy_uri.accept("RequestResponse", "Server")
4        msg = c1.receive("Client")
5        if msg.op == "GET":
6            resource_kind = parse_query(msg.value) # fun def omitted
7            c2 = None
8            try:
9                c2 = Conversation("ListResources")
10               c2.join("client")
11               registry_uri.invite(c2, "resource_registry")
12               c2.send("resource_registry", "request", resource_kind)
13               html_str = ""
14               def loop():
15                   msg = c2.receive("resource_registry")
16                   if msg.operator == "response":
17                       html_str = html_str + yaml2html(msg.value)
18                       loop()
19                   elif msg.operator == "completed":
20                       return
21               loop()
22               c1.send("HTTPClient", "sc200", html_str) # All went well
23           except Exception as e:
24               if c1.alive():
25                   c1.send("HTTPClient", "sc500", "internal error")
26               raise e
27           finally:
28               if c2 != None:
29                   c2.close()
30       else:
31           c1.send("HTTPClient", "sc501", "internal error")
32   except ConversationException as e:
33       print("Error({0})@{1}:{2}".format(e.errno, e.cid, e.strerror))
34   except:
35       print("Error({0}):{1}".format(e.errno, e.strerror))
36   finally:
37       if c1 != None:
38           c1.close();
```

Fig. 7. Conversation endpoint program for a service proxy program in Python (extract)

In Line 4, through c1, Proxy receives from User (denoted by its role name Client in the protocol), a message msg. The basic attributes of a session message include op, the operation name for the message (i.e. the message label or header), and the value array, the message payload. In Line 5, we check if the operation of msg is GET. We assume that the kind of resources is specified by the message value, parsed by the parse_query function and the result stored in resource_kind.

This example demonstrates the interleaving of multiple sessions in a single application. Here we introduce a second session in which Proxy now acts as client according to ListResources. Line 8 declares a nested try block for this session. In Line 9, we initialises a new session, using the class named Conversation. When creating a session, we specify the protocol name ListResources (taken to be the simplest version presented earlier, in Figure 1). In Line 10, after initialisation, Proxy "joins" the session as the client role specified in the protocol.

In Line 11, Proxy *invites* the remote registry_uri principal to this newly created session (to play the role resource_registry). The method returns when an acknowledgement is returned by the principal to accept the invitation. Now that both roles have joined, in Line 12, Proxy sends to Registry (role name `resource_registry`), a message with the `request` operation and the kind of resources it is interested in. Note the message format precisely follows the protocol.

The next part of the code gives a tail recursive routine for repeated data delivery, whose flow exactly matches that in the `ListResources` protocol. Lines 14–20 define a function `loop`. In its body, first in Line 15, the client receives a `msg` from Registry. Then we have two cases, depending on the operation of the message:

– If the operation is `response` (Line 16), a HTML-formatted version of the original message (which was specified in the protocol to have a YAML format) is appended to the string (Line 17), and the recursion is enacted (Line 18).
– If the operation is `completed`, the recursion is terminated (Line 19).

Line 21 executes this recursive function, and Line 22 returns the HTML request to User, concluding the inner try-block.

Line 23 catches exceptions. Line 24 checks if `c1` is alive (i.e. if it can still send a message), and if so, sends the Request-Response status code for an internal error before re-raising the exception. In this simple example, Line 30 handles the case when the request is not a `GET` by returning another error message. Finally Line 32 catches exceptions specific to sessions, signified by the exception class named `ConversationException`, whose content is printed in Line 33 (when an interrupt signature is specified in a protocol level, an endpoint program can use this signature to raise the interrupt, which can be caught in the same way). Line 33 shows that session exceptions contain the `cid` field, not present in standard exceptions (Line 35). Finally, either in the normal completion or not, Lines 27 and 36 clean up the sessions upon exiting their respective try blocks.

Discussions. We have illustrated above a simple use of sessions in communications programming. The use of sessions in programs makes it possible to build the application logic with a clear understanding on explicit conversation flows. These flows are clearly visible: by going through how conversation channels are mentioned in a given program (the red part in Figure 7), one can clearly capture these flows.

Having distinct flows of interactions explicitly expressed in your program help modular development, in the sense that one flow can be tweaked because e.g. we wish to offer better user experience, while keeping other flows intact. For example, we may consider a variation of the client in Figure 7, with more asynchronous interactions with the web server following more programmatic (e.g. Javascript-based) user-level interactions at the browser. A client can send data incrementally to the web server following repeated messages from the registry, which will be sent and displayed in the browser. We may also enrich the Request-Response protocol in Figure 7 to reflect the interactions at the user interface level. These refinements however do not affect the other protocol, for interactions between the client and the resource registry: so, in the program, we may only refine the interactions at `c1`, keeping those at `c2` intact.

Our purpose in our introduction to session programming in this section was to illustrate the core ideas of session programming, to see how it looks like to structure communications with (typed) sessions. There are other basic constructs for sessions, such as those for sending interrupts; creating a sub-session; inviting participants from the parent session in a child session; and others. Further, in practice, we often naturally wish to combine two or more consecutive sending actions, such as the invitation to join a session as a role and the initial sending action to that role. However the central idea is the same: to clearly present, in a communication program, how a flow of interactions – a session – proceeds through a sequence of program actions and their composition, possibly interleaved with actions in other sessions.

The resulting organisation of communication actions enable not only programs with a clear presentation of interaction structures, but also static validation of conformance to the underlying protocols through type checking; and its dynamic counterpart through finite state machine based protocols monitors. In the latter (dynamic) validation, it is assumed that we can identify the underlying session by inspecting a message, if that message belongs to a session. In this way the runtime messages also get organised, dividing numerous message exchanges in distributed computing environments into different chunks with a binding to underlying protocols. This is how sessions structure communication-centred computing.

4   Using Session Types

4.1   Session Types in Distributed Systems

Unlike in sequential computing, where a piece of software can often be regarded as a self-contained mathematical function, software in distributed computing environments evolve over long periods of time, interacting with other applications and services with disparate origins and histories. A piece of software interacts with other pieces of software, and their mutual interactions critically affect their behaviour to e.g. users. Because different endpoints should communicate with each other to realise a certain function, we need an infrastructure by which all this software can interact with each other. The global Internet is a typical and prominent example, which provides an infrastructure for communications in the shape of the TCP/IP protocol suite and, building on the end-to-end principle, enables diverse software and services to evolve and inter-relate with each other, creating the web of mutually dependent and evolving services. Partly overlapping with Internet but forming their own networks, we see many distributed computing environments designed and evolve, with different geographic expanses, shapes and functions, such as the corporate backbone networks, the backends of popular web services, and networked infrastructures for sciences and engineering.

Session types were introduced to structure distributed communicating processes. By different endpoints communicating with typed sessions, their interactions follow the stipulated scenarios, without inducing communication error: when a sender sends a message, the receiver can understand what it is, and in turn will send messages in an expected way. That is, we expect all parties to behave properly in their interactions following the protocols of sessions. It is then a natural question how we ensure proper communication behaviours of systems at run-time.

For example, we may realise typed sessions without having session information at run-time (for example, we may use a set of TCP connections to realise a session), with each program being type checked statically and whose session primitives invokes actions on such connections. In this case, there is no explicit session (wrt. the concept of session being proposed here – i.e. beyond that implicit to TCP) at run-time – except in our mind's eye. The freedom to realise sessions in this way is certainly the merit of having high-level abstraction in the shape of sessions assisted by static verification made possible by that very abstraction.

Another method is having sessions and protocols explicitly incorporated as part of the infrastructure in a distributed computing environment: a web of distributed runtimes, by which we can create and use sessions, become part of the infrastructure and applications use these runtimes to communicate with each other. Some of the practical motivations to use such a configuration include to track errors, to dynamically share protocols, and to optimise communication paths on the fly using information on sessions and their protocols. But the most prominent reason to choose this explicit approach is to insulate the specification, design and runtime behaviour of software systems in a distributed computing environment from low-level transport details. It leads to an environment where all or most communication behaviours in that environment are governed by explicitly declared protocols, and messages exchanged at runtime are marked by distinct sessions so that they can be multiplexed over communication channels and are checked against state machines induced by the underlying protocols (just as TCP and other transport and higher protocols are checked at endpoint network stacks). On this basis, we may build a machinery to assure high-level behavioural constraints such as conformance to security policies.

4.2   Using Session Types for End-to-End Cyberinfrastructure

Ocean Observatories Initiative [24], often abbreviated as OOI, is a large-scale NSF-funded project to build a cyberinfrastructure for observing oceans in the United States and beyond, with usage span of 30 years. It integrates real-time data acquisition, processing and data storage for ocean research (e.g. sensor arrays, underwater gliders, high-resolution under-water cameras), providing access for a wide ranging user community under different administrative domains. It consists of multiple marine networks where we lay cables over a large area under the sea, which are integrated by a distributed cyberinfrastructure. This cyberinfrastructure, called OOI CI (CI for CyberInfrastructure), is itself a network, consisting of distributed infrastructural services whose main sites are two large clouds but whose distributed components in the shape of containers also reside all over its distributed sites residing in hundreds of universities and marine institutions.

One of the central features of the OOI CI is its end-to-end nature, in the sense that its design allows and encourages scientists to register data (which often takes the form of real-time streaming data from sensors over different time scales) and data products (which are derivatives from raw data by application of models). Just as scientists publish their papers, they may as well publish their data and data products, shared by other scientists, as well as by teachers for educational purposes. In the same spirit, the OOI CI should allow an easy and well-regulated sharing of instruments and other resources, each under a specific administrative control. For example, a seabed camera owned by one institution may be used by a scientist in the other. Thus, in this system, multiple heterogeneous organisations and individuals participate, run their software (such as simulation models for sensor data) inside the system, and we need to ensure a high-level quality of usage including transparency, partly because marine data play a critical role at the time of calamity such as earthquakes and tsunami.

One of the architectural decisions of OOI CI is to regulate the behaviours of heterogeneous participants in the OOI CI by imposing high-level abstractions based on interaction patterns, which are in turn regulated by high-level policies through runtime monitors. The catalogue of interaction patterns will in turn assist developers to implement their distributed services with ease and clarity. Thus we need a descriptive means to write down these interaction patterns clearly and without ambiguity, use them for software development, and regulate communications behaviour of participating endpoints at runtime through induced protocol machines, augmented with regulation by policies on their basis. For the description of interaction patterns, the use of session types (and Scribble) is considered, building a framework to regulate interaction behaviour based on policies on its basis. This policy-based regulation is called "governance" by the OOI CI architects, conceived by Munindar Singh and the OOI CI architects, centring on the notion of commitments [11]. To use session types as a basis of regulating behaviour in this distributed computing platform, several technical challenges were identified, which include (restricted to those proper to session types):

- Can we accurately describe interaction patterns which are and will potentially be used in distributed applications in OOI CI?
- Can we ground them to programming? Can we help developers to build safe and robust systems with ease?
- Can we have a simple and efficient execution framework for these programs?
- Can we guarantee their communication safety at runtime? What would be the simplest mechanism?

The research team on session types in Imperial College London and Queen Mary, including the present authors, are contributing to the OOI CI development through, among others, the following technical elements:

- A protocol description language, *Scribble*, and development/execution environments centring on this language.
- A tool chain for protocol validation, endpoint projection, FSM translations, APIs and runtimes.
- Part of the monitor architecture based on the protocol machines (FSM) translated from protocols.

As we have already observed, Scribble is fully based on research on session types. The FSM translation is a direct application of the theory which links automata theory (communication automata) and session types, recently introduced in [10], where a session type can be directly translated into a communication automaton.

The development efforts are producing several interesting findings. For example, one of the methods for facilitating the use of session types for developers who are not accustomed to session types is to use the interface of the standard communication APIs such as RPC. These libraries were independently developed in the OOI CI to support application development based on traditional technologies: the idea is to replace them with distributed runtimes for session types. What we found is that this approach, where we implement libraries using session primitives, has rewarding practical merits in the tractability and transparency in engineering. For instance, each library is now a short scripting code by using the underlying session machinery, automatically monitored by the corresponding protocol. As one example, RPCs with diverse signatures are now based on a single parametrised protocol, and its interactions are checked by a generic monitor for general session types. This conversion is feasible because not even a single line of application code needs be changed: the resulting behaviour is the same, we can use the same interface file, with a formal foundation automatically assuring correctness of interactions. The layer for typed sessions is called Conversation Layer in OOI CI. As well as the extensive experiments on Conversation Layer itself, our development efforts are focusing on the governance functions to be realised on top of Conversation Layer.

5   Conclusion

In this work we have examined the motivations and backgrounds of the introduction of session types and associated programming methodology, together with illustration of how we may design and implement a program centring on session types. For organising communicating processes, there are other approaches which address different aspects of abstractions for communicating processes.

One basic approach centres on the notion of concurrent objects [33], where objects communicate with each other by sending messages to their object identities, starting from the actor model [1,15], which also gives one of the simplest forms of this paradigm. In concurrent objects in general, there is a strong integration of the idea of objects and concurrency, where concurrency is considered to be a default rather than an exception. While programming languages based on concurrent objects may not have treated sessions and session type beyond request-response patterns, the use of constraints on interaction patterns in such languages should certainly be feasible, as a recent work shows [14]. Similarly, the identities as found in actors and concurrent objects may as well be part of the session-based programming (for example, distributed infrastructures such as the OOI CI demand the use of identities for principals which act as endpoints of communications). Different experiments in such integrations will deepen our understanding on the relationships between these two paradigms. How the pursuit towards flexible programming abstraction in concurrent objects (e.g. reflection) may interact with the type-based approach in session types is another interesting future topic.

Concurrency and communication are a rich realm for which many different approaches exist. Occam-Pi [31] is a highly efficient systems-level concurrent programming language centring on synchronous communication channels, based on CSP and the π-calculus. Erlang [2] is a communication-centred programming language with emphasis on reliability whose central programming and execution paradigm is based on actors. Session types are an approach to structuring communications programs based on session abstraction and protocol description, with its formal basis in the π-calculus and its type theories. Protocols, arising as types for dialogue among endpoints, are used to constrain behaviour so that the resulting programs and runtime configurations are easy to understand and reason. For fully identifying its possibilities and limitations, we need to explore the use of typed sessions in various stages of software development, ranging from high-level modelling to execution, as well as formal specifications and verifications. Not restricted to session types, we need to identify a wide range of concrete methods usable to address these problems, as well as a unifying foundation for them, to reach a truly effective methodology for distributed computing systems.

We refer the reader to [12] for more detailed comparison of session type theory and session-based implementations against other related works.

Acknowledgements. We thank the reviewers for their comments, Dr Gary Brown for his collaborations on the Scribble project, and our colleagues in the Mobility Reading Group for discussions. This work is partially supported by the Ocean Observatories Initiative, EPSRC grants EP/F002114/1, EP/G015481/1 and EP/G015635/1, and EPSRC KTS.

References

1. Agha, G.: Actors: a model of concurrent computation in distributed systems. MIT Press, Cambridge (1986)
2. Armstrong, J.: Programming Erlang: Software for a Concurrent World. Pragmatic Bookshelf (2007)
3. Bergstra, J.A., Klop, J.W.: Algebra of communicating processes. Theoretical Computer Science 37, 77–121 (1985)
4. Bettini, L., Coppo, M., D'Antoni, L., De Luca, M., Dezani-Ciancaglini, M., Yoshida, N.: Global progress in dynamically interleaved multiparty sessions. In: van Breugel, F., Chechik, M. (eds.) CONCUR 2008. LNCS, vol. 5201, pp. 418–433. Springer, Heidelberg (2008)
5. Boudol, G.: Asynchrony and the pi-calculus. Technical Report 1702, INRIA (1992)
6. Capecchi, S., Giachino, E., Yoshida, N.: Global escape in multiparty sessions. In: FSTTCS. LIPIcs, vol. 8, pp. 338–351 (2010)
7. Cerf, V.G., Khan, R.E.: A protocol for packet network intercommunication. IEEE Transactions on Communications 22, 637–648 (1974)
8. Chen, T.-C., Bocchi, L., Deniélou, P.-M., Honda, K., Yoshida, N.: Asynchronous distributed monitoring for multiparty session enforcement. In: Bruni, R., Sassone, V. (eds.) TGC 2011. LNCS, vol. 7173, pp. 25–45. Springer, Heidelberg (2012)

9. Demangeon, R., Honda, K.: Nested protocols in session types. In: Koutny, M., Ulidowski, I. (eds.) CONCUR 2012. LNCS, vol. 7454, pp. 272–286. Springer, Heidelberg (2012)

10. Deniélou, P.-M., Yoshida, N.: Multiparty session types meet communicating automata. In: Seidl, H. (ed.) Programming Languages and Systems. LNCS, vol. 7211, pp. 194–213. Springer, Heidelberg (2012)

11. Desai, N., Chopra, A.K., Arrott, M., Specht, B., Singh, M.P.: Engineering foreign exchange processes via commitment protocols. In: IEEE SCC 2007, Los Alamitos, CA, USA, pp. 514–521. IEEE Computer Society (2007)

12. Dezani-Ciancaglini, M., de'Liguoro, U.: Sessions and Session Types: An Overview. In: Laneve, C., Su, J. (eds.) WS-FM 2009. LNCS, vol. 6194, pp. 1–28. Springer, Heidelberg (2010)

13. Dijkstra, E.W.: Letters to the editor: go to statement considered harmful. Commun. ACM 11(3), 147–148 (1968)

14. Dinges, P., Agha, G.: Scoped synchronization constraints for large scale actor systems. In: Sirjani, M. (ed.) COORDINATION 2012. LNCS, vol. 7274, pp. 89–103. Springer, Heidelberg (2012)

15. Hewitt, C.: Viewing control structures as patterns of passing messages. Artif. Intell. 8(3), 323–364 (1977)

16. Hoare, C.A.R.: Communicating sequential processes. Commun. ACM 21(8), 666–677 (1978)

17. Honda, K., Mukhamedov, A., Brown, G., Chen, T.-C., Yoshida, N.: Scribbling interactions with a formal foundation. In: Natarajan, R., Ojo, A. (eds.) ICDCIT 2011. LNCS, vol. 6536, pp. 55–75. Springer, Heidelberg (2011)

18. Honda, K., Tokoro, M.: An object calculus for asynchronous communication. In: America, P. (ed.) ECOOP 1991. LNCS, vol. 512, pp. 133–147. Springer, Heidelberg (1991)

19. Honda, K., Vasconcelos, V.T., Kubo, M.: Language Primitives and Type Discipline for Structured Communication-Based Programming. In: Hankin, C. (ed.) ESOP 1998. LNCS, vol. 1381, pp. 122–138. Springer, Heidelberg (1998)

20. Honda, K., Yoshida, N., Carbone, M.: Multiparty Asynchronous Session Types. In: POPL 2008, pp. 273–284. ACM (2008)

21. Milner, R.: A Calculus of Communication Systems. LNCS, vol. 92. Springer, Heidelberg (1980)

22. Milner, R.: Functions as processes. MSCS 2(2), 119–141 (1992)

23. Milner, R., Parrow, J., Walker, D.: A Calculus of Mobile Processes, Parts I and II. Info.& Comp. 100(1) (1992)

24. Ocean Observatories Initiative (OOI), http://www.oceanleadership.org/programs-and-partnerships/ocean-observing/ooi/

25. Pierce, B., Sangiorgi, D.: Behavioral equivalence in the polymorphic pi-calculus. Journal of ACM 47(3), 531–584 (2000)

26. Saltzer, J., Reed, D., Clark, D.: End-to-end arguments in system design. ACM Transactions in Computer Systems 2(4), 277–288 (1984)

27. Scribble development tool site, http://www.jboss.org/scribble

28. Scribble github project, https://github.com/scribble

29. Takeuchi, K., Honda, K., Kubo, M.: An Interaction-based Language and its Typing System. In: Halatsis, C., Philokyprou, G., Maritsas, D., Theodoridis, S. (eds.) PARLE 1994. LNCS, vol. 817, pp. 398–413. Springer, Heidelberg (1994)

30. Turner, D.N.: The Polymorphic Pi-Calculus: Theory and Implementation. PhD thesis, University of Edinburgh (1996)

31. Welch, P.H., Barnes, F.R.M.: Communicating Mobile Processes: introducing Occam-pi. In: Abdallah, A.E., Jones, C.B., Sanders, J.W. (eds.) Communicating Sequential Processes. LNCS, vol. 3525, pp. 175–210. Springer, Heidelberg (2005)
32. Yonezawa, A., Briot, J.-P., Shibayama, E.: Object-oriented concurrent programming in ABCL/1. In: OOPSLA, pp. 258–268 (1986)
33. Yonezawa, A., Tokoro, M.: Object-oriented concurrent programming: An introduction. In: Yonezawa, A., Tokoro, M. (eds.) Object-Oriented Concurrent Programming, pp. 1–7. MIT Press, Cambridge (1987)

From Linear Types to Behavioural Types and Model Checking

Naoki Kobayashi

The University of Tokyo

Abstract. This article reviews our past work on non-standard type systems for program analysis, which started from the motivation for static analysis of concurrent objects. We discuss how the notion of linear types has evolved to behavioral types and higher-order model checking.

1 Introduction

When I was a graduate student, my supervisor Akinori Yonezawa advised me to study linear logic [11] as theoretical foundations for concurrent objects [3, 49]. Since then, linear logic and linear types have been the main sources of our research ideas. To appreciate his insightful advice, in this article I summarize how our research topics evolved from linear logic and linear types to our more recent work on behavioral types [14,15,19] and higher-order model checking [21,26,28], and discuss their relationship.

When we started studying linear logic, there were two major, independent approaches to applying linear logic to programming languages: the linear logic programming approach (or proof search paradigm) [4,12] and the "formulas (of linear logic) as types" approach [1, 5, 7, 47]. These two approaches are rather independent and orthogonal. Motivated by Andreoli and Pareschi's pioneering work [4], we initially studied the former approach to provide foundations of concurrent objects [30,31], but later switched to the latter approach, as the latter provides fruitful techniques for analysis and verification of concurrent objects.

In the rest of this article, we first review our earlier work on linear types for concurrency in Section 2. We then explain how linear types evolved to behavioral types in Section 3. In Section 4, we show that recent program verification techniques based on higher-order model checking [21] can be considered a further extension of behavioral types. Section 5 concludes the paper. This paper reviews the evolution of linear types to behavioral types and higher-order model checking from a personal perspective, and is not intended to be an exhaustive survey of linear/behavioral type systems. A more extensive (but non-exhaustive) survey of linear/behavioral type systems can be found elsewhere [18].

2 Linear Types for Concurrency

For a proposition A, the conjunction $A \wedge A$ is equivalent to A in classical logic, but the (multiplicative) conjunction $A \otimes A$ is *not* in linear logic [11]. This resource-sensitiveness of linear logic has attracted attentions of programming language

G. Agha et al. (Eds.): Yonezawa Festschrift, LNCS 8665, pp. 128–143, 2014.

researchers, and various forms of linear types (where formulas of linear logic are viewed as types) have been studied [1,5,7,34,45,47]. We review here a linear type system [27] for the π-calculus [36,37,42], which is, to our knowledge, one of the first practical applications of linear types to message-passing-based concurrent programs.

We use the following variant of the (asynchronous) π-calculus [36,37,42] to discuss linear types for message-passing-based concurrent programs.

Definition 1 (processes). *We assume a countably infinite set of variables (used as channels), ranged over by x, y, z. The syntax of processes is given by:*

$$
\begin{array}{llll}
P \ (processes) ::= & \mathbf{0} & inaction \\
& | \quad x![y_1, \ldots, y_n] & output \\
& | \quad x?[y_1, \ldots, y_n].\, P & input \\
& | \quad (P \,|\, Q) & parallel\ composition \\
& | \quad (\nu x)\, P & channel\ creation \\
& | \quad *P & replication
\end{array}
$$

Just as the λ-calculus consists of only functions and their applications, the π-calculus consists of only communication channels and processes communicating through channels. The process $\mathbf{0}$ represents inaction. The process $x![y_1, \ldots, y_n]$ sends a tuple $[y_1, \ldots, y_n]$ on channel x. The process $x?[y_1, \ldots, y_n].\, P$ waits to receive a tuple $[z_1, \ldots, z_n]$ along channel x, binds $y_1, \ldots, y_n$ to $z_1, \ldots, z_n$, and then behaves like P. The processes $P \,|\, Q$ and $(\nu x)\, P$ represent parallel composition and channel creation respectively. The process $*P$ behaves like infinitely many copies of P running in parallel.

Various encodings of concurrent objects into π-calculus-like processes have been proposed [32,40,41]. By "concurrent objects", we mean an object (i.e., a state coupled with methods to manipulate it) with its own thread of control [48, 49]. For instance, Pierce and Turner [40] encoded a concurrent object as a parallel composition of a process representing the current state, and processes handling messages. For example, a counter class is expressed by the following process (called *Counter* below):

$$
\begin{array}{ll}
*newC?[init, r].\, (\nu st)\, (\nu read)\, (\nu inc) & \\
\quad (r![read, inc] & (*\ returns\ [read, inc]\ as\ the\ identity\ of\ the\ new\ object\ *) \\
\quad |\ st![init] & (*\ stores\ the\ initial\ counter\ value\ in\ st\ *) \\
\quad |\ *read?[r'].\, st?[n].\, (st![n]\,|\,r'![n]) & (*\ handles\ a\ read\ request\ *) \\
\quad |\ *inc?[r'].\, st?[n].\, (st![n+1]\,|\,r'![]) & (*\ handles\ an\ increment\ request\ *) \\
\quad)
\end{array}
$$

Here, we have assumed that the language has been extended with integers (which can be encoded in the π-calculus). The process above receives a request $newC![n, r]$ for creating a new counter object with the initial value n, and returns to r a tuple $[read, inc]$ of channels, on which the client can send requests for reading or incrementing the counter value. The counter value is stored in the channel st, and is read or updated by the processes $*read?[r'].\, \cdots$ and $*inc?[r'].\, \cdots$, which handle read/increment messages.

In the encoding above, each communication channel is used in a specific manner. For example, the channels r and r' are used just once for returning values. That property enables aggressive optimizations, like elimination of redundant messages [27]. For instance, consider a client process of the form:

$$Counter \mid (\nu r)\,(newC![n, r] \mid r?[c_{read}, c_{inc}].\,r'![c_{read}, c_{inc}] \mid P),$$

where r' is a channel and P is some process that does not use r. If r' is used just once for input in the process P, the process above can be replaced by $Counter \mid newC![n, r'] \mid P$. This is similar to tail-call optimizations in functional languages, in that it eliminates redundant communication to forward the result of a method invocation. As another source of optimization, observe that the channel st is used more than once, but that it holds at most one message at each state during execution. Thus, a one-place buffer can be used for implementing st, instead of an unbounded message queue [25];

Motivated by the above observations, various linear type systems for message-passing-based concurrent programs have been proposed [25, 27, 44]. We review the type system of [27] below.

The set of types is defined by:

$$\tau \text{ (types)} ::= b \mid [\tau_1, \dots, \tau_n]\ \mathbf{chan}_{(m_1, m_2)}$$
$$m \text{ (multiplicities)} ::= 0 \mid 1 \mid \omega$$

Here, b is a meta-variable for base types (like **int**, if the language is extended with integers). The type $[\tau_1, \dots, \tau_n]\ \mathbf{chan}_{(m_1, m_2)}$ describes channels used for exchanging a tuple of values of types $\tau_1, \dots, \tau_n$, at most m_1 times for input, and at most m_2 times for output.[1] The multiplicity ω means that channels can be used for arbitrarily many times. For example, in the process $Counter$ above, $read$, inc (in the ν-prefixes), and $newC$ (in the whole process) have the following types:

$$read : [[\mathbf{int}]\ \mathbf{chan}_{(0,1)}]\ \mathbf{chan}_{(\omega, \omega)}$$
$$inc : [[]\ \mathbf{chan}_{(0,1)}]\ \mathbf{chan}_{(\omega, \omega)}$$
$$newC : [\mathbf{int},$$
$$\qquad [[[\mathbf{int}]\ \mathbf{chan}_{(0,1)}]\ \mathbf{chan}_{(0,\omega)}, [[]\ \mathbf{chan}_{(0,1)}]\ \mathbf{chan}_{(0,\omega)}]\ \mathbf{chan}_{(0,1)}$$
$$\qquad]\ \mathbf{chan}_{(\omega, 0)}$$

The types describe the behavior of $Counter$ as follows.

- Upon receiving a $read$ request (with a reply channel of type $[\mathbf{int}]\ \mathbf{chan}_{(0,1)}$), the object sends an integer (at most) once as a reply. It never tries to receive a message from the reply channel.
- Similarly, upon receiving an inc request, the object sends a null tuple as a reply (at most) once. It never tries to receive a message from the reply channel.

---

[1] Because of a possibility of deadlock or divergence, the linear type system given below cannot ensure that channels are used *exactly* m_1 times for input and m_2 times for output.

$$\frac{NonLinear(\Gamma)}{\Gamma \vdash \mathbf{0}} \qquad \text{(LT-Zero)}$$

$$\frac{NonLinear(\Gamma)}{\Gamma + (x : [\tau_1, \ldots, \tau_n] \, \mathbf{chan}_{(0,1)}) + (y_1 : \tau_1) + \cdots + (y_n : \tau_n) \vdash x![y_1, \ldots, y_n]} \qquad \text{(LT-Out)}$$

$$\frac{\Gamma, y_1 : \tau_1, \ldots, y_n : \tau_n \vdash P \qquad m \in \{1, *\}}{(x : [\tau_1, \ldots, \tau_n] \, \mathbf{chan}_{(m,0)}) + \Gamma \vdash x?[y_1, \ldots, y_n]. P} \qquad \text{(LT-In)}$$

$$\frac{\Gamma \vdash P \qquad \Delta \vdash Q}{\Gamma + \Delta \vdash P \,|\, Q} \qquad \text{(LT-Par)}$$

$$\frac{\Gamma, x : [\tau_1, \ldots, \tau_n] \, \mathbf{chan}_{(m_1, m_2)} \vdash P}{\Gamma \vdash (\nu x : [\tau_1, \ldots, \tau_n] \, \mathbf{chan}_{(m_1, m_2)}) \, P} \qquad \text{(LT-New)}$$

$$\frac{\Gamma \vdash P}{*\Gamma \vdash *P} \qquad \text{(LT-Rep)}$$

Fig. 1. Typing rules for the linear type system

- Upon receiving a request for an object creation on *newC*, *Counter* sends back a pair of two channels (of types $[[\mathbf{int}] \, \mathbf{chan}_{(0,1)}] \, \mathbf{chan}_{(0,\omega)}$ and $[[] \, \mathbf{chan}_{(0,1)}] \, \mathbf{chan}_{(0,\omega)}$), on which clients can send (but not receive) request messages. Upon sending requests on those channels, clients can expect to receive at most one reply message.

Thus, linear types express more information about the behavior of processes than ordinary types. As indicated through the above example, they can ensure that certain processes behave like concurrent objects.

We now give a type system that assigns linear types to channels. A *type environment* is a map from a finite set of variables to types, represented in the form $x_1 : \tau_1, \ldots, x_n : \tau_n$. We use the metavariable Γ for type environments. When x is not in the domain of Γ, we write $\Gamma, x : \tau$ for the type environment Γ' such that $\Gamma'(x) = \tau$ and $\Gamma'(y) = \Gamma(y)$ if $x \neq y$. (Thus, when we write $\Gamma, x : \tau$, it is implicitly assumed that x does not occur in Γ.) A *type judgment* is of the form $\Gamma \vdash P$, which means that the process P can be safely executed under the assumption that each variable x is bound to a channel of type $\Gamma(x)$. Since types contain multiplicity conditions (on how often each channel can be used), "P being safely executed" means that P obeys those multiplicity conditions. For example, $x : [] \, \mathbf{chan}_{(0,1)} \vdash x![]$ is valid but $x : [] \, \mathbf{chan}_{(0,1)} \vdash x![] \,|\, x![]$ are not. The typing rules are shown in Figure 1. Here, the condition $NonLinear(\Gamma)$ in rules LT-Zero and LT-Out means that for every type binding $x : \tau$ in Γ, τ is either a base type or a channel type of the form $[\tau_1, \ldots, \tau_n] \, \mathbf{chan}_{(m_1, m_2)}$ with $m_1 \neq 1$ and $m_2 \neq 1$. The (partial) operations "$+$" and "$*$" on multiplicities, types, and type environments are defined by:

$$m_1 + m_2 = \begin{cases} m_2 & \text{if } m_1 = 0 \\ m_1 & \text{if } m_2 = 0 \\ \omega & \text{otherwise} \end{cases} \qquad *m = \begin{cases} 0 & \text{if } m = 0 \\ \omega & \text{otherwise} \end{cases}$$

$$b + b = b$$

$$[\tau_1, \ldots, \tau_n] \ \mathbf{chan}_{(m_1,m_2)} + [\tau_1, \ldots, \tau_n] \ \mathbf{chan}_{(m_1',m_2')}$$
$$= [\tau_1, \ldots, \tau_n] \ \mathbf{chan}_{(m_1+m_1',m_2+m_2')}$$

$$*[\tau_1, \ldots, \tau_n] \ \mathbf{chan}_{(m_1,m_2)} = [\tau_1, \ldots, \tau_n] \ \mathbf{chan}_{(*m_1,*m_2)}$$

$$dom(\Gamma + \Delta) = dom(\Gamma) \cup dom(\Delta)$$

$$(\Gamma + \Delta)(x) = \begin{cases} \Gamma(x) + \Delta(x) & \text{if } x \in dom(\Gamma) \cap dom(\Delta) \\ \Gamma(x) & \text{if } x \in dom(\Gamma) \setminus dom(\Delta) \\ \Delta(x) & \text{if } x \in dom(\Delta) \setminus dom(\Gamma) \end{cases}$$

$$dom(*\Gamma) = dom(\Gamma)$$

$$(*\Gamma)(x) = *(\Gamma(x))$$

Note that the operation "+" on types are partial: $[\tau_1, \ldots, \tau_n] \ \mathbf{chan}_{(m_1,m_2)} + [\tau_1', \ldots, \tau_{n'}'] \ \mathbf{chan}_{(m_1',m_2')}$ is defined only when $n = n'$ and $\tau_i = \tau_i'$ for every $i \in \{1, \ldots, n\}$.

The main difference from the usual (non-linear) type systems is that type environments cannot be shared between processes. For example, suppose that $x : [\mathbf{int}] \ \mathbf{chan}_{(0,1)} \vdash P$ and $x : [\mathbf{int}] \ \mathbf{chan}_{(0,1)} \vdash Q$ hold, which mean that *each of P and Q* uses x for sending an integer at most once. Then, we have $x : [\mathbf{int}] \ \mathbf{chan}_{(0,\omega)} \vdash P \,|\, Q$ (by using LT-PAR), but not $x : [\mathbf{int}] \ \mathbf{chan}_{(0,1)} \vdash P \,|\, Q$.

The condition $NonLinear(\Gamma)$ in rules LT-ZERO and LT-OUT ensures that each linear channel is used once for input and once for output (if there is no divergence or deadlock). Note that if we drop the condition, we would obtain, for example, $x : [[\mathbf{int}] \ \mathbf{chan}_{(0,1)}] \ \mathbf{chan}_{(1,0)} \vdash x?[y]. \, \mathbf{0}$, which ignores the channel y received through x, although the type of x suggests that y should be used for output.

Remark 1. Although the linear type system above has been *inspired from* linear logic based on the formulas-as-types approach, there is not so clear connection between the type system and linear logic (besides the fact that contraction and weakening are used in a controlled manner), unlike linear type systems for the λ-calculus [34,45,47]. Ignoring the operational semantics, however, one can observe some connections between the typing rules and inference rules of linear logic, as discussed below. We assume that readers have some familiarity with linear logic below; those who are not familiar with linear logic may safely skip the rest of this section. Let us encode channel types into linear logic formulas by:

$$[[\tau_1, \ldots, \tau_n] \ \mathbf{chan}_{(m_1,m_2)}] =$$
$$!_{m_1}(([\![\tau_1]\!] \otimes \cdots \otimes [\![\tau_n]\!] \multimap \mathbf{P}) \multimap \mathbf{P}) \otimes !_{m_2}([\![\tau_1]\!] \otimes \cdots \otimes [\![\tau_n]\!] \multimap \mathbf{P})$$

Here, $\mathbf{P}$ is the type of processes, and $!_m$ is defined as follows.

$$!_\omega A = !A \qquad !_1 A = A \qquad !_0 A = 1.$$

(The symbol "!" is the logical connective of linear logic and should not be confused with the constructor for output processes of the π-calculus.) The encoding of channel types above is based on the intuition that a channel can be viewed as a pair consisting of a function for receiving a message and a function for sending a message. The part $!_{m_1}((\llbracket \tau_1 \rrbracket \otimes \cdots \otimes \llbracket \tau_n \rrbracket \multimap \mathbf{P}) \multimap \mathbf{P})$ describes the former function (which takes a continuation as an argument) and the part $!_{m_2}(\llbracket \tau_1 \rrbracket \otimes \cdots \otimes \llbracket \tau_n \rrbracket \multimap \mathbf{P})$ describes the latter function.

Let us represent processes as terms of the λ-calculus.

$$\llbracket \mathbf{0} \rrbracket = \mathbf{0}$$
$$\llbracket x![y_1,\ldots,y_n] \rrbracket = \mathbf{let}\ (x_i, x_o) = x\ \mathbf{in}\ x_o(y_1,\ldots,y_n)$$
$$\llbracket x?[y_1,\ldots,y_n].\,P \rrbracket = \mathbf{let}\ (x_i, x_o) = x\ \mathbf{in}\ x_i(\lambda(y_1,\ldots,y_n).\,\llbracket P \rrbracket)$$
$$\llbracket P\,|\,Q \rrbracket = \mathbf{Par}\ \llbracket P \rrbracket\ \llbracket Q \rrbracket$$
$$\llbracket (\nu x)\,P \rrbracket = \nu^m(\lambda x.\,\llbracket P \rrbracket)\ \text{(where } m \text{ is } 0,\ 1,\ \text{or } \omega \text{ depending on the usage of } x)$$
$$\llbracket *P \rrbracket = *(\llbracket P \rrbracket)$$

Here, $\mathbf{0}$, $\mathbf{Par}$, ν and $*$ are treated as constants of the following types:

$$\mathbf{0}{:}\mathbf{P} \qquad \mathbf{Par}{:}\mathbf{P}\multimap\mathbf{P}\multimap\mathbf{P} \qquad \nu^m{:}(\llbracket[\tau_1,\ldots,\tau_n]\ \mathbf{chan}_{(m,m)}\rrbracket\multimap\mathbf{P})\multimap\mathbf{P} \qquad *{:}\mathbf{P}\multimap\mathbf{P}.$$

Then, each typing rule can be viewed as an (admissible) rule of a linear λ-calculus. For example, LT-OUT and LT-IN corresponds to the following type derivations in the linear λ-calculus.

$$\frac{\Gamma_1 \vdash x_o : (\llbracket\tau_1\rrbracket\otimes\cdots\otimes\llbracket\tau_n\rrbracket\multimap\mathbf{P}) \quad \Gamma_2\vdash(y_1,\ldots,y_m):\llbracket\tau_1\rrbracket\otimes\cdots\otimes\llbracket\tau_n\rrbracket}{\begin{array}{c}x_i:\mathbf{1},x_o:(\llbracket\tau_1\rrbracket\otimes\cdots\otimes\llbracket\tau_n\rrbracket\multimap\mathbf{P}),y_1:\llbracket\tau_1\rrbracket,\ldots,y_n:\llbracket\tau_n\rrbracket\vdash x_o(y_1,\ldots,y_m):\mathbf{P}\\ x:\mathbf{1}\otimes(\llbracket\tau_1\rrbracket\otimes\cdots\otimes\llbracket\tau_n\rrbracket\multimap\mathbf{P}),y_1:\llbracket\tau_1\rrbracket,\ldots,y_n:\llbracket\tau_n\rrbracket\vdash\llbracket x![y_1,\ldots,y_n]\rrbracket:\mathbf{P}\end{array}}$$

$$\frac{\begin{array}{c}\dfrac{\Gamma,y_1:\llbracket\tau_1\rrbracket,\ldots,y_n:\llbracket\tau_n\rrbracket\vdash\llbracket P\rrbracket:\mathbf{P}}{x_i:(\tau\multimap\mathbf{P}),x_o:\mathbf{1}\vdash x_i:(\tau\multimap\mathbf{P}) \qquad \Gamma\vdash\lambda(y_1,\ldots,y_n).\,\llbracket P\rrbracket:\tau}\\ \Gamma,x_i:(\tau\multimap\mathbf{P}),x_o:\mathbf{1}\vdash x_i(\lambda(y_1,\ldots,y_n).\,\llbracket P\rrbracket):\mathbf{P}\end{array}}{\Gamma,x:(\tau\multimap\mathbf{P})\otimes\mathbf{1}\vdash\llbracket x?[y_1,\ldots,y_n].\,P\rrbracket:\mathbf{P}}$$

Here, $\Gamma_1 = x_i{:}\mathbf{1},x_o{:}(\llbracket\tau_1\rrbracket\otimes\cdots\otimes\llbracket\tau_n\rrbracket\multimap\mathbf{P})$ and $\Gamma_2 = y_1{:}\llbracket\tau_1\rrbracket,\ldots,y_n{:}\llbracket\tau_n\rrbracket$ in the former derivation, and $\tau = \llbracket\tau_1\rrbracket\otimes\cdots\otimes\llbracket\tau_n\rrbracket\multimap\mathbf{P}$ in the latter one. By dropping terms, we can also view them as derivations in (intuitionistic) linear logic. $\square$

3   From Linear Types to Behavioral Types

As explained in the previous section, linear types describe more precise behaviors of concurrent programs than standard (non-linear) types, helping us reason about and optimize programs. They are, however, not precise enough for describing certain communication patterns. For example, recall the channel st in the *Counter* process. There can always be at most one message in the channel, but such a property cannot be expressed by the linear type system in the previous section: st is given type $[\mathbf{int}]\ \mathbf{chan}_{(\omega,\omega)}$, as it is used for input and output infinitely often.

We can express more precise information by extending the notion of linear types. Thanks to linearity, it became reasonable to talk about the *order* between each use of a channel. For example, the type $[\textbf{int}]\ \textbf{chan}_{(1,1)}$, which describes channels that can be used once for input and once for output, can be refined to the following types:

- $[\textbf{int}]\ \textbf{chan}_{?.!}$, which describes channels that can be used once for input *and then* used once for output.
- $[\textbf{int}]\ \textbf{chan}_{!.?}$, which describes channels that can be used once for output *and then* used once for input.
- $[\textbf{int}]\ \textbf{chan}_{!\,|\,?}$, which describes channels that can be used once for output and once for input in any order (possibly in parallel).

Based on this idea, the syntax of types is now extended as follows.

$$\tau\ \text{(types)}\ ::= b\ |\ [\tau_1,\ldots,\tau_n]\ \textbf{chan}_U$$
$$U\ \text{(usages)}\ ::= \textbf{0}\ |\ !.U\ |\ ?.U\ |\ (U_1\,|\,U_2)\ |\ *U$$

Here, the usage $\textbf{0}$ describes channels that cannot be used at all. The usage $!.U$ ($?.U$, resp.) describes a channel that can be used once for output (input, resp.), and then used according to U. The usage $U_1\,|\,U_2$ describes a channel that can be used according to U_1 and U_2 *possibly in parallel* (that is, the channel can be used either concurrently by two processes according to U_1 and U_2, or sequentially by a single process; thus, a channel of usage $?.\textbf{0}\|!.\textbf{0}$ may also be used according to $?.!.\textbf{0}$ or $!.?.\textbf{0}$). The usage $*U$ describes a channel that can be used according to U an arbitrary number of times, possibly in parallel. We often omit the trailing $\textbf{0}$ in usages, and write $!$ for $!.\textbf{0}$. The linear type $[\tau_1,\ldots,\tau_n]\ \textbf{chan}_{(m_1,m_2)}$ corresponds to the type $[\tau_1,\ldots,\tau_n]\ \textbf{chan}_{m_1!\,|\,m_2?}$, where $0U = \textbf{0}$, $1U = U$, and $\omega U = *U$.

For the example of *Counter*, the type of st is now refined to $[\textbf{int}]\ \textbf{chan}_{!\,|\,*(?.!)}$. From the usage $!\,|\,*(?.!)$, we know that there can be at most one message queued in the channel.

Typing rules for the extended type system are given in Figure 2. Here, we use the following (partial) operations on types:

$$b;b = b \qquad b+b = b \qquad *b = b$$
$$([\tau_1,\ldots,\tau_n]\ \textbf{chan}_\alpha);([\tau_1,\ldots,\tau_n]\ \textbf{chan}_U) = [\tau_1,\ldots,\tau_n]\ \textbf{chan}_{\alpha.U}\ (\text{where } \alpha \in \{!,?\})$$
$$([\tau_1,\ldots,\tau_n]\ \textbf{chan}_{U_1}) + ([\tau_1,\ldots,\tau_n]\ \textbf{chan}_{U_2}) = [\tau_1,\ldots,\tau_n]\ \textbf{chan}_{U_1\,|\,U_2}$$
$$*([\tau_1,\ldots,\tau_n]\ \textbf{chan}_U) = [\tau_1,\ldots,\tau_n]\ \textbf{chan}_{*U}$$

Note that the operation $([\tau_1,\ldots,\tau_n]\ \textbf{chan}_{U_1});([\tau'_1,\ldots,\tau'_m]\ \textbf{chan}_{U_2})$ is defined only if $[\tau_1,\ldots,\tau_n] = [\tau'_1,\ldots,\tau'_m]$, and U_1 is either $!$ or $?$. Those operations are pointwise extended to partial operations on type environments, as in Section 2. For example, we have:

$$(x:[\tau]\ \textbf{chan}_!);(x:[\tau]\ \textbf{chan}_U, y:[\tau']\ \textbf{chan}_{U'}) = x:[\tau]\ \textbf{chan}_{!.U}, y:[\tau']\ \textbf{chan}_{U'}.$$

Notice the difference between (LT-OUT)/(LT-IN) and (UT-OUT)/(UT-IN). The operation "+" on type environments has been replaced by ";", to take into

$$\emptyset \vdash \mathbf{0} \qquad\qquad\qquad \text{(UT-ZERO)}$$

$$\frac{}{(x : [\tau_1, \ldots, \tau_n]\ \mathbf{chan}_!); (y_1 : \tau_1 + \cdots + y_n : \tau_n) \vdash x![y_1, \ldots, y_n]} \quad \text{(UT-OUT)}$$

$$\frac{\Gamma, y_1 : \tau_1, \ldots, y_n : \tau_n \vdash P}{(x : [\tau_1, \ldots, \tau_n]\ \mathbf{chan}_?); \Gamma \vdash x?[y_1 : \tau_1, \ldots, y_n : \tau_n].\, P} \quad \text{(UT-IN)}$$

$$\frac{\Gamma \vdash P \qquad \Delta \vdash Q}{\Gamma + \Delta \vdash P \,|\, Q} \quad \text{(UT-PAR)}$$

$$\frac{\Gamma, x : [\tau_1, \ldots, \tau_n]\ \mathbf{chan}_U \vdash P}{\Gamma \vdash (\nu x : [\tau_1, \ldots, \tau_n]\ \mathbf{chan}_U)\, P} \quad \text{(UT-NEW)}$$

$$\frac{\Gamma \vdash P}{*\Gamma \vdash *P} \quad \text{(UT-REP)}$$

Fig. 2. Typing rules for the usage type system

account the temporal order. The type environment $x : [\tau_1, \ldots, \tau_n]\ \mathbf{chan}_?; \Gamma$ in rule (UT-IN) captures the fact that the process P is executed only after the input on x succeeds.

Example 1. $x : [\,]\ \mathbf{chan}_{?.!} \vdash x?[\,].\, x![\,]$ is obtained as follows.

$$\frac{x : [\,]\ \mathbf{chan}_! \vdash x![\,]}{x : [\,]\ \mathbf{chan}_{?.!} \vdash x?[\,].\, x![\,]} \ \text{UT-IN}$$

Note that $(x : [\,]\ \mathbf{chan}_?); (x : [\,]\ \mathbf{chan}_!) = x : [\,]\ \mathbf{chan}_{?.!}$ holds.
$x : [\,]\ \mathbf{chan}_{?.!}, y : [[\,]\ \mathbf{chan}_!]\ \mathbf{chan}_{?||} \vdash x?[\,].\, y![x] \,|\, y?[z].\, z![\,]$ is derived as follows:

$$\frac{\dfrac{x : [\,]\ \mathbf{chan}_!, y : [[\,]\ \mathbf{chan}_!]\ \mathbf{chan}_! \vdash y![x]}{x : [\,]\ \mathbf{chan}_{?.!}, y : [[\,]\ \mathbf{chan}_!]\ \mathbf{chan}_! \vdash x?[\,].\, y![x]} \qquad \dfrac{z : [\,]\ \mathbf{chan}_! \vdash z![\,]}{y : [[\,]\ \mathbf{chan}_!]\ \mathbf{chan}_? \vdash y?[z].\, z![\,]}}{x : [\,]\ \mathbf{chan}_{?.!}, y : [[\,]\ \mathbf{chan}_!]\ \mathbf{chan}_{?||} \vdash x?[\,].\, y![x] \,|\, y?[z].\, z![\,]}$$

Note that the temporal order between the input and output on x is correctly captured through the type of y. □

The usages of channels above can be considered a small subset of CCS [35], where there is only a single pair of an action (!) and a co-action (?). By using a larger subset of CCS [9, 14, 29, 44] (where more than one pair of actions is allowed), we can express even more precise properties of processes. Such types (including usage types) are often called *behavioral types*. They have been used to analyze various properties of processes, including deadlock-freedom, race-freedom, and information flow [2, 13, 14, 17, 19, 50].

Intuitively, behavioral types can be regarded as projections and abstractions of the behavior of a process to its channel-wise behavior. For example, consider the following type judgment:

$$x : [\,]\ \mathbf{chan}_{?.!}, y : [\,]\ \mathbf{chan}_! \vdash x?[\,].\, (x![\,] \,|\, y![\,]).$$

The type $[\,]\,\mathbf{chan}_{?.!}$ of x describes that x is used once for input and then once for output, ignoring the behavior on y (that y is used for output after x is used for input). In that sense, the type $[\,]\,\mathbf{chan}_{?.!}$ of x (the type $[\,]\,\mathbf{chan}_!$ of y, resp.) describes the *projection* of the behavior of the process on channel x (y, resp.). The behavior described by a type environment is also an *abstraction*, in the sense that it is an *overapproximation* of the actual behavior of a process. In the example above, the type environment does not tell us the causality between the input on x and the output on y; thus the type environment also describes $y![\,]\,|\,x?[\,].\,x![\,]$.

To analyze the behavior of a process, one can reason about its behavioral types, instead of the process itself. As a type (or a usage) is itself a process, such an analysis of the type can be viewed as model checking [10]. Let us define the reduction relation $U \longrightarrow U'$ on usages by the following rules.

$$\overline{!.U_1 \mid ?.U_2 \mid U_3 \longrightarrow U_1 \mid U_2 \mid U_3}$$

$$\frac{U_1 \equiv U_1' \qquad U_1' \longrightarrow U_2' \qquad U_2' \equiv U_2}{U_1 \longrightarrow U_2}$$

Here, $U_1 \equiv U_2$ is the least equivalence relation closed under the rules: $*U \equiv U \mid *U$, $\mathbf{0} \mid U \equiv U$, $U_1 \mid U_2 \equiv U_2 \mid U_1$, and $U_1 \mid (U_2 \mid U_3) \equiv (U_1 \mid U_2) \mid U_3$. The reduction relation can be considered a special case of the reduction relation for CCS, where there are only one pair (! and ?) of an action and its co-action. To see how the behavior of a process can be analyzed through the analysis of a usage, consider the usage $! \mid *(?.!)$ of the channel st in the process $Counter$. We can infer that there can be at most one output on channel st at every execution step, by checking how the usage $! \mid *(?.!)$ is reduced:

$$
\begin{aligned}
! \mid *(?.!) \;\; &\equiv \;\; ! \mid ?.! \mid *(?.!) &&\text{(by } *U \equiv U \mid *U) \\
&\longrightarrow \mathbf{0} \mid ! \mid *(?.!) &&\text{(by } !.U_1 \mid ?.U_2 \mid U_3 \longrightarrow U_1 \mid U_2 \mid U_3) \\
&\equiv \;\; ! \mid *(?.!) &&\text{(by } \mathbf{0} \mid U \equiv U) \\
&\longrightarrow \cdots
\end{aligned}
$$

As the usage $! \mid *(?.!)$ has just one state (where there is only one active output) up to the congruence $\equiv$, we know that at most one output can occur simultaneously on st.

The overall structure of the analysis is shown in Figure 3. A type system is first used to apply projection and abstraction to obtain simpler, abstract processes, and then model checking is used to check the behavior of the abstract processes. In the case of the type system above, the source program is a π-calculus process, while the abstract programs are written in a subset of CCS processes; note that the latter is more amenable to model checking. Compared with the linear types reviewed in Section 2, less abstraction is performed in the first phase thanks to the expressive power of types. Instead, the second step is more involved and requires model checking in general.

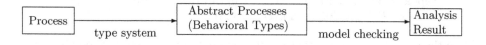

Fig. 3. Program Analysis by Behavioral Types

The same approach has also been applied to resource usage verification of functional programs with effects [15]. Here, the resource usage verification aims to check that functional programs access resources (such as files and networks) according to the specification (e.g., a read-only file is eventually closed after some reads, and no read/write occurs after the close operation). As in the behavioral type for the π-calculus, a type can be considered a projection (and over-approximation) of the behavior of a program to the resource-wise behavior. The syntax of types is given like:

$$
\begin{aligned}
\tau \text{ (types)} &::= b \mid \textbf{File}(U) \mid \tau_1 \rightarrow \tau_2 \mid \ldots \\
U \text{ (usages)} &::= \textbf{0} \mid a \mid U_1; U_2 \mid (U_1 \mid U_2) \mid U_1 \& U_2 \mid \alpha \mid \mu\alpha.U \mid \cdots \\
a \text{ (actions)} &::= \texttt{read} \mid \texttt{write} \mid \texttt{close}
\end{aligned}
$$

Here, α in the syntax of U denotes a variable (called a *usage variable*). The type $\textbf{File}(U)$ describes file pointers that should be used according to usage U. The usage $\textbf{0}$ means that the file should not be accessed at all, and the usage $\texttt{read}$ ($\texttt{write}$ and $\texttt{close}$, resp.) means that the file should be read (written and closed, resp.). The usage $U_1; U_2$ means that the file should be used according to U_1 and then U_2. The usage $U_1 \mid U_2$ means that the file can be used according to U_1 and U_2 in an interleaving manner. The usage $U_1 \& U_2$ means that the file can be used according to either U_1 or U_2, and $\mu\alpha.U$ means that the file can be used recursively according to the behavior α defined by $\alpha = U$. For example, $\mu\alpha.(\texttt{close}\&(\texttt{read};\alpha))$ describes the usage of a read-only file. The type system maps a program to the behavioral types that expresses resource-wise program behavior, and then model checking is performed to check that the resource-wise behavior is valid.

Example 2. Consider the following functional program M_1:

```
let rec repeat f x = if _ then () else (f x; repeat f x) in
let p = open_in "foo" in
  (repeat read p; close p)
```

Here, "_" represents a non-deterministic boolean value. The program first defines function `repeat`, which takes two arguments `f` and `x`, and repeatedly applies `f` to `x`. The program then opens file "foo" as a read-only file, and accesses them. By using the resource usage types above [15], the main body `repeat read p; close p` has type **unit** under the following type environment:

$$\text{repeat} : (\mathbf{File}(\text{read}) \to \mathbf{unit}) \to \mathbf{File}(\mu\alpha.(0\&(\text{read};\alpha))) \to \mathbf{unit},$$
$$\text{p} : \mathbf{File}(\mu\alpha.(0\&(\text{read};\alpha))); \texttt{close})$$

From the type of p, we know that p is indeed used as a read-only file pointer.   □

4   From Behavioral Types to Higher-Order Model Checking

As reviewed in the previous section, the shift from linear types to behavioral types has changed the role of type systems, from the whole analysis consisting of just one phase, to pre-processing of a program to obtain a simpler model (which is then model-checked in the next phase). The latter role can be shrunk further, by using more expressive models as inputs of model checking. In the case of the resource usage verification reviewed at the end of the previous section, the role of the type system was to extract, from higher-order functional programs (e.g. M_1 in Example 2), *first-order* programs (expressed in the form of usages; recall the usage $\mu\alpha.(0\&(\text{read};\alpha)); \texttt{close}$ in Example 2) that describe abstractions of resource-wise program behavior. Thanks to the decidability of higher-order model checking [38] (or, more precisely, the model checking of higher-order recursion schemes, which asks if the tree generated by a simply-typed, call-by-name, higher-order functional program with recursion satisfies a given property),[2] however, we can actually use *higher-order* programs to express resource-wise behavior.

For example, recall the (call-by-value) program M_1 in Example 2. From the above program, we can systematically (by using CPS transformation) construct the following (call-by-name) higher-order program M_2, which generates a tree describing how "foo" is accessed [21]:

```
let rec repeat f x k = br k (f x (repeat f x k)) in
let read' x k = read k in
let close' x k = close k in
    repeat read' p (close' p end)
```

Here, br is a binary tree constructor representing a non-deterministic choice, and close and read are unary constructors representing close and read operations respectively. The symbols end and p are nullary tree constructors, where the former represents termination of the program, and the latter represents a dummy parameter representing the function pointer p.[3] The following (infinite) tree is generated by the program above.

---

[2]   Higher-order model checking is a generalization of finite-state model checking [10] and pushdown model checking [43], in the sense that finite-state and pushdown model checking are reduced to model checking of order-0 and order-1 higher-order recursion schemes respectively.

[3]   A file pointer should actually be represented as a function when more than one file is accessed, and a more involved encoding is necessary: see [21].

Fig. 4. Program Analysis Based on Higher-Order Model Checking

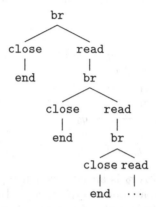

Thus, the program M_2 can be considered a projection of M_1 to the file access behavior. By using higher-order model checking [38], we can automatically check that the projection describes valid access behavior, i.e., that every path of the tree represents a valid access sequence.

The overall structure of the resulting analysis is shown in Figure 4. Compared with the approach using behavioral types (recall Figure 3), the first phase has been shrunk, and has been replaced by a simple program transformation [21]. The resulting analysis [21] is more precise than type-based one [15], and actually *complete* for the simply-typed λ-calculus with finite base types.

In Figure 4, the type system in the first-phase has been replaced by program transformation, but the role of type systems actually has not disappeared. Higher-order model checking [16, 38] (see also [22] for a survey on higher-order model checking) in the second phase is quite different from (but a generalization of) ordinary, finite-state model checking [10], and practical algorithms for higher-order model checking [20, 23] are based on reduction to type-checking problems [21, 26]. Thus, the role of type systems has just shifted from the first to the second phase.

We briefly explain how types help higher-order model checking (which asks if the tree generated by a given higher-order program satisfies a given property) by using the program M_2 above. Here, we wish to check that every finite path of the tree generated by M_2 is accepted by the automaton given in Figure 5. For that purpose, we can use the states of the automaton q_0 and q_1 as the type of trees every (finite) path of which is accepted from q_0 and q_1 respectively. Then, the tree constructors and the functions in M_1 are given the following types:

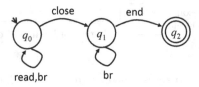

Fig. 5. A finite automaton that accepts valid access sequences for read-only files

$$
\begin{aligned}
\texttt{br} &: (q_0 \to q_0 \to q_0) \land (q_1 \to q_1 \to q_1) \\
\texttt{read} &: q_0 \to q_0 \\
\texttt{close} &: q_1 \to q_0 \\
\texttt{end} &: q_1 \\
\texttt{read'} &: q_0 \to \top \to q_0 \\
\texttt{close'} &: q_1 \to \top \to q_0 \\
\texttt{repeat} &: (q_0 \to \top \to q_0) \to \top \to q_0 \to q_0
\end{aligned}
$$

Here, a type of the form $\tau_1 \land \tau_2$ is an intersection type [6, 46], which describes a value that can be used as a value of type τ_1 and also as that of type τ_2. The type $\top$ denotes the empty intersection (that describes a value that cannot used at all). To see why the type $q_1 \to q_0$ is assigned to close, please note that if every path of a tree t is accepted from state q_1 (i.e., if t has type q_1), then every path of the tree $\texttt{close}(t)$ is accepted from state q_0, i.e., $\texttt{close}(t)$ has type q_0. Thus, close can be considered a function from type q_1 to type q_0.

Since the main body of M_2:

```
repeat read' p (close' p end)
```

has type q_0 under those type assumptions, we know that every finite path of the tree generated by M_2 is accepted by the automaton, which implies that the file "foo" is accessed in a valid manner by M_1.

As indicated in the example above, the types used for higher-order model checking [20,21,26] are intersection types, not linear types. The recent studies [23, 39], however, suggest that it is beneficial to combine the intersection types with game semantics. As game semantics is closely related to linear logic [8, 33], we can observe a trace of linear logic/types also in higher-order model checking.

The above approach has so far been applied mainly to functional programs. Work is however under way to apply it to verification of object-oriented and concurrent programs [24].

5   Conclusions

We have briefly reviewed our past work on type-based program analysis, which evolved from studies of linear logic and linear types as foundations for concurrent objects. Concurrent objects posed many challenges for theoretical work, e.g., on how we can statically ensure that a program really behaves like a concurrent object, and that concurrent objects do not suffer from deadlock or race. Those challenges served as a driving force for the development of linear and behavioral types for concurrent programs. In earlier linear type systems (such as the one reviewed in Section 2), program analysis (or verification) is carried out in "one-pass", through type inference. But in behavioral type systems developed later (such as those reviewed in Section 3), the overall analysis has been split into two phases (recall Figure 3), and the type systems focus on projection and abstraction of programs, leaving analysis of the abstracted programs to other methods such as model checking. The two phase structure has been re-organized in more recent work based on higher-order model checking (recall Figure 4). The first phase focuses on projection of a source program to another program that describes behaviors of interest (without abstractions), and the second phase checks the behavior of the program obtained by the projection. Type systems then take care of the second phase, by applying abstractions to deal with the infinite state space of the projected program. We hope this view helps further development of type-based program analysis/verification techniques.

Acknowledgment. I am sincerely grateful to Professor Akinori Yonezawa for his insightful advice that motivated me to study applications of linear logic. The work reviewed in this article would have been impossible without his initial advice and guidance. I would also like to thank anonymous referees for useful comments.

References

1. Abramsky, S.: Computational interpretations of linear logic. Theoretical Computer Science 111, 3–57 (1993)
2. Acciai, L., Boreale, M.: Responsiveness in process calculi. Theor. Comput. Sci. 409(1), 59–93 (2008)
3. Agha, G.: Actors: A Model of Concurrent Computation in Distributed Systems. MIT Press (1986)
4. Andreoli, J.-M., Pareschi, R.: Linear objects: Logical processes with built-in inheritance. New Generation Computing 9, 445–473 (1991)
5. Baker, H.G.: Lively linear lisp – look ma, no garbage? ACM Sigplan Notices 27(8), 89–98 (1992)
6. Barendregt, H., Coppo, M., Dezani-Ciancaglini, M.: A filter lambda model and the completeness of type assignment. J. Symb. Log. 48(4), 931–940 (1983)
7. Bellin, G., Scott, P.J.: On the π-calculus and linear logic. Technical Report ECS-LFCS-92-232, Department of Conputer Science, The University of Edinburgh (1992)
8. Blass, A.: A game semantics for linear logic. Ann. Pure Appl. Logic 56(1-3), 183–220 (1992)
9. Chaki, S., Rajamani, S., Rehof, J.: Types as models: Model checking message-passing programs. In: Proceedings of ACM SIGPLAN/SIGACT Symposium on Principles of Programming Languages (POPL), pp. 45–57. ACM Press (2002)
10. Clarke, E.M., Grumberg, O., Peled, D.A.: Model Checking. The MIT Press (1999)

11. Girard, J.-Y.: Linear logic. Theoretical Computer Science 50, 1–102 (1987)
12. Hodas, J.S., Miller, D.: Logic programming in a fragment of intuitionistic linear logic. Information and Computation 110(2), 327–365 (1994)
13. Honda, K., Yoshida, N.: A uniform type structure for secure information flow. In: Proceedings of ACM SIGPLAN/SIGACT Symposium on Principles of Programming Languages (POPL), pp. 81–92 (2002)
14. Igarashi, A., Kobayashi, N.: A generic type system for the pi-calculus. Theoretical Computer Science 311(1-3), 121–163 (2004)
15. Igarashi, A., Kobayashi, N.: Resource usage analysis. ACM Transactions on Programming Languages and Systems 27(2), 264–313 (2005)
16. Knapik, T., Niwiński, D., Urzyczyn, P.: Higher-order pushdown trees are easy. In: Nielsen, M., Engberg, U. (eds.) Fossacs 2002. LNCS, vol. 2303, pp. 205–222. Springer, Heidelberg (2002)
17. Kobayashi, N.: A partially deadlock-free typed process calculus. ACM Transactions on Programming Languages and Systems 20(2), 436–482 (1998)
18. Kobayashi, N.: Type systems for concurrent programs. In: Aichernig, B.K. (ed.) Formal Methods at the Crossroads. From Panacea to Foundational Support. LNCS, vol. 2757, pp. 439–453. Springer, Heidelberg (2003), http://www-kb.is.s.u-tokyo.ac.jp/ koba/papers/tutorial-type-extended.pdf
19. Kobayashi, N.: Type-based information flow analysis for the pi-calculus. Acta Informatica 42(4-5), 291–347 (2005)
20. Kobayashi, N.: Model-checking higher-order functions. In: Proceedings of PPDP 2009, pp. 25–36. ACM Press (2009)
21. Kobayashi, N.: Types and higher-order recursion schemes for verification of higher-order programs. In: Proceedings of ACM SIGPLAN/SIGACT Symposium on Principles of Programming Languages (POPL), pp. 416–428 (2009)
22. Kobayashi, N.: Higher-order model checking: From theory to practice. In: Proceedings of the 26th Annual IEEE Symposium on Logic in Computer Science (LICS 2011), pp. 219–224. IEEE Computer Society (2011)
23. Kobayashi, N.: A practical linear time algorithm for trivial automata model checking of higher-order recursion schemes. In: Hofmann, M. (ed.) FOSSACS 2011. LNCS, vol. 6604, pp. 260–274. Springer, Heidelberg (2011)
24. Kobayashi, N., Igarashi, A.: Model checking higher-order programs with recursive types. In: Felleisen, M., Gardner, P. (eds.) ESOP 2013. LNCS, vol. 7792, pp. 431–450. Springer, Heidelberg (2013)
25. Kobayashi, N., Nakade, M., Yonezawa, A.: Static analysis of communication for asynchronous concurrent programming languages. In: Mycroft, A. (ed.) SAS 1995. LNCS, vol. 983, pp. 225–242. Springer, Heidelberg (1995)
26. Kobayashi, N., Ong, C.-H.L.: A type system equivalent to the modal mu-calculus model checking of higher-order recursion schemes. In: Proceedings of LICS 2009, pp. 179–188. IEEE Computer Society Press (2009)
27. Kobayashi, N., Pierce, B.C., Turner, D.N.: Linearity and the pi-calculus. ACM Transactions on Programming Languages and Systems 21(5), 914–947 (1999)
28. Kobayashi, N., Sato, R., Unno, H.: Predicate abstraction and CEGAR for higher-order model checking. In: Proceedings of ACM SIGPLAN Conference on Programming Language Design and Implementation (PLDI), pp. 222–233 (2011)
29. Kobayashi, N., Suenaga, K., Wischik, L.: Resource usage analysis for the pi-calculus. Logical Methods in Computer Science 2(3:4), 1–42 (2006)

30. Kobayashi, N., Yonezawa, A.: ACL – a concurrent linear logic programming paradigm. In: Logic Programming: Proceedings of the 1993 International Symposium, pp. 279–294. MIT Press (1993)
31. Kobayashi, N., Yonezawa, A.: Asynchronous communication model based on linear logic. Formal Aspects of Computing 7(2), 113–149 (1995)
32. Kobayashi, N., Yonezawa, A.: Towards foundations for concurrent object-oriented programming – types and language design. Theory and Practice of Object Systems 1(4), 243–268 (1995)
33. Lafont, Y., Streicher, T.: Games semantics for linear logic. In: Proceedings of LICS 1991, pp. 43–50 (1991)
34. Mackie, I.: Lilac: A functional programming language based on linear logic. Journal of Functional Programming 4(4), 1–39 (1994)
35. Milner, R.: Communication and Concurrency. Prentice Hall (1989)
36. Milner, R.: Communicating and Mobile Systems: the Pi-Calculus. Cambridge University Press (1999)
37. Milner, R., Parrow, J., Walker, D.: A calculus of mobile processes, I, II. Information and Computation 100, 1–77 (1992)
38. Ong, C.-H.L.: On model-checking trees generated by higher-order recursion schemes. In: LICS 2006, pp. 81–90. IEEE Computer Society Press (2006)
39. Ong, C.-H.L., Tsukada, T.: Two-level game semantics, intersection types, and recursion schemes. In: Czumaj, A., Mehlhorn, K., Pitts, A., Wattenhofer, R. (eds.) ICALP 2012, Part II. LNCS, vol. 7392, pp. 325–336. Springer, Heidelberg (2012)
40. Pierce, B.C., Turner, D.N.: Concurrent objects in a process calculus. In: Ito, T. (ed.) TPPP 1994. LNCS, vol. 907, pp. 187–215. Springer, Heidelberg (1995)
41. Sangiorgi, D.: Typed π-calculus at work: a proof of jones's parallelisation transformation on concurrent objects. In: Fourth Workshop on Foundations of Object-Oriented Languages, FOOL 4 (1997)
42. Sangiorgi, D., Walker, D.: The Pi-Calculus: A Theory of Mobile Processes. Cambridge University Press (2001)
43. Schwoon, S.: Model-Checking Pushdown Systems. PhD thesis, Technische Universität München (2002)
44. Takeuchi, K., Honda, K., Kubo, M.: An interaction-based language and its typing system. In: Halatsis, C., Philokyprou, G., Maritsas, D., Theodoridis, S. (eds.) PARLE 1994. LNCS, vol. 817, pp. 398–413. Springer, Heidelberg (1994)
45. Turner, D.N., Wadler, P., Mossin, C.: Once upon a type. In: Proceedings of Functional Programming Languages and Computer Architecture, San Diego, California, pp. 1–11 (1995)
46. van Bakel, S.: Intersection type assignment systems. Theor. Comput. Sci. 151(2), 385–435 (1995)
47. Wadler, P.: Linear types can change the world? In: Programming Concepts and Methods. North-Holland (1990)
48. Yonezawa, A.: ABCL: An Object-Oriented Concurrent System. MIT Press (1990)
49. Yonezawa, A., Tokoro, M.: Object-Oriented Concurrent Programming. The MIT Press (1987)
50. Yoshida, N.: Graph types for monadic mobile processes. In: Chandru, V., Vinay, V. (eds.) FSTTCS 1996. LNCS, vol. 1180, pp. 371–386. Springer, Heidelberg (1996)

SALSA Lite: A Hash-Based Actor Runtime for Efficient Local Concurrency

Travis Desell[1] and Carlos A. Varela[2]

[1] Department of Computer Science, University of North Dakota,
Grand Forks, ND, USA
tdesell@cs.und.edu
[2] Department of Computer Science, Rensselaer Polytechnic Institute,
Troy, NY, USA
cvarela@cs.rpi.edu

Abstract. As modern computer processors continue becoming more parallel, the actor model plays an increasingly important role in helping develop correct concurrent systems. In this paper, we consider efficient runtime strategies for non-distributed actor programming languages. While the focus is on a non-distributed implementation, it serves as a platform for a future efficient distributed implementation. Actors extend the object model by combining state and behavior with a thread of control, which can significantly simplify concurrent programming. Further, with asynchronous communication, no shared memory, and the fact an actor only processes one message at a time, it is possible to easily implement transparent distributed message passing and actor mobility. This paper discusses *SALSA Lite*, a completely re-designed actor runtime system engineered to maximize performance. The new runtime consists of a highly optimized core for lightweight actor creation, message passing, and message processing, which is used to implement more advanced coordination constructs. This new runtime is novel in two ways. First, by default the runtime automatically maps the lightweight actors to threads, allowing the number of threads used by a program to be specified at runtime transparently, without any changes to the code. Further, language constructs allow programmers to have first class control over how actors are mapped to threads (creating new threads if needed). Second, the runtime directly maps actor garbage collection to object garbage collection, allowing non-distributed SALSA programs to use Java's garbage collection "for free". This runtime is shown to have comparable or better performance for basic actor constructs (message passing and actor creation) than other popular actor languages: Erlang, Scala, and Kilim.

Keywords: Concurrent Programming, Actor Model, Actor Languages, Fairness, State Encapsulation, SALSA, Erlang, Kilim, Scala.

1 Introduction

Actors model concurrency in open distributed systems [1, 2]. They are independent, concurrent entities that communicate by exchanging messages. Each actor encapsulates a state with a logical thread of control which manipulates

G. Agha et al. (Eds.): Yonezawa Festschrift, LNCS 8665, pp. 144–166, 2014.

it. Communication between actors is purely asynchronous. The actor model assumes guaranteed message delivery and fair scheduling of computation. Actors only process information in reaction to messages. While processing a message, an actor can carry out any of three basic operations: alter its state, create new actors, or send messages to other actors (see Figure 1). Actors are therefore inherently independent, concurrent and autonomous which enables efficiency in parallel execution [3] and facilitates mobility [4, 5].

This paper describes the development of a new runtime for SALSA called SALSA Lite. This runtime was designed to perform the basics of actor based computation, simple message passing and actor creation, as efficiently as possible (see Section 4). Then the rest of SALSA's advanced message passing constructs, remote message passing, remote actor creation, and actor mobility are built using this optimized core. The strategy is to separate the overhead of distributed communication, universal naming, mobile computation, and distributed garbage collection, so that SALSA programs that run locally on multi-core processors do not have to pay the performance price for distribution and mobility.

Because encapsulation and fairness are guaranteed by the language semantics, it was possible to create a highly efficient and simple runtime to execute lightweight actors. The runtime itself is also based on the actor model, and is similar in structure to E's *vats* [7, 8]. It assigns lightweight actors to *stages*, each of which have a single thread and combined mailbox for every assigned actor. A stage processes messages from its mailbox sequentially on its assigned actors using their message handlers, and actors send messages to other actors by placing them in the target actor's stage. In this runtime, the stage is essentially a heavyweight actor, and lightweight actors can be implemented as simple objects.

Using this approach, it is also possible to provide first class stage support, allowing SALSA developers to specify what stage actors are assigned to, and dynamically create new stages as needed. Furthermore, the stage runtime maps actor garbage collection to object garbage collection, allowing the use of Java's garbage collection without additional overhead for non-distributed non-mobile SALSA programs. Results show that for benchmarks testing actor creation and message passing, SALSA Lite is two times faster than Kilim, two to ten times faster than Scala, and over an order of magnitude faster than Erlang. Additionally, SALSA Lite does this while providing actor garbage collection and ensuring state encapsulation, in contrast to Kilim and Scala.

2   Related Actor Languages and Frameworks

This section describes three commonly used languages with actor semantics: Erlang, Kilim, and Scala.

2.1   Erlang

Erlang is a functional programming language which allows concurrency via processes that use the actor model [9]. Erlang's scheduler accomplishes fairness by counting the number of reductions, or function calls used by a process. When a

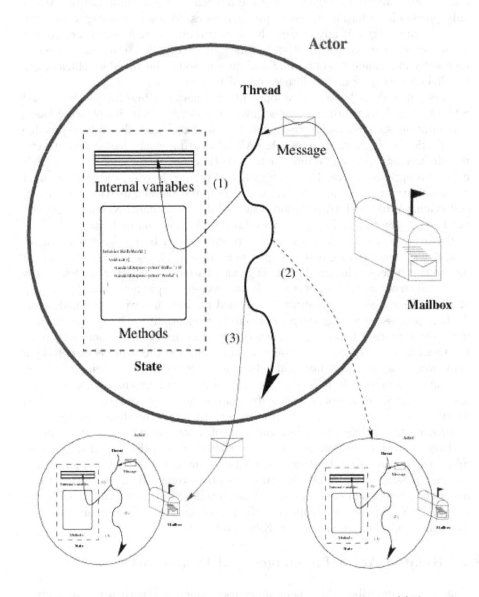

Fig. 1. Actors are reactive entities. In response to a message, an actor can (1) change its internal state, (2) create new actors, and/or (3) send messages to other actors (image from [6]).

process has made 1,000 reductions, it is paused and Erlang starts execution of a different process. This allows Erlang to scale to a large number of processes using a fixed number of actual processes without violating fairness.

The state of a process in Erlang can only be updated as the result of message passing. This coupled with safe message passing ensures state encapsulation. Safe message passing in Erlang is guaranteed by *single assignment*. Single assignment enforces that a value can be bound to a variable exactly once. As a consequence, all variables are immutable after their initial assignment. Since there is no way to directly update the state of other processes and variables passed in messages are immutable, there is no way to share mutable memory between Erlang processes.

2.2   Kilim

Kilim is an actor based message passing framework for Java. It uses byte-code transformation to convert specified Java objects into actors. Kilim actors use ultra-lightweight threads as well as safe, zero-copy message passing based on a type system [10]. Kilim's *weaver* transforms methods with a @pausable qualifier into continuation message passing. The resulting actor threads and continuation messages enable very fast context-switching via lightweight threads. Kilim uses a *linear ownership* type system to ensure that a message can have at most one owner at any time, which helps developers guarantee safe message passing.

However, Kilim requires users to explicitly copy Java objects when they are sent in messages, so it violates state encapsulation as actors can pass references to Java objects and access the same memory concurrently. Kilim actors can also be constructed with references to shared objects and access the mailbox and state of other actors directly. While having a reference to another actors mailbox allows actors to "send" messages, it also lets an actor "steal" messages from other actors' mailboxes. It also does not guarantee fair scheduling, as synchronous object method invocation and infinite loops may block an actor and the thread executing that and potentially other actors indefinitely, preventing it from processing further messages.

2.3   Scala

Scala provides a library `scala.actors`, heavily inspired by Erlang, to support the actor model. It supports synchronous and asynchronous message passing and fair scheduling by unifying threads and events [11]. However, it allows shared memory and synchronous execution of methods on other actors. While this can be desirable in some programs, it can also result in a violation of actor semantics as well as data inconsistencies. Similarly, objects passed within messages may be accessed by multiple actors simultaneously leading to a loss of state encapsulation. Allowing synchronous message passing can also cause deadlocks [12, 13].

Scala actors can be either heavyweight, with each actor using its own thread, or event-based, using a thread pool to provide fairness. It is possible to combine event-based and heavyweight actors in Scala. For event-based actors, Scala can use a single thread scheduler or a thread pool. Scala's thread pool scheduler will add a new thread to its thread pool if all worker threads are blocked due to long-running operations. This can be much more efficient than heavyweight actors, as the number of threads can typically remain constant if the worker threads are not continuously blocked. However, this implementation can still fail if enough actors are created that block worker threads, as the thread pool can run out of resources when the JVM cannot create any new threads.

3   The SALSA Lite Runtime

The SALSA Lite runtime was developed to execute the common case fast with the least amount of overhead. Message processing is accomplished via Java code, so in terms of the actor model the two most important common cases to execute fast are message sending and actor creation. Further, these need to be implemented in a way to protect state encapsulation and guarantee safe message passing.[1]

Figure 2 shows the runtime environment used by SALSA Lite. As the actor model provides a simple and efficient way to develop concurrent and distributed programs, the SALSA Lite runtime practices what we preach. It uses heavyweight actors (called *stages*) to simulate the execution of many concurrent lightweight actors in parallel, as with a heavyweight actor, each stage has its own mailbox and thread of control. Because of this, SALSA Lite actors are implemented as simple Java objects, consisting only of their state (object fields) and a reference to the stage they are *performing* or executing on, so other actors can easily send messages to them by placing those messages in their respective stage.

A drawback of this implementation is that if any message has an unbounded processing time, e.g., it enters an infinite loop or calls a blocking method invocation on an object like reading from a socket, the other actors on the same stage may starve. Currently, the solution to this problem is by creating an actor with its own stage, as described in Section 3.1, if it could potentially execute a message with unbounded execution time. This approach is also used by other performance focused actor implementaitons, such as `libcppa` [14].

Other implementations, which utilize thread pools (such as Scala) can also fall prey to this problem – if all threads in the threadpool are in an infinite loop or call a blocking method which never unblocks, actors waiting to process messages outside the thread pool will starve. Thread pools can also potentially cause significant performance overhead and can potentially cause the JVM to run out of resources when they cannot create new threads. Thread pools were examined for SALSA Lite, however they resulted in significantly worse performance. Further, they require each actor to also have some data structure to store their own individual mailbox, increasing memory requirements.

---

[1] *State encapsulation* refers to the inability to modify an actor's internal state other than indirectly by sending it messages. *Safe message passing* refers to the inability to missuse the message passing system in order to share memory and thereby break state encapsulation, e.g., by sending a reference to a mutable object in a message.

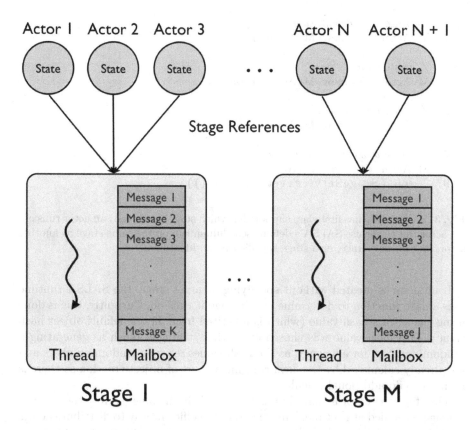

Fig. 2. The SALSA Lite runtime environment. Heavyweight actors called *stages* are used to process messages on multiple lightweight actors, simulating their concurrent execution. A stage will repeatedly get the first message from its mailbox and process that message on the message's target actor. Every actor is assigned to a stage. A Message sent to an actor is placed at the end of its assigned stage's mailbox.

Examining methods for automatically quarantining actors with unbounded message processing behavior to their own stages, or other methods for efficiently ensuring fairness at the runtime level remains an area of future research.

3.1 Actor Creation

Figure 3 gives an example of creating actors at different stages. The initial number of stages used can be specified at runtime, and these stages are identified 0 through $N-1$ where N is the number of stages. First class stage support can be used to create an actor at the same stage as another actor, a stage specified by its identifier, or its own new stage.

```
1:  //create on a default stage
2:  MyActor a = new MyActor();

3:  //create b on a's stage
4:  MyActor b = new MyActor() on (a);

5:  //create c on stage 3
6:  MyActor c = new MyActor() on (3);

7:  //create d on its own new stage
8:  MyActor d = new MyActor()
9:      on (StageService.getNewStage());
```

Fig. 3. SALSA Lite has first class support for which stage (or thread) an actor runs on. An actor can either use SALSA's default scheduling, run on the same stage as another actor, its own new stage, or a stage specified by an identifier.

If an actor is created without specifying a target stage, the SALSA runtime uses a hash function to determine which stage it runs on. Currently, this is done using the actor's hash value (which is inherited from Java's default object hash value). This hash value was chosen over other strategies (such as generating a random number) for efficiency, as the hash values serve as random numbers and are already calculated by the Java runtime as part of object creation so there is no need to do additional calculation.

The stage the actor is placed on is the actor's hash value modulo the number of stages specified at runtime. This makes for an efficient way to distribute actors over stages in a generally balanced and random way. Hashing actors to stages is particularly interesting as a research question, as it provides transparent parallelism of SALSA Lite programs, allowing the number of stages to be specified at runtime, independent of the application's code. Further, it makes it possible to examine different hashing functions with respect to their load balancing capabilities and performance.

This implementation also allows SALSA programs to intermingle lightweight and heavyweight actors without any additional overhead, as a heavyweight actor is simply an actor running at a stage without any other actors. Furthermore, actors which communicate frequently can be assigned to the same stage so they do not have to pay the price of context switching when passing messages, which can result in significant performance as shown by the ThreadRing and Chameneos-Redux benchmarks in Sections 4.1 and 4.2, respectively. In this way SALSA actors have location *translucency*: a developer can simply specify an initial number of stages and have the SALSA runtime determine what stage actors will be assigned to, or the developer can have first class control over the number of stages used, what actors are assigned to them, and can even change the number of stages dynamically.

3.2   State Encapsulation

State encapsulation, asynchronous communication, and fairness are the main semantic concerns in actor languages. As stated by Karmani et al., "Without enforcing encapsulation, the Actor model of programming is effectively reduced to guidance for taming multi-threaded programming on shared memory machines" [15]. Asynchronous communication is critical in preventing deadlocks and to facilitate the execution of concurrent systems on distributed environments. Finally, fair scheduling ensures the correctness of an actor system composed of several existing systems [16]. Without state encapsulation, asynchronous communication, and fairness, it is not possible to guarantee the correct execution of an actor-oriented program.

Many current actor system implementations use a language or framework that combines both object-oriented and actor-oriented programming [15], such as the ActorArchitecture [17], the Actor Foundry [18], JavAct [19], Jetlang [20], Kilim [10] and Scala [11]. However, the combination of objects, threads, and actors can lead to inconsistencies in the actor model implementation. For example, if an actor passes a reference to an object to another actor within a message, both actors can then access the memory of that object concurrently which can lead to race conditions, deadlock, or memory inconsistency; nullifying many of the benefits of the actor model. Some approaches, such as Kilim's, have attempted to address this issue by zero-copy isolation types [10], while others simply allow these inconsistencies. Erlang monitors the call stack and suspends actor processing, yielding to others if an actor takes too long to process a message [9], and Scala uses a thread pool which will spawn new threads if message processing becomes blocked [11]. In summary, it is very difficult to guarantee state encapsulation and deadlock freedom; and often complicated run time solutions are necessary to ensure fairness.

SALSA Lite guarantees state encapsulation during the compilation process. The SALSA lite compiler generates Java objects for each actor, which have all their state fields and methods flagged as private. The compiler generates two methods which take a message object and invoke the corresponding method or constructor on the actor, and these can only be invoked by that actor's controlling stage. Further, as SALSA Lite allows the use of Java objects, and the underlying implementation of actors and their references are objects, to prevent programmer confusion the compiler explicitly does not allow for methods to be invoked on actor references, and generates appropriate error messages. This guarantees state encapsulation of all actors.

3.3   Safe Message Passing

When a message is sent to an actor, it is placed in the mailbox of that actor's stage. Stages process messages in the same first-in, first-out manner as actors, except the messages are invoked on the target actor instead of the stage. As each actor is only assigned to a single stage, multiple messages will not be processed by an actor at the same time. Because this runtime is based on the actor model as well, there are very few synchronization points. The `LinkedList` of a stage's mailbox must be synchronized such that the thread will wait for new messages to be placed in the mailbox if it is empty, and incoming messages must be added to the mailbox one at a time. Inter-stage fairness follows from Java thread execution fairness. While the current implementation uses synchronization around the use Java's `LinkedList` class for a mailbox, performance may potentially be further improved by using lock-free data structures [14, 21–24], which will be investigated as future work.

When messages are sent, they must not allow direct access to the state of the actor sending the message, otherwise this would violate state encapsulation and distributed memory. One way to enforce this is by doing a deep copy on every argument passed in a message from one actor to another. However, this is not particularly efficient. Further, when an actor sends a message to another actor, the arguments of that message can either be references to other actors (whose state and references to objects and other actors do not need be copied) or objects, which do need to be copied. For a simple example, an argument to a message may be an `ArrayList` of actors. The `ArrayList` should be copied, but the actors (as well as the objects and actors referenced by those actors) it contains should not.

The SALSA Lite compiler uses static type checking and static method resolution which enable us to implement fast and safe message passing. In Java, primitives and immutable objects are passed by copy, while mutable objects are passed by reference. In order to sucessfully implement safe and efficient message passing in SALSA, primitives, immutable objects *and* mutable objects need to be passed by copy, while actors should be passed by reference.

Previous SALSA implementations use Java's default serialization interface, which would copy the entire message over a socket connection, which is not particularly efficient. In SALSA Lite, each stage only processes one message at a time, which allows the use of highly efficient and unsynchronized fast byte array input and output streams for the deep copy [25]. Further, as the SALSA lite compiler has static type checking, it can selectively copy only the message arguments which require it (mutable objects), by wrapping those particular arguments in a *deep copy* call.

Actors were implemented as Java objects extending a simple `Actor` class. SALSA disallows direct access to any fields within an actor, and these objects to allow message passing from other actors. These references are essentially immutable, so it is safe to share them between actors and objects. State encapsulation is enforced in SALSA utilizing the `writeReplace` and `readResolve` methods of Java's `java.io.Serializable` interface. The SALSA compiler provides a `writeReplace` and `readResolve` for each actor. When an actor is to be serialized, Java will call the `writeReplace` method and instead serialize the object returned by that method. When that object is read, its `readResolve` method will be called and the result of that method used as the unserialized object. This is used to hijack the serialization process of actors, preventing them from being copied. The `writeReplace` places the written actor into a hash table (using a hash function which generates unique values, separate from Java's default implementation which potentially has collisions), and returns an object with the hash value for that actor. The `readResolve` method takes the hash value of the serialized object, looks up the actor in the hash table and returns that actor. This approach also has further benefits in that it allows actor references to be tracked when actors are serialized to remote locations via migration in distributed applications.

3.4 Garbage Collection

Erlang provides garbage collection via a mark-and-sweep algorithm [26]. The actor implementation on the Kilim and Scala languages do not provide garbage collection at all. Using the description of actor liveness and garbage presented by Kafura et al. [27], an actor is garbage if:

- it is not a root actor.
- it cannot potentially send a message to a root actor.
- it cannot potentially receive a message from a root actor.

We can define an *unblocked* actor as an actor that is either processing a message or has messages waiting for it in its mailbox. A *potentially unblocked* actor is an actor that another unblocked or potentially unblocked actor has a reference to (and thus messages could be sent to it). Because of this, an actor is garbage if it is not potentially unblocked [28, 29].

All SALSA actors have static references to standard output, standard input, and standard error (via Java), so they all have references to root actors and objects. Therefore, in SALSA there cannot be active garbage, or garbage actors that repeatedly send messages to each other, since if an actor is processing messages, it can potentially send messages to root actors. Detecting live (non-garbage) actors is therefore reduced to reachability from potentially unblocked actors, also called *pseudo-roots* [28, 29].

In Java garbage collection, objects are collected if they are unreachable by a non-system thread. In SALSA Lite, the only non-system threads are the threads used by stages. In non-distributed programs, unblocked actors are always reachable by a stage thread, as the stage will have either a reference to the actor as it is processing a message, or a reference to a message in its mailbox which has a reference to that actor. As unblocked actors are always reachable by a stage thread, potentially unblocked actors are as well, because there will be a chain of references through other unblocked and potentially unblocked actors to every potentially unblocked actor. The only references to actors are in messages or in the state of an actor. If an actor is garbage, it is unreachable by any stage thread as there will be no messages to it in its stage mailbox and no unblocked or potentially unblocked actors will have a reference to it. Therefore it will be reclaimed by Java's garbage collector.

Because of this, the stage based runtime presented automatically maps local actor garbage collection to object garbage collection, allowing SALSA Lite to use Java's garbage collection to reclaim non-distributed garbage actors without additional overhead.

4   Performance Benchmarks

This section compares the performance of Erlang, Kilim, SALSA, and Scala with three different benchmarks. The ThreadRing benchmark measures the performance of message passing between concurrent entities (in this case, actors). Chameneos-Redux measures not only the performance of message passing, but also the fairness of scheduling for the concurrent entities. FibonacciTree measures the performance of message passing and actor creation, as well as the memory usage of many concurrent actors.

All experiments were run in a 2.93 GHz Intel Core 2 Duo MacBook Pro with 4 GB 1067 MHz DDR3 RAM, running Mac OS X 10.6.2. The Java version used was 1.6.0_17. The mean runtime for 25 experiments was used for all performance figures, and includes start up and shut down time (they were not run repeatedly within a JVM). The implementations of ThreadRing and Chameneos-Redux used by Java, Scala and Erlang were taken from the best performing versions at the *Computer Language Benchmarks Game*[2]. Scala 2.7.7, Erlang R14A, and Kilim 0.6 were used to perform the tests. The FibonacciTree has been used by SALSA in the past to test its performance, however it is not as well known as ThreadRing and Chameneos-Redux, so implementations were made for Erlang, Kilim and Scala using the same message passing strategy used by SALSA. Because of this it should be noted that there may be better performing implementations for Erlang, Kilim and Scala if written by an expert in those languages. However, the SALSA benchmarks were also programmed as typical programmers (e.g., see Appendix A and B for the SALSA code for the Fibonacci and ThreadRing benchmarks), and were not extensively optimized either.

4.1   ThreadRing

The specification for the ThreadRing benchmark states that 503 concurrent entities should be created and linked either explicitly or implicitly in a ring. Following this, a token should be passed around the ring N times. The ThreadRing benchmark provides a good measurement of the time to pass messages between actors. It also provides an interesting mechanism to examine the cost of context switching between actors (or threads), as only one is active at any given time while it is passing the token. Because of this, lightweight threading implementations which do not require context switching can provide significant speedup over heavyweight implementations.

Figure 4 compares the performance of Java, single stage SALSA, Kilim, Scala with a single thread scheduler (STS), typical Scala with a thread pool, and Erlang as the number of times the token was passed (message hops) was increased from 500 to 50,000,000. The runtime did not change much between 500

---

[2] http://benchmarksgame.alioth.debian.org/

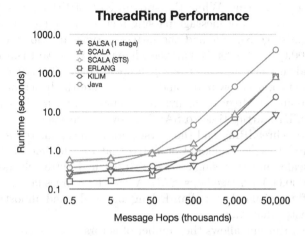

Fig. 4. The performance of Java, Kilim, Erlang, SALSA, and Scala for the Thread-Ring benchmark. SALSA used a single stage runtime, while Scala used a single thread scheduler (STS) and its typical thread pool runtime. Kilim had indistinguishable results for a single and double thread scheduler. The Java implementation used standard Java threads and the `java.util.concurrent.locks.LockSupport` class for a locking mechanism.

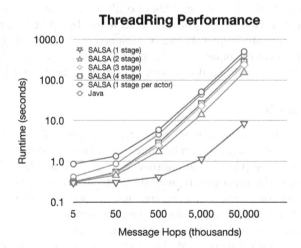

Fig. 5. The performance of SALSA using one to four stages, and to Java for the ThreadRing benchmark. This illustrates the high cost of thread context switching for this benchmark.

and 50,000 message hops, as the majority of this time was the startup cost of the runtime environment. While the startup cost of Erlang was the lowest, the performance overhead of message passing increased the fastest of the actor languages. Single stage SALSA had the fastest performance for message passing, and from 500,000 to 50,000,000 message hops had the lowest runtime. Single thread Scala had very fast message passing, however above 500,000 message hops it suffered from stack overflow and could not complete the benchmark, because the message passing strategy used involved recursion and method invocation. Kilim had a similar startup time to SALSA, however message passing was not as fast. The Java ThreadRing had the worst performance, due to its traditional heavyweight thread usage. It should be noted that the runtime in the figure is a logarithmic scale, and that single stage SALSA had extremely fast message passing; for 50,000,000 message hops, SALSA was three times faster than Kilim, and an order of magnitude faster than Erlang and Scala, and almost two orders of magnitude faster than Java.

As the SALSA runtime allows the number of actors in the system to be independent from the number of stages, or threads, used; Figure 5 shows the runtime of the ThreadRing benchmark using one to four stages, and a heavyweight version with one stage per actor. With multiple stages, the high cost of context switching becomes apparent, as the more stages there are, the more threads the message must hop through, causing more context switching. This is further demonstrated as the heavyweight SALSA ThreadRing performance matches the Java performance with some overhead (approximately 23%). As only there is only one message being passed at a time around the ring, when it is passed between actors on different stages, it will not continue to be passed until the context switches to that other stage. This also illustrates the benefit of having first class control over what stage processes what actor. In a SALSA application, actors which communicate frequently can be assigned to the same stage and thus not have to pay the cost of context switching when message passing. This is not possible using a thread pool based runtime, as is done in Scala and Erlang.

4.2   Chameneos-Redux

The Chameneos-Redux benchmark not only tests the speed of message passing, but also the fairness of concurrency scheduling. Two runs are done, one with an odd number of creatures (three) and another with an even number of creatures (ten). For each run, the creatures repeatedly go to a meeting place and meet (or wait to meet) another creature. Each creature has a color and upon meeting another creature both change their color to the complement of the creature they met. This tests the performance of message passing as there are many messages between the chameneos creatures and the meeting place. Additionally, it tests fairness of concurrency scheduling as with an unfair scheduler, some creatures will meet more than others.

Figure 6 compares the performance of Erlang, Killim, Scala and SALSA for the Chameneos-Redux benchmark, as the number of meetings was increased from 600 to 6,000,000. SALSA used a single stage runtime and a heavyweight runtime

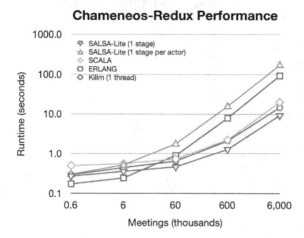

Fig. 6. The performance of Erlang, Kilim, SALSA, and Scala for the Chameneos-Redux benchmark. SALSA used both a lightweight runtime with a single stage and a heavy weight runtime which assigned each creature to its own stage. Only the thread pool version of Scala is shown as the benchmark had errors with a single thread scheduler. Kilim had indistinguishable results for both a single and double thread scheduler.

with one actor per stage. As with ThreadRing, the single thread scheduler in Scala had runtime errors due to stack overflow, so only the thread pool version of Scala is given. Again, Erlang was the quickest to start up, however its message passing was slower than both Scala and the single thread SALSA runtime. As the heavyweight SALSA Chameneos-Redux required context switching for each message passed between the creatures and the meeting place, its performance was very poor. As with the ThreadRing benchmark, single stage SALSA had the best runtime after startup costs became insignificant, being 1.75x faster than Kilim, 2.5x faster than Scala, and ten times faster than Erlang for 6,000,000 meetings.

Not only does the Chameneos-Redux benchmark test the speed of message passing between concurrent entities, it also provides a measure of the fairness of concurrency. With perfectly fair scheduling, each chameneos creature should have the same number of meetings. Figure 7 shows the standard deviation between the meetings of each chameneos creature for Chameneos-Redux with 6,000,000 meetings, run ten times for each language and runtime; for both the run with three creatures and the run with ten creatures. A lower standard deviation meant scheduling was more fair, as there was less difference in the number of times the creatures met. Both single stage SALSA and single thread Kilim were perfectly fair by processing messages in a first-in, first-out manner. Double thread Kilim had almost perfectly fair scheduling for an even number of creatures (10), and was almost perfect for an odd number (3). While a heavyweight Chameneos-Redux implementation in SALSA had the worst runtime, it had the

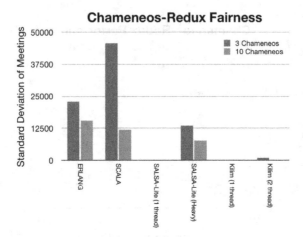

Fig. 7. The fairness of scheduling in Erlang, Kilim, SALSA and Scala. SALSA used both a single stage runtime and a multi-stage runtime that assigned each chameneos creature (and the meeting place) to its own stage. Kilim used both a single and double thread scheduler. The standard deviation between the meetings of creatures is shown, so a lower standard deviation is more fair concurrency. Single stage SALSA and single thread Kilim were perfectly fair with a standard deviation of 0.

next best fairness as it relied on Java's thread scheduling. Erlang and Scala had different fairness depending on the number of creatures. Erlang had better fairness for three creatures while Scala had better fairness with ten.

4.3   FibonacciTree

The last benchmark tested was a concurrent Fibonacci tree. This benchmark calculates the Fibonacci number using concurrent actors. A Fibonacci actor computes the Fibonacci number N by creating two child Fibonacci actors with the Fibonacci numbers $N - 1$ and $N - 2$, which create their own children and so on. If a Fibonacci actor is created with $N = 0$ it returns 0 to its creator, and if it is created with $N \leq 2$ it returns 1 to its creator. This benchmark not only tests the speed of message passing, but also the speed of creation of new actors. As this benchmark generates many actors, memory usage can be quite high. Because of this, Kilim, SALSA and Scala used the -Xmx and -Xms flags of the Java Virtual Machine to set the initial and maximum heap size to 2000MB, as the cost of allocating new memory has a significant effect on the runtime of the benchmark.

Figure 8 shows the performance of the FibonacciTree benchmark for SALSA with a single stage, one actor per stage, and a smart implementation that distributes subtrees across 4 stages, Kilim, Scala with a thread pool and a single thread scheduler, and Erlang. Both heavyweight SALSA and Erlang (which also uses a heavyweight actor implementation) failed after FibonacciTree(20), as no more resources were available to create new threads or processes.

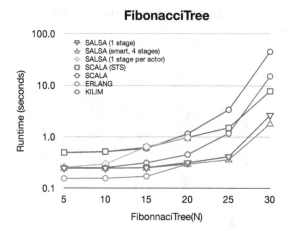

Fig. 8. The performance of the FibonacciTree for SALSA with a single stage, one stage per actor, and a smart implementation that placed subtrees across 4 stages, single thread scheduler and thread pool Scala, Kilim and Erlang. Both Erlang and heavyweight SALSA ran out of memory after FibonacciTree(20).

For FibonacciTree with $N > 20$, the smart implementation using four stages in SALSA had the best performance. This implementation shows the benefit of using first class stage support to split the FibonacciTree into closely sized subtrees[3] and assigning each of these to its own stage to be processed in parallel, improving performance by 44% over single stage SALSA (1.8 seconds to 2.6 seconds). Kilim was initially faster than Scala due to its faster startup time, however the single thread scheduler for Scala had the next best performance for larger Fibonacci numbers. Using the thread pool runtime of Scala had the worst performance. For smaller Fibonacci numbers, Erlang had the best performance until it ran out of resources, due to its fast startup time.

Scala with the single thread scheduler had the best memory usage, as it used recursion and method invocation on objects instead of actor creation and actual message passing, and thus had the interesting property of not requiring extra memory for larger Fibonacci numbers. Apart from this, SALSA had similar memory use for both a single and multi stage runtime, at 80MB for FibonacciTree(25) and 600MB for FibonacciTree(30). Kilim required the next least memory for FibonacciTree(25) and (30), around 180MB and 1530MB respectively. Scala required 300MB for FibonacciTree(25), and significantly more memory for FibonacciTree(30), reaching the imposed limit of 2000MB with a thread pool runtime.

---

[3] For FibonacciTree(30), stage 0 would be assigned FibonacciTree(28), stage 1 would be assigned FibonacciTree(27), stage 2 would be assigned FibonacciTree(27) and stage 3 would be assigned FibonacciTree(26).

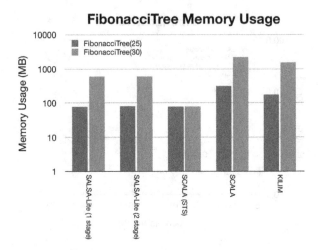

Fig. 9. Memory usage of FibonacciTree(25) and FibonacciTree(30) for SALSA with a single stage and the smart implementation with four stages, Kilim, and Scala with a single thread scheduler and thread pool. It should be noted that JVM memory usage was capped at 2000MB, and Scala with a thread pool could not allocate more than this amount of memory for FibonacciTree(30).

5   Discussion

This work describes an extremely efficient hash based runtime, in which actors are highly lightweight and independent from the threading mechanism used. The SALSA Lite runtime uses stages, similar to heavyweight actors, each with their own thread of control and mailbox, to simulate the concurrent execution of multiple lightweight actors. Each actor is assigned to a *stage*, either by an application developer using first class support to intelligently co-locate frequently communicating actors and give heavyweight actors their own thread, or by the SALSA Lite runtime. An added benefit of using this stage based runtime is that it automatically maps actor garbage collection to object garbage collection, and SALSA Lite can directly use Java's garbage collection for local (or non-distributed) concurrent programs.

Because of the stage based runtime and semantically guaranteed fairness and encapsulation, SALSA Lite significantly improved message passing performance and memory usage over earlier versions of SALSA. Results show that SALSA Lite's runtime is significantly faster than other existing actor implementations, two times faster than Kilim, between two and ten times faster than Scala, and over an order of magnitude faster than Erlang for the ThreadRing, Chameneos-Redux and FibonacciTree benchmarks. Additionally, with a similar result to single thread Kilim, SALSA Lite has perfect fairness using a single stage for the Chameneos-Redux benchmark. SALSA's memory usage was also less than Kilim and Scala using a thread pool scheduler, however not less than Scala's single thread scheduler which did not increase for larger FibonacciTree numbers due to its recursive method invocation, as opposed to actor creation based, strategy.

6 Future Work

While this paper describes SALSA Lite's non-distributed runtime and semantics in detail, SALSA also provides location transparency and mobility for distributed computing [5]. This lays the groundwork for extending the runtime presented with support for distributed applications with minimal overhead. Additionally, the strategy used for mapping actor garbage to local garbage will not work for distributed applications, so efficient distributed garbage collection is also required, e.g. [30, 31, 28].

Performance is limited by SALSA being implemented in Java. For example, in Section 4, Erlang consistently has the fastest startup time. While the Java implementation does have many benefits (like use of Java's libraries), it should be possible to have a significantly faster actor implementation if it was built up from a lower level, as done in ABCL [32] or libcppa [14]. This would also allow for a purely actor model implementation, and if developed in C or C++ would allow easy use of MPI, GPUs and many-integrated core accelerator cards, resulting in an actor language for high performance computing with the additional benefits of transparent parallelism and mobility.

Further, in work done by Plevyak et al. [33] and in systems like ABCL [32], compile and runtime optimizations are used to process messages using local non-parallel function calls when applicable. This can result in significant performance increases, as it utilizes the stack instead of the heap, and message passing typically requires the creation of an additional message object and passing information about the messages sender and potential receiver for return values. SALSA Lite currently utilizes the heap for all message passing, with each message requiring creation of a message object, which is slower than a pure object method invocation. Another area of future work is to investigate strategies for using the stack and method invocation when possible, e.g. when multiple actors are on the same stage and are passing messages to each other which do not require continuations.

Further, to guarantee fairness in this runtime, currently a programmer needs to identify actors which could potentially process unbounded messages and assign them to their own stages. While this significantly reduces overhead, it may be desirable to have the runtime automatically enforce fairness by quarantining actors with long running messages to their own stage. A future area of research is to evaluate ways of enforcing fairness without significant overhead; as many applications do not require this enforcement.

The SALSA Lite runtime uses a hash based strategy to determine what stages actors are assigned to. An interesting avenue of research would be examining other scheduling strategies for assigning actors to stages in an intelligent manner; for example, in the ThreadRing benchmark, there is no reason to divide the actors over multiple stages and suffer from context switching. The runtime presented also gives first class support for assigning actors to threads. Previous work with the Internet Operating System (IOS) has shown that dynamic reconfiguration of distributed SALSA programs can be used to improve performance [34, 35]. The stage based runtime can be extended to enable local mobility of actors, allowing actors to dynamically change what stage they are assigned to. It also may be possible to improve application performance through intelligent middleware that profiles the runtime and rearranges actors based on their communication patterns.

Acknowledgements. This work has been partially supported by the National Science Foundation under NSF CAREER Award No. CNS-0448407, and by the Air Force Office of Scientific Research under Grant No. FA9550-11-1-0332.

References

1. Hewitt, C.: Viewing control structures as patterns of passing messages. Artificial Intelligence 8, 323–364 (1977)
2. Agha, G.: Actors: a model of concurrent computation in distributed systems. MIT Press, Cambridge (1986)
3. Kim, W., Agha, G.: Efficient Support of Location Transparency in Concurrent Object-Oriented Programming Languages. In: Proceedings of Supercomputing 1995, pp. 39–48 (1995)
4. Agha, G., Jamali, N.: Concurrent programming for distributed artificial intelligence. In: Weiss, G. (ed.) Multiagent Systems: A Modern Approach to DAI. MIT Press (1999)
5. Varela, C., Agha, G.: Programming dynamically reconfigurable open systems with SALSA. SIGPLAN Not. 36, 20–34 (2001)
6. Varela, C.: Worldwide Computing with Universal Actors: Linguistic Abstractions for Naming, Migration, and Coordination. PhD thesis, U. of Illinois at Urbana-Champaign (2001), http://osl.cs.uiuc.edu/Theses/varela-phd.pdf
7. Miller, M.S., Shapiro, J.S.: Robust composition: Towards a unified approach to access control and concurrency control. PhD thesis, Johns Hopkins University (2006)
8. Miller, M., Tribble, E., Shapiro, J.: Concurrency among strangers. Trustworthy Global Computing, 195–229 (2005)
9. Armstrong, J.: Programming Erlang: Software for a Concurrent World. Pragmatic Bookshelf (2007)
10. Srinivasan, S., Mycroft, A.: Kilim: Isolation-typed actors for Java. In: Vitek, J. (ed.) ECOOP 2008. LNCS, vol. 5142, pp. 104–128. Springer, Heidelberg (2008)
11. Haller, P., Odersky, M.: Actors that unify threads and events. In: Murphy, A.L., Vitek, J. (eds.) COORDINATION 2007. LNCS, vol. 4467, pp. 171–190. Springer, Heidelberg (2007)
12. Vermeersch, R.: Concurrency in Erlang and Scala: The actor model (2009), http://ruben.savanne.be/articles/concurrency-in-erlang-scala
13. Varela, C., Agha, G.: What after Java? From Objects to Actors. Computer Networks and ISDN Systems: The International J. of Computer Telecommunications and Networking 30, 573–577 (1998); Proceedings of the Seventh International Conference on The World Wide Web (WWW7), Brisbane, Australia

14. Schmidt, D.C.T.C., Hiesgen, R., Wählisch, M.: Native actors–a scalable software platform for distributed, heterogeneous environments (2013)
15. Karmani, R.K., Shali, A., Agha, G.: Actor frameworks for the JVM platform: a comparative analysis. In: PPPJ 2009: Proceedings of the 7th International Conference on Principles and Practice of Programming in Java, pp. 11–20. ACM, New York (2009)
16. Agha, G.A., Mason, I.A., Smith, S.F., Talcott, C.L.: A foundation for actor computation. Journal of Functional Programming 7, 1–72 (1997)
17. Jang, M.W.: The Actor Architecture Manual. Department of Computer Science. University of Illinois at Urbana-Champaign (2004)
18. Astley, M.: The Actor Foundry: A Java-based Actor Programming Environment. Open Systems Laboratory. University of Illinois at Urbana-Champaign (1998–1999)
19. Rougemaille, S., Arcangeli, J.P., Migeon, F.: Javact: a Java middleware for mobile adaptive agents (2008)
20. Rettig, M.: Jetlang (2008–2009), http://code.google.com/p/jetlang/
21. Valois, J.D.: Lock-free data structures (1996)
22. Alexandrescu, A.: Lock-free data structures. C/C++ User Journal (2004)
23. Herlihy, M., Luchangco, V., Moir, M.: The repeat offender problem: A mechanism for supporting dynamic-sized lock-free data structures. In: Malkhi, D. (ed.) DISC 2002. LNCS, vol. 2508, pp. 339–353. Springer, Heidelberg (2002)
24. Herlihy, M., Luchangco, V., Martin, P., Moir, M.: Nonblocking memory management support for dynamic-sized data structures. ACM Transactions on Computer Systems (TOCS) 23, 146–196 (2005)
25. Isenhour, P.: Faster deep copies of java objects, http://javatechniques.com/blog/faster-deep-copies-of-java-objects/ (accessed: February 26, 2013)
26. Armstrong, J., Virding, R.: One pass real-time generational mark-sweep garbage collection. In: Baker, H.G. (ed.) IWMM-GIAE 1995. LNCS, vol. 986, pp. 313–322. Springer, Heidelberg (1995)
27. Kafura, D., Washabaugh, D., Nelson, J.: Garbage collection of actors. SIGPLAN Not. 25, 126–134 (1990)
28. Wang, W.: Distributed Garbage Collection for Large-Scale Mobile Actor Systems. PhD thesis, Rensselaer Polytechnic Institute (2006)
29. Wang, W.-J., Varela, C.A.: Distributed garbage collection for mobile actor systems: The pseudo root approach. In: Chung, Y.-C., Moreira, J.E. (eds.) GPC 2006. LNCS, vol. 3947, pp. 360–372. Springer, Heidelberg (2006)
30. Kamada, T., Matsuoka, S., Yonezawa, A.: Efficient parallel global garbage collection on massively parallel computers. In: Proceedings of the 1994 Conference on Supercomputing, pp. 79–88. IEEE Computer Society Press (1994)
31. Wang, W.-J., Varela, C., Hsu, F.-H., Tang, C.-H.: Actor garbage collection using vertex-preserving actor-to-object graph transformations. In: Bellavista, P., Chang, R.-S., Chao, H.-C., Lin, S.-F., Sloot, P.M.A. (eds.) GPC 2010. LNCS, vol. 6104, pp. 244–255. Springer, Heidelberg (2010)
32. Taura, K., Matsuoka, S., Yonezawa, A.: An efficient implementation scheme of concurrent object-oriented languages on stock multicomputers. ACM SIGPLAN Notices 28, 218–228 (1993)
33. Plevyak, J., Karamcheti, V., Zhang, X., Chien, A.A.: A hybrid execution model for fine-grained languages on distributed memory multicomputers. In: Proceedings of the 1995 ACM/IEEE Conference on Supercomputing (CDROM), Supercomputing 1995. ACM, New York (1995)

34. Desell, T., Maghraoui, K.E., Varela, C.A.: Malleable applications for scalable high performance computing. Cluster Computing, 323–337 (2007)
35. Maghraoui, K.E., Desell, T., Szymanski, B.K., Varela, C.A.: The Internet Operating System: Middleware for adaptive distributed computing. International Journal of High Performance Computing Applications (IJHPCA), Special Issue on Scheduling Techniques for Large-Scale Distributed Platforms 20, 467–480 (2006)

A   Fibonacci.salsa

A simple concurrent Fibonacci program in SALSA. The SALSA syntax is extremely similar to Java's syntax, and it can utilize all of Java's libraries (lines 9, 26). The **new** command creates a (concurrent) actor (lines 20 and 21), and <- sends asynchronous messages (lines 11, 20, 21). If a message or result of a message requires the result of another message (lines 11, 20, 21) it will not be sent until the required result has been sent with the **pass** statement (lines 16, 18, 20, 21), similar to a **return** statement. The constructor taking a array of arguments serves as an actor's **main** method.

```
1: behavior Fibonacci {
2:     int n;
3:
4:     Fibonacci(int n) {
5:         self.n = n;
6:     }
7:
8:     Fibonacci(String[] arguments) {
9:         n = Integer.parseInt(arguments[0]);
10:
11:         self<-finish( self<-compute() );
12:     }
13:
14:    int compute() {
15:        if (n == 0) {
16:            pass 0;
17:        } else if (n <= 2) {
18:            pass 1;
19:        } else {
20:            pass new Fibonacci(n-1)<-compute() +
21:                 new Fibonacci(n-2)<-compute();
22:        }
23:     }
24:
25:    ack finish(int value) {
26:         System.out.println(value);
27:     }
28: }
```

B   ThreadRing.salsa

A simple concurrent ThreadRing program in SALSA. A JoinDirector (line 20) is an actor that provides a method for waiting for a group of messages to complete before sending another message. After an actor completes a message, it sends a join message to the JoinDirector (lines 27 and 30), which will resolve after it has received a number of messages specified by sending a resolveAfter message (line 32). In this case, only after the JoinDirector receives threadCount messages, the forwardMessage will be send (line 33).

```
1: import salsa_lite.language.JoinDirector;
2:
3: behavior ThreadRing {
4:     ThreadRing next;
5:     int id;
6:
7:     ThreadRing(int id) {
8:         self.id = id;
9:     }
10:
11:     ThreadRing(String[] args) {
12:         if (args.length != 2) {
13:             System.out.println("Usage: java ThreadRing <threadCount> <hopCount>");
14:             pass;
15;         }
16:
17:         int threadCount = Integer.parseInt(args[0]);
18:         int hopCount = Integer.parseInt(args[1]);
19:
20:         ThreadRing first = new ThreadRing(1);
21:         JoinDirector jd = new JoinDirector();
22:
23:         ThreadRing next = null;
24:         ThreadRing previous = first;
25:         for (int i = 1; i < threadCount; i++) {
26:             next = new ThreadRing(i + 1);
27:             previous<-setNextThread(next) @ jd<-join();
28:             previous = next;
29:         }
30:         next<-setNextThread(first) @ jd<-join();
31:
32:         jd<-resolveAfter(threadCount) @
33:         first<-forwardMessage(hopCount);
34:     }
35:
36:     ack setNextThread(ThreadRing next) {
37:         self.next = next;
38:     }
39:
40:     ack forwardMessage(int value) {
41:         if (value == 0) {
42:             System.out.println(id);
43:             System.exit(0);
```

```
44:        } else {
45:            value--;
46:            next<-forwardMessage(value);
47:        }
48:    }
49: }
```

Past and Future Directions for Concurrent Task Scheduling

Robert H. Halstead

24 Louise Road, Belmont, MA 02478, USA
rhhalstead@alum.mit.edu

Abstract. A wave of parallel processing research in the 1970s and 1980s developed various techniques for concurrent task scheduling, including *work-stealing scheduling* and *lazy task creation,* and various ideas for supporting speculative computing, including the *sponsor model,* but these ideas did not see large-scale use as long as uniprocessor clock speeds continued to increase rapidly from year to year. Now that the increase in clock speeds has slowed dramatically and multicore processors have become the answer for increasing the computing throughput of processor chips, increasing the performance of everyday applications on multicore processors by using parallelism has taken on greater importance, so concurrent task scheduling techniques are getting a second look.

Work stealing and lazy task creation have now been incorporated into a wide range of systems capable of "industrial strength" application execution, but support for speculative computing still lags behind. This paper traces these techniques from their origins to their use in present-day systems and suggests some directions for further investigation and development in the speculative computing area.

1 Introduction

A first great wave of parallel processing research took place in the 1970s and 1980s as people began to think about inherent limits to the speed at which individual circuits can run and at which communication between circuits can operate, and began to recognize that parallel execution would be the ultimate route to achieving the highest performance. While that era did see the first construction of large-scale parallel computers and their use for certain really large computations, the programming effort required was heroic enough to prevent their use for all but a small set of really large computations. For everyday applications, the continuing rapid progress in uniprocessor clock speeds was enough to yield regular performance improvements and dissuade efforts to further improve performance using parallelism. Thus, techniques for parallelizing massive computations saw some practical application, but using parallelism for more modestly scaled applications remained of research interest only.

In the last ten years, however, this situation has started to change. Moore's Law continues to give us denser circuitry every year, but removing heat from processor chips has emerged as a major barrier preventing faster clock speeds. As

G. Agha et al. (Eds.): Yonezawa Festschrift, LNCS 8665, pp. 167–195, 2014.

a result, *multicore processors* capable of on-chip parallel processing have become the latest trend in processor chip architecture. Even consumer-grade personal computers are now sold with processor chips that have 2–4 cores, and more highly parallel chips are on the way soon.

The onus is now on application developers to restructure their applications to achieve higher performance by using more than one core. In the past, an application provider could simply wait a year for the next generation of faster computer hardware to come out, and all applications would automatically improve in performance. Now, the performance capabilities of processor chips continue to increase, but benefiting from those capabilities requires applications that can use multiple cores.

The computations that were parallelized for serious use during the first wave were generally large enough to be totally impractical for sequential execution and contained large amounts of potential parallelism that could be exploited with (somewhat) reasonable effort. These applications typically featured fairly uniform data parallelism at a fine-grained level, or else they could be decomposed into a large number of coarse-grained blocks of computation that could be executed without too much interaction between them. Many "everyday" applications are harder to decompose, but the advent of multicore processors has elevated the importance of finding parallelism in them, even if the total amount of parallelism found is not as large as in the earlier cases.

Commercially important compute-intensive applications that are not necessarily executed on large "data center" computers include engineering applications such as computer-aided design and simulation; data mining and analysis; 2-dimensional and 3-dimensional image processing for medical applications, graphic designers, gamers, and consumers; and many others. The importance of running these applications with high performance on multicore processors has revived interest in parallelization techniques that were investigated during the first wave but were never widely deployed because it was easier to just wait for the next generation of faster processors to achieve the next round of performance increases.

1.1 Achieving Parallel Execution on Multicore Processors

As a first approach to parallelizing a legacy application for execution on multiple cores, it is tempting to try decomposing the application into large-scale architectural modules, such as "parsing," "processing," and "output," assigning each module to a different core, and setting up a suitable connection, such as a pipeline, between the modules. While this approach may be appealing because it avoids extensive redesign of the application, it has serious scalability limitations as we look forward to processor chips with 8–16 cores or more. The number of large-scale modules that can be identified in an application grows with the size of the application code but not with the size of the application data, so further decomposing an application into more and more modules as the number of cores increases becomes more and more difficult. Moreover, it is very unlikely that the amount of processing required by the different modules will be well balanced, so there are likely to be performance bottlenecks and a majority of the cores may be poorly utilized.

To make efficient use of multicore processors and to be able to continue increasing in performance as processor chips become more powerful, an application really needs to be decomposed in a "data-parallel" manner with parallelism that scales with the size of the computation rather than the size of the application program source code. Since the applications that we are talking about are complex and heterogeneous, a flexible approach to exposing concurrency is required. The data parallelism of these applications will generally not be found in simple inner loops but in more complex and irregular patterns of access to large data structures. The communication and synchronization patterns of such computations usually cannot be mapped out in advance and must instead be managed at run time as they evolve.

The demands of this kind of concurrency are most easily satisfied using a shared-memory MIMD model that can support unplanned patterns of access to shared data at a reasonable cost. Fortunately, this is exactly the computing model that is supported by multicore processor chips. This happy coincidence has revived interest in techniques for shared-memory MIMD parallel computing. A particular discipline that is well suited to the multicore situation is the practice of annotating an application program to expose large amounts of potential concurrency and then letting a run-time task scheduler determine the actual parallel task schedule based on conditions at each moment during the execution of the application. Although there are certainly cases where automated program analysis tools can add annotations based on analysis of the concurrency opportunities in a program, our focus here is on manually placed annotations because this is pretty much the only viable strategy for parallelizing legacy applications of the kind that resisted parallelization in the past.

1.2   Overview of the Paper

This paper looks at a couple of techniques for task scheduling that were investigated in connection with the Multilisp [15,17] and Mul-T [27,28] projects during the first wave of parallel processing research and examines how these techniques are now being, or could be, put to work on multicore processors. A principal goal of these techniques is to reduce the cost of exposing concurrency while still enabling a good parallel execution order to be chosen efficiently at run time.

Although multicore processors are the technological trend that has brought interest back to these ideas, the ideas themselves are equally applicable in any shared-memory MIMD computing system, regardless of whether the processing cores are all on one chip or are distributed across multiple chips. Accordingly, we will informally use the terms "core" and "processor" somewhat interchangeably to mean "a device capable of executing a sequential stream of instructions."

We begin by examining *lazy task creation* implemented using *work-stealing schedulers*. These techniques address the problem of providing concurrency annotations that are inexpensive at run time and therefore can be used aggressively to expose a large number of concurrency opportunities in a program.

Work stealing and lazy task creation are now used in a wide range of systems for concurrent programming, of which perhaps the best known is the family of Cilk systems [6,25], including Cilk-5 [13], Cilk++ [24], and Intel Cilk Plus [19],

Later, we look at *speculative computing* using the *sponsor model*. These techniques are especially helpful for applications that include some kind of search. They provide additional opportunities for parallel execution by spawning and controlling the execution of computations whose results may be useful but are not certain to be needed. Speculative computing support should be thought of as building an additional layer of parallelism opportunities on top of the basic capabilities provided by lazy task creation and work-stealing schedulers. Speculative computing is still not widely used and there are many open issues regarding the best way to implement the sponsor model, but speculative computing opportunities occur in many important applications and improving our ability to use speculative computing is an important problem that deserves more investigation.

Section 2 of this paper gives some examples of parallel programming applications that do not involve speculative computing. Section 3 then discusses the task scheduling problem for such applications and explains the advantages of work stealing and lazy task creation for solving it. The section concludes with a review of how these technologies have been incorporated into contemporary systems. Section 4 discusses the nature of speculative computing and the new scheduling requirements that it entails. The sponsor model is briefly introduced and its strengths and weaknesses are discussed. The section concludes with a review of speculative computing support in some contemporary systems. Finally, Section 5 summarizes the paper and offers a vision of future parallel computing systems that integrate all of the scheduling technologies discussed.

2   Examples of Non-Speculative Parallel Computing

Concurrency in programs can be specified using various constructs, including Multilisp's `future` construct and the fork/join constructs of Cilk and various other languages. This section uses the `future` construct in a few examples of parallel computing that do not require speculative computation.

The expression (`future` X) is the main concurrency construct in Multilisp and Mul-T and may return a result before the evaluation of the expression X has completed [15]. In this case, the returned value is a *future* object that acts as a promise to deliver the value of X when it is known. When the evaluation of X yields a value, the future object *resolves* to that value. In this way, (`future` X) provides concurrency between evaluating X and executing the code that uses the value of X. It is natural to use `future` at all levels of recursion when exploring or operating on a large data structure; in this way, `future` allows the exposure of concurrency that scales with the size of the data.

Strict operations such as addition, which inspect their operands, may be applied to a future object but they *touch* the object, which means that they will block, if necessary, until the future object resolves. However, many operations such as parameter passing and construction of data objects are nonstrict and do not need to block if given an unresolved future.

2.1   Divide-and-Conquer Computations

Divide-and-conquer algorithms offer the most obvious opportunities for parallel computing. A trivial example, shown in Fig. 1, is the `psum-tree` procedure from [28] for summing a property of all leaves of a tree. This procedure uses `future` so that the leaf values for the left-hand child of a node can be summed concurrently with summing the leaf values for the right-hand child. Many divide-and-conquer computations have a similar structure and can be expressed in the same straightforward way. This style of concurrency is also easily expressed using fork/join constructs such as those in Cilk. In Cilk, the *reducer* construct, found in C++-based Cilk implementations, is often useful for combining tasks' results at the join point [24,25].

```
(define (psum-tree tree)
  (if (leaf? tree)
      (leaf-value tree)
      (+ (future (psum-tree (left tree)))
         (psum-tree (right tree)))))
```

Fig. 1. A simple parallel divide-and-conquer program

Many combinatorial enumeration computations, including the famous "N Queens" problem, as well as many dense matrix, exhaustive search, and sorting computations, also fit the divide-and-conquer paradigm.

2.2   Pipelined Computations

For another style of parallel computing, consider the program of Fig. 2, whose `p*` procedure multiplies two dense polynomials, using a representation where the polynomial $a_n x^n + \cdots + a_1 x + a_0$ is represented as a list of coefficients $(a_0\ a_1\ \ldots\ a_n)$. The `p*` procedure uses divide-and-conquer parallelism to multiply the first coefficient of x times the polynomial y concurrently with multiplying the rest of x times y, but the `pc*` and `p+` procedures use `future` to introduce a pipelined style of concurrency in which a caller of `pc*` or `p+` can begin to use the result of the call even before the full computation performed by the call has finished [16]. This pipelining is possible because the `cons` constructor operation is nonstrict and can return its value even before its arguments resolve. In this example as given, the tasks will be very small because the primitive + and * operations on numerical coefficients are fast; however, in other use cases where the coefficients are not simple numerical types, the granularity of the tasks will be coarser.

This pipelined style of computation is not expressible using simple fork/join constructs but it can be a prolific source of concurrency in computations that traverse data structures and build new data structures based on the information

```
(define (p* x y)        ; Polynomial x times polynomial y
  (if (null? x)
      '()
      (p+ (future (pc* (car x) y))
          (cons 0
                (future (p* (cdr x) y))))))

(define (pc* c y)       ; Scalar c times polynomial y
  (if (null? y)
      '()
      (cons (* c (car y))
            (future (pc* c (cdr y))))))

(define (p+ x y)        ; Polynomial x plus polynomial y
  (cond ((null? x) y)
        ((null? y) x)
        (else
          (cons (+ (car x) (car y))
                (future (p+ (cdr x) (cdr y)))))))
```

Fig. 2. A parallel program for multiplying dense polynomials

found. It is not difficult to imagine computations on sparse polynomials, tree rewriting, relational joins, and many others that use a similar concurrency style.

It is worth noting that if we used vectors of coefficients, rather than lists, to represent polynomials, this computation could be programmed using a straightforward divide-and-conquer algorithm. Nevertheless, other computations on inherently richer data structures can still benefit from pipeline parallelism.

2.3 Mostly Functional Programming

The parallel programming examples in Figs. 1 and 2 contain no side-effecting operations, which makes their correctness much easier to understand without considering the details of task scheduling. Generally, as many authors have noted, state-changing operations on objects shared between concurrent tasks bring about the possibility of nondeterminacy and difficulty in verifying that a program will behave correctly under all legal scheduling scenarios. For many computations, however, it is more natural and even more efficient to have some mutable objects that are shared between tasks. We can use the term *mostly functional programming* for a programming style that is largely free of shared mutable objects but does use them occasionally for important coordination purposes. Because it confines the potential nondeterminacy of a computation to a small number of interaction points, this style has much to recommend it for parallel programming, and for the rest of this paper we implicitly assume its use.

As a side note, clever ideas such as Cilk's reducer objects, mentioned above, can sometimes replace nondeterminacy-inducing shared objects, with great benefits to program understandability and reliability. We need as many clever ideas like this as possible.

3 Scheduling for Task-Based Parallel Computing

The requirements for exposing concurrency in an application for execution on a multicore processor are quite different from the classic requirements for thread-based execution using a threading library such as Pthreads [29]. The typical reason for using threads in an application is to ensure that some part of the computation can proceed, or remain responsive, even if another part of the computation is blocked or busy. For example, an application's developer may wish for the application's user interface to remain responsive even though the application is busy updating internal data structures or waiting for a network transmission to complete. Similarly, it may be desirable to continue making progress on a lengthy calculation even while waiting for user input or for one or more programmed input/output operations to complete.

In all of these situations, it is common to organize a computation into a set of threads so that each individual activity within the computation can proceed independently. In this model, it is important that all threads that are not blocked can proceed at some rate, because the whole idea of using threads is to keep all parts of the computation live and active as much as possible. This goal leads to the ideal of *fair scheduling* to guarantee that each unblocked thread can make progress.

3.1 Fair Scheduling Is Not Always Best

Fair scheduling is useful when working with threads, to ensure that semantically distinct parts of a computation can proceed independently, but it can be counterproductive if used for portions of a computation that has been subdivided to provide parallel work for multiple processor cores. Consider, for example, the divide-and-conquer scenario illustrated in Fig. 3, where each node except those at the bottom represents a subcomputation that recursively spawns two more subcomputations. This is the kind of task tree that could result from the psum-tree program of Fig. 1, for example.

If executed sequentially in the standard depth-first manner, this computation will require only $O(D)$ storage for the recursion stack, where D is the depth of the divide-and-conquer tree. If, however, each node is given its own thread and fair scheduling is used for the threads, the storage requirements of this computation will explode since the computation will effectively be performed breadth-first. Depending on the details, all nodes in the tree could be active simultaneously, leading to a storage requirement of $O(2^D)$.

The ideal execution order for this computation on a 4-core processor would involve spawning separate concurrent subcomputations for the first two levels of the tree in breadth-first fashion, so that there are four subcomputations ready to execute in parallel, and then unfolding the tree within each subcomputation

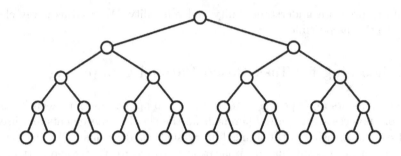

Fig. 3. A divide-and-conquer task tree

in depth-first fashion so as to economize on space usage. Assuming that each subcomputation takes about the same amount of time to execute, this execution order will achieve good utilization of all four cores while at the same time keeping the required storage from growing exponentially.

When using threads to expose concurrency, achieving this ideal execution order requires augmenting the application code with potentially complex tests to determine whether enough threads have been created yet, and to *throttle* the computation by suppressing thread creation and reverting to depth-first execution once enough threads have been created. This is unfortunate for several reasons. First, it mixes hardware-dependent scheduling code with the application code. It would be preferable to have the application code simply describe the computation to be performed, while scheduling details are handled by an orthogonal mechanism. Second, the scheduling code added to the application is fragile and depends on many assumptions. If the number of cores changes, the scheduling code needs to know the new number. If the subcomputations do not all take the same amount of time, the tree depth is not the same for all branches of the computation, or some subcomputations may become blocked waiting for actions by other subcomputations, it can be very difficult to know what decisions to program into the scheduling code. Moreover, if other parts of an overall application are also available to execute in parallel with this divide-and-conquer computation, this too affects the requirements for concurrency in ways that are difficult to address in the scheduling code.

3.2   Threads vs. Tasks

For all of the above reasons, it is better if the application code simply declares as many opportunities for concurrency as possible, and then an efficient scheduling mechanism uses this information to achieve the needed parallelism without causing excessive storage use. To avoid confusion with the thread model discussed above, let us call these basic units of concurrency "tasks."

3.3   Work-Stealing Schedulers

While fair scheduling has several important advantages for threads, it is not a desirable discipline for scheduling tasks. This fact has been recognized at least as far back as the work of Burton and Sleep [8], who described the problem with breadth-first expansion of a divide-and-conquer task tree, as well as its solution by defaulting to depth-first expansion but making pending tasks available to be "stolen" by idle processors. They in turn point to the AMPS project [21] as one of their sources of inspiration.

This work-stealing approach was also developed and implemented in the Multilisp project, and timing results for various benchmark programs were reported [15]. An impressive proof of bounds on the time and space requirements for computations scheduled using work stealing was published by Blumofe and Leiserson [7]. This work formed the basis for using work stealing in the Cilk system [6,25] and many systems that have followed.

In the basic work-stealing model, a program is thought of as containing various potential fork points at which one or more parallel tasks can be spun off if there are idle processors (or, in the modern case, processor cores) available to execute them. When execution reaches a fork point, a "work generator" object is pushed onto a double-ended queue, or deque, and then execution proceeds to the leftmost child node of the fork point, in exactly the same order as a sequential execution that would walk the task tree depth-first from left to right. Each processor has its own deque of work generators. Task execution on a processor may lead to further work generators being pushed onto the processor's deque, leading ultimately to a structure similar to that shown in Fig. 4.

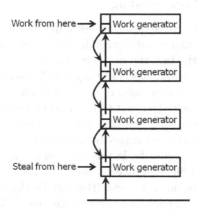

Fig. 4. A work generation deque used by a work-stealing scheduler

When a processor finishes executing a task, the processor uses the work generator at the tail of the deque (shown at the top in Fig. 4) to get the next task to execute. If the work generator is exhausted, it is popped off of the deque and the next work generator is used. If a processor is idle and its deque is empty, then it looks for work to steal from another processor's deque. When stealing, however, it removes the work generator from the *head* of the other processor's deque and uses it to generate work. This *steal* operation is shown in Fig. 5, which shows what happens when a *thief* processor P_2 steals work from a *victim* processor P_1. The steal entails some cost for synchronization and for increased cache-coherence and/or communication traffic, but it prevents a processor from lying idle.

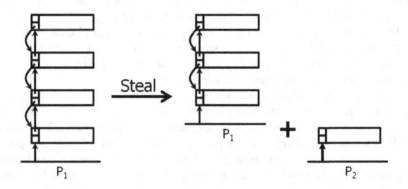

Fig. 5. A thief processor P_2 steals work from a victim processor P_1

3.4   Optimality of Work Stealing

Intuitively, it is best to amortize the cost of stealing by maximizing the size of the stolen unit of work. By taking stolen work from the head of a victim processor's deque rather than from the tail, the work-stealing strategy improves the chances of stealing a large unit of work, especially in a divide-and-conquer task tree such as that of Fig. 3. Stealing larger units of work also potentially improves locality of reference, since it can be hoped that the execution of a large block of work will be more self-contained, creating and later using its own private data structures.

While these hypothesized advantages are attractive, it is not obvious that they can be stated or proven rigorously. It was thus quite impressive when Blumofe and Leiserson [7] were able to prove useful time and space bounds for work stealing based on assumptions that are faithful to the character of many realistic applications. Their proof applies to computations that follow the "dag model of multithreading" in which a computation can be organized into a directed acyclic graph of tasks such as that shown in Fig. 6. The proof is further restricted to "fully strict" computations, which include fork-join computations but not certain task graphs that can occur in other types of computations. (For example, the pipeline-parallel polynomial multiplication program of Fig. 2 does not generate a fully strict task graph.)

Some key parameters of a computation can be defined based on the dag model:

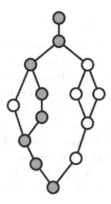

Fig. 6. A dag of concurrent tasks; the tasks on the critical path are shaded

- T_1, also known as the *work*, is the total number of instructions in the dag.
- T_∞, also known as the *span*, is the number of instructions in the critical path.

Based on these concepts, Blumofe and Leiserson proved worst-case bounds for the time T_P and space S_P required when the computation is executed using a work-stealing scheduler on P processors, with the following results:

$$T_P \leq T_1/P + O(T_\infty)$$
$$S_P \leq S_1 P$$

As an extra benefit, a bound on communication was also proven.

The equation for T_P contains the expected terms. Even if the work in the dag is divided evenly between all the processors, we cannot expect that the time T_P will be less than T_1/P because that would imply a speedup by a factor of more than P on P processors. Similarly, we cannot expect the time T_P to be less than T_∞ because that would require a magical ability to execute some of the operations on the critical path in parallel with each other, which would contradict the definition of a critical path. In this light, the result for T_P is really a very good result. Asymptotically, it is the best result that any scheduling algorithm could be expected to achieve.

Similarly, the guarantee that S_P is at most P times the required space on one processor is a very strong result. It implies that the storage that needs to be added to a system when processors are added is, at most, proportional to the number of processors. It is hard to imagine expecting a scheduling algorithm to do better than that.

While the assumptions made in this proof do not apply to every task-based parallel computation, in combination with empirical observations that work-stealing schedulers frequently lead to good parallel speedups, the proof does provide a lot of confidence that work stealing is a reasonable scheduling approach and shows that it is asymptotically optimal in an important set of cases.

3.5   Lazy Task Creation

The asymptotic benefits of work-stealing schedulers do not take away from the importance of implementing the primitive task-management operations efficiently. The cheaper the basic operations on the work deque can be made, the more aggressively a programmer can decorate an application program with potential fork points, exposing the largest number of opportunities for parellel execution. If we assume that a program has enough concurrency to keep all the available processors (or cores) busy most of the time, we can assume that steal operations will be comparatively infrequent, and thus the most important operations to optimize are those that push work generators onto the work generation deque and those that use and pop the work generators when no stealing is happening.

The Mul-T project [27], a successor to Multiisp, adopted a goal of making the pushing and popping of work for the `future` construct (see Section 2) "no more expensive than a procedure call." In a simple implementation, every time a (`future` X) expression is executed, a future object and a task to calculate X will both be created. The technique of *lazy task creation* optimizes this operation by deferring the creation of the future object and the task until a steal operation occurs. From the work-stealing perspective, sequential execution of (`future` X) proceeds directly into the evaluation of X, but the associated work generator creates the future object and spawns a task that executes the continuation of the `future` expression, using the future object as a proxy for the actual value of X. If no stealing occurs, these work generator operations will be skipped.

In addition to economizing on the cost of creating future objects, the lazy task creation implementation in Mul-T further reduced the cost of `future` by merging the work generation deque into the call stack and adopting a stack frame format for `future` expressions that includes linking and synchronization fields that enable cutting the stack during a steal operation and moving the base of the stack to a new processor [28]. Fig. 7 shows a call stack including several of these frames, and Fig. 8 shows how a steal operation is performed using this data structure.

The lazy task creation stack includes the minimum bookkeeping information that is needed for implementing the steal operation. This information consists of pointers associated with the stack that point to the work generator frames (referred to in [28] as *lazy continuations*) that are closest to the base and to the top of the stack, along with pointers in each lazy continuation that point to the next higher and lower lazy continuations in the stack. (The lazy continuations are shown as thick gray lines in the figures.) This doubly linked list of pointers to frames in the stack effectively implements the work generation deque.

When no steal occurs, processing of a `future` expression begins by simply building a lazy continuation on the stack and updating the pointers to link it into the doubly linked list, and ends by unlinking the lazy continuation and restoring the stack to its previous condition. A steal operation breaks the stack at the deepest lazy continuation, moving the base of the stack to the thief processor, creating the future object, and letting execution continue on the thief processor

Fig. 7. A lazy task creation stack including several work generator stack frames

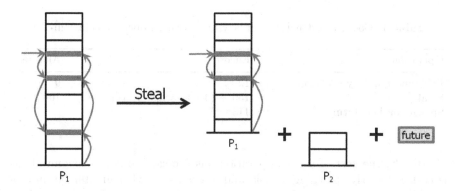

Fig. 8. A lazy task creation steal operation where thief processor P_2 steals work from victim processor P_1

using the future object as a proxy for the value that will be computed on the victim processor. When the victim processor finally returns from the bottommost stack frame on its stack, the value returned will be put into the future object. There is a potential race condition between popping a lazy continuation and having the same lazy continuation stolen by another processor. For this reason, a synchronization operation is needed when popping a lazy continuation; details are found in [28]. The lazy task creation concept can be generalized beyond the case of `future` to include any work-stealing implementation that defers the creation of synchronization objects until a steal operation occurs and integrates the work generation deque with the processor stack.

Lazy task creation for Mul-T was implemented both on an Encore Multimax multiprocessor and the MIT Alewife machine [1]. Table 1 gives the cost of the lazy task creation operations on each of these platforms [28]. (For low-level optimization reasons, the data structures supporting the lazy task creation stack were not organized exactly as in Fig. 7, but the overall concept was the same. Interested readers are referred to [28].)

The cost of the simple case, where a lazy continuation is created but never stolen, is 12 instructions on the Encore and 9 on Alewife, which was designed to support lazy task creation efficiently. This number is certainly within the same order of magnitude as the cost of a procedure call, suggesting that the Mul-T project at least came close to its performance goal for this operation. Compared with the cost of eagerly spawning a new task and enqueuing it for execution, which was 118 instructions on the Encore, we can see that the lazy task creation mechanism provided a major improvement in the minimum performance cost of concurrency annotations. (The Alewife implementation does not have a cost for eager task spawning because it used lazy task creation exclusively, and its cost for lazy task creation does not include a term that depends on the stack size because a stack representation was used that avoided the need to copy the base of the stack during a steal operation.)

Table 1. Cost (in instructions) of lazy task creation operations in Mul-T

Operation	Encore	Alewife
Push and pop lazy continuation	12	9
Steal	150 + (4 for each word copied)	100
Spawn non-lazy future	118	

Naturally, the cost of a steal operation has the same order of magnitude as the cost of eagerly spawning a task, and is even somewhat greater because of the additional complexity of taking apart an existing stack, but the numbers still show that we could afford to steal up to 50% of all lazy continuations and still pay a lower overall cost for parallelism management than if all tasks had been spawned eagerly. In a typical situation where the available concurrency exceeds the number of processors (or cores), the fraction of lazy continuations that are eventually stolen is usually far less than 50%, as shown by measurements of various example applications on Mul-T [28]. Thus, lazy task creation makes the exposure of concurrency cheap enough to allow programmers to aggressively expose large-scale, data-dependent concurrency in application programs.

The task graphs for computations that use **future** are not always "fully strict," so the optimality proof for work stealing by Blumofe and Leiserson [7] does not always apply to this case. Nevertheless, the performance measurements on Mul-T show reasonable behavior for the applications tested [28].

One disadvantage of the lazy task creation mechanism is that it leads to a "cactus stack" structure [18] when continuations are stolen. As implemented on the Encore and shown in Fig. 8, supporting this stack entails moving segments of stack from one memory address to another. Legacy subroutine libraries and calling conventions on standard processors do not anticipate stack frames being moved, and often store pointers to data on the stack which will become incorrect if a stack frame is moved. This becomes a problem if there is ever a call from inside a legacy library back out to application code that may include concurrency constructs [25]. Such calls can easily occur if a legacy library receives arguments that are pointers to callback procedures.

The Mul-T implementations did not use legacy libraries in this way, so they did not suffer from this limitation, but Cilk does allow application code to use legacy libraries. Early Cilk systems avoided the cactus-stack problem by forbidding program structures in which libraries call back into application code. Intel Cilk Plus [19] allows such callbacks at the cost of using multiple linear stacks to support the cactus stack [25], and the Cilk-M research prototype uses thread-local memory mapping to avoid moving stack frames to new virtual memory addresses [23].

3.6 Work Stealing and Lazy Task Creation Today

Task scheduling by work stealing has become mainstream, used by many systems including Cilk, Intel Threading Building Blocks, X10, Fortress, Phoenix, and others. Of these systems, Cilk has the longest pedigree, having originated in 1993 and evolved through many iterations to current systems including Cilk++ [24] and Intel Cilk Plus [19].

Cilk began as an extension of the C programming language, augmented with **spawn** and **sync** annotations to support fork-join concurrency, eventually adopting lazy task creation for task management [25]. The Cilk++ dialect [24], based on C++ rather than C, also introduced a simple cilk_for keyword for parallelizing loops, as well as *reducer hyperobjects* for combining results from parallel tasks without introducing locks. Cilk++ ultimately led to the Intel Cilk Plus product [19]. The various Cilk versions have served as the base for implementing large-scale applications such as the chess programs StarTech, *Socrates, and Cilkchess.

Intel Threading Building Blocks [33,32,20] uses a work-stealing model when tasks are spawned using the continuation-passing idiom. OpenMP also supports task parallelism by means of the task directive [4,9]. There is no fair scheduling guarantee for tasks, and tasks that are designated as "untied" are available to be moved between processors. This design opens the way for using a work-stealing scheduler, although the specification does not appear to require it [4].

Various research languages have also incorporated the work-stealing and lazy task creation concepts. Work stealing has been used in the XWS package [11] that was implemented for the X10 language [10]. Fortress [34,3] also provides fork-join parallelism based on tasks that are not scheduled fairly, and uses work stealing to move tasks between processors. Phoenix [35] uses lazy task creation in a parallel processing system in which processors can join and leave the computation dynamically.

One very useful property of scheduling by work stealing, exploited by these systems, is that when an application containing concurrency annotations runs on one processor, it runs in the same sequential order as an unannotated program. During application debugging, this property makes it easier to distinguish fundamental algorithmic bugs from bugs caused by race conditions: if an execution on one processor produces the same incorrect result that is produced by a parallel execution, then there is a bug in the basic algorithm. Otherwise, there is a problem with the way the concurrency annotations have been added. Race-detection tools such as Cilkscreen [24,25] capitalize on this property to detect potential data races just from sequentially executing an application with instrumented code. Programming in a mostly functional style (see Section 2.3) that minimizes the use of state changes to shared objects generally will also help avoid programming bugs caused by nondeterminacy.

4   Speculative Computing

The task management techniques discussed above are implicitly based on the assumption that all computations in a program are needed, and focus on how to exploit concurrency between those *mandatory* operations as effectively as possible. Many applications also have opportunities for parallelism by executing *speculative* computations that are not certain to be needed, but have some probability of being needed. Further performance improvements are often available by spawning speculative computations to execute in parallel with the rest of an application, without waiting for proof that the speculative computations will be needed. Supporting speculative computations in a parallel system without losing the benefits of a task-based, work-stealing scheduler presents several challenges, which are discussed in this section.

4.1   Sources of Speculative Parallelism

Opportunities for speculative parallelism are especially common in applications that involve searching or heuristics. The potential sources of speculative parallelism in applications fall into several related, and somewhat overlapping, categories. The following discussion follows the framework laid out by Osborne [30,31].

Multiple Approaches. Perhaps the simplest category of speculative parallelism involves trying multiple approaches or strategies for solving a problem in parallel. For example, many paths through a maze or graph can be tried in parallel, or different strategies for factoring an algebraic expression, solving an equation, or proving a theorem can be tried in parallel. These problems have the property that as soon as any of the alternative approaches succeeds, the others can be abandoned.

Multiple-approach speculative parallelism is often expressed using the *parallel AND* and *parallel OR* control structures. These operators have been defined in various ways, but a simple definition of parallel AND is that the expression (pand X_1 X_2 ... X_n) returns false if any of the operand expressions X_i returns false and otherwise returns the value of X_n. Parallel OR can be defined so that (por X_1 X_2 ... X_n) returns false if all the X_i return false, and otherwise returns the value of the first expression X_i that does not evaluate to false.

The corresponding sequential and and or operators traditionally work from left to right, evaluating operands until it becomes clear what the value of the and or or expression will be (for example, until a non-false operand value is found in an or expression). When this point is reached, evaluation of the remaining operands is skipped and the appropriate value is returned as the value of the and or or expression.

In the parallel case, we can extend the sequential execution order by considering the leftmost operand of pand or por to be a mandatory computation but also spawning speculative computations for the remaining operands. Considering the case of pand, if the mandatory operand finishes evaluating and yields a true value, then the leftmost remaining operand becomes mandatory; and if any operand (not necessarily the mandatory one) yields false, then the pand expression should return false and all of its remaining subcomputations should be canceled. Analogous reasoning applies to the por construct.

A very simple example of multiple-approach computation is the tree-equality problem [30], where a program must determine whether two trees have the same structure and equal values at their corresponding leaf nodes. (In this case, the term "multiple approach" is easiest to understand if we suppose that the problem to be solved is proving that the trees are *not* equal!) An obvious sequential implementation of this computation is shown in Fig. 9.

```
(define (tree-equal a b)
  (cond ((leaf? a) (leaf-equal? a b))
        ((leaf? b) false)
        (else
         (and (tree-equal (car a) (car b))
              (tree-equal (cdr a) (cdr b))))))
```

Fig. 9. A sequential procedure that tests for tree equality

Simply replacing and with pand leads to the speculative parallel version shown in Fig. 10. This parallel program actually has the capability of doing less work than the sequential version—for example, in the case where the car trees are equal and very large, while the cdr trees are trivially different—but of course it is also possible that the parallel version will do more work. This behavior is often seen in speculative computing situations.

The simple pand notation used here covers up many important issues that need to be addressed. For example, when executing mandatory and speculative operands of pand, further pand operators will be encountered, having their own mandatory and speculative operands. Eventually we may get a whole tree of

```
(define (ptree-equal a b)
  (cond ((leaf? a) (leaf-equal? a b))
        ((leaf? b) false)
        (else
         (pand (ptree-equal (car a) (car b))
               (ptree-equal (cdr a) (cdr b))))))
```

Fig. 10. A speculative parallel procedure that tests for tree equality

computations, where each arc in the tree is marked as either mandatory or speculative relative to its parent. How should we prioritize a computation that is reached by, say, a path that is labeled as mandatory-speculative-speculative relative to a path that is labeled as speculative-mandatory-speculative? This and many other important issues were noted by Osborne [30] and are briefly reviewed in the remainder of this paper. Osborne also described and studied a larger multiple-approach example: the EMYCIN benchmark originally developed by Krall and McGehearty [26].

Order-Based Speculation. A second speculative computing style may be termed "order-based" speculative computing [30,31]. This category includes branch-and-bound and alpha-beta pruning algorithms. Here, we are generally not looking for just any solution, but for a solution that is optimal according to some metric. Even if the algorithm finds a solution that looks pretty good, all other possible solutions need to be explored at least to the point where it becomes clear that they cannot possibly be better than an already found solution. Since many solutions will need to be explored, at least to some point, exploring these solutions can be a rich source of parallelism. Often there are heuristics that predict which solutions are likely to be the best, however. Exploration of those solutions needs to be given priority and not starved out by exploration of less promising solutions.

A classic example of this style of speculation is the branch-and-bound solution of the traveling salesman problem [30,31]. We may envision the solution of this problem as a tree-structured search problem similar to the "N Queens" problem, with a task responsible for further developing each partially developed path (typically by spawning more tasks), except that a task should be abandoned as soon as the cost of its path exceeds the cost of an already known complete path. Also, it is beneficial to focus system resources on the partial solutions that look most promising. Osborne used a heuristic of giving the highest priority to partial paths that have the lowest value for the total cost of the partial path divided by the number of nodes in the partial path [30].

Osborne also investigated problems that combine aspects of order-based and multiple-approach speculation such as the Boyer theorem-proving benchmark [14] and finding solutions for the Eight-puzzle, a children's sliding piece puzzle [30,31].

Speculative Precomputing. A third category of speculative parallelism involves precomputing values that may be needed in a computation, but are not yet known to be definitely needed. One example of this kind would be a producer-consumer situation where a producer produces a stream of values to be consumed by a consumer. If resources are idle, they can be used to continue executing the producer to produce more values even before it is known for sure that the consumer will demand them [30,31].

4.2 Requirements for Speculative Task Scheduling

Parallelism from speculative computations is of lower quality than that from mandatory computations because it is possible that a speculative computation will not contribute to the application's overall result. For this reason, scheduling should ensure that speculative tasks do not take resources from mandatory tasks that are available for execution.

Just as mandatory tasks have a higher worth than speculative tasks, some speculative tasks may have a higher worth than others, and scheduling should take these relationships into account. Measuring the worth of a speculative task is itself a challenging problem that could benefit from more research, but intuitively we expect it to depend on the probability that a speculative computation will prove to be necessary as well as the cost of the speculative computation. Both the benefit and the cost may only be known uncertainly, and as we saw above in the case of pand and por, the estimated worth of a computation may change as execution progresses and more information becomes available.

Considerable past research in speculative computing has focused on the idea of using garbage collection to keep an unneeded speculative computation from continuing and consuming unbounded resources [5], but this is not a very efficient way to focus computing resources on the most important tasks. When a speculative task becomes *irrelevant*—effectively, when its worth drops to zero—its execution should be stopped as soon as possible. Waiting for the next garbage collection is much too long.

Similarly, it is important to adjust scheduling policy on an ongoing basis to reflect changes in the estimated worth of speculative tasks, as well as changes in the number of available tasks at the various levels of worth. Low-worth speculative tasks should not use resources to the exclusion of higher-worth tasks, and speculative tasks should not use resources to the exclusion of mandatory tasks. Adherence to these principles may, for example, require processors to suspend execution of a speculative task when a mandatory or higher-worth speculative task becomes available. Garbage collection still has a role to play, but only for the final reclamation of resources for speculative tasks that are known to have become irrelevant.

These are not easy requirements to satisfy, especially because the scheduling operations involved must be efficient enough that they do not waste whatever benefit is gained by exploiting speculative computing in the first place. This is probably why there has not been much progress in supporting speculative computing in the parallel computing frameworks that are currently in wide use.

4.3   Applications at the System Level

Another reason for being interested in speculative computing support is that many of the speculative computing requirements, such as the ability to stop the execution of irrelevant computations and the ability to allocate resources between higher-worth and lower-worth computations, have analogs at the operating system level. Users interacting with a computer often ask for multiple computations to be performed. One computation may be the "foreground" job that is the user's primary focus at the moment, while others are "background" jobs that should execute as long as they don't interfere with the foreground job. Usually users want the foreground job to have first priority for computing resources, while background jobs should proceed as quickly as possible without slowing down the foreground job. This is not unlike a multiple-approach or precomputing scenario for speculative computing, though the relationships that need to be expressed are probably not as complex.

Also, users can change their minds and cancel a job after it has started, or a job may need to be canceled after an exception occurs in one of its subtasks. This is similar to the speculative computing case when a computation is found to be irrelevant.

Scheduling jobs on a server that has parallel processing capabilities also has points of similarity with speculative computing. Whenever these jobs have different priorities or deadlines, we will want the scheduling mechanism on the server to focus as many resources as possible on the highest-priority jobs and avoid starving them in favor of executing lower-priority jobs.

4.4   The Sponsor Model

One way to attack the problem of speculative parallelism is to represent the goal of each speculative subcomputation explicitly as an object that contains the information needed to make correct scheduling decisions. This approach was explored by Osborne [30,31] in the Multilisp project, who called these objects *sponsors* following the terminology introduced by Kornfeld and Hewitt [22]. The original sponsor concept was that a sponsor is a source of energy to run a computation, much as a research sponsor is the source of resources for carrying out a research project. The sponsor would monitor the sponsored computation, adjusting the resources allocated to it according to the results being generated by the computation as well as any pertinent news about other computations in the system.

Figure 11 illustrates the structure of a computation using the sponsor model. The sponsors are represented by the triangular objects in the diagram and the tasks are represented by rectangles. We can see that generally each speculative (or mandatory) subcomputation can consist of multiple tasks that are all governed by the same sponsor. Sponsors can also govern other sponsors that represent subcomputations of the sponsored computation. These subcomputations can be mandatory or speculative relative to the sponsored computation at the next higher level, which itself could be mandatory or speculative relative to the

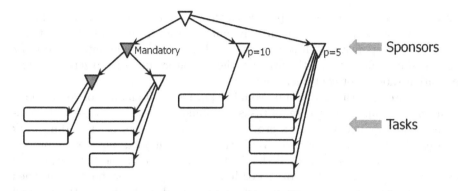

Fig. 11. A collection of speculative and mandatory tasks governed by sponsors

overall computation. In the figure, the sponsors of mandatory computations are shaded.

At this level of detail, the sponsor model is quite general and can represent pretty much any speculative computing scenario, but of course the sponsor model cannot be implemented without deciding what parameters are actually represented in the sponsor objects, how they are managed, and how they are used in scheduling decisions. This is one of the major areas in which the sponsor model needs further work, but for now let us suppose that each sponsor includes a numerical priority used for scheduling decisions, with larger priority values indicating computations of greater worth. In Fig. 11, these priority values are represented using the letter 'p'.

The investigation by Osborne [30,31] confined itself to studying multiple-approach and order-based speculation using numerical priorities of this kind, where a higher-priority task would completely pre-empt a lower-priority task (subject to possible time lags while the scheduling mechanism discovers that a pre-emptable lower-priority task exists). For example, in the traveling salesman solver the priority of each sponsor was set to the negative of that sponsor's partial path cost, divided by the number of nodes in the partial path. However, it is obvious that in some cases scheduling policies other than simple pre-emptive priority-based scheduling will be required, such as fair scheduling that allocates some percentage of effort between a sponsor's subcomputations. Further comments on this point appear in Section 4.6.

4.5   Using the Sponsor Model

In the presence of speculative computing and sponsors, the scheduling rules change. Within a sponsored subcomputation, we still prefer depth-first execution of tasks except when a steal occurs, but in addition, processors should always work on the highest-worth available tasks. This means that if a processor is busy with a task and a higher-worth task becomes available, work on the lower-worth task should be suspended so that the higher-worth task can be executed. Sponsors may also dynamically gain or lose priority, so task scheduling needs to be responsive to these events as well. Finally, if a computation loses its sponsorship—effectively, if the worth of the computation drops to zero—then its execution should not continue.

Taken literally, this philosophy could require a large amount of communication. In the simple case where all tasks are mandatory, scheduling-related communication only occurs when a processor becomes idle and needs to find work to steal from another processor. With the sponsor model, any time a processor creates new stealable work, it should determine whether another processor is currently executing a task of lower worth. If so, that processor should be notified to suspend execution of its current task so it can steal the higher-worth work and execute it instead. Shared data structures that indicate the priority level of tasks currently being executed, to support such notification decisions, can be expensive to maintain and access, increasing the cost of task-management operations that should be inexpensive, such as pushing a lazy continuation. Similarly, when a sponsor's worth changes, processors executing computations under that sponsor should reconsider whether to continue executing the same computation or switch to something different. To keep the cost of scheduling operations within reasonable bounds, it may be necessary to back off from the ideal scheduling policy for speculative computations and implement an approximate policy instead. The best way to accomplish this is a question that certainly needs further investigation.

When a new task is spawned, by default its sponsor should be the same as its parent task's sponsor. However, control structures that create speculative subcomputations need to extend the sponsor network to represent the relationship between the various speculative subcomputations.

Parallel AND/OR with Sponsors. Fig. 12 shows how the sponsor network should change when a parallel OR construct is encountered. (The ideas used in the case of parallel AND are similar.) A new sub-sponsor is created for each branch of the OR, and each of the new sub-sponsors is subordinated to the sponsor of the computation that has executed the parallel OR. The sub-sponsor responsible for the first subcomputation is made mandatory (relative to its parent sponsor) because it is known that this value will be needed in order to determine the value of the parallel OR. The other sponsors should be marked as speculative, with priorities that drop from left to right, since the second subcomputation is more likely to be needed than the third, and so on.

When any of the branches finishes, the other sub-sponsors should be updated accordingly. For example, if any branch yields a non-false value, then all tasks to its right should be downgraded to irrelevant, because it is known that their results will not be used. On the other hand, if the mandatory branch yields a false value, then the next branch to its right should be upgraded to mandatory (relative to the sponsor of the overall parallel OR computation).

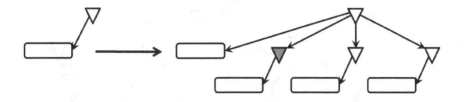

Fig. 12. Sponsor network generated by parallel OR operation

This discussion does not say what the priorities of the new sub-sponsors should be. Of course these priorities can be set using an arbitrary "one size fits all" strategy such as giving the highest speculative priority to the second operand, a lower priority to the third operand, and so on, but the por operator could also support annotations specifying the priorities to be used. It is hard to say more than this until a range of multiple-approach applications have been studied and the best priority structure for each has been determined.

Task Blocking and Sponsors. One of the problems that can occur with priority-based scheduling is the *priority inversion* problem when a higher-priority task H blocks waiting for a lower-priority task L to complete some action. In the Multilisp context, this could happen when H waits for the value of a future object that is being computed by L, or when H needs to obtain a lock that is currently held by L. In the sponsor model, this problem can be solved by having H's sponsor temporarily add its sponsorship to L, effectively elevating the priority of L [30,31]. Fig. 13 shows an example of this situation, where the priority 10 sponsor of a blocked task adds its sponsorship to a formerly priority 5 task (shown lightly shaded) that must execute before the blocked task can proceed.

Depending on how much is known about how to satisfy the condition that is blocking the high-priority task H, H's sponsor could add its sponsorship directly to a task that will satisfy the condition (as shown in Fig. 13) or to the sponsor of a whole subcomputation that will satisfy the condition. This latter situation could occur, for example, if H is waiting for a future object that will contain the result of a parallel OR computation. Given an effective mechanism for adjusting task schedules in response to changes in sponsor priorities, the above technique will automatically solve the priority inversion problem. It is important to note that this strategy does require enough bookkeeping so that any time a task blocks waiting for a condition to be satisfied, the task or sponsor that is responsible for satisfying the condition can be identified and sponsored so it will make progress.

4.6 Challenges for the Sponsor Model

Although the sponsor model is surely general enough to represent a wide range of speculative computing scenarios, some major challenges must be addressed before it can be put into widespread use.

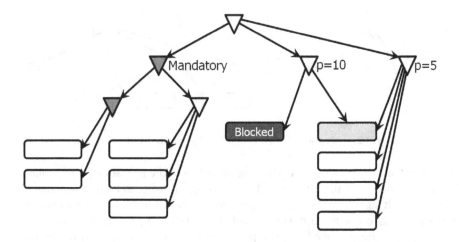

Fig. 13. Sponsor network generated when a task blocks, waiting for another task

The first of these challenges concerns the range of task scheduling policies that a sponsor can employ. The examples above have assumed a simple pre-emptive priority system: given two sponsors A and B, either A's tasks should always take precedence over B's, B's tasks should always take precedence over A's, or both are at the same level and therefore any ordering of A's tasks relative to B's is acceptable. However, in certain types of search, the optimal approach involves dividing processing resources fairly between A's tasks and B's, for example so that A's tasks will get a certain given percentage of the available resources and B's will get another given percentage. This can be the best approach when it is expected that one of two approaches to a problem could yield an answer fairly quickly but we don't know in advance which approach will be the best. In such a situation, we don't want to work exclusively on A's tasks for a long time if it turns out that B's tasks would have yielded an answer quickly. In addition to priority scheduling and fair resource sharing, are there other kinds of scheduling policies that also need to be implementable using the sponsor model? This question could use more thought.

There is also the question of what "resources" are controlled by sponsors. The discussion above implicitly assumes that processing time is the main resource of interest, so a sponsor is mainly in charge of monitoring and deciding how processing time is used. However, memory space is also an important resource that may need to be controlled in some situations.

The second challenge concerns the best way to represent a sponsor's attributes so it can be compared to other sponsors for scheduling purposes. Schedulers based on numerical priorities and real-time deadlines have often been built in the past. We can also consider defining the worth of a computation as a cost/benefit ratio, as discussed above. Each of these metrics has advantages and disadvantages, some of which are discussed by Osborne [30,31].

The third challenge involves defining the "combining rules" to use in the sponsor network when sponsors sponsor other sponsors. Whatever attribute values are chosen to characterize a sponsor, there has to be a rule for deriving the effective attribute values for every sponsor from its position in the network. For example, suppose sponsors have numerical priorities and there is a sponsor S_7 with priority 7 that has a child sponsor $S_{7,5}$ whose priority is 5 relative to S_7, and then there is another sponsor S_5 with priority 5 that has a child sponsor $S_{5,7}$ whose priority is 7 relative to S_5. Now if there is a task $T_{7,5}$ sponsored by $S_{7,5}$ and another task $T_{5,7}$ sponsored by $S_{5,7}$, what priority relationship should exist between these two tasks? A case can be made that $T_{7,5}$ should get priority because it is part of a higher-priority top-level computation, but this conclusion needs to be studied to determine whether it makes sense in general.

Correctly addressing the above challenges requires being able to explain how to handle a wide range of practical speculative computing problems by defining sponsor networks with the right attributes. For each of several important kinds of problems (branch and bound, alpha-beta pruning, parallel AND/OR, etc.) there should be an explanation of how to set up the sponsor network for that kind of problem, along with some kind of proof or demonstration that a good schedule will result.

In addition to defining the semantics of sponsors, as discussed above, an efficient implementation approach must be developed. This implementation must address challenges such as efficiently propagating sponsorship upgrades and downgrades through the sponsor network and efficiently notifying processors about the existence of high-priority work that they should steal. The basic efficiency benefits of work stealing and lazy task creation need to be preserved as much as possible, or else programmers will have to become stingier in identifying opportunities for parallelism, which in turn may result in less concurrency available to exploit.

A final challenge involves correctly closing down and deleting tasks that have become irrelevant. The details depend on the source language used for programming, but obviously there are situations, such as when a task holds a lock, in which it is not correct to just stop execution and delete all traces of the task as soon as it is declared to be irrelevant. One interesting idea is to use the mechanism for avoiding priority inversions to clean up a task's use of shared resources: any held locks or other resources that need cleaning up can have a pointer to the task which will clean them up if it continues to execute, and if these resources are ever needed elsewhere in the computation, that task (even if otherwise irrelevant) can be sponsored for as long as it takes to clean them up. Also, using a mostly functional programming style will help minimize the number of shared mutable objects that need this kind of treatment; for applications whose use of shared mutable objects is significant, a transactional approach to updating these objects may provide a good framework for doing the necessary cleanups when a computation is declared irrelevant.

It is probably best to rely on a garbage collector for the job of finally deleting the storage used by irrelevant tasks. This will ensure that a task is never deleted while there is still a chance that it might be reawakened to clean up a resource.

4.7 Speculative Computing Today

Most current systems provide some support for programming speculative computations, which testifies to the importance of this issue. The support that is provided in these systems is much simpler than the general sponsor model, however.

Cilk-4 introduced `inlet` and `abort` keywords [13,25] for speculative computing support, which is fairly important for the chess-playing applications that were one of the major showcases for the Cilk technology [12]. Inlets provide a way to execute computations in a parent task when a child task returns a value, and `abort` may be executed within an inlet procedure so that the arrival of a value from one subcomputation kills off other subcomputations rendered irrelevant by the arrival of that value. The Cilk runtime system thus provides a mechanism for killing irrelevant computations but does not provide control over how resources are allocated between competing speculative subcomputations.

Intel Threading Building Blocks [33,32,20] includes the concept of "enqueued" tasks, which are scheduled in a "first-come first-serve" order, which approximates fair scheduling. The availability of enqueued tasks along with "spawned" tasks which are executed in depth-first order provides a small amount of control over scheduling, which is potentially useful for speculative computing. Threading Building Blocks also includes the concept of "task_group_context nodes," which have some similarities with sponsors. Each task_group_context node is associated with a computation or subcomputation, and the nodes are organized into a tree whose structure mirrors the nesting of subcomputations. When an exception occurs in a subcomputation, the remaining tasks that belong to that subcomputation are canceled and then the exception is rethrown to the caller that is waiting for the subcomputation's result. Like Cilk's `abort` mechanism, this provides a way to cancel irrelevant computations but it does not provide control over how speculative computations are scheduled relative to each other.

Fortress [34,3] includes a `spawn` construct that creates threads that are scheduled fairly with respect to each other. Implicit tasks that are created within these threads are also scheduled fairly with respect to each other. This again provides a building block for speculative computing but with only a very limited degree of control over scheduling. X10 [10] also addresses the exception propagation problem by means of a `finish` statement that waits for all activity in a subcomputation to terminate. This statement serves as a point for rethrowing, if an exception was generated anywhere in the subcomputation.

Although not specifically aimed at speculative computing, there has been a whole subculture of research projects looking at how to share a multiprocessor between parallel jobs. The A-STEAL algorithm [2], developed in the Cilk research project, is an example. It divides the processors of a multiprocessor machine among the jobs that are asking for resources, adjusting the number of processors assigned to each job based on the job's demonstrated ability to fully use the processors assigned to it. Algorithms similar to A-STEAL could be an effective way to enable a set of speculative computations to share a machine with some degree of fairness.

There is a lot of evidence that speculative computing is an important idea, judging from the fact that every parallel processing system that has been put out for real, general-purpose applications includes at least some support for it. However, none of the systems surveyed provides a built-in capability for scheduling different tasks according to their worth. While there are still many important open questions about the sponsor model, it appears expressive enough to handle speculative computing requirements in a much more principled way than today's parallel computing systems. If reasonable answers can be found to the many open questions about sponsors, it would be very appealing to have a parallel computing system that uses lazy task creation to manage low-level tasks and uses sponsors for the higher-level management of speculative subcomputations. Such a structure could even provide benefits at the operating system level by providing a principled framework for allocating resources between tasks that belong to different user-level jobs. Can sponsors efficiently provide such a useful, general approach to the speculative computing problem? More investigation will be needed in order to find out.

5   Conclusion

With the advent of multicore processors, parallel computing has emerged after a long gestation period and is now a vital technology for improving the performance of many everyday applications. This development has brought renewed interest to various technologies, developed in earlier eras of parallel computing research, for exploiting shared-memory MIMD systems.

Effective and inexpensive task scheduling is one of the principal requirements for successful parallel computing. The space and time benefits of work-stealing scheduling and lazy task creation, developed and prototyped during the 1980s, have now been recognized and these approaches have been incorporated into systems that can handle "industrial strength" parallel computations.

While these ideas are effective for a wide range of applications, they do not fully address the needs of applications that involve search or heuristic problem solving. Achieving the best performance for these applications on a multicore or multiprocessor system requires exploiting speculative computing, in which some tasks are executed even before it is certain that their results will be required. Various contemporary systems for parallel computing incorporate features to support speculative computing, but these features are often ad hoc and provide only part of the control over scheduling that is needed in speculative applications.

The sponsor model is an old idea that offers a general and principled approach to speculative computing, but many details remain to be worked out before it can be deployed as an "industrial strength" computing technology. Perhaps a future survey of parallel computing technologies will be able to report that a combination of lazy task creation with the sponsor model has been developed into a truly powerful and efficient tool for scheduling the whole range of application programs on parallel machines.

Acknowledgments. The author very gratefully acknowledges the support by the symposium organizing committee that enabled him to participate in the symposium, as well as the efforts of the anonymous referees, whose comments have significantly improved this paper.

References

1. Agarwal, A., Bianchini, R., Chaiken, D., et al.: The MIT Alewife Machine: Architecture and Performance. In: 22nd Annual Int'l. Symp. on Computer Architecture, pp. 2–13 (1995)
2. Agrawal, K., Leiserson, C., He, Y., Hsu, W.: Adaptive Work Stealing with Parallelism Feedback. ACM Transactions on Computer Systems 26(3), 7:1–7:32 (2008)
3. Allen, E., Chase, D., Hallett, J., et al.: The Fortress Language Specification Version 1.0 (2008), http://research.sun.com/projects/plrg/fortress.pdf
4. Ayguade, E., Copty, N., Duran, A., et al.: The Design of OpenMP Tasks. IEEE Trans. on Parallel and Distributed Systems 20(3), 404–418 (2009)
5. Baker, H., Hewitt, C.: The Incremental Garbage Collection of Processes. MIT Artificial Intelligence Laboratory Memo 454, Cambridge, MA (1977)
6. Blumofe, R., Joerg, C., Kuszmaul, B., et al.: Cilk: An Efficient Multithreaded Runtime System. J. Parallel and Distributed Computing 37(1), 55–69 (1996)
7. Blumofe, R., Leiserson, C.: Scheduling Multithreaded Computations by Work Stealing. J. ACM 46(5), 720–748 (1999)
8. Burton, F.W., Sleep, M.R.: Executing Functional Programs on a Virtual Tree of Processors. In: Proc. of the 1981 Conf. on Functional Programming Languages and Computer Architecture, FPCA 1981, pp. 187–194 (1981)
9. Chapman, B., LaGrone, J.: OpenMP. In: Encyclopedia of Parallel Computing, pp. 1365–1371. Springer (2011)
10. Charles, P., Donawa, C., Ebcioglu, K., et al.: X10: An Object-Oriented Approach to Non-Uniform Cluster Computing. In: OOPSLA 2005, pp. 519–538 (2005)
11. Cong, G., Kodali, S., Krishnamoorthy, S., et al.: Solving Large, Irregular Graph Problems Using Adaptive Work-Stealing. In: International Conf. on Parallel Processing, pp. 536–545 (2008)
12. Dailey, D., Leiserson, C.: Using Cilk to Write Multiprocessor Chess Programs. J. Int. Computer Chess Assoc. 24(4), 236–237 (2002)
13. Frigo, M., Leiserson, C., Randall, K.: The Implementation of the Cilk-5 Multithreaded Language. In: ACM SIGPLAN 1998 Conf. on Programming Language Design and Implementation, pp. 212–223 (1998)
14. Gabriel, R.: Performance Evaluation of Lisp Systems. MIT Press, Cambridge (1985)
15. Halstead, R.: Multilisp: A Language for Concurrent Symbolic Computation. ACM Trans. on Programming Languages and Systems 7(4), 501–538 (1985)
16. Halstead, R.: Vista: un outil générique pour visualiser l'exécution de programmes parallèles. In: Proc. JFLA 1996, Journées Francophones des Langages Applicatifs, INRIA—Collection Didactique, pp. 3–24 (1996) ISBN 2-7261-0944-6 (in French)

17. Halstead, R.: Multilisp. In: Encyclopedia of Parallel Computing, pp. 1216–1222. Springer (2011)
18. Hauck, E., Dent, B.: Burroughs' B6500/B7500 Stack Mechanism. In: Proc. AFIPS Spring Joint Computer Conf., pp. 245–251 (1968)
19. Intel Corporation: Intel R C++ Compiler 12.0 User and Reference Guides (September 2010), Document Number 323271-011US (2010)
20. Intel Corporation: Intel Threading Building Blocks Reference Manual, http://www.threadingbuildingblocks.org/documentation.php
21. Keller, R., Lindstrom, G., Patil, S.: A Loosely-Coupled Applicative Multi-Processing System. In: NCC 1979, AFIPS Conf. Proceedings, vol. 48, pp. 613–622 (1979)
22. Kornfeld, W., Hewitt, C.: The Scientific Community Metaphor. IEEE Trans. on Systems, Man, and Cybernetics 11(1), 24–33 (1981)
23. Lee, I., Wickizer, S., Huang, Z., Leiserson, C.: Using Memory Mapping to Support Cactus Stacks in Work-Stealing Runtime Systems. In: PACT 2010, pp. 411–420. ACM (2010)
24. Leiserson, C.: The Cilk++ Concurrency Platform, J. Supercomputing 51(3), 244–257 (2010)
25. Leiserson, C.: Cilk. In: Encyclopedia of Parallel Computing, pp. 273–288. Springer (2011)
26. Krall, E., McGehearty, P.: A Case Study of Parallel Execution of a Rule-Based Expert System. Int'l J. of Parallel Programming 15(1), 5–32 (1986)
27. Kranz, D., Halstead, R., Mohr, E.: Mul-T: A High-Performance Parallel Lisp. In: ACM SIGPLAN 1989 Conf. on Programming Language Design and Implementation, pp. 81–90 (1989)
28. Mohr, E., Kranz, D., Halstead, R.: Lazy Task Creation: A Technique for Increasing the Granularity of Parallel Programs. IEEE Trans. Parallel and Distributed Systems 2(3), 264–280 (1991)
29. Nichols, B., Buttlar, D., Farrell, J.: Pthreads Programming: A POSIX Standard for Better Multiprocessing. O'Reilly, Sebastopol (1996)
30. Osborne, R.: Speculative Computation in Multilisp. Tech. Report MIT/LCS/TR-464, MIT Laboratory for Computer Science, Cambridge, MA (1989)
31. Osborne, R.: Speculative Computation in Multilisp. In: Ito, T., Halstead Jr., R.H. (eds.) US/Japan WS 1989. LNCS, vol. 441, pp. 103–137. Springer, Heidelberg (1990)
32. Reinders, J.: Intel Threading Building Blocks: Outfitting C++ for Multi-Core Processor Parallelism. O'Reilly, Sebastopol (2007)
33. Robison, A.: Intel Threading Building Blocks (TBB). In: Encyclopedia of Parallel Computing, pp. 955–964. Springer (2011)
34. Steele, G., Allen, A., Chase, D., et al.: Fortress (Sun HPCS Language). In: Encyclopedia of Parallel Computing, pp. 718–735. Springer (2011)
35. Taura, K., Kaneda, K., Endo, T., Yonezawa, A.: Phoenix: A Parallel Programming Model for Accommodating Dynamically Joining/Leaving Resources. In: ACM PPoPP 2003, pp. 216–229 (2003)

Controlling Concurrency and Expressing Synchronization in Charm++ Programs

Laxmikant V. Kale and Jonathan Lifflander

University of Illinois at Urbana-Champaign
{kale,jliffl2}@illinois.edu

Abstract. Charm++ is a parallel programming system that evolved over the past 20 years to become a well-established system for programming parallel science and engineering applications, in addition to the combinatorial search applications with which it started. At its earliest point, the precursor to Charm++, the Chare Kernel, was a purely reactive specification, similar to most actor languages. This paper describes the evolution of a series of concurrency control mechanisms that have been deployed in Charm++ to tame this unrestricted concurrency in order to improve code clarity and/or to improve performance.

1 Introduction

One of the challenges in parallel programming, especially in science and engineering applications, is resource management. This is especially true for dynamic and irregular applications, such as those involving dynamic adaptive mesh refinements. Newer machines, with issues of power and component failures, also create related challenges. A programming system supported by a smart adaptive runtime system that automates resource management is therefore desirable.

Charm++ is a concurrent-objects parallel programming system that has been used for programming science and engineering applications. With Charm++, one programs in C++, providing a few additional declarations to facilitate parallel mechanisms such as asynchronous method invocations. A Charm++ computation consists of a number of C++ objects that interact via asynchronous method invocations. An adaptive runtime system controls and dynamically changes assignments of objects to processors, and also chooses the sequence in which ready method invocations will execute on a given processor. These control mechanisms empowers the runtime to automate load balancing, as well as implement other resource management policies.

In this paper, we will focus on how concurrency and synchronization *within* an individual object is expressed. We present these concepts, which have been described in earlier literature [14,28] going over 20 years by us, in a pedagogical and historical sequence, with illustrations from recent case studies.

We begin this paper with a brief history of the beginning of CHARM++, to elucidate the evolution of its constructs, and to set the context for the description of concurrency control mechanisms in Section 3. From 1983 to 1985, a new parallel execution model for logic programming was developed, called the Reduce-Or

G. Agha et al. (Eds.): Yonezawa Festschrift, LNCS 8665, pp. 196–221, 2014.

process model [26]. This allowed a relatively novel combination of AND and OR parallelism. In particular, the main innovation was something called *consumer-instance parallelism*. Given a Horn clause such as p(X), q(Y), r(X,Y), this model was able to exploit independent-AND parallelism between p and q literals, the OR parallelism underneath p (as well as q), and also the parallelism between multiple instances of r created by incrementally joining solutions to p and q. This was accomplished by having the activation record for the clause as a persistent object. As each solution for p (or q) was returned to it, it combined them with the stored (already-received) solutions to q (or p), and fired a task for computing each instance (the so-called "consumer-instance") of r so created. Initially, as a part of a PhD thesis [25], this model was implemented in an interpreted mode, working with Prof. David Scott Warren. Later, byte-code compilation [41] and related optimizations were developed. However, for the theme of this paper, the interesting part is the runtime system itself. The runtime system needed to have a dynamic load balancer, to distribute all the goals across processors, especially as the distributed memory architectures (such as the "hypercubes", including NCUBE, and iPSC/2) were targeted. It also needed prioritization to focus the search on the most promising paths.

The main "applications" considered in the development of ROLOG (as the compiled implementation of Reduce-Or Process Model was called) involved combinatorial search, including N-queens, Knight's-tour, graph coloring, etc. [24,31]. Our interest shifted to the applications themselves, rather than the logic programming language used to express them. Consequently, the speed of finding a solution became an important goal in itself. These developments led to extraction of the runtime system into a separate entity, called the *chare kernel* [32]. This was a C-based parallel programming system. ROLOG itself was implemented on top of the chare kernel.

The term *chare* was borrowed from an earlier project on parallel implementation of functional languages called *RediFlow* [33] by Keller, Lindstrom, et al.; *chare* means a small task or a *chore* in old English. The activation records for evaluation of a Rolog Clause mentioned above can each be implemented as a chare. In the chare kernel, a chare was an object with its own ID; it was load balanced by the system, and it was possible to send messages to a chare.

One will recognize an ABCL-style concurrent object [49,50,9], or an "actor" in this description immediately [1], although we came to it from the functional language implementations, and macro-dataflow ideas. The *reactive kernel* and *Cantor* [4] were other relevant contemporary systems. However, the chare was clearly very similar to the notion of a concurrent object or an actor developed earlier by Agha [2] and Yonezawa [49] et al., which built upon Hewitt's earlier work [17]. The main differences, in retrospect, were minor up to this point: a C-based implementation, reflecting an efficiency orientation, and a focus on combinatorial search applications. From the language point of view, one difference was that, unlike actors, chares did not have access to their mailboxes. They simply executed every method anyone invoked on them.

There were potentially multiple invocations that were ready on a processor, stored in a prioritized message queue. The system picked the next message from this queue, invoked it on the named object, and it selected another message *only when it returned.* Any guards or internal synchronization within a chare were the responsibility of user's code within the method. This typically led to a lot of buffering and flags indicating what is ready and what is not. The reactive notation also affected the expression of the overall flow of control. A series of solutions to this problem constitute the focus of this chapter. We return to this theme in section 3, after reviewing the somewhat orthogonal but important developments within the Charm++ model in the next section.

Note that the chare kernel was developed before C++ had really taken off. So the language (called Charm by 1991), while object-based, was translated to C by a simple translator. In 1992, with increasing popularity of C++, a C++-based version was created, and it was called Charm++.

2   Charm++ and CSE Applications

In the early 1990's, the attention of CHARM++ developers shifted to applications in computational science and engineering (CSE), from the combinatorial search applications that were dominant earlier. In part because of the nature of these applications, and because of the pragmatic orientation that CSE applications necessitated, several new features and language constructs were developed that improved expressiveness of CHARM++ in comparison with the plain Chare Kernel as well as the Actor languages of that time.

The first of this was the notion of organizing the chares into indexed collections. This followed naturally from the need to support domain decomposition methods used in CSE. Consider a two-dimensional decomposition of a 2D domain in fluid dynamics. A single chare is responsible for one chunk of this decomposition. It needed to communicate (its borders) with the four neighboring chares. But what does "neighboring" mean? In the plain Charm of that time, one would have to create a network of chares, and pass IDs from one to the other in complex manner to ensure that everyone had the IDs of the four chares they needed. The need for an indexed organization was anticipated and developed in early work by Sanjeev Krishnan and Joshua Yelon [42,48]. These ideas were developed into the notion of a "chare array": an indexed collection of chares [37]. Although they were called "arrays", the index could be quite general, supporting sparse arrays as well as collections indexed by bit-vectors or even strings. A program (or more accurately, a computation) consisted of one or more chare array. These were typically created at the beginning of the computation by a "main" chare, but they could also be created dynamically in the middle of the computation.

Method invocation was directed to an individual member of the collection: A[i].foo(x,y) caused an asynchronous method invocation ("asynchronous" in that it returned immediately to the caller) being sent to the i'th member of the collection whose ID was represented by "A". The system took charge of global location management via a scalable scheme [37], so that it could identify the processor on which the named chare lived, and deliver the message to it.

For plain chares, their "seeds" (the messages containing the constructor arguments) were moved around by the load balancers; but once they took root (i.e. were installed on a processor, and executed their constructor), they were not allowed to migrate. For combinatorial search applications, where new chares were created all the time, this was a reasonable strategy. In contrast, chare array members were allowed to migrate. This allowed CSE applications to be load balanced dynamically. Observing that these applications tended to exhibit the *principle of persistence* [30], a suite of measurement-based load balancing strategies [8] were developed that periodically re-examine the load and migrate chares to restore balance. Research on such adaptive load balancers continues to date, and CHARM++ provides an excellent proving ground for new load balancing ideas.

The adaptive runtime system, of which the load balancers are a part, has continued to evolve. It now supports features such as automatic checkpointing [52,40], communication optimizations [34], fault tolerance, and power-and-temperature optimizations [43].

The CHARM++ model and all its constructs described so far do not have the notion of a "processor" in them. For the sake of practicality, processor-level constructs were added: the most basic of these mechanisms allowed specification on which processor to create a given chare. A more interesting example was a construct called *branch-office chare* [21] (later renamed *chare group*). A chare group consists of a set of chares such that there is exactly one chare (the "branch") on each processor. A regular chare, which does not know which processor it is on, can simply ask for a pointer to the local branch of a chare group, and invoke regular C++ methods on it. The members of the group can communicate with each other just as if they are chare array members—using the processor number as the index. This construct allowed development of many support libraries, including the load balancers mentioned above.

The base language described above does not have any global variables. Various types of global variables, based on specific modes of information sharing, were added early on to the language [44].

Several CSE applications have been developed using CHARM++. NAMD for biomolecular simulations was developed in mid 1990s and has continued to evolve with CHARM++. Other applications span topics such as computational astronomy [20], quantum chemistry and nanomaterials [35], agent-based simulation of contagion [5], etc. Also, several higher level languages have been developed using Charm++ [27].

2.1   Comments on the Charm++ Model

Fairness and Scheduling Strategy. By default, Charm++ processes pending method invocations in FIFO order. Also, method invocations by an object on itself are explicitly specified as either in-line or asynchronous by the programmer. This thus pushes the onus on fairness to the programmer; with FIFO, all the explicitly scheduled invocations will be executed fairly. However, Charm++ also supports prioritized queues, instead of (or in addition to) FIFO queues. In this case, the execution may not be fair. Again, the responsibility for ensuring non-starvation is mostly borne by the programmer. We have found this to be adequate for the applications we have developed so far. Further, the scheduler itself is pluggable component; so it is possible, for example, to replace it with one based on "lottery-scheduling" principles, where one selects between tasks randomly, with probabilities determined by the priority of the task.

Message Passing Semantics. In Charm++, messages are passed by value by default. If the serialization methods are implemented correctly for a user-defined type, a deep copy will be made of the data being serialized. However, if Charm++ is used with shared memory, data within a node can be passed by pointer if the programmer indicates that the data should be *conditionally* packed: only packed into a message when the data leaves the node. If a method invocation is marked as conditional, the programmer must ensure that the semantics are correct (e.g. the data is only read in that method).

3   Concurrency Control within a Parallel Object

The earliest version of Charm supported a fairly flat and reactive control structure. A chare was defined by a series of "entry points" (later called "entry methods" in Charm++), in addition to a set of data members and private methods. Its behavior is specified as a set of reactions: *if* the chare gets an invocation for its entry method A, it will execute the body of method A, and so on. The concurrency in such chares is unrestrained. Such a reactive specification does not allow a clear description of the life cycle of a chare. Also, it leads to a cluttered program, with buffers, flags and counters for keeping track of where the chare is in its life-cycle. This section, which is the main topic of the paper, describes three notational mechanisms for constraining the concurrency — specifying which of the many possible actions a chare can execute will be allowed to execute — and simplifying the expression of the life-cycle of a chare.

3.1   Dagger

The Dagger notation, developed around 1993 [13], allows specification of dependencies between computational actions and messages within a chare. A dag-chare is a special type of chare that supports such specification. A chare definition consists of a set of computational blocks called *when-blocks*. Each when-block is preceded by a list of dependencies. There are two kinds of dependencies: entry-method names, and condition variables. A condition-variable is set by calling `ready(condition-variable-name)`. A message sent to an entry method is not eligible to be looked at until it is *expected*. An entry method (named, say, EP) is marked as expected by calling `expect(EP)`. A when-block is ready to execute when all the condition variables in its dependency list are set and all the entry method invocations in its dependency list are both expected and received.

A when clause has the form: when g_0 , ... , g_k : { computation } where each g_i is either a condition variable or the name of an entry method.

The collection of when clauses defines a static dataflow graph. This graph both allows and constrains concurrency within an object. It is important to remember that all the actions within a chare take place on a single processor. So, when multiple actions within an object are described as "concurrent", it does not imply any parallel execution between them.

Consider the following code fragment, based on an example from the first paper about Dagger [12]. The data-flow graph corresponding to this chare definition is shown in Figure 1.

```
dag chare C {
    // ... declarations of local variables, condition variables,
    // ... entry methods and private methods

    when init: { ... Computation C0 ... ; expect(e1); expect(e2); }

    when e1: { ... Computation C1 ... ; ready(R); }

    when e2: {... Computation C2 ... ; expect(e3); }

    when R, e3 : { ... Computation C3 ... ; }
}
```

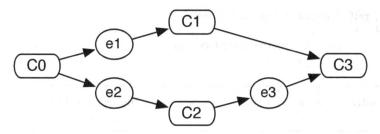

Fig. 1. Example dependency graph that could be expressed using the Dagger notation

The final computational block Computation3 is dependent on receipt of a message directed at entry method e3, but it also requires that condition variable R be set, and that the message for e3 be *expected*. Computation1 and Computation2 can be carried out in either order, depending on whether the message directed at e1 arrives before or after that directed at e2. Yet, they are not parallel computations: they both belong to the same chare, and therefore will be serialized in one of those two sequences. In general, the same behavior can be specified with different but equivalent graphs: for example the *expect(e3)* and *ready(R)* statement can be swapped in this example.

To describe a more concrete example, consider a formulation of martix-matrix multiplication where the row-blocks of the left matrix (say A), and column blocks of the right matrix (say B) are distributed among processors, using a distributed hash table (indeed, the earliest version of Charm supported distributed hash tables, which were simply called "distributed tables" [44]). The job of a particular chare is to request one block of rows from A, one block of rows from B, multiply them out, and send the result to be stored in another distributed table. Such a formulation may be useful in a context where dynamic balancing of block-multiplication tasks is necessary.

The "reactive" code for this chare, in plain Charm, is shown below. Note the use of counters and buffers (to store the row or column block that arrived earlier).

```
chare multiplyBlock
  int count;
  float *row, *column;

  entry init: (message Work *msg) {
    count = 2;
    Find(A, msg->rowNum, getRow, myChareID());
    Find(B, msg->colNum, getCol, myChareID());
  }
  entry getRow: (message TBL_REPLY *m) {
    row = m->data;
    if (--count == 0) matmul_block(row, col);
  }
  entry getCol: (message TBL_REPLY *m) {
    col = m->data;
    if (--count == 0) matmul_block(row, col);
  }
  ...
```

In contrast, the same code is expressed using the Dagger notation as shown below:

```
dag chare multiplyBlock
  entry init: (message Work *msg);
  entry getRow: (message TBL_REPLY *row);
  entry getCol: (message TBL_REPLY *col);

  when init: {
    Find(A, msg->rowNum, getRow, myChareID());
    Find(B, msg->colNum, getCol, myChareID());
    expect(getRow); expect(getCol);
  }
  when getRow, getCol: { matmul_block(row->data, col->data); }
```

The Dagger code makes the dependencies clear, avoids the use of counters, and automates the buffering required. The entry declarations associate message variables (which must have distinct names) with each entry method, so the buffered data (row, col) can be accessed in the subsequent when block.

We selected these examples from the first Dagger paper, to be faithful to the original syntax. Note that at that time, a message pointer was the only parameter an entry method was allowed to have. Modern Charm++, as well as the *Structured Dagger* notation we describe next, allow more general parameters for entry methods.

Synchronization mechanisms and, in particular, the inheritance anomaly (following the phrase coined by the Rosette system [47]) in concurrent object languages have been well studied in the literature [10]. One of the most comprehensive study of the problem and possible solutions was presented by Matsuoka and Yonezawa [39]. Our approach was to simply disallow inheriting "dagger" methods (called the body methods in some of the literature, analogous to the "run" threads of Java). Other sequential methods can be inherited just as in C++, because Chares are, after all, C++ classes. In practice, this has not been a hindrance in using the Dagger or SDAG (see next section) notation. Further, the focus of much of the related work in concurrent objects community was on expressing semantic constraints on individual methods. For example, a popular example of such a constraint was: a get method should not be executed on a bounded buffer object if the buffer is empty. In contrast, Dagger is designed to support expression of dependence graphs between computations and messages, and the ability to better express the life-cycle of an object.

3.2   Structured Dagger

In Dagger, we allow arbitrary dependencies (a DAG) to be represented between the entry methods or message receptions for a given parallel object in the system. Although this is very powerful, we found for many real applications of Dagger that a full dependency graph is not needed. The disadvantage of a full dependency graph is that there is no natural flow to the application's code. This makes comprehending the application code and flow of the parallel application difficult and unintuitive.

In Structured Dagger (SDAG, for brevity) [29] we limit the graphs that can be expressed to those constructed with single-entry single-exit (structured) blocks. This restricts one to a set of dependencies that are either sequenced (the default) or explicitly defined to be overlappable (i.e. they do not depend on each other). Although this reduces the set of graphs that can be represented, all the real applications we have found can be represented cleanly even with this limitation. For the cases that cannot be expressed using SDAG, one can fall back to the original reactive specification method. An example of a graph that cannot be expressed in Structured Dagger, without losing concurrency is shown in Figure 2 below.

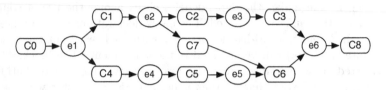

Fig. 2. An unstructured DAG that cannot be expressed in SDAG

In SDAG, the fundamental construct is a when statement that specifies a dependency on a incoming message or set of messages. In CHARM++, a message is targeted toward a method on a certain parallel object or chare in the system. So if we want to wait for a method invocation of void foo(int param), we could specify the following:

```
when foo(int param) { /* block1 */ }
/* block2 */
```

In this case, block1 will not execute until foo arrives, and because SDAG defines a sequence (i.e. program order) by default, block2 will not execute until foo arrives and block1 executes. Note, that SDAG constructs can be nested, so block1 can specify more when constructs or other SDAG constructs.

We can also wait on more than one method to arrive by simply specifying a list of methods that we are expecting:

```
when foo(int param), bar(int size, char str[size]) { /* block1 */ }
/* block2 */
```

Since SDAG defines a sequence by default, the following code will wait for foo to arrive, execute block1, then wait for bar to arrive and execute block2:

```
when foo(int param) { /* block1 */ }
when bar(int size, char str[size]) { /* block2 */ }
```

SDAG works by buffering any messages that are not *ready* to be received. A message is ready if a when statement that matches the incoming message has been executed by the SDAG runtime. If a when statement is encountered and no message has arrived that matches that declaration, a trigger is created that acts as a continuation that can be activated when the appropriate message(s) arrive. Thus, the "ready" statement and condition variables of the plain "Dagger" described in the previous section are not needed with SDAG, there use is replaced by relying on program order, and restricting the description to structured graphs.

If we have a set of statements that are overlappable (i.e. they can be executed in any order) we can override the default sequence enforced by using the overlap statement. For example, if foo(...) and bar(...) can actually be executed in any order according to the semantics of the application, we can declare the following:

```
overlap {
  when foo(int param) { /* block1 */ }
  when bar(int size, char str[size]) { /* block2 */ }
}
```

In general, we can specify a set of SDAG constructs in an overlap that can be executed without regard to ordering. Each nested construct within the overlap will be ordered separately — so an overlap relaxes the ordering to a partial order between a set of statements.

For many applications, we have found that we need to wait on a number of messages, all of the same type. An example of this is a typical near-neighbor interaction, were we wait for some defined number of neighboring elements to send data to this object. SDAG provides a convenient syntax for declaring this interaction pattern: using a for loop when the messages constitute a sequence, or a forall when the incoming messages are allowed to be processed in any order.

The following is an example of using a SDAG for loop:

```
for (i = 0; i < 4; i++)
  when updateGhostRegion(int d, int size, double buf[size]) serial {
    updateBoundary(d, size, buf);
  }
```

Using this code, we wait for each of the neighbors' data to arrive, execute some code (possibly performing an update or saving a pointer) when each arrives and continue only when all of them have arrived.

If the application we are writing is iterative, one possible problem with the above code is that we may not explicitly synchronize between iterations. If this is the case, a neighbor message for a subsequent iteration might arrive out-of-order with the current iteration. Note the above code does not have any way of specifying which iteration we are waiting on: we only wait on some method updateGhostRegion(...) to arrive.

To make this common case much easier, we allow a when trigger to wait on a certain *reference number* that can be included with a message. In SDAG, the first integer specified in the parameter list is the reference number for that message — and can be used to make the dependency more specific:

```
when updateGhostRegion[iter](int i, int d, int size, double buf[size])
```

In the above code, we wait on a specific class of the updateGhostRegion messages — ones that are marked with the reference number iter. So in an iterative application without explicit synchronization between iterations, we would write the following code, which is an example of how a 5-point stencil computation (Jacobi relaxation, for instance) could be implemented in SDAG:

```
serial {
  prepareGhostRegions();
  thisProxy(wrapX(x + 1),y).updateGhostRegion(iter, TOP, size, topReg);
  thisProxy(wrapX(x − 1),y).updateGhostRegion(iter, BOTTOM, size, botReg);
  thisProxy(x,wrapY(y − 1)).updateGhostRegion(iter, LEFT, size, leftReg);
  thisProxy(x,wrapY(y + 1)).updateGhostRegion(iter, RIGHT, size, rightReg);
}
for (i = 0; i < 4; i++)
  when updateGhostRegion[iter](int i, int d, int size, double buf[size]) serial {
    updateBoundary(d, size, buf);
  }
serial {
  int c = doCalc() < targetDiff;
  CkCallback cb(CkReductionTarget(Tile, checkConverged), thisProxy);
  if (iter % 5 == 1) contribute(sizeof(int), &c, CkReduction::logical_and, cb);
}
if (++iter % 5 == 0) {
  when checkConverged(bool result) serial { converged = true; }
}
```

In this code segment, while the stencil computation has not converged, we prepare the ghost regions for sending, and then send a message to each neighbor with the corresponding region copied into a buffer. Then, in the following for loop, we wait to receive 4 neighboring ghost regions that have a reference number corresponding to the current iteration iter. After receiving all 4 ghost regions, we run a compute kernel doCalc and then asynchronously contribute to a reduction that logically ANDs all the local convergence decisions. We exploit asynchronous reductions in CHARM++ by only contributing every 5 iterations and waiting for the result of the reduction 4 iterations later. In this way, the reduction is overlapped with the computation and we only block waiting to find out if the computation has converged every several iterations, instead of synchronizing every iteration. If the computation has converged, we set the local converged variable to true and stop executing the computation.

The serial construct simply specifies a sequential block of C++ code to be executed in sequence. The programmers have to explicitly mark these blocks of code due to the implementation details of how the SDAG code is parsed: our implementation does not actually parse all of C++ and serial allows us to mark which blocks the SDAG translator can safely ignore and pass to the C++ compiler directly.

If we want to wait on n method invocations (or n nested SDAG constructs, in general), but the order they are executed does not matter, we can use the forall construct in SDAG. The semantics are the same as overlap, but it is more convenient when we have n identical sequences that can be overlapped:

```
forall [iter] (0:10, 1)
  when recvData[iter](int param) { /* block1 */}
/* block2 */
```

In this case, we wait for 10 instances of recvData to arrive, each tagged with reference numbers from 0..9 (note the upper-bound on the range is exclusive: it defines a range [0, 10) with a stride of 1). The receives can arrive in any order and block1 will be executed for each one as they arrive. When they all arrive, block2 will be executed.

Fibonacci Example Using SDAG. Using SDAG we can define a pedagogical Fibonacci using the (inefficient) recursive algorithm in the following way:

```
entry void calc(int n) {
  if (n < THRESHOLD) serial { respond(seqFib(n)); }
  else {
    serial {
      CProxy_Fib::ckNew(n − 1, false, thisProxy);
      CProxy_Fib::ckNew(n − 2, false, thisProxy);
    }
    when response(int val)
      when response(int val2)
        serial { respond(val + val2); }
  }
};
```

In this example, we define a calc(...) method that calculates the n'th Fibonacci number by either sequentially calculating the Fibonacci number if n is small enough (for efficiency reasons), or creating two children chares, waiting for both their responses, and then adding them up. In either case, the respond function sends the answer to the parent. Using SDAG, we explicitly define the dependency on waiting for both the responses from the two children and SDAG buffers one of the responses until they both arrive and we can add them. Although this is a simple example, it demonstrates the power of SDAG— without this we would have to manually buffer the first response and add them up later.

3.3 Threads

Often in the middle of executing sequential code, some remote data is required to proceed with the computation. In CHARM++, this requires sending a message to a chare, waiting for a response, and then continuing execution. With SDAG this pattern can be expressed cleanly, but only if the waiting occurs at the top level entry method, because when blocks are allowed only in the entry methods).

```
entry void waitsForData(..) {
  serial {
    // some computation
    f(..);
    g(..);
  }
  when dataNeeded(...) serial {
    // continue execution with remote data
  }
}
```

Here, f and g may be regular methods or stand alone functions. This code works fine because the waiting happens at the top level. But if it is necessary to fetch remote data when the control is inside of (say) the function g, this is not supported by SDAG. Putting a when inside the body of g (g is regular C++ code), will just be flagged as a syntax error by the C++ compiler. In a SDAG entry, when a when statement is encountered, control typically *returns* to the Charm++ scheduler, with no trace of the ongoing work left on the stack itself. All the bookkeeping information about the pending when blocks and buffered messages is left in the SDAG data structures.

However, if we were to use a threaded model (assuming threads that are migratable) we can wait on remote data and then continue executing in the same context when the data arrives. CHARM++ supports this by allowing an entry method to be marked as threaded.

```
entry [threaded] void foo(..);
```

By declaring a method as such, the method will actually run in a user-level thread that is migratable. A thread is made migratable by allocating its stack using isomalloc, which allocates data with a globally-unique virtual address. The isomalloc function works by reserving the same virtual space on all processors [19,3].

We can then declare a certain entry method to be sync, which allows it to actually return data:

```
entry [sync] ReturnMsg* bar(..);
```

Then inside the implementation of the foo entry method, we can make a call to bar, wait for the result, and seamlessly continue execution when the data arrives:

```
Worker::foo(..) {
    // do some computation
    ReturnMsg* msg = remoteChare.bar(...);
    // continue execution when msg arrives
}
```

Further, the call to remoteChare.bar() doesn't need to be at the top level entry method. In the earlier example, this call could be inside the body of the C++ function g(), which still works, because when the call is made, the user-level thread simply suspends, with its stack intact.

Futures: Threads are useful for describing this interaction pattern, but we may want to overlap the computation with the communication. In the above example, once the sync entry method is invoked, we wait for the message from bar to arrive before we proceed. However, although we know we will need the data from bar, we may not need it immediately. A Future is an abstraction that allows us to declare a container that will hold the data at some future time. The future will only block when we try to "open" the container and access the data. Using futures, we can postpone waiting on the remote data until it is required for the computation.

The future construct was described, in the sense we use it, in the multiLisp system of Halstead [15], although multiple precursors existed before that. Taura, Matsuoka, and Yonezawa [46] extended ABCL to support the *future* construct as well.

The following code creates a CkFuture and passes it to an entry method:

```
Worker::foo(..) {
  // do some computation
  CkFuture ft = CkCreateFuture();
  remoteChare.bar(ft, ...); // call the remote chare with a future
  // continue execution
  ReturnMsg* msg = (ReturnMsg*)CkWaitFuture(ft); // wait on future
  // execute using the data from the remote chare
}
```

Here, we create a future that will hold the data that remoteChare.bar(...) will produce when it finishes execution. When we make the call to the remoteChare, we include the future, so it has a place to put its response. Then, when we actually need the data we can explicitly call CkWaitFuture(...), which will block if the remote data has not arrived.

Instead of using SDAG to express Fibonacci, we can express the same concurrency pattern using threaded methods and futures, as shown below. Note that since Charm++, as a C++ library, does not have a translator, except for parsing interface files and SDAG code, the method for accessing and setting futures is somewhat verbose.

```
void run(int n, CkFuture f) {
  if (n < THRESHOLD) result = seqFib(n);
  else {
    CkFuture f1 = CkCreateFuture();
    CkFuture f2 = CkCreateFuture();
    CProxy_Fib::ckNew(n−1, f1);
    CProxy_Fib::ckNew(n−2, f2);
    ValueMsg* m1 = (ValueMsg*)CkWaitFuture(f1);
    ValueMsg* m2 = (ValueMsg*)CkWaitFuture(f2);
    result = m1−>value + m2−>value;
    delete m1; delete m2;
  }
  ValueMsg *m = new ValueMsg();
  m−>value = result;
  CkSendToFuture(f, m);
}
```

Synchronization Mechanisms Based on Threads. The user level thread mechanism underlying Charm++ is designed to be used in a flexible manner. The API allows one to extract the (opaque) threadID of the currently running thread, to suspend the current thread (and thereby transferring control to the scheduler which may resume another ready thread), and to "awaken" a thread (which puts the threadID in the scheduler's queue of ready threads). This API can be used to implement customized synchronization mechanisms. As an example, a counting semaphore can be implemented as shown in the pseudocode below:

```
wait(x) {
    while (x->value == 0) { enqueue(x->waitingQ, CthThread()); CthSuspend(); };
    x->value--; }
signal(x) { x->value++; tid = dequeue(x->waitingQ); CthAwaken(tid);}
```

Note that this works because Charm++'s threads are cooperative (not pre-emptive), and each thread is confined to one core at a given time, until it is migrated by the load balancer. Thread migration does not happen while a thread is waiting in a queue, by convention.

3.4   Comparing Concurrency Control Mechanisms

So, should one use Dagger, SDAG, or threads in a given situation? The Dagger mechanism is historically and empirically been subsumed by SDAG by the Charm++ user community. The reasons are easy to discern and were alluded to earlier: a structured graph is adequate for most real applications, and when it is too restrictive, one can use the flat, reactive, entry methods of Charm++ to restore full concurrency. Using threads efficiently is more complicated. Again, statistically, most Charm++ users tend to prefer SDAG. Avoiding the (admittedly small) extra overhead of threads, and the need to predict stack sizes, combined with environment-dependent challenges of migrating threads for load balancing are some of the reasons why. Also, the cleaner separation of parallel and sequential code that SDAG engenders (via the "serial" construct) is often seen as a beneficial feature. On the other hand, some programmers find it beneficial to *not* have that separation, and so prefer using threads. In particular, if you are calling a function f from a threaded entry method, you do not have to know if this function is completely local, or if it may request and block for some remote data. That way, a function that is sequential today, may be modified by the writer of that function to become parallel later, without requiring a code-change in the caller's code. Threads are also useful when you need to block for some specific remote data when you are deep in the function-call stack.

The need for abstraction, especially arising out of supporting other programming models, is another reason for using threads. For example, AMPI [19] implements the well-known MPI abstraction on top of Charm++. To benefit from Charm++'s load balancers, AMPI maps multiple MPI "ranks" on a single processor. When one rank issues a receive call, and the data is not available, the implementation needs to suspend the execution of the calling rank, and resume execution on any other rank that is ready on that processor at that point. This blocking receive can be implemented using Charm++ threads. AMPI implements each user "rank" (which the user thinks of as an MPI process) as a user-level thread embedded in a Charm++ chare.

The specific issues that come up when one is trying to migrate a chare, in which a user-level thread or a DAG is embedded, are discussed in our earlier paper [51], which also presents detailed performance comparisons of the alternative methods.

4 Controlling Concurrency across Parallel Objects

The control structures described so far: threads, futures, Structured Dagger, etc., can be used to control and manage the concurrency and control flow within a chare. CHARM++ also has several mechanisms to enable chares to work together in various ways to increase efficiency and/or programmability.

4.1 Asynchronous Collective Operations

A simple example of this is allowing the use of asynchronous broadcasts and reductions (as shown in the 5-point stencil example) over a chare array, which can be sparsely populated and can grow and shrink over time without explicit synchronization. In addition, CHARM++ has a very efficient built-in algorithm to detect termination across the entire system: the state when no messages are in flight and all processors are idle [45]. The termination detection mechanism in CHARM++ is very easy to use, and only requires a single call to the system:

```
CkStartQD(CkCallback(...));
```

In the above snippet, whenever this call is made, the CHARM++ runtime starts its termination detection algorithm, and when it confirms quiescence, it triggers the callback, which allows the user to define an arbitrary endpoint to be notified (for instance, a entry method on a chare, or broadcast to a chare array).

An example where these features are very beneficial is adaptive mesh refinement (AMR). In traditional MPI (and thus, in any bulk-synchronous) implementations of AMR, remeshing is an expensive operation that requires multiple collective operations to determine when all the remeshing decisions are finished propagating based on the mesh criteria. In the CHARM++ implementation [36], one abstracts the computation (structured as blocks in an oct-tree) as a dynamic collection of blocks indexed by their position in the tree using a chare array. During remeshing, instead of using $\mathcal{O}(d)$ (where d is the depth of the propagation) expensive collective operations over all the processors to determine when remeshing is finished, we use point-to-point messages to propagate decision messages and then wait for termination to be detected by the system. A recent paper [36] shows that this methodology is highly-scalable and has many beneficial properties.

4.2 Queuing Policies

CHARM++ allows a priority to be set for an entry method invocation; such priorities are used to schedule a message when it arrives on the destination processor. Under the hood, CHARM++ maintains a queue of outstanding messages that execute in turn on each processor for the set of objects that live there. When a message arrives, it is placed in the queue to be executed in a certain order depending on its priority. Although message priorities are a heuristic, they can be very important for obtaining high performance.

Message priorities can be set very easily for an invocation by adding a single argument:

```
Worker::foo() {
    CkEntryOptions opts;
    opts.setPriority(100);
    remoteWorker.method(data, &opts);
}
```

Note that CHARM++ also allows priorities to be bit-vectors or other variable-sized fields, which is useful for state-space search applications [6].

In addition, CHARM++ allows the user to specify a queuing strategy that is used for the message when it arrives on the destination processor. By default, messages are enqueued in FIFO order, but this can be changed easily:

```
opts.setQueueing(CK_QUEUEING_LIFO);
```

An example where priorities make a high impact on application performance is dense LU factorization. In dense LU factorization, the matrix being factorized is decomposed into a 2D grid of blocks, which in the CHARM++ implementation [38] is encapsulated in a chare array. We can succinctly describe the parallel control flow of a non-pivoting LU in SDAG as follows:

```
 1  entry void factor() {
 2    for (step = 0; step < min(thisIndex.x, thisIndex.y); step++) {
 3      overlap {
 4        when recvL[step](blkMsg *mL) serial { L = mL; }
 5        when recvU[step](blkMsg *mU) serial { U = mU; }
 6      }
 7      serial {
 8        // Schedule the trailing update for sometime later with low priority
 9        CkEntryOptions opts;
10        opts.setPriority(calcPrioDepOnLoc(x,y));
11        thisProxy(x,y).processTrailingUpdate(step, &opts);
12      }
13      when processTrailingUpdate[step](int step) atomic {
14        updateMatrix(L, U);
15      }
16    }
17    if (x == y) serial {
18      thisProxy(x,y).processLocalLU();
19    } else if (x < y)
20      when recvL[step](blkMsg *mL) serial { thisProxy(x,y).processComputeU(mL); }
21    else
22      when recvU[step](blkMsg *mU) serial { thisProxy(x,y).processComputeL(mU); }
23  };
```

Each block goes through various phases as it executes depending on its location in the matrix. The most critical operation for unleashing concurrency is performing the diagonal factorization (line 18), which only depends on a few of the trailing updates (matrix-matrix multiplies) to be executed (lines 2-16) (each diagonal enables all the trailing updates below and to the right of the diagonal, but only the ones above and to the left of the next diagonal are required to start that computation).

Note in the above example when recvL and recvU arrive (lines 4-5) instead of immediately executing the trailing update that is available, we delay the execution by enqueuing a message in the local queue with low priority that will start the trailing update (see lines 9-11). In this example, we exploit CHARM++ prioritized scheduling to reduce the priority of an operation that might hamper work directly on the critical path from executing.

4.3   Memory-Aware Scheduling in LU

Another example of across-chare concurrency control also comes from LU factorization. When LU is being weak-scaled, as it often is for obtaining the top-500 benchmark results, it needs to run very close to memory limits to obtain maximum performance and reach the FLOP limit of DGEMM (the matrix-matrix multiplies that the trailing updates execute). The typical CHARM++ idiom is to send messages to a chare when the data is ready. However, for certain applications that are memory-sensitive, aggressively sending data when it is ready might exceed memory limits on the receiving end.

In our highly-scalable implementation of dense LU [38], we demonstrate how to exploit CHARM++ groups to control incoming messages by explicitly scheduling when messages arrive. For LU, instead of sending the block of data when it is ready on the sender-side, we notify the receiver that the data is ready and allow the receiver to determine which blocks to request based on what is ready and the optimized schedule it has computed that adheres to the dependencies natural in an LU computation. With this methodology, we are able to achieve high performance without exceeding memory limits or treating processors as first-class entities.

4.4   Charisma: Controlling Concurrency across Chares

Let us turn now, from the runtime schemes for across-chare concurrency control within a processor, to language-level mechanisms for controlling and expressing concurrency across chares, even when they are spread across multiple processors.

Note that Structured Dagger allowed clean expression of the life-cycle of a given chare, while still avoiding overly constraining the execution order, via the **overlap** and **forall** statements. However, the behavior of the program as a whole is not explicitly expressed; it remains an emergent property that needs to be inferred from the descriptions of behaviors many chares, possibly belonging to multiple chare arrays. Again, we built upon an empirical observation that a fixed, data-independent communication pattern among the chares is common in most (but certainly not all) applications. For instance, in such applications, which tend to be iterative, the content of messages and even their sizes may change from iteration to iteration, but the basic pattern of message-exchanges (the dataflow among the objects) remains the same. *Charisma* [18] is a notation developed to facilitate elegant expression of such applications.

Charisma also supports multiple indexed collections of chares, as Charm++, but their behavior is expressed by a collective script (hence we call it an *orchestration* language). This script is written in a special notation, while the sequential code in the form of plain methods of chares is kept in separate C++ files. The main statement in Charisma is a foreach statement.

```
foreach i in stencil[i]
    stencil[i].foo();
end-foreach
```

The code above asks all members of a chare array (stencil) to execute their method foo. More interestingly:

```
foreach i in stencil[i]
    q[i] <- stencil[i].bar(p[i-1]);
end-foreach
```

tells each chare stencil[i] to consume the parameter p[i-1] and produce the parameter q[i]. The charisma compiler connects producers and consumers by generating appropriate message-passing (Charm++ method invocations) code. The concurrency in Charisma is only constrained by data dependencies and program order. Without going into technical details, and simplifying the example, the following code fragment for the 5-point stencil computation illustrates Charisma.

```
foreach [i,j] in stencil
(top[i,j], bottom[i,j], left[i,j], right[i,j]) <- stencil[i,j].publishboundaries();
repeat
    foreach [i,j] in stencil
        (+error, top[i,j], bottom[i,j], left[i,j], right[i,j]) <-
            stencil[i,j].publishboundaries(top[i+1,j], bottom[i-1,j],
            left[i,j+1], right[i,j-1]);
until (error < THRESHOLD)
```

Values for the boundaries generated in previous iteration are consumed by the neighbors in the next iteration. The + symbol preceding error specifies a reduction (i.e. a commutative-associative operation). The operator for the reduction (here, max) is specified in the declarations, not shown here.

Although some applications, such as Barnes-Hut, are not amenable to Charisma, because of the data-dependent data-flow they exhibit, a substantial class of applications are expressible using Charisma. Charisma scripts are compiled into Structured Dagger programs.

5   Case Studies and Performance

In this section, we summarize two case studies to demonstrate that the concurrency control mechanisms, and specifically SDAG, lead to high performance code. These case studies are taken from our 2011 HPC Challenge submission, which won the class 2 award for programming language productivity [22].

5.1   LeanMD

LeanMD [23] is a molecular dynamics simulation benchmark written in CHARM++. It simulates the behavior of atoms using the Lennard-Jones potential to calculate the interaction between uncharged molecules. The benchmark is similar to the short-range non-bonded force calculation that NAMD calculates [7] and it also resembles the miniMD application found in the Mantevo benchmark suite [16] maintained by Sandia National Laboratory.

LeanMD is parallelized using a hybrid spatial and force decomposition. The three-dimensional space consisting of molecules is divided into equal-sized cells that hold a set of molecules using the cutoff distance r_c and a margin. During each iteration, the force calculation between a set of neighboring cells is assigned to another set of parallel objects called the *computes*. Using the forces that are sent to the computes, they perform the force integration and update the properties of the atom — namely acceleration, velocity, and position.

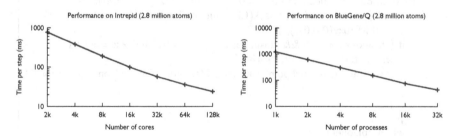

Fig. 3. Performance of LeanMD for the 2.8 million atoms system on Vesta (IBM BG/Q) and Intrepid (IBM BG/P)

Our code is very short (only 693 lines of code[1]) and it can be dynamically load balanced using many built-in strategies by CHARM++, can be checkpointed to disk or in-memory for fault tolerance, and is not sensitive to different shapes of simulation domains nor to the number of processors.

The following is a snippet of SDAG code that shows the parallel flow of control that describes the Cell object for LeanMD:

---

[1] The line count was generated using David Wheeler's SLOCCount.

```
array [3D] Cell {
  entry Cell();
  entry void run() {
    for(stepCount = 1; stepCount <= finalStepCount; stepCount++) {
      // send current atom positions to my computes
      serial { sendPositions(); }
      // update properties of atoms using new force values
      when reduceForces(vec3 forces[n], int n) serial { updateProperties(forces); }

      if ((stepCount % MIGRATE_STEPCOUNT) == 0) {
        // send atoms that have moved beyond my cell to neighbors
        serial { migrateParticles(); }
        // receive particles from my neighbors
        for(updateCount = 0; updateCount < inbrs; updateCount++) {
          when receiveParticles(const std::vector<Particle> &updates) serial {
            for (int i = 0; i < updates.size(); ++i)
              particles.push_back(updates[i]);
          }
        }
      }

      if (stepCount >= firstLb && (stepCount - firstLb) % lbPeriod == 0) {
        serial { AtSync(); } // periodically call load balancer
        when ResumeFromSync() { }
      }

      if (stepCount % checkptFreq == 0) { // periodically checkpointing
        serial { contribute(CkCallback(CkReductionTarget(Cell,startCheckpoint),
          thisProxy(0,0,0))); }
        if (thisIndex.x == 0 && thisIndex.y == 0 && thisIndex.z == 0) {
          when startCheckpoint() serial {
            CkStartMemCheckpoint(CkCallback(CkIndex_Cell::cpDone(),thisProxy))
            ;
          }
        }
        when cpDone() { }
      }
    }
  };
};
```

Figure 3 shows the scaling of LeanMD on BG/P and BG/Q — two IBM supercomputers. We achieve near-linear scaling and demonstrate that load balancing is beneficial for obtaining high-efficiency. The checkpoint (milliseconds) and restart time (100-200 milliseconds) for LeanMD is very low. As seen in the above snippet, using all these features of CHARM++ requires very little extra work by the programmer.

5.2   Dense LU Factorization

As described earlier, we have implemented a dense LU factorization library [38] in CHARM++ that fully conforms to the HPC Challenge [11] specification. Our implementation is a fully-composable library (it can share space and time with another parallel CHARM++ module) that allows for flexible data placement (by writing a simple block-to-processor function).

Our implementation has been scaled up to 8064 cores on Jaguar (Cray XT5 with 12 cores and 16GB per node) by increasing problem sizes to occupy a constant fraction of memory (75%) as we increased the number of cores used. We obtain a constant 67% of peak performance across this range. We also demonstrate strong scaling on Intrepid, an IBM Blue Gene/P machine, by running a fixed matrix size ($n = 96,000$) from 256 to 4096 cores. The results are shown in Figure 4.

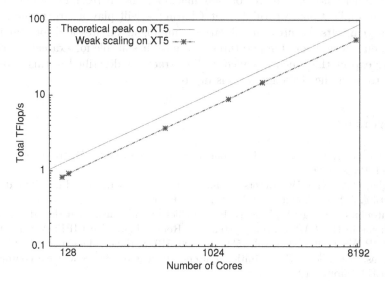

Fig. 4. Weak scaling (matrix occupies 75% of memory) from 120 to 8064 processors on Jaguar (Cray XT5)

6   Conclusion

We presented a historical overview of various mechanisms for controlling concurrency that have been developed for the Charm++ parallel programming system. Within a single chare (a message driven object), the mechanisms included Dagger, SDAG, and threaded entry methods based on migratable user-level threads. Of these, SDAG was seen to be the most beneficial and popular method, although threads combined with futures, and other synchronization mechanisms are very useful in somewhat narrower contexts. Mechanisms for coordination and control of concurrency across chares, and indeed across processors, were also discussed. These ranged from priorities, quiescence detection, memory aware scheduling, as well as Charisma, an orchestration languages that specifies the behavior of a collection of chares, when they are known to exhibit static data-flow. We included two case studies to demonstrate the raw performance attained by Charm++ using these methods.

Charm++ has become one of the few parallel programming systems developed in academia that has been successful as a production-quality system for a significant number of highly scalable parallel applications in Science and Engineering, in regular use by scientists on supercomputers in USA and elsewhere. In addition to being a programming language in its own right, it also forms a substrate for development of other high level languages, of which Charisma is an example. We expect that it will be used as a back-end by new programming languages that will be developed by us and others; in this context, its support for interoperability is very important.

As the field moves to more complex machines and increasingly sophisticated adaptive applications, we think that Charm++ will play a larger role in the coming years. Its features for tolerating component failures and for managing power, energy and core temperatures will make it suitable for exascale computers. We expect the concurrency control abstractions described in this paper to evolve to meet the challenges of this future.

References

1. Agha, G.: Actors: A Model of Concurrent Computation in Distributed Systems. MIT Press (1986)
2. Agha, G.A., Kim, W.: Actors: a unifying model for parallel and distributed computing. J. Syst. Archit. 45(15), 1263–1277 (1999)
3. Antoniu, G., Bouge, L., Namyst, R.: An efficient and transparent thread migration scheme in the PM^2 runtime system. In: Rolim, J.D.P. (ed.) IPPS-WS 1999 and SPDP-WS 1999. LNCS, vol. 1586, pp. 496–510. Springer, Heidelberg (1999)
4. Athas, W.C., Seitz, C.L.: Multicomputers: Message passing concurrent computers. IEEE Computer (August 1988)
5. Bisset, K., Aji, A., Marathe, M., Chun Feng, W.: High-performance biocomputing for simulating the spread of contagion over large contact networks. In: 2011 IEEE 1st International Conference on Computational Advances in Bio and Medical Sciences (ICCABS), pp. 26–32 (February 2011)
6. Booth, J.A.: Balancing priorities and load for state space search on large parallel machines. Master's thesis, University of Illinois at Urbana-Champaign (2003)
7. Brunner, R., Phillips, J., Kalé, L.V.: Scalable molecular dynamics for large biomolecular systems. In: Proceedings of SuperComputing 2000 (2000)
8. Brunner, R.K., Kalé, L.V.: Handling application-induced load imbalance using parallel objects. In: Parallel and Distributed Computing for Symbolic and Irregular Applications, pp. 167–181. World Scientific Publishing (2000)
9. Caromel, D.: Abstract Control Types for Concurrency (Position Statement for the panel: How could object-oriented concepts and parallelism cohabit). In: O'Conner, L. (ed.) International Conference on Computer Languages (IEEE ICCL 1994), pp. 205–214. IEEE Computer Society Press (August 1993)

10. Tomlinson, C., Singh, V.: Inheritance and synchronization with enabled-sets. In: ACM OOPSLA, pp. 103–112 (1989)
11. Dongarra, J., Luszczek, P.: Introduction to the HPC Challenge Benchmark Suite. Technical Report UT-CS-05-544, University of Tennessee, Dept. of Computer Science (2005)
12. Gursoy, A., Kale, L.: Tolerating latency with dagger. In: Proceedings of the Eigth International Symposium on Computer and Information Sciences, Istanbul, Turkey (November 1993)
13. Gursoy, A., Kalé, L.: Dagger: Combining the Benefits of Synchronous and Asynchron ous Communication Styles. In: Proceedings of the 8th International Parallel Processing Symposium (April 1994)
14. Gursoy, A., Kalé, L.: Dagger: Combining the Benefits of Synchronous and Asynchronous Communication Styles. In: Siegel, H.G. (ed.) Proceedings of the 8th International Parallel Processing Symposium, Cancun, Mexico, pp. 590–596 (April 1994)
15. Halstead, R.: Multilisp: A Language for Concurrent Symbolic Computation. ACM Transactions on Programming Languages and Systems (October 1985)
16. Heroux, M.A., Doerfler, D.W., Crozier, P.S., Willenbring, J.M., Edwards, H.C., Williams, A., Rajan, M., Keiter, E.R., Thornquist, H.K., Numrich, R.W.: Improving performance via mini-applications. Technical report, Sandia National Laboratories (September 2009)
17. Hewitt, C., Bishop, P., Steiger, R.: A universal ACTOR formalism for artificial intelligence. In: Proceedings of the International Joint Conference on Artificial Intelligence, pp. 235–245. SIAM (1973)
18. Huang, C., Kale, L.V.: Charisma: Orchestrating migratable parallel objects. In: Proceedings of IEEE International Symposium on High Performance Distributed Computing, HPDC (July 2007)
19. Huang, C., Zheng, G., Kumar, S., Kalé, L.V.: Performance Evaluation of Adaptive MPI. In: Proceedings of ACM SIGPLAN Symposium on Principles and Practice of Parallel Programming (March 2006)
20. Jetley, P., Gioachin, F., Mendes, C., Kale, L.V., Quinn, T.R.: Massively parallel cosmological simulations with ChaNGa. In: Proceedings of IEEE International Parallel and Distributed Processing Symposium 2008 (2008)
21. Kale, L.: The Chare Kernel parallel programming language and system. In: Proceedings of the International Conference on Parallel Processing, vol. II, pp. 17–25 (August 1990)
22. Kale, L., Arya, A., Bhatele, A., Gupta, A., Jain, N., Jetley, P., Lifflander, J., Miller, P., Sun, Y., Venkataraman, R., Wesolowski, L., Zheng, G.: Charm++ for productivity and performance: A submission to the 2011 HPC class II challenge. Technical Report 11-49, Parallel Programming Laboratory (November 2011)
23. Kale, L., Arya, A., Jain, N., Langer, A., Lifflander, J., Menon, H., Ni, X., Sun, Y., Totoni, E., Venkataraman, R., Wesolowski, L.: Migratable objects + active messages + adaptive runtime = productivity + performance a submission to 2012 HPC class II challenge. Technical Report 12-47, Parallel Programming Laboratory (November 2012)
24. Kale, L., Ramkumar, B., Saletore, V., Sinha, A.B.: Prioritization in parallel symbolic computing. In: Halstead Jr., R.H., Ito, T. (eds.) US/Japan WS 1992. LNCS, vol. 748, pp. 11–41. Springer, Heidelberg (1993)
25. Kalé, L.V.: Parallel architectures for problem solving. PhD thesis, State Univ. of New York, Stony Brook, USA (1985)

26. Kalé, L.V.: Parallel execution of logic programs: the REDUCE-OR process model. In: Proceedings of Fourth International Conference on Logic Programming, pp. 616–632 (May 1987)

27. Kale, L.V.: Programming Models at Exascale: Adaptive Runtime Systems, Incomplete Simple Languages, and Interoperability. The International Journal of High Performance Computing Applications 23(4), 344–346 (2009)

28. Kale, L.V., Bhandarkar, M.: Structured Dagger: A Coordination Language for Message-Driven Programming. In: Fraigniaud, P., Mignotte, A., Bougé, L., Robert, Y. (eds.) Euro-Par 1996. LNCS, vol. 1123, pp. 646–653. Springer, Heidelberg (1996)

29. Kale, L.V., Bhandarkar, M.: Structured Dagger: A Coordination Language for Message-Driven Programming. In: Fraigniaud, P., Mignotte, A., Bougé, L., Robert, Y. (eds.) Euro-Par 1996. LNCS, vol. 1123, pp. 646–653. Springer, Heidelberg (1996)

30. Bhandarkar, M.A., Brunner, R.K., Kalé, L.V.: Run-time Support for Adaptive Load Balancing. In: Rolim, J.D.P. (ed.) IPDPS 2000 Workshops. LNCS, vol. 1800, pp. 1152–1159. Springer, Heidelberg (2000)

31. Kale, L.V., Richards, B.H., Allen, T.D.: Efficient parallel graph coloring with prioritization. In: Queinnec, C., Halstead Jr., R.H., Ito, T. (eds.) PSLS 1995. LNCS, vol. 1068, pp. 190–208. Springer, Heidelberg (1996)

32. Kalé, L.V., Shu, W.: The Chare Kernel base language: Preliminary performance results. In: Proceedings of the 1989 International Conference on Parallel Processing, St. Charles, IL, pp. 118–121 (August 1989)

33. Keller, R., Lin, F., Tanaka, J.: Rediflow Multiprocessing. In: Digest of Papers COMPCON, Spring 1984, pp. 410–417 (February 1984)

34. Kumar, S.: Optimizing Communication for Massively Parallel Processing. PhD thesis, University of Illinois at Urbana-Champaign (May 2005)

35. Kumar, S., Shi, Y., Bohm, E., Kale, L.V.: Scalable, fine grain, parallelization of the car-parrinello ab initio molecular dynamics method. Technical report, UIUC, Dept. of Computer Science (2005)

36. Langer, A., Lifflander, J., Miller, P., Pan, K.-C., Kale, L.V., Ricker, P.: Scalable Algorithms for Distributed-Memory Adaptive Mesh Refinement. In: Proceedings of the 24th International Symposium on Computer Architecture and High Performance Computing (SBAC-PAD 2012), New York, USA (October 2012) (to appear)

37. Lawlor, O., Kalé, L.V.: Supporting dynamic parallel object arrays. In: Proceedings of ACM 2001 Java Grande/ISCOPE Conference, Stanford, CA, pp. 21–29 (June 2001)

38. Lifflander, J., Miller, P., Venkataraman, R., Arya, A., Jones, T., Kale, L.: Mapping dense lu factorization on multicore supercomputer nodes. In: Proceedings of IEEE International Parallel and Distributed Processing Symposium (May 2012)

39. Matsuoka, S., Yonezawa, A.: Analysis of Inheritance Anomaly in Object-Oriented Concurrent Languages. In: Agha, G., Wegner, P., Yonezawa, A. (eds.) Research Directions in Object-Based Concurrency. MIT Press (1993)

40. Ni, X., Meneses, E., Kalé, L.V.: Hiding checkpoint overhead in hpc applications with a semi-blocking algorithm. In: IEEE Cluster 2012, Beijing, China (September 2012)

41. Ramkumar, B., Kalé, L.V.: Compiled execution of the Reduce-Or process model on multiprocessors. In: The North American Conference on Logic Programming, pp. 313–331 (October 1989)

42. Krishnan, S., Kale, L.V.: A parallel array abstraction for data-driven objects. In: Proceedings of Parallel Object-Oriented Methods and Applications Conference, Santa Fe, NM (February 1996)

43. Sarood, O., Kalé, L.V.: A 'cool' load balancer for parallel applications. In: Proceedings of the 2011 ACM/IEEE conference on Supercomputing, Seattle, WA (November 2011)
44. Sinha, A., Kalé, L.: Information Sharing Mechanisms in Parallel Programs. In: Siegel, H. (ed.) Proceedings of the 8th International Parallel Processing Symposium, Cancun, Mexico, pp. 461–468 (April 1994)
45. Sinha, A.B., Kale, L.V., Ramkumar, B.: A dynamic and adaptive quiescence detection algorithm. Technical Report 93-11, Parallel Programming Laboratory, Department of Computer Science, University of Illinois, Urbana-Champaign (1993)
46. Taura, K., Matsuoka, S., Yonezawa, A.: An efficient implementation scheme of concurrent object-oriented languages on stock multicomputers. In: Proceedings of the 5th ACM SIGPLAN Symposium on Principles and Practice of Parallel Programming. ACM SIGPLAN Notices (June 1993)
47. Tomlinson, C., Kim, W., Scheevel, M., Singh, V., Will, B., Agha, G.: Rosette: An object-oriented concurrent systems architecture. In: Proceedings of the 1988 ACM SIGPLAN Workshop on Object-based Concurrent Programming, OOPSLA/E-COOP 1988, pp. 91–93. ACM, New York (1988)
48. Yelon, J., Kale, L.V.: Agents: An undistorted representation of problem structure. In: Huang, C.-H., Sadayappan, P., Banerjee, U., Gelernter, D., Nicolau, A., Padua, D.A. (eds.) LCPC 1995. LNCS, vol. 1033, pp. 551–565. Springer, Heidelberg (1996)
49. Yonezawa, A.: ABCL: An Object Oriented Concurrent System. MIT Press (1990)
50. Yonezawa, A., Briot, J.-P., Shibayama, E.: Object-oriented concurrent programming in ABCL/1. In: ACM SIGPLAN Notices, Proceedings of the OOPSLA 1986, vol. 21(11), pp. 258–268 (1986)
51. Zheng, G., Lawlor, O.S., Kalé, L.V.: Multiple flows of control in migratable parallel programs. In: 2006 International Conference on Parallel Processing Workshops (ICPPW 2006), Columbus, Ohio, pp. 435–444. IEEE Computer Society (August 2006)
52. Zheng, G., Ni, X., Kale, L.V.: A Scalable Double In-memory Checkpoint and Restart Scheme towards Exascale. In: Proceedings of the 2nd Workshop on Fault-Tolerance for HPC at Extreme Scale (FTXS), Boston, USA (June 2012)

MassiveThreads: A Thread Library for High Productivity Languages

Jun Nakashima and Kenjiro Taura

The University of Tokyo
Tokyo, Japan
{nakashima,tau}@eidos.ic.i.u-tokyo.ac.jp

Abstract. An efficient implementation of task parallelism is important for high productivity languages. Specifically, it requires a tasking layer that fulfills following requirements: (i) its performance scales to high core counts, and (ii) it is seamlessly integrated into a runtime system that performs inter-node communication and synchronization. More specifically, it should facilitate interactions between tasks and threads dedicated for inter-node communication. There have been many implementations that satisfy (i), but, to the best of our knowledge, none of such systems satisfy both requirements.

To address this issue, we propose a thread library called MassiveThreads. It provides not only lightweight threads and a scalable dynamic load-balancing mechanism among CPU cores, but also Pthread-compatible API and I/O semantics. In MassiveThreads, issuing a blocking I/O call triggers a user-level context switch instead of blocking the underlying OS-level thread. These features simplify interactions between tasks and communication threads by instantiating both of them on top of MassiveThreads.

1 Introduction

Current parallel programming languages and frameworks such as MPI[7] provide programming models based on the primitive abstraction of hardware. They achieve high performance by putting the burden of managing tasks and communication on programmers. The burden is becoming heavier as machines become larger, more heterogeneous, and more hierarchical.

To address this issue, there have been recently proposed many parallel languages that aim to improve both performance and productivity. Many of them provide a global address space and general *task parallelism*, in which tasks can be nested and created at arbitrary points of execution. This general form of task parallelism encompasses many syntactically different forms of parallelism supported in parallel programming languages, including fork-join, parallel recursions and parallel for loops.

The implementation of an application with task parallelism becomes simple and modular if there is an underlying thread package that can directly map multi-tasking primitives of the language to multi-threading primitives of the

G. Agha et al. (Eds.): Yonezawa Festschrift, LNCS 8665, pp. 222–238, 2014.

thread package. For example, if the underlying thread package is Pthreads, a task creation is directly translated into pthread_create. But instantiating a Pthread for each task creation performs poorly especially when a large number of tasks are created. To perform well when executing many fine-grained tasks, the underlying thread package should be lightweight.

A basic technique for implementing efficient task parallelism is known. Rooted back to Lazy Task Creation [8] proposed for a parallel Lisp, many systems are based on a similar principle of work-first and LIFO scheduling within each worker (underlying OS-level thread to execute tasks) and FIFO task stealing between workers. However, most of them assume applications running on single node machines.

Many high productivity languages such as X10[4] and Chapel[3] support task parallelism and work on distributed memory machines. If their runtime system can switch tasks trigged by communication, overlapping communication and computation — one of the important techniques to achieve good performance on distributed memory machines — can be easily written with the languages by simply creating many tasks.

One way to implement such runtime system is to integrate existing lightweight thread packages into a runtime system that communicates with other nodes, but it is complicated. Suppose a lightweight thread impletmented as a user-level thread performs a blocking I/O call. In this case, not the lightweight thread but the underlying OS-level thread is blocked until the I/O call finishes thus some degree of parallelism is lost. This issue can be addressed by yielding all the communication to a dedicated OS-level thread, but in this case synchronization between user-level tasks and the OS-level communication thread becomes a non-trivial issue.

Our approach is to eliminate the problem at its root: a thread package that is lightweight and can handle blocking I/O calls without blocking the underlying OS-level threads. By executing both a communication thread and lightweight threads for task paralleism on top of this thread package, integration into the runtime system can be simplified. Our proposed solution is implemented as a library called MassiveThreads, which we describe in this paper. This paper also describes the evaluation result of its performance.

2   Related Work

Comparing to OS-level threads, user-level threads have two major advantages. (1) User-level threads' overheads are much smaller since thread management does not require system calls, and (2) User-level threads can use scheduling policies optimized for specific applications. Such an application that can take advantage of user-level threads is a task parallelism runtime system. As described in previous section, efficient implementations of user-level threads for task parallelism on a shared memory machine is a well studied topic. There are many languages, frameworks, and libraries that support task parallelism by lightweight threads, such as Cilk[1], Java Fork/Join Framework[5], Intel Threading Building Blocks (TBB)[10], StackThreads/MP[12], Qthreads[14], and Nanos++[2].

Another application of user-level thread is for processing concurrent I/O. Mapping a thread for each connection is a naive way for implementing concurrent I/O processing, but OS-level thread is too heavyweight for this purpose. Capriccio[13] and StateThreads[11] provide user-level threads that can automatically switch the context triggered by I/O calls to leverage highly concurrent server implementations.

3 Design and Implementation

3.1 Design Overview

To make threads lightweight, MassiveThreads is implemented as a user-level thread library. In order to handle I/O calls without blocking the underlying OS-level threads, it automatically intercepts blocking I/O calls and switches contexts to other ready threads.

The MassiveThreads library is build as a shared library that provides the functions compatible with Pthreads. Therefore it can be used in place of Pthreads by simply linking it instead of Pthreads, or by dynamically loading at runtime by using environment variables. Thanks to this feature, existing communication libraries for Pthreads can easily run on top of MassiveThreads.

3.2 Definition of Terms

- "thread" means user-level thread managed by the MassiveThreads library
- "worker" means OS-level thread to execute user-level threads
- "deque" means double-ended queue

3.3 Thread Scheduling

Design. We chose work-first and LIFO scheduling within each worker and FIFO randomized work stealing between workers as MassiveThreads scheduling policy for two reasons. First, this scheduling policy is known to be efficient for recursive task parallelism. Most parallel constructs including fork-join and parallel for loop can be easily translated to recursive task parallelism. Therefore this scheduling policy can give the potential to execute most parallel constructs efficiently under the appropriately implemented compiler and the runtime system. The second reason is that the algorithm has no centralized components which may become a bottleneck with large number of cores.

Data Structure. The MassiveThreads library creates workers and binds them to CPU cores. Each worker thread has a deque called ready deque to store the ready user-level threads (Fig.1). Ready deque supports the following 3 operations.

- push: Insert a thread to the head by owner
- pop: Get a thread from the head and delete it from the deque by the owner worker
- take: Get a thread from the tail and delete it from the deque by non-owner worker

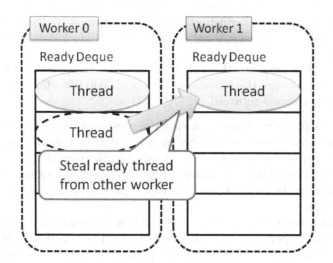

Fig. 1. Data Structure to Execute User-level Threads

Scheduling. When a new thread is created, underlying worker suspends a thread currently running, inserts it to the head of the ready deque by push operation, and executes the new thread immediately. When the current running thread is finished, the worker obtains a new thread using pop operation. If there is no thread in the ready deque, the worker tries to steal a ready thread from randomly chosen workers' ready deque using take operation.

Optimization. The MassiveThreads library is implemented to minimize context switching and thread creation overhead. This section describes some of these optimizations and their corresponding performance effects are shown in Section 4.

Avoid Using ucontext. On most Linux systems, portable user-level context switching library called ucontext can be used to implement user-level threads. We first use it for its portability, but found that its large switching overhead due to internal system calls for switching signal masks became a serious bottleneck. To address this issue, we implemented context switching routines that switch callee-saved registers only.

Ready Deque Implementation. To implement a ready deque, we followed similar approaches to Cilk[1] and Java Fork/Join Framework[5]. A ready deque consists of an array to store threads, two integers pointing the head and tail of the deque, and one spinlock. Following is the brief description of how it works.

- Push operation first stores a new thread to the array, and then increments the head pointer.
- Pop operation decrements the head pointer, and compares the head and tail pointers to check whether it is safe to return the result without locking. If it is safe result is returned without locking, otherwise lock is acquired to avoid conflicts.
- Take operation acquires the lock to serialize other operations, increments the tail pointer, and then checks conflicts with pop operation. If there is no conflict the result is returned.

To work the algorithm correctly, memory accesses order must not be changed. To meet this requirement we inserted memory barrier instructions and code snippets to suppress memory access re-ordering by the compiler.

With this algorithm push operation can be done without locking, and if there are more than one thread in the ready deque, pop operation can also be done without locking.

Additionally, we applied double-checked locking optimization to pop and take operations. Before pop and take, the number of threads in the ready deque is checked by comparing the head and tail pointer. If it is zero operations are aborted because there seems to be no thread available. This optimization improves the load balancing ability because it increases the amount of work stealing attempts per unit time by reducing the overhead of failed work stealing attempts.

Double-Checked Locking on Joining a Thread. Join function waits for the termination of a thread and returns the exit value of the thread. When a thread is terminated, its exit value is stored to the thread descriptor — an internal data structure to describe the thread. At the time the thread is joined by the other thread, the exit value is read and the descriptor is released. Thread termination and join function call can be occured at the same time, thus lock is required to avoid race conditions.

In order to support join function, a thread descriptor includes:

- Area to store the exit value
- An Integer to describe thread status (e.g. running, suspended, finished)
- A reference to the thread waiting for the termination
- A spinlock to avoid a race condition.

Before we applied double-checked locking optimization, join function is implemented as the following:

1. Acquire the lock of a target thread descriptor
2. Read the status
3. If it is already finished, read the exit value, release the descriptor, and return

4. Otherwise, set the reference to the currently running thread, suspend it, and then release the lock.
5. Read return value, release the descriptor, and return after the thread is continued

And thread termination is implemented as the following:

1. Acquire the lock of a target thread descriptor
2. Set the exit value
3. Set the status as finished
4. If the reference of suspended thread is set, resume it, and release the lock
5. Otherwise, get a thread from a ready deque and continue it, and release the lock.

This implementation acquires the lock 2 times for each thread join and termination. To reduce the number of attempts to acquire the lock, We applied double-checked locking optimization. Specifically, for thread termination, just after releaseing the lock the status is set to the another one called "ready to be released". For join function, before acquiring the lock the status is checked. If the status is ready to be released, it reads the exit values and releases the decsriptor without acquiring the lock. Before releasing the descriptor, it waits for status to change to ready to be released. Appendix A shows pseudocode of join operation and thread termination with double-checked locking optimization.

This optimization is effective for most task-parallel application because when a thread joins the other thread, usually it has already terminated.

Faster Thread-Local Storage Model. The MassiveThreads library internally uses thread-local storage to obtain worker-local information. There are 4 thread-local storage model: General Dynamic, Local Dynamic, Initial Exec, and Local Exec[6]. By default, General Dynamic model — the most general model in 4 models — is chosen. In General Dynamic model, access to the thread-local storage is compiled to a function call. We notice that this overhead takes up high percentage in thread creation and join overheads, because the thread-local storage is accessed very frequently. In order to reduce the overhead, we choose Initial Exec model — more restricted one than General Dynamic — through GCC compiler flags. In this model, access to thread-local storage is compiled to only a few instructions. This optimization has a drawback that the MassiveThreads library must be initially loaded. Thus runtime dynamic library loading mechanisms (e.g. dlopen) may not be used. But we believe this drawback is not serious, because most parallel applications do not load libraries dynamically, but libraries are linked with applications so that they are initially loaded.

3.4 Blocking I/O Call Handling

Currently this function only supports blocking I/O on network socket, thus in this paragraph, we use the socket-specific terms for explanation. But this implementation is essentially independent from the underlying I/O mechanism and

can be applied to other blocking I/O calls. This implementation looks similar
to that of Capriccio[13] or StateThreads[11], but is different in that it supports
working on multiple workers.

Data Structure. Fig.2 illustrates the data structures for I/O handling. To
manage the threads waiting for a file descriptor to become ready, The MassiveThreads library assigns two lists called "blocked lists" for each file descriptor. One of the blocked list is for read and the other is for write.[1] A blocked list
stores threads waiting for the file descriptor to become ready for the requested
operation, as well as the arguments to the requested I/O call.

To check the status of file descriptors, the MassiveThreads library uses *epoll*.
epoll is an I/O notification mechanism in Linux. To use epoll, file descriptors to
check should be registered to an epoll instance. After that the list of ready file
descriptors can be obtained using *epoll_wait* function. In order to distribute I/O
handling operations, each worker has its own epoll instance. File descriptors are
registered to one of the epoll instances.

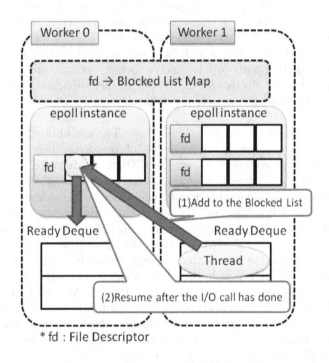

Fig. 2. Data Structure for I/O Handling

To look up the blocked lists from a file descriptor, there is a map from a file
descriptor to the corresponding blocked lists. It is implemented by a hash table

---

[1] In Fig.2, only one blocked list is shown for each file descriptor for simplicity.

and lookups to the map with different file descriptors can be done concurrently unless a hash collision occurs.

I/O Handling Procedures. I/O handling in MassiveThreads consists of three procedures, namely, registering a new file descriptor, performing the I/O call, and polling to resume blocked threads.

Registering a New File Descriptor. When a new file descriptor is created, two blocked lists are created and an association from the file descriptor to the lists is added to the map. Then it is registered to the *epoll* instance of the worker. To distribute I/O management loads, The worker is randomly chosen.

Performing the I/O Call. When the application performs a blocking I/O call, it is intercepted by MassiveThreads, and performed with non-blocking option. If I/O call fails because the file descriptor is not ready, then the worker puts the caller thread and the arguments of the I/O call to the corresponding blocked list (Fig.2 (1)), and then switches to the thread in the ready deque.

Polling to Resume Blocked Threads. When a worker has no thread to execute, it checks the status of the file descriptors using *epoll*. If there is a ready file descriptor with a non-empty blocked list, then the worker tries the I/O call again. If it now succeeds, the thread in the entry is put into the head of the ready deque of the worker (Fig.2 (2)). We choose this policy in order to minimize migrating threads between workers by running a thread which use a file descriptor on a worker that checks its status as possible.

4   Evaluation

First, in order to confirm the MassiveThreads library has enough performance for leveraging task parallelism implementation, we evaluated the overheads to create and join one thread and load balancing abillity. We also compared the performance with Cilk using pratical applications. Then, we evaluated how well blocking system call handling works through ping-pong benchmark with many concurrent connections.

4.1   Thread Create and Join Overheads

The overhead to create and join threads are especially important for fine-grained task parallelism. To evaluate them, we repeatedly create and join an empty (immediately finishing) thread using a single worker, and measured the overhead. The experimental setup is shown in Table 1.

Fig.3 shows the overhead to create and join one thread. For comparison, this figure also shows that of Cilk, Intel Threading Building Blocks (TBB), Qthreads, and Nanos++. The overhead of MassiveThreads is about 70 nanoseconds, which is close to that of TBB.

Table 1. Experimental Setup for Overhead and Scalability Evaluation

CPU	Xeon E7540 (2.0GHz) 4 Sockets
OS	Debian Linux 2.6.32
Compiler	GCC 4.6.0
Cilk	version 5.4.6
Intel TBB	version 3.0
Nanos++	version nanox-e3a0ce4 (included in Chapel 1.4) NX_SCHEDULE=cilk
Qthreads	version 1.7 sherwood scheduler QTHREAD_NUM_WORKERS_PER_SHEPHERD=1

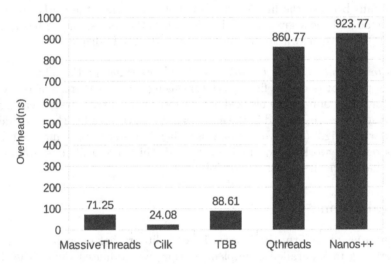

Fig. 3. Overheads to Create and Join One Thread

To see the overhead in more detail and to confirm the benefits of the optimizations described in Section 3.3 we broke down the overheads into 4 major parts: memory management (allocation, initialization, and release for thread descriptor and stack), context switching, operation to the ready deque, and synchronization on thread join. Fig.4 shows the breakdown in the stacked bar graphs. *Fullopt* in the figure shows the overhead with all the optimization enabled. The other four bars show the overhead with one optimization disabled: choosing faster thread-local storage model on *TLS*, double-checking for thread join on *Join*, double-checking for ready deque operation on *Queue*, and avoid using ucontext for *Context*.

Without using faster thread local storage (see *Fullopt* and *TLS*), memory management and synchronization overhead increase, because most functions read

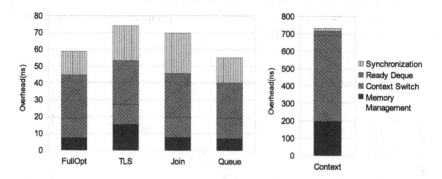

Fig. 4. Overhead Breakdown and Optimization Effects

worker-local data stored in the thread-local storage. When disabling double-checking for thread join (*Fullopt* vs. *Join*), synchronization overhead gets larger due to the extra atomic operation, while it is usually avoided when this optimization is enabled. Interestingly, ready deque operation overhead gets smaller when disabling double-checking for the ready deque operation (*Fullopt* vs. *Queue*). We are now investigating this case in order to reveal the cause and look for the opportunity to further performance improvement. When using ucontext instead of hand-written context switching functions (*Fullopt* vs. *Context*), the overhead jumps up to about 700 nanoseconds because of large increment of memory management and context switching overheads, because ucontext issues system calls every time on switching the contexts and on initializing the contexts for the new thread.

4.2 Load Balancing on Unbalanced Tree Search

To evaluate the scalability, we use Unbalanced Tree Search (UTS) Benchmark[9]. This benchmark measures the performance of searching highly unbalanced tree. The tree shape is highly unbalanced but contains sufficient amount of parallelism enough to fully utilize many CPU cores. Therefore, this performance reflects the performance of dynamic load balancing. We parallelize the reference implementation that performs depth-first search (*uts-dfs*) by creating threads recursively. As a dataset, we choose *T3L* tree (details are shown in Table 2).

Fig.5 shows the speedup of MassiveThreads, Cilk, and Intel TBB, Qthreads, and Nanos++ relative to a single core performance of each implementation.

Table 2. UTS Benchmark Dataset

Tree	Type	b_0	q	m	r	Depth	Nodes
T3L	binomial	2000	0.200014	5	7	17844	1.1×10^8

MassiveThreads speedup factor is approximately 21. Except for using 24 cores, the performance is close to that of TBB, which performs the best in existing frameworks used for the evaluation.

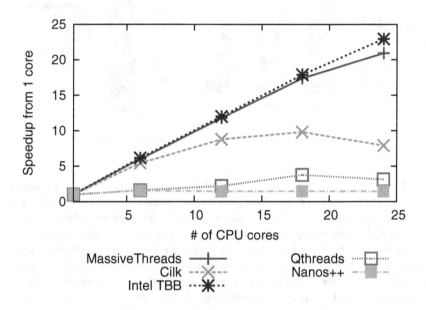

Fig. 5. Speedup of UTS Benchmark

4.3 Performance of Practical Programs

To see MassiveThreads performance for more practical applications, first we picked up programs from Cilk distribution that are non-interactive and can be directly translated to MassiveThreads (specifically, "abort" statement — task cancellaration in Cilk — cannot be directly translated). Then we ported them to MassiveThreads and evaluated the performance. Programs and their arguments are shown in Table 3. Fig.6 shows the relative performance compared to Cilk on a single core and 24 cores. In most program, MassiveThreads performances are similar to or little worse than Cilk. But in *bucket*, *fib* and *knapsack*, the MassiveThreads library has much worse performance than Cilk. We guess the reason is that the task granularity is too small to hide MassiveThreads overhead which is about 3 times larger than Cilk. On the other hand, in *cholesky*, *heat*, *lu* and *plu*, The MassiveThreads library outperforms Cilk on high number of cores, because it scales well enough to compensate its larger overhead.

4.4 Blocking I/O Performance

To evaluate the blocking I/O performance, we use ping-pong benchmark between 2 nodes. One node runs a server and the other runs a client. In this

Table 3. Benchmark Parameters on Practical Programs

Name	Commandline Arguments	Description
bucket	-n 10000000	Bucket sorting
cholesky	-n 6000 -z 40000	Cholesky decomposition of sparse matrix
cilksort	-n 400000000	Sorting
fft	-n 268435456	FFT
fib	44	Fibonacci
heat	-g 1 -nx 6000 -ny 6000 -nt 400	Heat diffusion solver using jacobi iteration
knapsack	-benchmark long	0-1 knapsack solver using branch-and-bound
lu	-n 8192	LU decomposition of dense matrix
matmul	6000	Cache-oblivious matrix multiply
plu	-n 8192	LU decomposition with partial pivoting
rectmul	-x 8192 -y 8192 -z 8192	Rectangular matrix multiply
spacemul	-n 8192	Dag-consistent matrix multiply
strassen	-n 8192	Strassen's algorithm

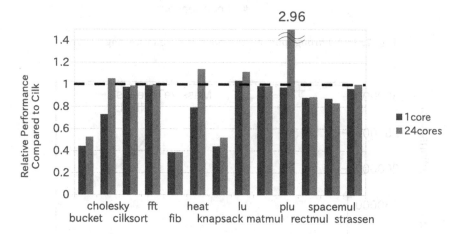

Fig. 6. MassiveThreads Relative Performance on Practical Programs

Table 4. Experimental Setup for Ping-pong

CPU	Xeon E5410 (2.5GHz) 4 Sockets
OS	Linux 2.6.26 (Debian)
Network	10Gbit Ethernet
C Compiler	GCC 4.4.1

benchmark, a server accepts TCP connections, and creates a thread for each connection. Threads in the server wait for a 1-byte message from the its connection. When a message arrives, the thread sends an acknowledgement. A client

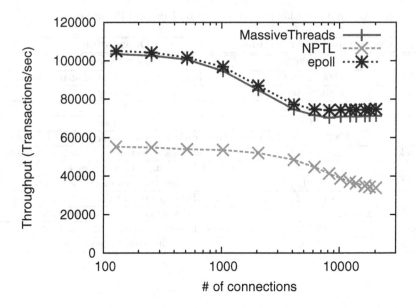

Fig. 7. I/O Throughput of Ping-pong Benchmark using 1 core

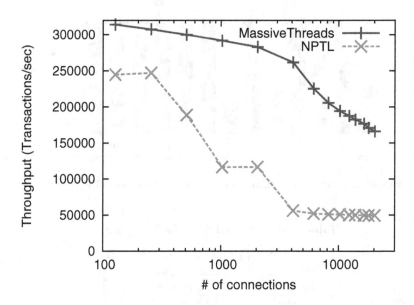

Fig. 8. I/O Throughput of Ping-pong Benchmark using 8 cores

establishes connections to the server. In order to limit message concurrency, connections are distributed among the predifined number of threads. Threads in the client randomly choose a connection, send a 1-byte message, and wait for the reply. In this experiment, we limit the concurrency to 128. We define a pair of the message and the reply as a transaction, and measured the throughput of transaction. The experimental setup is shown in Table 4. Fig.7 shows the throughput of MassiveThreads, NPTL (OS-level Pthreads on Linux), and single-threaded event-driven implementation using *epoll*. User-code for evaluation is common for both libraries. The MassiveThreads library outperforms NPTL and achieves close performance as *epoll*, which indicates MassiveThreads blocking system call handling works well enough to utilize *epoll* performance. Fig.8 shows the throughput using 8 cores. The MassiveThreads library achieves up to 4.5x better throughput than NPTL.

5   Conclusion and Future Work

In addition to good performance on single node, task parallel runtime system for distributed memory environment is required to interact with inter-node communication libraries. Our approach to address this issue is to implement a thread library called MassiveThreads, which can execute both tasks and communication threads on top of it. To achieve this, it supports context switches triggered by blocking system calls and has compatible API and semantics with Pthreads.

Evaluation results show the MassiveThreads library has competitive performance with existing task parallel implementations, and ping-ping benchmark result show user-level context switches triggered by system calls can multiplex blocking socket I/O calls from many threads better than OS-level Pthreads.

As future work we are going to the following:

1. Perform more in-depth performance analysis.
2. Support context switching for more types of blocking system calls or I/O calls for interconnects, and evaluate the benefits.
3. Evaluate MassiveThreads on distributed memory applications and study scheduling policies for good interactions between tasks and communication threads.

MassiveThreads source code is available under BSD license from this URL:

- http://googlecode.com/p/massivethreads

Acknowledgements. This work was supported by JSPS Grant-in-Aid for JSPS Fellows Grant Number 248391.

References

1. Blumofe, R.D., Joerg, C.F., Kuszmaul, B.C., Leiserson, C.E., Randall, K.H., Zhou, Y.: Cilk: An Efficient Multithreaded Runtime System. SIGPLAN Not. 30(8), 207–216 (1995)
2. BSC: Nanos++, http://pm.bsc.es/projects/nanox

3. Callahan, D., Chamberlain, B.L., Zima, H.P.: The Cascade High Productivity Language. In: Ninth International Workshop on High-Level Parallel Programming Models and Supportive Environments (HIPS 2004), pp. 52–60 (2004)
4. Charles, P., Grothoff, C., Saraswat, V., Donawa, C., Kielstra, A., Ebcioglu, K., von Praun, C., Sarkar, V.: X10: An Object-Oriented Approach to Non-Uniform Cluster Computing. In: OOPSLA 2005: Proceedings of the 20th Annual ACM SIGPLAN Conference on Object-Oriented Programming, Systems, Languages, and Applications, pp. 519–538. ACM, New York (2005)
5. Lea, D.: A Java Fork/Join Framework. In: JAVA 2000: Proceedings of the ACM 2000 Conference on Java Grande, pp. 36–43. ACM, New York (2000)
6. Drepper, U.: ELF Handling for Thread-Local Storage
7. Message Passing Interface(MPI) Forum: MPI: A Message-Passing Interface Standard. Technical report, Knoxville, TN, USA (1994)
8. Mohr, E., Kranz, D.A., Halstead Jr., R.H.: Lazy Task Creation: A Technique for Increasing the Granularity of Parallel Programs. IEEE Trans. Parallel Distrib. Syst. 2(3), 264–280 (1991)
9. Olivier, S., Huan, J., Liu, J., Prins, J., Dinan, J., wen Tseng, C.: UTS: An Unbalanced Tree Search Benchmark
10. Pheatt, C.: Intel®Threading Building Blocks. J. Comput. Small Coll. 23(4), 298–298 (2008)
11. Shekhtman, G.: State Threads for Internet Applications, http://state-threads.sourceforge.net/docs/st.html
12. Taura, K., Tabata, K., Yonezawa, A.: StackThreads/MP: Integrating Futures into Calling Standards. SIGPLAN Not. 34(8), 60–71 (1999)
13. von Behren, R., Condit, J., Zhou, F., Necula, G.C., Brewer, E.: Capriccio: Scalable Threads for Internet Services. In: SOSP 2003: Proceedings of the Nineteenth ACM Symposium on Operating Systems Principles, pp. 268–281. ACM, New York (2003)
14. Wheeler, K.B., Murphy, R.C., Thain, D.: Qthreads: An API for Programming with Millions of Lightweight Threads. In: IPDPS, pp. 1–8. IEEE (2008)

Appendix A: Join Implementation with Double-Checked Locking Optimization

```
// Data structure
typedef struct{
  void *return_value;
  int status;
  thread *waiter;
  mutex_t lock;
  ...
}thread;

// Join operation
void join(thread *th)
{
  void *ret;
  thread *this,*next;
  this=massivethread_self();
  // First check the status without locking
  if (th->status==FREE_READY){
    ret=th->return_value;
    mem_free(th);
    return ret;
  }
  // Then check with locking
  mutex_lock(&th->lock);
  if (th->status==FINISHED || th->status==FREE_READY){
    // Target is already finished
    ret=th->return_value;
    mutex_unlock(&th->lock);
    // Wait for the target ready to be freed
    while (th->status!=FREE_READY){}
    mem_free(th);
    return ret;
  }
  th->waiter=this;
  // Block currently running thread
  next=get_next_thread_from_ready_deque();
  switch_callstack(next);
  // Execute mutex_unlock with bollowing the other context's stack
  // in order to avoid collision of call stack
  mutex_unlock(&th->lock);
  switch_context(next);

  // Execution continues from here:
  mutex_lock(&th->lock);
  ret=th->return_value;
  mutex_unlock(&th->lock);
  // Wait for the target ready to be freed
```

```
    while (th->status!=FREE_READY){}
    mem_free(th);
    return ret;
}

void on_thread_termination(void *retval)
{
    thread *this,*waiter,*next;
    this=massivethread_self();
    mutex_lock(&th->lock);
    // Set return value and status
    this->return_value=retval;
    this->status=FINISHED;
    waiter=this->waiter;
    if (waiter!=NULL){
        // Continue the waiting thread
        switch_callstack(next);
        // Execute mutex_unlock with bollowing the other context's stack
        // in order to avoid collision of call stack
        mutex_unlock(&this->lock);
        // From here thread descriptor is ready to be freed
        this->status=FREE_READY;
        switch_context(waiter);
    }
    else{
        // Execute the other thread in the ready deque
        next=get_next_thread_from_ready_deque();
        switch_callstack(next);
        mutex_unlock(&this->lock);
        this->status=FREE_READY;
        switch_context(next);
    }
}
```

On Efficient Load Balancing for Irregular Applications

Masahiro Yasugi

Department of Artificial Intelligence, Kyushu Institute of Technology,
680-4 Kawazu Iizuka Fukuoka, Japan 820-8502

Abstract. This short essay overviews a history and a future perspective of dynamic load balancing for irregular applications. Since I write this essay for the Festschrift, I discuss ideas of load balancing from the point of view of concurrent objects as much as possible.

Keywords: load balancing, concurrent objects.

1 Introduction

In my doctoral work, I designed a concurrent object-oriented programming language ABCL/ST (ABCL/Statically Typed) based on ABCL/1 [32, 31] and implemented a concurrent object-oriented language system ABCL/EM-4 [28] for a highly parallel data-driven computer EM-4 [19].

In the computation/programming model for ABCL/1, computation is performed by a collection of autonomous, concurrently active software entities called *concurrent objects*, and the interaction between concurrent objects is performed solely via message passing. More than one concurrent object can become active simultaneously, and more than one message transmission may take place in parallel. Each concurrent object has its own single thread of control, and it may have its own memory, the contents of which can be accessed only by itself. Theoretical foundations for concurrent objects have been established by a series of studies in Actors [1], ABCM [20] (the computation model for ABCL/1), POOL [2], and calculi of asynchronous objects [15].

In a concurrent object-oriented language system ABCL/EM-4, the data-driven nature of EM-4 was well suited for efficient message handling. EM-4 consists of 80 PEs (Processing Elements) and the interconnection network. We can allocate a newly created concurrent object on a PE and exchange hardware-level packets between PEs to realize message passing. Interestingly, at the implementation level, I considered PEs as generalized, universal concurrent objects (i.e., abstract PEs). At present, I would like to call such generalized, universal concurrent objects *workers*, which handle implementation-level messages and change their roles according to ABCL-level concurrent objects. Usually, the abstract system consists of as many workers as there are PEs in the underlying computer system.

I also think that the concurrent object-based computation model is useful for implementing higher-level languages than concurrent object-oriented languages,

G. Agha et al. (Eds.): Yonezawa Festschrift, LNCS 8665, pp. 239–250, 2014.

where workers (as universal concurrent objects) actually run in parallel. It is useful for performance analysis as an execution model, and is useful for the design and verification of protocols (for high-level communication by exchanging messages). Concurrent objects have clear modularity; messages and their types (request/reply) are clear, and each concurrent object clearly has its own single thread of control and its own memory.

An actual computer system may have shared memory. The concurrent object-based computation model does not cover shared memory. Shared memory may serve as both an additional gift and a trouble. However, we can specify most interactions among workers without directly using shared memory; of course, shared memory can be used for implementing the concurrent object-based computation model.

Recently, as high-level languages that employ workers (as universal concurrent objects), I am interested in languages which support dynamic load balancing for irregular applications. In the rest of this short essay, I would like to overview a history and a future perspective of dynamic load balancing.

2   Load Balancing

With the growing popularity of parallel architectures including many/multi-cores, it has become important to ensure easy parallel programming for efficient parallel computing. An ultimate goal of programming/computing system research is to allow users to describe the computation at a higher level of abstraction and to automatically determine the details of how to perform the computation.

In many irregular applications, *static* partitioning of work with sufficient concurrency into parallel tasks (for present workers), each with an equal amount of work, is impossible. In such cases, dynamic load balancing, where a task (a piece of work) is dynamically allocated to an idle worker, is effective. Work stealing is a randomized technique that implements load balancing. An idle worker (thief) steals a task from another randomly selected loaded worker (victim). Usually, the number of workers does not exceed the number of underlying computing resources, such as cores and "hardware" threads (afforded by Simultaneous Multithreading (SMT) and Hyper-threading), so that workers actually run in parallel.

In general, work-stealing frameworks [26, 18, 27, 6, 7, 3, 8, 21, 23, 25, 16, 4, 5, 17, 13, 10, 11] work well with parallel divide-and-conquer (tree-recursive) algorithms, where workers, if necessary, exchange relatively large subdivided tasks near the root of the invocation tree in order to reduce the total work-stealing costs. It is well known that (nested) FORALL-style parallel algorithms can be converted into parallel divide-and-conquer (recursive) algorithms easily (almost automatically); for example, TBB [16]'s `parallel_for` template function recursively splits a given range into subranges. Examples of manual conversion for Cilk [8] can be found in our previous paper [29].

Work-stealing frameworks with parallel divide-and-conquer algorithms generally afford better cache locality than *work-sharing* approaches; when the `dynamic` schedule is specified on OpenMP's work-sharing loop construct, relatively small chunks of iterations are assigned to workers (called "threads in the team" in OpenMP) dynamically. Note that work-sharing with larger chunks (even with the guided schedule) is less tolerant of work imbalance among iterations.

2.1 Lazy Task Creation

LTC (Lazy Task Creation) [18] is one of the best implementation techniques for dynamic load balancing. LTC provides good load balancing for many applications including irregular ones; that is, it keeps all workers busy by creating plenty of "logical" threads and adopting the oldest-first work-stealing strategy.

In LTC, each worker spawns plenty of logical threads and schedules them internally and thus efficiently. An idle worker (thief) may steal (the continuation of) a logical thread from another worker (victim). That is, logical threads are used as tasks dynamically allocated to idle workers. When a logical thread recursively spawns offspring logical threads, the oldest-first work-stealing strategy is generally effective in making tasks larger.

In LTC, a newly spawned logical thread is directly and immediately executed like a usual call while (the continuation of) the oldest thread in the worker may be stolen by another idle worker. Usually, the idle worker (thief) randomly selects another worker (victim) for stealing a task. Cilk [8] employs this technique. LTC is originally invented for MultiLisp [12], where the *future* construct is used as in (+ (future E_1) (future E_2)). A *future* expression creates a logical thread, and the channel (or promise) of the result (which will be determined later) is passed to the continuation of the *future* expression. The result is waited for and extracted with an implicit *touch* operation.

A message passing implementation [6] of LTC employs a polling method where the victim detects a task request sent by the thief and returns a new task created by splitting the present running task. StackThreads/MP [23], OPA [25], and Lazy Threads [9] employ this technique. Although the thief may have to wait for a task for a long time, polling methods often improve performance by avoiding "memory barrier" instructions, as Indolent Closure Creation [21] improves Cilk's performance.

2.2 Cilk

Cilk [8] is a parallel programming language. It provides good load balancing by employing LTC [18].

In Cilk, the programmer specifies parallel functions (cilk procedures). The spawning of a parallel function is written as a C call with an additional spawn keyword. At the language level, a logical thread that executes the parallel function is created. At the implementation level, this child thread is executed immediately (prior to the parent), and (the continuation of) the parent thread becomes stealable for dynamic load balancing. The programmer writes a sync statement so that the parent thread waits for the completion of all spawned child threads. Note that sync statements are compiled away for *fast clones* [22] at the implementation level. Since each parallel function has `sync` as its implicit last statement, the child threads cannot survive longer than the parent thread. Thus, the termination of a parallel algorithm is simply detected as the completion of the corresponding parallel function invocation.

Note that Cilk can run on shared memory environments, but it cannot run on distributed memory environments. Since the continuation of the parent thread is implicit, explicit serialization/communication (for distributed memory) of the implicit continuation context is difficult.

Cilk employs a Dijkstra-like (and Dekker-like) protocol called the "THE" protocol for work stealing. When this protocol is implemented on modern parallel architectures that do not provide sequential consistency for shared memory, the owner (the potential victim) is forced to execute store-load memory barrier (fence) instructions when extracting its own potential tasks (logical threads in Cilk); this results in substantial overheads.

In Cilk, the pseudovariable `SYNCHED` is true if all spawned child threads are completed. `SYNCHED` was originally introduced to promote the reuse of a workspace[1] among child logical threads [22] and usually it cannot be used for the reuse of a workspace between parent and child logical threads.

2.3 Other Versions of Cilk

In 1995, a previous version of Cilk was published in [3]. This version of Cilk differs from the well-known version Cilk-5 [8] in the following manner:

- Each logical thread is nonblocking, which means that it can run to completion without waiting or suspending once it has been invoked.
- Programs must be written in explicit continuation-passing style; each logical thread must additionally spawn a successor thread (by `spawn_next`) to receive the children's return values when they are produced.
- When a thread spawns a new child thread, the parent-first approach is taken; i.e., the new child thread (rather than the parent thread) is pushed to the ready queue. Later, it will be popped or stolen. (More precisely, they use *levels* each of which corresponds to the number of `spawn`'s (but not `spawn_next`'s) to employ the ready queue as an array in which the Lth element contains a linked list of all ready threads having level L.)
- It can run on distributed memory computers. When threads are stealable, they have not been invoked and they have no continuation contexts. Implicit continuations in Cilk-5 may be expressed explicitly as such stealable new threads in [3]. Note that a thread may spawn as many threads as necessary, and creation of implicit Cilk-5 intrathread continuations can be mostly avoided.

Recently, MIT licensed Cilk technology to Cilk Arts, Inc. Cilk Arts developed Cilk++, which includes full support for C++, parallel loops, and superior interoperability with serial code. In July 2009, Intel Corporation acquired Cilk Arts.

---

[1] In this essay, *workspaces* mean arrays or any other mutable data structures.

Intel released its ICC compiler with Intel Cilk Plus for C and C++ and provided the GCC "cilkplus" branch C/C++ compiler.

In Cilk++ (and Cilk Plus), reducers and other Cilk++ hyperobjects are introduced, which enable lazy allocation of views (race-free reduction workspaces). That is, when the continuation of the parent thread is stolen, a new view of the reducer is allocated. This behavior can also be implemented with SYNCED in Cilk-5, but the use of reducers is easy to understand.

2.4   Tascell

Recently, we proposed a "logical thread"-free parallel programming/execution framework called *Tascell* as an efficient work-stealing framework [13]. Tascell implements *backtracking-based load balancing* with on-demand concurrency. A worker performs a computation sequentially unless it receives a task request with polling. When requested, the worker spawns a "real" task by temporarily "backtracking" and restoring its oldest task-spawnable state. Because no *logical threads* are created as potential tasks, the cost of managing a queue for them can be eliminated.[2] Tascell also promotes the long-term (re)use of workspaces (such as arrays and other mutable data structures) and improves the locality of reference since it does not have to prepare a workspace for each concurrently runnable logical thread.

The Tascell framework consists of a compiler for the Tascell language and a runtime system. This framework supports both distributed and shared memory environments. The Tascell compiler employs an extended C language as the intermediate language. In the first compilation phase, a Tascell program is translated into an extended C program with nested function definitions in order to implement *task-request handlers* and *dynamic winders*. In the second compilation phase, the extended C program with nested functions is compiled by an enhanced version of GCC [30] or by a translator into standard C [14]. These implementations provide lightweight lexical closures called "L-closures" which are created by evaluating nested function definitions, enabling a running program to legitimately inspect/modify the contents of its execution stack. Using elaborate compilation/translation techniques, we can delay the initialization of an L-closure until the L-closure is actually invoked, and we can use a private location as a register allocation candidate for an accessed variable to realize quite low creation/maintenance costs. Because the compiled Tascell program creates L-closures very frequently but calls them infrequently (only when spawning a task), the total overhead can be reduced significantly even with high invocation costs.

Idle workers request tasks from *loaded* workers. When receiving a task request, a loaded worker (victim) creates a new task by dividing the current running task,

---

[2] The effect is significant only when the cost of managing logical threads is relatively high (in expected time) as in Cilk-5. There are multithreaded languages and systems (such as StackThreads/MP [23] and OPA [25]) in which the cost of managing logical threads is quite low.

and returns the new task to the idle worker. When an idle worker (thief) receives a task, it executes the task and returns the result of the task.

In the current implementation of Tascell, each worker employs a single execution stack for multiple tasks. When a worker must wait for the result of a stolen task, it calls a C function which attempts to steal (and execute with the worker's stack) another task by dividing the stolen task.[3] When the result is available, the return to the "current" task is performed as the ordinary return in C; that is, the "current" task is managed (or "suspended") with C's call/return mechanism.

In Tascell, spawned tasks are managed. More precisely, a task request, the stolen (spawned) task, the result of the stolen task, and the ACK of the result are managed by both the victim and thief workers. A task and its result are represented by a task object.

Figure 1 shows a Tascell program that performs backtrack search for finding all possible solutions to the Pentomino puzzle. We defined a task object named pentomino. Several fields are declared as the search input. The field s is declared for storing the result. A Tascell worker that receives a pentomino task executes pentomino's task_exec body. In the task_exec body, Tascell worker can refer to the received task object by the keyword this.

In *worker functions*, which are specified by the keyword worker (like cilk procedures in Cilk), we can use Tascell's task division constructs. A parallel for loop construct can be used for dividing an iterative computation. It is syntactically denoted by:

```
for(int identifier : expression_from , expression_to) statement_body
    handles task-name (int identifier_from , int identifier_to)
    { statement_put statement_get}
```

This iterates $statement_{body}$ over integers from $expression_{from}$ (inclusive) to $expression_{to}$ (exclusive). When the implicit task-request handler (available during the iterative execution of $statement_{body}$) is invoked, the *upper half* of the remaining iterations are spawned as a new *task-name* task, whose object is initialized by $statement_{put}$. In $statement_{put}$, the actual assigned range can be referred to by $identifier_{from}$ and $identifier_{to}$. The worker handles the result of the spawned task by executing $statement_{get}$.[4] Note that a worker performs iterations for a parallel for loop sequentially unless requested; the worker does not create any logical threads and can (re)use a single workspace (such as a worker-local array) for a long time.

Parallel for statements may be nested *dynamically* in their $statement_{body}$. Therefore, multiple task-request handlers may be available at the same time.

---

[3] This saves the execution stack as in Leapfrogging [27]. TBB [16] employs a more general technique for saving the execution stack.

[4] Specifying a task definition and several statements to handle task objects makes Tascell programs more verbose than Cilk programs. These costs are necessary for more exact control of workspaces and distributed memory environment support.

```
task pentomino {
  out: int s; // output
  in: int k, i0, i1, i2;
  in: int a[12]; // manage unused pieces
  in: int b[70]; // the board, with (6+sentinel) × 10 cells
};
task_exec pentomino {
  this.s = search (this.k, this.i0, this.i1, this.i2, &this);
}

worker int search (int k, int j0, int j1, int j2, task pentomino *tsk)
{
  int s=0; // the number of solutions
  // parallel for construct in Tascell
  for (int p : j1, j2)
    {
      int ap=tsk->a[p];
      for (each possible direction d of the piece) {
        ... local variable definitions here ...
        if (Can the ap-th piece in the d-th direction be placed
            on the board tsk->b?);
        else continue;
        dynamic_wind // construct for specifying undo/redo operations
          { // do/redo operation for dynamic_wind
            Set the ap-th piece onto the board tsk->b and update tsk->a.
          }
          { // body for dynamic_wind
            kk = the next empty cell;
            if (no empty cell?) s++; // a solution found
            else // try the next piece
              s += search (kk, j0+1, j0+1, 12, tsk);
          }
          { // undo operation for dynamic_wind
            Backtrack, i.e., remove the ap-th piece from tsk->b and restore tsk->a.
          } // end of dynamic_wind
      }
    }
  handles pentomino (int i1, int i2) // Declaration of this and setting
                                     // a range (i1-i2) is done implicitly
    {
      // put part (performed before sending a task)
      { // put task inputs for upper half iterations
        copy_piece_info (this.a, tsk->a);
        copy_board (this.b, tsk->b);
        this.k=k; this.i0=j0; this.i1=i1; this.i2=i2;
      }
      // get part (performed after receiving the result)
      { s += this.s; }
    } // end of parallel for
  return s;
}
```

Fig. 1. A Tascell program that performs backtrack search for Pentomino

Each worker attempts to detect a task request by polling at every parallel `for` statement without heavy memory barrier (fence) instructions. When the worker detects a task request, it performs temporary backtracking in order to spawn a larger task by invoking as old a handler as possible.

We may use the `dynamic_wind` construct in order to specify how to perform undo-redo operations during the backtracking (undo) and the return from the backtracking (redo). In Figure 1, the worker employs a single workspace for representing a board with pieces (within `tsk`) unless it receives a task request; the *dynamic winder* temporarily removes pieces in order to restore a task-spawnable state near the root of the backtrack search tree so that the oldest *task-request handler* can spawn a larger task as `this` by copying the restored workspace (within `tsk`).

Our approach differs from LTC in the following manner:

- Our worker performs a sequential computation unless it receives a task request. Because no *logical threads* are created as potential tasks, the cost of managing a queue for them can be eliminated.
- In multithreaded languages, each (logical) thread requires its own workspace. In contrast, our worker can reuse a single workspace while it performs a sequential computation to improve the locality of reference and achieve a higher performance.
- When we implement a backtrack search algorithm in multithreaded languages, each thread often needs its own copy of its parent thread's workspace. In contrast, our worker can delay copying between workspaces by using backtracking.
- Our approach supports (heterogeneous) distributed memory environments (including mixed-endian environments) without using distributed shared memory systems.

Note that LTC assumes that the number of really created tasks (and steals) is incomparably smaller than the number of logical threads. Our approach also assumes that the number of really spawned tasks (and steals) is very small. This assumption justifies our approach, which accepts higher work-stealing (backtracking) overheads in order to achieve lower serial overheads than more conventional LTC such as Cilk.

Our approach is "logical thread"-free, but its ability to restore task-spawnable states without loss of good serial efficiency depends heavily on L-closures and the notion of lazy stack frame management [14, 30]. The idea of lazy frame management can also be applied to logical threads. Indolent Closure Creation [21] employs this idea for Cilk; its technique of using a shadow stack is similar to the lazy validation of an explicit stack in our transformation-based implementation [14] of L-closures. StackThreads/MP [23] enables each worker to manage logical threads within its execution stack by allowing the frame pointer to walk the execution stack independently of the stack pointer. (Our compiler-based implementation [30] of L-closures is based on generalization of this technique.) Moreover, our previous work [25] shows that the notion of "laziness" is effective for modern multithreaded languages with thread IDs and dynamically-scoped synchronizers.

Notice that Tascell's approach is to employ different semantics from multithreading rather than to reduce costs for multithreading. Tascell's approach enables further performance improvement by reusing a workspace and delaying copying between workspaces. This is the case in most multithreaded languages other than Cilk. In Cilk, a pseudovariable SYNCHED is provided, which promotes the reuse of a workspace among child logical threads [22].

2.5 Other Frameworks

WorkCrews [26], Leapfrogging [27], and Lazy RPC [7] take the parent-first strategy; at a fork point, a worker executes the parent thread prior to the child thread and makes the child stealable for other workers, and calls the child thread if it has not been stolen at the join point of the parent thread. Tascell uses a similar strategy; however, creations of stealable entities are delayed and mostly omitted.

Lazy Threads [9] realizes further optimization for spawning a thread by translating it into a *parallel ready sequential call*. It achieves a lower thread creation cost than the original LTC by avoiding operations for queueing a new thread. However, this technique can be applied only for consecutive forks. Furthermore, it is unclear how this technique can coexist with the *oldest-first* work stealing strategy.

We can find few pieces of recent work that make remarkable advances following the abovementioned techniques; for example, X10[4]'s thread (or activity) creation and synchronization are inspired by Cilk, and the fundamental parts of recent techniques [5, 17, 10, 11] are not beyond the abovementioned techniques. This means that the LTC/Cilk-originating ideas of "logical threads" for load balancing reach maturity.

3 Future Perspective

There is a research topic in Tascell. In Tascell, when a worker waits for the result of a stolen task, it tries to steal (and executes) another task of the task requester until the result is returned. This restriction is posed for saving the execution stack as in Leapfrogging [27]. This also limits the choice of tasks to steal and therefore might limit parallelism and cause tightly stealing workers. The use of multiple execution stacks for a single worker would alleviate the problem. In addition, the only temporary use of a constantly bounded execution stack would solve the problem; this means that continuations should be stealable.

For multithreaded languages (and Tascell with stealable continuations), the implementation for distributed memory is difficult mainly because the implicit stealable continuations are difficult to move to another node. The idea of Cilk++ hyperobjects, where the objects themselves can interact with steals, may be applied to this problem.

With the growing popularity of highly/massively parallel architectures, scalability and dependability will be very important properties of load balancing frameworks. Extending load balancing frameworks to support these properties would be required.

In a large scale shared memory system, preventing data races would become important. Type systems may be useful for preventing data races from occurring in the first place (e.g., based on [24]).

Recent computer architectures for high performance computing tend to exploit heterogeneity and hierarchy. Software systems also employ multiple programming languages and advanced features such as dynamic compilation. Load balancing frameworks and other frameworks should exploit these aspects for efficiency, meaning not only high performance but also low energy consumption. Clear modularity of concurrent objects can provide clear (extended) models for the design and verification of such complex systems.

References

1. Agha, G.: Actors: A Model of Concurrent Computation in Distributed Systems. The MIT Press (1987)
2. America, P., Rutten, J.: A layered semantics for a parallel object-oriented languages. In: de Bakker, J.W., de Roever, W.-P., Rozenberg, G. (eds.) REX 1990. LNCS, vol. 489, pp. 91–123. Springer, Heidelberg (1991)
3. Blumofe, R.D., Joerg, C.F., Kuszmaul, B.C., Leiserson, C.E., Randall, K.H., Zhou, Y.: Cilk: an efficient multithreaded runtime system. In: Proceedings of the Fifth ACM SIGPLAN Symposium on Principles and Practice of Parallel Programming, PPoPP 1995, pp. 207–216 (1995)
4. Charles, P., Grothoff, C., Saraswat, V., Donawa, C., Kielstra, A., Ebcioglu, K., von Praun, C., Sarkar, V.: X10: an object-oriented approach to non-uniform cluster computing. SIGPLAN Not. 40(10), 519–538 (2005)
5. Cong, G., Kodali, S., Krishnamoorthy, S., Lea, D., Saraswat, V., Wen, T.: Solving large, irregular graph problems using adaptive work-stealing. In: ICPP 2008: Proceedings of the 2008 37th International Conference on Parallel Processing, pp. 536–545. IEEE Computer Society (2008)
6. Feeley, M.: A message passing implementation of lazy task creation. In: Halstead, R.H., Ito, T. (eds.) US/Japan WS 1992. LNCS, vol. 748, pp. 94–107. Springer, Heidelberg (1993)
7. Feeley, M.: Lazy remote procedure call and its implementation in a parallel variant of C. In: Queinnec, C., Halstead, R.H., Ito, T. (eds.) PSLS 1995. LNCS, vol. 1068, pp. 3–21. Springer, Heidelberg (1996)
8. Frigo, M., Leiserson, C.E., Randall, K.H.: The implementation of the Cilk-5 multithreaded language. ACM SIGPLAN Notices (PLDI 1998) 33(5), 212–223 (1998)
9. Goldstein, S.C., Schauser, K.E., Culler, D.E.: Lazy Threads: Implementing a fast parallel call. Journal of Parallel and Distributed Computing 3(1), 5–20 (1996)
10. Guo, Y., Barik, R., Raman, R., Sarkar, V.: Work-first and help-first scheduling policies for async-finish task parallelism. In: 23rd IEEE International Symposium on Parallel and Distributed Processing (IPDPS 2009), pp. 1–12 (May 2009)
11. Guo, Y., Zhao, J., Cave, V., Sarkar, V.: Slaw: a scalable locality-aware adaptive work-stealing scheduler. In: 24th IEEE International Symposium on Parallel and Distributed Processing (IPDPS 2010), pp. 1–12 (April 2010)

12. Halstead, R.H.: New ideas in parallel Lisp: Language design, implementation, and programming tools. In: Ito, T., Halstead, R.H. (eds.) US/Japan WS 1989. LNCS, vol. 441, pp. 2–57. Springer, Heidelberg (1990)

13. Hiraishi, T., Yasugi, M., Umatani, S., Yuasa, T.: Backtracking-based load balancing. In: Proceedings of the 14th ACM SIGPLAN Symposium on Principles and Practice of Parallel Programming (PPoPP 2009), pp. 55–64 (February 2009)

14. Hiraishi, T., Yasugi, M., Yuasa, T.: A transformation-based implementation of lightweight nested functions. IPSJ Digital Courier 2, 262–279 (2006), IPSJ Transactions on Programming 47(SIG 6(PRO 29)), 50–67

15. Honda, K., Tokoro, M.: An object calculus for asynchronous communication. In: America, P. (ed.) ECOOP 1991. LNCS, vol. 512, pp. 133–147. Springer, Heidelberg (1991)

16. Intel Corporation: Intel Threading Building Block Tutorial (2007), http://threadingbuildingblocks.org/

17. Michael, M.M., Vechev, M.T., Saraswat, V.A.: Idempotent work stealing. In: Proceedings of the 14th ACM SIGPLAN Symposium on Principles and Practice of Parallel Programming (PPoPP 2009), pp. 45–54 (February 2009)

18. Mohr, E., Kranz, D.A., Halstead, R.H.: Lazy task creation: A technique for increasing the granularity of parallel programs. IEEE Transactions on Parallel and Distributed Systems 2(3), 264–280 (1991)

19. Sakai, S., Yamaguchi, Y., Hiraki, K., Kodama, Y., Yuba, T.: An architecture of a dataflow single chip processor. In: Proc. of the 16th Annual International Symposium on Computer Architecture, pp. 46–53 (June 1989)

20. Shibayama, E.: An Object-Based Approach to Modeling Concurrent Systems. Ph.D. thesis, Department of Information Science, The University of Tokyo (1991)

21. Strumpen, V.: Indolent closure creation. Tech. Rep. MIT-LCS-TM-580, MIT (June 1998)

22. Supercomputing Technologies Group: Cilk 5.4.6 Reference Manual. Massachusetts Institute of Technology, Laboratory for Computer Science, Cambridge, Massachusetts, USA

23. Taura, K., Tabata, K., Yonezawa, A.: StackThreads/MP: Integrating futures into calling standards. In: Proceedings of ACM SIGPLAN Symposium on Principles & Practice of Parallel Programming (PPoPP 1999), pp. 60–71 (May 1999)

24. Terauchi, T.: Checking race freedom via linear programming. In: Proceedings of the 2008 ACM SIGPLAN Conference on Programming Language Design and Implementation, PLDI 2008, pp. 1–10 (2008)

25. Umatani, S., Yasugi, M., Komiya, T., Yuasa, T.: Pursuing laziness for efficient implementation of modern multithreaded languages. In: Veidenbaum, A., Joe, K., Amano, H., Aiso, H. (eds.) ISHPC 2003. LNCS, vol. 2858, pp. 174–188. Springer, Heidelberg (2003)

26. Vandevoorde, M.T., Roberts, E.S.: WorkCrews: An abstraction for controlling parallelism. International Journal of Parallel Programming 17(4), 347–366 (1988)

27. Wagner, D.B., Calder, B.G.: Leapfrogging: A portable technique for implementing efficient futures. In: Proceedings of Principles and Practice of Parallel Programming (PPoPP 1993), pp. 208–217 (1993)

28. Yasugi, M.: A concurrent object-oriented programming language system for highly parallel data-driven computers and its applications. Tech. Rep. 94-7e, Department of Information Science, Faculty of Science, University of Tokyo (April 1994), Doctoral Thesis (March 1994)

29. Yasugi, M., Hiraishi, T., Umatani, S., Yuasa, T.: Parallel graph traversals using work-stealing frameworks for many-core platforms. Journal of Information Processing 20(1), 128–139 (2012)
30. Yasugi, M., Hiraishi, T., Yuasa, T.: Lightweight lexical closures for legitimate execution stack access. In: Mycroft, A., Zeller, A. (eds.) CC 2006. LNCS, vol. 3923, pp. 170–184. Springer, Heidelberg (2006)
31. Yonezawa, A. (ed.): ABCL: An Object-Oriented Concurrent System — Theory, Language, Programming, Implementation and Application. The MIT Press (1990)
32. Yonezawa, A., Briot, J.P., Shibayama, E.: Object-oriented concurrent programming in ABCL/1. In: Proc. of ACM Conference on OOPSLA, pp. 258–268 (1986)

Verifiable Object-Oriented Transactions

Suad Alagić and Adnan Fazeli

Department of Computer Science,
University of Southern Maine, Portland, Maine, USA
alagic@usm.maine.edu, adfazeli@gmail.com

Abstract. Unlike the existing object-oriented and other database technologies, database schemas in the technology developed in this research are equipped with very general integrity constraints specified in a declarative, logic-based fashion. These declarative specifications are expressed in object-oriented assertion languages and they apply to transactions that are implemented in a full-fledged, mainstream object-oriented programming language. The model of transactions is based on more advanced features of object-oriented type systems, the ownership model, and very general constraints. The main distinction in comparison with other database technologies is that transactions can be verified to satisfy the schema integrity constraints. The two main contributions of this paper are object-oriented schemas equipped with integrity constraints and static verification of transactions with respect to the integrity constraints. Solutions to these open problems have been out of reach so far. Furthermore, transaction verification is not only largely static, but it is also automatic, so that the subtleties of the underlying verification technology are hidden from the users. In addition to static verification, the technology offers dynamic enforcement of the integrity constraints when necessary. The overall outcome is a significant increase in data integrity along with run-time efficiency and reliability of transactions.

1 Introduction

This paper is addressing a major limitation of the current generation of object-oriented database systems. In fact, other widely used database technologies exhibit the same problem. The solution to this problem developed in this paper is based on recent developments in assertion languages and verification technologies. This represents a major departure from the technologies and tools that are commonly used in database systems.

The key issue in object-oriented database systems is management of persistent objects. Object-oriented languages have no support for persistent objects that would be suitable for databases. An object-oriented database schema specifies (collections of) persistent objects, and their types in particular. Complex actions on persistent objects are expressed as programs in an object-oriented programming language. A transaction is expected to start in a consistent database state and if successfully completed it must leave the database in a consistent state.

G. Agha et al. (Eds.): Yonezawa Festschrift, LNCS 8665, pp. 251–275, 2014.

The current generation of object-oriented systems is based on typed object-oriented programming languages. This is a source of a major discrepancy: data languages are declarative and mainstream object-oriented languages by themselves do not have such capabilities. Database schemas, the consistency requirements, and queries should be specified in a declarative style.

The current object technology has nontrivial problems in specifying even classical database integrity constraints, such as keys and referential integrity [10,17,20]. No industrial database technology allows object-oriented schemas equipped with general integrity constraints. In addition to keys and referential integrity, such constraints include ranges of values or number of occurrences, ordering, constraints that apply to inheritance, and the integrity requirements for complex objects obtained by aggregation [2]. More general constraints that are not necessarily classical database constraints come from complex application environments and they are often critical for correct functioning of those applications [3].

Object-oriented schemas are generally missing database integrity constraints because those are not expressible in type systems of mainstream object-oriented programming languages. Since the integrity constraints cannot be specified in a declarative fashion, the only option is to enforce them procedurally with nontrivial implications on efficiency and reliability. In a typed constraint-based database technology, the constraints would fit into the type systems of object-oriented languages and they should be integrated with reflective capabilities of those languages [22] so that they can be introspected at run-time. Most importantly, all of that is not sufficient if there is no technology to enforce the constraints, preferably statically, so that expensive recovery procedures will not be required when a transaction violates the constraints at run-time [2,3].

The idea of static verification of transaction safety with respect to the database integrity constraints has been considered in previous research [8,23,25,6] but it has not been implemented at a very practical level so that it can be used by typical object-oriented database programmers. The first problem is that object database technologies such as ODMG [9], Db4 [10], and Objectivity [20] are not equipped with general constraints, and even have difficulties in specifying keys and referential integrity [17]. This problem is resolved in this research by using an object-oriented assertion language such as JML [13] or Spec# [19]. An assertion language allows specification of schemas with general database integrity constraints (invariants) and transactions can be specified in a declarative fashion with preconditions and postconditions.

The ability to statically verify that a transaction implemented in a mainstream object-oriented language satisfies the database integrity constraints has been out of reach for a long time. Some of our previous results were based on a higher-order interactive verification system which is so sophisticated that it is unlikely to be used by database programmers. A pragmatic goal has been static automatic verification which completely hides the prover technology from the users. Automatic static verification of the object-oriented constraints is a major distinction with respect to our previous work [3,4] as well as with respect to other work [8,23,25,6]. Our goals are object-oriented schemas with general integrity constraints, transactions written in a mainstream object-oriented language, and their static verification that guarantees ACID properties in an implementation based on an object-oriented database management system. These goals represent a significant advancement of our previous results reported in [2].

A key observation is that if it is not possible to verify that transactions satisfy the schema integrity constraints, then it is not possible to truly guarantee the ACID properties of the transaction model. ACID stands for atomicity, isolation, consistency and durability. A serializable concurrent execution of a set of transactions has the property that it will maintain the schema integrity constraints only as long as the individual transactions by themselves (i.e., in isolation) satisfy those constraints [11]. This explains the relationship between the research reported in this paper and other research on object-oriented transactions. Most recent research on object-oriented transactions, such as [14,26,24], has been directed toward an apparatus for providing properties such as atomicity, isolation, and serializability that would replace the existing inadequate concurrent apparatus in object-oriented programming languages with respect to transactions. The integrity constraints (the C component) are not considered. Our research does exactly that.

The contributions of this paper are:

- Specification of object-oriented database schemas equipped with classical as well as more general integrity constraints not available in the existing database technologies.
- Schema modeling techniques based on abstraction, specification inheritance, and aggregation including the ownership model.
- A model of object-oriented transactions equipped with declarative specifications and techniques for automatic static and dynamic verification of transaction safety with respect to the schema integrity constraints.
- A complex object-oriented application that demonstrates the above techniques, verification of complex transactions in particular.
- A model of ACID transactions implemented on top of an object-oriented database management system that guarantees all ACID properties, the C component in particular.

This paper is organized as follows. We first specify (section 2) the basic features of our model of object-oriented transactions. General issues of concurrent transactions and the integrity constrains are discussed in section 3. In section 4 we present some key semantic concepts for modeling complex application environments and the associated transactions. Levels of consistency as they relate to the model of transactions and the ownership model are discussed in section 5. In section 6 we consider complex schemas equipped with a variety of general integrity constraints, including classical database constraints such as keys and referential integrity. This is followed by sample transactions with respect to schemas equipped with integrity constraints in section 7. In section 8 we elaborate the relationship between declarative specification of constraints and database queries. The impact of inheritance on the schema integrity constraints is discussed in section 9. Abstraction techniques for object-oriented schema are given in section 10. Dynamic constraint checking is the subject of section 11. The implementation issues related to the underlying database platform are discussed in section 12. Related research is summarized in section 13 and conclusions are given in section 14.

2   Transaction Model

Our main contribution is an implemented model of automatic verification of object-oriented transactions with respect to the object-oriented schemas equipped with constraints. To our knowledge this is the first time such a verification was possible for transactions written in a full-fledged mainstream object-oriented language and object-oriented schemas and transactions extended with very general constraints.

The components of our transaction model are more sophisticated features of the type system such as bounded parametric polymorphism, the ownership model, specification of the schema integrity constraints, pre and post conditions for transactions, and their automatic verification.

In our transaction model there exists an interface *Schema* and a class *Transaction*. Specific schemas implement the interface *Schema*.

A schema is a complex object, an aggregation of its components. A schema is the owner of its components. The ownership model of our transaction model allows constraints that apply to complex objects and their components. A particular case are integrity constraints that apply to complex schema objects. Objects with the same owner are modeled as peers. This in particular applies to components of a schema object.

Our model of transactions allows controlled updates of persistent objects in such a way that the constraints associated with complex objects, and schema objects in particular, are enforced. Independent updates of components of a complex object that might violate the integrity constraints that apply to the whole complex object are not allowed. Situations in which a transaction necessarily and temporarily violates the schema integrity constraints are carefully controlled in this model.

The relationship between a transaction object and a schema object is also modeled as a peer relationship. A transaction is not a component of a schema, and a schema is not a component of a transaction. There are multiple transactions accessing the same schema object and all of them cannot own the schema object. An object can have at most one owner. In addition, there are constraint-related reasons for modeling a transaction and its schema as peers to be elaborated in section 4. The basic features of the transaction model are represented in figure 1.

In our approach, the class *Transaction* is bounded parametric, where the bound type is the type of schema to which a specific transaction type is bound. This makes it possible for a particular transaction class to be compiled with respect to a specific schema type. The notation in the code given below follows

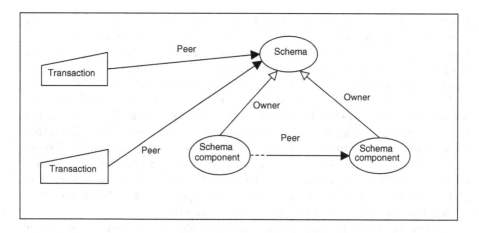

Fig. 1. Transactions and schemas

Spec#. $T!$ denotes a non-null object type, i.e., an object type that does not allow null references. The attribute [Peer] indicates that the relationship between a transaction object and its associated schema object is specified as the peer relationship. The attribute [SpecPublic] denotes private components that can be used as public only in specifications.

public interface Schema {...}

public class Transaction $<$T$>$ **where** T: Schema {
[**SpecPublic**][**Peer**] **protected** T! schema;
public Transaction(T! schema){ this.schema = schema;}
}

   Both schemas and transactions are equipped with very general logic-based constraints to be elaborated throughout the paper starting with sections 6 and 7.

3   Concurrent Transactions and Integrity Constraints

Our view is that a database schema should be equipped with explicitly specified integrity constraints that transactions acting on the database must satisfy. The database is acted upon by a set of concurrent transactions. A well-known fact is that concurrent executions of transactions may violate the database integrity constraints even if individual transactions do not.

   If individual transactions respect the integrity constrains, then obviously their *serial execution* will as well. That is, if the integrity constraints hold initially, they will hold after completion of the first transaction, and likewise they will hold after each subsequent transaction in a serial execution.

   However, *serial executions* are unacceptable for performance and database availability reasons. Database technologies are naturally based on concurrent transactions. Since concurrent transactions may violate the integrity constraints, they must be managed by a technology that allows only those concurrent executions that do not violate those constraints. From the viewpoint of database integrity, those concurrent executions are equivalent to serial executions. Such concurrent executions are called *serializable executions* [11].

A *concurrent execution* is *serializable* if it has an equivalent *serial execution*. Two executions are said to be equivalent from the viewpoint of integrity if they have the same ordering of conflicting actions. Two actions are conflicting if they are executed on the same object and at least one of them is an update. Various locking protocols have been invented and implemented to guarantee the serializability condition. The classical and the best known is *two phase locking*. Two phase locking is a pessimistic strategy and it is provably a sufficient condition for seralizability [11]. There are optimistic alternatives.

The beauty of the classical results on serializability is that they do not depend upon a particular form of the integrity constraints. But the underlying assumption is that whatever the integrity constraints are, each individual transaction in a concurrent execution is required to satisfy those constraints in isolation. Research on object-oriented transactions or the current generation of object-oriented database systems do not address this fundamental requirement. The reason is that there has been no technology to deal with more complex integrity constraints. This is precisely the main point of the research reported in this paper. We develop verification techniques that would guarantee that an object-oriented transaction satisfies the database integrity constraints.

The verification techniques for object-oriented transactions that we investigated belong to one of the following categories:

– *Dynamic enforcement of constraints*
  A representative of this type of technology is JML [13]. In this case schema constraints and transactions are specified in JML, and transactions are full-fledged Java programs. Database technologies enforce a few classical database constraints such as keys and foreign keys. JML allows much more general constraints. The main disadvantage is that violations are detected at run-time, where the implications may be non-trivial, such as invocation of expensive recovery procedures to maintain data integrity. In addition, dynamic enforcements of constraints in database systems comes with a siginificant cost. But very general constraints are specifiable and enforceable.

– *Static interactive reasoning*
  A representative of this type of technology is PVS [21]. The main advantage of this technology is that it is very general. PVS is a higher-order verification system that allows specifications of specialized logics suitable for transaction verification. Careful investigation of the transaction model shows that it is actually temporal in nature. This is why we developed transaction verification techniques in PVS that are based on a suitable temporal logic [3]. The main disadvantage of this technology is that it requires very sophisticated users and hence it is not likely to be directly used by ordinary database programmers. This technology has a complementary role in our transaction

verification environment. It is used to verify more general integrity constraints (such as temporal) that technologies based on object-oriented assertion languages cannot handle.

– *Automatic static verification*
This is the most appealing technology from the viewpoint of users. A representative of this technology is Spec# [15]. In our approach, schemas and transactions are specified in Spec# and transactions are full-fledged C# programs. In this technology the subtleties of the underlying prover technology are hidden from the users. Static automatic verification is attempted, with runtime checks generated as well. In addition, this particular technology comes with the ownership model that it is essential for a sophisticated model of object-oriented transactions. It also comes with features that allow controlled updates that might violate the integrity constraints. This technology is the focus of this paper because it is precisely what has been out of reach for many years: static verification of very general integrity constraints for transactions written in a mainstream, preferably object-oriented, programming language.

In the transaction verification technology presented in this paper static verification is complemented with dynamic checks. Dynamic checks are in fact necessary even if static verification succeeds. Static verification guarantees that the transaction code is correct with respect to the schema integrity constraints and the transaction specification in terms of its pre and post conditions. But if the schema integrity constraints or the transaction precondition do not hold at the transaction start, the results of static verification do not apply. In many situations checking the transaction precondition is possible only at run-time. For example, inserting an object into a database collection equipped with a key constraint requires checking that the key of the inserted element does not already exist in the database collection. This is why the transaction code must be written in such a way that it handles run-time exceptions caused by dynamic checks of constraints. In the absence of such exceptions, or if those exceptions are correctly managed, the transaction postcondition and the schema integrity constrains will hold at the transaction completion (commit) point. The key point about static verification is that if a transaction fails a static check, it should never be executed. This avoids major problems related to violation of the integrity constraints running a transaction that provably does not satisfy those constrains. The penalties of executing such a transaction are aborting a transaction and invoking expensive recovery procedures to restore database consistency.

4 Owners and Peers

In this section we consider the semantic modeling techniques for object-oriented database schemas explicitly supported in the technology presented in this paper. These techniques have not been considered in object database technologies such as ODMG [9], Db4 [10], and Objectivity [20], and hence have no proper support in those technologies.

In addition to inheritance, the key abstraction technique for modeling complex applications in this paper is aggregation. This abstraction is well understood in semantic data models, but in the object-oriented model it has specific implications. A complex object defined by aggregation is represented by its root object called the owner along with references to the immediate components of the owner specified as its representation fields. References to other objects do not represent components of that object. This way a complex object is defined as a logical unit that includes all of its components. Constraints that apply to objects defined by aggregation may now be specified in such a way that they refer both to the owner object and to the components defined by its representation fields. In a flight scheduling application developed in this paper, a flight scheduling object is defined as an aggregation of flights, planes and airports, as illustrated in figure 2.

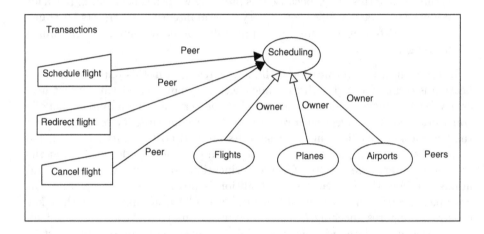

Fig. 2. Owners and peers in flight scheduling

The notion of ownership comes with a related semantic modeling notion. Objects that have the same owner are called peers. The relationship among objects flights, planes and airports is clearly not the ownership relationship. These objects are peers as they have the same owner, the scheduling object.

The peer relationship has a role that may be even independent from the notion of ownership. Consider the relationship of a transaction object and its associated schema object. As we already explained, a transaction and its associated schema are modeled as peers. Of course, we may view the overall application as the owner of the schema object and all the associated transaction objects.

In addition to the above abstractions, inheritance is naturally an essential modeling abstraction which we do not show in the above diagram. The model of this application includes inheritance hierarchies of different aircraft types and different airport types, as well as an inheritance hierarchy of different transaction types. The interplay of inheritance and constraints is discussed in section 9.

5   Levels of Consistency

The schema integrity constraints are typically violated during transaction execution and then the constraints are reinstated when the transaction is completed, so that the constraints should hold at commit time. The mechanism for handling correctly these situations is illustrated below by the structure of a transaction that closes an airport:

expose(flight scheduling){
close airport;
cancel all flights to or from the closed airport;
}

After the first action the referential integrity constraints are temporarily violated to be reinstated after the second action of cancelling all flights to or from the closed airport. The purpose of the **expose** block is to indicate that the schema object invariants may be violated in this block. Otherwise, the verifier will indicate violation of the schema invariants. In the **expose** block the object is assumed to be in a mutable state and hence violation of the object invariants is allowed. Outside of the **expose** block, assignments that possibly violate the invariants will be static errors. Different situations that may occur with respect to the object state and its satisfaction of the object invariants are summarized below:

- **Valid** object state – object invariants hold, updates must satisfy the invariants.
- **Mutable** object state - object invariants are not required to hold, updates are allowed to violate them
- **Consistent** object state – the object is in a **valid** state and
  - the object does not have an owner or
  - the owner is in a **mutable** state
- **Committed** object state – the object is in a **valid** state and
  - the object has an owner
  - the owner is also in a **valid** state.

When a transaction operates on an object, the implicit assumption is that the object is in a consistent state. This means that either the object does not have an owner to put restrictions on the object, or that the object has an owner, and the owner is in a mutable state, hence it allows update actions on the object. Since the object is in a consistent state, its state is valid and its components are thus in a committed state. In order to update the receiver and the states of its components, the receiver state must be changed to a mutable state using the *expose* block. This will also change the state of the components of the object from committed to consistent, so that methods can be invoked on them. The notions of valid, mutable, consistent and committed objects, and the effect of the expose statement, are illustrated in figure 3.

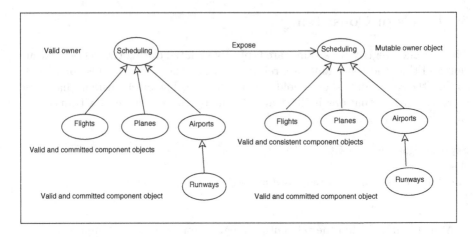

Fig. 3. Flight scheduling consistency states

There is an obvious alternative to viewing a transaction and its associated schema as peers: just omit any ownership or peer attributes. But in fact, using the peer relationship has important implications for transaction verification. A transaction is verified under the assumption that the schema integrity constraints hold when the transaction is started. If this condition is not satisfied, a transaction cannot be verified even if it is in fact correct with respect to the schema integrity constraints. So we really have to guarantee this condition.

Spec# adds an implicit precondition for peer consistency so that a transaction can assume this condition in its verification. This applies to in-bound parameters and the receiver of any method. The implicit postcondition for peer consistency also applies to all out-bound parameters and return values. The caller of a method is required to satisfy the peer consistency requirement. This means that an object and its peers must be valid, and their owner must be exposed first before an update is performed.

6   Constraints for Schemas

We now consider a specific schema in which the core object type is defined using the aggregation abstraction and the ownership model along with the associated integrity constraints. The *FlightScheduling* schema contains specification of three database collections: a list of airplanes, a list of airports, and a list of flights.

The schema *FlightScheduling* exhibits two cases of the aggregation abstraction as supported by the Spec# ownership model. The attribute [Rep] indicates that the lists of flights, airports and airplanes are components of the flight scheduling object which becomes their owner. The attribute [ElementsRep] indicates that list elements are also components of the flight scheduling object. These elements are then peers according to the Spec# ownership model. This has implications on invariants that can now be defined to apply to entire complex objects, i.e., including their components determined by the [Rep] and [ElementsRep] fields. These constraints are called ownership-based invariants.

public class FlightScheduling: Schema {

[**SpecPublic**][**Rep**] [**ElementsRep**] **private** List<Airplane!>! airplanes;

[**SpecPublic**][**Rep**] [**ElementsRep**] **private** List<Airport!>! airports;

[**SpecPublic**][**Rep**] [**ElementsRep**] **private** List<Flight!>! flights;
// constraints
}

In the collection of airplanes the key is *Id*, in the collection of airports the key is *Code*, and in the collection of flights the key is *FlightId*. The first referential integrity constraint specifies that each flight in the collection of flights refers to a unique airplane in the collection of airplanes. The remaining (omitted) referential integrity constraints specify that each flight in the collection of flights refers to a unique airport as its origin and a unique airport as its destination.

For presentation purposes, the notation in this paper is more mathematical than the Spec# notation. However, there is a direct correspondence between this notation and the Spec# notation.

invariant $\forall\{$int $i \in$ (0: flights.Count), int $j \in$ (0: flights.Count);
    flights[i].FlightId = flights[j].FlightId $\Rightarrow$ flights[i].Equals(flights[j]))$\}$;

invariant $\forall\{$int $i \in$ (0: flights.Count);
    $\exists$ **unique** {int $j \in$ (0: airplanes.Count); airplanes[j].Equals(flights[i].Airplane)$\}\}$;

A class is in general equipped with an invariant which specifies valid object states. The schema integrity constraints are specified above as class invariants. These assertions allow usage of universal and existential quantifiers as in the first-order predicate calculus, as well as combinators typical for database languages such as min, max, sum, count, avg etc. These constraints in the above schema refer to private components of the schema object. As explained earlier, the attribute [SpecPublic] means that these private components can be used as public only in specifications. Typically, such components will also be defined as public properties with appropriately defined *get* and *set* methods so that access to them can be controlled.

Spec# constraints limit universal and existential quantification to variables ranging over finite intervals. The above constraints contain specifications of half open intervals. The limitation that quantifiers are restricted to integer variables ranging over finite intervals was a design decision to sacrifice expressiveness in order to allow automatic static verification. This limitation is no problem in the application considered in this paper as the above schema shows.

The above schema contains non-null object types (indicated by the symbol *!*) that capture a very specific object-oriented integrity constraint. A frequent problem in object-oriented programs is an attempt to dereference a null reference. If this happens in a database transaction, the transaction may fail at run-time with nontrivial consequences. The Spec# type system allows specification of non-null object types. Static checking will indicate situations in which an attempt is made to access an object via a possibly null reference.

7   Sample Transactions

Each class that a schema refers to is also equipped with its constraints as illustrated below for the class *Flight*. The relationship between a flight object and the associated airplane object is defined as a peer relationship for the reasons explained in section 4. The invariants include the obvious ones: the origin and the destination of a flight must be different and the departure time must precede the arrival time. If the current time is greater than the arrival time or the current time is less than the departure time, the status of the flight must be idle. If the current time is greater than the departure time and less than the arrival time the flight status must be either flying, landing or takeoff.

invariant to $\neq$ from;

invariant departureTime < arrivalTime;

invariant DateTime.Now > arrivalTime $\Rightarrow$ this.flightStatus = FlightStatus.Idle;

invariant DateTime.Now < departureTime $\Rightarrow$ this.flightStatus = FlightStatus.Idle;

invariant DateTime.Now $\geq$ departureTime $\wedge$ DateTime.Now $\leq$ arrivalTime $\Rightarrow$
        this.flightStatus = FlightStatus.TakeOff $\vee$
        this.flightStatus = FlightStatus.Flying $\vee$
        this.flightStatus = FlightStatus.Landing;

The constraints specified in this section include some classical database integrity constraints such as keys and referential integrity, and in addition constraints that are not typical for the existing database technologies, object-oriented in particular. In fact, we are not aware of a database technology that allows constraints of the above variety.

To make the job of the verifier possible, specification of methods that change the object state, such as database updates, requires specification of the frame conditions. This is done by the *modifies* clause, which specifies those objects and their components that are subject to change. The frame assumption is that these are the only objects that will be affected by the change, and the other objects remain the same. An attempt to assign to the latter objects will be a static error.

Sample instantiations of the class *Transaction* by the flight scheduling schema are given below.

public class ScheduleFlightTransaction:
               Transaction<FlightScheduling> {

public Flight? scheduleFlight (string! flightId,
         string! toAirportCode, string! fromAirportCode,
         DateTime departure, DateTime arrival, Airplane! plane)

```
// constraints
{// transaction body }
}
```

Flight? in the above code is an explicit notation for a type that may contain a null value. The preconditions of the transaction *scheduleFlight* are that the flight id does not exist in the list of flights, that its origin (denoted *fromAirportCode*) and its destination (denoted *toAirportCode*) must refer to existing (valid) airport codes, and that the departure time precedes the arrival time. Valid airport codes are kept in a table *ValidCodes*. The transaction *scheduleFlight* modifies only the list of flights as specified in its **modifies** clause. The postcondition guarantees that the newly scheduled flight exists in the list of flights.

requires toAirportCode $\neq$ fromAirportCode;
requires $\forall$ {int i $\in$ (0: schema.Flights.Count);
       schema.Flights[i].FlightId $\neq$ flightId };
requires $\exists$ **unique** {int i $\in$ (0: schema.Airplanes.Count);
       schema.Airplanes[i].Equals(plane)};
requires $\exists$ **unique** {string code $\in$ ValidCodes.airportsCodes;
       code = toAirportCode};
requires $\exists$ **unique** {string code $\in$ ValidCodes.airportsCodes;
       code = fromAirportCode };
requires departure $<$ arrival;
modifies schema.flights;
ensures $\exists$ **unique** {int i $\in$ (0: schema.Flights.Count);
       schema.Flights[i].FlightId = flightId };

The first precondition of the transaction *cancelFlight* specifies that there exists a unique flight in the collection of flights with the given id of the flight to be deleted, denoted *flightId*. The second precondition specifies a requirement that the flight departure time is greater than the current time. The **modifies** clause specifies that this method modifies the collection of flights. The postcondition specifies that the cancelled flight does not appear in the list of flights.

requires $\exists$ **unique** {Flight flight $\in$ schema.Flights;
      flight.FlightId = flightId};
requires $\forall$ {Flight flight $\in$ schema.Flights;
      flight.FlightId = flightId $\Rightarrow$
      flight.departureTime $>$ DateTime.Now };

modifies schema.flights;

ensures $\forall$ {Flight! flight $\in$ schema.Flights;
      flight.FlightId $\neq$ flightId };

The precondition for the transaction *redirectFlight* are that the id of the flight to be redirected, denoted *flightId*, must exist in the list of flights, and that its status must not be landing. This transaction modifies just the list of flights. The postcondition ensures that the destination of the redirected flight has indeed been changed in the list of flights to *newDest*.

requires ∃ **unique** {Flight flight ∈ schema.flights;
    flight.FlightId = flightId ∧ (flight.FlightStatus ≠ FlightStatus.Landing)};
requires ∀ {Flight flight in schema.flights;
    flight.FlightId = flightId ⇒ flight.from ≠ newDest };

modifies schema.flights;

ensures ∀ {Flight! flight in schema.Flights;
    flight.FlightId = flightId ⇒ flight.to = newDest };

8 Constraints and Queries

Queries are pure methods. Pure methods are functions that have no impact on the state of objects, database objects in particular. Interplay of constraints and queries is illustrated below. The attribute [Pure] indicates a pure method and *result* refers to its result.

An example of a query (hence pure) method is *flightsDepartureBetween* which returns a list of flights whose departure time is within a given interval. The preconditions require that the time interval is not empty (i.e. the initial time is less than the end time) and that the initial time is greater than the current time. The postcondition ensures that the flights that are returned by this method have the departure times within the specified bounds.

[**Pure**] **public** List<Flight!>? flightsDepartureBetween
            (DateTime beginDateTime, DateTime endDateTime)
requires beginDateTime < endDateTime;
requires beginDateTime > DateTime.Now;
ensures ∀ {Flight! f ∈ result;
            f.departureTime ≥ beginDateTime ∧
            f.departureTime < endDateTime };
{// method body }

The body of this method is specified as a LINQ query given below:

```
// open db
IEnumerable<Flight> flights =
from Flight flight ∈ db
where flight.departureTime ≥ beginDateTime ∧
      flight.departureTime < endDateTime
select flight;
// close db;
```

A native query in Db4 Objects (details omitted) has the following form:

```
// open db
IList<Flight!>? flights =
db.Query<Flight!>(delegate(Flight! f) {
return (f.departureTime ≥ beginDateTime ∧
        f.departureTime < endDateTime); };
// close db;
```

9   Specification Inheritance

Specifications of constraints in a class are inherited in its subclasses. In addition, method postconditions and class invariants may be strengthened by additional constraints. Method preconditions remain invariant. This discipline with respect to inheritance of constraints is a particular case of behavioral subtyping [16]. It guarantees that an instance of a subtype may be substituted where an instance of the supertype is expected with no behavioral discrepancies.

Consider the class *Airport* given below in which an airport object is the owner of its list of runways, as well as of the specific runways in that list.

```
public class Airport {

[SpecPublic] private string code;
[Additive] protected int numRunways;
[SpecPublic] [Rep] [ElementsRep] protected List<Runway!>! runways;
// methods and constraints
}
```

The invariants of this class specify that that the number of runways must be within the specified bounds. In addition, there are ownership based invariants on flights in the take-off and landing queues in the runways. These are invariants that relate properties of the owner and its components and hence apply to the entire complex object of an airport. These constraints include a constraint that one and the same flight cannot be in two different queues belonging to different runways. In order to make it possible for subclass invariants to refer to the field *numRunways*, Spec# requires the attribute [Additive] in the specification of this field.

```
invariant numRunways ≥ 1 ∧ numRunways ≤ 30;
invariant runways.Count = numRunways;
invariant /* No multiple occurrences of the same flight in runways*/
```

Methods *addRunway* and *closeRunway* along with the associated constraints are specified as follows:

public virtual void addRunway(Runway! runway)
modifies runways, numRunways;
ensures ∃ {Runway! r ∈ runways; r.Equals(runway)};
{//code }

public virtual void closeRunway (Runway! runway)
modifies runways, numRunways;

ensures numRunways > 0;
ensures numRunways = **old**(numRunways) - 1;
ensures ∀ { Runway! r ∈ runways; !r.Equals(runway)};
{// code }

Consider now a class *InternationalAirport* derived by inheritance from the class *Airport*. The class *InternationalAirport* inherits all the invariants from the class *Airport*. In addition, it adds new invariants that are conjoined with the inherited ones. These additional invariants require that the number of runways is higher than the minimum required by an airport in general. Furthermore, an additional requirement is that there exists at least one runway of the width and length suitable for international flights. This is expressed using a model field *IntRunway*. The notion of a model field is explained in section 10 that follows.

public class InternationalAirport: Airport {
invariant numRunways ≥ 10;
invariant ∃ {Runway! r ∈ Runways; r.IntRunway };
// IntRunway is a boolen model field in Runway
// constructor, methods

public override void closeRunway (Runway! runway)
ensures numRunways ≥ 10;
ensures ∃ {Runway! r ∈ runways; r.IntRunway };
{// code}
}

Overriding of the method *closeRunway* demonstrates the rules of behavioral subtyping. One would want to strengthen the precondition of this method by requiring that there is more than one international runway at an international airport or else the invariant for the international airport will be violated. But that is not possible by the rules of behavioral subtyping. Otherwise, users of the class *Airport* would see behavior of the method *closeAirport* that does not fit its specifications in the class *Airport*. This would happen if the airport object is in fact of the run-time type *InternationalAirport*. The *modifies* clause cannot be changed either for similar reasons. But the postcondition can be strengthened as in the above specifications. The postcondition now ensures that the number of runways is greater than or equal to ten and that there exists at least one international runway after the method execution. These are specific requirements for international airports.

Specification inheritance has implications on behavioral subyping of parametric types that follow well-known typing rules for such types. For example, if we derive a schema *InternationlFlightScheduling* by inheritance from the schema *FlightScheduling*, *Transaction<InternationlFlightScheduling>* will not be a subtype of the type *Transaction<FlightSchedling>*, and hence not a behavioral subtype either.

A class frame is the segment of the object state which is defined in that class alone. A class frame does not include the inherited components of the object state. An invariant of a class will include constraints that apply to its frame, but it may also further constrain the inherited components of the object state. For example, an object of type *International Airport* has three class frames. These class frames correspond to classes *Object*, *Airport* and *InternationalAirport*.

The notions *valid* and *mutable* apply to each individual class frame. The notions *consistent* and *committed* apply to the object as a whole. So an object is consistent or committed when all its frames are valid. The *expose* statement changes one class frame from valid to mutable. The class frame to be changed is specified by the static type of the segment of the object state to be changed. For example, the body of the method *closeAirport* of the class *InternationalAirport* has the following form:

```
assert runways ≠ null;
[Additive] expose((Airport)this){
    runways.Remove(runway);
    numRunways--;
}
```

10 Abstraction

Typical classes in this application have private fields that are made public only for specification purposes. Examples are fields *code* and *runways* in the class *Airport*. Users of this class would clearly have the need to read the code of an airport, and some users would have the need to inspect the runways of an airport. On the other hand, these fields are naturally made private as users are not allowed to access them directly in order to change them.

The basic mechanism for exposing a view of the hidden object state is to use public pure methods. A related technique is to use public properties. A public property is defined as a pair of *get* and *set* methods. The constraints in the *set* method control correctness of an update to a backing private field. A property *Runways* of the class *Airport* is specified below.

```
public List<Runway!>! Runways {
get { return runways;}
[Additive] set
requires value ≠ null;
ensures runways = value;
```

ensures /*no multiple occurrences of the same flight in runways*/
{/* code */}
}

Property getters are pure methods by default. Properties represent a general abstraction mechanism as the value of a property returned by the method *get* need not just be the value of a backing field, but it may be computed in a more complex way from the hidden (private) components of the object state.

Another abstraction mechanism is based on model fields. A model field is not an actual field and hence it cannot be updated. The model fields of an object get updated automatically at specific points in a transaction. An example of a model field is *IntRunway* of the class *Runway* specified below.

model bool IntRunway {
satisfies IntRunway = (length $\geq$ 80 $\wedge$ width $\geq$ 10);}

Unlike pure methods, model fields do not have parameters. But they often simplify reasoning. The verifier checks that the *satisfies* clause can indeed be satisfied, i.e., that there exists an object state that satisfies this clause. The *satisfies* clause may depend only on the fields of *this* and the objects owned by *this*. The *satisfies* clauses may be weaker in superclasses, and strengthened in subclasses.

11   Dynamic Checking of Constraints

Static verification of a transaction ensures that if the transaction is started in a consistent database state (the schema invariants hold) and the transaction precondition is satisfied, the schema invariants and the postcondition of the transaction will hold at the point of the commit action. The application program that invokes the transaction must satisfy the above requirements at the start of the transaction, and will be guaranteed that the postcondition and the schema invariants will hold at the end of the transaction execution.

Static verification does not say anything about what happens if the schema integrity constraints or the transaction precondition are not satisfied. What it says is that the code of a successfully verified transaction is correct with respect to the integrity constraints. Violation of constraints may still happen at run-time given the actual data. For example, a transaction may be invoked with arguments that do not satisfy the precondition and hence the verification results do not apply. This is why the dynamic checks that Spec# generates are essential. JML does the same, but it does not offer automatic static verification of code. Run-time tests will generate exceptions indicating violation of constraints. The transaction must handle these exceptions properly. Static verification guarantees that in the absence of such exceptions the results of transaction execution will be correct with respect to the integrity constraints. This extends to concurrent serializable executions of a set of transactions that have been statically verified.

Explicit dynamic checks may be used to verify that the constraints hold at run-time. This is illustrated below with a dynamic check of the precondition of the transactions *addAirport* in which *a* denotes the airport that should be added. The precondition of *addAirport* is that an airport with the code of the new airport does not exist in the database. This can be checked only dynamically by querying the database and asserting that this condition is satisfied.

```
IList<Airport!>? airports =
db.Query<Airport!>(delegate(Airport! arp){
return (arp.Code = a.Code);}};
assert airports = null;
```

Ensuring that a new airport has been added to the database is accomplished by querying the database and asserting that the list of airports in the database with the new code is not empty and that the newly inserted airport is indeed in the database.

```
IObjectSet? airportsSet =
db.Query(typeof(Airport!));
assert ∃ unique {Airport! arp ∈ airportsSet; arp.Equals(a)};
```

12 Database Platform

The underlying database platform that we used in the implementation of the presented transaction model is Db4 Objects. Db4 is an open source object-oriented database management system. It manages persistent objects, offers multiple query languages, and two programming language interfaces for specifying transactions: Java and C#.

Research presented in this paper addresses precisely the limitations of the current generation of persistent object-oriented systems, and Db4 in particular. Db4 does not have an explicit notion of a schema and it does not have a transaction class. There are practically no constraints, especially of the kind presented in this paper. Consequently, the constraints are not enforced, and hence the fact that Db4 claims support for ACID transactions is not justified because of the C component.

Our research produces a much more sophisticated database technology that offers explicit types of schemas and transactions, very general constraints for both, and transaction verification. These specifications could be expressed in JML or Spec#, and the transaction code could be written in Java or C#. Enforcing constraints is done statically if Spec# is used, and it is dynamic in both JML and Spec#.

The role of PVS in our transaction verification environment is complementary. It is used to reason about more general schema and transaction constraints, such as temporal, which the two assertion languages cannot support. In addition, the

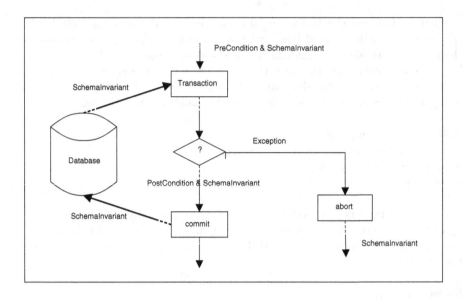

Fig. 4. Transaction execution

role of PVS is to show that some constraints are in fact provable, especially if static verification comes with difficulties.

Our technology truly supports ACID transactions. We rely on Db4 for implementation of atomicity, isolation and durability, and we guarantee consistency. In the actual implementation this is accomplished as follows:

- The precondition for the transaction invocation is that the transaction precondition and the schema invariant hold. This precondition will be the subject of static verification at the point of transaction call and it will be enforced dynamically if static verification is not possible.
- The above constraints are thus the precondition for the actual transaction action. The postcondition of the transaction action that is enforced is that the transaction postconditon and the schema invariant hold. This is the task of static transaction verification. The postcondition will be enforced dynamically as well.
- The above postcondition is the precondition for the transaction commit. The postconditon for the transaction commit is that the schema invariant holds.
- If an exception is raised and it is not handled by the transaction, the transaction action will be aborted. The postconditon of the transaction abort is that the schema invariant is reinstated. Figure 4 illustrates the above points.

Isolation of concurrent transactions is implemented as follows. When a transaction opens the database, it creates a private workspace. Accessing persistent objects for the first time brings them into the private workspace of the transaction. Updates of objects affect initially only the objects in the private workspace.

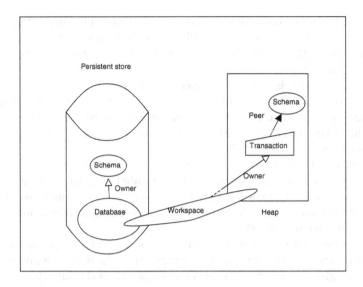

Fig. 5. Architecture

Since workspaces of individual transactions are private, updates that affect one workspace are inaccessible to updates of other transactions. Figure 5 illustrates some of the overall system architecture.

When a workspace is initially populated, the schema integrity constraints should hold for objects that are in the private workspace because they hold for the objects in the database. If that is not the case, the results on serializability and our verification techniques do not apply. During transaction execution the integrity constraints will typically be violated at some points. Static verification guarantees that the schema integrity constraints and the transaction postcondition will hold at the commit point. This is the property of the transaction code and hence the precondition of the transaction commit.

Atomicity is accomplished by installing all the changes recorded in the transaction workspace in the database so that either all of them are performed or none of them are. In the actual Db4 implementation a two phase write-ahead protocol is used to guarantee that all changes are made safely or none of them are.

There are two options supported by Db4 as far as the locking protocols are concerned. In a pessimistic strategy the private workspace consists of database objects and in-memory objects. In-memory objects are kept in separate workspaces and database objects are locked using a protocol that guarantees serializability (such as two-phase locking [11]). The locks will be held throughout transaction execution and released after a successful commit. In an optimistic protocol the private workspace will consist of in-memory objects only. Database objects will be accessed by multiple transactions and at commit time a concurrent execution will be checked for serializability.

The serializability check looks at the ordering of conflicting actions in the transactions log. The ordering of conflicting actions must correspond to some serial execution. If the serializability check fails at commit time, a suitable action must be performed, such as a rollback.

Once the commit is completed successfully, the updated objects in the database become available to other transactions. Successful verification guarantees that the objects in the database satisfy the integrity constraints. The D component of the notion of an ACID transaction will hold because committed changes will persist in the database.

The postcondition of the transaction abort is guaranteed by restoring the database objects and in-memory objects to the state before transaction execution so that the restored objects will satisfy the schema integrity constraints. Db4 has methods used in our implementation that rollback changes to persistent objects and refresh in-memory objects.

Our protocols differ from other similar protocols, and Db4 protocols in particular, in a fundamental way. They guarantee that the database integrity constraints will indeed be satisfied. To our knowledge, this is the only object-oriented technology that truly guarantees the C component of the notion of ACID transactions.

13   Related Research

General integrity constraints are missing from most persistent and database object models with rare exceptions such as [2,4,8]. This specifically applies to the ODMG model [9,5], PJama [18], Java Data Objects [12], and just as well to the current generation of systems such as Db4 Objects [10], Objectivity [20] or LINQ [17]. Of course, a major reason is that mainstream object-oriented languages are not equipped with constraints. Those capabilities are only under development for Java and C# [13,19]. In addition, none of the above technologies has support for the modeling techniques based on the ownership model.

A classical result [23] on the application of theorem prover technology based on computational logic to the verification of transaction safety is relational. Early object-oriented results include [8] and the usage of Isabelle/HOL [25]. A recent result [6] is relational and functional. In comparison with the above results and our own previous results, research reported in this paper produces object-oriented schemas with more general integrity constraints, transactions written in a mainstream object-oriented language, and their static verification that guarantees ACID properties in an implementation based on an object-oriented database management system.

Our previous results include techniques based on JML and PVS [3]. Our most recent results that apply to XML Schema constraints and the associated transactions are based on Spec# [2]. Reflective constraint management, static and dynamic techniques for enforcing constraints, and transaction verification technology are presented in [3,4,22]. The above techniques were applied to ambients of concurrent and persistent objects in [1].

A substantial amount of recent research has been directed toward a correct model and the required apparatus in object-oriented programming languages that would support the notion of a transaction [14,26,24]. These results are meant to resolve the mismatch between the existing concurrent object-oriented features of languages such as Java and C# and those required by the notion of ACID transactions. Unlike that research, research reported in this paper concentrates on the C component of ACID transactions. In addition, we also implement the D component of the ACID model based on the support of an object-oriented database management system [10].

14   Conclusions

The main contributions of this paper are solutions for two related problems that have been open so far:

- Lack of general schema integrity constraints in the existing object-oriented persistent or database technologies.
- Lack of a transaction specification and verification technology that would verify, preferably statically, that a transaction satisfies the schema integrity constraints.

The constraint-based technology allows specification of object-oriented schemas equipped with general database integrity constraints, transactions and their consistency requirements. The verification techniques presented in the paper allow largely static and automatic verification of transactions with respect to the specified constraints. A major advantage is that all the subtleties of the underlying verification and prover technology are completely hidden from the users. The implications on data integrity, efficiency and reliability of transactions are obvious and non-trivial.

Data integrity as specified by the constraints could be guaranteed. Runtime reliability of transactions is significantly improved. Expensive recovery procedures will not be required because the objects that violate the integrity constraints will never be committed to the database. The generated dynamic checks provide a significantly better control over exceptions raised by violation of the integrity constraints. In addition, more general application constraints that are not necessarily database constraints could be guaranteed. All of this produces a much more sophisticated technology in comparison with the existing ones.

The impedance mismatch between data and programming languages is to a great extent caused by different levels of abstraction of these two classes of languages. Data (query in particular) languages are largely declarative, and programming languages are largely procedural. A distinctive feature of the technology presented in this paper is declarative database programming in which the main emphasis is on writing a variety of constraints. The procedural code is in general simple, and thanks to recent extensions of object-oriented languages also largely declarative.

We demonstrated that an object-oriented model of transactions requires more advanced features of object-oriented type systems such as bounded parametric polymorphism and non-null object types. In addition, we showed that the ownership model is also essential for the transaction model. It allows specification of schemas using the aggregation abstraction and specification and enforcement of the integrity constraints that apply to complex objects. To our knowledge, no object-oriented persistent or database technology has the above features.

The model for schemas and transactions presented in this paper has been designed in such a way that it has a direct representation in Spec#. This makes Spec# verification technology directly applicable. Spec# limitations in expressiveness (like those for universal and existential quantification) presented no paricular problem in the application that we developed. But strictly speaking, the chosen application features a variety of temporal constraints that cannot be specified in Spec# in a temporal logic style. We use a different technology for specifying temporal constraints for schemas and transactions that complements the environment presented in this paper. That technology is based on a higher-order interactive verification system. While it is capable of expressing much more general constraints expressed in specialized logics, this technology requires very sophisticated users.

Automatic static verification (as in Spec#) is clearly a preferable verification technology from the viewpoint of the users. At this point that technology is still a prototype. The underlying architecture that separates the users view from the prover technology is very complex. Static verification sometimes comes with difficulties. However, while dynamic enforcement technology (as in JML) allows very general constraints, it comes with run-time penalties that are particularly pronounced in database applications.

References

1. Alagić, S., Anumula, A., Yonezawa, A.: Verifiable constraints for ambients of persistent objects. In: Advances in Software, vol. 4, pp. 461–470 (2011)
2. Alagić, S., Bernstein, P.A., Jairath, R.: Object-oriented constraints for XML Schema. In: Dearle, A., Zicari, R.V. (eds.) ICOODB 2010. LNCS, vol. 6348, pp. 100–117. Springer, Heidelberg (2010)
3. Alagić, S., Royer, M., Briggs, D.: Verification technology for object-oriented/XML transactions. In: Norrie, M.C., Grossniklaus, M. (eds.) Object Databases. LNCS, vol. 5936, pp. 23–40. Springer, Heidelberg (2010)
4. Alagić, S., Logan, J.: Consistency of Java transactions. In: Lausen, G., Suciu, D. (eds.) DBPL 2003. LNCS, vol. 2921, pp. 71–89. Springer, Heidelberg (2004)
5. Alagić, S.: The ODMG object model: does it make sense? In: Proceedings of OOPSLA, pp. 253–270. ACM (1997)
6. Baltopoulos, I.G., Borgström, J., Gordon, A.D.: Maintaining database integrity with refinement types. In: Mezini, M. (ed.) ECOOP 2011. LNCS, vol. 6813, pp. 484–509. Springer, Heidelberg (2011)
7. Benzaken, V., Doucet, D.: Themis: A database language handling integrity constraints. VLDB Journal 4, 493–517 (1994)

8. Benzanken, V., Schaefer, X.: Static integrity constraint management in object-oriented database programming languages via predicate transformers. In: Akşit, M., Matsuoka, S. (eds.) ECOOP 1997. LNCS, vol. 1241, pp. 60–84. Springer, Heidelberg (1997)

9. Cattell, R.G.G., Barry, D., Berler, M., Eastman, J., Jordan, D., Russell, C., Schadow, O., Stanienda, T., Velez, F.: The Object Data Standard: ODMG 3.0. Morgan Kaufmann (2000)

10. Db4 objects (2010), http://www.db4o.com

11. Eswaran, K.P., Grey, J.N., Lorie, R.A., Traiger, I.L.: The notions of consistency and predicate locks in a database system. Comm. of the ACM 19, 624–633 (1976)

12. Java Data Objects, Apache, http://db.apache.org/jdo/

13. Java Modeling Language, http://www.eecs.ucf.edu/leavens/JML/

14. Jagannathan, S., Vitek, J., Welc, A., Hosking, A.: A transactional object calculus. Science of Computer Programming 57, 164–186 (2005)

15. Leino, K.R., Muller, P.: Using Spec# language, methodology, and tools to write bug-free programs. Microsoft Research (2010), http://research.microsoft.com/en-us/projects/specsharp/

16. Liskov, B., Wing, J.M.: A behavioral notion of subtyping. ACM TOPLAS 16, 1811–1841 (1994)

17. Language Integrated Query, Microsoft Corporation, http://msdn.microsoft.com/en-us/vbasic/aa904594.aspx

18. Atkinson, M.P., Daynès, L., Jordan, M.J., Printezis, T., Spence, S.: An orthogonally persistent Java. ACM SIGMOD Record 15(4) (1966)

19. Microsoft Corp., Spec#, http://research.microsoft.com/specsharp/

20. Objectivity, http://www.objectivity.com/

21. Owre, S., Shankar, N., Rushby, J.M., Stringer-Clavert, D.W.J.: PVS Language Reference, SRI International. Computer Science Laboratory, Menlo Park, California, http://pvs.csl.sri.com/doc/pvs-language-reference.pdf

22. Royer, M., Alagić, S., Dillon, D.: Reflective constraint management for languages on virtual platforms. Journal of Object Technology 6, 59–79 (2007)

23. Sheard, T., Stemple, D.: Automatic verification of database transaction safety. ACM Transactions on Database Systems 14, 322–368 (1989)

24. Smaragdakis, Y., Kay, A., Behrends, R., Young, M.: Transactions with isolation and cooperation. In: Proceedings of OOPSLA 2007. ACM (2007)

25. Spelt, D., Even, S.: A theorem prover-based analysis tool for object-oriented databases. In: Cleaveland, W.R. (ed.) TACAS 1999. LNCS, vol. 1579, pp. 375–389. Springer, Heidelberg (1999)

26. Welc, A., Hosking, A.L., Jia, L.: Transparently reconciling transactions with locking for Java synchronization. In: Thomas, D. (ed.) ECOOP 2006. LNCS, vol. 4067, pp. 148–173. Springer, Heidelberg (2006)

Design and Implementation of a Mobile Actor Platform for Wireless Sensor Networks

YoungMin Kwon[1], Kirill Mechitov[2], and Gul Agha[2]

[1] Microsoft Corporation
One Microsoft Way
Redmond, WA, USA 98052
youngminkwon@gmail.com
[2] Department of Computer Science
University of Illinois at Urbana-Champaign
201 North Goodwin Avenue
Urbana, IL, USA 61801
{mechitov,agha}@illinois.edu

Abstract. *Wireless sensor networks* (WSNs) promise the ability to monitor physical environments and to facilitate control of *cyber-physical systems*. Because sensors networks can generate large amounts of data, and wireless bandwidth is both limited and energy hungry, local processing becomes necessary to minimize communication. However, for reasons of energy efficiency and production costs, embedded nodes have relatively slow processors and small memories. This makes programming sensor networks harder and requires new tools for distributed computing. We have developed *ActorNet*, an implementation of the *Actor model* of computing for sensor networks which facilitates programming by treating a sensor network as an *open distributed computing platform*. ActorNet provides a high-level actor programming language: users can write dynamic applications for a single cross-platform runtime environment with support for heterogeneous and physically separated WSNs. This shields application developers from some hardware-specific concerns. Moreover, unlike other programming systems for WSNs, ActorNet supports *agent mobility* and *automatic garbage collection*. We describe the ActorNet language and runtime system and how it achieves reasonable performance in a WSN.

1 Introduction

A *Wireless Sensor Network* (WSN) is a system of sensor nodes that collaborate with other nodes through wireless communication channels. A typical sensor node has one or more sensors, some data processing capabilities, a wireless communications channel, and an independent power source. With the utilization of the local processing capabilities and wireless communications, a sensor node can autonomously perform its tasks or collaborate with other nodes. Due to these unique features, WSNs have been proposed for applications such as environmental monitoring [33], structural health monitoring [8], intrusion detection [6], and target tracking [11].

G. Agha et al. (Eds.): Yonezawa Festschrift, LNCS 8665, pp. 276–316, 2014.

WSN application development remains a complex and challenging endeavor. The task is somewhat simplified by using a distributed middleware which can provide services such as localization [27], time synchronization [34], and data aggregation [40]. Despite the support offered by a middleware, programming WSN still poses difficulties. This is because of several reasons: embedded code is platform dependent; multiple applications cannot be concurrently executed; applications cannot be dynamically loaded; multiple WSNs cannot interoperate; and migration of processes is not supported.

Some of the problems we described above have been studied in the context of *open distributed systems*. In an open distributed system, adding new components may be added, existing components may be replaced, and interconnections between components may be changed. A platform which supports an open distributed largely should allow such evolution without impacting the functioning of the system. The *actor models* provides a suitable for building open distributed systems: it has a notion local components and interaction restricted through specified interfaces. Interaction in the actor model is based on asynchronous message passing; this prevents the direct manipulation of the internal state of one component by another.

In this paper, we implement a variation of an actor model, called *ActorNet* [2] to address some challenges in WSN programming. ActorNet provides a uniform computing platform for mobile agents, which we call *actors* [5]. ActorNet builds a single virtual network by interconnecting physically separated WSNs over the Internet. This virtual network removes the difficulties in interoperating multiple WSNs together. For example, an actor can track a seismic event while migrating thousands of miles through the Internet. The homogeneity of the computing environments provided by the interpreter layer of ActorNet simplifies interoperation. Because the underlying platform differences and the network differences are hidden from the actors, the same actor program can continue its tasks while migrating between different ActorNet platforms, e.g. a Mica2 sensor node and a PC. The ActorNet implementation is available with an open source license[1].

ActorNet consists of a language interpreter and a runtime system. The actor language supports powerful operations such as high-order functions, reflection, garbage collection, and tail recursion removal. The specific details of the underlying hardware and the operating system are hidden behind the high level operators of the actor language. The uniform computing environment also simplifies the application developments greatly as it precludes the need for different variations of programs for different platforms.

ActorNet runtime provides with a library of services such as virtual memory, application level context switching, garbage collection, and a communication stack machine. These services not only secure the necessary resources for ActorNet applications to run, but also enables ActorNet, as an application running on a sensor node, to coexist harmoniously with other native applications.

Unlike other WSN mobile agent frameworks based on a bytecode virtual machine [17], using an interpreter can greater power and flexibility. In particular,

---

[1] http://osl.cs.illinois.edu

the ActorNet interpreter facilitates reflective capabilities of the language. To support actor migration, we uniformly represent the state of an actor as a pair of a continuation [47] and a value to be passed to the continuation. This state representation, along with the reflection capability of the actor language (cf. [53]), endows actors with the *voluntary migration* capability. The mobility of actors enables fine-grained network reprogramming. The actors run only at required nodes and their migration does not disrupt the continuation of other actors' computation.

Organization of the paper. Section 2 discusses the problems we are trying to address. Section 3 describes our approach to addressing the problems identified. Section 4 provides a complete ActorNet example application to illustrate our approach. The detailed syntax and the semantics of ActorNet language is defined in Section 5. Section 6 describes the implementation of the interpreter and the runtime system of ActorNet. In Section 7 we evaluate the performance of the system. Section 8 examines the application of ActorNet mobile agents as the foundation of a *macroprogramming* system. Finally, we discuss the unique contributions of ActorNet in the context of related work on mobile agent systems and network reprogramming in Section 9. Concluding remarks and discussion of future work follow.

2 Motivation

Our research is motivated by our experience in building WSN applications which continues to require embedded systems programming and networking expertise. Domain experts are not usually embedded systems experts, as pointed out in [42]. We believe this has slowed down the adoption of WSNs. The difficulties can be summarized as follows:

- *Embedded code is dependent on the specific platform used.* Thus embedded systems programmers have to be familiar with the intricacies of the hardware, operating system, and programming language used for the particular embedded hardware and software that they are using. Moreover, it is difficult to adapt applications to new sensor platforms, even as new platforms are being continually developed.
- *Interoperation of multiple, possibly heterogeneous WSNs is not supported.* Many large scale events cannot be covered by a single WSN but require multiple WSNs; for example mapping the temperature of a city or recording seismic data observed across the globe may be facilitated by the cooperation of multiple WSNs. However, many WSN applications are designed only for a single or a handful of predetermined groups of sensors.
- *It is difficult to run multiple applications in a WSN.* As we move from dumb sensors to smart sensors with on board processing capabilities, embedded computers will be used to multitask. For example, it may process readings from different sensors and adapt the behavior of these applications based on the readings.

- *Remote reprogramming of sensors is tedious.* Because application images are preloaded on the nodes and the message formats are predetermined, a WSN cannot respond to dynamically changing requirements:
  - an application's coverage is bound to a predetermined set of sensors as nodes;
  - new nodes cannot dynamically join a WSN unless they are already programmed to do so; and,
  - even when applications potentially of interest are known in advance, given that memory on an embedded node is scarce, it is impractical to preload less-frequently used applications on a large number of nodes.

One approach to addressing the problem of dynamically changing requirements is to support *remote reprogramming*. Several network reprogramming systems have been developed including Deluge [22], over-the-air programming of Contiki [15], SOS [20], and Trickle protocol of Mate [31]. These systems install the whole image or replace some of the modules remotely injected from a central node. However, unless remote reprogramming supports fine grained targeting and inter-operation of heterogeneous application images, energy consumption considerations severely limit its usefulness.

A different *remote evaluation* approach has been proposed by Stamos et al. Instead of the traditional client/server architecture, server nodes in this remote evaluation framework provide a set of generic operations which allow remotely transmitted programs to run on a server using the generic operations and return the results [45]. The remote evaluation approach solves the scalability problem and can potentially reduce the communication load as well. However, some tasks can be better executed in a framework that not only allows program to be copied but migrates its state. Migrating an actor's state allows it to continue a computation on the destination platform. Actor migration enables to duplicate a program over the entire network. Moreover, the ability to migrate continuations can reduce the code size that needs to be migrated.

One of the design principles of a WSN is to build a large scale distributed system using cheap, even disposable, hardware. Naturally, problems arising from the limited resources follow. For example, Mica2 [13] node has only 4 kB of memory, which is a very tight limit even for a single application. To make matters worse, TinyOS [50], an operating system for the Mica nodes, does not support dynamic loading and unloading of applications. That is, the 4 kB of memory must be shared by *all* applications shipped on a node. These constraints pose a big impediment to the development and the maintenance of WSN applications. Some embedded computer operating systems support dynamic module/application loading: these include Contiki [15], Mantis [9], and SOS [20]. TinyOS, a popular operating system for WSNs, does not. According to a survey, TinyOS has the largest support community and the largest number of publications among operating systems for WSNs with 81% [29]. For this reason, ActorNet is implemented primarily targeting TinyOS; however, we believe porting ActorNet to other platforms may not be difficult: only a small fraction of the runtime system code is platform-dependent. ActorNet already provides support for two very diverse platforms: TinyOS on Mica2, and Linux on PC.

3   ActorNet Design

We now describe the overall design of the computing environment and highlight the issues that need to be addressed in its implementation. The principal features ActorNet provides are:

- A light-weight actor (mobile agent) programming language for WSN systems which powerful programming constructs such as higher-order functions, reflection, tail recursion removal, and garbage collection.
- Support for multiple concurrently actors which can execute on a node without interfering with each other.
- A library of useful services, including a virtual memory space on embedded nodes to dynamically load and run non-trivial actor programs and an application-level context switching mechanism to enable blocking I/O and fair scheduling.
- A virtual network platform that encompasses multiple physical WSNs and PC platforms without exposing the hardware and networking differences to the application.

3.1   Network Architecture Design

Simplifying the interoperation of multiple physically-distributed WSNs is one of the design goals of ActorNet. Toward this goal, ActorNet builds a single virtual computing environment for mobile actors that encompasses multiple WSNs. Specifically, this environment is constructed by interconnecting the base stations, or gateway nodes, of WSNs via an Internet overlay. Using the virtual environment, differences in the communication network as well as the underlying computing platform can be obscured from application-level actors. Being exposed to these differences, an actor program would have to prepare different sets of handlers for each hardware configuration, which results in duplicated code, unnecessarily complex implementations, and large application code sizes.

The proposed virtual environment spans two tiers of networks: an *ad hoc* wireless network and the Internet, as can be seen in Figure 1. These two network tiers feature vastly different topology, bandwidth, protocols, and performance characteristics. In *ad hoc* wireless networks, messages are locally broadcast to a node's neighbors, whereas most of the Internet consists of wired, point-to-point connections. The bandwidth differences between the two network types can be huge. Typical RF network devices used to interconnect wireless sensors can communicate at speeds ranging from 38.4 to 250 kbps, for 802.15.4 devices. However, in practice the communication speeds are much lower. For example, a 64-node WSN deployed on the Golden Gate Bridge took 12 hours to transport 90 seconds worth of high-frequency vibration data [26]. Finally, there is a multiple order of magnitude difference in performance of the hosts comprising the network: personal computers (PCs) and servers connected to the Internet typically have processors running at several GHz, whereas sensor nodes feature processors with maximum speeds of several MHz. These differences make developing applications that span both network types a challenging endeavor.

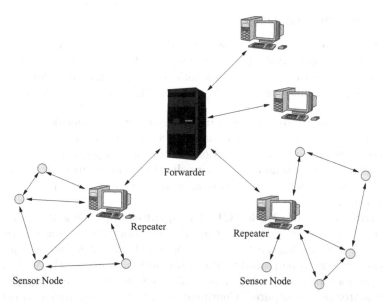

Fig. 1. ActorNet network architecture: the *forwarder* turns the Internet into a single-hop, broadcast overlay network, and the *repeaters* act as a bridge between it and the ad hoc wireless networks. This network architecture obscures the underlying network differences from the actor programs.

To hide the heterogeneity of the network from the actors, we represent the Internet a single hop broadcast network from the actor's viewpoint. Specifically, any messages transmitted from a *gateway node* connected to the Internet are forwarded to the other gateway nodes. In view of this network topology, the difference between the *ad hoc* network and the Internet is hidden from the actors. All ActorNet platforms connected to a forwarder node over the Internet can be regarded as a single hop neighbor. This virtual single-hop network extends the range of mobile actors to the global scale. That means, to an actor, a migration of thousands of miles through the Internet is no different from a local migration between two neighboring sensor nodes. As a solution for the network bandwidth differences, ActorNet provides a packet buffer at the gateway nodes, which compensates for temporary differences in the throughput of the two networks.

One of the merits of this network design is that existing agent coordination algorithms can be easily adopted. For example, *ant algorithms* use a reinforcement based on (computational) pheromones to guide the agent behavior. A notable example is the ant-based routing algorithm [14], which builds robust, adaptive end-to-end routes. In sensor networks, due to the intermittent nature of network connectivity, dynamic routing algorithms based on end-to-end route quality are preferable to static routing tables. With network design, building message routes across the WSNs does not differ from building them within a WSN.

3.2   Actor Language Design

The ActorNet programming language uses the syntax of the programming language Scheme [1], extended with actor operators. In this respect, it is similar to the actor language Rosette [51]. As mentioned earlier, the ActorNet programming language simplifies programming WSNs. This is accomplished by:

Platform independent execution: ActorNet naturally shields the platform differences from actors by functioning as a virtual machine.

Uniform messaging: Communication is platform independent: a simple send operator is used to send any type or volume of data to any destination node, even if the destination actor resides in a different WSN connected via an Internet gateway.

Continuation Passing Style (CPS) programming: The state of an actor is represented as a pair consisting of a *continuation*—a single parameter function representing the rest of the program [47], and a *reduction expression* whose *value* is to be passed to the continuation. Applying the value to the continuation produces a new actor state, and an actor repeatedly generates new states as it computes. Continuations allow a programmer to capture, send, and execute future computations, similar to the concept of *future type message passing* in the ABCL/1 concurrent programming language [56].

Actor Mobility: Because an actor program is represented as a data type, it is platform independent and can be migrated as source code.

Concurrency: Multiple actors may be concurrently executed on a single ActorNet node.

Note that the CPS representation of an actor's state supports *reflection* over the current state. This enables actors to migrate themselves at any stage of execution–by accessing the continuation and the value to be passed to the continuation, and send these to a new platform. To make the migration happen, an ActorNet platform needs to be ready to receive an actor's state and let it continue its execution. For this purpose, each ActorNet platform features a special-purpose built-in actor which receives such messages and creates a new actor to evaluate the message content. During the evaluation, the new actor's state is replaced with the actor state in the message.

3.3   ActorNet Platform Design

Running ActorNet platforms on sensor nodes presents its own unique difficulties. In this section, we describe the concerns in developing ActorNet platforms on extremely resource-constrained sensor platforms, such as Crossbow Mica2 sensor nodes (described below). Note that ActorNet would be much easier to implement on more powerful sensor platforms; we use a the Mica2 to demonstrate that our approach can be supported on a broad range of WSN devices.

Mica2 and TinyOS

The Crossbow Mica2 mote is built on an 8 MHz 8-bit ATmega128L CPU with 4 kB of SRAM, 128 kB of program flash memory, and 512 kB of serial flash [13]. The 4 kB SRAM space is shared by the stack, heap, and static variables of all TinyOS components and applications. This, in turn, places a tight memory constraint on applications. Application code, large constant tables, and log data are loaded in the flash memory units. As an application, ActorNet also has to share this 4 kB space, but because its data is actor programs, the small memory is the more restrictive to ActorNet compared to other applications. To address this fundamental problem, we designed a 56 kB virtual memory formed at the 512 kB serial flash memory. Usually, flash memory read operations are fast, but write operations are slow and expensive in terms of energy consumption. On Mica2 it takes ~15 ms to write a 128-byte page to flash.

Mica2 hardware is equipped with a CC1000 RF transceiver for single-duplex wireless communication. At the bit-level, TinyOS uses Manchester encoding [48], achieving a theoretical raw throughput of 38.4 kbps. In practice, a Mica2 node is able to transmit approximately 20 34-byte packets per second. Internally, TinyOS employs a *carrier sense multiple access* (CSMA) medium access control protocol called B-MAC [41], together with SEC-DED encoding and a 16-bit *cyclic redundancy code* (CRC) on each packet, which allows receivers to detect data corruption. In addition to the wireless transceiver, Mica2 units feature an RS-232 serial interface [46], allowing communication with PC-based applications through an interface board.

TinyOS is a lightweight operating system for the sensor nodes written primarily in NesC [19]. The system is structured as a collection of modules which are statically linked together based on a component specification. The modules consist of statically-allocated variables and three different types of program blocks: `command`, `event`, and `task`. Service requests are typically split-phase: a caller invokes a command, which returns quickly; once the request is satisfied, the service calls back to a corresponding event procedure in the caller. This communication pattern enables a higher application throughput as compared to simple blocking I/O. Long-running procedures are explicitly executed as *tasks*, which are scheduled in series and run to completion. Since only interrupts can preempt tasks or lower-priority interrupt handlers, if multiple processes must be run concurrently, they have to be explicitly segmented into a sequence of tasks.

In order to enable the mobility of actors, ActorNet supports dynamic loading and unloading of actor programs. Because an actor may allocate and deallocate memory during its computation, the dynamic unloading module must reclaim all the dangling memory made by the unloaded actor. As a general solution to this problem, we added a *Garbage Collection* (GC) mechanism to ActorNet. The GC mechanism is based on the mark and sweep GC algorithm, which is effective but induces an unpredictable latency with a large mean and a large variance. While the GC is running, most of the services are stopped, which can be critical for periodic sampling or communication services. The large variance in the latency also prevents an efficient task scheduling. As a remedy to these limitations, we

```
foo() {              int foo_a;           prebar() {
    int a;           int bar_a;               ...
    ...              prefoo() {               prefoo();
    read();              ...               }
    ...              }                     postbar() {
}                    postfoo() {              postfoo();
bar() {                 postread();        ...
    int a;              ...               }
    ...              }
    foo();
    ...
}
```

Fig. 2. Code examples with (left) and without (right) blocking I/O. read makes an I/O operation.

developed a multi-phase GC algorithm. Assuming that the virtual memory is lightly loaded and thus the mark phase is fast, we divided the sweep phase into multiple sub-phases and deallocated only fractions of the memory on each step. This partial deallocation reduces the slow flash memory write while maintaining the page hit ratio high. The multiple phase GC algorithm also reduces the mean and the variances of the GC latency, which results in a better scheduling.

Note that this garbage collection is constrained to local node resources, since the overhead costs involved with implementing distributed GC in a resource-constrained sensor network are prohibitive. In particular, garbage collection of actors is complicated by the fact that not only references from reachable actors have to be considered, but inverse references from potentially active actors must also be considered [52].

TinyOS achieves concurrency among applications through split-phase programming. More specifically, most of the I/O operations are supported only in the split-phase style. Although this style of programming increases throughput, the limited support of the blocking I/O makes it difficult to develop and maintain applications. For example, let us consider the code in Figure 2. The code on the left side is written with blocking I/O: bar calls foo and foo calls read which performs an I/O. Without blocking I/O, we must split the functions as in the right side of Figure 2: an application calls prebar and arranges an *I/O completed* event handler to call postbar. The problem is that every possible function call chain reachable to read should be divided into two parts like Figure 2. Furthermore one cannot use *stack allocated local variables* across the divided functions. That is, all such variables must be declared as static variables which take up space even after the functions are returned. The problem is even graver in ActorNet: any memory access can make a page fault which leads to a flash memory access, an I/O operation; split phasing on every memory access is practically impossible. To overcome these problems, we implement an *application level context switching mechanism*. The mechanism enables ActorNet to return control to TinyOS and regain control later with the same register, flags, and stack configurations. Using this mechanism, ActorNet enables blocking I/O for its actors. This mechanism also provides a seamless concurrent execution of ActorNet alongside other applications. The context switching mechanism is developed at the application layer to reduce the difficulty of porting it to other platforms.

The state representation of an actor can be structurally complicated. Specifically, there can be loops or multiple references in the list structure. Thus, sending and receiving the list data involves serialization and deserialization. One of the concerns in sending a message is that the message is locally broadcast to all the neighbors of the sender. Because there is a single sender with multiple receivers, it is computationally beneficial to allow higher computational load at the sender in order to lower the computational load at a receiver. To achieve this, we design a simple *communication stack machine*: a sender handles all the complexities of communication and makes a stream of data mixed with stack manipulation commands so that receivers can restore the data simply by running their stack machine following the commands.

4   Example

We provide a complete example application to illustrate the design of the Actor-Net platform before going into the details of the actor language and the platform implementation.

Consider an actor migrating through a WSN in search of a local temperature maximum—a typical environmental monitoring task. Searching for a local maximum point is a reasonable monitoring task for a WSN: for example, to detect a heat sink or a gas leak, one may want to find the local maximum point. An actor in this example autonomously selects its migration path based on the environmental information and reports the final result to a base station. The example demonstrates the high level of abstraction for WSN application development provided by ActorNet.

The steps in our *maxima search actor's* execution are as follows:

1. An actor A broadcasts to its neighbors a simple actor which measures the temperature at a node and sends back the result.
2. A determines the neighborhood maximum temperature and migrates itself to the corresponding node. When it migrates to another node, A records its point of origin so that it can forward the maximum temperature reading back along the path it followed.
3. When it arrives at a point with maximal temperature (i.e., where all the neighbors report a lower temperature), A migrates back to the base station. Upon arrival at the base station it prints out the temperature value. (Note that more information could easily be maintained and reported).

Because of expressiveness of ActorNet, we do not need any platform or OS support for multi-hop message routing. An actor locally broadcasts and moves itself to its neighbor with the greatest temperature, while constructing the return path as it migrates from node to node.

```
1  (rec (move path temp)  ;;return path, max temp
2   (seq
3     (send (list 0 measure (io 0)))  ;;broadcast measure actors to neighbors
4     (delay 100)  ;;wait for 10 seconds
5     ( (lambda (maxt)
6         (par
7           (cond (le (car maxt) temp)    ;;if it arrives at a maximal point
8                 (return migrate path temp)  ;;then return the temp along the path
9                 (move                  ;;else move to the highest temp. node
10                  (cond (equal path nil)
11                        (cons launch path)
12                        (cons (io 0) path))
13                  (migrate
14                    (cadr maxt)    ;;node id
15                    (car maxt))))  ;;temp
16            (setcdr (msgq) nil)))  ;;reset msgq
17        (max (cdr (msgq)) (list 0 0)))))  ;;find the max temp. and the node
```

Fig. 3. An actor program that migrates to a point of maximal temperature in a WSN and returns the temperature back to the base station

Consider a `migrate` function which makes an actor move to another node and then continue its execution. Recall that the state of an actor is a pair of a continuation and a value to be passed to the continuation. In ActorNet, an actor can easily migrate itself to a neighboring node, using the explicit state representation and sending its *current continuation*. There is a `launcher` actor running on every ActorNet platform that receives the messages sent to it as programs and evaluates them. The entire actor migration process is implemented using this very short `migrate` function:

```
1  (lambda (address value) ;; migrate
2    (callcc
3      (lambda (cc)
4        (send (list address cc (list quote value)))))))
```

The code for the temperature-search example, which utilizes this migrate function, is listed in Figure 3. The precise syntax and semantics of the language will be described in the next section, but this code excerpt illustrates the general structure of an ActorNet program and the compactness of the actor language. Note that a relatively complex application is implemented in under 20 lines of code.

The program first broadcasts a `measure` actor that reads a temperature at a remote node and sends back the reading. The sender then waits for 10 seconds and then checks its message queue, `msgq`, for the measurement. No other work is needed for synchronization. The `measure` actor can be encoded simply as

```
1    (lambda (ret) ;;measure
2      (send (list ret (io 1) (io 0)))).
```

The (io 1) system call returns a temperature reading and the call (io 0) returns the unique node identifier. A launcher actor running at a remote platform will evaluate this function with the return address, which is the (io 0) function call of the 3rd line of Figure 3. Although the measure actor in this example is simple, it could be an arbitrarily complex function. That is, an actor can easily distribute a complex piece of its code to run in other nodes and later collect the results in the form of messages. This example demonstrates the versatility of ActorNet as a concurrent computing environment for multiple actors.

Returning to Figure 3, the move function takes a return path and the current maximum temperature reading as its parameters. Migration occurs after evaluating the second parameter. Line 9 shows how the actor migrates to another node: it first appends its node id—(io 0)—to the return path and then migrates to the node where the greatest temperature was read. When the actor arrives at a point of the maximal temperature, it returns the temperature value using the return function, listed below.

```
1 (rec (return migrate path temp)
2   (cond (equal path nil)
3     (print temp)
4     (return migrate (cdr path)
5             (migrate (car path) temp))))
```

The return function is similar to move. It migrates across the nodes along the return path.

Note how easy it is to write a mobile agent program using the ActorNet platform. By providing simple-to-use and high-level features, ActorNet enables a rapid development of powerful WSN applications. Furthermore, because mobile agents operate autonomously, they can be used in resource-constrained sensor networks that do not provide many supporting services.

Finally, it is worthwhile to mention that this program does not require any routing services: the actor follows a steepest temperature ascent path, and it also maintains a return path by itself. Also note that the application does not require collecting the temperature reading from all nodes to a central node (usually done by a data dissemination process); instead the actor collects and processes the information while migrating in a sensor field. Even considering the data aggregation service, the saving in the amount of communication by the mobile agent approach is very significant.

5   Actor Language

We now formally describe the syntax and the semantics of the ActorNet actor language in *rewriting logic* [35, 38]. One of the merits of using rewriting logic is that it describes both the syntax and the semantics of a language together. The syntax is defined by its mix-fix definition of operators and the semantics is described by the deductions rules of a rewriting theory. Another benefit of using rewriting logic is that the descriptions are executable by rewriting engines, such as Maude [35].

5.1   Rewriting Theory

In rewriting logic, a *signature* Σ comprises a set S of *sorts*, a partial order relation $\leq$ of *subsorts*, and a $S^* \times S$ indexed set of *operators*. A Σ-*algebra* A_Σ is an algebra with an S indexed family of sets $\{A_s : s \in S\}$ such that $A_s \subseteq A_{s'}$ if $s \leq s'$, and constants $c \in A_s$ for each operator $c_{\emptyset \times s}$ of Σ, and functions $f : A_{s_1} \times \cdots \times A_{s_n} \to A_s$ for each operator $f_{s_1,\ldots,s_n \times s}$ of Σ. An interesting Σ-algebra is the *term algebra* T_Σ whose terms are $c \in A_s$ for $c_{\emptyset \times s}$, and $f(t_1,\ldots,t_n) \in A_s$ for $f_{s_1,\ldots,s_n \times s}$, where t_i is a term in A_{s_i}. The term algebra is a minimal Σ-algebra that has Σ-homomorphism to all Σ-algebras. The mix-fix operator definition of Maude eases defining the syntax of a language. However, for simplicity, we use the BNF notation where possible. For example, we write $\mathcal{P} ::= \langle \mathcal{V}, \mathcal{V} \rangle$ instead of $\langle \_, \_ \rangle : \mathcal{V} \times \mathcal{V} \to \mathcal{P}$ for pairs.

An *equational theory* is a pair (Σ, E) of a signature Σ and a set E of possibly conditional equations on the terms of T_Σ. We say that a Σ-algebra A_Σ is a *model* of a theory (Σ, E), and write $A_\Sigma \models (\Sigma, E)$ if A_Σ satisfies all equations in E. An equation e is a *theorem* of (Σ, E) if all models of (Σ, E) satisfy e. Theorems can be proved by applying the deduction rules of *reflexivity, symmetry, transitivity, congruence,* and *modus ponens*. Theorems can also be simply proved by applying *equational rewriting* under the termination and confluence conditions. The equational theory can be generalized in *membership equational logic*, where a *kind* is given to the equivalent class of sorts related by $\leq$, and the operators are indexed with kinds. Sorts are given to the terms through the *membership axiom*.

A *rewriting theory* is a four-tuple $\mathbb{R} = (\Sigma, E, L, R)$, where (Σ, E) is an equational theory and R is a set of labeled rewrite rules whose labels are from L. $\mathbb{R}$ describes the behaviors of a transition system, where the equivalent classes of terms represent the state of the system and the state transitions are described by applying the inference rules of *reflexivity, transitivity, congruence,* and *replacement*. A more detailed discussion of rewriting logic is presented in [35].

5.2   Syntax

In our actor language, everything is a value sort: numbers, symbols, pairs, lists[2], and all ActorNet program elements, such as actor programs, actor states, and actor configurations are values. Because these program elements have distinguishable structures, specific sorts are assigned to them through membership axiom.

Actor language has only one kind that all sorts belong to. Thus, in this paper, we drop the index from the sorts. Some examples of the sorts in S are $\mathcal{V}$ for values, which is the supersort of the other sorts, $\mathcal{N}$ for numbers, $\mathcal{S}$ for symbols, $\mathcal{P}$ for pairs, $\mathcal{L}$ for lists, $\mathcal{E}$ for expressions, $\mathcal{R}$ for environments, $\mathcal{A}$ for actor states, $\mathcal{K}$ for continuations, $\mathcal{M}$ for actor messages, and $\mathcal{C}$ for actor configurations. For each

---

[2] Lists are nested form of pairs ending with an empty list. However, because lists simplify the descriptions, we gave them a separate sort.

non-string sort T, we assume that there is a sort $T* \in S$ for the string of the sort. For example, $\mathcal{N}* \in S$ is a string of numbers. In this paper, we denote the variables of a sort with a small letter of that sort. We also suffixed the variables with s for their string sorts.

Examples of the constant operators for symbols $(\emptyset \to S)$ are `lambda, rec, cond, nil`. In this paper, we use the typewriter style font for the symbols. The constructor for pairs is $\mathcal{P} ::= \langle \mathcal{V}, \mathcal{V} \rangle$ and the constructor for lists is $\mathcal{L} ::= (\mathcal{V}*)$. A list indeed is a nested form of pairs. Thus, we equate them so that these terms belong to the same equivalent class.

$$\langle v, (vs) \rangle = (v\ vs).$$

The expressions $\mathcal{E}$ of the actor language have the well-known *S-expression* syntax defined as follows.

$$
\begin{aligned}
\mathcal{E} ::= \ &\mathcal{N} \mid \mathcal{S} \\
&\mid \ (\texttt{lambda}\ (\mathcal{S}*)\ \mathcal{E}_{body}) \\
&\mid \ (\texttt{rec}\ (\mathcal{S}\ \mathcal{S}*)\ \mathcal{E}_{body}) \\
&\mid \ (\texttt{cond}\ \mathcal{E}_{test}\ \mathcal{E}_{true}\ \mathcal{E}_{false}) \\
&\mid \ (\texttt{quote}\ \mathcal{V}) \\
&\mid \ (\mathcal{E}_{op}\ \mathcal{E}*),
\end{aligned}
$$

where $\mathcal{E}_{body}, \mathcal{E}_{test}, \mathcal{E}_{true}, \mathcal{E}_{false}, \mathcal{E}_{op}$ are expressions. When a value term is structured as above, it is given with a sort $\mathcal{E}$.

5.3 Semantics

In this section we describe the semantics of the actor language. First, we explain an informal semantics with examples, and then we describe the formal semantics of the actor system with a rewriting theory $\mathbb{R}$. In $\mathbb{R}$, the transitions of actor states and actor configurations are described as the deductions on the congruent terms modulo equations E.

Informal Semantics. Like the programming language Scheme, the ActorNet language uses prefix notation. For example (`add 1 2 3`) returns 6. Actor language has arithmetic operators like `add, sub, mul, div`, and logical operators like `and, or, not`. It also has a set of pair and list manipulation operators. For example (`cons 1 2`) returns a pair of 1 and 2, and (`car (cons 1 2)`) returns the first element 1, and (`cdr (cons 1 2)`) returns the second element 2. (`list 1 2 3`) returns a list $(1, 2, 3)$ which is equivalent to (`cons 1 (cons 2 (cons 3 nil))`). Note that (`cdr (list 1 2 3)`) is $(2, 3)$. There are assignment operators `setcar` and `setcdr` that set the first and the second elements of a pair.

An expression beginning with `lambda` is an anonymous function definition, where $\mathcal{S}*$ are zero or more names for the function parameters. To ease writing recursive functions, the actor language has the `rec` primitive, where $\mathcal{S}$ is for the name of the function and $S*$ is for the parameters. cond is used for branching expression: if $\mathcal{E}_{test}$ is evaluated to be true, $\mathcal{E}_{true}$ is evaluated; otherwise $\mathcal{E}_{false}$ is evaluated. Observe that this behavior is not the call by value semantics of the function application. quote is an operator that returns its parameter as a value without evaluating it. This operator is useful when we are sending a list as a data to another ActorNet platform. Without this operator, building a literal list is difficult because the interpreter regards the literal list as a function application and tries to evaluate all the elements. The seq operator is similar to the begin operator of the programming language Scheme: each expression is evaluated in turn, and the value of the last expression is returned.

The par, send and msgq are new actor operators not in Scheme. par creates new actors for each expression and makes the actors evaluate the expressions in parallel. The return value of the par expression is a list of the created actor ids. Note that these ids are initially known only to the creator, but they can be sent to other actors for the actor coordination, such as the join continuation [5]. While these actors remain in the same ActorNet platform, they share some parts of their environments so that they can communicate efficiently. If actors migrate to another platform, they can communicate via asynchronous messages. The send operator provides a simple mechanism to send messages to an actor. send makes a deep copy of the message and transmits it to the receiver to prevent any dependence on the source host. For example, (send (list 100 x)) sends all the data reachable from the variable x to an actor with id 100. An actor can access its message queue by calling the msgq operator, which returns the list of the messages the actor has received. ActorNet internally uses a recv method that receives the massage and collects it to the list returned by msgq. Note that msgq is one of the operators that makes our Actor language non-functional; it may return different values for different calls.

The callcc operator accesses the *Current Continuation* (CC)–an abstraction of the rest of the program remaining to execute [24]. For example, the CC of the expression (add 1 (mul 2 ↓ 3)) at the ↓ mark can be regarded as a single-parameter function c1: (lambda (x) (c2 (mul 2 x 3))), where c2 is an another single-parameter function (lambda (x) (add 1 x)). In general, the CC can be regarded as a stack of single-parameter functions. The operand of callcc is a single-parameter function to which the CC is passed.

In ActorNet, the state of an actor is a pair of a CC and a value to be passed to it. Because an actor can read its current continuation, it can duplicate itself or migrate to another platform voluntarily by sending its continuation-value pair to another ActorNet platform. By simply applying the continuation to the value, the sender's computation is continued on a new platform. Using these primitives we could easily and intuitively define the migrate function of Section 4.

Formal Semantics. The state of an actor is a pair of a continuation and a value to be passed to it. In the rewriting theory, the actor states are represented by an equivalent class of terms corresponding to the intermediate computations between the actor state transitions. The computation of an actor is a sequence of actor state transitions. The interaction between actors are captured by an actor configuration which is a snapshot of the whole actor systems. The actor configuration can be regarded as a soup of actor states and actor messages. The concurrent computations of actors are the transitions of the actor configurations.

Let us begin the formal semantics of Actor language with the *environment* ($\mathcal{R}$) which maps the identifiers to their values. An environment comprises two stacks of symbols and values. When a symbol is evaluated, it is looked up from the stack of symbols and the value at the corresponding index in the value stack is returned. $\mathcal{R}$ has three operations: a constant *emptyEnv*: $\emptyset \to \mathcal{R}$, an extend operation $[\_, \_]/\_ : \mathcal{S}* \times \mathcal{V}* \times \mathcal{R} \to \mathcal{R}$, and a lookup operation $\_[\_] : \mathcal{R} \times \mathcal{S} \to \mathcal{V}$. The equations below describe how environments are built. By the equations, the terms in the left side and the right side of $=$ are put to the same equivalent class of terms[3]

$$\text{emptyEnv} = (\textbf{env} \; () \; ())$$
$$[ss', vs']/(\textbf{env} \; (ss) \; (vs)) = (\textbf{env} \; (ss' \; ss) \; (vs' \; vs)).$$

We also assign the sort $\mathcal{R}$ to the lists structured as $(\textbf{env} \; (\mathcal{S}*) \; (\mathcal{V}*))$. The look up operation is also explained by the following equations.

$$(\textbf{env} \; (s \; ss) \; (v \; vs))[s] = v$$
$$(\textbf{env} \; (s' \; ss) \; (v \; vs))[s] = (\textbf{env} \; (ss) \; (vs))[s] \; \text{if} \; s \neq s'.$$

The second equation is a conditional equation: the equation is applied if the (in)equality following the *if* keyword holds.

Continuations ($\mathcal{K}$) are single parameter functions that represent the rest of the program. In the rewriting logic, we assign a sort $\mathcal{K}$ to the lists structured as follows.

$$\mathcal{K} ::= (\textbf{halt})$$
$$| \quad (\textbf{app} \; (\mathcal{V}*_{yet}) \; (\mathcal{V}*_{done}) \; \mathcal{R} \; \mathcal{K})$$
$$| \quad (\textbf{if} \; \mathcal{E}_{true} \; \mathcal{E}_{false} \; \mathcal{R} \; \mathcal{K}),$$

where $\mathcal{V}*_{yet}$ is a list of not yet evaluated parameters, $\mathcal{V}*_{done}$ is a list of already evaluated parameters, and $\mathcal{E}_{true}/\mathcal{E}_{false}$ are expressions to be evaluated when T/F are passed respectively.

A *state of an actor* is a pair of a continuation and a value: $\mathcal{A} ::= \langle \mathcal{K}, \mathcal{V} \rangle$. Any pair structured as such is assigned with a sort $\mathcal{A}$. An *actor configuration* ($\mathcal{C}$) is a set of actor states and actor messages. *Actor messages* is a list structured as $\mathcal{M} ::= (\textbf{mesg} \; \mathcal{N} \; \mathcal{V})$, where $\mathcal{N}$ is the recipient address and $\mathcal{V}$ is the message contents. The sort $\mathcal{C}$ of actor configurations is a supersort of $\mathcal{A}$ and $\mathcal{M}$, and has an associative and commutative constructor: $\_|\_ : \mathcal{C} \times \mathcal{C} \to \mathcal{C}$. That is, $\mathcal{C}$ is a soup of actor messages and actor states.

---

[3] In the rewriting logic, the equivalent classes can be regarded as states: the term rewriting occurs between the equivalent classes.

An *actor computation* is a transition of actor states by applying the deduction rules based on the following rewrite rules[4].

$$\lambda_1 : \langle\, (\texttt{if } e_{true} \ e_{false} \ r \ k)\,,\, \texttt{T}\,\rangle \rightarrow \langle\, k\,,\, eval(\,e_{true}\,,\,r\,)\,\rangle$$

$$\lambda_2 : \langle\, (\texttt{if } e_{true} \ e_{false} \ r \ k)\,,\, \texttt{F}\,\rangle \rightarrow \langle\, k\,,\, eval(\,e_{false}\,,\,r\,)\,\rangle$$

$$\lambda_3 : \langle\, (\texttt{app } (v \ vs) \ (vs') \ r \ k)\,\rangle \rightarrow \langle\, (\texttt{app } (vs) \ (vs') \ r \ k)\,,\, eval(\,v\,,\,r\,)\,\rangle$$

$$\lambda_4 : \langle\, (\texttt{app } ()\ ((\texttt{closure } (ss_{args}) \ r \ e_{body}) \ vs) \ r' \ k)\,\rangle$$
$$\rightarrow \langle\, k\,,\, eval(\,e_{body}\,,\,[ss_{args}, vs]/r\,)\,\rangle$$

$$\lambda_5 : \langle\, (\texttt{app } ()\ (\texttt{list } vs) \ r \ k)\,\rangle \rightarrow \langle\, k\,,\, (vs)\,\rangle$$

$$\lambda_6 : \langle\, (\texttt{app } ()\ (\texttt{car } (v \ vs)) \ r \ k)\,\rangle \rightarrow \langle\, k\,,\, v\,\rangle$$

$$\lambda_7 : \langle\, (\texttt{app } ()\ (\texttt{cdr } (v \ vs)) \ r \ k)\,\rangle \rightarrow \langle\, k\,,\, (vs)\,\rangle$$

$$\lambda_8 : \langle\, (\texttt{app } ()\ (k \ v) \ r \ k')\,\rangle \rightarrow \langle\, k\,,\, v\,\rangle$$

$$\lambda_9 : \langle\, (\texttt{app } ()\ (\texttt{callcc } (\texttt{closure } (s_{arg}) \ r' \ e_{body})) \ r \ k)\,\rangle$$
$$\rightarrow \langle\, (\texttt{halt})\,,\, eval(\,e_{body}\,,\,[s_{arg}, k]/r'\,)\,\rangle$$

λ_1 and λ_2 explain the transitions of the conditional expressions. If T is passed to the *if* continuation, e_{true} is evaluated; otherwise e_{false} is evaluated. We explain the *eval* operator in the next paragraph. λ_3 shows how the parameters to a function are evaluated sequentially: v, the first yet to be evaluated element, is removed from the continuation and its evaluation is passed to the resulting continuation. When all parameters are evaluated, they are applied to the function. λ_4 to λ_9 explain the parameter applications on different types of functions. λ_4 is for a user defined function. A user defined function is evaluated to be a *closure* structure. Thus, the application of parameters extends the environment with the parameters and evaluates the function body in the extended environment. λ_5, λ_6, and λ_7 are for primary operators. For simplicity, we show only the three primary operators for a list manipulation, but the rests are similar. λ_8 is for a continuation: if the function is a continuation, the parameter is passed to the continuation. Observe that the old continuation k' is ignored. λ_9 explains the callcc operator. The parameter to the callcc operator is a single parameter function which is evaluated to be a closure structure. In λ_9 the body of the single parameter function is evaluated in the environment extended with the continuation k.

In the rewrite rules above, we used an operator $eval(\, \_\,,\, \_\,) : \mathcal{E} \times \mathcal{R} \rightarrow \mathcal{V}$. *eval* evaluates the expression $\mathcal{E}$ in the environment $\mathcal{R}$. The following equations on the terms of the *eval* operator build an equivalent class of terms for the evaluation[5].

$$eval(\,s\,,\,r\,) = r[s] \tag{1}$$

$$eval(\,n\,,\,r\,) = n \tag{2}$$

---

[4] We simplified the rules by writing $\langle\, (\texttt{app } (vs) \ (vs') \ r \ k)\,,\, v\,\rangle$ as $\langle\, (\texttt{app } (vs) \ (vs' \ v) \ r \ k)\,\rangle$.

[5] The equational rewriting based on these equations on *eval* terms will produce their normal forms.

$$eval(\ k\ ,\ r\ ) = k \tag{3}$$

$$eval(\ (\texttt{closure}\ (ss_{args})\ r\ e_{body})\ ,\ r'\ ) = (\texttt{closure}\ (ss_{args})\ r\ e_{body}) \tag{4}$$

$$eval(\ (\texttt{lambda}\ (\ ss_{args}\ )\ e_{body})\ ,\ r\ ) = (\texttt{closure}\ (ss_{args})\ r\ e_{body}) \tag{5}$$

$$eval(\ (\texttt{quote}\ vs)\ ,\ r\ ) = (vs) \tag{6}$$

$$\langle\ k\ ,\ eval(\ (e_{func}\ es_{param})\ ,\ r\ )\ \rangle$$
$$= \langle\ (\texttt{app}\ (es_{param})\ ()\ r\ k)\ ,\ eval(\ e_{func}\ ,\ r\ )\ \rangle \tag{7}$$

$$\langle\ k\ ,\ eval(\ (\texttt{cond}\ e_{test}\ e_{true}\ e_{false})\ ,\ r\ )\ \rangle$$
$$= \langle\ (\texttt{if}\ e_{true}\ e_{false}\ r\ k)\ ,\ eval(\ e_{test}\ ,\ r\ )\ \rangle \tag{8}$$

Equation (1) shows that the evaluation of a symbol is the value looked up from the environment. Specifically, the equation means that the *eval* term and the terms involved in the look up operation are in the same equivalent class. Equation (2) to Equation (4) show that the evaluations of numbers, continuations, and closures are themselves. Equation (5) shows how user defined functions are converted to the closure structures. A closure is a list of the function parameter names, an environment, and the function body. When writing a program, referencing a function itself from its body are often necessary; for example, to make a recursive call. Although one can use the *Y combinator* [43] on the λ expression for this purpose, **rec** operator provides an easy access to the name of a function from its body. The following equation shows what **rec** means in terms of the Y combinator.

$$(\texttt{rec}\ (\ s_{fn}\ ss_{args}\ )\ e_{body}) = (Y\ (\texttt{lambda}\ (s_{fn})\ (\texttt{lambda}\ (ss_{args})\ e_{body}))),$$
$$\text{where}\ Y = (\texttt{lambda}\ (\texttt{f})\ (\ (\texttt{lambda}\ (\texttt{y})\ (\texttt{f}\ (\texttt{lambda}\ (ss_{args})\ (\ (\texttt{y}\ \texttt{y})\ ss_{args}))))$$
$$(\texttt{lambda}\ (\texttt{y})\ (\texttt{f}\ (\texttt{lambda}\ (ss_{args})\ (\ (\texttt{y}\ \texttt{y})\ ss_{args}))))\ ))$$

However, in the actual implementation, the **rec** term is transformed directly to a **closure** term like Equation (5) and its environment is extended with a mapping from the function name to the closure itself. Equation (6) shows that the evaluation of a **quote**'d list is the list content. The **quote** operator is useful when sending a list to another ActorNet platform; without it, the ActorNet node would regard the list as a function application with the function of the first element and the parameters of the rest of the elements. Equation (7) explains how a function application is converted to the *app* continuation. Similarly, Equation (8) shows how a conditional expression is converted to an *if* continuation. Observe that unlike *app* continuation the two parameters e_{true} and e_{false} of the *if* continuation are not eagerly evaluated: one of them is evaluated based on the evaluation of e_{test}.

Actors coordinate with others through the asynchronous message passing. These interactions are described as transitions of actor configurations which are a "soup" of actor states and messages. Actor configurations make transitions by applying the deduction rules based on the following rewrite rules.

$$\pi_1 : \langle\ k\ ,\ eval(\ (\texttt{par}'\ \langle\ (e\ es)\ ,\ (ns)\ \rangle)\ ,\ r\ )\ \rangle\ \rightarrow$$
$$\langle\ k\ ,\ eval(\ (\texttt{par}'\ \langle\ (es)\ ,\ (ns\ n)\ \rangle)\ ,\ r\ )\ \rangle\ |\ \langle\ (\texttt{halt})\ ,\ eval(\ e\ ,\ r'\ )\ \rangle,$$

where n is a fresh actor id and $r' = [\,\mathtt{msgq\ id},\ ()\,n\,]/r$

$\pi_2 : \langle\,(\mathtt{app}\ ()\ (\mathtt{send}\ n\ v)\ r\ k)\,\rangle\ \rightarrow\ \langle\,k\,,\ ()\,\rangle\ |\ (\mathtt{mesg}\ n\ v)$

$\pi_3 : \langle\,(\mathtt{app}\ (vs_{yet})\ (vs_{done})\ r\ k)\,\rangle\ |\ (\mathtt{mesg}\ n\ v)$

$$\rightarrow\ \langle\,(\mathtt{app}\ (vs_{yet})\ (vs_{done})\ r'\ k)\,\rangle\ \ \text{if}\ r[\mathrm{id}] = n,$$

where $r\ =\ (\mathtt{env}\ (ss\ \mathtt{msgq\ id}\ ss')\ (vs\ (vs_m)\ n\ vs'))$,
$r'\ =\ (\mathtt{env}\ (ss\ \mathtt{msgq\ id}\ ss')\ (vs\ (v\ vs_m)\ n\ vs'))$

$\pi_4 : \langle\,(\mathtt{if}\ e_{true}\ e_{false}\ r\ k)\,,\ v'\,\rangle\ |\ (\mathtt{mesg}\ n\ v)$

$$\rightarrow\ \langle\,(\mathtt{if}\ e_{true}\ e_{false}\ r'\ k)\,,\ v'\,\rangle\ \ \text{if}\ r[\mathrm{id}] = n,$$

where $r\ =\ (\mathtt{env}\ (ss\ \mathtt{msgq\ id}\ ss')\ (vs\ (vs_m)\ n\ vs'))$,
$r'\ =\ (\mathtt{env}\ (ss\ \mathtt{msgq\ id}\ ss')\ (vs\ (v\ vs_m)\ n\ vs'))$

$\pi_5 : \langle\,(\mathtt{halt})\,,\ v\,\rangle\ |\ c \rightarrow c\ \ \text{if}\ v\ \text{is}\ \mathcal{N},\ \mathcal{S},\ \mathcal{K},\ \mathcal{P},\ \text{or}\ \mathcal{L}\ \text{sort}$

π_1 shows how an actor creates other actors; **par** operator takes one or more expressions as its parameters and creates new actors for each expression to concurrently evaluate them. The return value from the **par** operator is a list of the new actor ids. To simplify the explanation, we introduced the following two helper equations.

$$eval(\,(\mathtt{par}\ es)\,,\ r\,)\ =\ eval(\,(\mathtt{par'}\ \langle\,(es)\,,\ ()\,\rangle)\,,\ r\,)$$
$$eval(\,(\mathtt{par'}\ \langle\,()\,,\ (ns)\,\rangle)\,,\ r\,)\ =\ (ns).$$

π_2 shows that **send** adds a message to the actor configuration. π_3 and π_4 specify that the message in the configuration is added to the message queue of the recipient actor. Finally, π_5 describes the demise of an actor: when an actor computation is completed, its state is removed from the configuration.

6   ActorNet Implementation

Based on the design proposed in Section 3 and the language definition of the previous section, we discuss the issues in implementing the ActorNet runtime platform.

6.1   ActorNet Network Implementation

ActorNet provides a single virtual WSN to actors by connecting physically separated multiple WSNs through the Internet. Recall that the uniform network structure of the virtual WSN is ensured by making the Internet a single hop broadcast network. ActorNet implements two services called *repeater* and *forwarder* to build the uniform network. The repeater bridges the communications between the Ad-Hoc wireless network and the Internet by passing all messages received from one network to the other. Meanwhile, the forwarder provides a single-hop broadcast overlay over the Internet by replicating the messages from each repeater to each of the others connected to it. The net effect of the repeater/forwarder architecture is transforming the individual physically-separated WSNs into a single-hop neighborhood.

Figure 1 shows the repeater/forwarder network architecture of ActorNet. Each repeater has a node called GenericBase through which the repeater can hear from and talk to its WSN. A repeater injects any message it hears from the Internet into its WSN and it sends any message it overhears from its GenericBase to the forwarder. On the other hand, a forwarder is listening to a TCP port for any connections. Once a connection is made, the client is registered to the forwarder until the connection is terminated. In summary, any message overheard by a repeater from its WSN is transmitted to the forwarder and then retransmitted to the other repeaters and ActorNet platforms running on PCs. Finally, the messages sent to the repeaters are injected into their WSNs.

The network bandwidth difference problem is currently handled by placing a large message buffer at the repeaters. The fast messages from the Internet are gathered at the buffer and then slowly retransmitted to the WSNs. However, as the number of clients to the forwarder is increased, the repeaters will constantly send messages to their WSNs. This will increase the chance of a network collision and drain the energy from the nodes near the GenericBase. In addition, the buffering solution is only valid while the input data rate to the buffer is smaller than its output rate. To address these problems, a smarter scheme that makes the repeaters selectively filter the messages can be used. The filtering is based on the actor computation model: when an actor is created, its unique id is known only to its creator, and as the parent or the children send messages with the new actor ids, others can communicate with the newly created actor. Thus, unless a messages with the actor id have passed through a *repeater*, no actors at the other side of the repeater know the existence of the new actor. Because every data is associated with its type in actor language, the actor id checking at the repeater can be effectively done by adding a new type for the actor ids. Observe that the actor ids stored in repeaters can be regarded as the receptionist names and the external actor names of the *actor configuration* [5]. Our actor configuration of Section 5.3 can be augmented with these actor names after this communication optimization is introduced.

6.2   ActorNet Language Implementation

Recall from section 3 that an actor state is a pair of a continuation and a value, and the computation of an actor is a series of actor state transitions made by applying a state's value to its continuation. In ActorNet, these state transitions are implemented by two core methods of actor language interpreter called eval and apply. apply takes the continuation and the value of an actor state as its parameter and produces a new actor state by applying the value to the continuation. eval takes an expression and an environment as its parameter and evaluates the expression within the environment. While evaluating an expression, the values of the identifiers are looked up from the environment that actually is a stack of identifier-value pairs. The environment stack is stored at a structure called *closure* when eval encounters a function definition, and is extended when the actual function parameters are applied to the function. The stack structure of environment and the use of closure ensure the lexical scoping rule when looking up the identifiers.

The tail recursion is a recursive call that does not necessarily result in a build up of state information on the stack [47]. Because actor programs use recursions for the loops, the tail recursion removal is crucial for actor programs; without it, the stack will grow for any simple loop implementations. ActorNet implemented only the basic tail recursion removal capability: the return addresses of function calls are eliminated, removing unnecessary growth of the stack. Although it is not a fully optimized capability, loops can be effectively replaced with parameterless functions. The return addresses are naturally eliminated through the use of the continuation in the actor computation.

The computation of an actor is explicitly managed as transitions of actor states. This explicit state management leads to a simple and notationally clean implementation of multi-threading capability. Because all the necessary information required to proceed the computation of an actor is stored in the actor state, the context switching is as simple as taking an actor state from a queue of actor states and then applying its value to its continuation. This mechanism is similar to the trampolining technique [47], except that ActorNet schedules the switching and the states are explicitly managed. Observe that the environments play the role of the stack, but they are essentially linked lists, as oppose to linear arrays, built on the virtual memory. This dynamic structure eliminates the stack management during the context switch.

6.3   ActorNet Platform Implementation

The current implementation of the ActorNet platform is implemented in only 30 kB of code and 2 kB of data. The code is stored in the Mica2's 128 kB flash memory unit, leaving 100 kB for other applications; the data is allocated in the 4 kB of SRAM space.

Figure 4 depicts a layered software architecture of ActorNet platform for a sensor node. A module does not know the modules above it, but it has access to all the modules below it, not just the ones immediately below it. In contrast, actors only use the interpreter module. Thus, the implementation details are hidden from the actor programs.

Virtual Memory. ActorNet provides a *virtual memory* (VM) subsystem which uses 64 kB of the 512 kB serial flash as the virtual memory. This address space is efficiently indexed by a 16-bit integer. The virtual address space is divided into 512 pages of 128 bytes each. In addition, 8 pages of SRAM (1 kB) are used as a cache for the virtual memory. While flash is not commonly used as a virtual memory store due to the limitation on the maximum number of writes it supports, typically about a million writes to each location, the relatively slow operating speed of sensor nodes and small data sizes of mobile actors mean that even long-term deployments of wireless sensors are very unlikely to approach this limit.

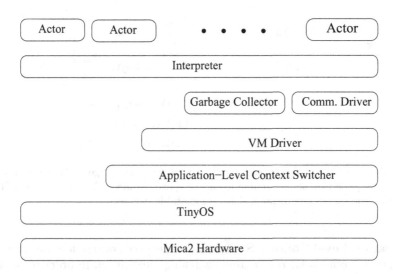

Fig. 4. Software architecture of ActorNet platform (Mica2 node). By making actors interact only with the interpreter layer, the platform differences are hidden from the actors.

An inverted page table is used to search the cached pages for a requested address. It is implemented as a priority queue that maintains the 8 most recently used pages. Hence, the page replacement follows the *Least Recently Used* (LRU) policy. Figure 5 shows the structure of a page. The 128 byte page is divided into a 112-byte data area, a 14-byte bitmap, a 1-bit dirty bit flag, a 4-bit lock count, and 11 bits of reserved space. Because the flash memory writes are slow, we used the dirty bit to avoid an unnecessary page writing. The lock count is used to prevent the VM subsystem from swapping out certain pages. For example, the communication driver of Figure 4 uses a set of static variables defined in a structure called `ComData`. Because this data has buffers shared with the TinyOS communication subsystem, its container page must be locked during transmit and receive operations. This is accomplished by calling the VM's `lock` procedure, subsequently followed by an `unlock` call.

Since there are 112 bytes of data area per page, the effective virtual memory space is 56 kB (512×112). In Figure 5, an allocation bitmap with 8-byte granularity is maintained at the end of each page. Note that the whole 4 kB SRAM space of the Mica2 is not large enough to hold the bitmap of all 56 kB of virtual memory space: $56kB/8 = 7kB$. Distributing the bitmap at each page has a disadvantage when searching for a free space, because the VM driver has to load each page from the flash to check the free space. On the other hand, it is crucial to save the precious SRAM space.

Evaluation based on the benchmark of recursively computing the nth Fibonacci numbers showed a page hit ratio of 95.00%. However, the page hit ratio rises to 99.06% if we consider only the page misses involving the flash-write operations.

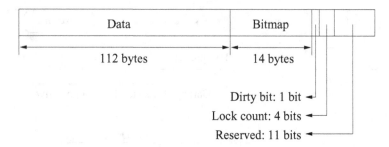

Fig. 5. ActorNet page structure. Including bitmaps in the page structure imposes a performance penalty when searching for a free space. However, having a smaller RAM space than the size of the bitmap, it is an inevitable decision.

Application-Level Context Switching. Figure 6 shows pseudo code of yield and resume methods for the context switching mechanism. In order to perform the context switching correctly, stack contents and register values must be preserved. We reserved a stack space for TinyOS and other applications by defining the stack[n] array in the stackBottom function. Register values including the *program counter* and *stack pointer* are stored and reloaded through the setjmp and longjmp system calls. The control flow for this mechanism is as follows.

1. When resume is called from TinyOS, it stores its register values in toTos. If this is the first time that resume has been called, stackBottom is called to allocate TinyOS stack space by defining stack[n] array. Following stack reservation, stackBottom initiates the ActorNet platform.
2. When ActorNet calls yield, the current register values are stored at the toApp variable and the control flow is returned from the setjmp call of the resume function. Note that control does *not* go back to the stackBottom function: the value of r in resume is 1 in this case.
3. When the resume function is called again from TinyOS, the register values are restored from the toApp variable and control flow is returned to the setjmp of the yield function.

The left side of Figure 6 shows the stack configuration with this mechanism. In the figure, the stack fills up from the bottom. The shaded area below the resume() is the stack space used by TinyOS. The white area below the stackBottom() is the additional stack space allocated to TinyOS in the stack[n] local variable. We use $n = 500$ for Mica2 platforms and $n = 5000$ for PC platforms. Note that the TinyOS stack is limited to this white area; while, in general, we cannot anticipate a stack usage, the applications running on a Mica2 are fixed when a binary image is loaded. This, combined with the fact that most TinyOS applications do not employ recursion, means that in most cases the stack usage is predictable. The shaded area above the stackBottom() is the stack space used by the ActorNet platform. The yield() line shows the top of the application stack when the yield is called.

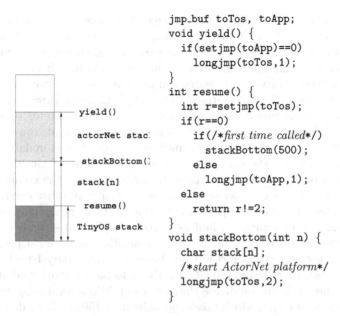

```
jmp_buf toTos, toApp;
void yield() {
    if(setjmp(toApp)==0)
        longjmp(toTos,1);
}
int resume() {
    int r=setjmp(toTos);
    if(r==0)
        if(/*first time called*/)
            stackBottom(500);
        else
            longjmp(toApp,1);
    else
        return r!=2;
}
void stackBottom(int n) {
    char stack[n];
    /*start ActorNet platform*/
    longjmp(toTos,2);
}
```

Labels on the figure:
- yield()
- actorNet stac
- stackBottom()
- stack[n]
- resume()
- TinyOS stack

Fig. 6. Application level context switching mechanism: stack[n] local variable provides a gap between the beginning of ActorNet platform stack (StackBottom) and the stack space for TinyOS. The yield and resume calls switch the stack pointer between these two regions accordingly.

In order to explore the utility of the context switching mechanism, let us consider the following NesC program for the **read**. Note that there is a spin-loop in the **read** function waiting for the **isFlashReadDone** variable to become true.

```
read() {
    ...
    while(!isFlashReadDone)
        yield();
    return flashData;
}
```

```
task loop() {
    resume();
    post loop();
}
```

With our context switching mechanism the **yield()** call in the **read** function causes control to exit from the **resume()** call of the **loop** task. Thus, TinyOS can schedule other tasks and process pending events. Later, when the **loop** task is scheduled again and the **resume** function is called, the computation continues from the **yield()** call of the **read** function as if it had just returned from the yield. Note that we do not need to divide the application program into two phases as in Figure 2. Hence the yield-resume mechanism improves the maintainability of applications.

Multi-Phase Garbage Collector. We implemented a scalable *mark and sweep* garbage collector [7,16] to reduce programming errors and to relieve the developers of the burden of manual memory management. Our actor language is a typed language: every data value is tagged with a byte for its type. Because there are only a handful of data types in the actor language, the rest of the bits can be used as marking flags. In fact, the garbage collector uses two bits for its marking and the communication stack machine uses another bit for serialization. Marking the reachability of a memory cell from any active actor states can be done easily because all actor states are explicitly managed. However, there are also temporary data produced by the actor language interpreter that are not yet bound to their state. To prevent them from being swept away, ActorNet manages a list of the temporary data until their actor state is updated.

In our experiments, the conventional mark and sweep GC can take as long as 10 seconds on Mica2 nodes. This delay can slow down the communication speed considerably, as flash write operations prevent any other computations, including radio communication, in TinyOS. Due to the memory limit, we cannot allocate enough communication buffers to cover the full 10 seconds of GC. We could squeeze the memory to make a communication buffer for 4 packets, but with the conventional GC algorithm this buffer can allow only 1 packet per 2.5 seconds. Instead, we redesign the GC algorithm to have a shorter latency.

To solve this problem, we divide the sweep step into several subphases. Each subphase clears 10 pages, which takes approximately 150 ms. If we disregard the mark phase, ideally, we can send as many as 26 packets per second, because ActorNet has a communication buffer for 4 packets. With the multi-phase GC algorithm, there is a transient time that the mark phase is finished, but the sweep phase is not completed for all pages. The memory allocated during the transient time needs a special care. Suppose that we do not mark the freshly allocated memory, then the memories allocated at not-yet-swept pages will be erroneously deallocated later. On the other hand, if we mark the fresh memory, the memories allocated at the already swept page will not be cleared in the next round of GC. To solve this problem, we implement a 2 bit marking scheme. In this scheme, we alternate the marking bit on each GC round and mark all freshly allocated memories with the current mark bit. Then, the freshly allocated memories will not be swept as they are marked, and the marking in the next round can be done correctly as it uses a different marking bit.

Communication Stack Machine. Sending and receiving a structured data involve data serialization and deserialization. Considering the sender/receiver imbalance, we built a stack machine for the communication. A sender traverses a structured data and sends a serialized stream of stack manipulation commands and data. The receivers can then reconstruct the data structure by simply following the stack commands.

A sender uses `encode` method to transmit a serialized stream of stack commands and data, and the receivers use `decode` method to restore the data. Both methods use a stack and an array called `adrsTable` to manage multiply referenced addresses.

The `encode` algorithm is done in two steps. In the first step, `encode` fills the `adrsTable` with the addresses of multiply referenced data. After this step,

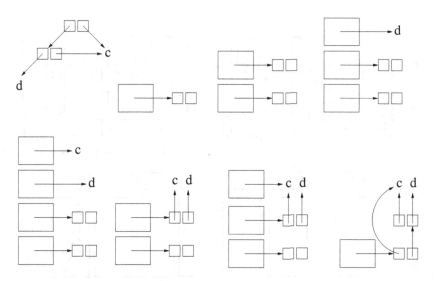

Fig. 7. A data structure to send (the first graph), and the stack configurations of a receiver (the next 7 graphs)

all data reachable from the parameter are marked. In the second step, encode generates a stream of stack commands and data while clearing the mark. The details of the second step are as follows:

1. If encode visits a marked non-pair data, it sends the type and the value of the data, and clears the mark. When decode receives the type tag and the value, it pushes the address of the value.
2. If encode visits a marked pair, it sends a TagPair tag, processes the two elements of the pair, and sends a CmdCons tag. decode creates a pair on receiving the TagPair as a place holder, and pushes the pair's address. It pops two elements from the stack and links them to the place holder beneath later when it receives the CmdCons.
3. If the marked data of cases 1) and 2) are in the adrsTable, encode sends a CmdSaveRef tag and the index of the data in the adrsTable. On receiving the CmdSaveRef, decode stores its top element at the index of its adrsTable.
4. Finally, if encode visits an unmarked data, it sends a TagRef tag and the index of the data in its adrsTable. On receiving the TagRef, decode pushes the address at the index of its adrsTable.

As an example of the serialization, suppose that we are sending the first graph of Figure 7. The sequence of data sent from encode is TagPair, TagPair, TagWord, d, TagWord, c, CmdSaveRef, 0, CmdCons, TagRef, 0, CmdCons, CmdEnd. From this stream of stack commands and data, decode replicates the same structure on its side. The 7 graphs from the second graph of Figure 7 show how the receiver stack changes.

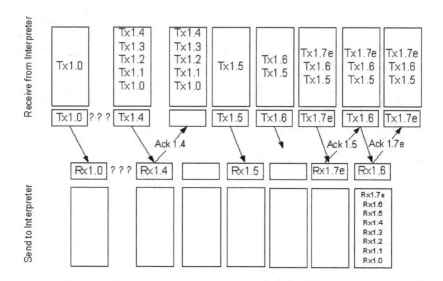

Fig. 8. Selective-repeat protocol for reliable actor migration

Reliable Communication. Execution and communication in a WSN is not always reliable. Many multi-agent applications do not depend on the reliability of a particular actor: the system simply waits for a timeout before launching another instance of a failed actor. Because reliable migration can increase communication cost and latency, the first release of ActorNet did not implement reliable migration. For other applications, however, time-outs to deal with a lack of reliable actor migration simply introduces unacceptable delays.

Two reliable communication methods have been implemented to provide reliable communication. The first is a *selective repeat protocol* based on the *sliding window* concept. This is similar to TCP, where the sender transmits all messages in an actor and then waits for the acknowledgments. Messages that have not been acknowledged are retransmitted. The receiver waits for an entire actor to be transmitted before it is added to the buffer for evaluation and execution. The other method is a simpler *stop-and-wait protocol* which sends one packet at a time and the sender blocks until the receiver acknowledges the packet. Under this protocol, every packet is retransmitted periodically until acknowledged. Figures 8 and 9 illustrate the behavior of these protocols.

We found the stop-and-wait protocol to be superior for environments with low packet loss rates (under 15%). This is because stop-and-wait has lower processor overhead, while selective repeat outperformed significantly in lossier environments. Both implementations are available in the ActorNet platform, and can be selected as appropriate for the application environment.

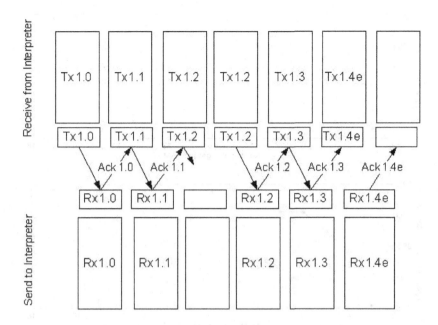

Fig. 9. Stop-and-wait protocol for reliable actor migration

7   Performance Evaluation

We now evaluate the experimental performance of the ActorNet platform. The focus of the experiments described here is to show that the overhead incurred by its constituent services is not prohibitive. Thus, ActorNet is a suitable platform for mobile agents in resource-constrained sensor networks. Our evaluation has three parts:

1. The page hit ratio of the virtual memory subsystem and its impact on system performance.
2. The performance of the multi-phase garbage collector.
3. The communication costs incurred by ActorNet.

7.1   Virtual Memory Performance

We use the benchmark of computing the nth Fibonacci number to evaluate the performance of the VM subsystem. A recursive version of this program is simple, but its exponential behavior is complex enough to carry out a performance evaluation.

As one might expect, as the page cache size increases, the page hit ratio increases. However, in a resource-limited computing environment such as a sensor node, we cannot increase the cache size indefinitely. We must consider a trade-off between the performance and the number of applications that can be run on the

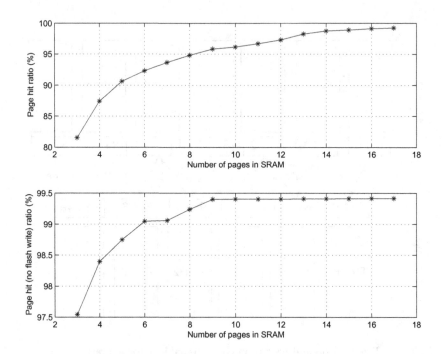

Fig. 10. Page hit ratio (top) and non-flash-write page hit ratio (bottom)

same platform (as not all applications use our VM). The first graph of Figure 10 shows the page hit ratio vs. cache size (number of pages in SRAM). Its shape is approximately concave and increases with cache size. After about 14 pages, the slope is almost flat. However, in the Mica2 platform, the flash write operations dominate the time spent in the VM subsystem. Hence, considering only the flash write operations as page-misses is a more accurate performance measure for the ActorNet platform. The second graph of Figure 10 shows the page hit ratio considering only the flash writes as a page miss. This graph shows a plateau after 9 cache pages (the current ActorNet implementation uses 8 cache pages). However, because of the lock count, when a message encoding or decoding task is running, it would use 7 cache pages. When there are 8 cache pages, the non-flash-write page hit ratio is 99.24%, while with 7 cache pages, the ratio becomes 99.06%.

7.2 Multi-Phase GC Performance

The slow flash write operation of the Mica2 poses a challenge for the garbage collection. As discussed earlier, the GC delay directly limits communication speed. In order to reduce the delay due to GC, we devised a multi-phase GC algorithm. We evaluate the performance of our multi-phase GC as a function of the number of pages swept per phase. The first graph of Figure 11 shows the number of flash

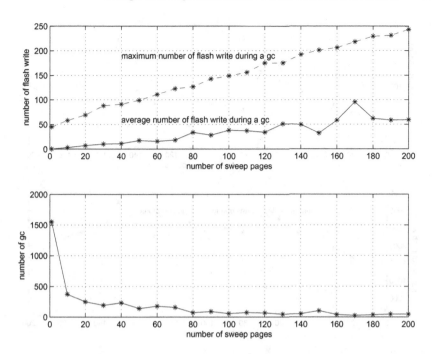

Fig. 11. The number of flash writes during a GC phase (top). The number of GC phases (bottom).

write operations during a GC phase. The solid line shows an average number of flash writes, which can be interpreted as the expected delay due to GC for each phase, and the dashed line shows the maximum number of flash writes, which can be interpreted as the worst case GC delay per phase. The two lines are roughly increasing functions of the number of pages swept, which agrees with intuition. The second graph of Figure 11 shows the number of times GC is called during an experiment. As expected, it is a decreasing function of the number of pages swept per phase. The current implementation of ActorNet sweeps 10 pages per phase; its average number of flash write operations is 3.02 per GC. If we choose the number of pages swept to be 100, then the average number of flash writes is increased to 38.19. That is, when 10 pages are swept per phase, each GC phase takes about 45.3 ms on average, and in the worst case it takes about 870 ms.

There is another merit of the multi-phase GC other than the reduced delay per GC phase. Because our memory reservation algorithm limits the search space for free memory within the interval of the last-swept pages, if the number of pages swept per phase is small, freshly allocated memory addresses are highly correlated in space and time. That is, the fewer the pages swept per phase, the higher the spatial and temporal locality of allocated data. The first graph of Figure 12 shows the number of mark operations during an experiment. Note that

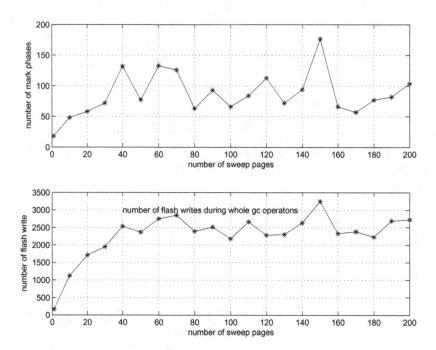

Fig. 12. The number of Mark phases called (top). The number of flash writes due to GC (bottom).

for each round of GC, there are a single mark phase and multiple sweep phases. Hence, the number of mark phases is an indicator of how efficiently the memory is used. The graph roughly shows that the number of GC rounds increases with the number of pages swept per phase. The second graph of Figure 12 shows the total number of flash writes made for GC during an experiment. Specifically, it shows an increasing, concave curve: when few pages are swept per phase, the related data tends to aggregate. Thus, related data is more likely to be found in the cache, which reduces the number of flash writes. However, sweeping too few pages at a time results in overly frequent calls to GC, as seen in the second graph of Figure 11.

7.3   Evaluation of Communication Performance

Next we evaluate the communication costs of the example application of Section 4. This application does not require a routing service: it follows a steepest ascent path of temperatures, and also maintains a return path by itself. Also note that it does not involve spanning tree based data dissemination; the program migrates through the network, rather than collecting all the data at a central node. When the gradient path is a straight line, and assuming that the nodes are uniformly distributed, the number of nodes involved in the experiment is proportional to $\sqrt{n}$ for a WSN of n nodes.

Table 1. The number of messages and the size of messages transmitted by the actor program of Figure 3

message	content size (byte)	number of messages
measure	107	4
temperature	27	1
move	$1629 + \text{hop} \times 8$	57+
return	$474 + \text{hop} \times 4$	17+

To assess the communication performance, we measured the number and size of messages while running the actor program in Figure 3. Table 1 summarizes the results. Broadcasting a measurement actor to neighboring nodes requires 107 bytes of data in 4 messages. Sending a temperature reading requires 27 bytes, which can be sent in a single message. 27 bytes for a simple temperature reading may look like an overhead. The overhead can be attributed to the type information, the list data structure, and the communication stack commands. However, they are necessary overheads to make actor messages generic and not application dependent. Observe that the measure actor is only 107 bytes long. A similar program that periodically samples the temperature and broadcasts the result is about 28 kB. In order to move an actor along the gradient ascent path, 1,629 bytes plus 8 bytes times the hop count thus far are necessary. The extra 8 bytes per hop account for the local variables stored during the migration (recursion). Note that as the actor migrates back to the base station, it discards the unnecessary pieces of its code. As such, the returning actor shrinks in size from 1,629+ bytes to 474+ bytes.

8   Case Study: Ambiance Platform

The ActorNet mobile agent framework is used as part of the macroprogramming system called *Ambiance* [42]. The goal of Ambiance is facilitate non-expert programmers in using pervasive computing devices in the environment, including WSNs. In the Ambiance system, users make "ubiquitous queries" called uQuery through a web interface. A uQuery is an aggregation of flow-independent specification of tasks whose comprising steps, such as primitive calls, loops, nested calls, and application-specific constructs, are converted to a task graph of concurrent active objects which can be executed concurrently. This makes Ambiance an *open system* where users and tasks can join or leave the system at any time.

In Ambiance, WSN computations are automatically converted to actor programs and executed on the ActorNet platforms deployed in the sensor network. Ambiance also uses a high level mobile agent system based on the meta-actor architecture by Mechitov et al. [37]. This system is focused on effectively scheduling and sharing middleware services for WSNs. For a given request, it runs matching algorithms on a repository of service implementations and node capabilities to find a feasible set of candidates, and optimally deploy the implementation to a fine-grained set of selected nodes.

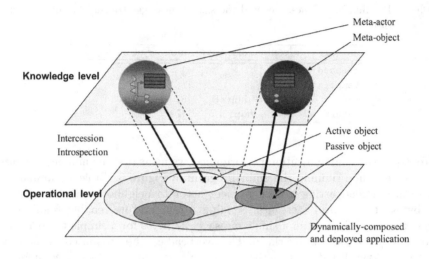

Fig. 13. Two-level adaptive object model architecture for controlling active objects in Ambiance

The Ambiance platform follows the architectural style of *Adaptive Object-Models* (AOM), which define a family of architectures for object-oriented software systems dynamically programmable by domain experts. AOMs are *meta-level architectures* that enforce separation of concerns, and in particular the separation of high-level logic from technical aspects of implementation. In other words, AOMs store the base object as used in the code alongside its meta-data description in terms accessible to the domain expert.

Ambiance further extend this architectural style to enable high-level specifications of global behavior by uncoordinated end-users through a specialized Web interface, and their translation into not only meta-objects, but also meta-*actors*, which control and customize the runtime behavior of both passive and active application objects. These meta-objects are dynamic, they have the capability to observe the application objects and the environment (*introspection*), and to customize their own behavior by analyzing these observations (*intercession*), as seen in Figure 13. This is a form of *reflection*, which allows a program to reason about and affect its own representation and behavior. Watanabe and Yonezawa [54, 57] introduced the notion of reflection in object-oriented concurrent computation model with message passing, which is in many respects similar to the actor model of Ambiance.

The key innovation with respect to the AOM architecture is the separation of the *knowledge level*, where the application, data, service definitions are represented, from the *operational level*, where actual low-level implementation of these objects and services are located and code execution takes place. Figure 14 provides an overview of the system decomposed into these two levels. Note that program representation and transformation environments exist entirely in the

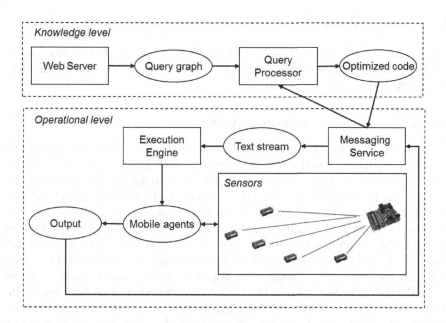

Fig. 14. Ambiance macroprogramming platform runtime

knowledge level, and are thus logically independent of the underlying execution framework used in the deployment environment.

At the operational level, a fine-grained mobile code deployment framework must be available on resource-limited, real-time distributed systems comprising the ambient infrastructure. The mobile code deployment platform is responsible for: 1) deploying and executing dynamically generated low-level code, 2) dynamically discovering and providing access to all sensor and computational resources in the system, and 3) implementing the elements of the service repository. In Ambiance, this role is filled by the ActorNet runtime.

ActorNet eases development by providing an abstract environment for lightweight concurrent object-oriented mobile code on WSNs. As such, it enables a wide range of dynamic applications, including fully customizable queries and aggregation functions, in-network interactive debugging and high-level concurrent programming on the inherently parallel sensor network platform. Moreover, ActorNet cleanly integrates all of these features into a fine-tuned, multi-threaded embedded Scheme interpreter that supports compact, maintainable programs— a significant advantage over primitive stack-based virtual machines used in other WSN-based mobile agent implementations. Mobile agents, called base-level actors in Ambiance, are automatically generated using templates in the knowledge level. The entire base-level application is then deployed as a system of cooperating mobile agents in the WSN, where each node is an ActorNet platform.

9   Related Work

There has been related work on WSNs in a number of areas, including mobile agents, intelligent agent systems, and database systems. We discuss this and other systems related work below.

9.1   Mobile Agent Systems for WSNs

Several attempts have been made to implement efficient mobile agent platforms on WSNs. With the proactive mobile agents, the flexibility in reprogramming and operating WSNs, and the energy saving due to the reduced amount of communication can be maximized. Mate [31] is one of the first mobile agent platform designed for WSNs. Sharing some of the same design goals as ActorNet, it is specifically targeted for highly memory restricted sensor nodes: its stack-based virtual machine operates on a Rene2 mote with only 16 kB of program memory and 1 kB of RAM. Mate features high-level instructions that result in a small code size and efficient code migration. Agilla is another mobile agent platform for WSNs [17]. Like Mate, Agilla is a stack-based virtual machine with special instructions for code mobility. Additionally, Agilla supports multiple applications running on a single node and features a Linda-like tuplespace that decouples data from the spatial constraints [12]. Unlike ActorNet, whose agents are written in a high-level language, programmability and code maintainability in these two systems pose a much greater challenge due to the low level of language abstraction.

Considering the programmability, there is a mobile agent platform for WSNs called SensorWare [10] that provides a high-level language abstraction. SensorWare supports an event-based Tcl-like script language. This high level language not only increases the programmability but also reduces the code size: the specific low-level details are removed by the high level of language abstractions. Currently, SensorWare is implemented only on more powerful platforms such as mobile phones or PDAs. However, with its code size of < 180 kB, it may not be directly applicable to current-generation sensor nodes, such as Mica2 or Telos, which have much tighter memory constraints. In contrast, ActorNet implements an interpreter for a high-level language in under 30 kB of code.

9.2   Intelligent Agent Systems for WSNs

Agent systems, in general, are concerned with high level issues such as negotiation or scheduling. Bryan et al. [30] have designed an agent system for target tracking in WSNs that addresses these high-level aspects of the system. In their system, a WSN is divided into non-overlapping regions called sectors, which are managed by statically assigned sector managers. The sector managers dynamically assign track managers which initiate a new target tracking task as new targets are detected. The tasks are described by alternatively selectable sequences of sub-tasks such that a schedulable plan for a new task can be dynamically built from the space of alternative choices of sub-tasks by negotiating the available resources with other task managers. However, specialized to a target tracking application, their system does not offer the flexibility usually associated with mobile agents. For example, a user has to reprogram the entire WSN loaded with the target tracking application to run different applications. Avoiding platform- and application-specific restrictions on the power of mobile agents is one of the distinguishing features of ActorNet, with its actors being able to take advantage of powerful programming abstractions such as higher-level functions and recursion to implement complex behaviors.

9.3   WSNs as a Data Provider

One of the main usages of a WSN is monitoring the area it is deployed. This task can be done by making the sensors push events to the servers or by making servers pull the data from sensors periodically or in response to the user's requests. In the pull model, WSNs can be seen as a data repository. Naturally, DataBase-like approaches have been developed. For example, with TinyDB [32], a user can easily read the sensor data by making a simple SQL-like query. In TinyDB, considering the efficiency, the sensor data are aggregated together on their way back to the base station. However, despite their efficiency and simplicity, the DataBase like approaches usually provide much less flexibility than mobile agent-based approaches such as ActorNet.

The approach TinyDB has taken on WSNs can be seen as a client/server system where the sensor nodes are the servers providing information in response to the requests from a central client. One of the problems, identified by James *et al* [45], in this client/server approach, especially when the server resources are limited, is that the server cannot provide enough interfaces that could satisfy all the requests of the client. Usually the set of the services a sensor node provides are statically determined when the node is deployed, but the kinds of requests to a WSN can dynamically change over time. Hence, the statically determined services may eventually fail to satisfy the dynamically changing requests. Observe that with a small storage and thus having only handful of fixed services, the utility of a WSN becomes worse as the size of a WSN becomes large. In other words, the efficiency and the scalability of a WSN can be restricted with this static approach. A technique called *Remote Evaluation* has been suggested to address this problem [45]. In this technique, a program is sent to a server to be evaluated remotely and the result is sent back to the client. This Remote Evaluation approach not only increases the flexibility of the server but also reduces the amount of the network communication between the server and the client.

Another approach similar to the Remote Evaluation technique is the work of Jagannathan [23]. His work is focused on the definition of languages for coordination in distributed environments. In his work, a continuation is transferred to a remote node instead of a program and its parameters. A continuation sent to a node can locally process the remotely located data to resolve the synchronization issues. Although we do not send continuations for this purpose, our notion of actor migration bears similarity with this mechanism.

9.4   Related Work in Other Aspects

The actors running on ActorNet are implementation of the Actor model. An actor is a self-contained computing element that communicates with other actors by asynchronous messages. The concept of the actors was proposed by Hewitt [21], and formalized as a transition system by Agha [5]. There are many implementations of the Actor systems including the work of Agha et al. [4], where the location of an actor computation is added to the actor programs to enhance the concurrency.

In developing applications for WSNs, reprogramming of sensor nodes has been a big problem that requires considerable amount of time and effort. For this specific problem, a network reprogramming protocol, called Deluge [22], has been developed. The protocol works like a distributed flooding algorithm [49]: each node compares the versions of the advertised images with its own. When a higher version exists it requests and installs the whole image from the winning advertiser. A practical difficulty is that the application images are often larger than the physical memory size. With this protocol, over-the-air reprogramming of a network becomes easy. However, when an upgrade is required on only a few nodes, Deluge is an overkill since it upgrades unnecessary parts of the network also. Moreover, running several distinct applications concurrently on a single network requires the creation of a large image containing all applications.

Since ActorNet was originally proposed in [28], it has been used as a base technology for other applications for WSNs. In the Ambiance system [42] and the shared middleware service system of Mechitov et al. [37], ActorNet serves as an end-computing platform. Karmani and Agha [25] developed a debugging tool for WSN applications based on ActorNet.

10   Future Research Directions

Although ActorNet provides many useful features not found in any previous sensor network programming platform, the current implementation still has several limitations. We describe several open problems.

One of the biggest challenges is *fault tolerance*: as message transmission in WSNs is via local broadcast, we cannot use a simple message acknowledgment mechanism for reliability. Several reliable communication mechanisms for ActorNet have been evaluated in [44], and we are currently investigating techniques to implement an efficient negative acknowledgment-based rebroadcast reliability mechanism.

ActorNet is a bare bones actor system and does not provide coordination mechanisms. The virtual memory and multi-tasking environments provided by ActorNet open the possibility for the more advanced *coordination mechanisms*. These could be as simple as *tuple spaces* [12] and *ActorSpaces* [3], or more complex ones such as *synchronizers* [18], which can be built on top of the existing distributed storage services for sensor networks [36].

Security is another concern for the mobile agents. Mobile agent platforms can prevent malicious agents performing an admission control against signed agent programs. However, this security checking is more challenging in ActorNet because the program is mixed with the states and is changing over time. However, actors work on isolated memory with well-defined and if the runtime ensures that the actor semantics is correctly implemented, security can be enhanced. Another possibility is to use memory management and garbage collection of actors to enhance security by limiting the temporal exposure of a node.

There are many resource management related issues that we have not considered in this work. For example, only a limited number of actors can operate with reasonable performance on as embedded systems have limited processing power and memory. This means that *resource arbitration* is necessary. Such resource arbitration must be *self-evolving* and *adaptive* to enable autonomic functioning of a WSN. In a way, this problem is analogous to the resource arbitration problem in clouds or in enterprise storage systems [55].

We have also not considered *energy consumption*. Energy is a critical constraint in WSNs and requires careful management. Some embedded nodes provide frequency scaling to conserve energy and this can interact with other behaviors of a node, further complicating energy management (e.g. see [39]).

Despite its limitations, we believe ActorNet provides powerful, efficient, scalable, and high level services for developing applications for WSNs. However, further research is needed to facilitate the broader use of actors for building WSN applications.

Acknowledgments. The authors gratefully acknowledge the support of this research by the National Science Foundation under grants CMS 06-00433, CNS 10-35773, NSF 10-35562, and NSF CMMI 09-28886; the Army Research Office under contract W911NF-09-1-0273, and Air Force Research Laboratory and the Air Force Office of Scientific Research, under agreement number FA8750-11-2-0084. The second author was also supported by the Vodafone graduate fellowship. Sergei Shevlyagin, a University of Illinois undergraduate student, contributed to the implementation of ActorNet's reliable communication protocol. The U.S. Government is authorized to reproduce and distribute reprints for Governmental purposes notwithstanding any copyright notation thereon.

References

1. Abelson, H., Dybvig, R.K., Haynes, C.T., Rozas, G.J., Adams, I.N.I., Friedman, D.P., Kohlbecker, E., Steele, J. G.L., Bartley, D.H., Halstead, R., Oxley, D., Sussman, G.J., Brooks, G., Hanson, C., Pitman, K.M., Wand, M.: Revised report on the algorithmic language scheme. SIGPLAN Lisp Pointers IV(3), 1–55 (1991), http://doi.acm.org/10.1145/382130.382133
2. ActorNet, http://osl.cs.illinois.edu/software/actor-net/
3. Agha, G., Callsen, C.J.: Actorspaces: An open distributed programming paradigm. In: Chen, M.C., Halstead, R. (eds.) PPOPP, pp. 23–32. ACM (1993)
4. Agha, G., Houck, C., Panwar, R.: Distributed execution of actor programs. In: Banerjee, U., Nicolau, A., Gelernter, D., Padua, D.A. (eds.) LCPC 1991. LNCS, vol. 589, pp. 1–17. Springer, Heidelberg (1992)

5. Agha, G.A., Mason, I.A., Smith, S.F., Talcott, C.L.: A foundation for actor computation. Journal of Functional Programming 7, 1–72 (1997)
6. Arora, A., Dutta, P., Bapat, S., Kulathumani, V., Zhang, H., Naik, V., Mittal, V., Cao, H., Demirbas, M., Gouda, M., Choi, Y.R., Herman, T., Kulkarni, S.S., Arumugam, U., Nesterenko, M., Vora, A., Miyashita, M.: A line in the sand: A wireless sensor network for target detection, classification, and tracking. Computer Networks, 605–634 (2004)
7. Azatchi, H., Levanoni, Y., Paz, H., Petrank, E.: An on-the-fly mark and sweep garbage collector based on sliding views. ACM SIGPLAN Notices 38(11) (2003)
8. Basharat, A., Catbas, N., Shah, M.: A framework for intelligent sensor network with video camera for structural health monitoring of bridges. In: Proceedings of Third IEEE International Conference on Pervasive Computing and Communications (PerCom (March 2005)
9. Bhatti, S., Carlson, J., Dai, H., Deng, J., Rose, J., Sheth, A., Shucker, B., Gruenwald, C., Torgerson, A., Han, R.: Mantis os: an embedded multithreaded operating system for wireless micro sensor platforms. In: Mobile Networks and Applications, pp. 563–579. Kluwer Academic Publishers (2005)
10. Boulis, A., Han, C.C., Srivastava, M.B.: Design and implementation of a framework for efficient and programmable sensor networks. In: International Conference on Mobile Systems, Applications, and Services. USENIX Association
11. Brooks, R.R., Ramanathan, P., Sayed, A.M.: Distributed target classification and tracking in sensor networks. In: Proceedings of the IEEE (2003)
12. Carriero, N., Gelernter, D.: Linda in context. Communications of the ACM 32, 444–458 (1989)
13. Crossbow Technology, Inc., http://www.xbow.com/
14. Dorigo, M., Caro, G.D., Gambardella, L.: Ant algorithms for discrete optimization. In: Artificial Life, pp. 137–172 (1999)
15. Dunkels, A., Gronvall, B., Voigt, T.: Contiki - a lightweight and flexible operating system for tiny networked sensors. In: IEEE International Conference on Local Computer Networks, pp. 455–462. IEEE Computer Society (2004)
16. Endo, T., Taura, K., Yonezawa, A.: A scalable mark-sweep garbage collector on large-scale shared-memory machines. In: Proceedings of the IEEE/ACM Conference on Supercomputing (1997)
17. Fok, C.L., Roman, G.C., Lu, C.: Rapid development and flexible deployment of adaptive wireless sensor network applications. Technical Report WUCSE-04-59. Washington University, Department of Computer Science and Engineering
18. Frølund, S., Agha, G.: A language framework for multi-object coordination. In: Nierstrasz, O. (ed.) ECOOP 1993. LNCS, vol. 707, pp. 346–360. Springer, Heidelberg (1993)
19. Gay, D., Levis, P., von Behren, R., Welsh, M., Brewer, E., Culler, D.: The nesc language: A holistic approach to networked embedded systems. In: Proceedings of Programming Language Design and Implementation (PLDI) (June 2003)
20. Han, C.C., Kumar, R., Shea, R., Kohler, E., Srivastava, M.: A dynamic operating system for sensor nodes. In: International Conference On Mobile Systems, Applications and Services, pp. 163–176. ACM (2005)
21. Hewitt, C.E.: Viewing control structures as patterns of passing messages. Journal of Artificial Intelligence 8, 323–364 (1977)
22. Hui, J.W., Culler, D.: The dynamic behavior of a data dissemination protocol for network programming at scale. In: Proceedings of the 2nd International Conference on Embedded Networked Sensor Systems, pp. 81–94. ACM Press (2004)

23. Jagannathan, S.: Continuation-based transformations for coordination languages. In: Theoretical Computer Science, vol. 240, pp. 117–146. Elsevier Science Publishers Ltd. (June 2000)
24. Kamin, S.N.: Programming Languages An Interpreter-Based Approach. Addison Wesley (1990)
25. Karmani, R., Agha, G.: Debugging wireless sensor networks using mobile actors. In: Real-Time and Embedded Technology and Applications Symposium, Poster Abstract (2008), http://hdl.handle.net/2142/4607
26. Kim, S., Pakzad, S., Culler, D., Demmel, J., Fenves, G., Glaser, S., Turon, M.: Health monitoring of civil infrastructures using wireless sensor networks. In: Proceedings of the 6th International Conference on Information Processing in Sensor Networks, IPSN 2007, pp. 254–263. ACM, New York (2007), http://doi.acm.org/10.1145/1236360.1236395
27. Kwon, Y., Mechitov, K., Sundresh, S., Kim, W., Agha, G.: Resilient localization for sensor networks in outdoor environments. In: International Conference on Distributed Computing Systems, pp. 643–652 (2005)
28. Kwon, Y., Sundresh, S., Mechitov, K., Agha, G.: ActorNet: An actor platform for wireless sensor networks. In: International Joint Conference on Autonomous Agents and Multiagent Systems, pp. 1927–1300 (2006)
29. Lajara, R., Pelegri-Sebastia, J., Solano, J.J.P.: Power consumption analysis of operating systems for wireless sensor networks. In: Sensors, vol. 10, pp. 5809–5826. IEEE (2010)
30. Lesser, V., Charles, L., Ortiz, J., Tambe, M.: Distributed sensor networks 15 (2007)
31. Levis, P., Culler, D.: Mate: A tiny virtual machine for sensor networks. In: International Conference on Architectural Support for Programming Languages and Operating Systems, San Jose, CA, USA (October 2002)
32. Madden, S.R., Szewczyk, R., Franklin, M.J., Culler, D.: Supporting aggregate queries over ad-hoc wireless sensor networks. In: Workshop on Mobile Computing and Systems Application (2002)
33. Mainwaring, A., Polastre, J., Culler, R.S.D., Anderson, J.: Wireless sensor networks for habitat monitoring. In: Proceedings of the First ACM International Workshop on Wireless Sensor Networks and Applications (WSNA) (2002)
34. Maroti, M., Kusy, B., Simon, G., Ledeczi, A.: The flooding time synchronization protocol. In: Sensys (2004)
35. Marti-Oliet, N., Meseguer, J.: Rewriting logic as a logical and semantic framework. In: Meseguer, J. (ed.) Electronic Notes in Theoretical Computer Science, vol. 4. Elsevier Science Publishers (2000)
36. Mazumdar, S.: Fast range queries using Pre-Aggregated In-Network storage. Masters' thesis, University of Illinois at Urbana Champaign (2004)
37. Mechitov, K., Razavi, R., Agha, G.: Architecture design principles to support adaptive service orchestration in wsn applications. ACM SIGBED Review 4, 37–42 (2007)
38. Meseguer, J.: Membership algebra as a logical framework for equational specification. In: Parisi-Presicce, F. (ed.) WADT 1997. LNCS, vol. 1376, pp. 18–61. Springer, Heidelberg (1998)
39. Moinzadeh, P., Mechitov, K., Shiftehfar, R., Abdelzaher, T.F., Agha, G., Spencer, B.F.: The time-keeping anomaly of energy-saving sensors: Manifestation, solution, and a structural monitoring case study. In: SECON, pp. 380–388. IEEE (2012)
40. Nagayama, T., Spencer, B.F., Agha, G., Mechitov, K.: Model-based data aggregation for structural monitoring employing smart sensors. In: International Conference on Networked Sensing Systems (2006)

41. Polastre, J., Hill, J., Culler, D.: Versatile low power media access for wireless sensor networks. In: Proceedings of the Second ACM Conference on Embedded Networked Sensor Systems (SenSys) (November 2004)
42. Razavi, R., Mechitov, K., Agha, G., Perrot, J.F.: Ambiance: A mobile agent platform for end-user programmable ambient systems. In: Advances in Ambient Intelligence, Frontiers in Artificial Intelligence and Applications, vol. 164, pp. 81–106. IOS Press (2007)
43. Reade, C.: Elements of Functional Programming. Addison-Wesley (1989)
44. Shevlyagin, S., Mechitov, K., Agha, G.: Implementation of fault tolerance in actornet. In: UIUC Department of Computer Science Undergraduate Research Symposium (2008)
45. Stamos, J.W., Gifford, D.K.: Remote evaluation. ACM Transactions on Programming Languages and Systems, 537–564 (1990)
46. Stevens, W.R.: Advanced Programming in the UNIX Environment. Addison Wesley (1992)
47. Sussman, H.A.G.J., Sussman, J.: Structure and Interpretation of Computer Programs, 2nd edn. The MIT Press (1996)
48. Tanenbaum, A.S.: Computer Networks, 4th edn. Prentice Hall (2003)
49. Tel, G.: Introduction to Distributed Algorithms, 2nd edn. Cambridge University Press (2001)
50. TinyOS, http://www.tinyos.net
51. Tomlinson, C., Kim, W., Scheevel, M., Singh, V., Will, B., Agha, G.: Rosette: An object-oriented concurrent systems architecture. SIGPLAN Notices 24(4), 91–93 (1989)
52. Venkatasubramanian, N., Agha, G., Talcott, C.L.: Scalable distributed garbage collection for systems of active objects. In: Bekkers, Y., Cohen, J. (eds.) IWMM-GIAE 1992. LNCS, vol. 637, pp. 134–147. Springer, Heidelberg (1992)
53. Watanabe, T., Yonezawa, A.: Reflection in an object-oriented concurrent language. In: Meyrowitz, N.K. (ed.) OOPSLA, pp. 306–315. ACM (1988)
54. Watanabe, T., Yonezawa, A.: Reflection in an object-oriented concurrent language. In: Yonezawa, A. (ed.) ABCL: An Object-Oriented Concurrent System. MIT Press (1990)
55. Yin, L., Uttamchandani, S., Palmer, J., Katz, R.H., Agha, G.A.: Autoloop: Automated action selection in the "observe-analyze-act" loop for storage systems. In: POLICY, pp. 129–138. IEEE Computer Society (2005)
56. Yonezawa, A., Shibayama, E., Takada, T., Honda, Y.: Modelling and programming in an object-oriented concurrent language ABCL/1. In: Yonezawa, A., Tokoro, M. (eds.) Object-Oriented Concurrent Programming. MIT Press (1987)
57. Yonezawa, A., Watanabe, T.: An introduction to object-based, reflective, concurrent computation. In: Agha, G., Wegner, P., Yonezawa, A. (eds.) Proceedings of the ACM SIGPLAN Workshop on Object-Based Concurrent Programming (1988)

Objects in Space

Wolfgang De Meuter, Andoni Lombide Carreton, Kevin Pinte,
Stijn Mostinckx, and Tom Van Cutsem

Software Languages Lab
Vrije Universiteit Brussel
Pleinlaan 2, 1050 Brussels, Belgium

Abstract. The paper presents a research agenda that we are currently executing for programming mobile applications that write and read information to and from passive RFID tags. Modern tags can host up to several kilobytes of information which makes it possible to store real software objects (in the object-oriented sense) that can even refer to each other. This gives the term 'spatial database' an entirely new meaning. The paper motivates the need for new programming language constructs that are specifically targeted towards representing objects on tags, designating specific tags in the application's proximity and keeping the internal status of the mobile application causally connected to its physical surrounding.

1 Introduction

In recent years, we have seen a steady growth in the penetration of smart phones in our society. Apart from being full-fledged computers, modern smart phones are also equipped with a plethora of sensors that can be used by application programmers. One such 'sensor' that is becoming a mundane feature is an RFID (Radio Frequency Identification) reader. Interestingly, RFID readers are not just sensors; they can also write information on the tags they encounter. This gives rise to a new type of mobile applications that we dub *Mobile RFID-Enabled Applications* or MoREnAs for short.

This paper analyses the difficulties that programmers face when writing well-functioning MoREnAs. We do so by considering MoREnAs as a particular kind of distributed application. However, instead of assuming a fixed (or fairly stable) set of communication partners, MoREnAs communicate with large volatile "clouds" of tags that happen to be in the communication range of a MoREnA at a particular moment in time. Our research hypothesis is that MoREnAs are best programmed in a distributed programming language that offers a rich set of features that are especially designed to handle a correct interaction with such clouds of tags.

Our research departs from a homegrown distributed language, called AmbientTalk. AmbientTalk has been originally conceived to program peer-to-peer mobile applications that run on networks that emerge spontaneously whenever users collocate. These networks are called mobile ad hoc networks or MANETs

G. Agha et al. (Eds.): Yonezawa Festschrift, LNCS 8665, pp. 317–340, 2014.

for short. Many problems of MoREnAs are inherited from the MANET case. Adopting existing solutions for these problems is therefore a logical thing to do. Our research agenda thus consists of extending AmbientTalk with features that are specifically targeted towards MoREnAs. These exhibit a number of properties that MANET applications do not exhibit: the fact that the communication partners come in vast amounts and the fact that they do not have any computational power whatsoever[1].

1.1   Scenario: Intelligent Kitchens

In order to give a concrete idea of the type of applications that we target, we start by outlining a potential scenario.

In this scenario we envision buying and using furniture in an IKEA-like furniture shop. Furniture configurations need to be selected and assembled from modular pieces. The typical setup is that customers walk through a show room in order to choose furniture from a particular product line ("a kitchen of the product line named Ångebakken", "a couch configuration of the product line named Zërikønt). After selecting a product line, various modular parts can be selected and composed in order to come up with one particular configuration that fits the needs of the customer. As soon as a concrete configuration has been composed, the necessary parts have to be collected at the exit of the shop. The parts have to be assembled at home.

In our scenario, users would run *a mobile shopping assistant application* that allows them detect the identity of the product lines that are involved in a particular show room. All assembly parts used in a show room contain an RFID-tag that stores a software object describing the assembly part. Based on the product line identities, the mobile application offers users a list of all the line's assembly parts and of a list of constraints that restrict their composability. It subsequently offers the ability to visually compose a particular configuration. After deciding on one particular configuration (e.g. a kitchen), the application enumerates the required assembly parts and generates a list of instructions on how to find those parts at the shop's 'self serve furniture area'. The customer collects his modular parts and proceeds to the cash register.

Once at home, *a configuration and installation application* displays a step-by-step assembly plan in order to assemble the chosen configuration. Moreover, while assembling, the application stores configuration information about that particular configuration onto the RFID tags that are built into those parts. Like this, a kitchen sink can "be told" that it is situated right below a certain cupboard. A door of a cupboard is programmed with the identify of "its" cupboard. A cupboard can be told that it is situated "on the left" of another cupboard, etc.

---

[1] Our work currently only deals with passive RFID tags. Active RFID tags are less interesting from an academic point of view since they are actually small computers; hence they fall under the MANET classification.

Third, *a mobile kitchen operation application* can be used to read and write information from and to the tags while one is using the kitchen. Cupboards can be programmed such that they know which tools they contain and so on.

Finally, the kitchen can also contain a number of *non-mobile kitchen application components* that monitor the "current state". For example, we could think of a software component built into a fridge which perpetually scans the tags attached to the products stored in the fridge. One particularly interesting application that we will use is the **RFID-Chef**. It is an application that is part of the kitchen counter. It assists a user while cooking. Figure 5 displays a screen shot of the application. Every time we put an ingredient on the kitchen counter, the RFID-Chef consults its database of recipes. The recipes that can become a candidate to be prepared are displayed. Recipes displayed in green are fully covered by the ingredients sitting on the counter. The amount of green is corresponds to the amount of surplus ingredients. Recipes displayed in red are nearly covered. The amount of red corresponds to the amount of ingredients that is still lacking.

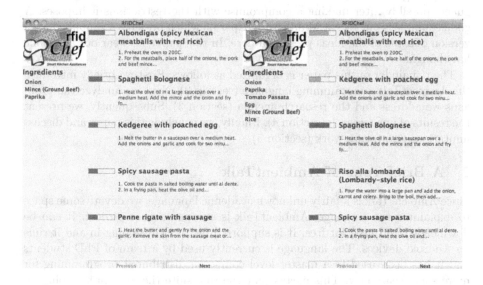

Fig. 1. Screenshot of the RFID-Chef

From a technological point of view, such applications are entirely feasible with todays technology. However, given the current state of the art in software technology, their construction is extremely intricate and tedious. This is explained in section 3. It forms the motivation for the rest of the paper.

1.2 Middleware vs. Programming Languages

In distributed programming research, we discern two different research methodologies. On the one hand there is the *middleware school* which tries to come up with novel concepts and abstractions that ease the construction of distributed applications. Usually, the abstractions are programmed in a mainstream language (e.g. Java). They are subsequently used by using the traditional abstraction mechanisms of that language (e.g. inheritance, composition, genericity). On the other hand there is the *programming language school* which typically designs an entirely new language or which extends an existing language with the novel abstractions. Here the focus is on trying to polish both the novel abstractions and the existing ones in order to form one coherent language.

In our research, we take a combined approach. From a purely academic point of view, we believe that the programming language approach is superior to the middleware approach because it results in cleaner, more orthogonal abstractions that can be studied in a laboratory setting [20]. When integrating middleware in an existing language, one often has to wrestle with the shortcomings of that language (e.g. the lack of reflection in Java) and this often influences the conceptual purity in a negative sense. Nevertheless, we do believe that we should also investigate how our novel abstractions can be applied to a mainstream language, possibly after making a compromise with the restrictions it imposes. A good example is our recent Middleware paper [2] which presents a simplified Java version of some of the ideas presented here. In this paper we wear our academic hat though.

The remainder of this paper is organized as follows. First we briefly introduce the AmbientTalk programming language (section 2). Next we analyze the problems we address and the research agenda (section 3). Subsequently, we present the results of our research (section 4). Finally, we conclude this paper and discuss limitations and future work (section 5).

2   A Brief Tour of AmbientTalk

Since AmbientTalk is a fairly unknown academic language, we devote some space to explaining the language. AmbientTalk is an open source project. It can be downloaded and used for free. It is supported by an Eclipse plug-in and it runs on Android devices. The language is currently used by a team of PhD students and it has been used in a master level course on distributed programming for quite some years now. This means that the tool suite (i.e. interpreter, plug-in, debugger) are fairly stable.

It is by no means our intention to cover the language entirely. It has been documented in several research papers [5,21] and in an online tutorial [18].

AmbientTalk features a concurrency and distribution model based on communicating event loops [15]. In this model, *event loops* form the unit of distribution and concurrency. Every event loop has a *message queue* and a single thread of control that perpetually processes messages from that queue. An event loop hosts regular objects. Within an event loop, object references are accessed using ordinary, synchronous message sending. An event loop can publish its objects (on the network). Other event loops can discover these published objects thereby obtaining a *remote object reference* (or *far reference*) to the object. Communication with a remote object happens by sending messages over the far reference.

The messages are then placed in the message queue of the event loop hosting the remote object. The event loop's thread handles these messages in sequence thus ensuring the hosted objects are protected against race conditions. A far reference operates asynchronously: a sender event loop will never wait for a message to be delivered, but immediately continues its computation. Figure 2 illustrates the communicating event loops model.

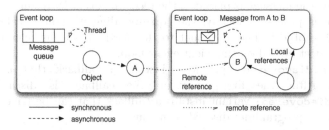

Fig. 2. The communicating event loops model

2.1   Service Discovery

Publishing an object on the network is done using the **export:as:** language primitive. It takes an object to be published and a *type tag*[2] to label the object. In the example below an object representing a printing service is published. The object is labelled with the Printer type tag, which was created using the **deftype** primitive. Notice that AmbientTalk is a prototype-based language, an object is created ex-nihilo using the **object:** primitive.

```
deftype Printer;

def printService := object: {
    def print(aDoc) {
        system.println("printing " + aDoc)
    } };

export: printService as: Printer
```

Clients have two ways to obtain a far reference to a remote object. Either they install discovery callbacks in order to react on the appearance of objects on the network, or objects are passed as arguments of messages sent over another far reference. Below is an example of a client interested in a printing service.

```
deftype Printer;

when: Printer discovered: { |farRef|
    farRef<-print(myDoc) }
```

[2] Type tags are a lightweight classification mechanism to categorize remote objects explicitly by means of a nominal type. They can best be compared to a topic in publish/subscribe terminology or marker interfaces in Java.

The **when:discovered:** primitive installs a block closure as a listener procedure (i.e. a callback). This procedure is triggered upon discovery of an object labeled with the Printer type tag on the network. When the callback is executed, the block closure receives a far reference to the remote printService object as an argument. The <- operator is used to send asynchronous messages over a far reference. In this case, the client sends a document to the printing service using the print message.

Intuitively, the message is placed in the receiving event loop's mailbox. When the message is processed locally, the corresponding method is called on the printService object. The argument to this method is a far reference to the document object hosted on the client event loop.

The **when:discovered:** primitive installs a callback that is executed only once. After the first execution the callback is discarded. The **whenever:discovered:** variant installs a callback that can be triggered many times, until the programmer discards it manually.

2.2   Fault Tolerance with Respect to Volatile Connections

When mobile devices move out of each others range, the event loops that are hosted on the different devices are disconnected from each other. Upon such a disconnection, all far references become disconnected and will start buffering incoming messages, as illustrated by figure 3. When the communication is reestablished, the far references are automatically rebound and all buffered messages are subsequently flushed to the message queue of the destination event loop.

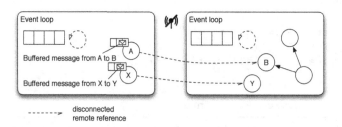

Fig. 3. Messages to disconnected objects are buffered until reconnection

The programmer can monitor the connectivity of far references by means of two primitives. **when:disconnected:** and **when:reconnected:** install callbacks that are triggered when a far reference is disconnected or reconnected. Here too, **whenever:disconnected:** and **whenever:reconnected:** variants exist that may be executed multiple times. In the example below, a print button is enabled or disabled depending on the availability of the service is unavailable.

```
whenever: farRef disconnected: {
    disablePrintButton() };
whenever: farRef reconnected: {
    enablePrintButton() }
```

2.3   Futures

By default, asynchronous message sends have no return value. *futures* can be used to alleviate this restriction. A future is a placeholder for the later return value, which may not yet be available. Initially, the future is said to be *unresolved*. Consider the example of a calculator service:

```
def calc := actor: {
    def add(x,y) {
        x + y
    } }

import /.at.lang.futures;
enableFutures(true);

def sumFuture := calc<-add(1,2);
```

The **actor:** primitive spawns a new event loop representing a calculator service with an add method. The **import** statement loads the futures library, after which it is enabled as the default for all asynchronous messages. Sending the add message to the calculator service now immediately returns a future which provides us with a handle on the eventual return value. Using the **when:becomes:** primitive, we can register a callback on a future, which is executed as soon as the future becomes resolved. The callback is given the actual return value of the message. Here is an example:

```
when: sumFuture becomes: { |result|
    system.println("the result was " + result);
} catch: { |exception|
    system.println("addition failed") };
```

The **when:becomes:catch:** function takes a future and two callback blocks (a callback and an errback). If the asynchronously invoked method returns a value, the future is *resolved*, and the callback is called with the return value. If the method instead raises an exception, the corresponding future becomes *ruined* and the errback is called with the exception.

2.4   Parameter Passing Rules

When sending a message across a far reference, objects are parameter-passed *by far reference*: the parameters of the invoked method are replaced by far references to the original objects.

There is one exception to the above parameter-passing rules: objects created as *isolates* (i.e. using `isolate:` instead of **object:**) are passed by (deep) copy rather than by far reference. Isolates are treated as lexically closed expressions. In other words, they are isolated from their lexical scope, which allows them to be copied across actor boundaries without losing information. The benefit of isolates is that the recipient actor will receive its own local copy of the isolate, avoiding further remote communication.

For the calculator example, it makes sense to represent e.g. complex numbers as isolates. The calculator service can then access the properties and methods using the regular synchronous dot operator:

```
def complexNumber := isolate: {
    def re := 0;
    def im := 0;
    def init(re, im) {
        self.re := re;
        self.im := im
    };
    def +(other) { self.new(re+other.re, im+other.im) } }
```

2.5   Summary

In brief, AmbientTalk is a distributed programming language that features objects that can be exported and discovered on MANETs. The fault tolerance that comes with its far reference semantics makes the language extremely well-suited for such networks. Temporal network disconnections are not felt by the programmer since far references transparently buffer messages. Objects never leave their hosting actor as they are passed by far reference. Isolates are used when a replication semantics is desirable. Local communication happens synchronously (using the ordinary dot operator). Remote communication happens asynchronously (using the left arrow). Futures are used to propagate back results.

3   Problem Statement and Research Agenda

The problem addressed by this paper is twofold. First, we currently lack abstractions to represent and interact with software objects that correspond to RFID-tags. Second, since RFID tags form large volatile clouds of devices, keeping a MoREnA's status consistent with the physical composition of such clouds leads to a highly event-driven system, which induces a number of programming problems.

3.1   Representing and Accessing Objects in Space

MoREnAs use RFID technology in a radically different way from existing RFID applications which typically are about stock management or item tracking. These applications use RFID tags as mere digital barcodes. They do not exploit the writable memory on these tags [16,6,14] and they typically assume the presence of an infrastructure in the form of a centralized backend database that associates every digital barcode with its semantics [10,7]. For MoREnAs such centralised infrastructure is absent. It should thus be possible to write the semantic information directly onto the tags. With the state of the art software technology, this is problematic. Developers of MoREnAs are currently forced to rely on extremely low-level abstractions in order to interact with RFID hardware; in most cases even directly with the hardware driver or bare tag memory level. The programmer must "manually" deal with the fact that communication with RFID tags is prone to many failures. E.g., on the Android platform, API documentation advice programmers to spawn a separate thread to cover this. As a consequence, dealing with these intermittent failures and interacting with the low-level abstraction layers offered by RFID vendors from within a general purpose programming language results in complex and brittle code. Apart from this problem, current APIs allow us to encode byte arrays but nothing more. As such, MoREnA programmers have to provide code that encodes their application objects into such (sequences of) byte arrays. Other abstraction levels have to be encoded manually on top of the machinery that sends these byte arrays back and forth between the MoREnA and the physical tags. Obviously, this is a level of abstraction that is even below the (already problematic) ORM (Object-Relational Mapping) level. In short, current technology does not offer a way to access and use tags in a conceptually clean object-oriented way.

3.2 Highly Event-Driven Nature

Since the set of tags in the range of an RFID reader is continuously fluctuating, it becomes impractical to use polling on the application level as the mechanism to detect the appearance and disappearance of tags. As a consequence, MoREnAs have to be conceived as event-driven applications from the ground up. Phenomena such as the appearance and disappearance of tags and the reception of acknowledgments from these tags become the driving forces of the application. This contribute to the highly event-driven nature of MoREnAs.

In such applications, it is no longer the programmer who steers the application's control flow. Instead, the control flow is entirely managed by a network of callbacks that get triggered as soon as an event is detected. Unfortunately, adopting an event-driven architecture, has the effect that the application logic becomes entirely scattered over different event handlers or callbacks which may be triggered independently [3]. This is a phenomenon that is known as *inversion of control* [8,17]. It engenders a number of unpleasant software engineering consequences. Unlike consecutive function calls, code triggered by different event handlers cannot use the runtime stack to make local variables visible to other event handlers. Because handing over state from one event handler to another no longer relies on parameter passing, these variables have to be made instance variables, global variables, etc. This is why in complex systems such an event-driven architecture becomes hard to develop, understand and maintain [11,9,13].

3.3   Problem Analysis

It was our goal to extend AmbientTalk with programming language constructs that tackle the above problems. We claim that there are three language aspects that need to be dealt with in order to render the engineering of such applications easier. We refer to figure 4 in order to make this vision more tangible.

Representation: First of all, the level at which data is written and read to and from tags should be raised drastically. Instead of dealing directly with bytes and byte arrays, we think it should be possible to communicate with tags by storing true *software objects* (in the object-oriented sense) on the tags. Furthermore, the RFID-reader itself should be hidden behind an object-oriented abstraction layer. Since it can operate independently from the rest of the application it should become an event loop.

Designation: Second, we need a technique for addressing and designating individual tags or groups of tags that belong together or that share some common characteristic. With the current software technology, we can only read all reachable tags into the memory of an application after which we need to manually loop over the read tags in order to select the ones that are needed. Only after this process we can start communicating with the tags in order to write or read data. This is obviously extremely error-prone: by the time we start communicating with a selected tag, the mobility of the application and the tags may already caused the tag to be unreachable. This problem may occur with large amounts of tags at the same time. Consider e.g. communicating with particular tags in a supermarket's racks. Writing correct code against such volatility requires a huge number of `if` tests and `try/catch` constructs. It would be so much easier if only we can use a declarative expression that allows us to specify which tags we want to communicate with. The concrete set of tags that satisfy this expression is extremely volatile as the MoREnA moves about. We envision a new "cloud" data type whose values correspond to such perpetually changing tag sets.

Synchronization: Having a new data type that perpetually represents the reachable (and selected) tags, it is our task to keep the internal state of a MoREnA consistent with the composition of the set. If e.g. a particular

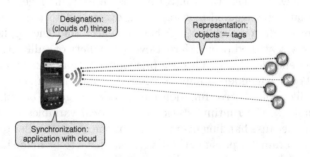

Fig. 4. Representation, Designation and Synchronization in MoREnAs

functionality of the application only makes sense when a certain group of tags is reachable, then that functionality should immediately be disabled as soon as one or more of the tags is no longer reachable. Conversely, the functionality should be re-enabled as soon as the tags come back into communication range. In other words, we want our application's internal status to be synchronised at all times with the status of the reachable part of the external world.

4   Research Results

We now present the three experimental enhancements of AmbientTalk. *Things* is the name for a new type of AmbientTalk object that represents a tag. *Ambient References* are used to query the "ether" for a cloud of desired tags. *Reactive Programming* is used to keep the internal state of the application consistent with the physical world. These are discussed in the following sections.

4.1   Representation: Things

It was our explicit goal to enrich AmbientTalk with the programming language constructs necessary to represent RFID tags and to keep the software representation of a tag (i.e. the "object" that lives in the MoREnA) as consistent as possible with the data that actually lives on the tag. To this extent, we extended the object system of AmbientTalk with a new type of objects called *things*. Remember from section 2 that AmbientTalk features objects and isolates. A thing is new type of remote object that is referred to by means of a far reference. The idea is to have a dedicated *RFID-actor* in every AmbientTalk virtual machine. This actor manages the things about which the actor knows that they exist on one of the tags it has encountered. The RFID-actor perpetually tries to keep its things as consistent as possible with the data that lives on the actual tags. The RFID-actor is causally connected to the hardware driver of the RFID reader. Every time the reader (re)discovers a tag, the thing is updated should the data on the tag be changed (possibly by another reader). Conversely, the data on the tag is updated should the thing be changed (by the MoREnA). In case the tag and the thing have both changed, an exception is thrown.

Here is how an application programmer creates a thing. The example is taken from a library MoREnA in which books contain a tag that stores information about the book as well as reviews written by users. Notice that the mere execution of this code does not involve communication with a tag yet.

```
deftype Book <: RFIDTag;

def aBook := thing: {
  def isbn := 123;
  def title := "My book";
  def reviews := Vector.new();
```

```
def setTitle(newTitle)@Mutator {
   title := newTitle };

def addReview(review)@Mutator {
   reviews.add(review) };
} taggedAs: Book;
```

The RFID-actor broadcasts any blank tag its reader discovers to the other actors in the system. As such, other AmbientTalk actors can discover blank tags in the following way. The code shows how a listener is installed that reacts to blank tags. As soon as a blank tag is discovered, the native `initialize` method is executed and it is this method that writes the thing on the tag. The result of this method is a future that resolves with a far reference `bookref` to the newly created thing when the tag was written successfully. Notice that the tag itself is represented by a far reference from the application actor to the thing residing in the RFID-actor.

```
deftype BlankTag < RFIDTag;

whenever: BlankTag discovered: { |tag|
   when: tag<-initialize(aBook)
     becomes: { |bookref|
        ... } }
```

This code shows how to use AmbientTalk's standard discovery mechanism for tags that are already initialized (possibly by another RFID-actor). The following code installs a listener that reacts to tags containing a `Book` thing.

```
whenever: Book discovered: { |bookref|
   ...
   whenever: bookref disconnected: {
      ... };
   whenever: bookref reconnected: {
      ... } };
```

Notice from the definition of the thing that some of its methods are annotated as `Mutator`. Execution of such methods by the RFID-actor will always cause a "dirty flag" to be set such that the actual tag becomes a candidate for updating as soon as it is in the communication range of the driver. For example, if a user adds a review message to a book object using the `addReview` method, the corresponding RFID tag will be updated as soon as it is in range.

Is is perfectly legal to refer to a thing from within another thing (e.g. a book that points to other books from the same author). References between things are also serialized (using the unique identifier of the RFID tag). Upon deserialization the respective far references are reconstructed. Some of these references may be disconnected depending on the availability of the corresponding RFID tag.

In brief, things are special objects that are maintained by a built-in RFID-actor. From the AmbientTalk perspective they are a special kind of isolates (see section 2) since copying their contents back and forth between the application and the tag cannot be combined with lexical scoping. Hence, things do not have a lexical scope. However, in contrast to isolates, things are referred to from within other virtual machines; i.e. they are referred to by far reference. Apart from this special status, things neatly fit into AmbientTalk and all its distributed programming features (such as the **when:** and **whenever:** primitives) are applicable to them as well. Things were developed in the context of Andoni Lombide Carreton's PhD work and we refer to the dissertation for more details [12].

4.2   Designation: Ambient References

As indicated before, we envision a MoREnA as an application that constantly moves about. Obviously, not all tags encountered will be relevant to a MoREnA or to the state in which a MoREnA finds itself. In order to give MoREnAs precise control over the tags it is interested in, we envision *an intentional object designation* feature that allows a programmer to declaratively express the kinds of things he wants to communicate with. This is where *ambient references* come into play. An ambient reference is create by an expression that describes the kind of things one is interested in. The expression is "perpetually" re-evaluated and therefore denotes a "cloud" of things that satisfy the expression. That cloud is the current status of the ambient reference.

For example, in the following code,

```
def books := ambient: Book
```

books refers to all things that correspond to a Book. Things appear and disappear from books as tags come and go. The following version of ambient references is a bit more interesting. The **ambient:where:** primitive takes a type tag and a predicate that can be used to filter things based on the status of their state variables. In the example, CSBooks corresponds to all computer science books encountered.

```
def CSBooks := ambient: Book where: { |b|
    b.cat == "Computer Science" };
```

Ambient Messages. Ambient references become interesting when they are used to convey *ambient messages*. These are messages sent asynchronously to an ambient reference. The messages are typically annotated with one of a predefined set of annotations. For example, the following example shows how a getShelf message is sent to all far references that belong to the ambient reference CSBooks. The @One annotation stipulates that the message only has to be sent once, to the first reference that was discovered by the ambient reference. The last line exemplifies the @Sustain annotation which stipulates that the message should be sent to all references that currently reside in the ambient reference *and* to all references that will in the future be discovered[3] as the content of the ambient reference

---

[3] AmbientTalk features machinery to cancel an ambient message as soon as we do not want it to be sent anymore.

changes due to user mobility. This implies that the precise number of receivers of that message cannot be determined upfront.

```
def shelfFuture := CSBooks <- getShelf()@One;

when: shelfFuture becomes: { |shelf|
  system.println("The book should be on shelf: " + shelf) };

CSBooks <- setShelf("5D")@Sustain;
```

We can combine different ambient message policies by grouping them in an array. For example, if `players` is an ambient reference in a mobile game, then `players <- askToVote(q)@[All,Expires(minutes(1))]` sends the `askToVote` message to all players belonging to the ambient reference (instead of just the first one discovered). The `Expires` annotation stipulates that we keep on broadcasting the message to newly appearing players for a total duration of 1 minute.

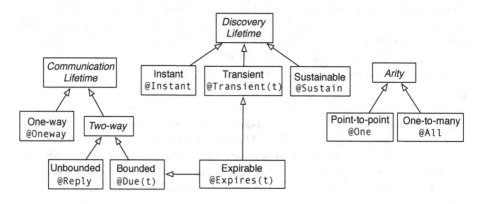

Fig. 5. Ambient Message Policies

Figure 5 summarizes ambient messages. Ambient messages have a *discovery lifetime*, a *communication lifetime* and an *arity*. The discovery lifetime corresponds to the amount of time that the interpreter needs to listen to new far references that should receive the message. `Instant` causes message to be sent to the currently reachable references. `Sustain` keeps on trying forever. `Transient(t)` puts a duration on the amount of time the ambient reference will try to send the message to newly discovered references. The communication lifetime specifies how long the interpreter waits for an answer. We can send the message without expecting an answer (i.e. `OneWay`) or we can wait for an answer to return, either indefinitely (i.e. `Reply`) or with a predetermined time limit (i.e. `Due`). Note that the `Due` annotation is used to prevent messages to be buffered indefinitely, for example, in case of a permanent disconnection. The arity is the number of recipients of the ambient message. For more details on ambient messages, we refer to the PhD work of Tom Van Cutsem [19].

The fact that ambient messages are sometimes sent to multiple objects may give rise to multiple results. As in standard AmbientTalk, these are returned by means of futures. The "cloud of futures" that results from sending an ambient message to an ambient reference is known as a *multi future*. The following example illustrates how sending a getBookInfo to all books discovered gives rise to a multi future books. Dedicated constructs such as **when:becomes:**, **whenEach:becomes:** and whenAll:**becomes:** allow us to install the appropriate listeners on such multi futures. The first one causes a block closure to be executed on the first future that is resolved. The second one executes its code for each future that is resolved (i.e. one by one). The final one executes its block only when all the futures of a multi future have been resolved. We refer to [19] for a more elaborate analysis as well as implementation details.

```
deftype Book < RFIDTag;

def books := ambient: Book;

whenEach: books <- getBookInfo()@Sustain becomes: { |infoAndRef|
    GUI.addToList(infoAndRef) }
```

Ambient references together with ambient messages can be referred to as *vague binding*. Ambient references were studied in great detail in the PhD work of Tom Van Cutsem [19]. Andoni Lombide Carreton first applied them to MoREnAs in his PhD [12]. We refer to both documents for more technical details.

4.3   Synchronization: Reactive Sets

AmbientTalk's RFID-actor takes care of sustaining the connection between tags and their corresponding things. However, we now show how using the concepts presented so far generate the following software engineering problems:

Inversion of Control. The control flow of the application is scattered across different event handlers. This results in applications in which the control flow is completely obfuscated. Explicitly orchestrating the interplay of these event handlers is nigh impossible, since the order in which they are triggered is beyond the developers control.

Explicit Dependency Management. Dependencies between causally connected objects need to be expressed explicitly in AmbientTalk. This implies that an object needs to know which objects are (possibly indirectly) causally connected to the environment, such that it can register an observer on these objects. This is detrimental to the evolution of the application since it implies that when an object becomes causally connected to the environment (i.e. its state is changed in an event handler), all users of the object need to register an additional dependency.

Superfluous Updates. One needs to explicitly register ones interest in changes to modules that are causally connected to the environment (e.g. the RFID reader). If these modules are not independent of one another, a single change to the environment may cause the dependent to be updated multiple times.

Premature Updates. Using an ad hoc mechanism to propagate updates implies that the order in which the various event handlers are triggered remains unspecified. Consequently, objects may be recomputed before all objects on which they depend are properly updated. Updating objects prematurely proves to be a subtle source of erroneous behavior.

We illustrate these problems by means of an AmbientTalk implementation of the RFID-Chef explained in section 1.1. The solution — Reactive Programming — will be explained by the second implementation of the RFID-Chef.

The RFID-Chef in Plain AmbientTalk. Every time an `Ingredient` tag (exported by the RFID-actor) is discovered, its corresponding thing is added to the set `AvailableIngredients`. Listeners are installed to monitor the connectivity status of the thing such that the set correctly represents the "currently visible" things.

```
def AvailableIngredients := ObservableSet.new();
whenever: Ingredient discovered: { |tag|
  AvailableIngredients.add(tag);
  whenever: tag disconnected:{AvailableIngredients.remove(tag)};
  whenever: tag reconnected: { AvailableIngredients.add(tag) } }
```

`AvailableIngredients` is an *observable set*. Such sets feature listener machinery (called **whenever:hasAdded:** and **whenever:hasRemoved:**) that allows reacting to the addition and removal of elements. Based on this set, we compute another set called `RecommendedRecipes` which consists of all recipes of which the ingredient list contains at least one of the present ingredients. The function `recipesForIngredient` queries a database of recipes given some ingredient i.

```
def RecommendedRecipes := ObservableSet.new();

whenever: AvailableIngredients hasAdded: { | ingredient |
  RecommendedRecipes.addAll(recipesForIngredient(ingredient)) };

whenever: AvailableIngredients hasRemoved: { | ingredient |
  RecommendedRecipes.clear();
  AvailableIngredients.each: { | i |
    RecommendedRecipes.addAll(recipesForIngredient(i)) } };
```

Notice that we cannot just remove a recipe when an ingredient disappears. This is because some of the other ingredients it uses may still be available. Hence, we clear the list of recommended recipes and we refill it again with the recipes for the ingredients that remain in `AvailableIngredients`. The code so far clearly illustrates the problem that the application suffers from **inversion of control**. The control flow is entirely determined by externally produced events. Inversion of control **contaminates the entire application** because dependencies need to be manually managed. The argument with `clear` illustrates that this is extremely error prone.

We are now ready to sort the recommended recipes according to how well they score. Given a `recipe` and the currently `availableIngredients`, then `recipeScore` generates a score based on the number of missing and the number of surplus ingredients for that recipe. `SortedRecipes` is an ordered set (which orders recipes based on a `recipeComparator` that compares the scores). The third expression initialises the sorted set and the last three expressions install the listener machinery needed to recompute the sorted set as soon as a recipe is added to or removed from the list of available ingredients. Notice that `recompSortedRecipes` has to clear the `SortedRecipes` manually. We cannot generate a new set because that would ignore all listeners installed on the original set.

```
def recipeScore(recipe, availableIngredients) { ... }

def SortedRecipes := ObservableSortedSet.new(recipeComparator)

SortedRecipes.addAll(RecommendedRecipes.map:{ |r|
  recipeScore(r, AvailableIngredients) })

def recompSortedRecipes(availableIngredients, recipes) {
  SortedRecipes.clear();
  SortedRecipes.addAll(recipes.map: { |r|
    recipeScore(r, availableIngredients) }) };

whenever: AvailableIngredients hasChanged: { |ingredient|
  recompSortedRecipes(AvailableIngredients, RecommendedRecipes)};
whenever: RecommendedRecipes hasChanged: { |ingredient|
  recompSortedRecipes(AvailableIngredients, RecommendedRecipes)};
```

We have installed one listener on `AvailableIngredients` and another one on `RecommendedRecipes` in order to recompute the sorted recipes. However, since `RecommendedRecipes` also depends on `AvailableIngredients`, a change in the ingredients will cause the recipes to be recomputed twice! This code illustrates a second problem of manually installing event handlers, namely the problem of **superfluous updates**.

Initializing the GUI is fairly boring. The code below uses AmbientTalk's access to the JVM in order to create a Swing component `RecipeForm` representing a recipe graphically, and a graphical `gui` that contains a panel `gui.TopRecipesPanel` that groups together all forms. `visibleRecipes` is an array of the 5 currently visible forms (w.r.t. scrolling).

```
def RecipeForm := jlobby.at.context.rfidchef.RecipeForm;
def gui        := jlobby.at.context.rfidchef.new();

def visibleRecipes[5] { RecipeForm.new() };
gui.TopRecipesPanel.addAll(visibleRecipes);
```

In the following, we register listeners on the previous and next buttons of the GUI. Clicking the buttons causes us to display the next or the previous 5 recipes. offset is the index in SortedRecipes of the first visible recipe.

```
def offset := 0;

gui.PreviousButton.addActionListener(object: {
    def actionPerformed(event) { offset := offset - 5;
                                 updateRecipes() } });
gui.NextButton.addActionListener(object: {
    def actionPerformed(event) { offset := offset + 5;
                                 updateRecipes() } });
```

The listener installed on SortedRecipes below ensures that the buttons are properly enabled (resp. disabled) in case more (resp. less) than 5 exist. This code shows a third problem of installing manual event handlers: since the variable offset is not observable, we have to implement **manual dependency management** code to correctly enable and disable the buttons every time we change offset.

```
def enableButtons(nrDisplayable) {
  gui.PreviousButton.setEnabled(offset != 0);
  gui.NextButton.setEnabled(offset + 5 < nrDisplayable) };

def capoffset(nrDisplayable) {
  while: { nrDisplayable < offset } do: {
    offset := offset - 5 } };

whenever: SortedRecipes hasChanged: {
  capoffset(SortedRecipes.size());
  enableButtons(SortedRecipes.size()) };
```

Finally, here is the method to update the 5 visible recipes. A range (starting at offset) of 5 recipes is extracted from the SortedRecipes and copied to the array of visible recipes, unless there are less than 5 recipes to show. On first sight, this is innocent code. However, if the updateRecipes happens to be triggered *before* capping the offset variable, an exception may be thrown (because it is out of range). Such **premature updates** may occur if the order of dependencies matters: we cannot control the order in which multiple event handlers (installed on an observable set) are triggered.

```
def updateRecipes() {
  def visibleRange :=
    SortedRecipes.range(offset,
                        min(offset + 5, SortedRecipes.size()));
  visibleRange.copyTo(visibleRecipes) };

whenever: SortedRecipes hasChanged: { updateRecipes() }
```

The RFID-Chef in Reactive AmbientTalk. The above code snippets clearly show that writing applications consisting of huge networks of collaborating event handlers soon gives rise to unmanageable code. In this code we explain how *reactive programming* alleviates this problem. We do so by showing how the RFID-Chef looks like in an experimental reactive version of AmbientTalk.

Reactive programming languages [1] feature so called *reactive values* and *event sources. Reactive values* change their value at regular time intervals. Suppose that x and y are variables containing a reactive value and suppose that we declare **def** z := (x + y) / 2. The idea of a reactive value is that z is automatically updated if either x or y changes. To this extent, reactive languages compile their programs into dependency graphs which are used to propagate changes through the program. Notice that the operator + is automatically *lifted* so that it automatically works on reactive values by recomputing its result as soon as one of its arguments changes. *Event sources* are objects that emit messages at irregular time intervals (e.g. depending on some externally produced IO-event or because they received an event from another event source).

Here is the reactive set AvailableIngredients. It grows and shrinks every time a tag is discovered by the built-in reactive value RFIDReader. This is an event source that emits tagRead and tagRemove messages every time a tag is discovered on the kitchen counter. The <<+ operator takes a regular object and an event source and registers the object to listen to the event source. Every time the event source emits a message, that message is relayed to the object. In our case, this gives rise to adding or removing the tag to the set of available ingredients.

```
def AvailableIngredients := makeReactive(Set.new());

def translator := object: {
  def tagRead(readerID, tag) { AvailableIngredients.add(tag) };
  def tagRemove(readerID, tag) {
    AvailableIngredients.remove(tag) } };

translator <<+ RFIDReader;
```

The following code illustrates the power of reactive programming. PromotedRecipes is a reactive set of sets. Every set it contains corresponds to the set of recipes that can be prepared with one of the ingredients. Notice that map: is a lifted method of the AvailableIngredients reactive set: every time the reactive set changes, map: is re-sent which gives rise to a recalculation of the PromotedRecipes set. RecommendedRecipes is the union of all promoted recipes. Notice that union is lifted again. Finally, SortedRecipes is a list of sorted recipes that automatically gets updated every time the AvailableIngredients set changes. An implementation technique of reactive languages — called *stratification* see [4] — guarantees that SortedRecipes is updated online once, even though it depends on two progenitors, one of which (i.e. RecommendedRecipes) depends on the other.

```
def PromotedRecipes := AvailableIngredients.map: { |ingredient|
    recipesContaining(ingredient) };

def RecommendedRecipes := union(PromotedRecipes);

def scoredRecipes(availableIngredients, recipes) {
    def scoredRecipes := SortedSet.new(recipeComparator);
    recipes.each: { |r| scoredRecipes.add(
        recipeScore(r, availableIngredients)) } }

def SortedRecipes := scoredRecipes(AvailableIngredients,
                                   RecommendedRecipes);
```

This code shows that we **no longer have to deal with explicitly managed inversion of control** thanks to default lifting semantics for functions and methods. The dependency graph is automatically constructed by the language instead of having to be constructed manually by a network of event handlers. Moreover, our code **no longer suffers from superfluous updates** in case of multiple dependencies. This is guaranteed by the stratification technique that is used to implement the language.

The initialisation of the GUI is omitted since it is identical to the non-reactive one. Here is the reactive code that updates the GUI. The variables NumRecipes, CappedOffset and VisibleRange all depend on reactive values and therefore also contain reactive values. The operators and methods used on the right hand side of the assignments are lifted by the language implementation. Because of the stratification, **premature updates are impossible**: all values change in the right order.

```
def NumRecipes := SortedRecipes.size();
def CappedOffset :=
    min(offset,((((NumRecipes - 1) /- displaySize)) * displaySize)

def VisibleRange := SortedRecipes.range(
    CappedOffset,
    min(CappedOffset + displaySize, SortedRecipes.size()));

def updateRecipes(visibleRange) {
    visibleRange.copyTo(visibleRecipes) };

updateRecipes(VisibleRange)
```

Finally, we show the code that takes care of enabling and disabling the buttons. The listing below shows the definition of a variable offset that is annotated with the @Reactive annotation. This means that the variable itself (as opposed to the value it may contain) is reactive. This allows us to assign values to the variable and at the same time write reactive expressions that depend on the changing state of such a reactive value. For example, the variable CappedOffset is defined in terms of offset. If offset were a variable containing a reactive value itself, then we would have ended up with a circular dependency. That is why offset is declared a reactive variable. Needless to say, we have to fill a reactive value with an ordinary value. To this extent, we provide the **snapshot**: primitive.

```
def @Reactive offset := 0;

gui.PreviousButton.setEnabled(CappedOffset != 0);
gui.NextButton.setEnabled(CappedOffset+displaySize < NumRecipes);

gui.PreviousButton.addActionListener(object: {
    def actionPerformed(event) {
        offset := (snapshot: CappedOffset) - displaySize } });

gui.NextButton.addActionListener(object: {
    def actionPerformed(event) {
        offset := (snapshot: CappedOffset) + displaySize } })
```

In contrast to the first version of the RFID-Chef, offset and CappedOffset can be used as reactive entities on the right hand side of expressions. Hence, there is no need to cover the lack of reactive variables with **manual dependency management** (as was the case in our first version of the RFID-Chef).

4.4 Discussion

In this section, we have explained three experimental language extensions that have been built on top of AmbientTalk. Together they implement the research vision on MoREnAs that we summarized in figure 4. The integration of things with ambient references is fairly well understood. We refer to Andoni Lombide Carreton's PhD for more details. The integration of these features with reactive programming is less well understood and still a topic of ongoing research. In our current implementation, reactive AmbientTalk uses "reactive sets" (as exemplified by the RFID-Chef) in order to represent perpetually changing clouds of things. An integration of reactive programming with ambient references is future work.

5 Conclusion

5.1 Limitations and Future Work

A problem that we have not considered yet is security. We are currently looking at using locking mechanisms for preventing eavesdropping and encryption of the serialized data on RFID tags to secure that data. However, it must be noted that the severity of these problems highly depends on the hardware and the setting used. We are also looking into transaction mechanisms to prevent inconsistencies that may arise when multiple devices concurrently access the same set of RFID tags. To this end, we are investigating a *leasing* mechanism where an application would get the right to exclusively access a tag for a specific period of time, using the tag's first memory block to store the necessary lease information.

Another limitation is the limited amount of writable memory on passive RFID tags. We have tested our implementation using RFID tags with up to 8 kbits of writable memory. This means that we can only store very small serialized objects on the tags. On the other hand, the technology is progressing and we can expect the storage on passive tags to steadily increase while the costs drop. This opens the door to use more standardized serialization formats as well, in our middleware implementation we convert Java objects to the JSON format [2].

Finally, we make the underlying assumption that all devices in the network attribute the same meaning to each type tag, i.e. we assume they define a common ontology to classify objects stored on RFID tags. This discovery mechanism also does not take versioning into account explicitly. For example, if the interface of objects of type Book from the example in section 4.1 is updated, older clients may discover the updated book objects, and clients that want to use only the updated interface may still discover older versions. Clients and services are thus themselves responsible to check versioning constraints.

5.2   Contributions

In this paper, we presented a research agenda for novel programming language support for mobile RFID-enabled applications, MoREnAs in short. We consider MoREnAs as extreme cases of distributed applications that have to deal with a dynamically changing set of communication partners. Hence, our starting point was to start from a distributed programming paradigm that provides some initial support, which needs to be extended to deal with vast volatile clouds of passive RFID tags. We chose to extend the ambient-oriented programming paradigm, a paradigm that is targeted to applications that run on dynamic mobile ad hoc networks and incorporates connection volatility into the heart of its computational model. We shortly described AmbientTalk as the concrete ambient-oriented programming language and research vehicle in which we are carrying out our experiments. We extended AmbientTalk to deal with three concerns that are hard to manage using a non-language approach (i.e. a middleware or a library) when implementing MoREnAs.

First, we aim to **represent** RFID-tagged real world objects as true software objects in an object-oriented system. It should be possible to seamlessly read and write these software objects from/to the memory of passive RFID tags. For this, we extended the prototype-based object model of AmbientTalk with a new kind of objects, which we call things. These things perpetually keep their internal state up to date when the RFID hardware reads out the memory of their associated passive RFID tags. Similarly, when their state is changed by a MoREnA, they autonomously attempt to store these changes onto the memory of their associated tags. Things are integrated into the asynchronous, event-loop based concurrency and distribution model of AmbientTalk.

Second, we propose to **designate** sets of tags that are related in a declarative manner, to prevent having to write extremely error-prone looping code over volatile clouds of tags. We have applied ambient references as an object-oriented abstraction to denote a set of perpetually fluctuating communication partners, such as passive RFID tags containing things. Ambient references support various messaging policies which are tailored to such volatile clouds of objects.

Third, the internal status of MoREnAs must be kept **synchronized** with its external surrounding, which turns MoREnAs into highly event-driven applications. Using traditional event-driven techniques such as callbacks to react on changes in the physical surrounding quickly becomes unmanageable when dealing with large volatile clouds of RFID tags. To automate this synchronization we introduced an orthogonal programming paradigm into AmbientTalk: reactive programming. By combining reactive programming with AmbientTalk we are able to declaratively specify sets of things that vary over time. New sets generated out of such reactive sets are automatically updated when the sets they depend on change (for example because the set of RFID tags in range fluctuates). Reactive sets are normal reactive values that cause dependent application code to be re-executed when their contents change.

These three objectives drive our research to come up with better integrating and more expressive novel language constructs. At the same time we try to carry over much of these ideas in mainstream programming technology, at the expense of conceptual purity, but with immediate usability as a bonus.

References

1. Bainomugisha, E., Carreton, A.L., Van Cutsem, T., Mostinckx, S., De Meuter, W.: A survey on reactive programming. ACM Computing Surveys (2012) (to appear)
2. Lombide Carreton, A., Pinte, K., De Meuter, W.: MORENA: a middleware for programming NFC-enabled Android applications as distributed object-oriented programs. In: Narasimhan, P., Triantafillou, P. (eds.) Middleware 2012. LNCS, vol. 7662, pp. 61–80. Springer, Heidelberg (2012)
3. Chin, B., Adsul, B.: Responders: Language support for interactive applications. In: Thomas, D. (ed.) ECOOP 2006. LNCS, vol. 4067, pp. 255–278. Springer, Heidelberg (2006)
4. Cooper, G.H., Adsul, B.: Embedding dynamic dataflow in a call-by-value language. In: Sestoft, P. (ed.) ESOP 2006. LNCS, vol. 3924, pp. 294–308. Springer, Heidelberg (2006)
5. Dedecker, J., Van Cutsem, T., Mostinckx, S., D'Hondt, T., De Meuter, W.: Ambient-oriented programming. In: Companion to the 20th Annual ACM SIGPLAN Conference on Object-Oriented Programming, Systems, Languages, and Applications, OOPSLA 2005, pp. 31–40. ACM, New York (2005)
6. Diekmann, T., Melski, A., Schumann, M.: Data-on-network vs. data-on-tag: Managing data in complex rfid environments. In: Proceedings of the 40th Annual Hawaii International Conference on System Sciences, HICSS 2007, p. 224a. IEEE Computer Society, Washington, DC (2007)
7. Floerkemeier, C., Roduner, C., Lampe, M.: RFID application development with the accada middleware platform. IEEE Systems Journal, Special Issue on RFID Technology 1(2), 82–94 (2007)

8. Haller, P., Odersky, M.: Event-based programming without inversion of control. In: Lightfoot, D.E., Ren, X.-M. (eds.) JMLC 2006. LNCS, vol. 4228, pp. 4–22. Springer, Heidelberg (2006)
9. Kasten, O., Römer, K.: Beyond event handlers: programming wireless sensors with attributed state machines. In: 4th Int. Symposium on Information Processing in Sensor Networks, p. 7. IEEE Press, Piscataway (2005)
10. Kefalakis, N., Leontiadis, N., Soldatos, J., Gama, K., Donsez, D.: Supply chain management and NFC picking demonstrations using the AspireRfid middleware platform. In: ACM/IFIP/USENIX Middleware 2008, pp. 66–69. ACM, New York (2008)
11. Levis, P., Culler, D.: Maté: a tiny virtual machine for sensor networks. SIGPLAN Not. 37, 85–95 (2002)
12. Lombide Carreton, A.: Ambient-Oriented Dataflow Programming for Mobile RFID-Enabled Applications. PhD thesis, Vrije Universiteit Brussel, Faculty of Sciences, Software Languages Lab (October 2011)
13. Maier, I., Rompf, T., Odersky, M.: Deprecating the Observer Pattern. Technical report, École Polytechnique Fédérale de Lausanne (2010)
14. Melski, A., Thoroe, L., Caus, T., Schumann, M.: Beyond EPC - insights from multiple RFID case studies on the storage of additional data on tag. In: Proceedings of the International Conference on Wireless Algorithms, Systems and Applications, WASA 2007, pp. 281–286. IEEE Computer Society, Washington, DC (2007)
15. Miller, M.S., Tribble, E.D., Shapiro, J.S.: Concurrency among strangers: programming in e as plan coordination. In: De Nicola, R., Sangiorgi, D. (eds.) TGC 2005. LNCS, vol. 3705, pp. 195–229. Springer, Heidelberg (2005)
16. Pais, S., Symonds, J.: Data storage on a RFID tag for a distributed system. International Journal Of UbiComp (IJU) 2(2), 26–39 (2011)
17. Petitpierre, C., Eliens, A.: Active Objects Provide Robust Event-Driven Applications. In: The 2002 International Conference on Software Engineering Research and Practice (SERP) (2002)
18. Software Languages Lab, Vrije Universiteit Brussel. AmbientTalk/2 tutorial, http://soft.vub.ac.be/amop/at/tutorial/tutorial
19. Van Cutsem, T.: Ambient References: Object Designation in Mobile Ad Hoc Networks. PhD thesis, Vrije Universiteit Brussel, Faculty of Sciences, Software Languages Lab (May 2008)
20. Van Cutsem, T.: Why programming languages (2011), http://soft.vub.ac.be/~tvcutsem/invokedynamic/node/11
21. Van Cutsem, T., Mostinckx, S., Boix, E.G., Dedecker, J., De Meuter, W.: AmbientTalk: Object-oriented event-driven programming in Mobile Ad Hoc Networks. In: Proceedings of the XXVI International Conference of the Chilean Society of Computer Science, SCCC 2007, pp. 3–12. IEEE Computer Society, Washington, DC (2007)

Towards a Substrate Framework of Computation

Kazunori Ueda

Department of Computer Science and Engineering, Waseda University
3-4-1, Okubo, Shinjuku-ku, Tokyo 169-8555, Japan
ueda@ueda.info.waseda.ac.jp

Abstract. A grand challenge in computing is to establish a substrate computational model that encompasses diverse forms of non-sequential computation. This paper demonstrates how a hypergraph rewriting framework nicely integrates various forms and ingredients of concurrent computation and how simple static analyses help the understanding and optimization of programs. Hypergraph rewriting treats processes and messages in a unified manner, and treats message sending and parameter passing as symmetric reaction between two entities. Specifically, we show how fine-grained strong reduction of the λ-calculus can be concisely encoded into hypergraph rewriting with a small set of primitive operations.

1 Introduction

It is fifty years since Carl Adam Petri formalized Petri Nets in his PhD thesis. Since then, we have seen a lot of proposals to capture and formalize the essence of concurrency. Yet, the world of concurrency and concurrent programming is not like its sequential counterpart where Turing machines and the λ-calculus are the two established formalisms. This indicates two things: one is that the world of concurrency has more aspects to address than the sequential world, and the other is that we don't understand concurrency in sufficient depth yet.

The author's research career started with the design of a concurrent programming model, where he reengineered the nuts and bolts of logic programming (such as first-order terms and unification) to have a simple model of communication and synchronization as an improvement over previous attempts [16]. In the resulting model, Guarded Horn Clauses (GHC), processes work on data structures equipped with logical (single-assignment) variables. Processes communicate by instantiating logical variables by unification and observing their values by matching (one-way unification). The dataflow synchronization mechanism provided by one-way unification was widely recognized as the highlight of concurrent logic programming. However, another key highlight of concurrent logic programming is that first-order terms with logical variables were expressive enough to represent sequences of messages with reply boxes (necessary to encode Concurrent Objects) and channel mobility (exactly in the sense of the π-calculus). This is in sharp contrast with many other concurrency formalisms in which communication is heavily studied but data structures are not treated as primary issues.

G. Agha et al. (Eds.): Yonezawa Festschrift, LNCS 8665, pp. 341–366, 2014.

It is worth mentioning that the development of the concurrent logic programming paradigm and Guarded Horn Clauses proceeded in parallel with the development of Concurrent Objects in early 1980's, partly stimulated by each other. Both shared the high level goal of establishing a concise model of message-passing concurrency but with somewhat different focuses: Concurrent Objects were designed at a higher level of abstraction, that is, in terms of objects and messages, while concurrent logic programming languages were designed as a substrate model consisting of a smallest possible set of primitive constructs and still allows the *encoding* of Concurrent Objects and operations on them [17].

In spite of the nice properties and the expressive power of Guarded Horn Clauses, it was felt that we could treat processes and data in a more unified manner. Communicating fine-grained processes may form process structures (such as lists or grids of processes) that act as autonomous, concurrent data structures, but process structures and ordinary data structures had to be handled very differently.

With this motivation, the author designed LMNtal a decade ago as his second model of concurrent programming based on a small class of *graph rewriting*, where nodes represent processes or data and edges represent one-to-one channels or links. In fact, nodes are nothing more than atomic logical formulas and edges are nothing more than zero-assignment logical variables (i.e., variables that will never get concrete values). First-order terms, which are trees with constructors and variables, are represented using relations by employing one $(n + 1)$-ary relation for each n-ary constructor.

It turned out that LMNtal was almost backward compatible with concurrent logic languages. LMNtal also allowed interpretation as a linear logic programming language [23]. Nevertheless, the real challenge of LMNtal was to have a formalism that could be understood without deep technical knowledge in computer science (such as logic and categories). The adoption of graphs, a widespread mathematical notion, as the basic structure is motivated exactly by this goal. The versatility of the graph data structure became evident when our publicly available LMNtal implementation was tailored into a model checker that used LMNtal as a modeling language for state transition systems in general [25].

The present paper is concerned with our next step of language evolution. We have already incorporated *hyperlinks* (links interconnecting multiple points) in addition to one-to-one links so that it may better cover a broader range of computational models. The resulting language, HyperLMNtal [26], has much in common with Bigraphical Reactive Systems [14], and its versatility and viability seem to be worth exploring in depth to establish it as a substrate model of computation.

The rest of the paper is organized as follows. Section 2 briefly describes LMNtal with some examples. Section 3 describes how LMNtal evolved to Hyper-LMNtal. Section 4 discusses static analysis techniques that reveal two important properties of programs, capabilities of links and multiplicities of nodes. As one of the most challenging case studies, Section 5 presents a fine-grained encoding

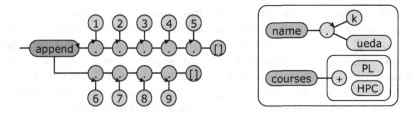

Fig. 1. LMNtal graphs: A tree-shaped graph with one free link (left) and a hierarchical graph with two membranes (right). An arrowhead indicates the first argument and the ordering of links.

of the full reduction of the lambda calculus into HyperLMNtal and how the type system of Section 4 gives further computational structures to the encoding.

2 LMNtal: A Model and Language Based on Graph Rewriting

This section reviews LMNtal briefly. Technical details and relation to other formalisms can be found in [23].

LMNtal embodies the view that computation is manipulation of graphs, which in our setting consist of (i) *atoms*, (ii) *links* for one-to-one connectivity, and (iii) *membranes* that can enclose atoms and other membranes and can be crossed by links. Connectivity and hierarchy are the two major basic structuring mechanisms in both real worlds and cyberworlds including computing, society, biological systems and body of knowledge. The purpose of LMNtal is to provide a concise programming and modeling language that allows us to represent the two mechanisms simultaneously and manipulate them in a direct manner. Figure 1 shows some graphs that can be manipulated by LMNtal.

The choice of links and membranes as structuring mechanisms allows programming with sets and graphs. Although sets and graphs are less common than arrays, records and pointers as programming language constructs, they are more standard and commonly used in the rest of the world and in mathematics in particular. As a formalism of concurrency, an important feature of LMNtal is that it provides a well-defined notion of atomic actions: graph rewriting by a single rule application is always done atomically.

2.1 Basic Syntax

The syntax of LMNtal is defined as in Fig. 2, where the syntactic constructs not used in this paper are omitted for simplicity.

The two syntactic categories, *link names* (denoted by X_i) and *atom names* (denoted by p) are presupposed. *Processes* are the principal syntactic category and consist of hierarchical graphs and rewrite rules. In the concrete syntax, capitalized names represent links, while other names (e.g., those starting with lowercase letters, numbers, and non-alphanumeric symbols) represent atoms.

A process P must observe the following *link condition*: Each link name in P (excluding link names occurring in rules) may occur *at most twice*. A link whose name occurs exactly once (twice) in P is called a *free link* (*local link*) of P, respectively. The T's are *process templates* that are used in rewrite rules and handle local contexts, namely contexts within particular membranes.

(Process) $P ::= \mathbf{0} \mid p(X_1, \ldots, X_m) \mid P, P \mid \{P\} \mid T :\text{-} T$

(Process template) $T ::= \mathbf{0} \mid p(X_1, \ldots, X_m) \mid T, T \mid \{T\} \mid T :\text{-} T \mid \text{@}p \mid \$p$

Fig. 2. Syntax of LMNtal

$\mathbf{0}$ stands for an inert process (represented as an empty symbol in the concrete syntax), $p(X_1, \ldots, X_m)$ stands for an atom with m links, and P, P stands for parallel composition called a *molecule*. Note that links of an atom are totally ordered and that multiple links between atoms are allowed as well as links connecting the same atom. $\{P\}$ is called a *cell* and stands for a process enclosed by a *membrane* $\{\ \}$. $T :\text{-} T$ stands for a rewrite rule, which is applied to processes located at the same place of the hierarchy formed by membranes. The two T's are called the *head* and the *body* of the rule, respectively. A rewrite rule is subject to several syntactic conditions [23]. Most notably, a link name occurring in a rule must occur exactly twice in the rule.

The reserved atom name, $=$, is called a *connector*. The process $X = Y$ short-circuits the link X and the link Y. A *rule context*, denoted by $\text{@}p$, matches the (possibly empty) multiset of all rules within a membrane, while a *process context*, denoted by $\$p$, is to match all processes other than rules within a membrane.

2.2 Operational Semantics

The operational semantics of LMNtal (Fig. 3) consists of structural congruence defined by (E1)–(E10) and the reduction relation defined by (R1)–(R6). (E4) stands for α-conversion. (E9)–(E10) are the interaction rules between atoms/cells and connectors.

Computation proceeds by rewriting processes using rules collocated in the same place of the nested membrane structure. (R1)–(R3) are standard structural rules, while (R4)–(R5) are the mobility rules of $=$. The central rule of LMNtal is (R6), in which θ is to map process contexts into actual processes. For programs that do not use membranes, (R6) degenerates to a simpler form: $T, (T :\text{-} U) \longrightarrow U, (T :\text{-} U)$.

2.3 Extended Syntax and Examples

A rule may be prefixed by a rule name and two @'s.

(E1) $\mathbf{0},P \equiv P$ (E2) $P,Q \equiv Q,P$ (E3) $P,(Q,R) \equiv (P,Q),R$

(E4) $P \equiv P[Y/X]$ if X is a local link of P

(E5) $P \equiv P' \Rightarrow P,Q \equiv P',Q$ (E6) $P \equiv P' \Rightarrow \{P\} \equiv \{P'\}$

(E7) $X = X \equiv \mathbf{0}$ (E8) $X = Y \equiv Y = X$

(E9) $X = Y,\ P \equiv P[Y/X]$ if P is an atom and X occurs free in P

(E10) $\{X = Y,\ P\} \equiv X = Y,\ \{P\}$ if exactly one of X and Y occurs free in P

(R1) $\dfrac{P \longrightarrow P'}{P,Q \longrightarrow P',Q}$ (R2) $\dfrac{P \longrightarrow P'}{\{P\} \longrightarrow \{P'\}}$ (R3) $\dfrac{Q \equiv P \quad P \longrightarrow P' \quad P' \equiv Q'}{Q \longrightarrow Q'}$

(R4) $\{X = Y,P\} \longrightarrow X = Y,\ \{P\}$ if X and Y occur free in $\{X = Y,P\}$

(R5) $X = Y,\ \{P\} \longrightarrow \{X = Y,P\}$ if X and Y occur free in P

(R6) $T\theta,(T :\!- U) \longrightarrow U\theta,(T :\!- U)$

Fig. 3. Structural congruence and reduction relation of LMNtal

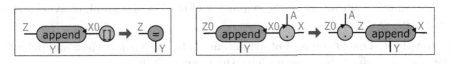

Fig. 4. Reaction rules for append

An abbreviation called a *term notation* allows an atom b without its final argument to occur as the kth argument of a, to mean that the kth argument of a and the final argument of b are interconnected. For instance, `f(a)` is the same as `f(A),a(A)`. This can be written also as `f=a` because `f(A),a(A)` is congruent (i.e., convertible in zero steps) to `f(A),A=A1,a(A1)` (by (E9) of Fig. 3), to which we can apply the abbreviation twice to obtain `f=a`. A list with the elements A_i's can be written as $X = [A_1, \ldots, A_n]$, where X is the link to the list.

Example 1. Two lists can be concatenated using the following two rules:

```
append(X0,Y,Z), '[]'(X0) :- Y=Z.
append(X0,Y,Z0), '.'(A,X,X0) :- '.'(A,Z,Z0), append(X,Y,Z).
```

This form makes it explicit that there is no distinction between predicate symbols and constructors, but we can write it also in a more familiar, Prolog-style form:

```
append([],Y,Z) :- Y=Z.
append([A|X],Y,Z0) :- Z0=[A|Z], append(X,Y,Z).
```

Figure 4 shows a diagrammatic representation of the two rules, where the arrowheads indicate the first arguments of atoms and the ordering of arguments.   □

Some atoms such as '+' are written as unary or binary operators. Parallel composition (e.g., $P_1, P_2, \ldots, P_n$) can be written also in a period-terminated form (e.g., $P_1.\ P_2.\ \ldots\ P_n.$).

Example 2. The dining philosopher problem can be represented as a circular graph with philosophers and forks:

```
phi(L1,R1), fork(+R1,+L2),  phi(L2,R2), fork(+R2,+L3),
phi(L3,R3), fork(+R3,+L4),  phi(L4,R4), fork(+R4,+L5),
phi(L5,R5), fork(+R5,+L1).

fork(+X,+L), phi(L,R) :- fork(-X,+L), phi(L,R). % grab left fork

fork(-X,+L), phi(L,R), fork(+R,+Y) :-
fork(-X,+L), phi(L,R), fork(+R,-Y).              % grab right fork

fork(-X,+L), phi(L,R), fork(+R,-Y) :-
fork(+X,+L), phi(L,R), fork(+R,+Y).              % release forks
```

Each link represents a philosopher's access to a fork, and the atoms '+' and '−' indicate the availability of the fork. The LMNtal model checker constructs and visualizes the state space of the model, where the state space construction algorithm takes advantage of the symmetry of the circular graph to avoid state space explosion. ☐

Example 3. One of the uses of membranes is to encapsulate rules and delimit their scope of effect. Suppose we have the following rule:

```
{module(m),@m}, {use(m),$p,@p} :- {module(m),@m}, {$p,@p,@m}
```

The first cell stands for a rule set repository with a module name, while the second cell stands for a "test tube" that requires the rules in the module m. This rule causes a new copy of @m, which is the content of the module m, to be loaded to other cells containing use(m). ☐

The rest of this subsection is about how to specify operations on primitive datatypes.

We note that numbers in LMNtal are unary atoms such as 8(X), where X is connected to the atom referring to the number. To specify operations on primitive types such as integers, the two constructs, *typed process contexts* and *guards*, are introduced. While the process matched by an ordinary process context is determined by the membrane it belongs to (i.e., hierarchy), the process matched by a typed process context is determined by the graph structure (i.e., connectivity) and the atom name inside the structure. For instance, the guarded rule

```
p(X), $n[X] :- int($n), $n>0 | p(Y), $n[Y], p(Z), $n[Z].
```

means that, when a unary atom p is connected to a positive integer, that two-atom molecule will be duplicated. The guard constraint int($n) requests that $n[X] is a typed process context (with one free link) representing an integer atom, and the constraint $n>0 requests that the value of the integer is positive.

Available type constraints other than **int** include **unary** (standing for unary atoms) and **ground** (standing for non-hierarchical connected graphs with exactly one free link). Note that **int** is regarded as a subtype of **unary** which in turn is a subtype of **ground**. A rule containing typed process contexts can be viewed as a *rule scheme* that represents a set of rules without guards.

3   Incorporating Hyperlinks

The design decision of LMNtal to feature one-to-one links rather than hyperlinks came from the observation that multi-point connectivity could be encoded
using membranes. However, membranes are a general construct that can be used
to enclose processes and rules for localized reactions and are somewhat heavyweight for representing just multi-point connectivity or multisets. Also, program variables in most computational models and languages represent possibly
shared data, and efficient and succinct encoding of those program variables is of
practical importance. This motivated us to incorporate hyperlinks into LMNtal.
The main driving force was to build an efficient encoding of Constraint Handling Rules (CHR) [6], a constraint programming language syntactically close to
LMNtal.

The first step towards HyperLMNtal was the design of the hyperlink construct. Since the design and implementation of LMNtal was quite stable, it was
considered ideal if the extension could be made smoothly without changing the
basic framework of the language and its implementation or affecting the performance of existing applications. The two design choices we have made are the
following:

- *Distinguish between links and hyperlinks.* Although hyperlinks could be regarded as subsuming links, we maintain the distinction between them. Each
  link connection has exactly one partner, and this property is not only a fundamental program invariant but also utilized by the implementation of links
  in many ways, including the access to partners and the garbage-collection of
  partners.
- *Treat hyperlinks as atoms with local names.* Having decided that hyperlinks
  are a syntactic category different from links, we must decide whether to
  incorporate something totally new or something close to an existing category.
  We already observed that links are local names shared by exactly two atoms
  [23], and this suggests that hyperlinks should be treated as local names
  shared by any number of atoms. This can be realized by providing a construct
  to create a unary atom with a fresh local name, because unlike link names,
  unary atoms can be copied and discarded in our extended syntax.

Now we describe the constructs provided for hyperlink manipulation. A fresh
local name can be created by a **new** guard construct as:

H :- new($x) | B

where the hyperlink name $x can be used in B. The scope of x (i.e., the set of
atoms that can access x) is B initially, but it may extend to other atoms in the
course of graph rewriting, as is the case with local names of the π-calculus.

To check if an argument of an atom is a hyperlink, we write:

H :- hlink($x) | B

where `$x` occurs in H. Because `hlink` is a subtype of `unary`, the equality and inequality of hyperlinks can be checked using guard constraints '`==`' and '`\==`'.

Motivated by Linear Logic, we allow hyperlinks to be written in the form $!X$ (X capital), in which case either of the guard constraints `hlink` and `new` is implicitly provided, depending on whether the hyperlink occurs in the head or not.

The most characteristic operation is the *fusion* of two hyperlinks,

$$H \ \text{:-} \ \dots \ | \ !X \ \text{><} \ !Y, \ B.$$

which is a hyperlink version of the connector '`=`' and interconnects two hyperlinks by fusing two hyperlink names. In the abstract syntax, `><` will be denoted as ⋈.

Another characteristic operation is to obtain or check the *cardinality* (i.e., number of endpoints) of a hyperlink:

$$H \ \text{:-} \ \text{num(}!X,\$n\text{)} \ | \ B$$

where `!X` occurs in H and `$n` is bound to the current cardinality of `!X`.

The shorthand notation illustrated below allows a hyperlink to occur more than once in the head of a rule to represent sharing:

Example 4

```
a(!X), b(!X), c(!X) :- .
```

is the same as

```
a($x), b($x0), c($x1) :-
   hlink($x), hlink($x0), hlink($x1),
   $x==$x0, $x==$x1 | .
```

This rule removes three unary atoms a, b, c if they share the same hyperlink, in which event the cardinality of that hyperlink is reduced by three.   □

4   Analyzing HyperLMNtal Programs

Since graphs are highly general data structures, programming with graphs will greatly benefit from tools and techniques for analyzing and understanding the properties and the behavior of programs.

With this motivation, we have developed a model checker for LMNtal and its integrated development environment (IDE)[25] and found them extremely useful for analyzing the state space of nondeterministic concurrent systems. The model checker can presently handle systems with a half billion states with various optimization techniques and shared-memory parallel processing. The LMNtal model checker was later extended to handle hypergraphs.

HyperLMNtal as a programming language requires no declarations of any kind (variables, types, procedures, etc.), and could be positioned as *a scripting language for model checking* in the sense that it allows concise description and quick development of small- to medium-scale models. To analyze hypergraph rewriting, however, static analysis will also play an important rôle because we are far less familiar with computing with hypergraphs than computing with lists and trees. It will also identify important subclasses of programs that are more legitimate or likely to be correct than others.

With this in mind, we describe two static analysis techniques that address aspects of program properties in a clear way. Our goal here is not to analyze programs as precisely as possible; rather, we are concerned with extracting simple properties by abstracting others. Chemistry suggests that the fundamental properties of graphs are those about (chemical) atoms and those about bonds, and we follow this metaphor. For the sake of simplicity, henceforth we focus on Flat HyperLMNtal, a fragment of HyperLMNtal without membranes, and call Flat HyperLMNtal simply as HyperLMNtal.

4.1 Assigning Polarities and Capabilities to Links and Hyperlinks

Let a *port*, denoted by $\langle a, i \rangle$, stand for the ith argument of an atom a, which is an endpoint of a link or a hyperlink. Firstly, we are interested in which port of an atom may be connected to which port of the same or another atom. This information will lead to a type system that deals with graph structures based on a local view. Although the connectivity information alone may not capture the global shape of data (e.g., whether a grid forms a square or a rectangle; whether a list is terminated by a nil or not), it addresses local properties of structures with sharing (i.e., more than one path leading to a single atom) and cycles.

Secondly, we may be interested in the rôle of each port. Informally, by a rôle we mean the polarity or capability of a port, where a polarity stands for the direction of access (i.e., whether the port is used for sending data or receiving data), information flow, or ownership (i.e., whether the port of an atom is used to access data it owns or is used to be accessed by its owner), while a capability additionally stands for whether the port of a hyperlink has exclusive access to the partner(s) or shares them with others. We focus on this second aspect of ports, namely their polarities and capabilities.

Technically, we choose to represent the capability of a port using a real number between -1 and $+1$ inclusive. The capability value $+1$ means that the port stands for an exclusive, full ownership of (or exclusive reference to) the partner atom(s), while a value $0 < c < 1$ stands for a non-exclusive, partial ownership (or shared reference). The value -1 stands for a sole source or access point of data available to the partner(s). A hyperlink with a -1 port and several positive fractional ports is a *directed hyperarc* of a specific kind called a *backward hyperarc* [7] (Fig. 5), and can be represented by a family of pointers pointing to the atom with the -1 port. A value $-1 < c < 0$ represents a partial source and appears when a partial ownership is returned through that port. The value 0 stands for an inactive port not connected to anywhere else.

This notion of capability inherits the author's capability type system designed for a class of Flat GHC programs [21], except that the system described in the present paper simplifies the original one thanks to the unified treatment of processes and data and by focusing on individual (hyper)links. The use of fractions in type systems later appeared in [3] and subsequent papers with different settings. Our type system is unique in that it uses negative as well as positive

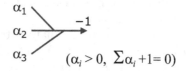

$$(\alpha_i > 0, \ \Sigma \alpha_i + 1 = 0)$$

Fig. 5. A backward hyperarc with three owners

fractions, enjoying symmetry around zero. Historical account of fractional type systems can be found in [19].

The capability type system for (Flat) HyperLMNtal consists of the constraints given in Fig. 6, where a capability type c is formulated as a function from the set of ports to the closed interval $[-1, +1]$. To be useful, our type system is necessarily polymorphic because capabilities are very often split and passed to atoms with the same name, that is, they keep decreasing in the course of recursion. The polymorphism is realized by suffixing each atom in a rule $l :\!\!- r_1, ..., r_n$ as $l_s :\!\!- r_{1,s.1}, ..., r_{n,s.n}$, where a suffix s is a sequence of indexes, and $s.i$ means appending an index i to s. Atoms with the same name and different suffixes are subject to the same constraints but may adopt different solutions.

The first constraint, (Conn), represents the relationship between the ports of a connector and a fuser.

The key advantage of our formulation is that the central type constraint on a (hyper)link is exactly *Kirchhoff's current law* (KCL), i.e., the capabilities of the endpoints of a (hyper)link sum up to 0.

Constraint (Coop) states that

- if a left-hand side occurrence of L has a positive capability, all the left-hand-side occurrences must have positive capabilities and jointly act as the source of data in the rule, and
- otherwise exactly one of L's occurrences in the right-hand side must have a negative capability and act as a single source of data.

In other words, it states that that a hyperlink L represents a backward hyperarc (if $k = 0$) or transforms a backward hyperarc into another backward hyperarc (if $k \geq 1$) by using the rule. Note that the capability of a hyperlink occurrence on the left-hand side of a rule must be negated because the left-hand side acts as a template of rewriting. This constraint states also that the capability of a hyperlink port should be nonzero. The non-zero condition is to disallow the "silent" participation to and withdrawal from a hyperlink.

Constraint (Link) states that the capability of a link should be either 1 or -1 (i.e., non-fractional). We could allow a singleton hyperlink with a zero capability as was done in [21], but will not discuss it here.

Although we have installed the suffix system to allow polymorphism, Occam's razor tells us that type inference as an explanation of program properties should

- prefer maximally general solutions to those with unnecessary constraints and

(Conn) If $(X_1 =_s X_2) \in Q$ then $c(\langle =_s, 1 \rangle) + c(\langle =_s, 2 \rangle) = 0$;
   If $(X_1 \bowtie_s X_2) \in Q$ then $c(\langle \bowtie_s, 1 \rangle) + c(\langle \bowtie_s, 2 \rangle) = 0$

Let a link or a hyperlink L occur $n \, (\geq 1)$ times in P and Q at $p_1, \ldots, p_n$, of which the occurrences in P are at $p_1, \ldots, p_k$ $(k \geq 0)$. Then

(KCL) $-c(p_1) - \cdots - c(p_k) + c(p_{k+1}) + \cdots + c(p_n) = 0$ (Kirchhoff's Current Law)

(Coop) If $k = 0$ then $\mathcal{R}(\{c(p_1), \ldots, c(p_n)\})$;
   If $k \geq 1$ then $\mathcal{R}(\{-c(p_1), c(p_{k+1}), \ldots, c(p_n)\})$;
   where $\mathcal{R}$ is a 'cooperativeness' relation:

$$\mathcal{R}(S) \stackrel{\text{def}}{=} \exists s \in S\big(s < 0 \wedge \forall s' \in S \setminus \{s\} \, (s' > 0)\big)$$

(Link) If L is a link then $c(p_k) \in \{-1, 1\}$ for $1 \leq k \leq n (= 2)$

Fig. 6. Capability constraints imposed by a rule $P :\text{-} Q$

- prefer least polymorphic (i.e., most uniform) solutions to those that give different types to each instance of atoms with the same name.

As an example, we first consider polarizing **append** (Sect. 2.3) in a monomorphic setting.

Example 5. The constraints imposed by (KCL) and (Conn) on **append** in a monomorphic setting are as follows:

$c(\langle \text{append}, 1 \rangle) + c(\langle [], 1 \rangle) = 0$ by X0
$c(\langle \text{append}, 3 \rangle) + c(\langle \text{append}, 2 \rangle) = 0$ by =
$c(\langle \text{append}, 1 \rangle) + c(\langle ., 3 \rangle) = 0$ by X0
$c(\langle \text{append}, 3 \rangle) = c(\langle ., 3 \rangle)$ by Z0
$c(\langle ., 2 \rangle) = c(\langle \text{append}, 1 \rangle)$ by X
$c(\langle ., 2 \rangle) + c(\langle \text{append}, 3 \rangle) = 0$ by Z

This is satisfiable with the following solution satisfying (Coop) and (Link) also:

$c(\langle \text{append}, 1 \rangle) = 1, \quad c(\langle \text{append}, 2 \rangle) = 1, \quad c(\langle \text{append}, 3 \rangle) = -1,$
$c(\langle [], 1 \rangle) = -1,$
$c(\langle ., 2 \rangle) = 1, \quad \text{and } c(\langle ., 3 \rangle) = -1, \quad (\text{no constraints on } c(\langle ., 1 \rangle))$

which intuitively means an **append** reads its first and the second arguments and writes to the third argument. However, this is not the only satisfying assignment, and another solution is:

$c(\langle \text{append}, 1 \rangle) = -1, \quad c(\langle \text{append}, 2 \rangle) = -1, \quad c(\langle \text{append}, 3 \rangle) = 1,$
$c(\langle [], 1 \rangle) = 1,$
$c(\langle ., 2 \rangle) = -1, \quad \text{and } c(\langle ., 3 \rangle) = 1, \quad (\text{no constraints on } c(\langle ., 1 \rangle)).$

The latter solution makes practical sense. A '.' here can be thought of an *active message* that activates **append** which generates another '.' that may act on the subsequent procedure connected to the third argument of **append**. This message-oriented scheduling policy was studied and implemented in the logic programming context [20], but our framework which does not distinguish between predicate symbols and constructors provides more uniform treatment of different reduction strategies.   □

A set D of atoms is said to *dominate* the left-hand side of a rule if all the atoms in the left-hand side can be reached (by following directed (hyper)links) from the atoms in D. In the case of the above example, the atom **append** dominates the left-hand sides in the first solution, while '.' and [] dominate the left-hand sides in the second solution. One may wish to interpret dominators as procedures and non-dominators as data.

An example involving hyperlinks will be described in Section 5.6.

The capability type system turns hypergraphs into directed hypergraphs and allows them to be represented using one-way pointers. The type system thus provides key information for compiler optimizations even when undirected links are a more natural tool for modeling purposes (e.g., when directed links break symmetry). It will also help deeper understanding of graph structures and debugging.

We have confirmed that most simple LMNtal programs allow uniform polarization that gives the same polarity vector to atoms with the same name. We have found exceptions as well:

Example 6. A program constructing a fullerene (C_{60}) structure does allow polarization but needs two different polarity vectors for c:

```
dome(L0,L1,L2,L3,L4,L5,L6,L7,L8,L9) :-
    p(T0,T1,T2,T3,T4), p(L0,L1,H0,T0,H4), p(L2,L3,H1,T1,H0),
    p(L4,L5,H2,T2,H1), p(L6,L7,H3,T3,H2), p(L8,L9,H4,T4,H3).

dome(E0,E1,E2,E3,E4,E5,E6,E7,E8,E9), /* top half */
dome(E0,E9,E8,E7,E6,E5,E4,E3,E2,E1). /* bottom half */

/* icosahedron -> fullerene */
p(L0,L1,L2,L3,L4) :- X=c(L0,c(L1,c(L2,c(L3,c(L4,X))))).
```

It is easy to see that there is no uniform (monomorphic) solution because exactly half of the 180 ports provided by the 60 ternary carbon atoms must be positive, namely 1.5 ports per atom.   □

Thanks to the algebraic formulation, it is rather straightforward to prove the subject reduction property:

Theorem (subject reduction). If a program $P : c$ and $P \longrightarrow Q$ then $Q : c$.

4.2   Composition Analysis

Many programs that handle data structures enjoy beautiful invariants with respect to the size of data. The **append** program is a typical example, where the

Fig. 7. Size space of the dining philosopher program

recursive rule just changes connectivity and preserves all the atoms, while the base case rule loses two atoms, append and []. The possibly non-terminating dining philosopher program preserves the total number of atoms, while the composition of the '+'s and the '−'s keeps changing. This suggests that composition analysis (exactly in the sense of chemistry) could be a useful tool to analyze properties about the number of atoms.

Remarkably, properties about the increase and decrease of atoms in state transition systems have been studied in depth in the field of Petri Nets [1]. Boundedness of the number of tokens at each place is a fundamental property of Petri Nets and is analyzed by forming a reachability graph of possible markings. The possible markings of unbounded Petri Nets can be represented using coverability graphs, which over-approximates possible markings of unbounded Petri Nets using the ordinal number ω, and much work has been done on the algorithms for constructing coverability graphs [5][15].

Now notice that place/transition nets, the most basic form of Petri Nets, are exactly multiset rewriting systems; they are different representations of the same thing. Note also that graph rewriting degenerates to multiset rewriting simply by forgetting about links. Thus, it is almost trivial to have a multiset rewriting system corresponding to a given LMNtal program and analyze its state space that captures just the composition of atoms.

Example 7. Figure 7 shows the state space of the dining philosopher program with respect to the number of atoms, which was visualized by our LMNtal IDE. The multiplicities of atoms are indicated by suffixes as in chemical formulae. The shape clearly indicates that the number of available forks is reduced one by one, possibly leading to deadlock, while it may be increased by two at a time.   □

Example 8. Let us consider append again. The polarization of links establishes an interpretation of the initial graph such as

    X = append([1,3,5,7,9],[11,13,15])

as a binary tree. Composition analysis tells that, upon termination, there will be a single list consisting of the initial elements. Now notice that the preorder traversal of the above tree, modulo append and [], visits the list elements in increasing order, and the second rule of append is exactly a tree rotation operation that does not affect preorder traversal (modulo append and []).

The same line of argument applies to establish the associativity of append:

```
X = append(append([1,3,5],[7,9]),[11,13,15])
X = append([1,3,5],append([7,9],[11,13,15]))
```

Each of the above graphs is obtained by rotating the two `append` atoms at the top of the other graph, which preserves preorder traversal modulo `append` and `[]`.   □

5   Encoding the Pure Lambda Calculus into HyperLMNtal

> *Substitutions is the éminence grise of the λ-calculus.*
> —*Abadi et al. (1991) [2]*

> *The usual implementation of functional programming languages based on a weak evaluation paradigm (no reduction inside a lambda), betray the very spirit, i.e., the higher-order nature, of lambda-calculus.*
> —*Asperti (1998)*

One of the most significant challenges in the (Hyper)LMNtal project has been to have a concise encoding of the λ-calculus. This may sound surprising, but it was a real challenge because HyperLMNtal's connection to the λ-calculus was far less obvious than to concurrency calculi such as the π-calculus and the ambient calculus [27]. The encoding of the λ-calculus is significant because the λ-calculus and λ-terms play fundamental rôles not only in functional languages but in the treatment of variable binding, scoping, and substitutions that appear in various formalisms.

The core of the λ-calculus is β-reduction, $(\lambda x.M)N \rightarrow M[x \mapsto N]$, but the definition of substitutions used here is far from simple and provoked various alternative formulations. In particular, "to replace all the free occurrences of x by copies of N" does not necessarily reflect actual implementation, which may share the representation of N whenever possible but must sometimes make copies of N (e.g., when applying another λ-term to N).

One of the formalisms aiming at the precise representation of the λ-calculus is the λσ-calculus [2], which provides two syntactic categories, λ-terms and explicit substitutions, and gives rewrite rules to both.

Another approach to formalizing the λ-calculus is to adopt graph representation of λ-terms; a bound variable can most naturally be represented as an edge (or a hyperedge) that connects the defining and applied occurrences of the same variable. Most previous work in this approach adopted Interaction Nets [8] to represent and manipulate graphs ([9][11][12], to name a few). Many of the encodings of the λ-calculus into Interaction Nets pursued optimal sharing or efficiency, and resulted in more or less involved representation of λ-terms to achieve the objective. One notable exception is the encoding by Sinot [18], which addressed the simplicity of the encoding, but it focused on the weak λ-calculus that did not evaluate the body of λ-abstractions. Indeed, as KCLE [12] suggests, encoding of the pure calculus can be much less concise (in terms of the number of rules involved) than the encoding of the weak calculus. Weak λ-calculi may be appropriate for the foundations of functional languages, but the applications of the λ-calculus as a whole call for *strong* (or *pure*) λ-calculi as well.

This raises one question: Is there any *concise* graph-based encoding of the *pure* λ-calculus? With Interaction Nets, YALE [11] proposes a relatively simple solution but still needed to simulate "boxes" for scope management. So the next question is: To obtain a more concise encoding (appropriate, say, for an undergraduate text), what additional constructs should be included to the graph rewriting framework?

A concrete answer to these questions was given using LMNtal by presenting a fine-grained and highly nondeterministic encoding of the pure λ-calculus (with open terms) and discussing its properties [24]. Although the membrane construct of LMNtal provides powerful functionalities such as the copying of the graph enclosed by a membrane, the encoding used membranes only to represent and manipulate fresh local names, called *colors*, so that each rewrite step could be executed in (almost) constant amortized time. Thus the encoding was essentially not specific to LMNtal, and the evolution of LMNtal to HyperLMNtal gives us another chance of bringing insights on what constructs are most basic for concise encoding. The purpose of this section is to describe our encoding of the pure λ-calculus into typed HyperLMNtal whose hyperlink manipulation is significantly more restricted than that of untyped HyperLMNtal. Since each of the proposed rewrite rules is simple and well-motivated, the proposed method is expected to serve not only as an encoding but as a fine-grained reformulation of the pure λ-calculus.

5.1   Representing λ-terms in HyperLMNtal

Now we describe our encoding of the λ-calculus into (Flat) HyperLMNtal. Our starting point was the encoding into Interaction Nets. Interaction Nets is a non-hierarchical graph rewriting formalism with strong syntactic conditions, and HyperLMNtal can be considered as a model and a language that extends Interaction Nets by alleviating their syntactic conditions and introducing hyperlinks. Of various encodings into Interaction Nets, Sinot's encoding [18] is one of the simplest in the sense that it dispenses with the explicit management of free variables in each λ-abstraction. However, the method is to compute weak head normal forms (terms of the form $xM_0 \ldots M_n$ ($n \geq 0$) or $\lambda x.M$, where M and M_i are not necessarily in normal form) and the computation is serialized using a control token navigating over the λ-graph. Our goal, in contrast, is to encode the basic reduction semantics of the pure λ-calculus, preserving and manifesting nondeterminism inherent in the formalism.

5.2   Representing λ-terms

First of all, we define the encoding from a λ-term L into an LMNtal process. The result must have exactly one free link (say R), which is connected to the atom referring to L. So the translation function $\mathcal{T}$ receives as arguments the λ-term L and the free link name R.

- When L is a variable x, it is represented as a unary atom with the name x connected to R via a binary atom $\mathtt{fv}$ indicating a free variable:

$$\mathcal{T}(x, R) \stackrel{\text{def}}{=} \mathtt{fv}(x, R) \quad (= R = \mathtt{fv}(x)).$$

- When L is a λ-abstraction $\lambda x.M$, let k (≥ 0) be the number of free occurrences of x in M, and $\mathcal{T}_x(M, [R_1, \ldots, R_k], R)$ be a process obtained from $\mathcal{T}(M, R)$ by removing all unary atoms x and their tags $\mathtt{fv}$ and changing them into free links $R_1, \ldots, R_k$. (For example, $\mathcal{T}_x(x, [R_1], R) = R = R_1$.) Then

$$\mathcal{T}(\lambda x.M, R) \stackrel{\text{def}}{=} \mathtt{lambda}(R_0, R', R), \ \mathcal{T}_x(M, [R_1, \ldots, R_k], R'),$$
$$connect[R_0, R_1, \ldots, R_k],$$

where $connect[R_0, R_1, \ldots, R_k]$ is a process with free links R_0, R_1, ..., R_k defined as follows:

$$connect[R_0] \stackrel{\text{def}}{=} \mathtt{rm}(R_0)$$
$$connect[R_0, R_1] \stackrel{\text{def}}{=} R_0 = R_1$$
$$connect[R_0, R_1, \ldots, R_n] \stackrel{\text{def}}{=} \mathtt{cp}(R_1, R_0', R_0), \ connect[R_0', R_2, \ldots, R_n] \ (n \geq 2).$$

- When L is an application MN:

$$\mathcal{T}(MN, R) \stackrel{\text{def}}{=} \mathtt{apply}(R_1, R_2, R), \ \mathcal{T}(M, R_1), \ \mathcal{T}(N, R_2).$$

Bound variables are encoded into LMNtal links, but because of the Link Condition of LMNtal, bound variables not occurring exactly twice requires the branching or termination of links. We employ a unary atom $\mathtt{rm}$ (remove) to terminate unused bound variables and a ternary atom $\mathtt{cp}$ (copy) to bifurcate links. The encoding of a bound variable with more than two occurrences forms a tree of $\mathtt{cp}$'s, but the form of the tree does not count for our encoding and its properties. For example, a combinator $\mathbf{I} = \lambda x.x$ is represented as

```
lambda(X,X,Result)     (= Result = lambda(X,X))
```

where $\mathtt{Result}$ is the free link name representing the result. The Church encodings of natural numbers, $\lambda fx.f^n x$ ($n \geq 0$), can be represented as

```
0: lambda(rm,lambda(X,X),Result)
1: lambda(F,lambda(X,apply(F,X)),Result)
2: lambda(cp(F0,F1),lambda(X,apply(F0,apply(F1,X))),Result)
```

and so on.

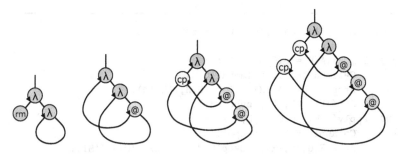

Fig. 8. Graph representation of the Church numerals $0, 1, 2, 3$, where '@' stands for apply

5.3 Reaction Rules with Color Management

Figure 9 shows a complete set of rules that encodes the pure λ-calculus using our λ-term representation, in which cpc stands for a complement of cp and hereafter denoted as $\overline{\text{cp}}$. Intuitively, an atom a is said to be a complement of b if they may cancel each other. Likewise, topc and subc are the complements of top and sub and will be denoted as $\overline{\text{top}}$ and $\overline{\text{sub}}$.

The first rule, beta, performs "bare" β-reduction, that is, performs parameter passing without copying the argument even when it is referenced more than once. Rule beta alone is sufficient if all formal parameters are used exactly once; otherwise we need reaction rules for the atoms cp, $\overline{\text{cp}}$, rm, and $\overline{\text{rm}}$ (11 rules following beta) to destroy or copy graph structures incrementally. The final four rules are for the color management described next.

The ternary cp's in λ-terms are first converted to quinternary cp's by Rule c2c. The additional third and fourth arguments form a pair of complementary circuits for distinguishing between cp's with different origins (i.e., cp's copied from the ones belonging to different λ-abstractions) when copying nested λ-abstractions. The additional information is called a *color* after the Petri Net terminology. Let us focus on the circuit formed by the third arguments and come back to the other circuit formed by the fourth arguments later. Each color is represented using a hyperlink that interconnects all atoms sharing that color.

Colors form tree-shaped partial order. Two colors in the supercolor-subcolor relationship are interconnected by an atom sub. The topmost color is connected to the atom top. Figure 10 shows a graph structure consisting of one cp with a top color, one cp and one $\overline{\text{cp}}$ with the complementary pair of a subcolor, and one cp and two $\overline{\text{cp}}$'s with the complementary pair of another subcolor.

Each quinternary cp is given a top color initially. Rule c2c creates an independent top color cell for each cp, but whether to create independent top color cells or share a single top color cell does not affect the correctness of our encoding.

Graph copying starts when beta reduction takes place and a cp on the formal parameter side meets apply, lambda, or fv in the argument term. Figure 11 depicts important rewrite rules related to cp's.

```
beta@@ H=apply(lambda(A, B), C) :- H=B, A=C.

l_c@@  lambda(A,B)=cp(C,D,!L,!M) :-
         C=lambda(E,F), D=lambda(G,H),
         A=cpc(E,G,!L1,!M1), B=cp(F,H,!L2,!M),
         sub(!L1,!L2,!L), subc(!M1), .
a_c@@  apply(A,B)=cp(C,D,!L,!M) :-
         C= apply(E,F), D= apply(G,H),
         A=cp(E,G,!L,!M1), B=cp(F,H,!L,!M2), !M=jn(!M1,!M2).

c_c1@@ cpc(A,B,!L1,!M1)=cp(C,D,!L2,!M2), sub(!L1,!L2,!L) :-
         A=C, B=D, sub(!L1,!L2,!L), !L1 >< !M1, !L2 >< !M2.
c_c2@@ cpc(A,B,!L1,!M1)=cp(C,D,!L2,!M2), top(!L2) :-
         C=cpc(E,F,!L1,!M11), D=cpc(G,H,!L1,!M12), !M1=jn(!M11,!M12),
         A=cp(E,G,!L2,!M21), B=cp(F,H,!L2,!M22), !M2=jn(!M21,!M22),
         top(!L2).
f_c@@  fv($u)=cp(A,B,!L,!M) :- unary($u) |
         A=fv($u), B=fv($u), !L >< !M.

l_r@@  lambda(A,B)=rm :- A=rmc, B=rm.
a_r@@  apply(A,B)=rm :- A=rm, B=rm.
c_r1@@ cp(A,B,!L,!M)=rmc :- A=rmc, B=rmc, !L >< !M.
c_r2@@ cpc(A,B,!L,!M)=rm :- A=rm, B=rm, !L >< !M.
r_r@@  rmc=rm :- .
f_r@@  fv($u)=rm :- unary($u) | .

promote@@ subc(!L1), sub(!L1,!L2,!L3) :- !L2 >< !L3.
join@@ !Y=jn(!X,!X) :- !X >< !Y.
c2c@@  A=cp(B,C) :- A=cp(B,C,!L,!M), top(!L), topc(!M).
gc@@   top(!L), topc(!L) :- .
```

Fig. 9. HyperLMNtal encoding of the pure λ-calculus

When a `cp` meets an `apply`, it copies the partner, splits itself, and proceeds to the copying of the `apply`'s two arguments. In this case, the color of the split cp's remains unchanged (Rule `a_c`).

When a `cp` meets a `lambda`, it copies the partner and splits itself in the same manner, but in this case it turns into a complementary pair of cp and $\overline{cp}$. Furthermore, the complementary pair is made to have different colors as described below (Rule `l_c`).

The hyperlink `!L` on the left-hand side of `l_c` stands for the current color. The right-hand side creates a subcolor `!L2` and its complement `!L1`. A $\overline{cp}$ moving anticlockwise (in the representation of Fig. 8) from the x side of a λ-term $\lambda x.M$ and a cp moving clockwise from the M side are given the same color held by the first and the second arguments of `sub`, respectively.

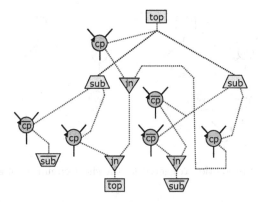

Fig. 10. Coloring `cp` atoms. Non-circular atoms and dotted edges form a circuit for color management.

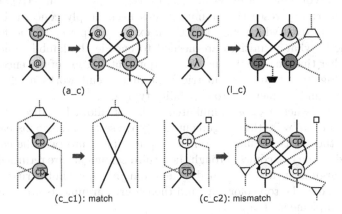

Fig. 11. Reaction rules for `cp` atoms. A white triangle stands for `jn`; a white trapezoid stands for `sub`; a black trapezoid stands for $\overline{\text{sub}}$; and a white square stands for `top`.

As can be seen from the Church numerals example, the link representing the bound variable of a λ-abstraction is either terminated by `rm` or is split using zero or more `cp`'s and connected to some places in the body. Accordingly, each $\overline{\text{cp}}$ will eventually meet, and is annihilated by, either an `rm` or a `cp` with the complementary color (possibly after crossing and copying `cp`'s with the top color). When a $\overline{\text{cp}}$ meets a `cp` with the top color, it copies the partner using `c_c2`, splits itself, and proceeds.

In contrast, a `cp` may not meet a $\overline{\text{cp}}$ with the complementary color, because it may *escape* the scope of the λ-abstraction through a link representing nonlocal variables. The color of a `cp` that has escaped must be changed back to the original color. This is done using **promote**, which fuses a subcolor with its supercolor by removing the atom `sub` when all the $\overline{\text{cp}}$'s of the subcolor disappear (Fig. 12). This promotion mechanism was realized using membranes in our first encoding [24], where the emptiness checking of membranes was used in an essential way.

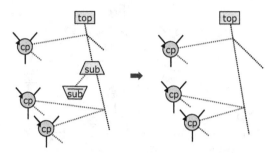

Fig. 12. Color promotion triggered by the short-circuiting of sub and $\overline{\text{sub}}$

Based on this experience, a cardinality operator of some sort was considered an indispensable construct for hyperlinks, and was incorporated into HyperLMNtal.

The concurrency research community has been deeply concerned with the choice of primitives which may affect the expressive power of the formalism. Thus, exactly what primitives are needed to encode the lambda calculus is a central rather than marginal issue. The major contribution of the encoding presented in Fig. 9 is that a symmetric hyperlink circuit works nicely for color management and is amenable to capability typing.

Recall that, when a cp is annihilated, it is not allowed to discard the color capability carried by its third argument in a typed setting; the cp instead returns it through the fourth argument. When a cp is copied into two, the capabilities distributed to the two copies through their third arguments are returned through the fourth arguments and are joined by an atom jn defined in the rule join. The initial cp's carry the top color top, and their fourth arguments are connected to $\overline{\text{top}}$, the complement of top.

A similar mechanism is implemented for the $\overline{\text{cp}}$'s sharing the same subcolor; the third arguments of the $\overline{\text{cp}}$'s are connected to the first argument of sub, while their fourth arguments are connected, possibly via jn's, to the complementary atom $\overline{\text{sub}}$. From Fig. 10, one can observe that a hyperlink circuit between a sub and a corresponding $\overline{\text{sub}}$ form a circuit involving $\overline{\text{cp}}$'s and containing jn's on the $\overline{\text{sub}}$ side. When the $\overline{\text{cp}}$'s are short-circuited, the jn's will detect the identity of two hyperlinks and join their capabilities. The sub and the $\overline{\text{sub}}$ will establish one-to-one connection eventually, when they annihilate each other and triggers promotion. Similarly, observe from Fig. 10 that a top and a corresponding $\overline{\text{top}}$ form a circuit involving cp's, which also contains sub's on the top side and jn's on the $\overline{\text{top}}$ side, which is symmetric if the sub's and the jn's are ignored.

Rule promote is applied asynchronously with other rules; it is not necessarily applied as soon as all the $\overline{\text{cp}}$'s of some color disappear. The delay of promote simply delays the reaction between cp's and $\overline{\text{cp}}$'s (using c_c1 and c_c2) and does not cause wrong reactions by affecting the applicability of other rules.

Of the remaining rules, f_c copies global free variables. This rule contains a side condition, unary($u), that specifies that the first argument of fv is connected to some unary atom, which will be copied in the right-hand side because

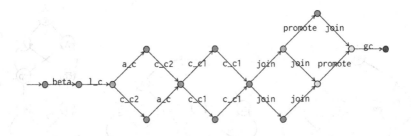

Fig. 13. State space of the omega combinator

$u occurs twice there. Rules `l_r`, `a_r`, `c_r1`, `c_r2`, `r_r`, and `f_r` are to delete any partner that an `rm` or an `r̄m̄` may encounter. Rule `gc` is to delete a topmost color not referenced any more.

5.4 Examples

From numerous examples we have run using our LMNtal system, we pick two well-known λ-terms to illustrate our encoding.

Example 9. The omega combinator $\Omega = (\lambda x.xx)(\lambda x.xx)$ is a beautiful λ-term that involves copying. Figure 13 shows the state space of Ω encoded into HyperLMNtal, where `beta` is allowed to be used only once for the purpose of our analysis. Figure 14 shows some of those states. Graph (G1) is the initial state decorated with colors by `c2c`. The only rule applicable to (G1) is `beta`, which yields (G2). Now λ reacts with `cp` and is split into two ((G3)). (G4) is obtained from (G3) by `a_c` and `c_c2` (in either order). Now the two complementary pairs of `cp` and `c̄p̄` are canceled by two applications of `c_c1`, and the resulting (disconnected) graph, (G5), consists of Ω (left) and a graph of used colors (right), where the Ω graph came with a color representation different from (G1). The color graph will be erased by `join`, `promote` and `gc`.

When we do not restrict the number of β-reductions, the encoding turns out to have infinitely many states (unlike Ω in the original λ-calculus which has only one state) because the erasure of the garbage graph may be delayed arbitrarily long. □

Example 10. The exponentiation of Church numerals seems to be an important test of λ-calculus encodings because the extremely simple encoding of m^n, $\lambda mn.nm$, involves exponential amount of graph copying. It is important also because it requires the evaluation of the bodies of λ-abstractions.

The program in Fig. 15 reduces to

$$R = \underbrace{\texttt{apply(fv(s),apply(fv(s),...,apply(fv(s)},\texttt{,fv(0))...))}}_{81 \text{ times}}$$

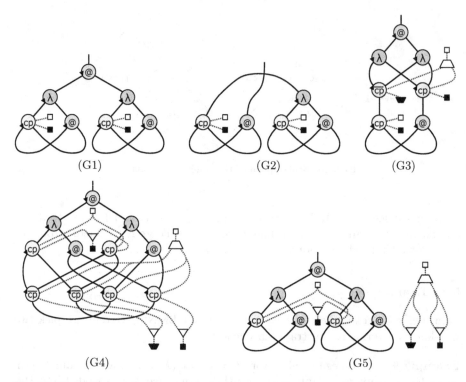

(G1)   (G2)   (G3)

(G4)   (G5)

Fig. 14. Reduction of the omega combinator. a white square stands for top; a black square stands for $\overline{\text{top}}$; a white trapezoid stands for sub; a black trapezoid stands for $\overline{\text{sub}}$; and a white triangle stands for jn.

that stands for $s^{3^{3^{2^2}}}(0)$. The encoding is highly nondeterministic, reflecting the fine-grainedness of the encoding. Even the computation of R = apply(n(2),n(2)) (2^2) has 2874 possible states. □

5.5   Properties of the Encoding

The encoding described above decomposes β-reduction into many small microsteps that allow asynchronous, out-of-order execution. The adequacy of the encoding is therefore not obvious; recall that the confluence and termination of the $\lambda\sigma$-calculus was not obvious, either [4][13]. Furthermore, because of the asynchrony, the "meaning" of an intermediate state of graph reduction broken into microsteps is far from obvious.

To address the above problems, in [24] we proposed to interpret graphs using λ-terms with additional binder constructs corresponding to rm and cp atoms, and established several important properties of the (original) encoding through well-known properties of the λ-calculus. Exactly the same technique can be used to establish the properties of the encoding described in this paper because the two encodings differ only in the *representation* of colors that is abstracted in the

```
N=n(2) :- N=lambda(cp(F0,F1),lambda(X,apply(F0,apply(F1,X)))).
N=n(3) :- N=lambda(cp(F0,cp(F1,F2)),
                   lambda(X,apply(F0,apply(F1,apply(F2,X))))).
R = apply(apply(apply(apply(n(2),n(2)),n(3)),fv(s)),fv(0)).
```

Fig. 15. Church numerals and their exponentiation

extended λ-term representation of graphs. We do not repeat the technical details but mention that the encoding enjoys the following properties, whose proofs can be found in [24]:

1. *Preservation of strong normalization*: If a λ-term M is strongly normalizing, the HyperLMNtal encoding of M is strongly normalizing.
2. *Soundness*: If an HyperLMNtal encoding G of M reduces in 0 or more steps to G' which is an encoding of some term M', then $M \longrightarrow^* M'$.
3. *Completeness*: If G is a HyperLMNtal encoding of M and $M \longrightarrow^* M'$, then there is a HyperLMNtal encoding G' of M' such that G can be reduced to G' in 0 or more steps.

Most previous encodings into Interaction Nets used two kinds (i.e., two colors) of copying tokens. Two colors sufficed in [18] because it did not evaluate bodies of λ-abstractions. YALE and KCLE computed normal forms, but did so by explicitly managing nonlocal variables, which added certain complexity. Although not for computing normal forms, Lang's encoding [10] employed many colors, where colors were represented as sequences of fresh names. Color comparison was based on whether one color was a prefix of the other, whose practical cost is yet to be studied. Lamping's optimal sharing [9] also employed many colors (called *levels*), and further employed tokens called croissants and brackets (both coming with many colors as well) to achieve sharing and complicated level management. Our encoding pursues a different direction: the size of the rewrite system. Color hierarchy implemented using hyperlinks lead to a rewrite system that added only a few rules to the rules for handling all possible pairs of atoms that may meet.

Our rewrite system could be slimmed down further. Rule c2c can be dispensed with by starting with colored cp atoms. Rules l_r, a_r, c_r1, r_r, f_r (i.e., all rules involving rm and $\overline{\text{rm}}$ except c_r2), plus gc are just for garbage collection and tidying up the tree of cp's, and could be dispensed with. (Rule c_r2 cannot be removed because it kills $\overline{\text{cp}}$'s whose cardinality is counted.) This leaves us only nine essential rules, beta, l_c, a_c, c_c1, c_c2, f_c, c_r2, promote, and join, which suffice for the full evaluation of colored λ-term representation.

5.6   Typing the Encoding

The encoding described in this section is designed to allow capability typing. We omit the typing constraints but show a well-typing of atom ports:

$$c(\langle @, 1\rangle) = c(\langle @, 2\rangle) = 1, \quad c(\langle @, 3\rangle) = -1,$$
$$c(\langle \lambda, 1\rangle) = -1, \quad c(\langle \lambda, 2\rangle) = 1, \quad c(\langle \lambda, 3\rangle) = -1,$$
$$c(\langle \mathtt{cp}, 1\rangle) = c(\langle \mathtt{cp}, 2\rangle) = -1, c(\langle \mathtt{cp}, 5\rangle) = 1,$$
$$c(\langle \mathtt{cp}, 3\rangle) > 0, \quad c(\langle \mathtt{cp}, 4\rangle) < 0, \quad c(\langle \mathtt{cp}, 3\rangle) + c(\langle \mathtt{cp}, 4\rangle) = 0,$$
$$c(\langle \overline{\mathtt{cp}}, 1\rangle) = c(\langle \overline{\mathtt{cp}}, 2\rangle) = 1, \quad c(\langle \overline{\mathtt{cp}}, 5\rangle) = -1,$$
$$c(\langle \overline{\mathtt{cp}}, 3\rangle) > 0, \quad c(\langle \overline{\mathtt{cp}}, 4\rangle) > 0, \quad c(\langle \overline{\mathtt{cp}}, 3\rangle) + c(\langle \overline{\mathtt{cp}}, 4\rangle) = 0,$$
$$c(\langle \mathtt{rm}, 1\rangle) = 1, \quad c(\langle \overline{\mathtt{rm}}, 1\rangle) = -1,$$
$$c(\langle \mathtt{jn}, 1\rangle) > 0, \quad c(\langle \mathtt{jn}, 2\rangle) > 0, \quad c(\langle \mathtt{jn}, 3\rangle) < 0,$$
$$c(\langle \mathtt{jn}, 1\rangle) + c(\langle \mathtt{jn}, 2\rangle) + c(\langle \mathtt{jn}, 3\rangle) = 0,$$
$$c(\langle \mathtt{sub}, 1\rangle) = -1, \quad c(\langle \mathtt{sub}, 2\rangle) < 0, \quad c(\langle \mathtt{sub}, 3\rangle) > 0,$$
$$c(\langle \mathtt{sub}, 2\rangle) + c(\langle \mathtt{sub}, 3\rangle) = 0,$$
$$c(\langle \overline{\mathtt{sub}}, 1\rangle) = 1, \quad c(\langle \overline{\mathtt{top}}, 1\rangle) = 1, \quad c(\langle \mathtt{top}, 1\rangle) = -1$$

Ports constrained by inequalities and zero-sum constraints are polymorphic ports for hyperlinks. The above constraints give us an interpretation that

- @ works on λ in Rule beta,
- cp and rm work on @, λ, $\overline{\mathtt{cp}}$, $\overline{\mathtt{rm}}$, and fv in Rules a_c, l_c, c_c1, c_c2, c_r1, f_c, a_r, l_r, c_r2, r_r, and f_r,
- $\overline{\mathtt{top}}$ works on top in Rule gc,
- $\overline{\mathtt{sub}}$ works on sub in Rule promote, and
- jn works by itself.

Thus, the capability typing provides all atoms (except jn) with active or passive rôles in reaction, and this directionality information should be useful in an optimized implementation of our encoding.

6   Conclusion

We have shown that programming with controlled use of links and hyperlinks provides us with a uniform framework of concurrent and non-deterministic computation that allows (among other things) concise and fine-grained encoding of the strong λ-calculus. The encoding shows that the carefully chosen set of hyperlink operations (equality checking and fusing) are powerful enough to express multiset operations necessary to encode the scope management of the λ-calculus.

The simple capability type system with a $[-1, +1]$ real-valued type domain gives interpretation of hyperlinks as backward (directed) hyperlinks. The type constraints are formulated around Kirchhoff's current law, and could be solved rather easily using SAT (for links) or SMT (for hyperlinks) solvers. Although we advocate distinguishing between links and hyperlinks syntactically, the distinction is for practical reasons, since the capability type system is powerful enough to automatically infer which ports and hyperlinks are used as (and can be implemented as) links. The capability type system seems to advocate a symmetric program structure with respect to capability management; that is, hyperlink capabilities split into fractions in a tree-like manner should eventually be joined in the tree-like manner.

Our ongoing work includes the encoding of Bigraphical Reactive Systems into Flat HyperLMNtal, in which hyperlinks are used in a much more sophisticated way. Two major directions of future work are (i) to apply the proposed type system to aggressive compiler optimization and (ii) to develop a verification framework for programs based on hyperlink rewriting.

Acknowledgments. The author is indebted to the present and past members of the LMNtal group for fruitful discussions and building the (Hyper)LMNtal system on which the present work was successfully based. He would like to thank anonymous referees for their careful reviewing and useful comments. This work is partially supported by Grant-In-Aid for Scientific Research ((B) 23300011), JSPS, Japan.

References

1. van der Aalst, W., Stahl, C.: Modeling Business Processes: A Petri Net-Oriented Approach. The MIT Press, Cambridge (2011)
2. Abadi, M., Cardelli, L., Curien, P.-L., Lévy, J.-J.: Explicit Substitutions. Journal of Functional Programming 1(4), 375–416 (1991)
3. Boyland, J.: Checking Interference with Fractional Permissions. In: Cousot, R. (ed.) SAS 2003. LNCS, vol. 2694, pp. 55–72. Springer, Heidelberg (2003)
4. Curien, P.-L., Hardin, T., Lévy, J.-J.: Confluence Properties of Weak and Strong Calculi of Explicit Substitutions. J. ACM 43(2), 362–397 (1996)
5. Finkel, A.: The Minimal Coverability Graph for Petri Nets. In: Rozenberg, G. (ed.) APN 1993. LNCS, vol. 674, pp. 210–243. Springer, Heidelberg (1993)
6. Frühwirth, T.: Constraint Handling Rules. Cambridge University Press, Cambridge (2009)
7. Gallo, G., Longo, G., Pallottino, S., Nguyen, S.: Directed Hypergraphs and Applications. Discrete Applied Mathematics 42(2-3), 177–201 (1993)
8. Lafont, Y.: Interaction Nets. In: Conference Record of the Seventeenth Annual ACM Symposium on Principles of Programming Languages (POPL 1990), pp. 95–108. ACM (1990)
9. Lamping, J.: An Algorithm for Optimal Lambda-Calculus Reductions. In: Conference Record of the Seventeenth Annual ACM Symposium on Principles of Programming Languages (POPL 1990), pp. 16–30. ACM (1990)
10. Lang, F.: Modèles de la β-réduction pour les implantations. Ph.D. Thesis, École Normale Supérieure de Lyon (1998)
11. Mackie, I.: YALE: Yet Another Lambda Evaluator Based on Interaction Nets. In: Proc. Third ACM SIGPLAN International Conference on Functional Programming (ICFP 1998), pp. 117–128. ACM (1998)
12. Mackie, I.: Efficient λ-Evaluation with Interaction Nets. In: van Oostrom, V. (ed.) RTA 2004. LNCS, vol. 3091, pp. 155–169. Springer, Heidelberg (2004)
13. Melliès, P.-A.: Typed λ-Calculi with Explicit Substitutions Not Terminate. In: Dezani-Ciancaglini, M., Plotkin, G. (eds.) TLCA 1995. LNCS, vol. 902, pp. 328–334. Springer, Heidelberg (1995)
14. Milner, R.: The Space and Motion of Communicating Agents. Cambridge University Press, Cambridge (2009)

15. Reynier, P.-A., Servais, F.: Minimal Coverability Set for Petri Nets: Karp and Miller Algorithm with Pruning. In: Kristensen, L.M., Petrucci, L. (eds.) PETRI NETS 2011. LNCS, vol. 6709, pp. 69–88. Springer, Heidelberg (2011)
16. Shapiro, E.Y., Warren, D.H.D., Fuchi, K., Kowalski, R.A., Furukawa, K., Ueda, K., Kahn, K.M., Chikayama, T., Tick, E.: The Fifth Generation Project: Personal Perspectives. Comm. ACM 36(3), 46–103 (1993), (This is actually a collection of single-authored articles, and my article (pp. 65–76) was originally titled "Kernel Language in the Fifth Generation Computer Project")
17. Shapiro, E., Takeuchi, A.: Object oriented programming in Concurrent Prolog. New Generation Computing 1(1), 25–48 (1983)
18. Sinot, F.-R.: Call-by-Name and Call-by-Value as Token-Passing Interaction Nets. In: Urzyczyn, P. (ed.) TLCA 2005. LNCS, vol. 3461, pp. 386–400. Springer, Heidelberg (2005)
19. Suenaga, K., Kobayashi, N.: Fractional Ownerships for Safe Memory Deallocation. In: Hu, Z. (ed.) APLAS 2009. LNCS, vol. 5904, pp. 128–143. Springer, Heidelberg (2009)
20. Ueda, K., Morita, M.: Moded Flat GHC and Its Message-Oriented Implementation Technique. New Generation Computing 13(1), 3–43 (1994)
21. Ueda, K.: Resource-Passing Concurrent Programming. In: Kobayashi, N., Babu, C. S. (eds.) TACS 2001. LNCS, vol. 2215, pp. 95–126. Springer, Heidelberg (2001)
22. Ueda, K., Kato, N.: LMNtal: A Language Model with Links and Membranes. In: Mauri, G., Păun, G., Jesús Pérez-Jímenez, M., Rozenberg, G., Salomaa, A. (eds.) WMC 2004. LNCS, vol. 3365, pp. 110–125. Springer, Heidelberg (2005)
23. Ueda, K.: LMNtal as a Hierarchical Logic Programming Language. Theoretical Computer Science 410(46), 4784–4800 (2009)
24. Ueda, K.: Encoding the Pure Lambda Calculus into Hierarchical Graph Rewriting. In: Voronkov, A. (ed.) RTA 2008. LNCS, vol. 5117, pp. 392–408. Springer, Heidelberg (2008)
25. Ueda, K., Ayano, T., Hori, T., Iwasawa, H., Ogawa, S.: Hierarchical Graph Rewriting as a Unifying Tool for Analyzing and Understanding Nondeterministic Systems. In: Leucker, M., Morgan, C. (eds.) ICTAC 2009. LNCS, vol. 5684, pp. 349–355. Springer, Heidelberg (2009)
26. Ueda, K., Ogawa, S.: HyperLMNtal: An Extension of a Hierarchical Graph Rewriting Model. Künstliche Intelligenz 26(1), 27–36 (2012), doi:10.1007/s13218-011-0162-3
27. Ueda, K.: Encoding Distributed Process Calculi into LMNtal. Electronic Notes in Theoretical Computer Science 209, 187–200 (2008)

Event-Based Modularization of Reactive Systems

Somayeh Malakuti[1] and Mehmet Aksit[2]

[1] Software Technology Group, Technical University of Dresden, Germany
somayeh.malakuti@tu-dresden.de
[2] Software Engineering Group, University of Twente, The Netherlands
m.aksit@utwente.nl

Abstract. There is a large number of complex software systems that have reactive behavior. As for any other software system, reactive systems are subject to evolution demands. This paper defines a set requirements that must be fulfilled so that reuse of reactive software systems can be increased. Detailed analysis of a set of representative languages reveals that these requirements are not completely fulfilled by the current programming languages and as such reuse of reactive systems remains a challenge. This paper explains Event Composition Model and its implementation the EventReactor language, which fulfill the requirements. By means of an example, the suitability of the EventReactor language in creating reusable reactive systems is illustrated.

Keywords: reactive system, object-orientation, aspect-orientation, event modules, reuse anomaly, evolvability.

1 Introduction

Reactive systems are the ones that can respond to external events [1]. Conceptually, one can assume that a reactive system is composed of a non-reactive part and a reactive part; the reactive part responds to the event calls that are published by the non- reactive part. There may be many forms of responses, such as collecting data, filtering data, verification of certain properties, interpretation, displaying information, taking corrective measures on the non-reactive part, etc.

As for any other software system, reactive systems are subject to evolution demands. By the term evolution, we refer to a large set of change request possibilities on an existing system, such as bug fixes, performance improvement requests, introduction of new functions, integration with other systems, etc. Generally, in case of evolution demands, software engineers face correctness and reuse challenges. The correctness challenges are considered out of scope of this paper; we refer to [2] for more details on this topic.

This paper focuses on the reuse challenge that is defined as the ability to maximum reuse of code without unnecessary redefinitions. We consider it a **reuse anomaly** if the evolution demands cannot be localized to the relevant parts of the implementation, and have ripple modification effects on parts of the system that are irrelevant to the demand. Naturally, there has been a vast amount of publications on reactive systems [3]. For example, some publications have focused on the definition and application of patterns and

G. Agha et al. (Eds.): Yonezawa Festschrift, LNCS 8665, pp. 367–407, 2014.

architectural styles such as Observer pattern [4], MVC pattern, Publisher-Subscriber style [5], etc. There have been studies which address the problem of expressive specification and efficient implementation of domain specific events, for example for database updates. Some studies have focused on specific applications of the reactive part for example for the purpose of visualization. Similarly, there have been extensive studies on control algorithms and deriving the control calls on the non-reactive part [6]. There have been publications on some applications of reactive systems and the related architectures for example for run-time verification and control, fault-tolerant systems. Last but not least, we want to refer to the studies on reactive systems which have focused on the linguistic constructs of the programming languages so that reactive systems can be easily implemented, verified and/or reused [7–9, 3].

In this paper, we refer to this last category of research activities. In particular, we investigate and research to find answers to the following two questions in relation to the evolution of reactive systems: a) To which extent the current languages help to avoid reuse anomalies? b) Which kinds of linguistic abstractions are still needed to avoid reuse anomalies? To be able to answer these questions, this paper first identifies a set of reuse and language requirements that must be fulfilled by a language to avoid reuse anomalies, and then it evaluates a set of representative languages with respect to these requirements.

This paper discusses the suitability of Event Composition Model [10, 8] to achieve reusability in structuring reactive systems. Event Composition Model considers **events** and the **reaction** to the events as the core abstractions of computations, and introduces **event module** to modularize a set of correlated events and the reactions to these events. Event Modules have well-defined event-based interfaces, which help to keep event modules loosely coupled to each other and to other modules. New kinds of events, reactions and event modules can be programmed, and new compositions of event modules can be defined by reusing the existing event modules. We discuss the EventReactor language, which implements Event Composition Model. By means of an example, this paper illustrates that Event Composition Model is suitable in eliminating the reuse anomalies defined in this paper.

This paper is organized as follows: Section 2 provides a definition of reactive systems, and outlines the reuse and language requirements that must be fulfilled to avoid reuse anomalies. Section 3 identifies reuse anomalies in a representative set of languages. Section 4 explains Event Composition Model. Section 5 discusses the EventReactor language by means of an example, and Section 6 illustrates its suitability in achieving reusable implementations by means of a set of evolution scenarios. Section 8 explains the compiler of the EventReactor language, and Section 9 outlines the conclusions and future work.

2   Reactive Systems

2.1   Definitions

A reactive system is generally defined as a system that responds to external events [1]. As shown in Figure 1, conceptually, one can assume that a reactive system is composed of a *non-reactive* part and a *reactive* part, although in implementations such a clear separation is not always the case.

The reactive part responds to the *event calls* that are published by the non-reactive part; there may be many forms of responses, such as collecting data, filtering data, verification of certain properties, interpretation, displaying information, taking corrective measures on the non-reactive part, etc. Here the term *event* refers to any relevant state change in the execution of the non-reactive part of the system. The exact implementation of publishing of an event can be various such as direct call, event-propagation mechanisms as defined in the Observer and Publisher-Subscriber patterns [4], implicit invocations as in aspect-oriented languages [11], etc. The reactive part accordingly may regulate the execution of the non-reactive part through *control calls*. The event and control calls convey the necessary information between non-reactive and reactive part.

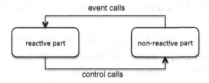

Fig. 1. Typical concepts in reactive systems

It is possible to merge the reactive and non-reactive parts within a single code block. However, in this paper, we are particularly interested in reactive system architectures, where these parts are organized as separate modules. In the literature of reactive systems, clear separation of these parts are generally claimed to be necessary. For example, in control systems, it is desired that the controlling system (reactive part) is separated from the system being controlled (non-reactive part).

Nowadays, there is a large number of systems with reactive behavior; self-adaptive systems [12], runtime verification systems [13], and fault-tolerant systems [14] are examples. Self-adaptive systems can adapt their structure/behavior in response to the changes in the environment. In these systems, the reactive and the non-reactive part can correspond to adaptation mechanisms and the system to be adapted, respectively. In these systems, event calls are means to represent the changes in the environment, and control calls are means to represent the adaptations that must be performed on the system. Runtime verification systems check the execution trace of software to reason about its behavior, for example, to detect the violation of certain security properties. The system under verification and the system that verifies form the non-reactive and reactive parts, respectively. The state changes in the system under verification (e.g., invocations on a method, construction of an object) are regarded as event calls; various actions (e.g. reporting an error) can be performed by the reactive part in case failures are detected. Fault-tolerant systems usually adopt a similar mechanism as runtime verification systems to detect the failures in the non-reactive part, and heal it from the failures. In these systems, event calls are means for abstracting necessary information from the execution trace of software, and control calls are means to heal the software from failures for example by initializing a recovery action.

The architecture that is shown in Figure 1 is mostly suitable in representing a single feedback-loop based control system[1]. Control systems can be organized in more complex ways such as peer-to-peer control, distributed control, hierarchical control, etc. Nevertheless, for now, we consider the architecture shown in the figure sufficient enough to identify the essential concepts in reactive systems.

2.2 An Illustrative Example: Recoverable Process

In this paper, we particularly focus on fault-tolerant systems as an illustrative case for reactive systems. We make use of Recoverable Process [15] as an illustrative example, which aims at making processes fault-tolerant by monitoring the processes to detect their failures, and by restarting a failed process along with other processes that are semantically related to it. This technique assumes that after recovery, processes can continue their normal operation.

Figure 2 is a UML class diagram representing the concerns of Recoverable Process. *AppProcess* represents a child process, and has the attributes *pid*, *name*, *status*, *init* and *kill*. The attribute *pid* is the unique identifier of the child process, which is generated by the operating system. The attribute *name* is the developer-specified name of the child process. The attribute *status* is the execution state of the child process, which can either be *running*, *terminated* or *under-recovery*. The attributes *init* and *kill* are the methods that create or kill the child process, respectively. The events *initiated* and *killed*, which are shown as operations in the figure, occur if the child process is created or killed, respectively.

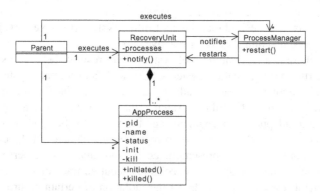

Fig. 2. The concerns of Recoverable Process

The concern *RecoveryUnit* represents a group of child processes that must be recovered together. *RecoveryUnit* detects the failures in the corresponding child processes,

---

[1] http://en.wikipedia.org/wiki/control_theory

and publishes an event to the concern *ProcessManager* to inform the failures. Consequently, *ProcessManager* recovers the corresponding child processes by changing their status to *under-recovery*, restarting them by invoking the methods *kill* and *init*, and setting their status back to *running*. The concern *Parent* represents the parent process of *AppProcess*. It creates the child processes, and publishes the event *initiated* for each of them.

As depicted in Figure 2, *Parent* and *AppProcess* belong to the non-reactive part of Recoverable Process, where *RecoveryUnit* and *ProcessManager* belong to the reactive part. *AppProcess* communicates with *RecoveryUnit* by publishing the event *killed*. The invocations on the methods *kill* and *init* on *AppProcess* are control calls that are issued by *ProcessManager*. The reactive part has a hierarchical architecture, in which *ProcessManager* responds to the event calls from *RecoveryUnit*.

We apply Recoverable Process to an example media-player software to make its processes fault-tolerant. An abstract block diagram of the media-player software is shown in Figure 3. The software is structured around four processes *Runner*, *MPCore*, *Audio* and *Video*, which execute the modules *Main*, *Core*, *Libao* and *Libvo*, respectively. The nesting of blocks shows that the parent process *Runner* has spawned the other processes as children. The arrows in the figure represent the messages that are exchanged among processes. We would like to apply Recoverable Process for the **global recovery** of media-player software, i.e. if *MPCore* is destroyed, *MPCore* along with *Audio* and *Video* are restarted, because the latter two child processes cannot continue their operation as well.

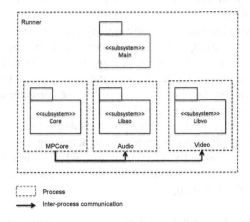

Fig. 3. An abstract block diagram of the media-player software

2.3   Language Requirements for Reusable Reactive Systems

Like many software systems, reactive systems are generally subject to continual evolution demands, which may influence various parts of the system. For example, the media-player application may evolve such that a new child process called *UserInterface*

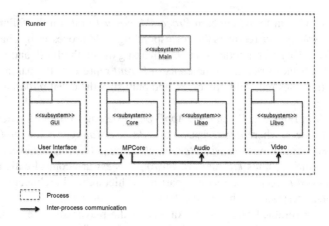

Fig. 4. An abstract block diagram of the evolved media-player software

is added, which executes the code related to interactions with users. Figure 4 shows the block diagram of the evolved media-player.

This evolution demands *RecoveryUnit* and *ProcessManager* to take the new child process into account for the global recovery. Likewise, the reactive part may evolve such that **local recovery** is supported for the individual child processes *UserInterface*, *Audio* and *Video* if the are destructed unexpectedly. Local recovery increases the overall availability of the media-player application [15], because other child processes can continue their execution.

Evolution demands may cause the software engineers to deal with both reuse and correctness challenges. We define the reuse challenge as to be able to maximum reuse of code without unnecessary redefinitions. A correctness challenge is to assure the correctness of software systems after the implementation of the new requirements. In this paper we mainly focus on the reuse challenges. For the correctness challenges of the evolution of reactive systems, we refer to [2].

The linguistic constructs of the adopted programming language and the chosen implementation technique play an important role in achieving reusability in the implementations of reactive systems. By referring to the field of control theory and Figure 1, to eliminate the irrelevant ripple modification effects for each element of the figure, a language must fulfill the following goals:

- The language must facilitate the evolution of the structure and/or the semantics of the non-reactive part with minimal impact on event calls, control calls, and the reactive part. Such an evolution may be demanded for example due to new application requirements, changes in hardware components, improvements in algorithms, etc.
- The language must facilitate the evolution of the event calls for example by introducing new event calls and/or by modifying the existing ones with a minimal impact on the reactive and the non-reactive part of the software.
- The language must facilitate the evolution of the structure and/or the semantics of the reactive part with minimal impact on event calls, control calls and the

non-reactive part. Evolution of the reactive part can be due to new monitoring and control requirements, improvements in control algorithms, etc.

- The language must facilitate the evolution of control calls with a minimal impact on the reactive and the non-reactive part of the software.
- The language must facilitate the evolution of the architecture, for example, from single feedback loop control architecture towards multiple feedback loop architecture, hierarchical architecture, etc.

We consider it a **reuse anomaly** if the adopted language is not expressive enough to fulfill the above-mentioned goals. Reuse anomaly causes the implementation of an evolution demand have ripple modification effects on the parts of the system that are irrelevant to the evolution demand. In the following, we outline a set of language requirements that we consider necessary to improve the reusability of reactive systems:

- **Events:** Depending on the application domain, reactive systems may need to deal with different kinds of events. For example, Recoverable Process shown in Figure 2 is applied to process-related events. More example of events are: an invocation of a method on an object, calling a function, beginning or ending of a thread of execution, a success or failure of a verification operation, triggering a diagnosis operation, committing a recovery action, excessive usage of a resource, excessive increase of temperature, etc. The kinds of required events are not fixed and cannot be anticipated always. This implies that a language must offer suitable means to define new events of interest and/or flexibly modify the existing ones when necessary. Otherwise, one has to provide workarounds to map the desired events into the set of events supported in the language; such mappings may increase the complexity of implementations. For example, although processes are the basic means of structuring operating systems, process-related events may not be directly available to the application programmers and as such they must be introduced if necessary.
- **Event calls:** The non-reactive part may consist of various different elements; for example, it may consist of application modules developed in different languages, middleware, OS and hardware elements. For instance, in the media-player software example, the process-related events may be generated by software modules implemented in different languages. It is a common practice for example that the GUI process is implemented in Java, whereas the other processes are implemented in C. This implies that event calls may be issued from various different kinds of sources, and a language must provide means to represent these calls and to receive them. Otherwise, the usability of the language for implementing various kinds of reactive systems is hindered, and/or one has to provide workarounds to map the desired event calls to the ones supported by the language. Such workarounds complicates the implementations.
- **Reactive parts:** To improve the reusability of reactive parts, we claim that a language must fulfill the following two requirements:
  - **Selection of event calls:** The language must offer dedicated constructs to identify and select the event calls of interest. Since the kinds of events and event calls cannot be fixed, the offered constructs must be expressive enough to cope with the diverse set of events and event calls. In addition, the language must

facilitate defining the specification of event calls of interest separately from the reactions to them, so that both the specifications and reactions can be reused independently. For instance, the event calls generated by the child processes shown in Figure 3 must be processed by Recoverable Process, in case fault tolerant software is required.

- **Reactions to event calls:** The language must offer sufficient means to program the desired reactions to the selected event calls. Since the reactive part of systems are generally defined as state-machines, it may be desirable to adopt a domain specific language (DSL) that directly support state-based formalisms. To support evolution of state machines, the DSL must be equipped with the suitable abstractions and composition operators. Naturally, to program the reactive part, other kinds of formalisms and consequently different kinds of DSLs may be also desirable.

- **Control calls:** The kinds of necessary control calls are not fixed and cannot be anticipated always. The language must offer a rich set of interaction possibilities to implement control calls including event-based communication. For example in Recoverable Process, the type of control calls depend on the characteristics of the processes to be recovered, and as such loose coupling among these may be necessary.

- **Architectural constraints:** The interactions between the non-reactive and reactive parts may be constrained in various ways. For example, if both global recovery and local recovery are applied to the media-player software, it may be necessary to define architectural constraints to coordinate global and local recovery strategies. An example constraint is that local recovery for a child process must not be executed if the child process is being restarted during the global recovery.

A language must offer suitable constructs to specify the necessary architectural constraints, and the specifications must be separated and modularized from the reactive and non-reactive parts. Otherwise, the implementation of the architectural constraints scatters across and tangles with these parts, which consequently, increases their complexity and decreases their reusability for different architectural configurations.

3   Reuse Anomalies in Reactive Systems

In the following, we discuss implementation alternatives of reactive systems in a representative set of languages, and explain the extent to which the reuse requirements that are mentioned in Section 2 are fulfilled.

3.1   Object-Oriented Implementation of Reactive Systems

There are various ways that one may implement reactive systems in an object-oriented (OO) language. In the following, we explain two typical cases.

Monolithic Implementation: In this approach, the reactive and non-reactive parts are not clearly separated from each other. The event and control calls are implemented via explicit method calls among the corresponding objects. The state machine behavior of the reactive part can be implemented through the use of *IF-THEN-ELSE*-like statements. *IF-THEN-ELSE* like statements have a serious limitation in that the event and control calls must be defined a-priori. Each newly introduced unanticipated event and/or control call requires recompilation of the code [16]. This is an error-prone activity and against the minimal impact requirements presented in the previous section.

Implementation Using Design Patterns: To increase the reusability of implementations, one may adopt combination of various design patterns [4]. For example, the state-machine behavior of the system can be implemented using the State pattern. The Observer pattern can be used to implement the event calls; the Decorator pattern can be used to dynamically extend the semantics of the methods of an object through the use of so-called decorator objects; this pattern can be useful for instance to introduce new event calls per method when necessary. The Strategy pattern can be used to change the implementation of an object dynamically, for example to adapt the implementation of reactive part.

Using design patterns to increase reuse, however, has a number of limitations. First, to cope with the new reuse demands, implementations must be extended with the mechanisms that are needed for each pattern. In the most extreme case, each object or even each method of an object must be prepared for extension. This creates unnecessary overhead in case extensions are not used as anticipated.

Second, the incorporated patterns may not be always suitable for the new evolution requirements. For example, assume that State pattern is adopted in the reactive part. In this case, the introduction of a new event call has a ripple effect on the reactive part, because the interface of every state object has to be extended to handle the new event. If a new state has to be introduced, the existing state objects must be modified to include transitions to the newly-defined state. Consequently, there will be ripple modification effect on the whole state-machine.

As another example, both Decorator and Strategy patterns assume a fixed set of interfaces for each object. This is because, decorations/variations are encapsulated by an object which dispatches the calls to the dynamically installed implementation objects. In this case, the interface of the encapsulating object is fixed at compile time. If necessary, one may overcome this problem by using an additional pattern, such as the Command pattern. However, this may complicate the implementation because in the Command pattern, the message passing of the call has to be implemented in the application and as such the language runtime is by-passed. Also, type conversion problems may arise in passing the command objects with new call arguments.

3.2 Aspect-Oriented Implementation of Reactive Systems

Aspect-Oriented (AO) programming languages [11, 17] offer various constructs, which may help in overcoming some of the problems that appear in the OO implementation of reactive systems.

The key concepts in AO programming languages are join points, pointcut predicates, advices and aspects. Join points are identifiable state changes in the execution of so-called base programs. Examples are execution of methods, creation of objects, and throwing of exceptions. Pointcut predicates are linguistic constructs for querying the join points of interest from the program. Advice is a program code that is executed when the corresponding join point is activated. An advice is bound to a set of join points through pointcut predicates. In most AO languages, the combination of an advice and its pointcut predicate forms an aspect.

In an AO implementation of reactive systems, base programs represent the non-reactive part, join points and the activation of join points can be regarded as a means to define event calls. Pointcut predicates are means to define the semantics for selecting event calls, and advices are means to define the reactive part, which are bound to event calls through pointcut predicates. Control calls can be defined by accessing the corresponding base objects from aspects, and by changing the flow of executions and/or data values in the base objects. A hierarchical architecture is facilitated if an AO language allows defining aspects on aspects.

There is a large number of AO languages introduced in the literature. In the following we evaluate AspectJ [11], some of its relevant extensions [18–21], and the Compose* [17] language. AspectJ is a widely-used language among the AO languages. There are many other AO languages whose features are similar to the ones of AspectJ; we therefore assume that the shortcomings of AspectJ are representative for them. Compose* will be evaluated due to its distinctive features such as language-independence and its support for some domain-specific languages for the advice code.

AspectJ: With respect to the supported events, a predefined set of join points in Java programs are supported by AspectJ. Consequently, if a new set of events are required which are not included in this set (e.g. process destruction), software engineers have to provide workarounds to map the desired event calls to the supported join points. As it is studied in [22, 8], such workarounds increase the complexity of programs, reduce their reusability and may lead to the implementations that are not correct.

With respect to the supported event calls, naturally the event calls can only be issued from Java programs. However, as it is usually the case in embedded systems, non-reactive part may be implemented in multiple languages, which means that to implement the reactive part using AspectJ, software engineers have to provide various workarounds. As we studied in [23], a solution would be to redefine the reactive part such that it is implemented in AspectJ and AspectC [24], for example. This solution would however suffer from reuse anomaly because the reactive part has to be redefined if the non-reactive part evolves with different languages. Moreover, software engineers have to provide means to compose aspects that are implemented in various languages, so that the overall functionality of the reactive part is achieved. The lack of a standard composition mechanism for this matter leads to ad-hoc and arbitrary implementations of compositions, which might not be reusable for different kinds of applications.

With respect to selection of event calls, AspectJ offers a fixed set of pointcut predicates to designate the event calls of interest. The problems with fixed set of pointcut predicates with a limited expression power are well-studied in the literature [25]; one has to provide workaround code to express the desired event selection semantics in the base software and/or advice code. Such code complicates the implementations and causes the code for selecting event calls gets tangled with the code implementing the non-reactive and/or reactive parts. Another problem in AspectJ is that the code for binding the advice code to the pointcut predicates is tangled with the advice code, which reduces the reusability of the advice code for different applications.

With respect to the reactions to event calls, DSLs are not supported in AspectJ. Consequently, one has to make use of the imperative Java language to implement the reactive part, possibly by adopting design patterns. This, however, leads to the same problems explained for the OO implementations of the reactive part.

As stated previously, reactive systems may be organized hierarchically; for example, the concern *RecoveryUnit* represents a reactive part for which a higher order reactive part is defined through the concern *ProcessManager*. To implement such hierarchal structures, the adopted AO language must support defining aspects on aspects. AspectJ offers the *adviceexecution* pointcut predicate that picks out join points representing the execution of advices. Since advice code is not named in AspectJ, *adviceexecution* cannot distinguish among advices within an aspect to select the join points related to a specific advice. As a workaround, one has to rewrite an advice by putting its original body in a method and invoke this method from within the advice. By this way, AspectJ pointcut predicates can be used to select the event calls corresponding to the invocation and/or execution of this method. This solution, however, suffers from the reuse anomaly because the aspect has to be redefined; moreover, it increases the complexity of aspect code.

In AspectJ, one can adopt the existing composition operators such as *declare precedence*, scoping pointcut predicates such as *cflow* and *within*, and/or higher level aspects to define architectural constraints and the coordination semantics between the reactive and non-reactive parts. The precedence rules can be defined separately from the corresponding aspects. However, adopting the scoping pointcut predicates and/or higher level aspects may cause the redefinition of the corresponding aspects; consequently, reuse anomaly can be experienced if the architecture evolves.

Let us illustrate a set of reuse anomalies that can be experienced if AspectJ is adopted to implement our Recoverable Process example. Here, we aim at providing a reusable implementation by modularizing each concern that appear in Recoverable Process. Listing 1 shows an excerpt of the abstract aspect AppProcess, which represents the concern *AppProcess*. The aspect defines the attributes pid, name, status, init and kill, as it is specified by *AppProcess* depicted in Figure 2. The pointcut predicates e_Initiated and e_Killed are to select the state changes corresponding to the initialization and destruction of a child process, respectively. After the pointcut e_Initiated is activated, the attribute status is initialized with the value 'running'. After the pointcut e_Killed is activated, the attribute status is initialized with the value 'terminated'. We assume that the information about the unique identifier of the child process, and the methods that construct or destruct the child process are abstracted from the base program via pointcut arguments, and are assigned to the attributes pid, init and kill. The assignments to the attributes are performed by the advice code and the helper methods in Listing 1.

```
 1  public abstract aspect AppProcess {
 2    public int pid;
 3    public String name;
 4    public String status;
 5    public Method init;
 6    public Method kill;
 7    abstract pointcut e_Initiated(...);
 8    abstract pointcut e_Killed(...);
 9    after(...): e_Initiated(){ initiated();}
10    after(...): e_Killed(){ killed();}
11    public void initiated(){ status="running"; ...}
12    public void killed(){ status="terminated"; ...}
13  }
```

Listing 1. Modular representation of the concern *AppProcess*

Each child process of interest is represented as a sub-class of `AppProcess`. For example, Listing 2 shows an excerpt of the aspect `MPCoreProcess` to represent the child process *MPCore* of the media-player software. Since the join point model of AspectJ does not support the join points representing process construction and destruction, we are obliged to provide the workaround methods `initMPCore` and `killMPCore` in the class `Main`, whose invocations represent the construction and destruction of *MP-Core*, respectively. The pointcut predicates `e_Initiated` and `e_Killed` are defined to select these invocations. The other child processes must be defined likewise.

```
 1  public aspect MPCoreProcess extends AppProcess{
 2    ...
 3    pointcut e_Initiated(...): call (* Main.initMPCore(..));
 4    pointcut e_Killed(...): call (* Main.killMPCore(..));
 5    ...
 6  }
```

Listing 2. Modular representation of the process *MPCore*

Listing 3 shows the aspect `GlobalRecovery` that defines a recovery unit for the global recovery of the media-player software. The method `getProcesses` specifies the processes *MPCore*, *Audio* and *Video* as the elements of the recovery unit. This is achieved by retrieving the corresponding instance of the aspect `AppProcess` via the operator `aspectOf` of AspectJ. The method `getInitiator` specifies the child process `MPCoreProcess` as the initiator process, whose destruction causes the recovery unit be restarted. the pointcut predicate `e_processfailed` selects the join points indicating that the *MPCore* process is killed. The advice code is provided as a means to inform the destruction of *MPCore*; this is done by invoking the dummy method `notifyFailure`.

Listing 4 defines the aspect `ProcessManager`, which represents the concern *ProcessManager* of Recoverable Process. The aspect reacts to the events generated by a recovery unit, and restarts the processes forming the recovery unit. The pointcut `notified` selects the invocations of the method `notifyFailure` defined within `GlobalRecovery`. The advice code first re-initializes the initiator process, then retrieves all other processes forming the recovery unit, kills and re-initializes them.

```
1  public aspect GlobalRecovery{
2    public AppProcess[] getProcesses(){
3      return new AppProcess[]{
4        MPCoreProcess.aspectOf(),
5        AudioProcess.aspectOf(),
6        VideoProcess.aspectOf()};
7    }
8    public AppProcess getInitiator(){return MPCoreProcess.aspectOf(); }
9    pointcut e_processfailed (AppProcess p):
10      call(* AppProcess.killed()) &&
11      target(p) && && if(p == MPCoreProcess.aspectOf());
12   after (AppProcess process): e_processfailed(process){notifyFailure();}
13   public void notifyFailure(){}
14 }
```

Listing 3. Modular representation of the global recovery unit

```
1  public aspect ProcessManager{
2    pointcut notified (GlobalRecovery ru):
3      call(* GlobalRecovery.notifyFailure())&& target(ru) ;
4    after(GlobalRecovery ru): notified(ru) {
5      //invoke init method of
6      //the initiator process via reflection
7      ...
8      for (AppProcess p: ru.getProcesses())
9        if (p != ru.getInitiator()){
10         //invoke kill method via reflection
11         //invoke init method via reflection
12       }
13     }
14 }
```

Listing 4. Modular representation of the concern *ProcessManager*

Let us assume that the media-player software evolves such that the functionality of representing user interface is no longer handled by the child process *MPCore*. Instead, a new child process named *UserInterface* is introduced, which executes the module *GUI* as depicted in Figure 4.

This new child process must be taken into account for global recovery. In addition, to improve the availability of the media-player software, we would like to also apply Recoverable Process for the local recovery of *UserInterface*. This means that if this child process is destroyed, it must be restarted individually, while other child processes can continue their operation.

To implement the above-mentioned evolutions, we have to extend the media-player software with new methods indicating the construction and destruction of the *User-Interface* child process, and must provide a sub-class of the aspect AppProcess to represent this child process. In addition, the aspect GlobalRecovery in Listing 3 must be extended to consider this child process.

To implement the local recovery, we must define a new recovery unit, say named as LocalRecovery, which only consists of *UserInterface*. The functionality to restart child processes is the same for both local and global recovery, as such we would like to reuse the aspect `ProcessManager`. As a possible solution, we may consider extending the pointcut predicate `notified` in the aspect `ProcessManager` to select the corresponding joint points in `LocalRecovery` too. Since in future it may be demanded to change the set of applied recovery strategies, for example, by removing global recovery and adding local recovery for each child process, we would like to avoid redefining `ProcessManager` for each evolution, and make it as reusable as possible.

To this aim as shown in Listing 5, we define `RecoveryUnit` as the base class for the aspects representing recovery units. Listing 5 also shows the evolved implementation of `GlobalRecovery` and the implementation of the aspect `LocalRecovery`. We also have to redefine the pointcut `notified` in the aspect `ProcessManager` to let it interact with `RecoveryUnit`; this is shown in Listing 5.

As this example shows, a change in the architecture of Recoverable Process let us experience reuse anomaly as we were obliged to apply several redefinitions in the implementations to make them more reusable for possible future evolutions.

```
1  public abstract aspect RecoveryUnit{
2    public abstract AppProcess[] getProcesses();
3    public abstract AppProcess getInitiator();
4    pointcut e_processfailed (AppProcess p) :
5      call(* AppProcess.killed()) &&
6      target(p) && destroyedProcess(AppProcess);
7    abstract pointcut destroyedProcess (AppProcess x);
8    after (AppProcess process): e_processfailed(process) {notifyFailure();}
9    public void notifyFailure(){}
10 }
11 public aspect GlobalRecovery extends RecoveryUnit{
12   public AppProcess[] getProcesses(){
13     return new AppProcess[] {
14             MPCoreProcess.aspectOf(),
15             UserInterfaceProcess.aspectOf(),
16             AudioProcess.aspectOf(),
17             VideoProcess.aspectOf()};
18     }
19   public AppProcess getInitiator(){ return MPCoreProcess.aspectOf(); }
20   pointcut destroyedProcess(AppProcess x) :
21     target(x) && if(x == MPCoreProcess.aspectOf());
22 }
23 public aspect LocalRecovery extends RecoveryUnit{
24   public AppProcess[] getProcesses(){
25     return new AppProcess[]{ UserInterfaceProcess.aspectOf() }};
26   public AppProcess getInitiator(){ return UserInterfaceProcess.aspectOf();}
27   pointcut destroyedProcess(AppProcess x) :
28     target(x) && if(x == UserInterfaceProcess.aspectOf());
29 }
30 public aspect ProcessManager{
31   pointcut notified (RecoveryUnit ru):
32     call(* RecoveryUnit.notifyFailure())&& target(ru) ;
33   ...
34 }
```

Listing 5. Evolved representation of the concerns

During the global recovery of the media player software, the process *UserInterface* is killed and re-initialized. LocalRecovery detects the destruction of *UserInterface* during the global recovery, and notifies it to ProcessManager, which consequently re-initializes the process *UserInterface* again. To prevent having two processes running as *UserInterface*, we must define a constraint between local and global recovery strategies: if a process is killed during global recovery, it must not locally be re-initialized.

We have various alternatives to express this constraint. For example, we can compose GlobalRecovery and LocalRecovery such that LocalRecovery does not publish a failure event if *UserInterface* is killed during the global recovery. This constraint can be represented as the clause "!cflow(adviceexecution() && within(RecoveryUnit))", which must be conjuncted to destroyedProcess of the aspect LocalRecovery in Listing 5. However, this solution causes the specification of architectural constraints gets tangled with the aspect LocalRecovery, which increases the complexity of the aspect, and makes it fragile to the evolution in the architectural constraints. Another alternative implementation is to encode this constraint in the aspect ProcessManager, which suffers from the same problems.

Assume that the architectural constraint evolves such that if the global recovery fails to successfully restart *UserInterface*, local recovery must still be applied to this process. To increase reuse, we would like to define this constraint modularly via aspects. For this, we have to replace ProcessManager with two aspects, named as ProcessManager4GR and ProcessManager4LR, so that it is possible to distinguish between the action for the global and local recovery. Second, the aspects GlobalRecovery and LocalRecovery must be redefined so that the method notifyFailure is invoked from within them, instead of from their base class.

Listing 6 shows an excerpt of the aspect ProcessManager4GR. Here, line 11 initializes a process and assigns the result of initialization to the variable result. If the initialization succeeds, the unique identifier of the process, which is generated by the operating system, is returned; otherwise the return value is -1. In lines 12 and 13 if the result equals -1, the helper method failedRecovery is invoked with the name of the failed process as its argument.

Listing 6 defines the aspect Coordinator that modularizes the architectural constraint. It selects the invocations of the method failedRecovery on the instances of ProcessManager4GR. If the failed process is *UserInterface*, it invokes the method notifyFailure on the aspect LocalRecovery. Consequently, the recovery is performed for the process *UserInterface*.

As the example implementation of Recoverable Process in AspectJ shows, several helper methods in the base program and aspects were defined to overcome the limited join point model of AspectJ; examples are the methods initMPCore and killMPCore that are referred to in Listing 2, and the methods initiated, killed and notifyFailure in Listings 1 and 3, respectively. Moreover, avoiding reuse anomaly in AspectJ is a challenge, because the concerns cannot properly be separated and modularized. Consequently, evolution demands, for example changes in the base program and architectural constraints, have ripple modification effects on several parts of the implementation, and cause redefinition of the parts that are irrelevant to the evolution demands.

```
1  public aspect ProcessManager4GR{
2    pointcut notified (GlobalRecovery ru):
3      call(* GlobalRecovery.notifyFailure())&& target(ru);
4    after(GlobalRecovery ru): notified(ru){
5    //invoke init method of
6    //the initiator process via reflection
7      ...
8      for (AppProcess p : ru.getProcesses())
9        if (p != ru.getInitiator()){
10         //invoke kill method via reflection
11         int result = //invoke init method via reflection
12         if (result == −1)
13         failedRecovery(p.name);
14       }
15     }
16     protected void failedRecovery(String name){}
17  }
18  public aspect Coordinator{
19    pointcut notified (String name):
20      call(* ProcessManager4GR.failedRecovery(String)) && args(name);
21    after(String name): notified(name){
22    if (name.equals("UserInterface"))
23      LocalRecovery.aspectOf().notifyFailure();
24  }
25  }
```

Listing 6. A modular representation of the coordination concern

AspectJ Extensions: Several extensions are proposed to overcome the limitations of AspectJ; however, they still fall short to fulfill the requirements outlined in Section 2.3. In the following, we briefly discuss a relevant set of these extensions.

There have been attempts to extend the join point model of AspectJ with new elements. For example in [20], the so called *loop join point* is introduced. Unfortunately, such extensions do not change "the fixed set of elements feature" of the join point model. EJP [26] facilitates specifying arbitrary Java code blocks as event calls. Here, a new join point can be declared as a special kind of method interface. In the code where a join point must be activated, a reference to the corresponding join point declaration is made. In case multiple languages are adopted in the implementation of the non-reactive part, such an approach may become too limited since it works only with Java based implementations. IIIA [26] is another approach which has the same shortcomings as EJP in case multiple languages are adopted.

Tracematches [18] adopts the regular expression formalism over AspectJ pointcuts to express the expected sequence of event calls. The advice code is executed when the sequence matches at runtime. Although Tracematches extends the expressive power of AspectJ's pointcut language in binding to event calls of interest, it still limited to the expressive power of regular expressions. As it is extensively studied in the runtime verification community [27], the expressive power of other kinds of formalisms, such as temporal logics or state machines, may be needed to bind to the desired event calls.

Association Aspects [19] facilitates parameterizing aspects with a group of objects, which has a fixed length; it also offers pointcuts predicates to select join points that are activated on such a group of objects. Although this improves the expressive power of AspectJ pointcut language, the pointcut expressions are not defined separately from the aspect implementation, and the same implementation cannot be reused for two different groups of objects with different length.

A vision to extend AspectJ to define event calls and reactions to event calls is proposed in [21]. This approach distinguishes between event call declaration and aspect declaration blocks. The former facilitates programming composite event calls over the primitive event calls that are defined in the AspectJ join point model, and/or other composite event calls. The aspect declaration block selects the specified event calls of interest and define reactions to them. Inherited from AspectJ, this proposal also suffers from a fixed set of primitive events that can be published from Java programs, lack of support for DSLs, and the same set of problems in defining architectural constraints.

Compose*: Compose* [17] is a platform-independent language, which can be used to enhance the composition mechanisms of the Java, C and .Net languages. The join point model of Compose* includes the event calls that correspond to the incoming and outgoing messages to and from objects. To react on the incoming and/or outgoing messages, Compose* defines the notion of *filters* which are attached to objects. Each filter has a type that implements its functionality. A group of correlated filters are defined as a *filter module*, which is a unit of reuse. The pointcut predicates in Compose* are termed as *superimposition specification*, which are expressed using a Prolog program. Superimposition specifications facilitate selecting the objects of interest (i.e. the non-reactive part) and composing the corresponding filter modules with these objects.

Since the join point model of Compose* is also fixed, the same problems that were discussed for AspectJ may appear. Although the Compose* compiler supports multiple base languages, it is limited to one language at a time for its Java and C implementations, and it does not facilitate abstracting event calls from the non-reactive part implemented in multiple languages. In Compose*, this shortcoming has been overcome in the .Net languages.

Filter modules can be regarded as a means to modularize the reactive part; since filter modules are defined separately from superimposition specifications, the reuse possibilities of filter modules are enhanced in comparison to AO languages where advice code and pointcut predicates are integrated under a single linguistic abstraction.

By means of filter types, Compose* facilitates defining domain-specific advice code. In [28], we defined the E-Chaser language [28], which is an extension to Compose*, and showed the possibility to define domain-specific filter types for the runtime verification domain.

Compose* supports one instantiation strategy; i.e. individual instances of filter modules are created for each individual object on which the filter module must be superimposed. This reduces the reusability of the reactive part if they must process event calls that are triggered by more than one object.

The set of filters that are grouped within a filter module provide the actual functionality of the reactive part. Filters cannot publish event calls; consequently, the reactive part must be implemented as one monolithic module, which increases the complexity of implementations and reduce their reusability.

3.3   Languages Supporting Event-Based Communication

Due to the inherent event-based communication of the non-reactive part with reactive part, one may consider adopting programming languages that provide dedicated constructs that support event-based communications. In the following, we discuss reuse anomalies in a representative set of these languages.

Event-Delegate Mechanism of C#: The OO languages usually offer an event-delegate mechanism to facilitate implementation of event-based applications. This sections evaluates the event-delegate mechanism of C#, nevertheless the discussions can be generalized for the other event-delegate mechanisms that have similar characteristics.

In the event-delegate mechanism of C# [29], new event types and their attributes can be defined via special kinds of classes, which extend class *System.EventArgs*. To facilitate the binding of event publishers to event consumers, C# provides a pointer-like mechanism named as *delegate*, which is a type that references a method; any method that matches the delegates signature, which consists of the return type and parameters, can be assigned to the delegate. This facilitates binding various event consumer methods to an event. Events are published by instantiating the corresponding event type, and invoking the corresponding delegate. As a result, the event consumer methods that are bound to that delegate are invoked to process the event.

The non-reactive part of the system can be implemented as classes that define event types along with necessary delegates, and publish the necessary information as events. The reactive part can be implemented as classes that define methods whose signature matches the desired delegates; these methods implement the functionality to process the events. Although new kinds of events can be programmed, they can only be published from programs that are written in C#. As for AspectJ, there is a lack of support for DSLs to implement the reactive part.

Although event-based communication facilitate loose coupling of the non-reactive and the reactive parts, the types of events that are processed by the reactive part is fixed by the signature of methods that are defined in the reactive part. The lack of support for quantifying over events, may reduce the reusability of the reactive part; for example, if it must be reused to process multiple different types of events published from various sources. Moreover, the need for explicit binding of the reactive part to the non-reactive part also reduces the reusability of implementations. For example, if new events and event calls are introduced, the reactive and the binding parts must be redefined accordingly.

The evolution of architecture of system may also have ripple modification effects on various parts of programs. For example, if system evolves such that there are multiple reactive parts processing one event, it may be necessary to define the event processing order. C# does not provide dedicated constructs for this matter; hence, programmers are obliged to provide workaround code in the non-reactive, binding and/or reactive parts. Such workarounds scatter across and tangle with multiple classes and consequently reduces the reusability of implementations for various kinds of architectures. More complex constraints, such as conditional reactions to a specific set of events, must be implemented within the methods in the reactive parts. This reduces the reusability of reactive part for architectural configurations.

EScala: EScala [30] is an extension to the Scala [31] language with object-oriented events. EScala supports *implicit events*, which correspond to the join points in AO languages and marks language-specific execution points, such as the beginning or the end of the execution of a method. These events can be selected by the available pointcut predicates. The EScala language also facilitates defining so-called *imperative events* which are similar to the C# events; these must be explicitly published from within application classes.

EScala combines the idea of event-based programming from C#-like languages, and AO languages to define events at the interface of objects. However, the limitations discussed for AspectJ and C# are valid for EScala. For example, although new kinds of imperative events can be defined, these are limited to the base software events as implemented in Scala. Moreover, similar to C# and AspectJ, the implementation of constraints among multiple reactive part may scatter across and tangle with the reactive part, and consequently may introduce reuse anomalies. DSLs are not supported to implement the reactive part; last but not least, the pointcut predicates have limited expression power to select the event calls of interest. Consequently, complex selection semantics must be programmed in the reactive part, which increases the complexity of implementation and reduces its reusability.

Ptolemy: In Ptolemy [32], the execution of arbitrary expressions can be identified as events. Ptolemy facilitates defining event types for abstracting over such events. Events must explicitly be published by binding an event type to an expression in the base program. Ptolemy allows handler methods to be declaratively registered for a set of events using one succinct pointcut predicate. Handler methods and pointcut predicates can be regarded as a means to define reactive part and their binding to events, respectively.

Although new kinds of event types and events can be defined, Ptolemy is limited to support programs implemented in Java. As for AspectJ, the pointcut language of Ptolemy has a limited expressive power to select the events of interest; i.e. queries can only be expressed over event types. Consequently, if needed, complex binding semantics must be expressed as a part of handler methods, which will reduce the reusability of these methods in case different binding semantics are needed.

Handler methods and pointcut expressions are defined within one class. Such a tight coupling of handler methods to the specification of events of interest, reduces the reusability of handlers for different events. The necessary interaction constraints must be programmed as part of handler methods. This may reduce the reusability of handler methods in case different constraints are needed due to evolution requirements.

3.4 Dedicated Languages

In addition to the general-purpose languages explained in the previous sections, there are diverse sets of DSLs that can be adopted for implementing reactive systems. Examples are the languages developed for the domain of runtime verification [28, 33, 13, 34].

In [10], we performed an extensive study of the available languages for the domain of runtime verification, and identified that they significantly fall short to fulfill the requirements mentioned in Section 2.3. Except for the E-Chaser languages [28], these DSLs support a limited set of events and event calls, which can be published from a single implementation languages. Consequently, if the non-reactive part evolves with different implementation languages, multiple DSLs must be adopted to implement the reactive part, without a standard means to compose these DSLs.

The DSLs developed for the domain of runtime verification do not facilitate modularizing various concerns that appear in the reactive part. Moreover, they support a fixed architecture for reactive systems, and do not offer means to express architectural constraints such as ordering and conditional execution of the reactive parts. Last but not least, these languages do not facilitate defining hierarchal architectures for reactive systems.

4 Event Composition Model

In [8, 10] we proposed Event Composition Model, which offers a set of novel concepts to effectively modularize and compose concerns that typically appear in runtime verification systems. This paper explains the core concepts of Event Composition Model and their suitability in structuring reusable reactive systems.

Figure 5 is a UML class diagram, which depicts the core concepts of reactive systems in terms of the concepts introduced by Event Composition Model. Here, we assume that a **reactive system** consists of a set of **non-reactive part** and **event module**.

We regard **events** as the core concept for implementing reactive systems. In Event Composition Model, events are typed entities. Event Composition Model distinguishes between **base events**, which represent the events that are published by the non-reactive part, and **reactor events**, which represent the events that are published by event modules. An **event type** defines a set of **attributes** for the events. Application-specific and domain-specific attributes can be defined for each type of event.

Event modules facilitate modularizing a group of related events and the reactions to them. In the literature, module is defined as a reusable software unit with well-defined interfaces and implementation. The implementation is encapsulated, and the interfaces of the module are points of interaction with its environment. Event modules adhere to this definition in the following ways.

To facilitate reuse, event modules are identifiable and referable by their unique **names**. An event module has an **input interface**, which specifies the set of events of interest to which the event module must react. One important difference between the input interface of modules in programming languages and the input interface of event modules is that in programming languages input interfaces are invoked explicitly, whereas in event modules invocations are implicit. The explicit invocation means that programmers write code for invoking the input interface of a module. In

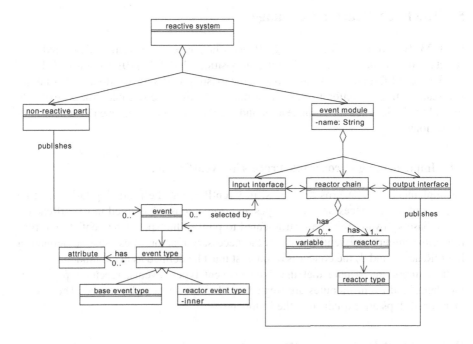

Fig. 5. A representation of reactive systems in Event Composition Model

contrast, implicit invocation [22] means that there is no need for such code; when an event of interest occurs, the corresponding event module is activated by the language environment.

The implementation of an event module is termed as **reactor chain**, which contains a set of **reactors** and **variables**. Each reactor processes (a subset of) the events specified in the input interface of the event module. Reactors are typed entities; a **reactor type** is a domain-specific type that defines the semantics in processing the events of interest. The input interface and implementation of an event module are separated from each other, and yet bound to each other so that the implementation can process the specified input events.

While processing an input event, a reactor may publish new events, which are termed as **reactor events**. These events have a special attribute named as **inner** that keeps a reference to the input event being processed by the reactor. This facilitates maintaining necessary information about the casual dependency of events. An event module has an **output interface**, which defines the set of events that are published by the event module to its environment. The output interface of an event module bound to (a sub-set of) reactor events that are published by the reactors. The events published by an event module are available in the execution environment, and can be selected by other event modules. This facilitates composing multiple event modules with each other to form a hierarchy. The event modules in higher levels of the hierarchy can implement and modularize the composition constraints among the event modules residing at the lower levels of the hierarchy.

5   The EventReactor Language

In [8, 23, 10], we introduced the EventReactor language[2], which offers dedicated constructs to define the concepts of Event Composition Model. In [10], we illustrated how
the features of EventReactor improves on the existing DSLs for the domain of runtime
verification. In this section makes use of our illustrative Recoverable Process example
to explain the features of EventReactor and their suitability to achieve reusable implementations.

5.1   Implementing Recoverable Process in EventReactor

To implement the concerns of interest in EventReactor, the following tasks must be
carried out: a) the necessary event types and events must be defined in EventReactor;
b) the base software must be instrumented to publish the specified events to the runtime environment of EventReactor; c) the necessary reactor types must be defined in
EventReactor; and d) the concerns of interest must be defined as event modules.

It is important to note that the defined event types, events, reactor types, reactor chains and event modules are treated as libraries and can be reused. The above-
mentioned steps are explained in the following.

Defining Event Types and Events: Event types are data structures that define a set of
static and dynamic attributes for events. The former includes the set of attributes whose
values do not change and are known at the time an event is defined in the framework.
The latter defines the set of attributes whose values are known at the time an event is
published during the execution of software. EventReactor offers a dedicated language
to programmers to define the event types of interest. As Listing 7 shows, EventReactor also makes use of this language to define three built-in event types `EventType`,
`BaseEventType` and `ReactorEventType`.

The data structure `EventType`, which is the super data structure for all event types,
defines `publisher`, `thread`, `stacktrace`, and `returnflow` as dynamic attributes. The attribute `publisher` refers to the element that publishes the event; the
attribute `thread` refers to the thread of execution in which the event is published; the
attribute `stacktrace` refers to a report of the active stack frames at a certain point in
time during the execution of a software; the type `StackTrace` is defined by Event-
Reactor to keep the list of active stack frames. The attribute `returnflow` specifies
the changes that must be applied to the flow of execution of the publisher after an event
is successfully processed. The type `Flow` is defined by EventReactor as an enumeration with the fields `Continue`, `Exit` and `Return`. The field `Continue` means that
the flow of execution must not be changed. The field `Exit` means that the execution
of program must terminate. The field `Return` means that the flow of execution must
return to the publisher.

---

[2] http://sourceforge.net/projects/eventreactor/

```
1  eventtype EventType {
2      dynamiccontext:
3          publisher: Object;
4          thread: Long;
5          stacktrace: StackTrace;
6          returnflow: Flow;
7  }
8  eventtype BaseEventType extends EventType {}
9  eventtype ReactorEventType extends EventType {
10     dynamiccontext:
11         inner: EventType;
12 }
```

Listing 7. The specification of built-in super event types

Since Event Composition Model distinguishes between base events (i.e. published by non-reactive part) and reactor events, EventReactor also provides the data structures `BaseEventType` and `ReactorEventType` to represent these two categories of events. The data structure `ReactorEventType` defines the attribute `inner` to maintain a reference to the event whose processing causes a reactor event to be published.

As the concern *AppProcess* in Figure 2 shows, two events *initiated* and *killed* must be defined for each child process of interest. These events indicate the creation and the destruction of a child process, respectively. Listing 8 shows the specification of the event type *ChildProcessEvent*. Here, the attributes `PID` and `parent` represent the unique identifier of the child process and its parent, which is generated by the operating system. The events `MPCoreInitiated` and `MPCoreKilled` are defined of the type `ChildProcessEvent` to represent the initialization and destruction of the child process *MPCore*. The other events of interest are defined likewise.

```
1  eventtype ChildProcessEvent extends BaseEventType{
2      dynamiccontext:
3          PID: long;
4          parent: long;
5  }
6  event MPCoreInitiated instanceof ChildProcessEvent{}
7  event MPCoreKilled instanceof ChildProcessEvent{}
```

Listing 8. The specification of a user-defined event type

Publishing Events: To publish an event, it is necessary to initialize its attributes and inform the runtime environment of EventReactor of the event. The API of EventReactor offers two routines for this matter. In the first one, the information about the event is provided as a comma-separated list of attributes and their values. This API is useful if the base software is implemented in a language other than Java. The second API is useful if the events are published from a Java program. In this case, EventReactor generates Java classes from the specification of events; such a class defines the name of the event and both the static and dynamic attributes specified for the event. To publish an event, the corresponding Java class must be instantiated, the attributes specified in the part `dynamiccontext` must be initialized, and finally the instantiated object must be sent to the runtime environment of EventReactor.

```
1  public class MPCoreClass{
2      void initMPCore() {
3          ...
4          int processID= \\ create the child process MPCore
5          ...
6          MPCoreInitiated event = new MPCoreInitiated();
7             event.initializeDynamicAttribute("publisher", parentPID);
8             event.initializeDynamicAttribute("thread",CurrentThread.ID);
9             event.initializeDynamicAttribute("stacktrace",CurrentThread.stacktrace);
10         event.initializeDynamicAttribute("PID",processID);
11         event.initializeDynamicAttribute("parent", parentPID);
12            EventReactor.publish(event);
13     }
14     void killMPCore(){...}
15 }
```

Listing 9. An excerpt of *MPCoreClass*

In the media-player example, the parent process is the only publisher of events of interest; consequently, the runtime environment of EventReactor is executed in the parent process by its main thread of execution. For each child process of interest, we extend the media-player software with a class that defines two methods: one for initiating the child process, and one for killing it. From within these methods, the events that are defined for the child process are published to the runtime environment of EventReactor. The media-player software is also changed such that the parent process invokes these methods when needed. Listing 9 shows an example of such a class for the child process *MPCore*, in which two methods `initMPCore` and `killMPCore` are defined.

Defining Auxiliary Information for Control Calls: As Figure 2 shows, the concern *AppProcess* has two attributes *init* and *kill*, which represent the methods that are used by the media-player software to create or kill a child process, respectively. These methods are invoked by *ProcessManager* to perform recovery. The necessary information about these methods must also be defined in EventReactor. The compiler of EventReactor is extendable with new kinds of specifications, providing that suitable generators are provided to translate them to Prolog facts and queries. Using this feature of EventReactor, we provide a specification language to define the method of interest in EventReactor. Listing 10 shows an excerpt of such specifications for the child process *MPCore*.

```
1  Method void initMPCore() In Class MPCoreClass
2  Method void killMPCore() In Class MPCoreClass
```

Listing 10. An excerpt of the specification auxiliary

Defining Reactor Types: EventReactor offers a dedicated language to define the reactor types of interest. Each reactor type is defined via a so-called action class and a specification of meta information. The action class, which is implemented in Java, provides the functionality of reactor type in processing input events. The specification of meta information defines the name of the reactor type, the name of its action class, the name and type of reactor events that are published by the reactor type, and the parameters of the reactor type.

```
1  reactortype React {
2      reaction = ReactClass;
3      events = { parameters.name: ReactorEventType};
4      parameters = {name: String};
5  }
6  reactortype RestartProcess {
7      reaction = RestartProcessClass;
8      parameters = {processes: List};
9  }
```

Listing 11. The specification of the reactor types

To implement our running example, we provide two reactor types: React and RestartProcess, whose specification is depicted in Listing 11. The sole function of React is to publish a reactor event when it receives an event to process. The name of the reactor event must be provided as an argument to the reactor type. The reactor type RestartProcess restarts a group of child processes that is specified as the parameter of the reactor type. Listing 12 shows the implementation of the class ReactClass, which provides the functionality of the reactor type React.

```
1  public class ReactClass extends ReactorAction {
2      String name;
3      @Override
4      public void initialize(Context context) throws Exception{
5          if (this.getParameters("name") == null)
6          {
7              throw new Exception("The required parameter \"name\" is not
8              initialized");
9          }
10         ...
11     }
12     @Override
13     public void execute(Event event, Context context) throws Exception{
14         ReactorEventType result = new ReactorEventType();
15         result.initializeStaticAttribute("name", name);
16         result.initializeDynamicAttribute("inner",event);
17         result.initializeDynamicAttribute("publisher",context.getEventModule());
18         ...
19         EventReactor.publish(result);
20     }
21 }
```

Listing 12. The implementation of an action class

This class extends `ReactorAction`, which is the base action class provided by EventReactor, and provides two methods `initialize` and `execute`. The former is executed when the corresponding reactor is instantiated, for example to initialize the parameters of the reactor. The latter is executed when the corresponding reactor receives an event to process. These methods can access the instances of the corresponding reactor, reactor chain and event module via their argument `context`.

In Listing 12, the method `initialize` ensures that the parameter `name` is initialized by the corresponding reactor. The method `execute` creates a reactor event, sets the name of the reactor event, initializes the attribute `inner` with `event` whose processing causes the reactor event be published, specifies the corresponding event module as the publisher, and finally publishes the reactor event. For the sake of brevity, the implementation of other reactor types is not discussed.

Defining the Non-reactive Part: In implementing Recoverable Process, we require to represent the child process of interest as *AppProcess*. The actual representation of child processes is provided by the operating system, and may not be directly accessible to programmers. To achieve implementations that are abstract from a specific platform and operating system, it is possible to adopt event modules to provide an abstract representation of the non-reactive part. An abstract representation of child processes of interest by means of event modules is explained in this section.

EventReactor offers a dedicated language to define the event modules and reactor chains of interest. To increase the reusability of implementations, reactor chains are defined as separate modules, so that they can be reused as the implementation of multiple event modules. Event modules are packaged within in so-called event packages. Listing 13 defines the event package `Processes` in which event modules are defined to represent the child processes of the media-player software. Line 3 selects the event named as `MPCoreInitiated` that represents the initialization of *MPCore* during the execution of the media-player software. Likewise, line 4 selects the event named as `MPCoreKilled` that represents the destruction of *MPCore* during the execution of the media-player software.

Lines 5–6 select information about the method `initMPCore` whose execution in the media-player software initializes the child process `MPCore`. This method is defined in the EventReactor language as shown in Listing 10. Likewise, lines 7–8 specify information about the method `killMPCore` whose execution in the media-player software terminates the child process `MPCore`. The events and methods for other child processes of the media-player software must be defined similarly.

Lines 11–13 define the event module `MPCoreProcess` to represent the child process *MPCore*. Here, the events selected by `e_inited` and `e_killed` are grouped as the input interface of the event module. The reactor chain `AppProcessImpl` is specified as the implementation of this event module. The selected events and methods are passed to the reactor chain as its arguments. As the output interface, the event module publishes the events `inited` and `killed`. Since there is only one child process as *MPCore* in the media-player software, the event module is specified to be instantiated in a singleton manner. The other child processes of interest must be specified in a similar way.

```
1  eventpackage Processes{
2     selectors
3        e_inited = {E | isEventWithName(E, 'MPCoreInitiated')};
4        e_killed = {E | isEventWithName(E, 'MPCoreKilled')};
5        m_init = {M | isMethodWithName (M, 'initMPCore'),
6                      isClassWithName (C, 'MPCoreClass'), isDefinedIn(M, C)};
7        m_kill = {M | isMethodWithName (M, 'killMPCore'),
8                      isClassWithName (C, 'MPCoreClass'), isDefinedIn(M, C)};
9        ...
10    eventmodules
11       MPCoreProcess := {e_inited, e_killed} <−
12                        AppProcessImpl (m_init, m_kill, e_inited, e_killed) −>
13                        {inited: ReactorEventType, killed: ReactorEventType};
14       AudioProcess := ...
15       VideoProcess := ...
16 }
```

Listing 13. The specification of the child processes of interest

Listing 14 defines the reactor chain `AppProcessImpl` to implement the functionality of the concern *AppProcess*. Here, the parameters `pinit` and `pkill` represent the methods that create or kill a child process, respectively. The parameters `pinited` and `pkilled` represent the events indicating that a child process is initiated or killed, respectively. As Figure 2 shows, the concern *AppProcess* has a set of attributes and events. These attributes and events are represented via the variables and reactors in the reactor chain, respectively.

```
1  reactorchain AppProcessImpl (pinit:Method,pkill:Method,pinited:Event,pkilled:Event) {
2     variables
3        init : Method = pinit;
4        kill : Method = pkill;
5        pid : Integer;
6        status : String;
7     reactors
8        reportInitiated : React = (event.name == pinited.name) =
9           { status = 'running'; pid = event.PID; reactor.name = 'inited'; };
10       reportKilled : React = (event.name == pkilled.name) =
11          { status = 'terminated'; pid = −1; reactor.name = 'killed';};
12 }
```

Listing 14. The specification of the reactor chain *AppProcessImpl*

Lines 3–4 define the variables `init` and `kill` and initializes them with the corresponding parameters of the reactor chain. Line 5 defines the variable `pid` of type `Integer`, which will maintain the unique identifier of the corresponding child process. Line 6 defines the attribute `status`, which will maintain the state of the corresponding child process. Lines 8–9 define the reactor `reportInitiated` of type `React`, which only processes the input events represented by `pinited`. In the body of this reactor, the value `'running'` is assigned to the attribute `status` of the reactor chain, the unique identifier of the created process is retrieved from the attribute `PID` of the selected event and is assigned to the attribute `pid` of the reactor chain, the value 'inited' is specified as the name of the event that will be published by the reactor. As a result, upon the occurrence of the event pinited, the event inited is published by the reactor, and the specified values are assigned to the attributes of the reactor chain.

Lines 10–11 define the reactor reportKilled of type React, which specifies the event pkilled to be of interest. As it is specified in the body of the reactor, upon the occurrence of pkilled, the value 'terminated' is assigned to the attribute status, the value -1 is assigned to the variable pid of reactor chain, and the value 'killed' is specified as the name of the reactor event.

At runtime when the child process *MPCore* is created in the media-player software, the event MPCoreInitiated is published to the runtime environment of EventRe-actor by the code depicted in Listing 9. The runtime environment first checks whether the event kind is known in the language. Since it is so, it creates a single instance of the event module, instantiates the reactor chain AppProcessImpl for it, and initializes the attributes of the reactor chain as it is specified. The reactor ReportInitiated receives the event, and since the event is of interest, the reactor assigns the specified values to the variables defined in the reactor chain, and publishes the reactor event inited. Afterwards, the event is received by the reactor ReportKilled, but the reactor ignores it because it is not of interest.

Defining the Reactive Part *RecoveryUnit*: Listing 15 defines the GRUnit event pack-age in which an event module is defined to represent a recovery unit for the global recov-ery of the media-player software. This recovery unit must group all the child processes, and it must report a failure when the child process *MPCore* is killed.

```
1  eventpackage GRUnit{
2    selectors
3      e_killed = {E | isEventWithName(E, 'killed'),
4        isEventModuleWithName (EM, '*.MPCoreProcess'), isPublishedBy(E, EM)};
5      em_mpcore = {EM | isEventModuleWithName (EM, '*.MPCoreProcess')};
6      em_audio = ...
7      em_video = ...
8    eventmodules
9      GlobalRU := {e_killed} <-
10               RecoveryUnitImpl ({em_mpcore, em_audio, em_video})
11               -> {failure : ReactorEventType};
12 }
```

Listing 15. The specification of the global recovery unit

Lines 3–4 of Listing 15 select the event killed that is in the output interface of the event module MPCoreProcess, and name it as e_killed in the event package. Line 5 selects the event module MPCoreProcess. Likewise, lines 5–7 select other event modules representing the other child processes of the media-player software. Lines 9–11 define the event module GlobalRU. The event e_killed is specified as its input interface, and RecoveryUnitImpl is specified as its implementation. The list of selected child processes is passed to the reactor chain RecoveryUnitImpl. The event module publishes a reactor event named failure as its output interface.

Listing 16 defines the reactor chain `RecoveryUnitImpl` to implement the functionality of the concern *RecoveryUnit*. The reactor chain receives the list of corresponding child processes in its parameter `processLst`. In the body of the reactor chain, the variable `processes` is initialized with `processLst`, and the reactor `reportFailure` is defined of type `React`. The name of the reactor event that will be published by `reportFailure` is specified as `'failure'`.

```
1  reactorchain RecoveryUnitImpl (processLst: List) {
2    variables
3      processes : List = processLst;
4    reactors
5      reportFailure : React = { reactor.name = 'failure'; };
6  }
```

Listing 16. The specification of the reactor chain *RecoveryUnitImpl*

At runtime if the child process *MPCore* is killed, the event `killed` is published by the event module `MPCoreProcess`. As a result, a single instance of the event module `GlobalRU` and its reactor chain is created and the event is provided to the reactor `reportFailure`, which consequently publishes the reactor event `failure` as it is specified in line 5 of Listing 16.

Defining the Reactive Part *ProcessManager*: Listing 17 defines the event package `ProcessManager` in which event modules are defined to represent the concern *ProcessManager* of Recoverable Process. Lines 3–5 select the recovery unit `GlobalRU` and the event published by it. Lines 7–8 define the event module `RestartAll`. It takes the event selected by `e_global_failure` as input interface and binds the reactor chain `ProcessManagerImpl` to it. The value of the attribute `processes` that is defined in the implementation of `GlobalRU` is passed as the argument; the event module does not publish any event as its output interface.

Listing 18 defines the reactor chain `ProcessManagerImpl` to implement the functionality of the concern *ProcessManager*. The reactor chain receives the list of processes to be restarted via its `processes` parameter. These are, in fact, expected to be event modules whose implementation is the reactor chain `AppProcessImpl`. Line 3 defines the reactor `restart` of type `RestartProcess` and assigns `processes` to the parameter `processes` of the reactor type.

```
1  eventpackage ProcessManager{
2    selectors
3      e_global_failure = {E | isEventWithName(E, 'failure'),
4        isEventModuleWithName (EM, '*.GlobalRU'), isPublishedBy(E, EM)};
5      em_global = {EM | isEventModuleWithName (EM, '*.GlobalRU')};
6    eventmodules
7      RestartAll := {e_global_failure} <-
8                    ProcessManagerImpl(em_global.processes) -> {};
9  }
```

Listing 17. The specification of a process manager

```
1  reactorchain ProcessManagerImpl(processes: List){
2      reactors
3          restart : RestartProcess = {reactor.processes=processes};
4  }
```

Listing 18. The specification of the reactor chain *ProcessManagerImpl*

At runtime, if the event failure is published by the event module GlobalRU the reactor Restart is informed of the event, and restarts the child processes that form the recovery unit. For this matter, the reactor retrieves the necessary information about the methods that kill and re-initialize a child process from the attributes init and kill of the corresponding instance of AppProcessImpl, and invokes them.

6   Reusable Implementations in EventReactor

By means of a set of evolution scenarios, this section illustrates how the EventReactor language supports reusable implementations of Recoverable Process.

6.1   Evolution of the Non-reactive Part and Event Calls

As it is explained in 3.2, assume for example that the media-player software evolves such that the functionality of representing user interface is no longer handled by the child process *MPCore*. Instead, a new child process named *UserInterface* is introduced, which executes the module *GUI*.

Through event modules, we can modularly extend the implementation explained in the previous section with an abstract representation for *UserInterface*. Listing 19 shows the definition of the event module UIProcess. In contrary to the AspectJ implementation, no redefinition of the modules is required, and the AppProcessImpl reactor chain is reused with suitable arguments to provide the implementation of the event module.

In is worth mentioning that EventReactor is extensible with new event types, events and auxiliary information for control calls. The set of events and auxiliary methods that must be defined for this matter are similar to the ones explained in Sections 5.1.

```
1   eventpackage UserInterfaceProcess { selectors
2     e_inited = {E | isEventWithName(E, 'UIInitiated')};
3     e_killed = {E | isEventWithName(E, 'UIKilled')};
4     m_init = {M | isMethodWithName (M, 'initUI'),
5                      isClassWithName (C, 'UIClass'), isDefinedIn(M, C)};
6     m_kill = {M | isMethodWithName (M, 'killUI'),
7                      isClassWithName (C, 'UIClass'), isDefinedIn(M, C)};
8     eventmodules
9     UIProcess := {e_inited, e_killed} <-
10                     AppProcessImpl (m_init, m_kill, e_inited, e_killed) ->
11                     {inited: ReactorEventType, killed: ReactorEventType};
12  }
```

Listing 19. The specification of the child process *UIProcess*

```
1  eventpackage GRUnit{
2    selectors
3      e_killed = ...
4      em_mpcore = ...
5      em_audio = ...
6      em_video = ...
7      em_ui = {EM | isEventModuleWithName (EM, '*.UIProcess')};
8    eventmodules
9      GlobalRU := {e_killed} <−
10               RecoveryUnitImpl ({em_mpcore, em_ui, em_audio, em_video})
11               −> {failure : ReactorEventType};
12 }
```

Listing 20. The evolved specification of the global recovery unit

The child process *UserInterface* must be considered in the global recovery too. Therefore, inevitably, we must extend the implementation in Listing 15 to include *UserInterface*. Listing 20 shows the evolved implementation of the `GlobalRU` event module. Here, we define line 7 to select the event module `UIProcess`, and we modified line 10 to include the selected event module in the arguments of the reactor chain `RecoveryUnitImpl`. As this listing shows, in contrary to the AspectJ implementation, such an extension can easily be performed by adapting the arguments of the reactor chain *RecoveryUnitImpl*, without the need for changing the internal implementation of this reactor chain.

```
1  eventpackage LRUnit{
2    selectors
3      e_uikilled = {E | isEventWithName(E, 'killed'),
4        isEventModuleWithName (EM, '*.UIProcess'), isPublishedBy(E, EM)};
5      em_ui = {EM | isEventModuleWithName (EM, '*.UIProcess')};
6    eventmodules
7      LocalRU := {e_uikilled} <− RecoveryUnitImpl({em_ui})
8               −>{failure : ReactorEventType};
9    }
10 eventpackage UIProcessManager{
11   selectors
12     e_local_failure = {E | isEventWithName(E, 'failure'),
13               isEventModuleWithName (EM, '*.LocalRU'), isPublishedBy(E, EM)};
14     em_local = {EM | isEventModuleWithName (EM, '*.LocalRU')};
15   eventmodules
16     RestartUI := {e_local_failure} <− ProcessManagerImpl(em_local.processes)−> {};
17 }
```

Listing 21. The specification of a local recovery unit and its process manager

To improve the availability of the media-player software, we would like to also apply Recoverable Process for the local recovery of *UserInterface*. Listing 21 defines `LocalRU` to modularly represent a recovery unit containing the *UserInterface* child process, and defines the event module `RestartUI` to modularly represent the local recovery of this child process. In contrary to the AspectJ implementation, the extensions were applied modularly without the need for redefining the implementations. Besides, the separation of reactor chains from the interfaces of event modules as well as the support for parametric reactor chains help to improve the reusability of the implementation further. Here, the `RecoveryUnitImpl` and `ProcessManagerImpl` reactor chains are reused with suitable arguments.

6.2   Evolution of the Reactive Part and Event/Control Calls

The event modules `GlobalRU` and `LocalRU` in Listings 20 and 21 both specify the child process *UserInterface* as an element of their recovery unit. Assume that at run-time the child process *MPCore* fails. As a consequence the global recovery kills and re-initializes the child processes *Audio, Video, UserInterface*. When the child process *UserInterface* is killed for the global recovery, the event `failure`, which is specified in lines 3–4 of Listing 17, is detected and the child process *UserInterface* is re-initialized for the local recovery. As a result, there will be two processes running as *UserInterface*.

To overcome the above problem, we want to extend the implementation of the reactive part of our example with a constraint: If the global recovery is being executed on a group of processes, these processes must not be recovered locally. Listing 22 defines the event package `RecoveryConstraint` in which this constraint is specified.

EventReactor facilitates defining the desired constraints among the event modules `RestartAll` and `RestartUI`, separately from the corresponding event modules, in the part `constraints` of the event package. In line 6, the operator `ignore`, which is a predefined composition operator in EventReactor, indicates that the event module `em_RestartUI` must ignore the events that are published during the execution of the event module `em_RestartAll`.

```
1  eventpackage RecoveryConstraint{
2      selectors
3          em_restartAll = {EM | isEventModuleWithName (EM, '*.RestartAll')};
4          em_restartUI = {EM | isEventModuleWithName (EM, '*.RestartUI')};
5      constraints
6          ignore(em_restartUI, em_restartAll);
7  }
```

Listing 22. The specification of an architectural constraint

More complex constraints can be defined as event modules, and dedicated reactor types can be defined for their implementation. As another evolution case, assume that if the global recovery fails to re-initialize *UserInterface*, the local recovery must still try to do so.

To implement this case, we need to define a new event call from the event module *RestartAll*, indicating that the restart operation for a child process is failed. In EventReactor, such an event will be a reactor event, which must be published from within the reactor `Restart` in Listing 18. To define such a reactor event, we need to extend the specification and implementation of the reactor type `RestartProcess`. Listing 23 shows the evolved specification of this reactor type, which indicates that the reactor event `failed` of the type `RecoveryResult` is published if the reactor fails to restart

a child process. The event type `RecoveryResult` must also be defined in EventReactor similarly to the other events types of interest. In short, it has an attribute named as
`processName` in its dynamic context, which specifies the name of the child process
that the reactor type aims to restart.

We also need to modify the event module `RestartAll` so that it publishes the
event `failed` as its output interface to it environment. Listing 24 shows the evolved
event module `RestartAll`.

```
1  reactortype RestartProcess {
2      reaction = RestartProcessClass;
3      events = { failed: RecoveryResult};
4      parameters = {processes : List};
5  }
```

Listing 23. The evolved specification of the reactor type *RestartProcess*

```
1  eventpackage ProcessManager{
2      selectors
3      ...
4      eventmodules
5      RestartAll := {e_global_failure} <-
6              ProcessManagerImpl(em_global.processes) -> {failed: RecoveryResult};
7  }
```

Listing 24. The evolved specification of a process manager

After these preparations, we can modularly extend the implementation of the reactive part of our example to coordinate the global and local recovery. Listing 25
defines the event module `Coordinator` for this matter. Here, lines 3–4 select the
event `failed` that is published by the event module `RestartAll`. Line 5 selects the
event module `UIProcess`. Lines 7 defines the event module `Coordinator`, specifies `e_failure` as its input interface, and the reactor chain `CoordinatorImpl` as
its implementation. The argument `'UserInterface'` of the reactor chain indicates
the name of the child process of interest, and the argument `em_ui` represents the child
process.

```
1  eventpackage Coordination{ selectors
2      e_failure = {E | isEventWithName (E, 'failed'),
3          isEventModuleWithName (EM, '*.RestartAll'), isPublishedBy(E, EM)};
4      em_ui = {EM | isEventModuleWithName (EM, '*.UIProcess')};
5      eventmodules
6      Coordinator := {e_failure}<- CoordinatorImpl ('UserInterface', em_ui)->{ };
7  }
```

Listing 25. The specification of a complex architectural constraint

Listing 26 defines `CoordinatorImpl`, which receives the name of the child process of interest and a reference to the event module representing it as its parameters.
In the body of the reactor chain, we reuse the reactor type `RestartProcess` to

define the reactor `restart`. This reactor processes only those events whose attribute `processName` is equal to `failedProcess`. In the body of the reactor, the parameter `process` is assigned to the parameter `processes` of the reactor. At runtime, if the event module `RestartAll` publishes the event `failed` for the child process *UserInterface*, the event module `coordinator` will be instantiated, and the reactor chain `CoordinatorImpl` will restart the child process.

```
1 reactorchain CoordinatorImpl (failedProcess, process){
2   reactors
3     restart : RestartProcess = (event.processName ==failedProcess)
4       {reactor.processes = {process};}
5 }
```

Listing 26. The specification of the reactor chain *CoordinatorImpl*

7   Evaluation

The concepts introduced by Event Composition Model, which are implemented in the EventReactor language, facilitate achieving reusability in the implementation of reactive systems, in the following ways:

– **Events:** As we explain it in 8, the compiler of EventReactor automatically detects a set of general-purpose events, such as method invocation and execution, and defines them in EventReactor. As it is shown in the previous section, new event types and events can be defined according to application demands. This feature helps to overcome the problem of "fixed join point model" that exists in the current AO languages, as such facilitates defining process-related events without the need for workaround helper methods.

– **Event calls:** Events can be published from programs implemented in different languages; for non-Java programs, Java-JNI [35] must be adopted to provide events to the runtime environment of EventReactor. The specification of event modules and reactor chains are independent of the implementation language of base program. As we extensively studied in [10], this feature helps to increase the modularity of implementations if the base program is implemented in multiple languages and/or its implementation language changes in due time. As we have shown in [8, 36], to some extent, they are also independent of the distribution of base program. This increases the reusability of specifications if the distributation of base program changes.

– **Reactive parts:** Abstractions over the non-reactive part and the reactive part of reactive systems can be implemented and modularized as event modules. This facilitates localizing the changes within the corresponding event modules. For example the evolution of the non-reactive part by introducing the child process *UserInterface* could effectively be handled by introducing new modules `UIProcess`, `LocalRU` and `RestartUI` in Listings 19 and 21.

  • **Selection of event calls:** When new event types and events are defined, the EventReactor compiler automatically generates Prolog expressions from the specifications of event types and events. As shown in Listing 13, the generated expressions can be used in the event packages to select the events of interest. If more complex queries to select events are needed, they can be expressed and modularized via event modules. In [10], we show the possibility to adopt regular expressions to define the expected order of events. Since EventReactor is extensible with new reactor types, it is possible to define and adopt domain-specific languages to express complex queries. These features of EventReactor help to tackle the problems with limited expression power of pointcut predicates and workaround code, which are experienced in the current AO languages.

- **Reactions to event calls:** By means of reactor types, DSLs are supported to program the implementation part of event modules; examples are the reactor types `RestartProcess` and `React` in Listings 11. Since EventReactor is open-ended with new DSLs, it can be reused for implementing reactive systems in various domains.

  The separation of the interfaces of an event module from its implementation (i.e. reactor chains), and the modularization of the reactor chains facilitate reusing them for multiple event modules. Examples are the reactor chains `AppProcessImpl` and `RestartProcess`, which are reused in Listing 19 and 26. The explicit interfaces of event modules facilitate localizing the corresponding changes to interfaces, without influencing the implementations; for example in Listing 15, we could localize the changes in the interface of event module `GlobalRU` to take the *UserInterface* process into account.

- **Control calls:** To reduce the coupling of reactive to the non-reactive part in making control calls, EventReactor facilitates selecting necessary information to make control calls, and enables programming event modules with this information. This is shown, for example, in Listing 13, in which the necessary information about the methods `initMPCore` and `killMPCore` is selected and is provided to the event module `MPCoreProcess` as arguments.

- **Architectural constraints:** The event-based interface of event modules helps to keep the event modules loosely-coupled from each other and from the non-reactive part. The possibility to select the events that are published by event modules helps to flexibly change the architecture of the reactive part. For example in Listing 25, we extended the reactive part with the new module `Coordinator`, to manage the interference among other event modules. The possibility to define the composition constraints using the available keywords separately from the corresponding event modules (see Listing 22), or modularizing complex constraints via event modules (see Listing 25) increases the reusability of event modules for different architectures, without the need for redefining them.

8   The Compiler of EventReactor

In [10], we explain the runtime behavior of EventReactor is processing events. In this section, we briefly explain the compiler of EventReactor.

Figure 6 provides a global overview of the compiler of EventReactor. The major functionality of this compiler is similar to the compiler of Compose* aspect-oriented

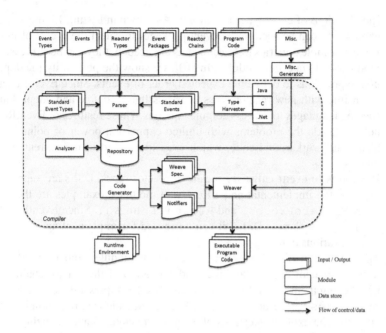

Fig. 6. An overall view of the EventReactor compiler

language, which is explained in several articles [37, 38]; therefore, we avoid detailed discussion. The modules of the compiler make use of a shared *Repository* to exchange information among each other.

8.1   Input and Output of the Compiler

As shown at the top of the Figure 6, the compiler receives the specifications of *Event Types*, *Events*, *Reactor Types*, *Event Packages* and *Reactor Chains* as its input. In addition, the compiler receives *Program Code*, which represents the base software publishing programmer-defined events and/or the base software from which the list of standard events must be extracted.

EventReactor is open-ended with new kinds of information that are needed for implementing RE techniques. The input *Misc.* indicates the specification of such information, and *Misc. Generator* represents a tool that generates Prolog facts and expressions from the specifications and stores them in *Repository*. This tool is not part of standard EventReactor compiler, and must be provided by programmers.

As its output, the compiler creates the runtime environment of the program and modifies *Program Code* such that it announces standard events to the runtime environment. These are shown as *Runtime Environment* and *Executable Program Code* in Figure 6, respectively.

8.2 Parsing

The specifications are input to the module *Parser*, which performs the following tasks:

1. It checks that the specifications are syntactically correct.
2. It checks the correctness of cross references within the specifications.
3. From the specification of reactor types, it extracts and defines the specified reactor types in *Repository*.
4. From the specification of event modules, it extracts and defines the specified output events in *Repository*.
5. It generates Prolog facts and Prolog query expressions from the statically available information in the specifications. These expressions facilitate selecting events and auxiliary information based on the static and dynamic attributes that are defined for them.
6. It stores data records representing these Prolog facts and query expressions and a reference to the original specifications in *Repository*.

In addition to programmer-defined specifications, *Parser* receives the specification of *Standard Event Types* which is provided by EventReactor itself, and generates Prolog facts and query expressions from them and stores them in *Repository*.

The module *Type Harvester* is adopted from the Compose* compiler. This module parses *Program Code* and converts it to a common internal representation to which Java, .Net and C programs can be converted. Among others, this representation contains the following information: a) the static structure of the program code in terms of the classes defined in the program; b) the interfaces that are implemented by each class; c) the methods and attributes defined in each class; and d) the methods that are invoked by the classes.

For each method invocation in *Program Code*, *Type Harvester* defines two events of the event type *MethodBased*; one representing the state change before the invocation, and one representing the state change after the invocation. For each method definition, it creates two events of the event type *MethodBased*; one representing the state change after the invocation and immediately before the execution of the method, and one representing the state change after the execution of the method, which terminates normally. *Type Harvester* specifies the code segments in *Program Code* from which the events must be published. This information is provided as the specification of *Standard Events* to the module *Parser*, which generates Prolog facts from them and stores them in *Repository*.

8.3 Analysis

Although events occur at runtime, the data records stored in *Repository* facilitate performing various static checks on the specifications. The following checks are performed by the module *Analyzer* and the results are stored in *Repository*:

1. It evaluates the specified Prolog query expressions against the Prolog facts stored in *Repository*, selects the data records that match the queries, and maintains a link between the Prolog query expressions and the selected data records in *Repository*.

2. It checks whether a selected data record refers to an event that is specified as the input interface of multiple event modules. If it is so and the order in which the event modules must process the event is not specified via the operator *precede*, it shows a warning to programmers.

3. If the constraint *ignore* is specified for two event modules, say *A* and *B*, *Analyzer* tags the reactors that are bound to *A* as conditional so that they ignore the events that are published during the execution of the reactors bound to *B*. This modification is stored in *Repository*.

8.4   Code Generation

The final step of the compilation is the generation of the executable program and the runtime environment of EventReactor. If not disabled by the programmer, the compiler generates code to publish the standard events to the runtime environment of Event-Reactor. For this matter, *Code Generator* creates the modules *Notifier* as part of the runtime environment of EventReactor, which inform the runtime environment of the occurrence of the specified standard event. *Code Generator* retrieves the data records corresponding to the specified standard events from *Repository*, and identifies the code segments from which the standard events must be published. This information is provided as *Weave Specification* to the module *Weaver*, which also receives *Program Code* as input and inserts invocations to *Notifier* in specified places in *Program Code*.

9   Conclusion and Future Work

We discussed the need to achieve reusability in the implementation of reactive systems, and identified five reuse requirements. We evaluated a representative set of languages, and identified that the implementation of reactive systems in these languages significantly suffers from various reuse anomalies. As a result of this evaluation, we concluded that reuse anomalies can be avoided if a language facilitates a) defining open-ended kinds of event calls, b) publishing these event calls from various kinds of elements that form the non-reactive part, c) defining various semantics for selecting event calls of interest, d) defining desired reactive parts, e) defining open-ended kinds of control calls, and f) defining various kinds of architectural constraints modularly.

We introduced Event Composition Model, whose concepts respect the above requirements. Event Composition Model considers events as the core concepts in implementing reactive systems, and introduces a novel kind of module termed as event modules to modularize the reactive part and/or abstractions over the non-reactive part. Event modules communicate with each other and with the non-reactive part via events, which helps to achieve loose coupling among the modules.

The EventReactor language can be compared to language-agnostic AO languages since it can be integrated with different base languages through events. Since events can be gathered from various places in the base program, event modules can be adopted to modularly implement crosscutting concerns. Unlike current AO languages, EventReactor is open-ended with new (domain-specific) event types and events, as well as DSLs to express the functionality of event modules. These facilitate representing domain-specific concerns in their DSL, without the need for designing an AO DSL from scratch.

Composition of event modules with each other is a means to compose the concerns that are implemented in different DSLs.

As future work, we would like to extend the EventReactor language with various composition operators such as inheritance for event modules and selectors. We would also like to adopt EventReactor for implementing other kinds reactive systems such as self-energy-adaptive software systems [39]. Event Composition Model does not fix possible implementation of its concepts. For example, in the current implement of EventReactor, reactors are composed with each other within a reactor chain in a sequential manner. A language may also implement parallel composition of reactors. Likewise, a language may support more complex predicate-based instantiation strategy of event modules. As future work, we would like to extend EventReactor to support other alternative implementation of the concepts of Event Composition Model.

Acknowledgments. We acknowledge the support of Prof. Yonezawa in the development of Composition Filters Model and the Compose* language. Event Composition Model and the EventReactor language are the successors of the Composition Filters Model and the Compose* language, respectively.

References

1. Harel, D., Pnueli, A.: On the Development of Reactive Systems. In: Apt, K.R. (ed.) Logics and Models of Concurrent Systems, pp. 477–498. Springer, New York (1985)
2. Güleşir, G.: Evolvable Behavior Specifications Using Context-Sensitive Wildcards. PhD thesis, University of Twente, Enschede (2008)
3. Salvaneschi, G., Mezini, M.: Reactive Behavior in Object-Oriented Applications: an Analysis and a Research Roadmap. In: AOSD 2013, pp. 37–48. ACM (2013)
4. Gamma, E., Helm, R., Johnson, R., Vlissides, J.M.: Design Patterns: Elements of Reusable Object-Oriented Software. Addison-Wesley Professional (1994)
5. Clements, P., Bachmann, F., Bass, L., Garlan, D., Ivers, J., Little, R.: Documenting Software Architectures: Views and Beyond. Addison-Wesley Professional (2002)
6. Basten, T., Hamberg, R., Reckers, F., Verriet, J.: Model-Based Design of Adaptive Embedded Systems. Springer (2013)
7. Boussinot, F.: Reactive C: An Extension of C to Program Reactive Systems. Software: Practice and Experience 21(4), 401–428 (1991)
8. Malakuti, S.: Event Composition Model: Achieving Naturalness in Runtime Enforcement. PhD thesis, University of Twente (2011)
9. de Roo, A., Sözer, H., Aksit, M.: Verification and Analysis of Domain-Specific Models of Physical Characteristics in Embedded Control Software. Information and Software Technology 54(12), 1432–1453 (2012)
10. Malakuti, S., Akşit, M.: Event Modules: Modularizing Domain-Specific Crosscutting RV Concerns. In: Chiba, S., Tanter, É., Bodden, E., Maoz, S., Kienzle, J. (eds.) Transactions on AOSD XI. LNCS, vol. 8400, pp. 27–69. Springer, Heidelberg (2014)
11. Kiczales, G., Hilsdale, E., Hugunin, J., Kersten, M., Palm, J., Griswold, W.G.: An Overview of AspectJ. In: Lindskov Knudsen, J. (ed.) ECOOP 2001. LNCS, vol. 2072, pp. 327–353. Springer, Heidelberg (2001)
12. Salehie, M., Tahvildari, L.: Self-adaptive Software: Landscape and Research Challenges. ACM Trans. Auton. 4(2), 14:1–14:42 (2009)

13. Delgado, N., Gates, A., Roach, S.: A Taxonomy and Catalog of Runtime Software-Fault Monitoring Tools. IEEE Transactions on Software Engineering 30(12), 859–872 (2004)

14. Koob, G.M., Lau, C.G.: Foundations of Dependable Computing: Paradigms for Dependable Applications. Springer (1994)

15. Sozer, H.: Architecting Fault-Tolerant Software Systems. PhD thesis, University of Twente (2009)

16. Ingalls, D.H.H.: A Simple Technique for Handling Multiple Polymorphism. In: OOPLSA 1986, pp. 347–349. ACM (1986)

17. Compose, http://composestar.sourceforge.net/

18. Pavel, C.A., Allan, C., Avgustinov, P., Christensen, A.S., Hendren, L., Kuzins, S., Moor, O.D., Sereni, D., Sittampalam, G., Tibble, J.: Adding Trace Matching with Free Variables to AspectJ. In: OOPSLA 2005, pp. 345–364 (2005)

19. Sakurai, K., Masuhara, H., Ubayashi, N., Matsuura, S., Komiya, S.: Association Aspects. In: Proceedings of the 3rd International Conference on Aspect-oriented Software Development, pp. 16–25. ACM, Lancaster (2004)

20. Harbulot, B., Gurd, J.R.: A Join Point for Loops in AspectJ. In: AOSD, pp. 63–74. ACM (2006)

21. Bockisch, C., Malakuti, S., Katz, S., Aksit, M.: Making Aspects Natural: Events and Composition. In: AOSD 2011, pp. 285–299. ACM (2011)

22. Steimann, F., Pawlitzki, T., Apel, S., Kästner, C.: Types and Modularity for Implicit Invocation with Implicit Announcement. ACM Transactions on Software Engineering and Methodology 20, 1:1–1:43 (2010)

23. Malakuti, S., Aksit, M.: Evolution of Composition Filters to Event Composition. In: Proceedings of the 27th Annual ACM Symposium on Applied Computing, SAC 2012, pp. 1850–1857. ACM (2012)

24. AspectC, http://www.cs.ubc.ca/labs/spl/projects/aspectc.html

25. Ostermann, K., Mezini, M., Bockisch, C.: Expressive Pointcuts for Increased Modularity. In: Gao, X.-X. (ed.) ECOOP 2005. LNCS, vol. 3586, pp. 214–240. Springer, Heidelberg (2005)

26. Hoffman, K., Eugster, P.: Cooperative Aspect-Oriented Programming. Sci. Comput. Program. 74, 333–354 (2009)

27. Khurshid, S., Sen, K. (eds.): RV 2011. LNCS, vol. 7186. Springer, Heidelberg (2012)

28. Malakuti, S., Bockisch, C., Aksit, M.: Applying the Composition Filter Model for Runtime Verification of Multiple-Language Software. In: ISSRE 2009, pp. 31–40. IEEE Press, Piscataway (2009)

29. Microsoft Corporation. C# language specification, http://msdn.microsoft.com/en-us/vcsharp/aa336809.aspx

30. Gasiunas, V., Satabin, L., Mezini, M., Núñez, A., Noyé, J.: EScala: Modular Event-Driven Object Interactions in Scala. In: AOSD 2011, pp. 227–240. ACM (2011)

31. Odersky, M.: Programming in Scala: A Comprehensive Step-by-Step Guide. Artima Inc. (2008)

32. Rajan, H., Leavens, G.T.: Ptolemy: A Language with Quantified, Typed Events. In: Vitek, J. (ed.) ECOOP 2008. LNCS, vol. 5142, pp. 155–179. Springer, Heidelberg (2008)

33. Chen, F., Roşu, G.: MOP: An Efficient and Generic Runtime Verification Framework. In: Object-Oriented Programming, Systems, Languages and Applications(OOPSLA 2007), pp. 569–588. ACM Press (2007)

34. Havelund, K.: Runtime Verification of C Programs. In: Suzuki, K., Higashino, T., Ulrich, A., Hasegawa, T. (eds.) TestCom/FATES 2008. LNCS, vol. 5047, pp. 7–22. Springer, Heidelberg (2008)

35. Java-JNI, http://download.oracle.com/javase/1.5.0/docs/guide/jni/spec/jniTOC.html

36. Malakuti, S., Aksit, M., Bockisch, C.: Runtime Verification in Distributed Computing. Journal of Convergence: An International Journal of Future Technology Research Association International 2(1) (2011)
37. de Roo, A., Hendriks, M., Havinga, W., Durr, P., Bergmans, L.: Compose: A Language- and Platform-Independent Aspect Compiler for Composition Filters. In: International Workshop on Academic Software Development Tools and Techniques (2008)
38. Nagy, I.: On the Design of Aspect-Oriented Composition Models for Software Evolution. Phd thesis, IPA (May 2006), ISBN: 90-365-2368-0
39. Malakuti, S., te Brinke, S., Bergmans, L., Bockisch, C.: Towards Modular Resource-Aware Applications. In: VariComp 2012, pp. 13–17. ACM, New York (2012)

From Actors and Concurrent Objects to Agent-Oriented Programming in simpAL

Alessandro Ricci and Andrea Santi

DISI, University of Bologna
via Venezia 52, Cesena (FC), Italy
{a.ricci,a.santi}@unibo.it

Abstract. Today we are witnessing a fundamental turn of software towards concurrency, distribution and interaction in every-day programming. This calls for introducing further abstraction layers on top of mainstream programming paradigms, to tackle more effectively the complexities that such turn implies. To this purpose, *agent-oriented programming* can be framed as an evolution of actors and concurrent objects, introducing a further level of *human-inspired* concepts for programming software systems. In that perspective, a program is conceived like an organization of human workers (agents), proactively doing some tasks and working together inside a possibly distributed environment—sharing resources and tools. In this paper we describe a new programming language called simpAL which allows for investigating agent-oriented programming as a general purpose paradigm for developing software systems.

1 Introduction

Pushed by the evolution of hardware architectures (e.g. multi-core, many-core, mobile platforms) and network availability, the fundamental turn of software towards concurrency, distribution and interaction is having a strong impact on everyday programming. As stated in [58], *the free lunch is over*: concurrent and distributed programming are no more a matter of specific application domains (e.g. high-performance computing) only, but are more and more issues to take into the account in mainstream programming. Besides, modern software systems are more and more complicated by reflecting more and more demand from the real-world. Since the real-world is inherently concurrent, we inevitably incorporate concurrency in software systems.

This caused a big tide on concurrency, and the consequent development of libraries, frameworks and fine-grained mechanisms on top of existing languages specifically tailored to harness the power of multi-core, many-core and cloud-core architectures in programs. However, we argue that the free lunch is over also for *conceptual modeling* and *abstraction*. That is, besides mechanisms we need programming models and languages that make it possible to *think concurrent*, to exploit concurrency, decentralization of control and interaction as first-class dimensions of program design and development.

G. Agha et al. (Eds.): Yonezawa Festschrift, LNCS 8665, pp. 408–445, 2014.
© Springer-Verlag Berlin Heidelberg 2014

To this purpose, a main reference is the research on *object-oriented concurrent programming* developed in 1980s and 1990s in particular [65,6,16]. At that time, we were still free lunching so-to-say and the context of such research was not really mainstream programming but high-performance computing and parallel programming. The actor computing model [5] and concurrent objects [65,2] were among the main results and target of investigations, along with the development of several new programming languages and frameworks based on the actor and the concurrent object idea [65,6].

Actors provide a clean and sound foundation for unifying objects[1] and concurrency [2]. An actor can be defined as an object encapsulating a control flow, with a mailbox where messages are enqueued [1]. The model is based on the *reactivity principle* [35]. An actor reacts to the arrival or availability of a message in the mailbox, by selecting and executing a corresponding method (handler). The execution of the method is atomic and may cause the update of the current state of the actor, the delivery of messages and the creation of other actors.

Actors are getting a momentum today, as far as one considers their injections in terms of libraries and frameworks developed on top of existing programming languages [36], or directly supported by new languages (e.g. DART [26], with isolates). However, as remarked in [39] (pag. 444): *"although the simplicity of the actor model is appealing, [..] problems with message order, message delivery, and coordination between sequences of concurrent actions also help us appreciate the programming value of more complex concurrent languages"*. This is a fundamental problem when assuming a software development perspective.

One possible way to address this problem is to introduce *ad hoc* programming abstractions to tackle specific issues, without changing the basic computing model. Examples are synchronisation constraints [4] and synchronizers [22]. This approach has the merit to keep the clean foundation of the basic model, but it makes the overall programming model quite complex and the integration of the features not clear [50].

Another way to tackle the problem is to directly extend the basic computational and programming model. This is what has been done by the notion of concurrent objects as introduced by ABCL family [63,62]. In fact, the concurrent object model enriches the basic actor one with features targeted to raise the level of abstraction in modelling and programming systems and finally simplifying them. Examples of such features are the *past/now/future* type message passing, the *ordinary* and *express* mode message passing, the *waiting* mode with the selective receive [62].

Following this perspective, the vision of *agent-oriented programming* proposed in this paper can be framed as a conceptual extension of actors and concurrent objects in particular, where a further *human-inspired* abstraction layer is added [51,57]. Such an abstraction layer draws inspiration from concepts, models and even existing languages developed in *agents and multi-agent systems* [32].

Actually, agents have been introduced and developed mainly in the context of Distributed Artificial Intelligence (DAI). This strongly influenced both the idea

---

[1] As defined in modern OOP.

of agent-oriented programming – originally introduced in [57] – and the further development of agent programming languages [11,12]. The focus has been mostly on theoretical aspects, in particular related to agent reasoning capabilities.

Our work aims at introducing a further perspective about agent-oriented programming, taking programming paradigms – in particular concurrent and distributed programming – and software development as *the* reference context. The general objective is to explore agent-oriented programming as a general-purpose programming paradigm, in the same track of actors and concurrent objects. To this end, we conceived a new programming language and platform called simpAL. The aim of this paper is to provide an overview of the main concepts characterizing the simpAL model and language, discussing its key features to deal with some relevant issues in design and programming. The first ideas about this viewpoint and about the simpAL project have been already sketched in a previous paper [49]. Here instead we discuss their development and maturation that lead to the current version of the simpAL programming language and platform.

The remainder of the paper is organized as follows: In Section 2 we provide a brief background about agents and multi-agent systems focused on the key aspects that are interesting for this paper. In Section 3 we describe the main concepts on which simpAL is based. In Section 4 we move from the concepts to the programming language, describing the key points that characterize simpAL programming and in Section 5 we briefly report about some aspects that concern the current implementation of simpAL platform and tools. In Section 6 we discuss some key aspects of the approach, compared to actors and concurrent objects in particular. Finally, in Section 7 we provide an overview of related works and in Section 8 we conclude the paper by sketching open issues and future work.

2 Motivations and Background – Agents as a Modelling and Programming Paradigm

The notion of agents and multi-agent systems appeared in many different computer science contexts – main examples are Distributed Systems, Artificial Intelligence, (Agent-Oriented) Software Engineering and (Agent-Based) Modeling & Simulation. Two key features that characterize the agent abstraction in spite of the specific contexts are:

- **Autonomy** — agents are autonomous entities, encapsulating a state, a behaviour and the control of such a behavior.
- **Interaction as a main design dimension** — a (not naive) system is designed in terms of a dynamic set of agents that interact and cooperate either by exchanging messaging using some Agent Communication Language (ACL) or by acting and perceiving events from the *environment* where they are logically situated.

The notion of Agent-Oriented Programming was introduced at the beginning of the 1990s with a seminal paper by Shoham in a AI context [57]. In spite of the AI-oriented perspective, the paper conceived Agent-Oriented Programming as an evolution of the OO paradigm towards an *cognitive* and *societal* view of computation. In this view, agents are specialization of objects with mental components (such as beliefs, intentions, goals) and the capability of interacting with other agents with high-level speech-act based ACL. That work was the root of many Agent Programming Languages (APL) and platforms developed in the two subsequent decades [11,12,15], still in the of context of Agents and Multi-Agent Systems. Main examples include AgentSpeak(L) [45] and Jason [14], 3APL [21] and 2APL [20], GOAL [31], Jadex [44], JaCaMo [10]. All these languages are directly or indirectly based on the BDI (Belief-Desire-Intention) agent architecture [46] and are especially targeted to the development of intelligent agents and multi-agent systems based on them. The main reference context is Distributed AI.

In the context of Agent-Oriented Software Engineering (AOSE) [33] agents have been proposed as high-level software components, conceptually extending objects with high-level features, such as autonomy and high-level communication based on speech acts. Such works lead to the development of platforms and frameworks that make it possible to design and implement multi-agent systems on top of mainstream OO languages – a main example is JADE [8], based on Java. The value of agents and multi-agent systems in this case is explored more at the architectural level, as an effective approach for designing complex distributed systems.

The simpAL project has been conceived with a different (but related) objective, which is to explore the value of agents and related concepts as first-class abstractions to tackle the complexities affecting modern *programming*—related to concurrency, asynchronous programming, distribution, and so on. In other words, our objective is to explore the value of agents as a modelling and programming paradigm, conceptually extending actors and concurrent objects.

Key Features and Contribution. Compared to actors and related extensions, the agent-oriented approach as implemented in simpAL provides the following key features and improvements:

- **Integrating reactivity and proactivity** – actors and objects are based on the reactivity principle [37], founded on message passing. Agents integrates reactivity with a first-class support to *proactivity*, i.e. they act (and react) in order to achieve some explicit *task*. Tasks are first-class concepts of the model.
- **Interaction model based on actions and observations** – people interact both by direct communication and by acting and perceiving in a shared environment, by doing actions that cause some observable effect which can be perceived indirectly by other people, possibly in a different timeframe. Actually, the usefulness of uncoupled models of interaction – based e.g. on events and patterns like the observer – is well-known also in software engineering and programming. In the agent model adopted in simpAL, this kind of interaction is adopted at the foundational level, along with direct communication.

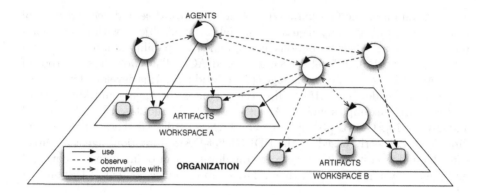

Fig. 1. Abstract view of a simpAL program

- **Human-inspired modelling and programming** – actors promote a modelling approach where everything is modelled as an (autonomous) actor and every interaction can be modelled in terms of message passing. Agent-oriented approaches have a stronger view about autonomy, promoting a modelling approach which forces to clearly separate in a system what can be suitably modelled as an autonomous entity – encapsulating the control of activities – and what is better modelled as an non-autonomous entity – part of the environment manipulated by such activities. Such a modelling approach can be labelled as *human-inspired* since it promotes a view about any system as an organization of people (agents) interacting in the same organization environment – sharing and co-using resources and tools – so as to accomplish both individual tasks and cooperative tasks at the system level.

These points will be discussed in detail in the remainder of the paper.

3   The simpAL Model – An Informal Overview

simpAL main concepts are based on the A&A (Agents and Artifacts) conceptual model [41] and the BDI (Belief-Desire-Intention) agent architecture [46,45,13]. A program in simpAL is conceived as an *organization* of *agents* working & interacting inside a common *environment*, composed by dynamic set of *artifacts* located in *workspaces*, distributed over the organization nodes (see Fig. 1). In particular:

- An **agent** is a computational component that encapsulates the *control* of activities, which are oriented to accomplish some *tasks*. Agents are both *proactive* and *reactive*. Proactive means that they have an explicit notion of task to be fulfilled and actions are continuously selected and performed to achieve tasks. Reactive means that in general, in order to fulfil a task, agents can process asynchronous events that occur in the environment where they are situated and to messages communicated by other agents (including themselves).

- An **artifact** is a non-autonomous component that encapsulates a set of *operations* that can be triggered by agents, and an observable state – represented by a set *observable properties* – which may be observed by interested agents. Artifacts represent the basic building blocks to design and compose the environment which is shared and used by agents to do their tasks. Examples of computational entities that can be properly modeled as artifacts are a simple counter, a bounded buffer, and a blackboard.
- **Workspaces** are logical containers of agents and artifacts, running on some specific node of the network. So the overall (dynamic) set of agents and artifacts of a simpAL organization is partitioned into one or multiple workspaces, possibly running on different nodes of the network. Workspaces make it possible then to explicitly define the logical topology of a simpAL organization, to handle the logical/physical distribution of an application.

A simpAL program is called an *organization* since agents participate to the system by playing some specific *roles*, that actually define their responsibilities in terms of tasks to accomplish.

3.1 The Agent Computational Model and Control Architecture

In a very abstract view, an agent is an autonomous component that continuously selects what actions to do in order to fulfil its tasks and execute them, eventually changing its state and the environment where it is situated. Action selection is driven by both the tasks the agent aims at fulfilling, its current internal state and the state of the environment which is observing, including messages sent by other agents.

The computational model of an agent in simpAL is based on the following first-class concepts:

- **Tasks** – representing the description of the jobs that agents have to do. At runtime, agents can instantiate tasks as instances of some task type, and assign them to other agents.
- **Plans** – representing modules that encapsulate the procedural knowledge about *how* to accomplish tasks. At runtime an agent has a (possibly dynamic) set of plans that can be used to accomplish tasks that are assigned to it.
- **Beliefs** – representing the knowledge that an agent has about its state and the observable state of the environment which is using. Beliefs in simpAL are like variables, having a value and a type—ranging from primitive data types, objects instances of classes[2], or references to specific simpAL abstractions (agents, artifacts, tasks, etc.).

---

[2] In the simpAL language, a subset of Java is used to define the OOP layer.

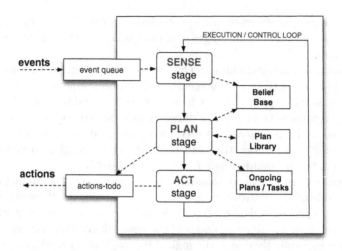

Fig. 2. An abstract view of the architecture of an agent and its execution cycle

Based on these concepts, the abstract architecture of an agent is composed of (see Fig. 2):

- a *belief-base*, which is the long-term private memory of the agent, storing the beliefs;
- a *plan library*, storing the current set of plans available for doing tasks;
- a set of plans in execution, called *intentions* – the agent can carry on multiple intentions at the same time;
- an *event-queue*, where inputs from the environment/other agents are asynchronously enqueued.

The behaviour of the agent is governed by an execution cycle called *control loop*. It is inspired to the reasoning cycle of BDI agents [46] and can be framed as an extension of the the basic *event loop* found in actors [38]. Next page shows an abstract version of the control loop in pseudo-code. According to that, the behaviour of an agent can be conceived as a loop continuously executing three stages in sequence:

- A **sense** stage, in which an event is removed (if available) from the external event queue and processed, updating the agent internal state.
- A **plan** stage, in which the set of actions to do in the current cycle is selected, given the current state and intentions of the agent. First, for each new assigned task, a plan for executing the task is selected from the plan library (if available) and instantiated and added to the list of intentions. Then, actions are selected by checking every intention. If a plan in execution is completed, i.e. the related task is fulfilled, then the intention is dropped from the list.
- An **act** stage, in which the selected actions are executed. Actions can be either *internal*, i.e. just updating the internal state of the agent (e.g. updating

---

Algorithm 1. simpAL Agent Control Loop

```
 1: BB ← BB₀  /* Belief-base */
 2: PL ← PL₀  /* Plan library */
 3: EQ ← []   /* Event queue */
 4: TD ← []   /* Task todo list */
 5: IL ← []   /* List of intentions (i.e. plans in execution) */
 6: while true do
 7:                                                    ▷ SENSE stage
 8:     ev ← ⊥
 9:     if EQ ≠ [] then
10:         < ev, EQ >← PICKEVENT(EQ)
11:         < BB, TD >← UPDATEAGENTSTATE(ev, BB, TD)
12:     end if
13:                                                    ▷ PLAN stage
14:     if TD ≠ [] then
15:         for td ∈ TD do
16:             pl ← SELECTPLAN(td, BB, PL)
17:             IL ← IL ∪ {NEWINTENTION(pl, td, BB)}
18:         end for
19:         TD ← []
20:     end if
21:     AL ← []
22:     for in ∈ IL do
23:         if TASKFULFILLED(in) then
24:             IL ← IL \ {in}
25:         else
26:             for < et, c, ac >∈ ACTIONRULES(in) do
27:                 if MATCH(et, ev) ∧ HOLD(c, BB) then
28:                     AL ← AL ∪ {ac}
29:                 end if
30:             end for
31:         end if
32:     end for
33:                                                    ▷ ACT stage
34:     for ac in AL do
35:         < BB, IL, TD, PL >← EXECUTE(ac, BB, IL, TD, PL)
36:     end for
37: end while
```
---

the value of a belief, dropping a plan in execution, creating a new task todo); or *external*, i.e. triggering the execution of an operation on an artifact and communicating with other agents. For external ones, the completion of an action (with success or failure) may arrive in the future, as an asynchronous event enqueued in the event queue. In the former case, such an event is immediately enqueued with the execution of the stage itself.

From a conceptual point of view the execution cycle of an agent is *never blocked*: it is continuously looping on these stages, possibly without choosing any action

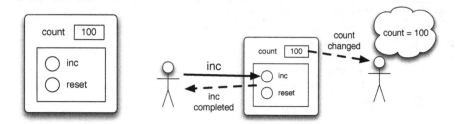

Fig. 3. *(Left)* A representation of an artifact, with in evidence its usage interface: the operations (inc and reset) and one observable property (count). *(Right)* Agents interacting with the artifact, executing an action and perceiving its observable state.

to perform if there are no active tasks or whether there is nothing to do in current tasks in execution.

3.2   A Computational Model for Artifacts

Artifacts have a simpler architecture than the agents' one, more similar to monitors as introduced in concurrent programming. Fig. 3 shows a pictorial representation of an artifact, representing a simple counter. Similarly to objects and tools used by humans, artifacts provide a *usage interface* which is exploited by agents to use and observe them. Such an interface includes:

– A set of **operations**, that correspond to the set of *atomic* actions available to agents for using the artifact. So the repertoire of an agent's actions at runtime depends on the artifacts that the agent knows and can use. In the counter example, inc and and reset are the two operations provided by the artifact. An agent that wants to use the counter has an inc action and reset action in its action repertoire.
– A set of **observable properties**, as variable-like information items storing those properties of the artifact that may be perceived and exploited by the agents using it. In the counter example, the artifact has a single count property, whose value is currently 100.

Besides an observable state, an artifact can have also an internal (hidden) state composed by state variables, which can be accessed and updated by operations.

In action/operation execution, there is no transfer of control between an agent and the used artifact. However, from a logical point of view, the execution model of an action over an artifact is *synchronous*. When an agent does an action (in the act stage of the control loop) corresponding to an operation in an artifact, such operation is executed logically in a separate control flow. An event is then explicitly generated when (if) the operation/action completes or fails, fetched by the agent control loop in the sense stage. So the agent can properly react to action completion or failure.

The way in which agents using an artifact perceive its observable state is event-driven, making the *observer pattern* directly part of the basic interaction model. In particular, an agent which is observing/using an artifact for doing its tasks, automatically has a belief about the current value of each artifact's observable property. Every time an observable property of the artifact is updated by the successful execution of an operation, a proper event is generated and asynchronously notified to all the agents using that artifact. The event is eventually fetched in the sense stage of the control loop and the corresponding belief updated with the new value.

Artifacts can be observed and used concurrently by multiple agents, automatically enforcing all the constraints that are necessary for avoiding interferences. To that purpose, operation execution in artifacts is *atomic*: operations are executed in a mutually exclusive way and the changes to the observable state of the artifact (properties) are made observable atomically, only after operation completion. Changes are perceived by agents observing the artifact only when an operation completes (with success).

Then, for implementing *coordination artifacts* – i.e. artifacts providing coordination functionalities – it is necessary to have operations whose execution overlap in time, but without interferences. To that end, operations can be explicitly suspended waiting for some conditions, allowing then other operations to be triggered and executed. A concrete example (a bounded buffer) will be given in next sections.

It is worth remarking that if an agent executed an action over an artifact and the corresponding operation is suspended or it has still to be completed, the agent control cycle is not blocked—so the agent is always ready to perceive events coming from its environment.

4 The simpAL Programming Language

In this section we introduce the key elements of the simpAL programming language using a simple program implementing a producer-consumer architecture (see Fig. 4). The program implements a simpAL organization composed by three workspaces (main, producers, consumers). In the producers workspace, some producer agents have the task of producing continuously some items that are consumed by a couple of consumer agents, in the consumers workspace. A bounded buffer artifact, located in the consumers workspace, is used as a tool by the producers and consumers to coordinate their activity. Producer agents must stop the production as soon as the user stops it through a GUI, represented by an artifact in the main workspace. Consumer agents must stop their activities either in the case that the total number of items processed is greater than a certain value or if the user issues a stop by means of the GUI. A shared counter is used by consumers to keep track of the total number of items processed. Finally, a manager agent in the producers workspace has the responsibility of creating the producer agents and eventually to inform them if more items need to be produced, during the producing task.

In the following we proceed bottom-up, first introducing the programming of agents and artifacts as basic components of a program, and then the definition of the organization, used to specify the overall structure of the program.

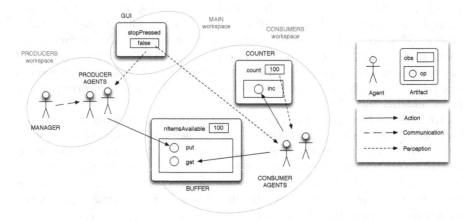

Fig. 4. An abstract view of the producers-consumers example with in evidence the agents and artifacts involved

4.1   Programming Agents

The principle of separation between interface and implementation is pervasively adopted in the language. Accordingly, the agent programming model is characterized on the one side by *roles*, representing the interface of agents in terms of what they are capable to do, their skills in terms of *task types*. On the other side by *agent scripts*, containing the implementation of concrete plans useful to accomplish the tasks related to one or multiple roles.

Defining Agent Types: Roles and Tasks. Tasks are first-class entities of the language. They can be instantiated given a *task type* and then assigned to some agent in order to fulfil it. Task types are used to define the information

```
1   role Producer {
2
3       task Booting { }
4
5       task Producing {
6
7           input-params {
8               numInitialItemsToProduce: int
9               bufToUse: Buffer
10          }
11
12          understands {
13              newItemsToProduce: int
14          }
15      }
16  }
```

```
1   role Consumer {
2
3       task Consuming {
4
5           input-params {
6               maxItemsToProcess: int
7           }
8
9           output-params {
10              totItemsProcessed: int
11          }
12
13      }
14  }
```

Fig. 5. Definition of roles in simpAL: the Producer role *(left)* and the Consumer role *(right)*

and structure of the tasks. A role collects the description of one or multiple task types and is used to define the *type* of an agent, representing the set of agents that are able to fulfil those specified types of tasks.

Fig. 5 shows the definition of the Producer and Consumer roles, part of the example. Each task type is defined by a name and the declaration of a set of typed input/output parameters, representing information about the task to do, specified by agents at runtime. In the example, the role Producer has two types of tasks, Booting and Producing. The task Producing is characterized by a couple of input parameters, indicating the initial number of items to be produced (maxItemsToProduce) and the buffer artifact to be used (bufToUse). The role Consumer has a task, Consuming, which has also an output parameter, totItemsProcessed – reporting the number of items processed by the consumer in doing the task.

Besides input/output parameters, the definition of a task type can include a set of predefined attributes to refine task type specification. Among the others, understands makes it possible to specify messages that can be sent to the agent performing the task. In the example, Producer agents can be told about the value of newItemsToProduce belief, which is of integer type. A further attribute, not shown in the example, is talks-about, which makes it possible to specify messages that can be sent by the agent assignee of the task.

Defining Agent Structure and Behaviour: Scripts and Plans. A script represents a module of agent behavior, implementing some role. It can contain both the definition of a set of *plans* useful to accomplish the task types defined in the role, and a set of beliefs that are shared among the plans. By loading a script, an agent adds the declared beliefs to its belief-base and the plans to its plan library.

In the example, the SimpleProducer script shown in Fig. 6 has three plans – one for the Booting task type and two for Producing – and a couple of global beliefs, testing and itemMaker. The first is a boolean flag, while the latter can store the identifier of an ItemMaker artifact.

Plan Definition and Action Rule Blocks. The definition of a plan includes the specification of the type of task for which the plan can be used (e.g. Producing) and a plan body, containing a specification of the procedural knowledge that the agent can use in order to accomplish the task. Multiple plans can be specified for the same type of task (e.g. Producing). In that case, an attribute context: *Cond* makes it possible to specify the condition over the belief base that must hold at runtime in order to consider the plan *applicable*. When a task is assigned, the first plan in the plan library which matches the task type and which is *applicable* is selected and instantiated. In the SimpleProducer script, when a Producing task is assigned to the agent using this script, the two different plans are chosen depending on the value of the testing belief.

The plan body is represented by an *action rule block*, denoted by { . . . }. Action rule blocks are meant to be the basic module to encapsulate the definition of

```
1   agent-script SimpleProducer implements Producer in ProdConsModel {
2
3     itemMaker: ItemMaker
4     testing: boolean
5
6     plan-for Booting {
7       new-artifact ACMEItemMaker() ref: itemMaker
8       testing = false
9     }
10
11    plan-for Producing context: !testing {
12      #completed-when: is-done jobDone || is-done stopNotified
13      #using:  console@main, gui@main
14
15      noMoreItemsToProduce: boolean = false
16      nItemsProduced: int = 0
17      nItemsToProduce: int = numInitialItemsToProduce
18
19      println(msg: "num items to produce: "+nItemsToProduce);
20      {
21        #to-be-rep-until: nItemsProduced >= nItemsToProduce || stopPressed
22        #using: itemMaker, bufToUse
23
24        newItem: acme.Item
25
26        makeItem(item: newItem);
27        put(item: newItem) on bufToUse;
28        nItemsProduced = nItemsProduced + 1
29      };
30      println(msg: "job done") #act: jobDone
31
32      when changed stopPressed in gui@main => {
33        println(msg:"stopped.")
34      } #act: stopNotified
35
36      every-time told newItemsToProduce => {
37        println(msg: "new items to produce: "+newItemsToProduce);
38        nItemsToProduce = nItemsToProduce + newItemsToProduce
39      }
40    }
41
42    plan-for Producing context: testing {
43      #using: console@main
44      println(msg: "this is a test")
45    }
46  }
```

Fig. 6. Definition of a script in simpAL: the `SimpleProducer` script

behaviour which may need to integrate and mix the *autonomous* execution of some workflow of actions along with *reactions* to some events or condition over the state of the agent. An example is given by the plan for `Producing` (lines 11-40). The plan repeatedly creates new items by using an `ItemMaker` artifact and insert them in the buffer, until the number of items to produce specified in the task is achieved (lines 19-30). Both `bufToUse` and `numInitialItemsToProduce` are input task parameters. Besides, every-time a message about new items to produce is received, the agent must promptly react and consider the updates (lines 36-39). Also, the producing process must be stopped when a stopped event generated by the GUI is perceived (lines 32-34).

The definition of an action rule block includes: a (possibly empty) set of local beliefs, i.e. beliefs whose scope is the block, as a kind of short-term memory, and a set of *action rules*, each one specifying *when* to execute *what* action. Action rule blocks can be nested, making it possible to structure the behaviour inside a plan – this point will be discussed extensively in next sections.

A set of pre-defined attributes (denoted by symbols starting with #) can be specified at the beginning of the block to declare further information affecting *how* the block will be executed. A main one is `#using:`, which specifies the list of the identifiers of the artifacts used inside the block (e.g., lines 13, 22 in the `SimpleProducer` script). An artifact inside a block can be used/observed only if explicitly declared. At runtime, when entering a block where an artifact is used, automatically the observable properties of the artifact are continuously perceived and their value is stored in corresponding beliefs in the belief base—updated in the sense stage of the agent execution cycle. Another important attribute is `#completed-when:Cond`, which makes it possible to specify the condition *Cond* for which the action rule block execution can be considered completed with success. Other attributes will be described in next sections.

Action Rules: Events, Conditions, Actions. The action rule model has been conceived to be expressive enough to specify any pattern of actions and reactions. In the most general case, an action rule is of the kind:

$$ev \; : \; cond \; \texttt{=>} \; act \; \texttt{\#act:} \; tag$$

meaning that the specified action *act* labelled as *tag* can be executed every time the specified event *ev* occurs and the specified condition *cond* holds.

The event template *ev* can refer to: a change to the observable properties of an artifact currently used by the agent (`changed` *obs-prop*); the success or failure of the execution of an action (`done` *tag*, `failed` *tag*) or of a task (`done` *t*, `failed` *t* – where *t* is a belief denoting a task); the arrival of a message sent by other agents (`told` *msg*). The event template *ev* can be omitted, meaning that the triggering of the rule is based solely on the condition.

The condition *cond* is a boolean expression over the agent belief base (including plan local beliefs). Some predefined predicates over actions and tasks can be used: `is-done` *tag* / `is-failed` *tag* to check is an action has been completed with success or has failed; `todo` *tag* to check if an action has never been selected and executed yet. For tasks, predicates with the same names are available.

An example of action rule block including some action rules follows:

```
1  {
2      c1, c2, c3: Counter
3      log: Console
4      v: int = 0
5
6      !todo a1 => inc() on c1 #act: a1
7      !todo a2 => inc() on c2 #act: a2
8      is-done a1 && is-done a2 => v = v + 1 #act: a3
9      done a3 : true => inc() on c3
10     changed count on c3 : count on c3 > 2 => println(msg: "alarm") on log
11  }
```

This block is composed of five local beliefs (c1, c2, c3, log and v—lines 2–4) and
five action rules (lines 6–10). The resulting behaviour is to immediately request
an inc operation on two counter artifacts. Then, as soon as both the actions
(labelled as a1 and a2) have been completed, the belief v is incremented and
(in sequence) a third counter – referenced by the belief c3 – is incremented.
Besides, every time the observable property count on the counter referenced by
c3 is updated and its value is greater than two, then a message is printed on the
console referenced by log.

Some syntactic sugar is provided to ease the implementation of frequently
used patterns of actions. One is the *sequence* of actions. A sequence or *chain* of
actions is defined by a list of actions a_i, where: *(i)* the action a_k can be executed
only when the completion of action a_{k-1} is perceived; and *(ii)* any action a_i must
be executed only once. This can be specified as a simple list of actions (with no
event or condition specified) using ; as separator. If the sequence is composed
of a single action, then that action can be selected and executed immediately,
but only once.

An example of sequence of actions is shown in the plan for the task Producing,
in Fig. 6. The plan first prints a message on a console (line 19), then a nested
block (lines 20-29) is executed and, when the block has been completed, then
the last message is printed (line 30). The block (lines 20-29) contains a sequence
(lines 26-28), in which: first an item is created by executing a makeItem operation
over the ItemMaker artifact. Then the item is inserted in the buffer by means of
the put action. Finally, when the put succeeded, the number of items produced
is incremented.

A block can contain also multiple independent sequences, which are carried
on in parallel. An example is given in the ManagerScript script, shown in Fig. 8.
The script implements the Manager role, who is responsible in the example of
setting up the producer agents. The plan SetupProducers has two sequences
(lines 8-11 and lines 13-16), each one creating a Producing task and assigning
it to a new producer agent.

Some syntactic sugar is provided also on the reaction side. The when keyword
can be used to specify rules that must be triggered *only once* in the lifespan of
the action block:

```
when ev : cond => act #act: tag
when ev => act #act: tag
when cond => act #act: tag
```

when rules are translated in flat ones by simply adding a further condition in *cond* that make the rule applicable if the action *tag* is still todo. An example is shown in the **Producing** plan of the **SimpleProducer** script (lines 32-34). When a change of the observable property **stopPressed** in the GUI artifact is perceived, then the agent must react, printing a message. Another example – without the event specified, with only the condition – is shown in the **Manager** script (Fig. 8, lines 18-20). Only when both the tasks previously created and assigned to the two agents have been successfully completed, a message is printed on the console.

Besides **when** rules, **every-time** rules are triggered *every time* some event / condition holds:

```
every-time ev : cond => act #act: tag
every-time ev => act #act: tag
every-time cond => act #act: tag
```

An example is provided in the **Producing** plan, lines 36-39. Every-time a message about the new threshold is told, the agent must react and update the total number of items to produce.

Action Rule Block Management: Nesting, Interruption, Completion and Repetition. Actions include also the instantiation of a new action rule block, to support *nested blocks*. At runtime, for each intention (i.e. plan in execution), a stack of action rule blocks is managed. Whenever an internal action instantiating an action rule block is executed, the block is pushed on top of the stack. That internal action is then considered completed as soon as the action rule block is completed, and then the block is removed from the stack.

Besides being useful to structure the set of rules, block nesting makes it possible to realize an *interrupt* behaviour. For instance:

```
1    counter: Counter
2    nInterrupts: int = 0
3    ...
4    println(msg: "this ");
5    println(msg: "can be");
6    println(msg: "interrupted")
7
8    when changed count in counter => {
9      println(msg: "interruption!");
10     nInterrupts++
11   }
```

In this example, the sequence of printing actions can be interrupted in any point as soon as the agent perceives that the observable property **count** has changed. When (if) this occurs, the block in lines 8-11 is pushed on the stack. Blocks pushed by reactions – like in this case – are tagged by default as *hard-blocks*. This means that when selecting actions in the plan stage, if a hard-block is at the top of the stack, only the rules of this block are considered, and the rules of other blocks below in the stack are ignored. In other words, hard-blocks cannot be interrupted by rules not belonging to the block.

```
1   agent-script SimpleConsumer implements Consumer in ProdConsModel {
2
3     consumed: int
4
5     plan-for Consuming {
6       #using: console@main, gui@main
7       consumed = 0;
8       {
9         #using: counter@consumers, buffer
10        #to-be-rep-until: (count >= maxItemsToProcess) || stopPressed
11
12        item: acme.Item;
13        get(item: item);
14        do-task new-task ProcessItem(item: item);
15        inc()
16      };
17      println(msg: "consumer done - num items processed: "+consumed);
18      totItemsProcessed = consumed
19    }
20
21    plan-for ProcessItem {
22      #using: console @ main
23      consumed = consumed + 1;
24      println(msg: "processed "+item)
25    }
26
27    task ProcessItem {
28      input-params {
29        item: acme.Item
30      }
31    }
32  }
```

Fig. 7. The SimpleConsumer script

```
1   agent-script ManagerScript implements Manager in ProdConsModel {
2     plan-for SetupProducers {
3       #using: console@main
4
5       prodA: Producer
6       prodB: Producer
7
8       t1: Producing = new-task Producing (numInitialItemsToProduce: 20000,
9                                           bufToUse: buffer@consumers);
10      new-agent SimpleProducer() init-task: new-task Producer.Booting() ref: prodA;
11      assign-task t1 to: prodA
12
13      t2: Producing = new-task Producing (numInitialItemsToProduce: 20000,
14                                          bufToUse: buffer@consumers);
15      new-agent SimpleProducer() init-task: new-task Producer.Booting() ref: prodB;
16      assign-task t2 to: prodB
17
18      when is-done t1 && is-done t2 => {
19        println(msg: "job done by both.")
20      }
21    }
22  }
```

Fig. 8. Definition of a script in simpAL

Blocks pushed on the stack by pure actions (rules without the event/condition) are by default tagged as *soft-blocks*. In that case, when selecting actions in the plan stage, if a soft-block is at the top of the stack, also the other blocks in the stack are considered. For instance:

```
1    counter: Counter
2    nInterripts: int = 0
3    condition: boolean
4    ...
5    println(msg: "this ");
6    if (condition){
7       println(msg: "can be");
8       println(msg: "interrupted")
9    }
10
11   when changed count in counter => {
12      println(msg: "interruption!");
13      nInterrupts++
14   }
```

Here if is a pre-defined simpAL internal action, pushing on the stack the block specified in the "then" arm if the condition holds. In this case the block specified in lines 6-9 is soft and can be interrupted. The attribute hard/soft can be explicitly specified using the pre-defined #hard-block and #soft-block.

Among the other attributes influencing action selection in the plan stage, an important one is #atomic. This can be used to specify that, when a block with this attribute is instantiated in a plan in execution, then the selection of action rules must be restricted to that intention, until the block is completed. In other words, only this plan in execution must be carried on.

The completion of a block is defined by the #completed-when: attribute. If this attribute is not explicitly specified by the programmer, then some different cases are considered by default, depending on the content of the block. If the block contains only one or multiple sequences of actions – no reactions – then the condition implicitly defined in #completed-when: is the completion with success of the last action of every sequence. In other words, the block completes when all the sequences of actions complete. Instead, if the block contains at least one reaction, i.e. an action rule with the event/condition specified, then the default value for #completed-when: is false. In this case the block is meant to be never completed—this is useful, for instance, in *maintenance* tasks.

Finally, proactive tasks typically account for repeatedly executing some set of actions. In simpAL this can be expressed declaratively, by means of some attributes of an action rule block: #to-be-repeated and #to-be-rep-until:*Cond*. The former says that once completed, the action rule block should be re-instantiated on the stack. The latter is a variant in which the block is re-instantiated until the specified condition holds. In the example, this attribute is used both in Producing and Consuming plans. In the former case (line 21), it is used to specify that the block should be repeated until all the items have been produced or a stop command on the GUI has been issued. In the latter case (line 10), the block is repeated until the count observable property of the counter shared by the consumers achieved the desired value or, again, the GUI issued a stop.

More about Actions. The repertoire of actions that an agent can perform includes a pre-defined set of actions useful to change its internal state. An example is given by the belief-assignment action, used to assign a new value to a belief. Values can be also *plain old* Java objects: the language provides internal actions to instantiate objects (`new-object`) and invoke methods. It is worth remarking that the OOP layer is used only to define and reuse data structures: Java mechanisms and classes related to concurrency, time and I/O are obviously not considered—being modelled by the agent-oriented layer.

Other examples of internal actions include those working with tasks: to create new tasks (`new-task`), to assign them (`assign-task`, `do-task`) and manage their in execution (`suspend-task`, `drop-task`, etc.). An example is shown in the plan for the task `SetupProducers`, in the `ManagerScript` (Fig. 8). Two instances of the `Producing` task are created (line 8-9 and line 13-14) and assigned to agents by means of the `assign-task` action.

Some pre-defined actions can be defined as *communicative actions*, since they involves the communication with other agents. The `tell` action can be used to send a message about the value of some belief. For instance, in the plan for the `SetupProducers` task in the `ManagerScript` (Fig. 8), the manager could send a message to a producer as follows:

```
1   prodA: Producer
2   ...
3   t1: Producing = new-task Producing (numInitialItemsToProduce: 20000,
    bufToUse: buffer@consumers);
4   ...
5   assign-task t1 to: prodA
6   ...
7   tell t1.newItemsToProduce = 10
```

The receiver of the message in `tell` is omitted, since it is implicitly the assignee of the task. It is worth noting that communications are necessarily bound – or, *contextualised* – to tasks: the basic idea is that any message exchange can occur only in the context of some task.

Also actions assigning tasks to *other* agents are communicative. An example is shown in line 11 and 16 of the `ManagerScript` in Fig. 8.

Besides pre-defined actions, the repertoire of an agent's action is *open*, since by definition it includes the operations of artifacts that an agent may want to use. The complete syntax of these kinds of action is:

$$op\,(Params)\ \text{on}\ art$$

where *op* is the name of the operation provided by the artifact referred by *art*, specifying *Params* as parameters. The reference *art* can be either a belief or directly a literal (e.g. `gui@main`) denoting the identifier of the target artifact. The target artifact can be omitted when it can be deduced at compile time by the name of the operation and the artifacts declared in the `#using:` attribute.

Finally, some pre-defined actions at the language level are just a syntactic sugar for referring operations on predefined artifacts. Main examples are `new-artifact` and `new-agent`, which can be used respectively to dynamically create a new artifact and spawn a new agent. These are operations provided by a pre-defined *workspace artifact*, available by default in every workspace, providing functionalities for its management. In the example, `new-artifact` is used in the `Booting` plan (line 7, Fig. 6) to create a new `ItemMaker` artifact. Instead, `new-agent` is used in the `SetupProducers` plan of the `ManagerScript` to spawn producer agents. Another example of pre-defined artifact – available by default in the `main` workspace – is `console`, which is used in the example to print messages on standard output (`println` operation).

Structuring Complex Plans. Complex plans can be modularized by breaking them into sub-plans and corresponding sub-tasks, that can be instantiated and managed by pre-defined actions mentioned in previous section. An example is reported in the script of the consumer shown in Fig. 7. The processing of the item is represented by a *private* task type `ProcessItem` defined in the script (lines 27–31), as well as a plan for handling it (lines 21–25). The sub-task is assigned at line 14 by means of the `do-task` action, after having successfully retrieved an item from the buffer. As soon as the action completes – that happens when the self-assigned sub-task is completed – the counter is incremented.

4.2   Programming Artifact-Based Environments

The programming model of artifacts is simpler than the agents' one, more similar to the model used for classic passive entities, such as monitors or objects. Analogously to the agent case, also for artifact programming we separate the abstract description of the artifact functionalities from their concrete implementation. The former is specified by *usage interfaces* – examples are `Counter` shown in Fig. 9 and `Buffer` shown in Fig. 10. Usage interfaces define the *type* of artifacts.

The definition of a usage interface includes the name of the interface, a set of observable properties and the declaration of a set of operations. Observable properties are similar to variables, characterized by a name, a value and a type. The parameters declared by operations are keyword based—for instance, `put` has a parameter called `item`. On the agent side, when invoking the operation (i.e. executing an action), the parameters must be specified with the keyword, in any order. A parameter can be declared to be an *action feedback*, i.e. an output parameter which is computed by the operation and returned to the agent (e.g. `item` parameter in `get` operation) when the operation (action) has completed. An operation can include multiple output parameters.

The implementation of an artifact is defined in *artifact templates* – examples are `CounterImpl` in Fig. 9 and `BoundedBuffer` in Fig. 10. Like classes in OOP, artifact templates are a blueprint for creating instances of artifacts. As already mentioned, on the agent side, the `new-artifact` action can be used to create a new artifact, specifying the template, the initial parameters and a belief where to store the reference to the artifact created, e.g.:

```
myCount: Counter
...
make-artifact Counter(startCount: 10) ref: myCount
...
```

The definition of an artifact's template includes a name, the declaration of the implemented artifact model, the concrete implementation of operations and the definition of internal (non observable) state variables, that can be accessed by operations. In templates, the observable properties are not re-declared, being already declared in the usage interface.

```
1  usage-interface Counter {
2
3    obs-prop count: int
4
5    operation inc()
6
7  }
```

```
1  artifact CounterImpl implements Counter {
2
3    init (startValue: int) {
4      count = startValue;
5    }
6
7    operation inc() {
8      count = count + 1;
9    }
10
11 }
```

Fig. 9. Usage interface (`Counter`) and template implementation (`CounterImpl`) of a counter artifact

```
1  usage-interface Buffer {
2
3    obs-prop nElems: int;
4
5    operation put(item: acme.Item);
6    operation get(item: acme.Item #out);
7
8  }
```

```
1  artifact BoundedBuffer implements Buffer {
2
3    elems: acme.Item[];
4    numMaxElems: int;
5    first: int;  last: int;
6
7    init (maxElems: int) {
8      numMaxElems = maxElems;
9      elems = new acme.Item[numMaxElems];
10     first = 0; last = 0; nElems = 0;
11   }
12
13   operation put (item: acme.Item) {
14     await nElems < numMaxElems;
15     nElems = nElems + 1;
16     elems[last] = item;
17     last = (last + 1) % numMaxElems;
18   }
19
20   operation get (item: acme.Item #out) {
21     await nElems > 0;
22     nElems = nElems - 1;
23     item = elems[first];
24     first = (first + 1) % numMaxElems;
25   }
26 }
```

Fig. 10. Usage interface (`Buffer`) and template implementation (`BoundedBuffer`) of a bounded buffer

```
1   org-model ProdConsModel {
2
3       workspace producers {
4           manager: Manager
5       }
6
7       workspace consumers {
8           buffer: Buffer
9           counter: Counter
10          consA : Consumer
11          consB : Consumer
12      }
13
14      workspace main {
15          gui: GUI
16      }
17  }
```

```
1   org ProdCons implements ProdConsModel {
2
3       workspace main {
4           gui =
5               new-artifact SimpleGUI(title:"Simple GUI")
6       }
7
8       workspace producers {
9           manager =
10              new-agent ManagerScript() init-task:
11                  new-task Manager.SetupProducers()
12      }
13
14      workspace consumers {
15          counter =
16              new-artifact CounterImpl(startValue:0)
17          buffer =
18              new-artifact BoundedBuffer(maxElems:10)
19          consA =
20              new-agent SimpleConsumer() init-task:
21                  new-task Consuming(maxItemsToProcess:15000)
22          consB =
23              new-agent SimpleConsumer() init-task:
24                  new-task Consuming(maxItemsToProcess:15000)
25      }
26  }
```

Fig. 11. An example of an organzation model (**ProdConsModel**) and of a concrete organization implementing it (**ProdCons**)

Operation behavior is given by a simple sequence of statements, in pure imperative style, using classic control flow constructs, assignment operators, etc. As mentioned previously, Java is used as a language for defining data structures. So objects as well as primitive values can be used in expressions and as value of variables and observable properties, and method invocation appears among the statement of the language. For instance, in the **BoundedBuffer** implementation, the class **acme.Item** (not shown) is used to represent the elements produced and consumed by agents, and stored in the buffer.

Besides classic statements, specific primitives are introduced to synchronize operation execution. For instance, the **await** statement allows for suspending the operations until the specified condition is met. An example of use is in the implementation of the **put** and **get** operations of the bounded buffer. The former is suspended until the buffer is not full, the latter until the buffer is not empty. As in the case of monitors, only one operation can be in execution: so if multiple suspended operations can be resumed a certain time, only one is selected. This feature is useful in particular to implement *coordination artifacts*, i.e. artifacts explicitly designed to provide also coordinating/synchronizing functionalities to the agents sharing and concurrently using them.

Operations may complete with success or fails. Correspondingly the agent who issued the operation will eventually receive an action completion event with success or an action failure event.

4.3   Defining the Organization

The global structure of a simpAL program and its initial configuration are specified by the notion of *organization*. The *organization model* contains the description of the topology of the organization in terms of a set of workspaces, each possibly including the name (identifier) and the type of some agents and artifacts that are known to be part of that workspace.

As an example, Fig. 11 shows the definition of the ProdConsModel organisation model, composed by three workspaces: producers, consumers, and main—the latter is available by default in every organization. The workspace producers is declared to host an agent called manager playing the role of Manager (not shown). The workspace consumers is declared to host a couple of agents called consA and consB playing the role of Consumer, along with a Counter artifact called counter and a Buffer artifact called buffer. The main workspace hosts a gui artifact of type GUI. An organization can contain further agent/artifact instances created at runtime, besides those statically declared in the organization model. The static case is useful anyway to specify the identifier of those elements whose name and type must be known at the organizational level, at *compile time*. In other words, to define global symbols that can be resolved and checked in scripts that explicitly declared to play a role inside an organization of this type (e.g. SimpleProducer script which declares to implement the Producer role inside the ProdConsModel). By doing so, the symbols and identifiers declared in the organization model can be referred as literals also in the script (e.g., gui@main in #using: attribute) and then checked at compile time.

The definition of a concrete organization accounts for specifying the concrete instances of agents and artifacts declared in the org model (see Fig. 11, on the right). For artifacts, the artifact template is specified, possibly including also the value of some initialization parameters. For agents, the initial script to be loaded must be specified, along with the initial task to do.

Finally, a simpAL program can be launched by specifying a configuration file specifying further deployment information, such as the Internet address of the workspaces defined in the program [56]. An example of deployment file for the producer-consumer organization is:

```
1   org ProdCons
2   org-id my-test-app
3   workspace-addresses {
4       main = localhost
5       producers = localhost:1000
6       consumers = 137.204.107.188
7   }
```

In this case, the program will be distributed transparently among three simpAL nodes, in two different hosts.

5   simpAL Implementation: Platform and Tools

An important aspect of our investigation related to agent-oriented programming concerns also the design of the technologies. In particular, we are interested to

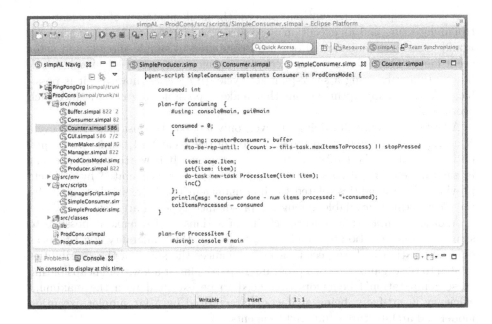

Fig. 12. IDE Overview

explore both how the new abstraction layer can be supported by platforms and tools, and how it would impact on the deployment, debugging and profiling of programs.

The current prototype of simpAL platform[3] has been developed in Java and includes a compiler, a runtime – including an infrastructural layer for the execution of distributed programs – and an Eclipse-based IDE. The compiler is based on the Xtext language development framework[4] and it produces binaries that can be read and executed by the simpAL runtime. Such a runtime map the logical level of concurrency defined in a program into the physical one, like it happens in other modern actor-based technologies [7,28,36].

In simpAL programs, the execution of agents is concurrent, as well as the execution of operations on distinct artifacts. This is at the logical level. It is then responsibility of the runtime platform to effectively map these concurrent entities and activities on the physical processors available in the systems. This is currently done by exploiting a pool of threads, whose size is strictly related to the number of such processors. This makes it possible to have a certain degree of scalability and finally running effectively programs composed by a very large number of agents (and artifacts) on the same node, like simple objects in OOP programs.

---

[3] Available as an open-source project here: http://simpal.sourceforge.net
[4] http://www.eclipse.org/Xtext/

A critical aspect of the runtime concerns the implementation of the agent control architecture and its execution cycle (described in Section 3). In principle, it would introduce a substantial overhead compared to simple threads and actor event loops. This is because, in theory, an agent (interpreter) is never blocked, but continuously doing a sense-plan-act cycle. In practice, however, it is possible to foresee many optimizations that make it possible to greatly reduce such overhead.

A first one accounts for doing the cycle only *by need*. For instance, if in a cycle N no rules are selected, then the execution of the cycle N+1 can be postponed until an event can be fetched from the event queue. It is worth remarking that in simpAL *temporal events* can be modelled as events generated by artifacts providing functionalities related to time management. An example is given by the *clock* artifact, available among the pre-defined types of artifacts.

Another optimization concerns chains of actions, which make it possible to simplify action selection in the plan stage. Finally, the availability of artifacts as dual abstraction with respect to agents enhances the space of the possibilities related to the organization of a program. In particular, it allows for encapsulating those computational behaviors that need to be executed with the maximum efficiency in artifacts, being artifacts characterized by a far simpler execution model and architecture compared to agents.

The infrastructural layer supports the distributed deployment and execution of programs that span over multiple workspaces on different network nodes. Actually many important issues have not been considered so far – such as the (distributed) garbage collection of agents and artifacts – and will be considered in future work.

Finally, the IDE has been conceived and developed exploiting the Eclipse tool ecosystem. It includes typical features of Eclipse-based IDE, such as a project-manager and file editors with features such as context-assist, code completion, template proposals, cross-referencing. Fig. 12 shows a screenshot of the IDE in action.

6   Discussion

In this section we discuss some key aspects of simpAL and agent-oriented programming, compared to actors and concurrent objects in particular.

6.1   From a Reactivity to a Proactivity Principle

A distinguished feature of the computational and programming model of agents in simpAL is the *proactivity principle*, compared to the *reactivity* one defined for actors. Agents act (and react) because they have a task to do, not necessarily because they received a message. Conceptually, the activity of a simpAL agent is *state-driven*, not event-driven. In fact, they keep on selecting actions until the task has been fulfilled – in spite of the task allocation event. Tasks may be assigned by means of message passing, but this is not necessarily the only case.

This makes it possible to reduce the gap between design and implementation. Task-oriented decomposition and division of labor is a common strategy used to design concurrent programs. At that level, tasks are not messages, but the description of a unit of work to be done — which may involve the adoption of some interaction protocol or some further decomposition in subtasks and related coordination. By adopting tasks as a first-class concept also at the level of the computation/programming model, we keep this level of abstraction alive.

6.2   Integration of Autonomous and Reactive Behavior

In the most general case, a plan must integrate both the execution of some pre-defined workflow of actions *and* reactions handing asynchronous events that are relevant for the task. The plan model in simpAL aims at making it possible to easily specify in a modular and simple way strategies that include both actions and reactions. From the execution point of view, this is supported then by the control loop, which defines the agent execution cycle.

This makes it possible to tackle two main issues that affect in general asynchronous programming, i.e. *inversion of control* and *asynchronous spaghetti*. A comprehensive discussion about this aspect can be found in [50] – in the following we report just some glances.

Events without Inversion of Control. In Object-Oriented Programming, *inversion of control* (IoC) refers to the method used in frameworks to execute user's application code [34]. The framework plays the role of the main program in coordinating and sequencing application activity, controlling the execution also of components encapsulating the business logic of the application.

In concurrent programming, this method is often used to realize the asynchronous interaction among parts executed by different threads of controls [27]. In these cases IoC occurs when, instead of calling blocking or long-term operations for waiting the occurrence of certain events, a program merely registers its interest to be resumed on certain events (e.g. an event signaling a pressed button), by installing proper handlers (callbacks) in the execution environment. The program never calls these event handlers itself. Instead, the execution environment dispatches occurred events to the installed handlers. Thus, the control over the execution of program logic is "inverted."

All approaches based on inversion of control suffer from the following two problems [27]: *(i)* the interactive logic of a program is fragmented across multiple event handlers (or classes, as in the state design pattern [23]) and *(ii)* control flow among handlers is expressed implicitly through manipulation of shared state [17].

In simpAL there is no inversion of control. The control is logically encapsulated in the agent control loop. Event handlers are modeled directly by action rules, which are evaluated and possibly selected and related actions executed by the same logical control flow, i.e. the agent control loop.

Avoiding *asynchronous spaghetti*. Also in pure actor-based solutions there is no inversion of control: the control flow is encapsulated by the event loop,

```
1    public class TestActor extends Actor {
2
3        int first = -1;
4        boolean ignore = false;
5
6        @message
7        public void printLowest(ActorName s1,  ActorName s2, String item) {
8            send(s1,"request",item,self());
9            send(s2,"request",item,self());
10           ignore = false;
11       }
12
13       @message
14       public void stop() {
15           ignore = true;
16           call(stdout,"print","Stopped.");
17       }
18
19       @message
20       public void reply(Integer value) {
21           if (!ignore) {
22               if (first == -1) {
23                   first = value;  /* first value received */
24               } else {
25                   /* both values available */
26                   int lowest = (value < first ? value : first);
27                   call(stdout,"print","Lowest: "+lowest+"\n");
28               }
29           }
30       }
31   }
```

Fig. 13. The simple example implemented in ActorFoundry

which repeatedly fetches a message from the mailbox and executes the corresponding method. However, in that case the logic of a plan used to accomplish some task must be necessarily fragmented into a set of handlers that are related to the messages to be received. In other words, the criteria that can be used to modularize the complex behavior of an actor must be related to message handling [50]. In simpAL, the strategy needed to accomplish some task can be encapsulated into a plan, without fragmentations. The plan of a complex task can break the task in sub-tasks, self-assigned through do-task but encapsulating the logic of the sub-task management and aggregation of task results in the same plan.

Let's consider a simple example. Suppose that we want to implement an actor/agent whose job is to get the prices of two items by interacting with some external services and to print to output the lowest price. Besides, the actor/agent should be able to react to a *stop* input by the user—in that case the actor/agent must print a stop message. We want that (i) the two requests are carried on in parallel, and (ii) there is a prompt reaction to used input.

A solution based on actors – using the pure (simplest) model - is shown in Fig. 13, implemented in ActorFoundry [36], a well-known actor framework based on the JVM. The printLowest message handler sends the requests to the two service actors. Then the actor waits either for replies or for a stop message. The reply handler is called each time the actor receives the response by a service

```
1    plan-for PrintLowest {
2
3      #using: cons, gui, s1, s2
4      #completed-when: is-done print || is-done stop
5      p1,p2: int
6
7      {
8        request(item: id, reply: p1) on s1
9        request(item: id, reply: p2) on s2
10     };
11     {
12       if (p1 < p2){
13         println(msg:"Lowest: "+p1) on cons
14       } else {
15         println(msg:"Lowest: "+p2) on cons
16       }
17     } #act:print
18
19     when changed stopPressed in gui => {
20       println(msg: "Stopped.") on cons
21     } #act:stop
22   }
```

Fig. 14. The same example implemented in simpAL

actor. If both replies have been received, then the lowest value can be computed and the message can be printed to output. If a stop is received, a flag (`ignore`) is set, in order not to process messages arriving later.

in spite of the simplicity of the example, the behaviour of the actor must be necessarily fragmented into (at least) three message handlers. Such a decomposition is *not* suggested by design principles to improve modularity, but is enforced by the message flow. In other words, the `reply` handler is not really a module storing a self-contained reusable part of the strategy; it can be more correctly conceived as the *continuation*[5] of a single conceptual module, started with the `printLowest` handler.

It is worth noting that `call` in ActorFoundry is a built-in mechanism implementing an RPC-like messaging on top of the basic actor communication model. In this case it is used to interact with the `stdout` predefined actor; RPC-like messaging is not useful to solve the problem in this case—e.g., by using `call` when doing the requests before computing the lowest value because it would sequentialize the computation.

A sketch of a plan in simpAL implementing this behaviour is shown in Fig. 14. The services are represented in this case by a couple of artifacts – referenced by the `s1` and `s2` parameter of the `PrintLowest` task. The action block in lines 7-10 executes the two requests in parallel and implicitly completes when both the actions (each corresponding to a sequence of a single action) have been completed, carrying thier results in `p1` and `p2` integer variables. After the completion of this block (note the `;` at line 10), a further block printing the lowest value is executed. The reaction to user input is modelled by a rule triggered when the a

---

[5] A solution based on continuations as first-class linguistic construct will be described later.

```
1   behavior Test {
2     boolean ignore = false;
3
4     void printLowest(Service s1, Service s2, String item ){
5       join { s1<-request(item); s2<-request(item); } @ computeLowest (token);
6     }
7
8     void computeLowest(Object values[]){
9       if (!ignore){
10        int v0 = (Integer)values[0];
11        int v1 = (Integer)values[1];
12        if (v0 < v1){
13          standardOutput <-println("Lowest: "+v0);
14        } else {
15          standardOutput <-println("Lowest: "+v1);
16        }
17      }
18    }
19
20    void stopMsg(){
21      standardOutput <-println("Stopped. ");
22      ignore = true;
23    }
24  }
```

Fig. 15. The simple example implemented in SALSA

change to the **stopped** observable property is observed (lines 19-21). As specified at line 4, the action rule block representing the plan body can be considered completed either when the lowest value is printed or the stop is processed. In this case, the strategy is fully encapsulated in a single plan, whose structure follows quite faithfully the high-level description of the strategy. In particular: *(i)* the continuation behaviour after receiving the replies from the two services is written just after the block storing the two request actions; *(ii)* the prompt response to user input is guaranteed by the reaction to **stopPressed**, which – if triggered – interrupts the sequence of actions and causes the main body to complete. The code is not polluted by explicit **if**-based tests to check if a stop has been issued or not.

The actor solution can be improved by exploiting *join continuations* [2], which are provided by some actor languages and frameworks. Essentially, join-continuations make it possible to express in a single handler workflows of actions implementing a divide-and-conquer pattern, whose management is in charge of a continuation actor automatically created by the runtime. SALSA [60] is an actor language providing first-class continuations. Fig. 15 shows an implementation of the example in SALSA. In the **printLowest** message handler, the join continuation (line 5) sends the two **request** messages to the service actors and then, as soon as both the replies about the requests are available, a **computeLowest** message is sent back to the actor. On the one side, this solution improves the previous actor one since the structure of the workflow of actions is encapsulated in a single place (the **printLowest** handler). On the other side, *(i)* the programmer is still forced to break the code in multiple handlers corresponding to messages that are received; *(ii)* the semantics of behaviour mixing join continuations and

```
1    print_lowest(S1,S2,Item) ->
2      io:format("started~n", []),
3      S1 ! {request, Item, self()},
4      S2 ! {request, Item, self()},
5      receive_first_reply().
6
7    receive_first_reply() ->
8      receive
9        {reply, N} -> receive_second_reply(N);
10       stop -> io:format("Stopped~n", [])
11     end.
12
13   receive_second_reply(N1) ->
14     receive
15       {reply, N2} -> io:format("Lowest:~p~n", [min(N1,N2)]);
16       stop -> io:format("Stopped.~n", [])
17     end.
```

Fig. 16. The simple example implemented in Erlang

reactions to events could be tricky to grasp. In the example, the actor correctly reacts to a stop message (`stopMsg`) even in the middle of the workflow specified by the join continuation, so before that the `computeLowest` message has been received. Like in the previous actor solution, an explicit test must be used in the `computeLowest` handler to check if a stop has arrived.

A more high-level solution – similar to simpAL's one – can be conceived by using concurrent objects and ABCL [64], exploiting (i) the selective message reception and the waiting mode—to wait for replies inside an handler after sending the requests; and *(ii)* the express mode message passing—to promptly react to the stop message, possibly interrupting object current activities. The availability of an explicit selective receive is found also in modern hybrid actor-based approaches like Erlang [7] and Scala actors [29], unifying event-driven behavior with a thread-like one. Fig. 16 shows a solution of the problem using Erlang, which is a classic approach provided by any framework supporting asynchronous message passing. The body of the actor – represented by the `print_lowest` function – is decomposed in two functions, `receive_first_reply` and `receive_second_reply`, each one doing a selective receive. This decomposition is not strictly necessary in this case—both the receives could be packed inside the `print_lowest`. Compared to the simpAL solution, here we have to manage the explicit exchange of messages and – depending on the design – the handling of the `stop` message may need to be replicated.

Task Decomposition and Atomic Blocks. Fig. 17 shows a solution in simpAL of the same toy example in which a task/plan decomposition is exploited. A SubTask task is used to encapsulate the interaction with services and the computation and printing of the lowest value. Then, the main plan creates an instance of the sub-task and self-assigns it. In this case there are two plans in concurrent execution inside the agent, that may interleave their actions. The execution of individual actions (including the evaluation of expressions related

```
 1   plan-for PrintLowest {
 2
 3     t: SubTask = new-task SubTask(serv1: s1,     1    plan-for SubTask {
 4                                  serv2: s2,      2
 5                                  it: id);        3      #using: s1, s2, cons
 6     {                                            4
 7       #using: gui, cons                          5      p1,p2: int
 8       #completed-when: is-done t ||              6      {
 9                        is-done stop              7        request(item: it, reply: p1) on serv1
10       do-task t                                  8        request(item: it, reply: p2) on serv2
11                                                  9      };
12       when changed stopPressed in gui => {     10      {
13         #atomic                                 11        if (p1 < p2){
14                                                 12          println(msg:"Lowest: "+p1) on cons
15         println(msg: "Stopped.") on cons        13        } else {
16         if (!is-done t){                        14          println(msg:"Lowest: "+p2) on cons
17           drop-task t                           15        }
18         }                                       16      }
19       } #act:stop                               17    }
20     }
21   }
```

Fig. 17. The example in simpAL with subtasks

to action parameters) is guaranteed to be atomic—occurring in the act stage of the agent control loop. Even if multiple actions are scheduled to be executed in the same execution cycle, they are executed in sequence in the act stage. So no low-level races can occur, e.g. for actions accessing to the same beliefs—declared at the agent script level, which are shared by plans in execution. However, this does not prevent high-level races to occur, involving the interleaving of groups of actions. This can be avoided by exploiting the #atomic attribute in action blocks. In the example, as soon as the action rule block in lines 12-20 is pushed on top of the intention stack (when a stopPressed is perceived), only actions from this intention are chosen in the agent execution cycle (as explained in Subsection 4.1). So no interleaving can occur with actions selected from the plan in execution for SubTask.

6.3   Asynchronous & Synchronous Interaction and Indirect Communication

Even if asynchronous message passing can be adopted as unique foundational interaction model, the use of synchronous interactions and high-level coordination mechanisms/patterns – such as tuple spaces [24] – can strongly simplify programming in many cases. For this reason, almost any actor framework provides mechanisms to enrich the basic asynchronous message passing model. The simplest example is given by RPC-like interaction, which is implemented by means of mechanisms such as continuation actors [4] or now type message passing [63] or directly by specific primitives such as call in ActorFoundry [36]. More complex examples include synchronizers [22] and actor spaces [3] for supporting uncoupled communication.

In simpAL this general issue is tackled at the computation/programming model level, by introducing artifacts (i.e., the environment) as a further first-class computational abstraction aside agents. This makes it possible to define a general notion of *action* and *observable state*. Actions allow for expressing synchronous interactions in a natural way. The notion of observable state makes it possible to uniformly and elegantly implement the observer pattern and related even-driven/uncoupled communication.

Coordinating Agent Actions with Artifacts. Artifacts make it possible to adopt a further coordination style among agents besides direct message passing, that is *environment-based coordination* [47,42]. As such, an artifact can be designed to function as a *coordination medium* [18] *(i)* enabling the indirect interaction among agents and *(ii)* enforcing some coordination laws managing the dependencies among actions executed by agents. This makes it possible to *encapsulate* coordination strategies inside artifacts (functioning as *coordination artifacts* [42]), instead of distributing the burden of coordination among the participants. In agent literature this is called *objective* coordination (vs. subjective one) [40] and was strongly inspired by the works on coordination models and languages [25].

Objective coordination implies a form of centralization (either conceptual or practical) in coordinating agents—being the coordination medium *the* entity where such coordination is encapsulated. So not every problem can be effectively solved by adopting this style—in same cases, full decentralization of coordination (i.e., subjective coordination) is a better solution [40]. This is the reason why simpAL supports both styles.

It is worth remarking that the `await` primitive in artifact programming model (Subsection 4.2) is a *necessary* mechanism for implementing coordination artifacts. In fact, the synchronization of concurrent actions – which is the basic step of coordination – implies that the execution of actions inside an artifact would overlap, but without violating the artifact mutual exclusion property. So `await` allows for suspending current action execution, allowing other actions to be executed. This is analogous to the condition variable mechanism in *monitors*—in simpAL the condition can be directly specified as a parameter of the `await` primitive, instead of using condition variables.

6.4   Static Typing

simpAL is a statically and strongly typed programming language. In particular, agents and artifacts are typed—roles are used to define the types of agents, while usage interfaces are used for artifacts.

This makes it possible to enact a wide spectrum of compile-time checks on how agents and artifacts are implemented and how they interact. For instance, on the agent side we can check that if a script S has been declared to implement some role R, then S must implement at least one plan for each type of task T described in R. Then, given the identifier of an agent a of some type R, then only instances of tasks whose type is included in R can be assigned to a.

Generally speaking, the usefulness of typing goes far beyond error checking [43]. It is an effective tool for improving the modelling and design of a program, making it more extensible, reusable, etc. For instance, the definition of a *sub-typing* relationship between roles would make it possible to conceive a sound *principle of substitutability* [61] also for agents. A first discussion about these points can be found here [52]: a more comprehensive treatment, including the definition of formal type system, will be considered in future work.

7   Related Work

simpAL is – on the one side – strongly related to existing agent programming languages – especially to Jason [14] and its integration with CArtAgO environment framework [48], which have been an important source of inspiration. On the other side, the language is deeply different from existing approaches in AI since it has been designed from scratch with software development in mind. The aim is to bring inside an agent-oriented programming language the same robustness, usability and flexibility which is found in mainstream programming languages.

Besides existing agent programming languages in (D)AI context, our work is related to existing frameworks and platforms that allow for developing agent-oriented programs exploiting existing programming languages. Among these, JADE [9] which has been introduced in Section 2, is one of the most used Java-based FIPA[6] compliant platform for developing agent-based software. JADE makes it possible to write agent programs in Java, where agents communicate using FIPA ACL as a standard high-level agent communication language. The model adopted for defining agent is based on *behaviors*, which share some similarities with the notion of plan adopted in simpAL. Besides agents, recently JADE model has been extended with a notion of *service* which is quite similar to the notion of artifact used in simpAL and in A&A, as non-autonomous components providing operations to agents.

In the context of concurrent programming, the agent-oriented abstractions in simpAL can be seen as a conceptual extension of the concept of actors and concurrent objects [63,2]. The extension concerns introducing specific first-class concepts to improve the structuring of autonomous behaviors (tasks, plans), the integration of task-oriented and event-driven behaviors, the separation of concerns related to autonomous (agents) and non-autonomous (environment) entities. The aims of raising the level of abstraction to be adopted in modelling and programming with respect to the pure actor model makes simpAL strongly related to the ABCM model and the ABCL language family [62] in particular. Like the Concurrent Object abstraction, also agents have an explicitly anthropomorphic nature. Also, some features that concern the agent programming model in simpAL have a clear correspondence in ABCL and not in the actor model. Examples are given by the waiting modality with selective receive and the express mode in message passing provided by ABCL. In simpAL, corresponding features are provided by the plan model, which integrate actions and reactions.

In concurrent programming the notions of actor and agent are often used as synonyms, to generically refer to active entities that exchange asynchronously

---
[6] Foundation for Intelligent Physical Agents, http://www.fipa.org

messages and are reactive, in particular react to messages received in input by other agents. An example is given by recent works exploiting the F# functional language – and its asynchronous programming model – to implement agent-based concurrency and agent-oriented programs on top of functional programs [59]. Always in the context of concurrent programming, a notion of agent is used also in the Clojure language [30], as a state-full, reactive, non-autonomous entity which is used as a simple concurrency mechanism to manage the execution of asynchronous I/O operations. A common issue which is considered very important by these approaches as well as in simpAL is the the availability of some programming support for easily integrating thread-based and event-driven behavior. This is a central point tackled also in the implementation of actors as a library on top the Scala language [29].

Finally, simpAL is related to our previous work simpA [55], a Java-based framework for developing concurrent programs using agent-oriented abstractions. simpAL can be considered an evolution of that work, *(i)* introducing a new language instead of relying on a framework based on existing technologies, and *(ii)* adopting a different computational model for agents, inspired to BDI.

8   Conclusion and Future Work

The simpAL language introduces a basic agent-oriented abstraction layer over the actors and concurrent objects, aimed at raising the level of abstraction in programming concurrent systems. The work is just the first step allowing for investigating and exploiting agent-oriented programming as a programming paradigm, and many further issues are worth to be explored from this starting point.

Different kinds of improvements can be devised about the basic agent and artifact model. A main one is the generalization of the task model to consider also *cooperative tasks*. In the current model tasks are *individual*: they can be assigned to a single agent – the task assignee – and communication can occur only between the task assigner and the task assignee. This basic model is not effective to represent tasks that involve multiple agents, working together and playing different roles in the same task. This model can be extended to capture directly these kinds of tasks, making it possible to specify also interaction protocols among agents playing the different roles. Another main improvement is the introduction of sub-typing and inheritance for agents (for roles, scripts) and artifacts (for artifact models, templates) for better supporting extensibility and reuse.

Besides these improvements, a main objective of our ongoing and future work is the definition of a unified model that makes it possible to integrate in a clean and sound way agent-oriented abstractions – based on the simpAL model – and object-oriented programming. First results about this direction are described here [53,54] and concerns a language and system called ALOO[7]. ALOO artifacts and objects have been unified in a single object model, which essentially extends

---

[7] ALOO is the short version of simpAL-OO, which means simpAL integrated with OOP.

the original OOP one with artifacts features. So an ALOO program is an organization of agents and objects. Also the agent abstraction in ALOO is a simplified version compared to simpAL one, so as to keep the model as simple as possible, yet preserving the key features of the agent abstraction. This language will make it easier to define a formal semantics to study more rigorously the properties (and problems) of the computational model. Some initial investigations about this point have been done in the past using the simpA framework [19].

References

1. Agha, G.: Actors: a model of concurrent computation in distributed systems. MIT Press, Cambridge (1986)
2. Agha, G.: Concurrent object-oriented programming. Commun. ACM 33(9), 125–141 (1990)
3. Agha, G., Callsen, C.J.: Actorspace: an open distributed programming paradigm. SIGPLAN Not. 28(7), 23–32 (1993)
4. Agha, G., Frolund, S., Kim, W., Panwar, R., Patterson, A., Sturman, D.: Abstraction and modularity mechanisms for concurrent computing. IEEE Parallel Distributed Technology: Systems Applications 1(2), 3–14 (1993)
5. Agha, G., Hewitt, C.: Concurrent programming using actors. In: Yonezawa, A., Tokoro, M. (eds.) Object-oriented Concurrent Programming, pp. 37–53. MIT Press, Cambridge (1987)
6. Agha, G., Yonezawa, A., Wegner, P. (eds.): Research Directions in Concurrent Object-Oriented Programming. The MIT Press (1993)
7. Armstrong, J.: Erlang. Communications of the ACM 53(9), 68–75 (2010)
8. Bellifemine, F., Caire, G., Poggi, A., Rimassa, G.: Jade: A software framework for developing multi-agent applications. lessons learned. Information & Software Technology 50(1-2), 10–21 (2008)
9. Bellifemine, F.L., Caire, G., Greenwood, D.: Developing Multi-Agent Systems with JADE. Wiley (2007)
10. Boissier, O., Bordini, R.H., Hübner, J.F., Ricci, A., Santi, A.: Multi-agent oriented programming with jacamo. Science of Computer Programming 78(6), 747–761 (2013)
11. Bordini, R., Dastani, M., Dix, J., El Fallah Seghrouchni, A. (eds.): Multi-Agent Programming Languages, Platforms and Applications, vol. 1, 15. Springer (2005)
12. Bordini, R., Dastani, M., Dix, J., El Fallah Seghrouchni, A. (eds.): Multi-Agent Programming Languages, Platforms and Applications, vol. 2. Springer (2009)
13. Bordini, R.H., Hübner, J.F.: BDI agent programming in AgentSpeak using *jason* (Tutorial paper). In: Toni, F., Torroni, P. (eds.) CLIMA 2005. LNCS (LNAI), vol. 3900, pp. 143–164. Springer, Heidelberg (2006)
14. Bordini, R., Hübner, J., Wooldridge, M.: Programming Multi-Agent Systems in AgentSpeak Using Jason. John Wiley & Sons, Ltd. (2007)
15. Bordini, R.H., Dastani, M., Dix, J., El Fallah Seghrouchni, A.: Special Issue: Multi-Agent Programming, vol. 23 (2). Springer (2011)
16. Briot, J.-P., Guerraoui, R., Lohr, K.-P.: Concurrency and distribution in object-oriented programming. ACM Comput. Surv. 30(3), 291–329 (1998)
17. Chin, B., Adsul, B.: Responders: Language support for interactive applications. In: Thomas, D. (ed.) ECOOP 2006. LNCS, vol. 4067, pp. 255–278. Springer, Heidelberg (2006)

18. Ciancarini, P.: Coordination models and languages as software integrators. ACM Comput. Surv. 28(2), 300–302 (1996)
19. Damiani, F., Giannini, P., Ricci, A., Viroli, M.: A calculus of agents and artifacts. In: Cordeiro, J., Ranchordas, A., Shishkov, B. (eds.) ICSOFT 2009. CCIS, vol. 50, pp. 124–136. Springer, Heidelberg (2011)
20. Dastani, M.: 2apl: a practical agent programming language. Autonomous Agents and Multi-Agent Systems 16(3), 214–248 (2008)
21. Dastani, M., van Riemsdijk, M.B., Dignum, F.P.M., Meyer, J.-J.C.: A programming language for cognitive agents goal directed 3APL. In: Dastani, M., Dix, J., El Fallah-Seghrouchni, A. (eds.) PROMAS 2003. LNCS (LNAI), vol. 3067, pp. 111–130. Springer, Heidelberg (2004)
22. Frolund, S., Agha, G.: Abstracting interactions based on message sets. In: Ciancarini, P., Wang, J. (eds.) ECOOP-WS 1994. LNCS, vol. 924, pp. 107–124. Springer, Heidelberg (1995)
23. Gamma, E.: Design patterns: elements of reusable object-oriented software. Addison-Wesley Professional (1995)
24. Gelernter, D.: Generative communication in Linda. ACM Transactions on Programming Languages and Systems 7(1), 80–112 (1985)
25. Gelernter, D., Carriero, N.: Coordination languages and their significance. Commun. ACM 35(2), 97–107 (1992)
26. Google. Dart programming language specification, Online document, available at: http://www.dartlang.org/docs/spec/ (last retrieved: April 12, 2012)
27. Haller, P., Odersky, M.: Event-based programming without inversion of control. In: Lightfoot, D.E., Ren, X.-M. (eds.) JMLC 2006. LNCS, vol. 4228, pp. 4–22. Springer, Heidelberg (2006)
28. Haller, P., Odersky, M.: Scala actors: Unifying thread-based and event-based programming. Theoretical Computer Science (2008)
29. Haller, P., Odersky, M.: Scala actors: Unifying thread-based and event-based programming. Theoretical Computer Science 410(23), 202–220 (2009)
30. Hickey, R.: Agents and asynchronous actions (in clojure), Online document, available at: http://clojure.org/agents (last retrieved: September 1, 2011)
31. Hindriks, K.V.: Programming rational agents in GOAL. In: Bordini, R.H., Dastani, M., Dix, J., El Fallah Seghrouchni, A. (eds.) Multi-Agent Programming: Languages, Platforms and Applications, vol. 2, pp. 3–37. Springer (2009)
32. Jennings, N.R.: An agent-based approach for building complex software systems. Commun. ACM 44(4), 35–41 (2001)
33. Jennings, N.R., Wooldridge, M.: Agent-oriented software engineering. Artificial Intelligence 117, 277–296 (2000)
34. Johnson, R.E., Foote, B.: Designing reusable classes. Journal of Object-Oriented Programming 1(2) (1988)
35. Karmani, R.K., Agha, G.: Actors. In: Padua, D.A. (ed.) Encyclopedia of Parallel Computing, pp. 1–11. Springer (2011)
36. Karmani, R.K., Shali, A., Agha, G.: Actor frameworks for the JVM platform: a comparative analysis. In: Proceedings of the 7th International Conference on Principles and Practice of Programming in Java, PPPJ 2009, pp. 11–20. ACM, New York (2009)
37. Kay, A.C.: The early history of smalltalk. In: Bergin Jr., T.J., Gibson Jr., R.G. (eds.) History of programming languages—II, pp. 511–598. ACM, New York (1996)
38. Miller, M.S., Tribble, E.D., Shapiro, J.S.: Concurrency among strangers. In: De Nicola, R., Sangiorgi, D. (eds.) TGC 2005. LNCS, vol. 3705, pp. 195–229. Springer, Heidelberg (2005)

39. Mitchell, J.: Concepts in Programming Languages. Cambridge University Press (2002)
40. Omicini, A., Ossowski, S.: Objective versus subjective coordination in the engineering of agent systems. In: Klusch, M., Bergamaschi, S., Edwards, P., Petta, P. (eds.) Intelligent Information Agents. LNCS (LNAI), vol. 2586, pp. 179–202. Springer, Heidelberg (2003)
41. Omicini, A., Ricci, A., Viroli, M.: Artifacts in the A&A meta-model for multi-agent systems. Autonomous Agents and Multi-Agent Systems 17(3), 432–456 (2008)
42. Omicini, A., Ricci, A., Viroli, M., Castelfranchi, C., Tummolini, L.: Coordination artifacts: Environment-based coordination for intelligent agents. In: Jennings, N.R., Sierra, C., Sonenberg, L., Tambe, M. (eds.) AAMAS 2004, vol. 1, pp. 286–293. ACM (2004)
43. Pierce, B.C.: Types and programming languages. MIT Press, Cambridge (2002)
44. Pokahr, A., Braubach, L., Lamersdorf, W.: Jadex: A BDI reasoning engine. In: Bordini, R., Dastani, M., Dix, J., Seghrouchni, A.E.F. (eds.) Multi-Agent Programming. Kluwer (2005)
45. Rao, A.S.: AgentSpeak(l): BDI agents speak out in a logical computable language. In: Perram, J., Van de Velde, W. (eds.) MAAMAW 1996. LNCS, vol. 1038, pp. 42–55. Springer, Heidelberg (1996)
46. Rao, A.S., Georgeff, M.P.: BDI Agents: From Theory to Practice. In: First International Conference on Multi Agent Systems, ICMAS 95 (1995)
47. Ricci, A., Piunti, M., Viroli, M.: Environment programming in multi-agent systems: an artifact-based perspective. Autonomous Agents and Multi-Agent Systems 23, 158–192 (2011)
48. Ricci, A., Piunti, M., Viroli, M., Omicini, A.: Environment programming in CArtAgO. In: Bordini, R.H., Dastani, M., Dix, J., El Fallah-Seghrouchni, A. (eds.) Multi-Agent Programming: Languages, Platforms and Applications, vol. 2, pp. 259–288. Springer (2009)
49. Ricci, A., Santi, A.: Designing a general-purpose programming language based on agent-oriented abstractions: the simpAL project. In: Proc. of AGERE! 2011, SPLASH 2011 Workshops, pp. 159–170. ACM, New York (2011)
50. Ricci, A., Santi, A.: Programming abstractions for integrating autonomous and reactive behaviors: an agent-oriented approach. In: Proc. of AGERE! 2012, pp. 83–94. ACM, New York (2012)
51. Ricci, A., Santi, A.: A programming paradigm based on agent-oriented abstractions. International Journal on Advances in Software 5, 36–52 (2012)
52. Ricci, A., Santi, A.: Typing multi-agent programs in simpAL. In: Dastani, M., Hübner, J.F., Logan, B. (eds.) ProMAS 2012. LNCS, vol. 7837, pp. 138–157. Springer, Heidelberg (2013)
53. Ricci, A., Santi, A.: Concurrent object-oriented programming with agent-oriented abstractions the aloo approach. In: Proc. of AGERE! 2013, ACM, New York (2013)
54. Ricci, A., Santi, A.: Concurrent OOP with agents. In: Proceedings of the 4th Annual Conference on Systems, Programming, and Applications: Software for Humanity, SPLASH 2013. ACM, New York (to appear, 2013), Extended abstract
55. Ricci, A., Viroli, M., Piancastelli, G.: simpA: An agent-oriented approach for programming concurrent applications on top of java. Sci. Comput. Program. 76, 37–62 (2011)
56. Santi, A., Ricci, A.: Programming distributed multi-agent systems in simpAL. In: Flavio, D.P., Giuseppe, V. (eds.) Proceedings of the 13th Workshop on Objects and Agents (WOA 2012). CEUR Workshop Proceedings, vol. 892, Sun SITE Central Europe, RWTH Aachen University (2012)

57. Shoham, Y.: Agent-oriented programming. Artificial Intelligence 60(1), 51–92 (1993)
58. Sutter, H., Larus, J.: Software and the concurrency revolution. ACM Queue: Tomorrow's Computing Today 3(7), 54–62 (2005)
59. Syme, D., Petricek, T., Lomov, D.: The F# asynchronous programming model. In: Rocha, R., Launchbury, J. (eds.) PADL 2011. LNCS, vol. 6539, pp. 175–189. Springer, Heidelberg (2011)
60. Varela, C., Agha, G.: Programming dynamically reconfigurable open systems with salsa. SIGPLAN Not. 36(12), 20–34 (2001)
61. Wegner, P., Zdonik, S.B.: Inheritance as an incremental modification mechanism or what like is and isn't like. In: Gjessing, S., Chepoi, V. (eds.) ECOOP 1988. LNCS, vol. 322, pp. 55–77. Springer, Heidelberg (1988)
62. Yonezawa, A.: ABCL – an object-oriented concurrent system. MIT Press series in computer systems. MIT Press (1990)
63. Yonezawa, A., Briot, J.-P., Shibayama, E.: Object-oriented concurrent programming in ABCL/1. In: Meyrowitz, N.K. (ed.) Conference on Object-Oriented Programming Systems, Languages, and Applications (OOPSLA 1986), Portland, Oregon, pp. 258–268. ACM (1986)
64. Yonezawa, A., Shibayama, E., Takada, T., Honda, Y.: Modelling and programming in an object-oriented concurrent language ABCL/1. In: Yonezawa, A., Tokoro, M. (eds.) Object-oriented Concurrent Programming, pp. 55–89. MIT Press, Cambridge (1987)
65. Yonezawa, A., Tokoro, M. (eds.): Object-oriented concurrent programming. MIT Press (1987)

Author Index